Libraries
at Large

*The Resource Book Based on the
Materials of the National
Advisory Commission
on Libraries*

Libraries
at Large

TRADITION,
INNOVATION, AND
THE NATIONAL INTEREST

Edited by
DOUGLAS M. KNIGHT *and*
E. SHEPLEY NOURSE

R. R. BOWKER COMPANY, NEW YORK & LONDON 1969

Published by the R. R. Bowker Co. (A XEROX COMPANY)
1180 Avenue of the Americas, New York, N.Y. 10036
Copyright © 1969 by Duke University, Durham, North Carolina
This work is based, in large part, on studies funded by the United States Office of
Education to assist the National Advisory Commission on Libraries in its deliberations.
No copyright is claimed for chapter 11, chapter 12, and appendixes A-D.
No copyright is claimed for chapter 10 by the Library of Congress staff.
All rights reserved.
Standard Book Number: 8352–0223–2
Library of Congress Card Number: 70–79429
Printed and bound in the United States of America

NATIONAL ADVISORY COMMISSION ON LIBRARIES SUMMARY OF OBJECTIVES AND RECOMMENDATIONS

The fundamental recommendation of the National Advisory Commission on Libraries, on which further recommendations are based, is that it be declared National Policy, enunciated by the President and enacted into law by the Congress, that the American people should be provided with library and informational services adequate to their needs, and that the Federal Government, in collaboration with State and local governments and private agencies, should exercise leadership assuring the provision of such services.

Objectives for Overcoming Current Inadequacies

* Provide adequate library and informational services for formal education at all levels.

* Provide adequate library and informational services for the public at large.

* Provide materials to support research in all fields at all levels.

* Provide adequate bibliographic access to the nation's research and informational resources.

* Provide adequate physical access to required materials or their texts throughout the nation.

* Provide adequate trained personnel for the varied and changing demands of librarianship.

Recommendations for Achieving the Objectives

1. Establishment of a National Commission on Libraries and Information Science as a continuing Federal planning agency.

2. Recognition and strengthening of the role of The Library of Congress as the National Library of the United States and establishment of a Board of Advisers.

3. Establishment of a Federal Institute of Library and Information Science as a principal center for basic and applied research in all relevant areas.

4. Recognition and full acceptance of the critically important role the United States Office of Education currently plays in meeting needs for library services.

5. Strengthening State library agencies to overcome deficiencies in fulfilling their current functions.

PREFACE

by DOUGLAS M. KNIGHT

At the time this book goes to press, indications are favorable for early establishment of a strong permanent National Commission on Libraries and Information Science—a basic recommendation of the National Advisory Commission on Libraries
which I served as Chairman. This is only one already evident result of the Advisory
Commission's deliberations during its active period from establishment by Executive
Order in September 1966, through submission of its Report in July 1968 to the President's Committee on Libraries, and finally to the formal presentation of its Report to
President Lyndon B. Johnson on October 15, 1968.

This book, *Libraries at Large,* is itself one tangible outcome of Advisory Commission activity, representing the combined efforts of Duke University, the R. R. Bowker
Company, members of the Commission and its several study groups, and many other
diverse individuals within and without the library world. The resultant theme is the
same one that characterized the work of our Commission from the beginning—namely,
a concern that every individual in our society be provided with library and informational
services adequate to his current and emerging needs. Confronting this goal requires a
recognition of inevitable change, and we have questioned *status quo,* recognizing at the
same time the differing pace and character requisite for the implementation of designs
in the adaptability to change. The national interest demands simultaneous sympathy
with people in pockets of illiteracy and people in the vanguards of intellectual achievement.

To question today's library is to question our world—an act of high fashion at the
moment, full of cliché, urgency, and promise. A library, after all, is one of the neat
symbols of continuity, order, even rigidity and confinement, in a disordered world. To
question it is to play the child, if we do so negatively, and to play the modest prophet if
we have the great purposes of renewal in mind, and if we search in the library, as everywhere in our society, for "new styles of architecture, a change of heart."

But why should renewal be a major issue? Are not preservation and reference adequate functions for the library, just as the analysis and ordering of knowledge might be
adequate for a university? The answer is "no" to both questions and for the same reason; like every other institution today, the university and the library inhabit a world of

radical and constant change. The issues for the next fifty years are above all those of how to shape that change wisely and for the greatest human benefit.

The major problem we face as we look at libraries is, then, not unique to them; it is rather the basic question of all design, one which plagues airports, hospitals, or super-highways. In each case the question is the same: Is some mechanical purpose to be served, or is man the design center? It is impossible for any modern traveler to escape the image of an airport like O'Hare, so clearly created to accommodate planes and so defiant of people and their needs. Without exaggeration, at an airport like Dulles one can see man served by a system designed for his human purposes; at O'Hare one must simply endure the opposite.

The same issue of design has become tragically urgent for whole cities; one can leave a bad airport, but he may have to inhabit urban sprawl and smog. Again the question: Are we to serve man, or has he become incidental to some set of mechanical limits which define the modern city? In slightly different form we see the same puzzle in the structure of modern colleges and universities. Without realizing it, they have radically modified and diffused—even fragmented—their social order in the years since World War II. Year by year we did not give a name, or even much conscious attention, to this shift, but it has been moving students, faculty, alumni, and trustees into new orbits of belief and action. Now we must relate ourselves to one another in patterns that recognize the lessons of the last quarter of our century, use them, grow beyond them. Some have tried to pretend that the universities could, or should, retreat from these new orbits of action. But for the universities, as for our libraries, the real problem is far more important and far less negative. How can we keep the great traditional functions of a university or a library alive and *at the same time* relate those functions to the best of what is new, both in need and in technique for meeting the need?

Take the simplest example from the university world—a basic shift in the teaching of foreign languages, brought on by the urgencies of World War II and then sustained by the results of that war. We needed actually to speak unusual and exotic languages, and so we learned the techniques of teaching them; then we found ourselves in a post-war world where the speaking of two languages was a daily necessity for millions of Americans. Without the war and a permanent shift in our international relationships, I doubt that we would yet have learned how to teach those languages with full effectiveness. The stress of a particular time brought about a permanent improvement in our educational pattern.

Behind the obvious change stands a whole complex of changes that have led us to basic reformations of design in university curriculum, as a constructive use of our world revolution rather than an attempt to ignore or deny it. In the university world (and a shift there has great meaning for the future of libraries), we have become both more intensive and more extensive—intensive in our treatment of each field, extensive in the development not only of new disciplines but of new relationships to society. We do not yet have the organization to handle these new levels of duty, but we are working with them; in time our effective means will catch up with the facts of what we are doing.

Behind these and a host of other changes of texture and direction in our society stands one major need, which is being attempted and yet denied by us every day. This is the need to humanize and civilize our enterprises, and particularly those which have grown large, mechanized, routine. It is the need to ask what greatness truly is if we dare to speak of "a great society," or true "law and order," if those are to be our terms of reference. If we cry out for identity and freedom (and who does not?), we must ask how we identify and free ourselves without trampling our neighbor, or putting him in bondage. No matter what our idiom or our medium, we all ask a variant of one question: How do we become more perceptive as we become more powerful, more genuinely responsive to others as our own lives become more privileged?

This is a basic moral issue for our time, and in reckoning with it the library is both a means and an end. How do we define wisdom, acquire it, and use it? A library is not simply designed to communicate information. The information must be organized first or the library cannot exist at all; and in the fact of organization is the fact of valuing. The library of the future, by whatever names we know it, will be more sophisticated than that of the past in a hundred different ways, but in this one essential it will not change. To make knowledge available is to organize it; and to organize it we must make judgments about what is important, what is trivial, and what is useless.

In this book, as in the deliberations of the National Advisory Commission on Libraries itself, we have described some of today's inadequacies and the many ways in which new kinds and levels of organization might be brought to bear on the age-old job of structuring knowledge so that it can illuminate lives. Evidence is presented from many disciplines and points of view, which we hope will provide continuing resource for the job ahead—the future research that is needed and the decision-making in implementation of new designs. The user orientation is strikingly consistent throughout this diversity of resource material. It is the underlying theme of *Libraries at Large.*

Each of us involved in the original Commission work, and later in the Duke University Library and Information Science Publication Project, owes a great debt, not only to the specialized studies of library resources and development which undergird this book, but to the hundreds of individual conversations and suggestions which have occurred so freely and generously. They have lent us confidence, not only in the need for the Advisory Commission's study in the first place, and the thorough documentation provided in this book, but in the validity of the specific recommendations included in the Commission's unanimous Report, which appears here as the concluding chapter 12.

Everyone has his own solution for the ills of our time—argument, legislation, violence, fond attempts to recover a past that never really existed. In these pages we raise the quiet voice of the original National Advisory Commission on Libraries for understanding, learning, action based on judgment, and the creation of new institutions firmly based in the best of what we have. This is the challenge to libraries—that they play an active role in creating a society which is humane but not merely genteel, stable but not merely conventional. As they do so, they will establish the same pattern for themselves; and so they will become fully a part of the society they strengthen.

DOUGLAS M. KNIGHT
President, Duke University

CONTENTS

PART III. *Government Involvement in Library and Informational Services: Roles, Relationships, and Potentialities*

LIST OF TABLES

Tables in Chapter 2, Section B.2

Tables in Chapter 2, Section C.2

LIST OF FIGURES

Figures in Chapter 5, Section D

Figures in Chapter 11

Figure in Appendix F-3. C

Libraries
at Large

PART I

Users and Uses of Library and Informational Services in a Changing Society

CHAPTER I

SOCIAL CHANGE AND THE LIBRARY: 1945–1980[1]

by DAN LACY
Senior Vice President
McGraw-Hill Book Company

FORCES IMPELLING SOCIAL CHANGE

The two most dynamic forces impelling the social changes that affect the library are probably the changing population patterns and the radically increased social investment in scientific and technical research and development. The purpose of this paper is to sketch these trends and their impact on education, social organization, and national policy, and then to discuss society's changing needs for communication, the implications of current technological development, and the library's emerging responsibilities. The library has an active role to play in an era of new social emphasis.

POPULATION SHIFTS

Following a long period of relatively slow growth, the population of the United States leaped forward in the years following World War II as millions of men returned from the armed services to found families. The dynamics of growth may be seen in the annual number of births. Throughout the 1920's this figure averaged just under 3 million for the United States. It declined with the coming of the Depression and averaged only 2.5 million for the 1930's. The deferral of marriages and the absence of husbands continued to depress the birth rate even after the return of prosperity in wartime. In 1945 there were still only 2,858,000 births in the United States.

This pattern changed sharply in 1946 and 1947, when there were 3,426,000 and 3,834,000 births, respectively. The number of births increased steadily year by year until it reached a peak of 4,268,000 in 1961. Since then the birth rate has declined, slowly at first and then more rapidly, reaching a figure of 3,629,000 in 1966.

This massive wave of births, coupled with a declining death rate, brought about an enormous postwar population increase. The increase from 1920 to 1930 was only 17.2 million, or 16.2 percent. The population estimate for 1945 was 140,468,000, but then the figure climbed steeply to 151.3 million by 1950. The 1950's saw a further increase to 179.3 million, or 18.5 percent. The estimated population for 1967 is 200 million, for a total postwar increase of 59,532,000, or over 40 percent.

The meaning of this startling increase is not clear, however, without analysis by

[1] *This paper is from a special study of the same name commissioned by the National Advisory Commission on Libraries and performed by the National Book Committee in 1967.*

generations, for it has been almost wholly an increase in the number of children and youths. Only in 1967 did the earliest of the postwar generation become 21. The number of persons under 20 has grown from an estimated 46,795,000 in 1945 to 77,815,000 in 1966, an increase of 66.3 percent as compared with 27.1 percent for the population over 19, which has grown only from an estimated 92,827,000 to 118,042,000. There have been actual declines in certain sectors of the adult population. For example, there are today fewer people in the age bracket 30–35 than at any time since the early 1930's.

One consequence of this oscillation of birth rates is that the extremely rapid growth in the number of children and young people requiring educational and related services has come at precisely a time when the number of persons ready to enter such professions as librarianship and teaching has been at its lowest in decades. This mismatching of generations is a principal cause of the manpower shortage in schools and libraries. It will largely correct itself, given adequate salary support, over the next ten or fifteen years.

Changes in the number and age distribution of the population have not, however, been the only dramatic population changes in the United States. Almost equally dramatic are the changes in geographic and occupational distribution. There have been massive movements in the postwar decades from rural and small town areas to metropolitan areas, from core cities to suburbs, and from the South and Middle West to Florida, the Southwest, and the Pacific Coast.

Between 1950 and 1960 the net outward migration from the Dakotas, Virginia, West Virginia, the Carolinas, Georgia, Tennessee, Kentucky, Alabama, Mississippi, Arkansas, Louisiana, Oklahoma, Texas, Montana, Wyoming, New Mexico, Alaska, and Hawaii was more than 1.5 million; this figure has been even larger for the years since 1960. Because much of this migration consisted of young adults who were parents or potential parents, it was doubly significant as a population factor. The birth rates of the states from which they departed fell, and the population of the states to which they came rose swiftly from an increase in births as well as from immigration. In such states as West Virginia, Arkansas, and Mississippi, the annual number of births in the 1950's and 1960's was actually below that of 1940, and in a number of other states the increase was relatively slight. In contrast, in California the number of births went from 114,000 in 1940 to 247,000 in 1950 and 372,000 in 1960; in Florida it went from 37,000 to 66,000 to 115,000 in the same years. The impact on schools, libraries, and similar services of the massive postwar increase in the birth rate was heavily concentrated in areas whose resources were already strained to provide for in-migrants.

A considerable part of the migrant flow consisted of retired persons, increasing in numbers and in affluence, who sought the warmer climates of Florida, Arizona, and California. A second and very important part consisted of highly trained young men and women, skilled in the new technologies, who were drawn to aerospace and electronic industries. These industries, handling few or no heavy materials, did not have to concentrate in ports or transportation centers or near mines or other sources of raw materials. In fact, these industries were impelled to choose locations that helped them to attract skilled people—pleasant suburbs, resort areas, places with outstanding cultural and research opportunities.

A third and tragically important part of the migration consisted of unskilled and semiliterate agricultural laborers, mostly Negro, Puerto Rican, or Mexican, made useless by the introduction of new machinery and chemical weed-killers and pesticides, who were driven by the hundreds of thousands from the farms on which they had worked to become ill-adapted and almost helpless residents of the ghettos of large northern core cities. The Negro rural population declined from 5,650,000 in 1950 to 5,057,000 in 1960, and has fallen even more sharply subsequently. The Negro urban population rose in the same period from 9,393,000 in 1950 to 13,792,000 in 1960, and has continued to rise rapidly. Even these figures conceal the full impact of the migration, for it was not to urban areas generally but very specifically to the core cities of large northern and Pacific

Coast states. The nonwhite population of Manhattan grew from 20.5 percent in 1950 to 25.1 percent in 1960. In Chicago the nonwhite population rose to 23.6 percent; in Los Angeles, to 16.8 percent. Baltimore, Cleveland, Detroit, Newark, Philadelphia, and St. Louis were more than 25 percent Negro in 1960; Washington was more than 50 percent. In all of these cities the Negro population has continued to grow rapidly.

The migration of displaced agricultural laborers to central cities of metropolitan areas was paralleled by a migration of more prosperous families from the central cities to the suburbs. This shift was due in part to affluence, in part to a desire to avoid proximity to the new central-city residents, in part to the general movement from central cities of businesses that were not compelled to be there and that were seeking more pleasant, cheaper, and more efficient locations. These parallel population movements produced a truly revolutionary change in the character of nearly all major cities, redefining the clientele of all their services, greatly increasing the demands for those services, and reducing or limiting the financial resources to support them.

The bare statistics convey little of the human reality represented by these vast movements of population. One needs rather to think of this generation of immediately postwar children, whose arrival at every stage of their growth, though known for years ahead, seemed always to catch society unprepared—the double shifts in schools, the inadequate buildings, the jammed libraries, the desperate scramble to get into inadequately enlarged colleges, and the adult amazement at the mass, even the existence, of a teen-age generation.

The human reality lay, too, in the dying areas of marginal hill farms and mountain coal-mining towns, where long unemployment and deadening poverty left the remaining population in a bleared and empty aimlessness, drifting confused and untrained into an unfamiliar time. It lay in the newly bulldozed acres of glistening suburbs in which tens of thousands of young families reared their children in brigades of uniform age, but in rootless communities in which all institutions had to be created anew. As the children were brigaded in the grandfatherless suburbs, so were the elderly brigaded in the childless retirement communities, dislodged at an age of slow adjustment from all that was familiar, confronting in affluent loneliness the emptiness of a rootless community of another kind.

Perhaps most poignantly of all, the human reality existed in the stark despair of the millions made useless on the farms and in the mines, who were driven to cold and indifferent cities and there set apart by race and by peasant ignorance of city ways and city jobs. They drifted into crowded and ill-served ghettos and were reduced to anarchy by the shattering of the network of personal, family, church, and occupational ties that had shaped their rural lives. They were plagued with unemployment, poverty, and the frustrated search for some door opening out into a hopeful future.

All of these displaced millions, in different ways, have needed new institutions to serve them: new in location, plant, resources, and staff—and often radically new in orientation and purpose.

RESEARCH EMPHASIS

Thus the clientele of libraries has been undergoing a great increase in numbers, a radical change in age distribution, and a vast churning across the land; but at the same time the body of knowledge to be made available through libraries has been transformed with equal rapidity. Until the twentieth century the increase of knowledge proceeded almost fortuitously, impelled by the curiosity of individuals rather than by the policy of governments or the programs of universities. Research began to play a central role in the functions of colleges and universities only gradually as the nineteenth century progressed; only in a few areas directly related to agriculture, mining, or defense had the state systematically devoted itself to the increase of knowledge, and then in only a very limited way. True, many businesses of the nineteenth and early twentieth centuries had been founded on or had profited by particular inventions, and a few, like General Electric in its relations with Steinmetz, systematically sought new inventions; but none gave attention to the basic sciences, and none devoted any substantial resources to advancing even the most immediately useful applied technology.

World War II changed this pattern in a revolutionary way. The demonstrated results of applying massive research and development funds to the achievement of predetermined objectives were overwhelming and reached their dramatic climax with the explosion of the atom bomb. Paced by Government programs in the fields of defense and space exploration, society as a whole devoted enormous sums in the postwar decades to scientific research and technical development. An average annual investment for these purposes was $15 billion. This was more than the entire gross national product of all but a few nations and more than that of the United States itself only a few decades before. For the first time in the history of the world, a nation deliberately mobilized all its relevant resources to achieve radical and comprehensive technological innovation as rapidly as possible.

One consequence was an enormous and rapid increase in the amount of recorded information produced, especially in the fields of the physical and biological sciences, engineering, and medicine. The number of books published in these fields increased from 1,576 in 1940 to 4,933 in 1965; the number of journals rose proportionately. Even more of a problem in documentation was presented by the countless thousands of unpublished research reports in which many advances in science were recorded. The flood of new material facing every scholarly or technical library was revolutionary in its volume and complexity. Furthermore, wholly new levels of library resources had to be provided in universities, in Government agencies, and in major corporations to sustain this research; libraries became highly focused, providing intense and immediate coverage of specific areas of advancing knowledge.

But there were other, and in the long run even more important, consequences for libraries deriving from this massive research and development effort. One was the immediate impact on the economy. Decades or generations might elapse in earlier centuries before the average man experienced in his daily life the consequences of a new scientific discovery. Copernicus, Galileo, Newton, Lavoisier, Darwin, and Maxwell might discover as they would, yet the peasants and artisans of the world went about their work in age-old ways. But most of the billions of dollars for research and development spent by the United States in every recent year has gone not into the relatively inexpensive endeavors of pure scientific research but into development—into the immediate application of the results of research to practical economic life. A new chemical with special properties is scarcely discovered before it is widely marketed as a herbicide, displacing thousands of agricultural laborers from their tasks of chopping weeds. The principles of a digital computer are devised, and within a decade hundreds of thousands of men and women are at work making, servicing, programming, and using these marvels.

In contrast to earlier days, when only a very small proportion of the population needed to be familiar with advanced scientific knowledge or its technological implications, now millions, even tens of millions, of men and women have to master in varying degrees aspects of the new knowledge. One result has been the necessity of extending post-high-school training to half or more of the youths of the country. More than five times as many of our young people now receive college training as did before World War II. The proportion receiving postgraduate and professional training has increased even more dramatically.

A second result is that the corpus of knowledge that most men employ in their daily work is based on the changing technology and hence itself changes rapidly, requiring the frequent, indeed nearly continuous, retraining of professional, technical, and managerial personnel. This training takes place on the job, through professional journals and books, in formal training programs, and through postgraduate courses.

As another consequence of scientific development, the domination of the daily lives and occupations of the general public by the advanced technology has excluded from full participation in society those who do not share the technology. The untrained face dwindling job opportunities, increasing poverty in the midst of affluence, impotence in a world of enormous power. Their geographic displacement into large cities where they are disoriented and even more helpless has already been described. The enormous Federal expenditures undertaken to accelerate scientific and technical progress and to disseminate and apply the advanced technology have had the unintended result of stripping of their usefulness and place in society the millions who do not share in the command of this new technology. The more advanced our knowledge and the wider the circle of those who participate in it, the more hopelessly frustrating is the lot of those who do not.

MANIFESTATIONS OF SOCIAL CHANGE

EDUCATION

The most directly measurable impact on libraries arising from the combined effects of population changes and the growth and applicability of scientific and technical knowledge has come in the field of education. The most obvious development has been the increase in school enrollments as a result of population growth. As one goes up the educational ladder through high school, college, and professional and graduate schools, one finds high proportions of the relevant age groups enrolled. The elementary school enrollment, public and private, increased from 21.1 million in 1940 to 22.2 million in 1950, 32.4 million in 1960, and 35.1 million in 1965. High school enrollment fluctuated from 7.1 million in 1940 to 6.5 million in 1950, 9.6 million in 1960, and 13.0 million in 1965. College and university enrollment went from 1.5 million in 1940 to 2.7 million in 1950, 3.2 million in 1960, and 5.7 million in 1965. Since students are by far the most intensive users of libraries in our population, these increases have imposed a major additional workload on libraries.

The enrollment increase was not equally distributed, however. Enrollments in the states with a heavy outward migration of population (e.g., Arkansas, Mississippi, or West Virginia) increased little if at all, especially in the lower grades, and in many school districts enrollment declined. Conversely, the increases were disproportionately large in those states (like California, Arizona, and Florida) with heavy in-migrations. Suburban areas had enrollments that multiplied many times over. Correspondingly, white enrollment dropped precipitately in core northern cities, while Negro and Puerto Rican enrollments rose with almost equal speed.

It is further characteristic of this increase in enrollment that it has largely been absorbed in new institutions or in institutions radically transformed in size and objectives. Between 1955 and 1966, 758,459 new elementary and secondary classrooms were constructed. Since 1945, 315 new junior colleges and 278 new degree-granting institutions have been created. In addition, hundreds of institutions that had previously served as small colleges primarily for the training of elementary school teachers were transformed into general liberal-arts colleges, or even universities, and doubled or tripled in size. As a result, only a very small part of the increase in college enrollment came in institutions with strong library resources. Most of the millions of additional college students were in institutions whose libraries either were very weak in relation to their new responsibilities or else were being created from the beginning.

Moreover, many of the new colleges were not built on rural or isolated campuses but in urban areas, and most of their students lived at home rather than in dormitories.

This was particularly true of the new junior and community colleges. A consequence was that the students relied on the resources of the nearest public library more than on the resources of the college library, which might be distant from the homes in which they studied.

But the changes in education were by no means numerical only. Our surprise that the Russians anticipated us in space exploration dramatically supported those who in the ten years after the war had been complaining that American education was insufficiently demanding. Following the shock of the first sputnik in 1957, there was a national outcry for a greater emphasis on science, mathematics, and modern foreign languages. Reinforced by the National Defense Education Act of 1958, this demand led to a substantial broadening of the high school curriculum and a raising of standards.

Meanwhile, the curricula of colleges and universities were feeling the impact of the massive and organized support of scientific and technical research, as well as the global extension of American interests. New departments and courses in area studies, in less-familiar languages, and in developing areas of science were created in hundreds of institutions, each asserting its demand for library resources.

Especially noteworthy was the increase in postgraduate enrollment. The number of institutions offering the Ph.D. degree increased from 98 in 1938 to 218 in 1964, and the number of doctoral degrees conferred rose from 3,290 in 1940 to 16,467 in 1965. The support of research at this level imposed incomparably heavier demands on libraries than the support of undergraduate instruction and required the building up of dozens of major new research libraries and hundreds of specialized collections.

SOCIAL ORGANIZATION

The increase in population and the explosive growth of science have expressed themselves not only in this radical and unprecedented expansion of our educational effort. They have also resulted in an enormous increase in the complexity of our social organization and hence of the processes of communication necessary to sustain it. As I pointed out on an earlier occasion:

> Another consequence of the more complex organization of society rising from the wider and more elaborate use of the new technology is that the patterns of everybody's daily behavior are much more completely determined socially. Very many Americans work for very large corporations or governmental agencies with intricate internal organization, and the concept of the "organization man" as one whose whole life is determined by the necessities of adaptation to the corporate organism of which he is a part has become a cliché of our current speech. Yet the social determination of the working activities of the self-employed or the worker for the small company is almost equally great. The individual owner of a small filling station is as definitely "fixed" in the vast pattern of the automotive industry and as dependent on its vagaries as the assembly-line worker at General Motors or the worker in the small independent plant that produces a single GM component on contract. The successful doctor or lawyer, though in private practice, plays a role in the vast network of people and institutions that serve our health or maintain the lawful patterns of our lives, to which he must adapt as much as the executive in an oil company. The truth is that it is our society itself that has become vast and interwoven, and we must each fulfill his role in its intricate ecology whether working alone or as a corporate employee with thousands of fellows.
>
> It is pointless to deplore this more highly organized character of contemporary life. It is simply a fact that the enormous sources of power made available to us can be used only by a society with an extremely high degree of specialization of economic functions; it can only work with, as it were, a highly "orchestrated" performance. Anarchy and disorganization society cannot tolerate; the population has grown too large in relation to the resource base to be sustained except by con-

tinuous and well-organized activity. In modern wars the principal cause of death is likely to be not combat but starvation resulting from the disorganization of economic activity.

It is obvious that for each person to perform usefully in so highly organized yet so fluid a society, he must receive a constant flow of information that will enable him to adapt his behavior to the changing requirements. In large part, this information consists of orders or instructions, like those to a locomotive engineer telling him at what hour and minute he is to report at what terminal to take what train where. But even within large corporations, specific instructions have become less and less adequate to bring the activity of employees into the necessary pattern. Certainly they will be far less adequate in the future, as more and more jobs capable of being governed by fixed instructions will be taken over by machines. Increasingly the necessary coordination will be obtained by preparing the employee with sufficient training so that he has a high level of insight into the purposes of his work and will independently make the desired decisions when confronted with unforeseeable circumstances. This method of achieving social adaptation is most complete, of course, in respect to the self-employed professional like the doctor or lawyer. He receives no "orders," yet his long professional training, the careful implantation of professional ethics, and the steady flow through professional journals and meetings of new information means that members of the profession, confronted with a given situation—a contract to be drawn or an appendix to be removed—will respond to it in a more or less uniform or at least similar way and will discharge effectively the social role required of them. More and more it is by similar means that the more responsible employee within a large corporation fits his work to the corporation's needs.

This method of achieving social coordination is far more expensive of communication, and of communication of a higher order, than achieving coordination by instruction from above. It means that each participant in the common endeavor must understand the whole endeavor and be kept currently informed of the entire changing situation so that he can continuously make his own proper adaptation to it. And he must understand the purposes of the general enterprise and share its values to a degree that will impel him to make the adaptation. These needs will exist whether the enterprise that must be organized is a small business firm or the entire society. Such very large enterprises as our major corporations or the armed services have undertaken elaborate internal programs of training, indoctrination, and current information in order to achieve the higher level of coordination now required. In a precisely similar way society itself, to sustain its extremely complex present organization, needs and largely has achieved a massive flow of information whose principal purpose is to enable individuals to fit themselves meaningfully to society's needs and to achieve a sharing of values that will give them a common motivation.[2]

The principal burden of communication required to sustain the interconnectedness of contemporary society has, of course, fallen on the media of current information: newspapers, magazines, technical journals, broadcasts, and especially the less formal flow of data within organizations. But no small part of it falls on public, professional, corporate, and college libraries as reservoirs of the information we all need to sustain our functions in relation to a complex, changing, and highly integrated society.

NATIONAL POLICY

The devotion of enormous resources to research and development has also brought with it a surge of national power. This has manifested itself in ways that have the most serious consequences for our national future and for that of civilization generally. Heavy responsibilities are imposed on our means of communication generally and perhaps especially on libraries.

2 Dan Lacy, Freedom and Communications (2nd ed.; Urbana: University of Illinois Press, 1961, 1965), pp. 18–20.

One of these consequences is that the United States Government has an unprecedented capacity to change the entire course of history. We are dramatically aware of this in connection with atomic weapons and their potential for global destruction. But it is almost equally true in other ways. The pace of American industry gulps natural resources at a destructive rate and pours forth pollutants that stain the air and rivers and lakes of a continent. For the first time men have a major capacity to alter for good or ill the whole natural environment within which they live. American power strides across the globe, and in the farther reaches of Asia American food and medicines save and American weapons kill. Medical skills can prolong human life and alter genetic inheritance. Satellites span the sky, and men may soon reach the moon. An abundance of goods pours forth that for the first time in history allows most of a nation to live in affluence. To an extent never before dreamed of, the human future, for good or ill, will be shaped by human decision. Our judgments of policy carry a burden of responsibility never before borne by human judgment.

At the same time that our burgeoning power has endowed our policy decisions with such awful importance, it has removed the grounds for their determination from our common experience. In the Depression of the late 1930's one could understand unemployment: it was the common experience of ourselves and our friends and neighbors. In the same way the issues that were fought over in the Revolution and the Civil War, no matter how complex they were, lay for the most part within the daily ambit of responsible men. But now the facts crucial to our most critical policy decisions can be known, by all but a few, only at second hand. In the course of our ordinary activities, who can gain knowledge of Vietnamese politics or the internal tensions of Communist China or the convolutions of Russian policy? Who knows from his own experience the facts on which to base decisions as to atomic arms control or the development of defensive missiles or economic aid to India?

In our political decisions we all react not to a real world of our own knowing but to an envisioned world, an image of the world created in our minds by the media of communication in which we are immersed. It happens moreover that for most of the issues most crucial to us, the sources of that image, the information on which it must be based, are derived from or controlled by the Government. This is true with respect to many aspects of nuclear energy (especially as related to weaponry), to almost every aspect of national defense, and to the more critical problems of international relations. Hence the task of forming an accurate image of a complex and distant problem about which we need to make a judgment is made doubly complex, not only by its inherent difficulty, but by the preponderant influence on the image of the very agencies of Government about whose activities we need to form an opinion. The implications for all our media of communication, including libraries, are obvious.

But if public judgment on public issues has become more difficult, it has also become more determinative. In earlier days of the Republic fundamentally important decisions were taken without substantial public participation and with a minimal pressure from public opinion. This was true of the Constitutional Convention, which met in secret, and of the great diplomatic decisions in the nation's early days, decisions of which the general public was hardly aware. With the increasing effectiveness of the news media, it has become progressively easier to arouse a militant, if not necessarily well-informed, opinion on any issue, an opinion so powerful that it narrowly defines the freedom of choice of the Government. Today the politically possible choices of an Administration on such issues as the Vietnam War are limited by what would be acceptable to a sensitized and clamorous public opinion. Our opinions, and hence the sources of information on which they are based, have become of crucial importance because the Government, in facing the decisions that quite literally determine life or death, can no longer be wiser than we are.

IMPLICATIONS FOR COMMUNICATION

The constellation of social changes so sketchily described above has imposed enormous demands on all our means of disseminating information. It has become a challenge to sustain the enlarged formal education programs, to keep fresh the knowledge and skills of all professionals, to operate our complex economy and society, and to enforce our political decisions. Society has responded with an enormously increased machinery of communication. The role of the library has been affected both by the increased demand for the communication of information and by changes in the pattern of the other means of communication with which it shares the response to that demand.

The four postwar developments in communications having the most important implications for the library appear to be:

1. The creation and widespread distribution of inexpensive paperbound books.
2. The great growth of news magazines and their replacement of the newspaper as the dominant printed news medium.
3. The rise of television.
4. The development of a new technology in information storage, retrieval, and dissemination.

THE MASS AUDIENCE

Paperbound books are an old invention, but their modern distribution through magazine sales channels was initiated in the late 1930's. An immediately promising development was inhibited by wartime limitations, but the manufacture of large quantities of paperbacks for Government use in the armed forces and in overseas distribution gave an opportunity to improve their physical production. The publishing industry was ready to go into paperbacks on a large scale as soon as the war ended, and by the mid-1950's paperback publications had achieved a major nationwide position.

Initially emphasis was given to the publication of popular informational books, light fiction, Westerns, and detective stories. It was found, however, that the public was ready to buy almost any good book in large quantities if inexpensively priced, and soon most successful books were appearing in paperback within one to two years after their original appearance in hard covers.

Paperbounds initially were published by magazine companies, like Dell and Popular Library, or by companies like Pocket Books, Bantam, and New American Library, which produced only mass-market paperbounds. In either case they sought their market through national magazine distributors, through magazine wholesalers in individual marketing areas, and through newsstands, tobacco shops, railway and bus stations, supermarkets, and other retail outlets in which books had not been traditionally sold. In the mid-1950's traditional book publishers entered the paperback field with books that were printed in smaller editions, that were somewhat better printed and bound, and that sold at higher prices in traditional bookstores. Initially the paperbounds produced by such publishers were aimed primarily at a college market and were rather formidably erudite.

As the years passed, the distinction between these two types of paperbacks became blurred. Mass-market paperbacks now reproduce the classics in millions of copies, seek out schools and colleges as a major market, and overlap in price those produced in more traditional patterns. The confluence of these two streams of paperbacks results in the issuance of about 8,000 titles a year, the availability in paper of about 45,000 works, and an annual sale of about 350 million copies. Substantially all the world's standard literature now exists in inexpensive editions, together with an impressive proportion of standard historical, philosophical, and critical works and an array of basic surveys in all fields of science. As mentioned above, most popular new books appear in inexpensive editions within one to two years of their original publication.

Though many libraries have made significant use of paperbacks in their own services, the principal significance to them of the growth of paperbacks has been to provide an alternative means of access to books, thus relieving libraries of pressures to perform certain services. The two most obvious examples are the provision of light fiction, mysteries, and Westerns to the general public and the provision of material for outside reading assignments of students. The convenient availability of recreational reading on the newsstands has lessened the demand on libraries to provide routine fiction. This is one of the factors that has tended to direct the function of the library away from recreation and toward information and study. It is reflected in the radical shift in the proportions of fiction and nonfiction circulation since the war and in the tendency of circulation figures to rise less rapidly than other measures of public library service.

The availability in inexpensive editions of standard literary and historical works not only has permitted their much wider use in teaching, but has relieved the college library in particular of the necessity of stocking and circulating multiple, sometimes a hundred or more, copies of each of numerous works assigned on class reading-lists, thus freeing staff and book funds for more extensive services.

Television and the rising dominance of newsmagazines have shared in two developments with major implications for libraries. One development is the greater range, vividness, and immediacy of information available to the general public. The other is the centralization of sources of information and values. Actually the weekly magazine with a substantial news content antedates even the Civil War, and the modern weekly newsmagazine is a product of the 1920's. The real impact of the magazine as a national news medium came with transportation and production developments of the recent postwar decades. For tens of millions of Americans, by the mid-1960's three or four national newsmagazines had superseded the twenty-five hundred different local newspapers as their principal printed source of national and international news.

Magazine coverage of news, especially of social, economic, cultural, and foreign events, was much more extensive and perceptive than that of all but a handful of daily papers. The newsmagazines helped to create on the part of tens of millions of Americans at least a superficial familiarity with categories of affairs of which previous generations had been almost entirely ignorant.

Perhaps even more significant was the fact that most Americans of high school education or better were now tending to look to national rather than local sources of news. It is true that the local newspapers had relied on national press associations as a central source of news, so that the same AP or UPI dispatch might be printed in hundreds of local newspapers. But the press-service stories were narrowly factual and objective. Placement in the paper, headlines, treatment, and editorial comment were all determined locally. The result was that people in different cities, and even those within individual cities that had competing newspapers, might receive quite divergent impressions of events or conditions. Today most Americans with high school or better education are likely to receive their impressions of national or international events from one of a very few sources, each presenting the news vividly and compellingly, few hesitating to editorialize heavily in its presentation, and all of which have substantially similar general concepts.

This trend toward the blanketing of the country by a penetrating and persuasive depiction of the current world emanating from a few closely similar national sources was enormously strengthened by the postwar development of television. The impact of this invention came suddenly in the postwar years, when technical skills and materials were released. A considerable national network of television stations was in existence by 1950, and by 1955 the nation was blanketed. Widespread sale of sets followed: two thirds of all homes had TV sets by 1955, nearly nine tenths by 1960; and today more homes have television sets than have bathtubs or flush toilets.

Estimates of the amount of time the average American spends in front of his television set are probably unreliable, but they suggest that this activity, or inactivity, consumes more time than any other thing that Americans do except for sleep and their jobs. Three networks provide almost all of this bath of communication in which we are immersed—three networks almost indistinguishable in general outlook and character—and only in larger cities does a resident typically have even this range of choice. Television, even more than the newsmagazines, means that one nearly uniform image of the world is created for us and that it is immediate, vivid, and compelling.

Television has affected libraries in many ways. It has become the predominant leisure-time activity of Americans, and its impact on reading was widely feared at first. The time devoted to TV has been taken primarily from radio-listening, movie-going, and simple idleness, but some of it, no doubt, has indeed been taken from reading. The reading displaced by television was probably of a very light recreational character: murderers and cattle rustlers have been pursued across the cathode-ray tube rather than across the page. Television has joined with paperbounds in diminishing the importance of the library as a center for light recreation, freeing its resources to respond to demands for information and other needs not readily served by the newsstand or the television set.

Television has undoubtedly done a great deal to stimulate these more-demanding calls on the library. Viewers by the tens of millions have seen with their own eyes glimpses of war in Korea, the Middle East, and Vietnam; racial confrontations in the South and in northern ghettos; the spoilage of rivers and lakes and forests; the takeoff of space flights; the new wonders of science; and indeed the whole range of changes and problems with which we are confronted. They have seen political conventions in session and come into intimate contact with hundreds of candidates for office. A consequence has been a far greater awareness of and concern for events beyond the daily lives of individuals than we have ever known. This is reflected in the much higher proportion of citizens voting than in pretelevision days, in the intensity of public opinion, and (in a degree relatively pitifully small but absolutely quite large) in the stimulation of further serious inquiry that brings citizens to the library. Some libraries themselves have made a moderately effective use of television as a means of informing the public of the library's resources and of promoting their use.

THE INDIVIDUAL AUDIENCE

But the more profound implication for the library lies in the transformation of the communications environment within which we all live. The net effect of all the social and technological innovations of the last generation has been not only to increase enormously the quantity of information disseminated and the number of people reached, but also to increase enormously the power and influence of the communicators. Primitive forms of communication tend to be one-to-one—the face-to-face dialogue, the personal letter—and some modern technological devices (e.g., the telephone) continue to serve this sort of personal communication. But, in general, every technical or social advance in communication, from the invention of printing onward, has tended to amplify the power of the speaker, to make it possible for him to reach a larger and larger audience.

The ratios of listeners to one speaker, or readers to one writer, have been astronomically increased by the latest generation of social and technical communications, which have at the same time made possible a more vivid and compelling presentation than was ever possible with earlier means. The author who could reach hundreds in the days before printing could reach thousands after Gutenberg, hundreds of thousands after the invention of the steam-powered press and machine-produced paper, and millions with paperback production and modern book-publishing techniques. Until our century a speaker could not be heard beyond the natural range of his voice, and an audience of a few thousand was enormous. First radio and then television have given him access to audiences that easily number in the tens of millions. And they have offered an immediacy that print cannot give, an immediacy heightened in the case of television by a visual sense of personal presence.

Mass publishing, motion pictures, and network radio and television have combined to create the typical pattern of communication of our generation; it links single sources of information or ideas with audiences of millions, or tens of millions, and enables communicators to utilize all the resources of sound and image to create a persuasive illusion of immediate, even intimate, contact. The number of speakers who can gain access to this enormously powerful instrument is limited by its nature. Anyone can talk to his friends or write a letter; almost anyone has a chance, if he seeks it, to address a group face to face; many can speak over local radio stations or write letters to the editor of the local newspaper. But obviously only a handful of people can gain access, or choose those who have access, to the microphones, cameras, and presses of the truly mass media. While the number of communicators is severely restricted by the new technology, the power granted to the centers of communication is enormous and unprecedented. There has never been anything remotely like it before in human history.

Almost alone among the devices of our society in reversing this ratio and linking the single reader or listener or seeker to myriad sources of information, ideas, and inspirations among which he can choose, rather than linking the single voice or image to an audience of millions, is the library. It is our one major communications device that deals with an audience as individuals and communicators as a collection rather than the other way about. As such, it is the specific complement of the mass media.

This is by no means a theoretic consideration. In the exceptionally complex and elusive reality that we confront in Vietnam, for example, we are all necessarily dependent on a reflected image of the actualities of that distant land in arriving at our views of public policy. For most Americans that image is shaped primarily by network television and a few national magazines, and to a lesser degree by the more pallid press association reports. There may be no conscious bias in any of these media, yet at best they can present only a superficial depiction of a most complex actuality. And the picture they present will be heavily influenced by the view of reality held by the Government, which, of course, the Government hopes all will share. Statements of high officers of the Government are in themselves newsworthy and have ready access to the mass media, and the Government is usually the most authoritative and often the only source of facts. Hence, though there may be debate, even heated controversy, over how to respond to the situation in Vietnam, or rather to the image of that situation shared by most Americans, there is little difference about the image itself. The framework within which the problem is conceived is fixed.

Shallow and superficial though the mass-media-created image may be, it is vividly implanted. It would be most difficult for any Administration to alter course and respond to any conception of the Vietnam reality radically different from that now commonly accepted. And quite apart from the rightness or wrongness of any conception of the Vietnam reality or of any comparable situation, *no* conception of it that has been given currency by the mass media can avoid being an oversimplification. There is an almost inescapable tendency to overreact in one way or another to an image that has been oversimplified from reality.

It is, of course, idyllic to assume that all or most or even many of those whose views have been shaped on the simple and uniform pattern of the mass media will resort to the library for extensive reading to amplify, correct, and provide detail for their image of world affairs. And certainly if even one percent of those who read about Vietnam in

Time or see it discussed on TV were to call on libraries for more serious books on the subject, library service would collapse under the burden. Some dozens of books have been published on Vietnam in the last few years, several of them excellent. Yet very few indeed have sold more than 15,000 copies, and most fewer than 5,000. To serve more than 100 million adults, I would guess, there are probably no more than 10,000 or 15,000 copies of significant books on Vietnam in American public libraries—hardly more than enough to lend a copy to every ten-thousandth adult.

But it is extremely important that the library be available and be greatly strengthened to offer its diversity to the lone inquirer, to the small but leavening number who will seek to shape a more valid image of the realities we must encounter—the writers, the speakers, the leaders who will guide our nation's response. And with every further and inevitable strengthening of the mass media, satisfying the lone inquirer will become yet more necessary.

TECHNOLOGICAL DEVELOPMENTS

The final set of changes in communications media with major implications for the library is the development of new technologies in recording, storing, retrieving, and reproducing documents and the information they contain. So dazzling is this new technology that it has led to predictions that the traditional library will be replaced by new kinds of information systems operating independently of the library, or that the library itself will be transformed into a very different kind of institution. Prophets of the library of the future have envisioned its holdings as embodied in microforms, in tapes, or in the memory cores of computers. They have assumed that its users will communicate, by dialing or similar devices, the identification number of the document and perhaps of the page or passage they wish to consult, the subject on which they want information, or perhaps even the question to which they want an answer. The library, operating through computers, would display on cathode-ray tubes or print-out the desired information or passages or references in consoles at the library itself or at remote terminals in a home, office, study, or laboratory. Connections between libraries would enable a user of one to draw on the resources of all of those so linked.

The technology for such miracles is indeed, for the most part, available. The microreproduction of documents can be carried to incredible degrees. The memory capacity of computers has been enormously increased, and immediate access to any part of the memory without awaiting the relatively slow scanning of tapes has been made possible. Cathode-ray display and almost instant hard-copy reproduction, even at a great distance, are now within our technical capacity. Great ingenuity has been shown in developing systems for indexing documents and for identifying them or portions of them in terms of subject or other characteristics so that they can be instantly retrieved when the proper clues are provided.

Elsewhere in this book, particularly in chapter 7, there is a detailed consideration of the new technology available for library and related purposes. However, it is appropriate here to consider some of the broader implications for the library of the new communications technology as one of the major transforming forces in our society.

The most widely discussed potential impact—the transformation of library collections into microform or digital-computer memories and the use of computer technology for retrieval—will probably be the least significant and the least likely to occur on a large scale. Assumptions that such a transformation will occur are likely to ignore or give insufficient weight to three considerations. One is that a majority of users of most libraries are not seeking specific information or specific brief passages but rather the opportunity to read a text at leisure, whenever they choose, in attractive and portable format capable of being read without access to special equipment. Service to this majority of readers will require that most of the holdings of most libraries will need to be retained in more or less conventional forms capable of being removed and read elsewhere, even if the same holdings are also incorporated in an information storage and retrieval system. This will mean that the cost of transforming the collections into newer formats is usually an addition to, rather than a replacement of, other costs, thus eliminating the economies that might be hoped for.

Another neglected consideration is that the major part of the task of finding desired documents or facts is now accomplished by casual visual inspection, by browsing on the part of the user or the library staff. Any system that makes a collection of documents inaccessible for this sort of inspection enormously increases the task of subject analysis, indexing, and bibliographical control necessary for its effective use. For example, a secretary or file clerk can make do with rather inefficient and disorderly files so long as she can hunt through them herself; but if they are to be microfilmed, the most careful arrangement, insertion of headings, and indexing are necessary to retain their utility. Since the cost of such controls, even at their simplest, is normally the principal cost of administering a collection, any further increase is likely to far more than offset any possible savings in cost through reduction to a more easily stored form.

The third consideration is that the principal benefit the typical user wants from an information retrieval system is not assurance that it has identified and included all the documents that may relate to his interests, but rather assurance that it has *excluded* all documents except the minimum necessary to serve his purposes. The swift and feeble-minded patience of the computer is perfectly adapted to searching a collection of documents and identifying all those that have certain predesignated characteristics, thus assuring the inquirer (if the cataloging has been thoroughly done) that he knows about *everything* in the collection in any way relating to his subject. But this very undiscriminating thoroughness means that the computer will dredge up in the process vast quantities of only superficially or nominally relevant junk. Narrowing the search is achieved by multiplying the number of descriptors (terms used to define more precisely the kind of documents sought). Even when this technique is carried to its maximum practical limits, it is characteristic of computer-based information retrieval systems that they tend to overwhelm the inquirer with unusable masses of repetitious citations or other data.

To date, such systems have usually been applied to very limited bodies of documents (rarely more than 100,000 and usually much fewer), of relatively homogeneous content, that are available to a small class of users, all of whom are experienced in the techniques of computer search. If such systems were to be developed in order to embrace documents numbered in the tens or hundreds of millions rather than tens of thousands, covering an infinite range of subjects, and used by an unlimited body of inquirers seeking unpredictable combinations of information in unpredictable ways, the problems would almost certainly become not only vastly larger but of an altogether different kind. In particular, the propensity of automated retrieval systems to retrieve comprehensively and undiscriminatingly would become an uncontrollable disaster. Imagine the problem of devising limiting descriptors that would yield from the holdings of the Library of Congress appropriate citations and data for a student doing a thesis on Lincoln's foreign policy or on the second day of the Battle of Gettysburg, or even for an inquirer who wanted to know something as simple as the date of Lincoln's death!

But if the computer is most unlikely to replace the traditional library, it and other creatures of the new technology will nevertheless affect the library's functions in many important ways. One is in the daily conduct of business. It seems quite clear that it will be possible to devise systems that will enable the library's acquisitions, cataloging, circulation, inventory, and statistical work to be automated, with important increases in efficiency. It also seems clear that these systems, if compatible among libraries, as they will surely be, can contribute greatly to the ease of centralized cataloging and bibliographical control, with important savings for all. Similarly, as facsimile transmission becomes cheaper, it may replace many interlibrary loans and make rare holdings in central libraries much more accessible.

Less directly, the new technology will greatly amplify the range of research capability in organizing and making inductions from masses of raw data. This may make tractable for research purposes manuscript collections, census returns, ephemeral publications, and other materials now rarely used. In other ways this may also impose demands on research libraries that cannot now be easily anticipated.

Perhaps the most important consequence, for libraries, of the new information technology is that its use in Government and in business makes it possible to organize and administer programs of an otherwise impossible complexity. The balance between littleness and bigness has been markedly shifted by the computer. Hitherto the obvious efficiencies of large-scale operation have been offset by the cost and the cumbersomeness of large-scale administrative overhead, with the result that maximum efficiency in any undertaking has been achieved at some median point of size. Computer technology can lower the cost and greatly improve the effectiveness of large-scale operation, placing the point of maximum efficiency much higher on the scale of complexity.

Every increase in the complexity of society, in turn, multiplies the creation and the consumption of information, placing new demands on all media of communication, including libraries. The larger corporations, the more extensive technological enterprises, the vaster Governmental operations, and the more complex and sophisticated social interrelations generally will all produce and use great quantities of documents. The future will require a higher level of informational content for participants in society generally.

Finally, it should be pointed out that many of the above-mentioned obstacles to more extensive use of computers for the actual storage and retrieval of information (as distinguished from bibliographical control) derive from the fact that we are trying to transform into computer-usable form information originally expressed in ways and in physical forms essentially incompatible with the computer. In part this is a matter of simple physical format: it is enormously, indeed prohibitively, expensive to incorporate texts into a computer manually by keyboarding or punch-card devices. Optical scanners might be able to perform this task economically, but they are likely to be defeated by the enormous variety of type faces, ideographs, formulas, symbols, and graphs used in texts originally prepared for other purposes with no thought of their use in an optical scanner.

In part the difficulty relates to the physical form of symbols used. Western languages are recorded in alphabets in ways intended to suggest the pronunciation of each word. Some Oriental languages are expressed in ideographs not associated with spoken words but, originally at least, with the appearance of the object or act referred to. The incompatibility of these two systems impedes East-West communication; observe, for example, the difficulties in the input of Chinese ideographs into a typewriter or linotype machine conceived for alphabetic language. Quite similarly, both alphabetic and ideographic systems are incompatible with efficient computer input, which needs no suggestions of pronunciation or appearance and cannot without waste incorporate the excess baggage of symbolic devices used for these purposes in writing and printing.

In part the difficulties are more fundamental. Speech, including its written form, relates to the reality to which it refers in the same way the human mind does. It is ambiguous and imprecise, metaphorical and suggestive, laden with emotional overtones, implicative and connotative rather than explicit and denotative. In other words, it describes not reality but the human apperception of reality. The literal-minded computer is at a loss in understanding and handling this essentially poetic instrument. It needs symbols that mean one thing and one thing only, that do not change their meanings, and that are each the only symbol used for the particular referent. The need for this sort of language was not born with computers; it accounts for the special languages of the sciences and professions, the Latin names for plants and animals, the Latin and Greek terminology of medicine, the symbols of mathematics and logic. But the computer makes the need acute: it cannot deal with the living human being who has a bank account, or even efficiently with the spelled-out name that identifies him, but only with a unique number that identifies one account and one account only. It cannot efficiently translate from one language to another when neither has the qualities of precision and stability required for a compatible set of one-to-one relations with the same aspects of reality.

Many of the inefficiencies of the computer for data storage and retrieval systems arise from its having to deal with data that have already been expressed in ways suited to conventional language and unsuited to the computer. It can realize its true efficiency only when dealing with data expressed from the beginning in appropriate form. This is increasingly the case now. By substituting numerical symbols for words, all sorts of transactions can be recorded, analyzed, and recalled, and the recordings can be transmitted entirely within a computer system. Only specialized kinds of information, susceptible to this degree of abstraction, can be handled in this way. For those kinds of information we will increasingly skip the whole inefficient process of recording in written or printed symbols for human speech and will use the computer directly.

Hence the future will see increasingly enormous banks of data (like census returns) embodied from the beginning in computers and not input at second hand from printed documents. The custody of these data banks is a librarylike function and one of rapidly increasing importance; whether it can more effectively be performed by libraries or by more specialized institutions will depend in part upon the degree to which a computer capacity will have been developed by libraries for administration, cataloging, and bibliographical purposes.

EMERGING LIBRARY RESPONSIBILITIES

This swift review has endeavored to describe the recent social changes that have defined the principal responsibilities of libraries today and shaped the context within which libraries operate. Perhaps five principal responsibilities emerge:

1. To support formal education, from prekindergarten through graduate and professional schools.
2. To sustain the increasingly complex operations of the Government and the economy of the country.
3. To provide opportunities for continuing self-education and retraining.
4. To play a role in the reintegration into the society of groups now largely isolated and excluded by their lacks in education and training.
5. To provide resources for an informed public opinion and for personal cultural and intellectual growth and individuation.

DEMOGRAPHIC TRENDS

Most of the trends described in earlier sections of this report will undoubtedly continue through the foreseeable future, and their impact on the library will simply be emphasized rather than altered. There are certain developments, however, that will be new or will take a somewhat new direction.

One is the reversal of the trend toward an annually increasing number of births. From a peak level of about 4.3 million births annually from 1957 through 1961, the number has declined annually, with increasing speed, to 3,806,000 in 1965 and 3,629,000 in 1966. Beginning in 1968, this will be reflected in a decline in the number of children entering the first grade. Over the following eight years, to 1976, the number of elementary school students enrolled will first level off and then significantly decline. The decline in births will, however, be reversed as the children of the postwar decade mature to parenthood; by the end of the 1970's this counterdevelopment will have reversed the trend, and elementary school enrollments will again be moving up.

For the decade of the 1970's, however, we shall have a breathing spell in the race to provide elementary school facilities. This does not necessarily mean a lessening in the need for better library resources in the elementary school. On the contrary, the pressures for better, more comprehensive, and more individualized instruction at the elementary school level are reasonably certain to do far more than offset the leveling-off and eventual temporary decline in enrollments. Indeed relief from the pressure of the need for new buildings and of shortages of professional personnel should make it possible to achieve goals of elementary school library service that are now unattainable.

The impact of birth-rate changes on the high school will be delayed. It will be 1976 before the number of children reaching high-school-entering age will begin to decline, and near the end of the decade before the total number of high-school-age students reverses its present growth. Meanwhile, for a number of years to come there will continue to be a rapid growth in secondary school enrollments, augmented by a probable further increase in the already extremely high proportion of high-school-age persons who are actually enrolled.

No such leveling-off of college enrollments is in early prospect. Through the 1970's the number of youths of college-entering age will continue to increase from year to year, and there is every reason to suppose that the proportion of them participating in post-high-school education will continue its marked increase. It is quite probable that by the late 1970's we shall have at least ten million students pursuing formal education after high school. A considerable part of this enormous force, however, will probably be enrolled in technical schools of a variety of sorts, and there will probably not be a proportionate increase in traditional formal college education.

Over the next decade the postwar population boom and the revolutionary educational developments of the last two decades will for the first time have their effect on the makeup of the adult population. Between 1967 and 1977 the first children of the postwar era—about forty million of them—will become adults. They will be adults whose whole life experience will be radically different from that of earlier generations. In particular, they will be far better educated and culturally far more sophisticated than any earlier generation. About fifteen million of them will have been to college. A decade hence, the number of college-educated men and women in their twenties in this country will be twice as great as the entire population of Sweden today.

The coming-of-age of this generation will have a vast impact on the American cultural world. In literature, music, art, ballet, and theater there has already been a surge of audience growth, even when the educated adult population was growing only slowly. The sudden influx of these millions of sophisticated young people will enormously increase the audience for higher-level cultural experiences and will elevate and enlarge the demands on public libraries.

NEW SOCIAL EMPHASIS

Meanwhile, the swift movement toward a highly technical, science-based society will not only continue but will be accelerated. The consumption of scientific, technical, and professional information in the society will be enormous. The needs for library resources for the administration of Government agencies and corporations and for the practice of professions will continue to grow. So will the need for access to the resources of libraries for continuing self-education. The shift from activities governed by habit and word-of-mouth communication to activities involving the use of print and other formal media of communication will be even more pronounced.

But the continued emphasis on high-level training and extensive reliance on complex written materials will make all the more complete and oppressive the exclusion of the uneducated and semiliterate from full participation in society. Perhaps the most dramatic of all the probable developments of the next decade relating to libraries, and to educational institutions and services generally, will arise from the necessity of grappling really seriously with the problem thus presented.

We have already become painfully aware of the existence of quite literally tens of millions of such men and women and children as they have been dislodged from the plantations and farms of the South, the mines of Appalachia, the sugar plantations of Puerto Rico, and similar areas where their poverty had been hidden and their labor had value that gave them a social function. Palliative welfare appropriations have been made, a beginning recognition of special education needs has come with the enactment of the Elementary and Secondary Education Act of 1965, and there have been some experiments in adapting libraries to the special needs of this group.

To date, however, the efforts to integrate the excluded poor, whether white or Negro, into the advancing technological society have been small and feeble. The situation in the larger northern core cities has continued to disintegrate into ever more frightening chaos. Almost certainly in the coming decade far more large-scale efforts will be made to achieve this integration as the present situation becomes totally intolerable.

This will require not only more money but a rather radical redesign of some of our social institutions and programs. Our educational system, broadly defined to include libraries, has always assumed the continuing existence of a large class of workers having limited need for literacy. Until the latter nineteenth century we were quite content that almost all Negroes and many whites should be totally unschooled. Even after universal education, at least through the elementary school level, became a uniformly accepted and usually achieved goal, there was no serious commitment to giving the entire population training that could enable them to play skilled roles in the developing technological society. Indeed there was an active opposition to education for the "lower" classes, especially for Negroes, that might make them dissatisfied with the performance of unskilled labor for meager pay.

Library services and educational opportunities above the elementary school level that were available to the unskilled laboring classes were intended to provide exceptional youths with the opportunity to escape from that class. They continued to represent the values, the vocabularies, and the attitudes of the cultured class. A Negro or immigrant child who learned the Latin and algebra of the high school and went on to college, who found in the library an opening door to a world of the highly literate mind, left his own cultural environment and joined another. He left his cultural home to join the more privileged world; the educated society did not reach out to encompass him. The children with whom he grew up mostly stayed where they were. The society of the time, through its schools and libraries, had no intention of transforming the great class of illiterate or semiliterate ill-paid workers, for whom society had a great need; indeed any effort to elevate this whole class of workingmen would have met active social resistance.

Now the whole problem has changed. Schools and libraries can no longer function as a means of providing a ladder by which bright and ambitious "lower-class" youths can climb out into the middle class. They need to be instruments to transform the whole class itself, since society no longer has a need or a role for unskilled labor. This means that these institutions can no longer merely passively offer the vocabulary, skills, and values of the educated class to those willing to adopt them. It means that these institutions themselves, on a massive scale, must enter into the lives and relate to the values of the whole population that has hitherto lived beyond their scope. This will present a profound challenge to all social service agencies in areas of poverty, including libraries. The changes in core-city school and public libraries over the next decade will need to be quite radical in character.

THE CHALLENGE

The total impact of the rapid and massive sweep of social change within which we live will obviously be to increase the nation's quantitative demand for library services at all levels. But more importantly, it will spotlight the seriousness of that demand. As our society becomes increasingly information-based, as the mastery of complex bodies of information becomes more essential to every aspect of its management, and indeed to individual functioning within the society, the library will become a more essential operating component of society. From an institution with rather general educational, cultural, and recreational aims, functioning—however worthily—somewhat on the margins of our central concerns, the library will increasingly become a part of our essential machinery for dealing with these concerns.

The greater seriousness, the greater centrality, of the library's role will justify, indeed will require, a much larger public support. But it will also impose a much heavier responsibility upon libraries and the library profession: a responsibility to use the new technology wherever it is useful, to raise and broaden professional standards, to develop broad and imaginative patterns of national cooperation, and to express in daily operations a keen and pervasive sense of the library's enlarged social commitment.

CHAPTER II

THE NONSPECIALIST AND PRESPECIALIST USER OF LIBRARY AND INFORMATIONAL SERVICES

Early in the deliberations of the National Advisory Commission on Libraries it became clear that the members wished to try to identify the nation's needs for library and informational services. Their focus was on people: the users of these services and those who should be induced to become users, the people who need services that are not readily available to them, and the people who provide these services. The Commission concluded that there were basic commonalities characterizing all users, in spite of great diversity, and that the total picture should be reflected in its objectives (see chapter 12, section C).

Education, inextricably bound with research impact, emerged as the most potent force that has affected and will continue to affect every kind of need for library and informational service. This is obvious of course in formal education and very advanced specialized research, less so perhaps with respect to the general public. Chapter 3 of this book discusses the specialized needs of the scholarly user, the scientific research user, and the professional user. The present chapter is devoted to the needs of the undifferentiated general public and of the students (and faculty) at the prespecialist levels of formal education. As it turns out, the needs of the nonspecialists and prespecialists are sometimes highly specialized in fact.

Chapter 2 consists of six separate but related papers organized into three sections. Section A presents evidence of the librarian's view of public library use, section B presents the user's view of public libraries, and section C describes library functions in support of elementary, secondary, and undergraduate college education.

A. THE LIBRARIAN'S VIEW OF PUBLIC LIBRARIES

Although not intended to be comparable, two different studies commissioned by the National Advisory Commission on Libraries shed light on what the library profession itself thinks about the users and uses, present and potential, of public libraries in the shifting society of the United States. Both reports appear below, constituting section **A** of chapter 2.

The similarities in the results are notable, and not only in the more obvious respects; e.g., financial and personnel problems, impact of education, failure to attract the disadvantaged. Both also show some broad awareness of social forces, and both urge shattering traditional attitudes and experimenting with new alignments.

It should be noted that the two respondent groups are quite different. The first is a nationwide sample of 134 public librarians, no doubt somewhat select in terms of interest and enthusiasm; the second is a very select group of 14 experts in the profession, not all of whom have had public library experience. The front-line public librarians appear considerably more willing to initiate new ventures toward the goal of serving, and even creating, user needs than the experts give them credit for. This suggests a lively participative role for public librarians in implementing a national policy of services that truly meet the nation's needs.

1. SOCIAL FACTORS
AND PUBLIC LIBRARY USE:
OPINIONS OF PUBLIC LIBRARIANS[1]

A questionnaire survey entitled "Major Social Changes Affecting Library Service in the United States" was conducted as part of the same study that produced chapter 1 of this book. There were four respondent groups: public librarians, school librarians, college librarians, and members of the Board of the National Book Committee. Only the results of the public librarian survey are discussed in this section, which concentrates on the librarian's view of what public libraries are doing, could do, and should do to serve the needs of the people in a changing society.

Of a total of 272 questionnaires sent to selected public libraries of all sizes, nationwide, 134 were returned and analyzed under considerable time pressure. Highlights of this reponse are summarized in Table 2A–1.1, and the regional distribution is shown in Table 2A–1.2; all states were represented, with the exception of Alaska, the District of Columbia, Hawaii, Kentucky, Nevada, South Dakota, and West Virginia. The response of 13 out of 38 state library agency heads is included in the analysis.

USER CONSIDERATIONS

Shifts in Clientele

Most of the public libraries in this survey (107 out of 134) have experienced growth in the population of their service areas since 1955—an increase of no less than 10 percent, and in a few cases of 100 percent (Table 2A–1.3). Only 7 cited a population decline; 20 cited no change. It does not appear, however, that many public libraries have attracted a notably increased share of their increasing numbers of potential clients over the last decade, although 98 have noted some growth in the proportion of the population they are reaching with library services (Table 2A–1.4). Surely they are serving increased numbers. Of 117 public librarians who estimated their clientele, well over half felt that at least 40 percent of their service area population were, if not registered borrowers, at least users of the library.

Some interesting relationships between population rise and library use can be gleaned from the questionnaires. For example, in Scranton, Pennsylvania, a decline in

[1] *From* Social Change and the Library: 1945–1980, *a study by the National Book Committee commissioned by the National Advisory Commission on Libraries in 1967. The questionnaire survey of public librarians was conducted by Virginia H. Mathews, Staff Associate, National Book Committee.*

city population of 10 percent was paired with a rise of 5–10 percent in the percentage of library users; in Dallas the library-user percentage of growth was higher than the percentage of growth in population of the area. Circulation in the 19 major libraries in Idaho was up 93 percent. There had been a recent regional planning commission survey in Cuyahoga County, Ohio, showing that 45.9 percent of the sample questioned had used the library within six weeks of the interview.[2]

Of 129 libraries responding to the question, all but 5 noted a shift in the use of library facilities. The majority said that more people are using the main or central library facility; 68 noted more use of branches, as opposed to 15 who thought that branches are less used; more use of bookmobiles was cited by 56 libraries, less use by 31. Study center extensions were more used in 20 cases, less in one; 14 libraries noted more use of deposit station or drop, while 30 noted less use.

Responses to the question "Has there been a change in the character of the clientele you now serve as compared with 1955?" were fascinating in their sameness from all parts of the country. There were 97 libraries that said "Yes," they have noticed a change; 12 said "No." The nature of the change? Among the differences cited, the most frequent was more businessmen users. Also, more adults generally from all walks of life, especially men; more students of all ages; more lower-class, low-income children and adults; more preschool children and fewer elementary-school-age children as schools develop good school libraries at the elementary level, and yet more high school students, though many presumably have relatively good libraries at their schools. There appear to be fewer readers of light fiction and people using the library for recreational purposes, as opposed to more using it for cultural enrichment and purposeful self-development.

Increased use by students enrolled in community or commuter colleges was noted everywhere. One librarian pinpointed the high point of the "student use upsurge" as between 1955 and 1962, with a "leveling-off period" from 1962 to 1965. Student use now, though increasingly heavy from both college and high school students, seems to be balanced by the upsurge of other kinds of adult use. Users of the library were characterized at one end of the spectrum as being more sophisticated, seeking specialized material, and at the other end as being of lower educational attainment and requiring new kinds of simple, easy-to-read materials. More middle- and upper-income-level users were noted in many places, as were blue-collar high-skill workingmen. The comment was made over and over that better school libraries are changing the program of children's work and its target audience; middle-class children will use school libraries, and public library emphasis will turn to preschool programs, especially those geared to lower economic groups.

Library use patterns have been changing (Table 2A–1.5). According to respondent opinion, all kinds of people seem to be using the library more: young people, older people, women, men. Frequency of use; number of books, periodicals, paperbacks, records, tapes, and films borrowed; attendance at recreation and information programs; and use of reference services were characterized as "More" for all the above groups, except for older people, who show less use of reference service. No categories of library-goers use notably more fiction, and young people and men demand less fiction, women patrons about the same amount, and older people slightly more. Information and recreation programs for all categories show a rise, and several respondents added films and large-type books to the other categories given them.

The present clientele of the public library was seen as more purposeful by all of the 126 people who answered the query concerning characteristics of clients: better educated, taken as a whole, by all but 6 respondents; more cultured by all but 12 respondents; and more at home in the library by all but 7 of those who replied. In commenting

---

2 *This result is rather heartening when compared with the nationwide public apathy revealed in the poll of adults conducted for the National Advisory Commission on Libraries and reported in section B.2 of this chapter. It suggests some notable regional differences, an impression borne out by the regional hearings held by the Commission.*

on this question, many cited greater sophistication in library use, more demand for depth service, and more awareness of what to expect of a good library. Many also cited the mobile nature of the population and the decentralization of research as positive factors in providing more vocal supporters of tax support for good library service.

Meeting User Needs

There was a firmly checked "No" from 105 respondents in answer to the question "Do you feel that your library has responded quickly enough and fully enough to the needs of the disadvantaged?" Most of those who checked "Yes" (23) qualified their reply in some way: "Quickly," yes, so certainly not "fully" or "enough"; "Yes," but without any visible success so far, etc. The greatest success and evidently the greatest effort, among those who felt they had made any effort worthy of mention, was with the children, usually the preschool children, of the poor. One librarian in a medium-sized city with a critical poverty problem commented, "Anyone who answers 'Yes' to this question is nuts!" But both the need and the desire for the public library to try to cope effectively were apparently foremost in the minds of nearly every respondent.

The majority of librarians (123) felt that they had indeed made progress in making the library more user-oriented; 6 said "No" but in such a way as to indicate it wasn't for the lack of honest effort; 87 have cut complex routines; 64 have longer open hours, with from 60 to 75 hours a week mentioned frequently; 51 have more evening hours; and 86 mentioned taking resources and services where the people are. One state librarian expressed the opinion that all local facilities built in the future should be built with easy entrance for the elderly and handicapped in mind. A number of people mentioned new services to prisoners, nursing homes, and shut-ins. Others mentioned development of a common card for all libraries in an area, no card needed at all, orientation programs, returns to any library agency of materials borrowed from any other, no fines, and a more people-oriented staff. One library mentioned using volunteer community welcomers at the door to find out in general the kind of service wanted and to take the would-be patron to the right helper or department.

PROGRAMS AND SERVICES

Functions and Philosophy

The great majority of respondents thought that the library's cultural, self-renewal, and recreational functions have improved, but many of these felt that they have not kept pace with the reference and information function. All but 7 people out of 129 responding felt that the cultural, self-renewal, and recreational functions will gain in importance in the decade ahead, as material needs are met and education generally is upgraded.

Some interesting answers were given in reply to the question of whether there had been any change, in the past decade, in the philosophy of program and service of the library staff: 113 said "Yes"; 17 thought "No." There is extraordinary unanimity as to the nature of the change, though expressed in many different ways: "Much less attention to library routines, more attention to people"; "A more people-oriented staff"; "We feel an urge to go out of the library, meet the people where they are"; "Library must change its methods and develop services to meet changing community needs"; "Library has an obligation to seek users, not wait for them to come!"; "We've become user rather than staff oriented"; "More concerned with the needs of the individual"; "Library more involved in social questions, more willing to experiment, communicate, innovate"; "Change from passive stance to dynamic one"; "Emphasis on *ideas* as the library's stock-in-trade rather than types of materials"; "There is growing awareness among librarians that some other agency may in time replace us if we cannot perform effectively."

Special Programs

Asked about an increase in indirect services, outreach programs involving other agencies, 109 public librarians said "Yes"; 84 libraries are involved with adult education, 40 of these with literacy programs; 78 with antipoverty agencies or programs; 54 with health and welfare agencies; 34 with employment. Also mentioned were literacy and job-development programs with the labor department, programs and collections at a variety of neighborhood sites, day-care centers, a thrift shop (Spanish-speaking), a clubhouse for senior citizens, bookmobiles to factories and plants. Many mentioned programs with migrants, Head Start children and parents, Neighborhood Youth Corps and Job Corps youngsters.

As for changes in the number of individuals seeking reading guidance, 77 respondents noticed an increase in those who seek personal guidance, as compared with 31 who noted a decrease, 8 who saw no change, and 18 who did not respond to the question. The response suggests that the increase may be influenced by the fact that more people are motivated to read for cultural background and self-improvement, rather than for pleasure, and by the concomitant fact that there is more staff available to help them. A wider selection of books to choose from, availability of leisure time, intellectual stimulus, and wider interests may also be factors. Comments from among the 31 librarians who saw a decrease in requests for general personal guidance mentioned shortage of competent staff, a higher level of sophistication among readers ("They know what they want"), and reading advice from many other sources (clubs, church, adult classes) as factors decreasing the patron's need for guidance.

The majority of public librarians surveyed apparently felt they had *not* really undertaken any special program (group or individual) for young people that would help them to use books, records, films, and other materials in the development of opinions and values. About one fourth of the respondents had planned young adult programs that stressed "the importance of a wide range of viewpoints in forming opinions," and that they hoped had helped young people to "orient themselves to responsibility" and to "gain some perspective." A number of others expressed hope that they might do this in future, when appropriate staff and budget might make it possible. A few extensive programs mentioned regular discussion groups, film series, creative writing, and other youth activities.

The programming of library materials and services via radio and TV (as opposed to "plugging" library use) is disappointingly meager among the 134 libraries queried. There were 84 Noes compared with 38 Yeses, and 7 more said they used radio as a library medium; 21 "haven't tried"; 50 have no staff to do this professionally; 38 mentioned that this is not a priority for staff time and money. Several expressed disillusionment: "Have tried with no results," presumably having based the effort on the expectation that listeners and viewers would come to the library after the treatment.

On the other hand, those librarians who seem to view the use of radio and TV as an extension of program appeared pleased with their efforts and eager to do more. Richmond, Indiana, has "reached the middle-class, book-oriented public through radio, but not the lower class—yet." Columbia, Missouri, has sponsored programs about interesting people, places, events, and lets viewers know that follow-up is available in the library. Another library, which is trying, said honestly, "We haven't yet learned to promote ideas, just the library." In Nashville, Tennessee, the library owns and operates the FM station and programs ten hours each day. The several libraries that work at it seemed to be saying, "It is very important if you really want to reach people you don't reach in any other way."

The final question of a series on programs and services: "Have pressing needs from certain segments of your clientele caused you to go overboard on any one aspect of program?" Of 127 replying, 105 said "No"; 22 said "Yes"; only a few gave explanations. "Demands from business and industry," said several, with the implication that he who pays the piper calls the tune. "Demanding and vocal college-bound students and their parents" was another comment. One thoughtful librarian mused: "We have gone overboard on physical plant, building new branches instead of making the ones we have better by building up materials and services."

MATERIALS

Respondents were asked to comment on a series of questions about materials: their selection, the types used, and their organization.

Methods of Selection

The great majority of public librarians in this survey, 102, reckoned that more time is being spent in book selection now, as compared with 1955; 17 thought less; 12, the same; only 3 did not respond to the question. Most felt that the increase in the volume of published material and the addition of new types of material, plus the more specialized requirements of more users, necessitated more time spent. Others noted that selection, though more important, is becoming less time-consuming. "Processing centers have improved book selection—librarians have more time for it." One large-city system comments, "With more funds available we tend to be more inclusive, less selective. . . . We used to ask, 'How much will this book be used?' Now we ask, 'Should this book be available in this library?'" Another says, "I see no reason why all books should be reviewed in every library."

Asked if the selection function in libraries will become more or less important, or at least different, 79 said "More"; 7, "Less"; 11, "The same"; and 29, "Different." More books, more money, more people, more selection, was the rationale of most of those who said "More"; the "more" and "different" groups usually cited nonprint-materials selection as complicating the selection process, too. A large-metropolitan-system librarian, however, submitted this thoughtful answer: "Selection will become less important—it is evident that book selection in similar libraries is 80 to 90 percent identical, and a great deal of time is wasted. . . . We are moving toward less time devoted to book selection by most librarians, and more time to individual service. . . . Our book collection has had to increase from 100,000 to 800,000 in just eight years." The "different" category also produced several replies suggesting that fewer and more specialist librarians would be involved in selection and that the situation would of course be profoundly affected by coordination and systems developments.

Asked to characterize the selection of nonbook, nonprint materials, librarians were given four possibilities: innovative and enthusiastic, 24; competent and balanced, 63; uneasy and sporadic, 41; nonexistent, 8. Several implied with wry humor that "competent and balanced" was giving their library the benefit of the doubt, and that probably "uneasy and sporadic" came closer to unvarnished truth!

The involvement of nonlibrarians in the selection of all materials was cited as greater than formerly by 67 public librarians; 61 thought not. Patrons, faculty members, staffs of other community agencies, and other specialists were mentioned as participants. In one research-oriented city a committee of scientists advises on the purchase of scientific material. In another, men from industry have helped in the choice of technical books. Yet at the less sophisticated end of the spectrum several who spoke for small libraries that have only recently established book selection as the librarian's professional task wrote their Noes with feeling! It is in fact the widely diverse interpretations, reactions, and responses to such queries that underscore the unbelievable range and variety of institutions we refer to when we talk of "the public library."

Types Needed and Used

Respondents were asked to make an educated judgment as to what percentage of books and other materials in their libraries were used, for reference or circulation, more than ten times a year. For the most part, numbers of responses to each choice were quite evenly divided (Table 2A–1.6). More interesting than just the straight estimates, however, were the comments of those who broke their figures down between central library and branches. One librarian who is especially wise and experienced said that the "turnover" of materials would be about 15 percent in the main library and more like 40 percent in the branches. Several echoed this spread, reflecting as it does the more popular, frequently used holdings of neighborhood branches.

The great majority of respondents cited a greater and growing need for more books and other materials at both ends of the spectrum; i.e., the very elementary and the highly specialized, with a slight edge to the latter. There were 98 who said they were meeting this need by cooperative purchasing arrangements with other libraries, thus permitting heavy overemphasis or omission of certain specialized areas; 65 indicated they were continuing to provide for "average," or "middle-of-the-road," demands. Use of the state library to supplement was mentioned, as were interlibrary loan, duplicate pay collections, and regional centers. Several said that they were buying more heavily at both ends of the spectrum, where the greatest needs are, and buying less for the average reader.

It appears that in some cases (only 87 librarians responded) significant amounts of money are being allocated to support new programs. Percentages of budget for new materials for these programs are reported in Table 2A–1.7. Programs appear to be most frequently of the outreach variety, addressed to the needs of the disadvantaged or the handicapped.

Asked for the single factor that has most affected the type of material "you buy now as compared with 1955," respondents produced many varieties of answers, all fascinating in their individuality. Most boiled down to: (1) the needs of student users, all ages; (2) the needs of business and industry and of other research and specialized information users; (3) the needs of the undereducated, especially in large and medium-sized cities. But the faint beginnings of the swing back may be discernible in the wistful statement of one librarian, who said, "We cut out light fiction and romance, and now as we serve the old, retired, and homebound, we wonder . . ." One librarian expressed a philosophic-operational shift that seems to fit many colleagues: "Our library now anticipates needs, especially in nonfiction, instead of just responding to requests." This same librarian, from the Deep South, cited as the single factor most affecting the type of materials bought: "the shift from rural-agricultural to urban-diversified . . . more management-level people."

Radical changes over the past ten years in the types of materials used by both high school and college students were noted by 120 respondents. Most attributed this phenomenon to "better teaching with emphasis on independent study and original sources." Others felt that "more kinds of materials accessible" and "more individual responsibility for one's own learning" were more cogent factors than "more unrequired reading," though 47 checked the latter in addition to other possibilities. The general upgrading of education all along the line was a comment volunteered often by respondents.

The group of questions on types of materials included this one: "What kinds of materials would you like to have that you cannot find?" Overwhelmingly the librarians of the country—coming closer to unanimity perhaps than anywhere else on the questionnaire—wrote in the need for easy-reading material with adult content for the functionally illiterate adult. Other interesting needs included collections of information, organized by topic, about legislation in the various states; books for children with reading and learning problems; simply written technical books; popular material in foreign languages; new junior books in science and technology; simple, beginning, how-to-do-it books for adults, "the nonstudent amateur"; good reprints of standard titles; and many more. Good inexpensive 8 mm films were mentioned, more periodicals on microforms, more large-print titles.

Organization and Processing

In this set of questions respondents were asked, "Have you any idea of the total percentage of time spent by all professional librarians in your operation on clerical tasks and technical procedures?" Their response is summarized in Table 2A–1.8. "Have you taken any recent steps to change this percentage?" There were 12 Noes and 118 Yeses. Of the latter, the great majority (105) have made fuller use of clerical and technical personnel; 90 have cut and eliminated some steps; 39 have entered into centralized processing, and 45 into automated procedures that have helped to professionalize the librarian's work. Time has been used "for planning," "for training staff," or "to absorb the growing volume of work." In general terms, 73 saw the time released used on programs and services for individuals, 48 on work with groups, 44 on administration, and 32 on work with agencies.

Significant changes in the handling and processing of materials in the near future? Again there was some consensus among the write-ins, with frequent mentions of processing at source by publisher or jobber and of acquisitions, bookkeeping, cataloging, processing, all centralized and computerized on a national, state, and regional basis. Commented one person, "Our cataloger is an expensive luxury." A significant change will be more informal processing in poverty areas, said one knowledgeable librarian, who continued, "It will require intensive work to persuade authorities to allocate savings effected by automated processing to expansion and improvement of services . . ."

Several other respondents mentioned the possibility of having paperbacks and some other types of materials treated as expendable and given away by the library. The computer-based book catalog was seen as a great help by many. All the comments were couched in terms of serving the user better and shucking off, as far as possible, traditional functions and routines: "We're going to quit worrying about little things and concentrate on big ones."

ADMINISTRATION

Interlibrary Cooperation

"Do you think that different types of libraries will need to define and perhaps limit their functions more sharply in relation to each other and the clients in their service area?" In response to this question 103 public librarians said "Yes"; 19 said "No." The comments were *most* interesting, and should all be reproduced here, but these are a few samples:

> We will work out a division of labor, I hope. For example, public libraries may turn all service to children and young people over to the schools and concentrate their efforts on service to adults.

> None but the largest libraries will be able to continue to try to be all things to all users; limitations of responsibility and specialization of collections must be worked out.

> Better school libraries release the public library to give service to more adults.

> Our biggest problem: to define role of the public library *vis-à-vis* the school libraries and to make decisions as to the value of many small branches vs. a few large ones.

> Function of the library will be determined by the relationship with other libraries in the area . . . duplications of certain materials and types of services are becoming impossible.

> We must define and perhaps limit function, but must preserve the integrity of knowledge and be concerned with the completely unbounded nature of human curiosity.

> Officials are beginning to ask more questions regarding the functions and clientele of the several types of libraries.

Some of those who said "No" seemed to interpret the question as suggesting a limiting of client service, and others thought the question meant *limit* in a sense of fewer resources rather than reorganized ones. Of 124 responding, 71 had entered into a variety of formal (legal) sharing or mutual-benefit arrangements in the past year; 53 had made no formal contracts but described a variety of informal ones in progress.

Budget Determination

Only 54 respondents thought that the social and economic importance of libraries was well enough established to seek to base budgets on realistic needs rather than traditional use and performance bases; 69 said "No"; "but it's coming," added several. "Too many city officials and citizens still do not view the library as an effective force in the community." "Boards, staff, and public cling to the traditional role of the library." "The war on poverty has been a tremendous opportunity for the library to become involved in cooperative efforts of many community agencies and to understand the interrelationship of people, institutions, and political realities." "Yes," says one notably successful librarian, "how else would you take care of long-range plans and dreams?" Apparently some conceive and convey the dreams more vividly than others!

The questionnaire asked for write-ins on the basis for budget determination. Some comments were: "Political moxie." "Theoretically determined by performance budgets, but actually by value judgments made by the Board and Mayor and Council." "We ask for what we think we can get; they give us as little as they think they can get away with." And a wide variety of others, all or most of which are depressing. Seventy-four libraries are experimenting with program-oriented budgets or have done so, often without success.

Personnel

Response to the set of questions on personnel indicates that 115 public librarians have attempted or are currently attempting task analysis and redefinition of goals within their libraries. Table 2A–1.8 shows the estimated time-distribution of library professionals in clerical and technical activities. There the question was asked within the context of materials processing, but the response here, where over-all personnel planning is the context, is quite consistent. Of 113 responding, 107 have found that a number of tasks once performed by professional librarians can be satisfactorily performed by others: technicians, 70; professionals in some other field, 54; and clerical help, 99. Several mentioned college graduates without special professional training, library trainees, and volunteers.

About half (58) of those answering the question have revised, de facto or formally, their ratio of professional librarians to other staff. Now it is one professional librarian to four nonlibrarians, said 46; one professional to three nonlibrarians, said 29. Several mentioned a ratio of one-to-five or more, up to ten. Others apparently cried, "In this library it's all academic—we can't get them anyway, and we do the best we can with what we can get."

Asked to check some positions they felt required a person with a library school degree or library training (Table 2A–1.9), nearly all respondents indicated that they would require it for the director; a high percentage would also require it for the director of in-service training programs. Conversely, most people felt that both the job of personnel director and public relations director could be filled by excellent nonlibrarian practitioners in those fields. Community coordinators could, according to nearly half the respondents, be nonlibrarians also, provided they understood library service philosophy and program potentials.

Finally, in this group of questions, librarians were asked what they thought would be the effect of an influx into the library profession of a large group of upwardly mobile young people, drawn from the lower classes by a profession with such obvious middle-class credentials. The free-response comments were mostly enthusiastic and expressed the view that this would enhance the profession. A few had demurs, however, expressed as fear that these young people, and young people from all classes generally, might be looking for "a snug harbor from which to watch the world go by." Many seemed to like the idea that these young people would tend to "make the library more of a cross between an educational and a social service institution." One noted, "These people will want to do a good job, not out of a need for self-sacrifice, but out of a need for self-respect, for making a contribution by choice to the society." Another, "If they are bright, enthusiastic, iconoclastic, and think *à la* the Peace Corps, or even the hippies, it will be the best thing that ever happened."

Many expressed the view that "libraries of the future will no longer serve mainly the middle class," and that we need "creative young people who are responsive to human beings, alive to the future as well as the past." All young people coming in will "question present methods, have less patience with routines, have more interest in community needs and service, and have lower standards in book selection."

IMPRESSIONS OF SOCIAL FACTORS

Major Stresses

Asked which set of societal pressures had affected their library most keenly, respondents checked as many as they felt applied to their situation. Not surprisingly, educational stresses were most keenly felt by 112; next was population, felt as a real pressure by 94. Occupational, social and philosophical, communications and documentation, and political pressures were each checked by 40-odd respondents. Research and knowledge, however, drew a slightly higher response: 61.

Demands by students and special subject users—which require a quantum jump in funding, space, and staff—combined with the inability of taxing jurisdictions to obtain more money, have perhaps made financial stresses the most pressing in practical terms. The creation of new community colleges and technical institutes with very limited libraries has placed a new kind of curriculum-related burden on local public libraries; adults engaged in upgrading education, often job-related, have necessitated sweeping changes in book selection and use of available funds.

At the same time, the lower educational level of some users has required changes in provision of materials at the other end of the scale. A regional library in Appalachia put its problem succinctly:

> As a library in a rural mountain area, with a steadily decreasing population and economy, we are very conscious of the changes produced by the flight to the city, the struggle to convert from the old rural economy to some kind of economic basis in small industry, cooperatives, new crops including tourism and recreation. The tremendous social changes produced by distribution of consumer goods and services on a national scale have thrown out of kilter the old tax base of real estate. Most public service institutions are still caught in this vise.

From a large city comes this comment:

> Population stresses, particularly the migration of middle-class families to the suburbs, the bypassing of the city as a place to live for middle-class residents, have helped to generate a variety of financial stresses and other concerns that bear directly upon our library. These are imposing limits in terms of facilities, services, collections, new programs, and staffing patterns. Our library is a creature of city government, and our problems and limitations reflect those of the city itself. Large segments of a metropolitan area's population call upon city services without concern for or even recognition of boundaries of financial support or responsibility. The tax bases of many large cities are strained . . . serious problems arise in connection with new and needed programs for the city's own underprivileged areas.

"What one social phenomenon of the past ten years or so, whether listed by us or not, has given you the most worry and trouble in day-to-day operational terms?" Amazingly, this completely open-ended question elicited worry and deep concern about one phenomenon above all others: lessening of respect for public property or the rights of others by young people, especially expressed in mutilation and theft of books and other materials. This concern was expressed from all parts of the country, in cities and small towns and rural areas.[3] One librarian referred to it as "increased criminal or antisocial behavior in libraries." Others commented that while there had always been some of this, there has been a marked and frightening increase in the past few years.

Obsolescence of tax structures, the pressure of faster communications, the radical right, and the growing influence of conservative pressure were mentioned by a number of librarians. Others were most concerned about the apathy of the citizenry concerning library service; the quantity, type, means, and transmission of information and the implications thereof; and the inability to reach out with services in areas of critical social need, such as the ghettos.

Respondents were next asked to dwell upon the social phenomenon that had given them the most concern in philosophical terms. These replies were varied, thoughtful, and in many cases spoke highly of the intellectual level at which the leadership of the library profession operates. One big-city librarian wrote, "Man in conflict with himself as a result of the dichotomy of affluence and poverty, highly complex technology, and inability to define his role as a citizen of his community and the world." A state librarian expressed deep concern about "two-faced attitudes toward race, I mean acceptance of Negroes in jobs on the basis of their qualifications but unwillingness to accept them otherwise; i.e., fear that they might come to the staff Christmas party, etc. . . . also a tendency to prejudge the capabilities of Negro patrons." Still other philosophical concerns include these:

I'm concerned that people are too willing to accept what is said by an expert or the communications media, and are unwilling to explore for alternatives.

The mass media with their pressure for promoting the Single View probably have represented the greatest threat to public libraries' consistent philosophy of the right of the individual to find out for himself. . . . Pressures on Library Board and librarians to provide only the majority point of view, the latest best seller or TV craze, the book that offends no one, the religion, morality, or politics that are innocuous or blandly commercial.

Our apparent inability to find useful ways to serve new people in the city.

The complete indifference of even the educated part of the community to the great social problems of today. The Negro problem: "We have no Negroes in our city; we are not interested." Peace: "War brings prosperity, and anyhow, our wars are in defense of property." Poverty: "Any man around here can get work if he wants it."

Another librarian commented, "Making readers out of nonreaders often equals trying to make rational out of emotional beings." Perhaps, she thinks, this is a disservice in a society that seems to give less respect and value to rational behavior! The impression emerges clearly from a careful reading of these statements that the best of our librarians are concerned, committed, and intelligent people, determined to use their profession in the full service of society and its beset individuals.

Response to Stress

Most librarians felt that their greatest success in meeting social pressures or opportunities was in the area of student need. "Meeting student and research need," said one librarian succinctly, speaking for many of his colleagues. Many southern librarians spoke with some degree of satisfaction of the full racial integration of their libraries. "We are more relevant," was another comment. Said one suburban, fast-growing library, "We have integrated the library into the teen culture of the community without driving

3 *This evidently nonregional problem came up also in the regional hearings of the National Advisory Commission on Libraries, sometimes within the context of the role of inexpensive copying machines in libraries and at least once with reference to the copyright dilemma (see chapter 6).*

out the adults." Several librarians were pleased with the success they felt in "reorienting service to serve a broader cross-section of the community." Only a few libraries said that they had been in some degree successful in supporting unit poverty programs, especially in relation to Head Start and other preschooler programs, and job-training programs. "Success?" commented one tired librarian, "Just coping with sheer numbers!"

With few exceptions the librarians queried felt that they had grappled least successfully with service to the disadvantaged, of all ages. Many people feel discouraged. "So little response." "So much effort and not commensurate with the meager successes." New adult service programs of all kinds, but especially those for the adult poor, were mentioned as one of the failures. "We have failed to become a resource to which lower-income groups turn automatically, as do many among middle- or upper-income groups."

One articulate state librarian put it this way:

We have had no effect on the Negro who is about to riot in the streets; we have never had him as a patron. We haven't, I think, done much either for the middle-class suburbanite who may someday have Negro grandchildren, be part of a tightly organized society controlled by "experts," find himself faced with hostility and hatred from the rest of the world . . . see his children rebel and abandon the values he has tried to teach them . . . is confused and discouraged that nothing seems to be going as it should.

A thoughtful small-town librarian whose single-industry town has had a traumatic changeover period said, "We have not known how to restore faith and hope—or even interest—to the people of the community who have been hurt by change." Another problem cited: "There is still a large group of non-library-users in the middle class." Concern for service, or lack of it, to the elderly and retired is growing, too.

As for innovations and progressive steps, two state librarians who responded took satisfaction in having involved themselves, other members of their staffs, and librarians in the state in workshops and conferences on aging, city and state government, and contemporary social problems—all opportunities "to grow up and out" and "to relate the library to the reality of today's world and to prod librarians into being a more relevant part of that world." Other respondents were proud of abolishing nuisances, blocks to free use of the library: "We have abolished a number of small charges for various library services . . . all LP records were in a pay collection . . . there was a rental charge for films." A variety of new services and efficiencies in library housekeeping were mentioned; but, "sponsorship of an international poetry forum," said one big-city librarian.

The Future

Greatest challenge—or most pressing problem—between now and 1975? Many respondents saw it, stripped to basics, as getting the library fully recognized as a social force, an agency for change that will be regarded as an integral part of the community development team. "Money," said almost all. "Changing services fast enough to meet changing needs." Said one: "Public, school, junior college, and small college libraries will be on the bottom side of a widening gap—with large university and research libraries handling the real information science revolution." Expressed another way: "The difference between research libraries with their banks of computers and information storage machinery and libraries like ours will widen . . . public libraries in areas like this one will continue to be book oriented." Working out a system for all kinds of service for all people, at a cost within the limits of possibility, is nothing less than the heart of the problem.

The public library respondents were also asked to respond freely on how they were going to tackle the challenge. "Remain flexible"; "revise constantly"; "work on all fronts at once." "Seek to bypass local constituency and have favorable decisions made at the Federal and possibly state levels." "If necessary, chuck all the sacred traditions of library science and embark on programs which assure that the library, or the community collection of books, is a continuing part of the thought of more and more people . . . we need to improve our distribution, our ways of getting what someone needs."

"We will tackle it by contracting with consultants for specialized skills." "Train nonprofessionals, preferably college graduates who for some reason are not going to library school, to work with books and people." "By working harder to improve state and Federal support for libraries, and assisting the city in programs for reevaluation of tax base." Or from a state library: "I hope librarianship will devote more time and energy to working more with social service agencies in attempting to reach people, perhaps alter or build physical facilities to accommodate book-related activities, use college graduates extensively, take materials and services to people, reduce red-tape regulations and really cooperate among themselves to get at the nonusers. Here is a major task."

And: "We are going to work with the children of the deprived, cooperate with all agencies working with them; open library facilities in quarters used by agencies serving the deprived. . . . The library system must become like the highway system: interstate, some U.S. highways, some state, some local streets and roads; the user must be able to enter any one of these and have access to the resources of all of them." "We will try pilot programs for leisure time, intellectual stimulation as a substitute for TV boredom, as demonstrations to win financial support." Said one experienced library leader: "I would like to see a complete realignment of library services . . . [based on] a thorough study of all types of libraries related to the requirements of all kinds of people who need resources and services at all levels."

Two or three just took a look at the question, noted the date, and wrote gleefully, "By retiring!"

Further evidence of the unusually voluminous and thoughtful free response produced in this survey can be found in the public librarians' response to the final questionnaire item. Let yourself go, and write about libraries in the future, says the last question—and they did! Some don't like the look of the future much: "I'm obsolete!" said one particularly intelligent, active, and reasonably youthful librarian in the Middle West. A few voiced fears that computers would take over, and books, personal services, and person-to-person contact would be a thing of the past. "The humanistic role of the library will receive less attention . . . the intellectual in the library faces the same fate as the intellectual in the educational process: we need him, but is he really welcome?"

But most respondents were not too worried. A good many expressed in different ways the expectation of seeing two very different types of public libraries. "I would like to see neighborhood book collections, open a few hours every day, within reach of the very old and the very young, who cannot drive; more complete circulating and reference within thirty minutes' drive: telephone, teletype, telephoto, should make all the resources of the world available there." "I believe that more kinds of people, as well as more people, will be using them—maybe no more 'regular library-users' but people who take for granted the occasional use; after all, we don't use an auto mechanic every week."

And another: "Small public libraries will tend to become reading centers no longer attempting to provide a full range of services . . . those seeking information will depend on regional center libraries that are interconnected with all retrieval sources." "Libraries will be multimedia cultural centers . . . people will come for mental and spiritual revitalization more than just to take things out or get the facts . . . *information center* is much too narrow a term for this institution." And if we don't plan it this way, people will want it enough to make it happen anyway—as many libraries happened in the first place! Listen: "Libraries will be bright, large, busy, efficient, and mediocre. Small private libraries will begin to spring up in some places."

Almost everyone who commented about the future agreed that more people will use libraries and more of everything in them. "Libraries will have more books than ever—in addition to tapes, microfilms, etc." "Some and perhaps many libraries will be open twenty-four hours a day; Sunday opening will be routine." "Information will be important, of course, but recreation and humanistic culture and leisure are becoming more important in general life and must be considered." "Libraries will become cultural service-stations and will be used by as many people as are now frequenting supermarkets and gas stations." "Large media complexes will serve all types of patrons without designation as public or college." Many librarians saw the public library growing into more of an adjunct to the formal education system, with informal emphasis on continuing self-development.

Who will run them? "Management experts will manage libraries; automation will deal with circulation, acquisitions, cataloging, leaving librarians free for service." "Children's libraries will work with visuals, tapes, programmed reading gadgets." "First-rate people who understand the role of the library in society and translate it into action . . . a variety of specialists will be used, and so will many college graduates with good reading background, who will be given basic courses in library philosophy and in-service training." "The staff will include the neighborhood motherly type who likes people and enjoys introducing them to books and ideas, the computer programmers, indexers, reference librarians, and readers' advisors."

"We will no longer lend anything but will 'give' or 'sell' a copy of whatever is wanted in the form of print-out from film or electronic storage . . . librarians will be responsible for what goes in, and anybody will be able to learn how to 'get it out.' " "The staff will be a team: administrative, business, technical, educational, PR, political science, group work. The business of the library will be ideas and information in every form." "Librarians will be concerned, even at their own risk, with people thinking and knowing . . . and the library will welcome the concern of people who are doubtful, uncertain, confused."

By way of conclusion to this brief report of the survey of public librarians, it is appropriate to quote from one respondent who has given much thought, much agonizing reappraisal, to the functions and capabilities of public libraries, James E. Bryan of the Newark Public Library, Newark, New Jersey:

> Increasingly literate population will require larger and more specialized collections and services. Most libraries will remain book centered. People will continue to read more for "point-of-view" and general information than for "isolated facts." "Isolated facts" and bibliographic locating will be satisfied by centralized computer stations with outlets in regional or area libraries. Use of nonbook materials (films, slides, tapes, etc.) will increase. Libraries will provide teaching machines connected with central program banks and supply more programmed instruction. In smaller communities public libraries will tend to become "little cultural centers" with increasingly wider cultural programs of lectures, exhibits, and participation activities. There will be centralized acquisitions processing centers for large geographical areas. There will be more experimentation with branch and neighborhood agencies involving other community services. The trend toward specialization and systems will continue. There will be more referral.
>
> These libraries will require as managers broadly trained and educated generalists with a good sense of educational and cultural goals. More subject specialists will be needed. Staff will have more training in interview and counseling techniques and procedures and will be more "outreach" oriented. More specialists in such fields as publicity, community relations, business management will be required.

TABLE 2A–1.1

SUMMARY HIGHLIGHTS OF AN OPINION SURVEY ON
SOCIAL FACTORS AND THE PUBLIC LIBRARY

(134 public librarians)

Summary highlights

1. Population growth in their library service areas was noted by 79 percent of 134 public librarians from all types of communities nationwide; 5 percent noted a decline; the rest noted little or no change. Of 117 who estimated their clientele, well over half felt that at least 40 percent of their population were, if not registered borrowers, at least users of the public library.

2. Shifts in the character of their clientele were noted by 97 public librarians, the most frequently cited being more businessmen, more students, and more low-income children and adults. More use of various public library services by young people, older people, men, and women appears to be the trend, except for a decline in fiction use by men and young people.

3. Nearly all the respondents felt they had made some progress in making public libraries and services more user-oriented, but 105 believed they had not responded fully enough or promptly enough to the needs of the disadvantaged.

4. Over the past decade a change in the public librarian's philosophy of program and service was noted by 113 respondents, such changes being in the direction of an actively people-oriented service. Consistent with this philosophy are the frequently cited attempts at outreach programs and at meeting the demands for personalized guidance.

5. Public librarian response on the types of books and other materials to meet user needs emphasized the diversity of clientele—more sophisticated students, more specialists from business and industry, and more undereducated. The greatest problem librarians have encountered in purchasing material is the lack of easy-to-read material with adult content.

6. Public librarians tend to favor interlibrary cooperation and specialization; 103 of 122 respondents think different types of libraries in a service area will need to define and limit their functions. Out of 124 respondents, 71 had entered into a formal sharing or mutual-aid agreement in the preceding year.

7. The administration of public libraries appears to be traditional with respect to budget determination, although 74 of the public librarians have experimented with program-budgeting. Personnel experimentation appears more promising, for 115 have attempted task analysis and 107 found that tasks once performed by professional librarians did not require training in library science.

8. Pressures on the public library stemming from the social force of educational developments were cited by 112 librarians as being most notable; population was the second most frequently cited impact. Free-response comments by the public librarians suggest that many have a broad social awareness and desire to respond to social pressures through innovative approaches and active attempts to serve the individual needs of their constituency.

SOURCE: Social Change and the Library: 1945–1980, *a study by the National Book Committee, commissioned by the National Advisory Commission on Libraries in 1967. All the tables in chapter 2, section A.1, are based on the questionnaire survey of public librarians conducted by Virginia H. Mathews.*

TABLE 2A–1.2

REGIONAL DISTRIBUTION OF PUBLIC LIBRARY QUESTIONNAIRE RESPONDENTS

(Total N = 134)

STATE	N	STATE	N
Alabama	1	Missouri	4
Alaska	0	Montana	2
Arizona	1	Nebraska	2
Arkansas	4	Nevada	0
California	7	New Hampshire	1
Colorado	2	New Jersey	5
Connecticut	3	New Mexico	1
Delaware	1	New York	13
D. C.	0	North Carolina	4
Florida	6	North Dakota	2
Georgia	4	Ohio	8
Hawaii	0	Oklahoma	3
Idaho	3	Oregon	2
Illinois	5	Pennsylvania	5
Indiana	2	Rhode Island	2
Iowa	1	South Carolina	1
Kansas	3	South Dakota	0
Kentucky	0	Tennessee	2
Louisiana	6	Texas	1
Maine	1	Utah	1
Maryland	2	Vermont	1
Massachusetts	2	Virginia	1
Michigan	3	Washington	4
Minnesota	5	West Virginia	0
Mississippi	2	Wisconsin	3
		Wyoming	2

TABLE 2A–1.3

ESTIMATES OF POPULATION CHANGE IN PUBLIC LIBRARY SERVICE AREAS SINCE 1955

ESTIMATED PERCENTAGE OF POPULATION CHANGE	*Number of librarians citing*[*]	
	GROWTH	DECLINE
10%	32	6
25%	40	1
50%	19	–
75% or more	15	–
No response	1	–
TOTAL N	107	7

[*] *No population change was cited by 20 respondents.*

TABLE 2A–1.4

ESTIMATES OF PUBLIC LIBRARY USERS IN RELATION TO TOTAL POPULATION

(User defined as registered borrower, client of special programs, or reference user)

ESTIMATED PERCENTAGE	NUMBER OF LIBRARIANS
Of total present service area population who are public library users	
10%	9
25%	46
40%	39
50% or more	23
No response	17
TOTAL N	134
Of growth in public library user proportion since 1955*	
Less than 5 %	5
5%	13
10%	21
15%	11
20%	5
25%	3
35%	2
50%	6
60%	1
100%	1
No estimate of degree of growth	30
TOTAL N citing growth	98

* Only 2 respondents cited a decline, both by 10%; 10 cited no change; 24 did not respond.

TABLE 2A–1.5

CHANGING PATTERNS IN CURRENT PUBLIC LIBRARY USE AS PERCEIVED BY LIBRARIANS

ITEM	Number of librarians citing			NO RESPONSE
	MORE	LESS	SAME	
Characteristic of young people				
Frequency of use	107	6	7	14
Number of books	89	13	10	22
Fiction	26	42	32	34
Reference use	114	1	1	18
Periodicals	105	1	8	20
Paperbacks	86	0	6	42
Records and tapes	82	4	7	41
Recreation and information programs	44	10	23	57
Other: films	7	0	0	127
large-type books	1	0	0	133
Characteristic of women				
Frequency of use	60	7	44	23
Number of books	59	12	39	24
Fiction	40	32	34	28
Reference use	63	3	42	26
Periodicals	62	8	37	27
Paperbacks	60	2	27	45
Records and tapes	68	2	23	41
Recreation and information programs	42	8	20	64
Other: films	8	0	1	125
large-type books	1	0	0	133
Characteristic of men				
Frequency of use	84	3	24	23
Number of books	68	10	30	26
Fiction	20	43	37	34
Reference use	97	4	11	22
Periodicals	80	4	23	27
Paperbacks	61	2	25	46
Records and tapes	67	2	21	44
Recreation and information programs	35	6	26	67
Other: films	8	0	1	125
large-type books	1	0	0	133
Characteristic of older people				
Frequency of use	72	7	35	20
Number of books	57	11	38	28
Fiction	44	19	36	53
Reference use	38	5	54	37
Periodicals	43	7	46	38
Paperbacks	36	7	37	54
Records and tapes	43	4	36	51
Recreation and information programs	46	5	19	64
Other: films	6	0	0	128
large-type books	3	0	0	131

TABLE 2A–1.6

FREQUENCY OF USE OF PUBLIC LIBRARY HOLDINGS

(Educated judgment of librarians)

ESTIMATED PERCENTAGE OF LIBRARY'S BOOKS AND OTHER MATERIALS USED FREQUENTLY*	NUMBER OF LIBRARIANS
Less than 15%	1
15%	25
25%	38
40%	28
50%	23
More than 50%	10
No response	9
TOTAL N	134

* More than ten times per year for reference or circulation.

TABLE 2A–1.7

FUNDS DEVOTED TO MATERIALS IN SUPPORT OF NEW PUBLIC LIBRARY PROGRAMS

PERCENTAGE OF MATERIALS BUDGET*	NUMBER OF LIBRARIANS
None	10
1–5%	27
6–10%	24
11–20%	10
21–30%	9
31–40%	2
41–50%	2
More than 50%	3
No response	47
TOTAL N	134

* Spent last fiscal year.

TABLE 2A–1.8

DISTRIBUTION OF PUBLIC LIBRARIAN TIME
DEVOTED TO CLERICAL AND TECHNICAL ACTIVITIES

ESTIMATED PERCENTAGE OF PROFESSIONAL TIME PER LIBRARY	Number of librarians citing	
	CLERICAL TASKS	TECHNICAL PROCEDURES
Less than 10%	9	8
10%	56	40
25%	30	33
40%	8	10
More than 40%	2	12
"Too much"	2	2
No response*	27	29
TOTAL N	134	134

* Evidently some respondents in the total group who made no attempt to estimate the time distribution are trying to change it; 118 cited recent steps to change it, and 12 indicated no such steps.

TABLE 2A–1.9

OPINIONS ON PUBLIC LIBRARY POSITIONS
THAT REQUIRE LIBRARY TRAINING

POSITION REQUIRING LIBRARY TRAINING	Number of librarians		
	YES	NO	NO RESPONSE
Library director	120	3	11
Director of in-service training	95	21	18
Community coordinator	63	46	25
Personnel director	23	93	18
Public relations director	11	106	17

2. PUBLIC LIBRARY USE AND POTENTIAL USE: OPINIONS OF SELECTED EXPERTS IN LIBRARIANSHIP[4]

Additional insight into the way librarians view current library service to nonspecialist general users and to prespecialist student users—both groups often highly and diversely specialized in fact—is gained from another survey done for the National Advisory Commission on Libraries. There is nothing strikingly new, at least to those who are well-informed on library matters, in the results reported here, and the respondent group is very small, but the urgency of current inadequacies in both understanding and meeting the needs of the public at large is reinforced by this evidence. Furthermore, the

4 From The Use of Libraries and the Conditions That Promote Their Use by The Academy for Educational Development, Inc., one of the special studies commissioned by the National Advisory Commission on Libraries during 1967. Harold Mendelsohn was Director of the study; Karen Wingerd was Research Assistant.

desirability of sophisticated multidisciplinary research and the establishment of experimental models in such areas as library use, manpower utilization, technological application, and cooperative ventures emerges rather clearly. The reader may find some clues to the traditional attitudes of the library profession that a number of forward-looking librarians, themselves influenced by the traditions, believe should be changed.

Fourteen of a select list of twenty nationally recognized specialists in librarianship finally participated in this study.[5] Twelve of these were interviewed personally, the other two by mail. All responded to a comprehensive questionnaire, prepared by Dr. Harold Mendelsohn, designed to elicit opinions and judgments on factors that will contribute significantly to determination of the roles American libraries are to play in the future.

THE IMAGE OF THE ACADEMIC LIBRARY

Most of the survey was oriented toward public libraries and their various educational and social functions; but some very brief attention was given to college and university libraries, which share some educational users with the public libraries. Because of the high prestige value of the academic and their reputation as models of excellence for other libraries—factors that often conceal the problems many academic libraries face —this part of the survey is reported first. (For the problems of academic libraries in their research library context, see chapter 3, section A; for their undergraduate student context, see section C.2 of the present chapter.)

Primarily, the college or university library is seen as a top-drawer institution that trades in intellectual commodities for two distinct audiences exclusively: graduate students and scholars-researchers. This type of library is idealized as the noble paragon of libraries, which affords service primarily to the intellect—the stretching of the mind. Secondarily, the college or university library is viewed as a most important adjunct to curricula. It is a resource "without which colleges and universities could not function." Thirdly, the college or university library, like the large metropolitan library, is viewed as a model for all other libraries to emulate, as well as a major resource to which other libraries can go for both aid and counsel.

This rather exaggerated positive view of college and university libraries is reflected in the performance ratings the respondents to this survey, 14 experts in librarianship, attributed to this type of institution. Here, 4 of the 14 rated their performance as excellent, 7 rated them good, and only 3 rated them fair. No one gave a poor assessment for the way this class of libraries is doing its job. Perhaps the fact that 10 of the 14 specialists in the sample had work experience in college and university libraries has something to do with their predominantly favorable assessments of these institutions. Here is an illustration of the positive disposition of the experts: "From my own experience I know here is where you are getting imagination and top-quality brains. There is a lot of pioneering and interest. Publishing is going on. There's a lot of experimentation and good leadership."

It should be pointed out that the overall positive view librarians hold of college and university libraries is not an unequivocal one. Apparently, in assessing academic libraries, the respondents were mostly mindful of the large, well-funded, high-status institutions. They did indicate considerable criticism of the smaller, poorer, lower-status college libraries. In particular, they emphasized that junior college and community college libraries have inadequate means of serving the needs of both students and faculty.

[5] *A description of the 14 library-expert respondents follows.* Sex: *9 men, 5 women;* age: *10 aged fifty or over;* education: *4 doctorate degrees, 6 master's degrees, 4 bachelor's degrees;* duration of library experience: *10 with twenty years or more;* type of library experience: *10 college and university library, 6 special library, 4 small-city public library, 3 middle-sized-city public library, 4 large-city public library, 2 public school library;* self-evaluation: *6 administrators primarily, 3 teachers primarily, 3 researchers primarily, 2 librarians primarily. In the role of library user these respondents indicated use of different libraries for different purposes, including their own personal libraries; public, university, and specialized libraries were most frequently mentioned.*

There is a low level of academic libraries serving in colleges and universities in the South. The needs of the present generation of teen-agers and the more technical and sophisticated needs of today are not being met. Junior colleges, community colleges, and satellite campuses are not getting adequate service.

Junior and community college libraries are doing the worst job. They simply have inadequate collections.

Respondent comments on improving academic libraries concentrated mostly on upgrading the smaller ones through injections of additional funds for improved facilities, better collections, and higher-quality personnel. The latter was stressed most frequently. Several suggested setting up more and better systems of interlibrary communication and cooperation.

Some recommendations were made for the future of academic libraries:

1. More automation.
2. Increased collections to keep up with increased enrollments.
3. Increased leadership with regard to publication and consulting services, teaching methods, and library research.
4. Consolidation as the one main campus information resource.
5. Establishment of a national network of library information exchanges to avoid duplication of materials and services.
6. Work toward general stimulation of student's interests beyond curriculum.

Respondent suggestions for bringing these recommendations into being are summarized here as a four-point program:

1. Reevaluate and redefine the goals and objectives of the academic library.
2. Upgrade personnel and gear services to the needs of the academic community.
3. Communicate goals, services, and need to the academic community, alumni, and voters.
4. Obtain enough money from Federal, state, local, and private sources to fund improvements where they are needed most.

THE EXPECTED FUNCTIONS OF CONTEMPORARY PUBLIC LIBRARIES

The remainder of this paper reports opinions on public libraries (summarized in Table 2A–2.1)—their functions and potential in serving user needs. Although many of the fourteen specialists agreed that the community-size criterion is not a suitable one by which to evaluate the functions of public libraries, they nevertheless did use these three categories of communities in making their assessments of public libraries:

Small communities (population 50,000–100,000).
Middle-sized communities (population 100,000–1,000,000).
Large communities (population over 1,000,000).

The consensus among the respondents was that all public libraries should serve three functions mainly: (1) provision for the education-information needs of the community, (2) provision for its cultural needs, and (3) provision for its recreational needs. The focus of concern among experts hinges on the mechanism whereby such needs are actually met and the adequacy of these mechanisms. Here it was indicated by a number of these library experts that it is foolish for public libraries across-the-board to attempt to be all things to all men. Rather, it was suggested that public libraries should attempt to confine themselves to specific targets and to limited but well-pursued programs within their limitations of funds, matériel, and personnel. The following observation illustrates this particular point of view: "If libraries tend to be poor, the reason is that they are trying to serve everyone. They should set one or two major goals to serve one or two major sectors and give everything they have—top staff, top money— to this effort."

Small Communities: Response to Popular Demands, Interdependence

As one respondent explained, "The larger the community, the more the libraries have to do." Generally speaking, these librarian experts manifested far less expectation for the smaller-community public libraries than they did for the rest. The one key set of expectations for these libraries voiced by the respondents was that they should try their best to react to popular demands. They should function in ways that are best suited to the make-up of a given community. Thus, if the community is made up of industry mainly, its public library should be an information resource primarily; or if the community is predominantly suburban, its public library should serve as sort of a community cultural center.

There was a divergence of opinion about whether public libraries in smaller communities should stick to providing routine services or should try to provide auxiliary services, such as lending records, holding art shows, providing children with storytelling. The formula offered here was, "If they can afford to—let them."

In all, not much more than routine service can be expected from smaller-community public libraries according to the results of this survey. The low level of expectation becomes reflected in the relatively low esteem in which these libraries are held. Of the 14 respondents, 9 rated the performance of this class of public libraries as fair, 3 rated it as good, and 2 did not make an assessment. No one gave either the "excellent" or "poor" assessment.

The primary reasons behind the tepid evaluations are based on reported inadequacies in this class of library's funding, facilities, resources, personnel, and imagination. The following quotations are illustrative:

> The tax base is too small. They can't attract good people. They lack strong leadership.

> Obviously they need better staffs. Too often these sized libraries are run by non-professionals. They are a little too much tradition-bound. They should be more imaginative—offer more outgoing services; be more community oriented—take more initiative.

Three suggestions for improvement dominate the opinions expressed. First, and most important, is the suggestion that public libraries in smaller cities stop trying to go it alone. Instead, it is proposed that they integrate themselves more closely into state systems and enter into cooperative sharing exchanges with larger libraries all over the country.

> There must be more cooperation, especially in acquisition, ending or minimizing duplication. More cooperation in pooling special' materials and sharing professional personnel.

> They can be improved by working with the state library and particularly with larger libraries that are neighbors to facilitate the availability of books not owned locally or that are not in mass demand.

Second, is the suggestion for more financial assistance.

> Federal and state governments must recognize that small libraries need more financial support. There must be better integration of small libraries into larger library units which can generate better financial support. Only Federal funds will make this feasible. These libraries need more money, larger quarters, and better staff. More money.

However, the experts believe that requests for extra funding should be justified in terms of the improved services that will result. Thus, efforts should be focused on tailoring services to needs, communicating these to the public, and then requesting more money. This adds up to the over-all need for better public relations.

Small libraries must convince the public that quality service can be furnished economically and that it is desirable from an educational point of view. They have to get outside consultants to come in to look over the situation from the point of view of what services are needed and how much money will be needed to support these services. They need to demonstrate their value to the community in order to get support.

Middle-sized Communities: Some Specialization, Some Independence

In essence, public libraries in middle-sized locales are seen by the respondents as being far more autonomous than those in smaller places. Following through on the theme of "The larger the community, the more the libraries have to do," the experts viewed these libraries as beginning to offer specialized services, particularly in the key area of filling information-education needs.

Response to the survey suggests that rather than trying to coordinate their services with neighboring and state systems, public libraries in the middle-sized class should complement various college and university libraries, technical libraries, and business and industrial libraries in their locales. On the whole, the respondents believe that public libraries in middle-sized cities can very well serve as essential components of the total information-resources available in their areas.

These libraries are expected to gear their activities much more closely to the diverse needs of their communities than are smaller libraries. In this regard, the respondents placed particular stress on the needs of technology and business, of disadvantaged groups, and of students.

They should have ready access to a rich variety of printed materials that are geared to sharply changing needs of modern society. There is a need for increased capacity to serve in a growing industrial and technological society. It is urgent that they find flexible, imaginative ways to bring the library service to both low-literacy groups and to students.

The library experts gave more favorable performance ratings to middle-sized public libraries than they did to smaller ones. Although none gave an excellent rating to the former, 6 rated them as good, 6 as fair, and 2 made no evaluation. None of the 14 classified them as doing a poor job. Comments praising these libraries mentioned their pioneering spirit in attempting to be innovative and the quality of their personnel.

They have been in the forefront of developing the "center-of-interest" concept rather than concentrating solely on "materials."

Much of the impetus for library improvement has come from libraries of this size.

They have very good people, who are dedicated and doing a very good job.

Those experts who assessed public libraries serving middle-sized communities as fair faulted them most often for their parochialism and lack of understanding of the new needs of their respective communities, especially the needs of the disadvantaged.

They are still trying to serve everyone rather than concentrating on the special needs of special subpopulations.

They haven't yet managed to develop specialized programs tailored to the needs of a more varied clientele. They tend to have a number of people who today are classed as "disadvantaged." They simply have to provide services which will appeal to this group.

In too few instances have they broken away from the classical style of library service in dealing with socially disadvantaged people. They haven't taken advantage of the skills of social workers and other professionals in helping groups of this kind.

Only one or two respondents suggested the cliché "more money," "more space," "more personnel" formulas for improving public libraries in the middle-sized city. Most believed instead that the resources already at hand must be studied and modernized in order to develop the imaginative new services that changing communities demand. Heavy stress was placed on conducting self-evaluative research, on assessments of manpower utilization, and on the adoption of modern systems and automated approaches in the services to be rendered. These interview excerpts are exemplary of the positions taken on these scores:

"I think they need careful study of their work processes." "What is needed is increased automation of all types." "They should adopt more systems approaches." "I recommend closer examination of work procedures. They need more efficient use of manpower to offer the services needed by the community."

Large Communities:
Diversification and Specialization, Coordination and Leadership

Large metropolitan-based public libraries were seen as highly diversified and specialized institutions that are sensitized to the most varied and often exotic needs of the gigantic communities they seek to serve. In essence they are viewed as prototypical pacesetters in librarianship—as major resources of research and experimentation in the field to be emulated by smaller libraries in their regions and throughout the land.

Metropolitan public libraries are expected most often to provide highly specialized information services to the panoply of subgroups that make up our huge metropolitan centers. Such public libraries are expected to develop and maintain specialized collections in science, technology, business, social science, drama, music, international affairs, ethnic minorities, and the like. They are expected to be both imaginative and comprehensive in the services they offer. Furthermore, our major public libraries are seen as focal points around which many activities of smaller libraries can be developed and, most importantly, coordinated. Thus, the metropolitan public library must serve not only as a major information-resource for the varied subpublics of our largest cities, but also as an input mechanism for bettering the jobs to be performed by smaller libraries.

How well do the experts see the major public libraries of America fulfilling these expectations? Two rated the job performance of major metropolitan public libraries as excellent, 5 rated it as good, 7 rated it as fair, and none rated it as poor. Again a division of opinion, with half the group being more favorably disposed and the rest remaining less favorably disposed to our metropolitan-based public libraries. Respondent evaluation of our largest public libraries seemed to depend mainly on the individual's impressions of how well a particular institution is able to cope with the enormous pressures that are applied to it. Frequent allusions were made to specific libraries as examples of high performance.

The New York, Philadelphia, Boston, Detroit, and Brooklyn public libraries—in their own styles—are doing good jobs. New York at Lincoln Center—with the idea of a branch devoted to the whole business of dance, music, and theatre—is doing a marvelous job. The Brooklyn library is good for its community.

There are exceptional cities like New York and Boston which are doing excellent jobs even while being overwhelmed by demands for all kinds of services.

They are doing a good job. This is my personal opinion based on my contacts and my experiences in the field.

More critical comments on the larger metropolitan-based public libraries show disappointment with their seeming lack of success in reaching significant sectors of the urban population.

The main failure with the metropolitan library is that its branch system has not reached the urban poor.

I don't think they have caught up with the needs of social unrest and the technological and sophisticated needs of the present generation.

They have to develop a greater variety and many more imaginative programs for dealing with the minority groups. They have to develop more sophisticated methods of service for the scholars and scientists.

They need to provide books, films, and audiovisual aids designed specifically for near-illiterates to encourage and help them and also provide more industrial and technological books. They have to keep in touch with the needs.

For the most part, the respondents stressed the same suggestions for improvement for both large and middle-sized public libraries. For the large libraries, modernization, automation, and better utilization of personnel were emphasized.

PROBLEMS AND GOALS OF PUBLIC LIBRARIES

The response of the fourteen experts in librarianship in evaluating what services our contemporary public libraries as a whole do best and least well in providing is summarized in Table 2A–2.2. In capsule, the experts believed that what public libraries have been doing routinely throughout the past they continue to do best currently. In responding to new demands and keeping pace with the growing urban problems of our time, public libraries were considered to be generally less effective—failing to reach out to those who might benefit most from their services. Inadequacies were also noted in our public libraries' attempts to meet the needs of intellectuals and at fulfilling roles as major information, adult education, and general cultural resources.

Extending the Community Role of the Public Libraries

To what extent can the public library become more integrated into the actualities of contemporary life? To what extent can it contribute to the amelioration of hard-core social problems like juvenile delinquency and adult self-education?

The consensus was that the public library *can* affect these kinds of social problems, but not alone and not directly. No respondent believed that public libraries by themselves could prevent juvenile delinquency or educate school dropouts, but most of the fourteen agreed that if public libraries could take on more active roles in their communities in setting up cooperative lines of communication with other educational and social agencies, much indeed could be accomplished toward solving social problems. Here the key seems to lie in encouraging libraries first to shed their usual autonomous, remote social roles and then to get together directly with the total community social welfare–educational establishment in cooperative communitywide problem-solving efforts. The key phrase here is "community involvement."

They can accomplish cooperation through periodic but regular conferences with school administrative personnel, directors of social settlement houses, and other community leaders.

There is a need for public libraries to ally themselves with community colleges. They aren't yet really in touch with the new junior colleges, and college reflects the new social needs. I don't see many libraries working with music centers or art centers to provide a totality of culture.

I see the need for cooperation with all sorts of community agencies and programs, such as poverty and the aging. Cooperation with businessmen's groups. The libraries must *participate*. They must go beyond saying, "We have books."

There are certain limitations that restrict libraries from engaging in these undertakings. Perhaps the most critical one noted by the library experts is the traditional image of the library that is shared by library personnel and community alike. It was pointed out by some of the respondents that libraries cannot be expected to be primary social-educational agencies. The best they can be expected to do is to serve as secondary backup resources to the major ongoing agencies and programs that serve the community more directly.

Coping with the Administrative Problems of the Public Libraries

Table 2A–2.3 shows that the most pressing problem facing the administrators of today's public libraries is what the respondents called the manpower crisis, the shortage of trained personnel. Other problems involve the need for more and better space, more adequate financing, more and better book acquisition opportunities, elimination of archaic procedures, and improvements in salaries. These may be directly or indirectly related to the one major problem that was noted as offering the greatest threat to the very existence of public libraries—the inability of these institutions to attract and to keep trained professional personnel.

The manpower crisis in our public libraries is due to a complex of factors that, according to the respondents in this survey, spell out one thing—libraries lack an attractive image in the manpower marketplace. Most of the experts in the sample put the blame squarely upon the public libraries themselves for this state of affairs; for example: there is no precise definition of what jobs library personnel are required to perform; the libraries have not been putting a premium on creativity, imagination, and innovativeness; institutions training library personnel have leaned too much in the direction of "how-to-do-it"; public libraries have not overcome their overbearing routine work; the salaries offered by libraries are generally below those offered in business and industry. Here are some excerpts from the response:

The fault is with library education. It's mostly a how-to-do-it orientation. Traditional library service is seen as lacking vision and therefore does not appear to be a valuable service.

The librarian's job has become less of a scholarly one.

The library is regarded by many school counselors and by the public as too much of a sheltered workshop.

There must be adequate plans for effective and efficient expenditure of public funds so that efficient and effective use of such can be determined. I see little evidence of this point of view in library management.

What trained personnel there is is being misused.

We haven't been able to unload the heavy burden of routine tasks that wear everyone down in the business.

Salaries are not commensurate with education requirement. In many cases we have not defined our jobs carefully enough. We need to do extensive research so that we can make precise job information available.

A four-pronged program emerges for coping with the problems, and the first aspect calls for additional financial support from Federal, state, and local sources.

Get more grants in aid from the Federal Government. The states will put up some money if the Federal Government gives them a boost.

The second aspect is concerned with libraries taking the initiative to redefine their goals, to streamline their procedures, and to embrace automation so that better use can be made of the trained personnel that is available presently.

There must be more efficient use of available technical services which will release trained librarians for real public service.

Perhaps what is needed is a multimillion dollar demonstration center which could define libraries' limitations and activities.

I believe three things are needed:
1. A reclassification and restatement of the public library (and its goals) as an active agency.
2. Increased emphasis on public librarianship in the schools.
3. Not to draw away from but to embrace the new technological computer changes.

Management can study methods and procedures of work; it must make more use of computers.

The third aspect of the program for public library improvement is concerned with upgrading library education to cope with the changing needs of our contemporary communities and the public libraries that seek to serve them.

There must be an increase in training agencies and more efficient use of library personnel.

Library schools should face up to the problem of recruiting and training more people.

Library education must be improved. We must get some top-notch brains on library school faculties—especially we must get nonlibrarians. We must emphasize research in library education programs—but not particularly in library research. We must get support for library school students just as we do for prospective teachers.

The final suggestion is to develop sound public relations programs that will acquaint communities with their public libraries, what they have to offer, and what their problems are.

There must be an educatonal campaign to educate the public about what libraries can do for them. Trustees and city government are not educated to library needs.

We've got to generate much stronger voter support at Federal and state levels. There must be more public understanding of the crucial importance of imaginative librarians. There must be more dramatic impact on the political mind.

USERS AND USES OF PUBLIC LIBRARIES

For the most part, impressions of who uses or does not use public libraries as voiced by the 14 experts in librarianship jibe with the research findings, based on the literature and a social survey of attitudes, presented in section B of this chapter. Both personal observation (12 of the respondents) and familiarity with the literature (9 of the respondents) were cited as bases for their comments. In commenting on general research on library usage, incidentally, the consensus was "fair to poor": 1 rated it excellent, 2 rated it good, 6 rated it fair, 3 rated it poor, and 2 made no effort at assessment.

This group of experts tends to see library users mainly as children, students, and middle-aged, middle-class, better-educated professionals and businessmen—those seeking information more often than "traditional" general reading. Services are not truly responsive to the entire public. All but one respondent cited as at least fairly accurate the claim that public libraries today cater mostly to elites.

Nonusers are generally considered to be that majority of the public which is not particularly book-oriented—mostly the less well educated, the minority groups, the poor, and those whose leisure activities do not normally include literary material. The respondents also pointed to the minority book-oriented subpublic among nonusers, the persons who buy their own books, the scholars and specialists who both need and have access to highly specialized sources of information. Most of the fourteen librarians put the "blame" for nonusage upon an indifferent public that is essentially a non-book-reading one, but a number placed some responsibilities directly upon the libraries, who have failed to reach these nonusers with offers of new, meaningful, and useful services oriented directly to their particular needs.

How satisfied are the American people with their public libraries? The survey reported in section B.2 of this chapter shows that for the most part American adults are more or less indifferent about their public libraries. The select experts in this survey read the public's pulse quite similarly. Half rated the public as only fairly satisfied, and the remaining half claimed that a high degree of indifference (neither satisfied nor dissatisfied) characterizes the outlook of the public as it pertains to their libraries.

The respondents noting a relative lack of public satisfaction made comments concerning the libraries' inability to keep up with public needs. These quotations are illustrative:

Libraries are too self-protective. They are afraid to go out on a limb and try new things that might attract more people.

People just aren't getting good service.

Neither the public nor the libraries show any great desires to change, to redo, to innovate more suitable services.

Most users have never experienced "excellent" library service.

It was also noted that compared with other public institutions (e.g., schools, hospitals, protective services), there is an observed lack of interest among the people.

Changes in both public library users and library usage were cited by nine respondents. Increases were noted in numbers of students and persons with specialized interests using public libraries, and two librarians noted some instances of increases in numbers of lower-income persons who patronize public libraries. The differences in usage cited most often refer to drops in general reading and circulation and increases in the use of reference-information services. Also noted was some observed increase in public usage of nonbook library services (e.g., borrowing tapes, records, art reproductions, etc.).

Some quotes from interviews indicate opinions on the social forces that have influenced changes in library usage:

This growing need for information followed the Russian sputnik launching. The realization that they were better than we were. This touched off our knowledge and information explosion.

We are becoming more and more a scientific, computerized, and mechanized society.

Our ever-increasing emphasis on specialization requires new skills and increased knowledge.

It has been a gradual process. The big change came following the war and the tremendous increase in the availability of paperbacks and television.

I think these changes occurred because of the increased accessibility of fiction and nonfiction in paperback.

POTENTIAL FOR THE FUTURE

Motivation of Users

With near unanimity the respondents agreed that nonusers can be attracted to use public libraries if the institutions themselves go out of their way to uncover the needs of the people and then adjust their programs and services accordingly. The keynote word here, as used by one expert, is "outreach." Public libraries, it was suggested, cannot expect nonusers to come to them simply because—like the great mountain peaks—they are there. Public libraries must adjust themselves to actual public needs and then actively reach out in imaginative ways to attract the nonuser.

We need more "outreach." More storefront libraries in the slums, participation of the culturally deprived in the planning of library collections, services, etc.

We must go to "them." We must be concerned with need and use rather than with circulation. We have to put outlets where the state of public education demands them.

This is very difficult to do, and it may not be the libraries' job alone—with one exception. If you demonstrate that you have a service that can fit people's needs, you are more likely to have people recognize them by themselves than if you simply announce that you have all those goodies.

Libraries must offer more imaginative services and improved facilities that are more closely related to real needs. They must actually demonstrate what libraries can do as part of all-inclusive culture.

The respondents referred to the fact that many public library systems are currently actively engaged in reaching out to publics that are not normally users. There was mention of efforts being made to reach the poor and minority populations by the public libraries of New York City and its boroughs and by libraries in Newark, Kalamazoo, Milwaukee, Baltimore, Los Angeles, and Cleveland. Typically, these are demonstration programs where staff members make direct neighborhood contacts, open up storefront branches, run essay and art contests, and stock collections that may be of particular interest to potential patrons. Apparently librarians believe that the success of these efforts varies, and that it is too early to determine how effective these outreach efforts actually are.

Other efforts at motivating nonusers were cited by some respondents as being rather successful, but no general guidelines are identifiable thus far.

An unspecified number of school demonstration programs that are now in progress throughout the country. These demonstrations have been concerned with creating ideal school libraries with the infusion of what one expert termed a good chunk of money, the hiring of imaginative personnel, and the involvement of teachers and school administrators with librarians.

The Minneapolis effort, which is described as utilizing sound public relations techniques via the mass media to inform the public of the services that that city's public library has to offer to all its citizens.

National Library Week, which uses the instrumentalities of mass publicity to generate usage.

Opinions on Facilities

The respondents were asked to react to a rather lengthy statement that read as follows:

Again, some critics of libraries claim that various innovations have made obsolete our classical concepts of permanent library buildings as merely housing collections of books and papers. They claim that investing funds in building new library plants or refurbishing or expanding old ones are wasteful.

Instead they suggest that funds could well go into subsidizing such things as paperback books that could be sold to the public at cost; or that these monies could be used to develop and distribute home microdot storage and retrieval systems; or buildings that are only partially used at present, such as schools, governmental buildings, parish buildings and the like. Please describe how you feel about the argument that more funds should be invested in physical library plants, rather than in the alternatives that were presented. Please state the reasoning behind your thinking.

For 11 of the 14 respondents the notion of not funding library buildings but investing money in other means of distribution instead was generally unacceptable. This did not mean that traditional library buildings should be supported merely because this has been the pattern of old, but rather that funds should be used to create imaginative new, functional facilities that essentially will convert libraries into true information centers. This cannot be done by using other public facilities, which at most represent stopgaps. Automated information storage, retrieval, and reproduction systems were seen as instruments to enhance the functions of the new library-information facility, not as a substitute for it. At the same time, the efficacy of these systems was viewed as lying in the future but not as being practical in the present.

These alternatives cannot substitute for library buildings. They are only supplementary. The cost of microdot storage is so great that it is a long way off. All these things are useful, but they do not substitute for the physical library.

A library plant can be a major information source in many ways so long as it is constructed imaginatively and its connections with all information and communication agencies are made stronger.

Buildings are reflections of programs. We need imagination in constructing varied-purpose rooms for film viewing, studying, and language-teaching.

I don't like the alternatives given because they seem to make the public library even more invisible than it is, but on the other hand, "visibility" is not a huge Roman tomb in the middle of the city called "The Library." I would think that buildings have to follow the determination of the library's objectives.

First, the possession of paperback books is quite different from having access to a total collection representing a multitude of interests and points of view. Second, the automation that is being developed is going to give us a certain flexibility we do not now have. Its achievements thus far are limited, and the leaders in the field of automation are not claiming miracles.

However, three respondents expressed their agreement with the statement, mentioning that radically different distributive innovations are needed. One expert put it this way:

I agree with the critics—at least partially—because major innovations in consumption in other areas seem to have resulted from new marketing and distribution techniques (e.g. supermarkets).

Another made this stronger comment:

Less money should be spent on library buildings as such and more should be spent on microdot and paperbacks and television transmission. In a few years you will be able to dial the telephone and get reproductions on a home TV screen. This is very close. This is where the money should go.

A National Policy

"In your opinion what should be the elements that go into an American National Policy which would promote increased usage of current library facilities and of additional facilities and resources that might be provided in the future?" The library experts were asked to respond to this question. Collectively, the replies reflect both the concerns of these experienced librarians and their hopes for bettering library services in the future. The experts agreed that there is need for a concerted nationwide effort to reexamine the roles of our libraries, to reorient these roles according to needs that have been delineated via empirical research, to experiment with imaginative new methods and techniques, to train and attract qualified personnel, and to adopt modern methods that have been proved effective. In short, these respondents appear to believe that it is time for our libraries to shed tradition and to step into the actual arena of contemporary happenings.

By way of conclusion to this brief report, it is appropriate to summarize some approaches to identifying the people's needs and the libraries' needs, and to motivating the active roles of both, as suggested by the fourteen library leaders. First, heavy stress should be placed on consolidating and coordinating library activities through state, Federal, and private library-oriented agencies. Second, the need for extensive sound research, evaluation, development, and experimentation should be emphasized. Third, attention should be focused on the adaptation of modern technologies to library functions. And fourth, effort should be directed toward persuading voters to support new library programs and services already empirically demonstrated as effective.

TABLE 2A–2.1

SUMMARY HIGHLIGHTS OF AN OPINION SURVEY ON USE OF PUBLIC LIBRARIES

(14 experts in librarianship)

Summary highlights

1. The experts tended to hold academic libraries in higher esteem than public libraries.
2. Although the experts generally felt that the size of a community is not a proper criterion by which to evaluate the function of a public library, they were able to categorize libraries by size of community when expressing judgments.
3. The experts generally emphasized modernization, automation, and better utilization of personnel as areas that can contribute to improvement of the operation of large and middle-sized libraries.
4. The experts felt that public libraries generally best provide services such as (1) basic adult general reading and circulation, (2) general children's reading and circulation, and (3) general and special reference service, particularly to students.
5. The experts generally agreed that the public libraries do less well in (1) providing services to minority and disadvantaged individuals and groups; (2) providing services to special groups such as scientists, innovators in the arts, etc.; (3) providing reliable up-to-date information and research material; and (4) providing community cultural and adult education services.
6. The experts believed generally that libraries do a better job of the kind of things they have traditionally done than they do in coping with the newer opportunities and needs of the modern urban community.
7. Practically every expert mentioned the lack of trained personnel as an important problem of the libraries, and most ranked this as the most critical problem.
8. Of 12 respondents, 9 rated general research on library usage as fair to poor rather than good or excellent.
9. In general, the experts agreed that there has been a considerable expansion in the use of the public libraries by students.
10. To 11 of the 14 experts the idea of investing in new means of distribution of library materials (subsidized paperback books, information retrieval systems, etc.) in place of expanding library buildings in the future was generally unacceptable.

SOURCE: The Use of Libraries and the Conditions That Promote Their Use, *a study by The Academy for Educational Development, Inc., commissioned by the National Advisory Commission on Libraries in 1967.*

TABLE 2A–2.2

OPINIONS ON INADEQUACIES IN PUBLIC LIBRARY SERVICES

(14 experts in librarianship)

CURRENT PUBLIC LIBRARY SERVICES	NUMBER OF MENTIONS
Provided best	
Basic adult general reading and circulation	8
General children's reading, storytelling, and circulation	7
General reference and guidance	6
Special reference services for pupils and students	5
Special information and reference services for specialized subgroups	4
Extension services (e.g., bookmobiles)	2
Film showings	1
Coordinating area resources	1
Avoiding censorship	1
Provided least well	
Reaching minority groups, the disadvantaged	8
Reaching special groups such as scientists, technical community, the avant-garde	5
Furnishing dependable up-to-date information and research material	4
Provision of community cultural and adult education services	3

SOURCE: The Use of Libraries and the Conditions That Promote Their Use, *a study by The Academy for Educational Development, Inc., commissioned by the National Advisory Commission on Libraries in 1967.*

TABLE 2A–2.3

OPINIONS ON ADMINISTRATIVE PROBLEMS OF PUBLIC LIBRARIES

(14 experts in librarianship)

ADMINISTRATIVE PROBLEM	*Number of mentions*	
	PROBLEM	MOST URGENT PROBLEM
Manpower shortage; lack of trained personnel	13	12
Lack of proper buildings; inadequate space, facilities	7	2
Lack of financing	5	2
Book acquisition	5	3
Archaic procedures	4	1
Inadequate salaries	2	1

SOURCE: The Use of Libraries and the Conditions That Promote Their Use, *a study by The Academy for Educational Development, Inc., commissioned by the National Advisory Commission on Libraries in 1967.*

B. THE USER'S VIEW OF PUBLIC LIBRARIES

The National Advisory Commission on Libraries was fortunate to have documentation available to it on the use of public libraries and the attitudes of the public at large toward their libraries. This new evidence bears out what the public librarians already know, as seen in the preceding section, about the impact of education on library use and about their failures to reach portions of their potential clientele. This evidence also suggests that the job of attracting these people, as many public librarians seem determined to do, will require persuasive skill indeed—most adult nonusers, on a national average, could think of no way they could be enticed into using library facilities.

The purpose of this section is to present the evidence of public library use and nonuse in order to demonstrate the need for more broadly conceived research in this area and to provide some insight on the basis of current knowledge. It consists of two papers: the first is a review of the literature, and the second reports the results of a national poll of adults.

1. THE RECORD OF PUBLIC LIBRARY USE AS SUGGESTED BY A REVIEW OF THE LITERATURE[6]

There is some evidence of the ways people actually do use their libraries, and this portion of chapter 2, section B, is devoted to a discussion of this evidence as reported in the literature. Library specialists tend to agree that research that has been done on library use is fragmented, redundant, and inadequate, and that far more sophisticated studies, drawing on the expertise of many disciplines, must be done to provide the foundation for broad-based planning in meeting society's needs for library and informational services. Thus it is relevant to explore the record; highlights of this review, reported in the following pages, are summarized in Table 2B–1.1.

First, a few comments on the methodology, which apply both to the public library material appearing here in section B.1 and to the discussion of the literature on academic library use in section C.2. In order to examine the research that was being done on library usage contemporarily, this literature search was confined to large-scale studies that were conducted (with one exception) in the years 1949 to 1967. Only literature available through customary channels (e.g., interlibrary loans, journals, published reports that were generally available to the public) was examined, thus eliminating privately conducted and circulated research from the investigation. The search was confined to primary studies of people who were purported to be users of public, college, and university libraries, and no effort was made to cover usage of Federal, state, public school, or specialized libraries. Standard reference sources pertaining to public and academic libraries were used to locate the materials, and also library specialists both within and outside the University of Denver were canvassed for suggested materials. Only studies whose units of measure were people—rather than books, registration cards, or circulation rates—were included for analysis. Studies pertaining to library facilities, personnel, administration, or management were excluded. The sources selected for examination are referenced throughout this paper.

Five questions about the users of public libraries provided the structure for this study: (1) Who uses public libraries? (2) Why do these individuals use libraries? (3)

6 *From* The Use of Libraries and the Conditions That Promote Their Use *by The Academy for Educational Development, Inc., one of the special studies commissioned by the National Advisory Commission on Libraries during 1967. Harold Mendelsohn was Director of the study; Karen Wingerd was Research Assistant.*

Who does *not* use public libraries? (4) Why do these particular people *not* use public libraries? (5) What can be done to motivate people to use libraries?

Two questions may be raised about the literature that attempts to identify library users. First, what techniques, measures, and criteria are used to define users? Second, what information is available about users? Several methods have been used to define users of libraries.[7] One of the commonest is to define a user in terms of an individual's actual registration with a public library. A second method of defining users entails counting the call slips on all materials checked out in a library by particular individuals. Users may also be defined as individuals calling on the library at least once a year. Finally, users may be defined as individuals using the library at least once a month.

The difficulty presented by these several approaches to defining users is evident in the literature on libraries. None of the researchers appear to be aware that what they term "user" is not necessarily comparable to what is termed "user" by some other researcher. The problem of definition of users is compounded when the researcher fails to indicate what criteria he is employing to identify the users of library materials in his own particular study.

WHO USES PUBLIC LIBRARIES?

The available data on library users may be classified according to the type of library used, and this paper is confined to public libraries only. A survey of the literature on use of academic libraries appears in section C.2 of the present chapter.

The classic study of the public library is Berelson's *The Library's Public,* published in 1949. Berelson indicated that there were 7,400 libraries in 1949, offering services to a population of 100 million people. The public libraries then contained over 125 million volumes. About 25 million people were registered with the public libraries. Today the picture is slightly different. Approximately 6,783 public libraries and 3,676 branch libraries serve a population of 199 million. About 52 million individuals (26 percent) are registered with these institutions.[8]

A glance at these figures reveals that the number of people served by libraries in 1965–66 is almost twice as many as those who were offered service in 1949. However, the number of libraries in 1965 had not doubled with the increases in population. This may be due either to increased efficiency in information storage and retrieval systems in libraries or to the fact that libraries, like other public institutions (schools), have simply not kept pace with population changes. The fact remains that some 20 million Americans have no access to public library services. As discussed later in this report, those 20 million people may be significant because they are characterized by a unique set of socio-economic attributes.

In addition to sheer gross numbers, public library users may be identified and studied according to age, education, sex, occupation, economic status, marital status, race, and residence.

Age

The Berelson study reports that children and young adults, especially those of school age, use the library more than any other age group. Both relative to the numbers in the total population and in relation to the total number of library users, they are the largest portion of the library clientele. According to Berelson's 1949 study, juveniles make up about twice as large a proportion of library registration as they do of the population at large. The figure for juvenile users is slightly larger today. Current surveys indicate that of the 52 million individuals using libraries, at least 50 to 70 percent are juveniles. In a two-day study in Youngstown and Mahoney counties in Illinois, researchers found that 68 percent of the library users were juveniles.[9]

The predominance of juveniles in the public library clientele suggests that the use of

7 B. Berelson, The Library's Public (*New York: Columbia University Press, 1949*).
8 Statistics on Public Libraries (*Washington, D.C.: American Library Association, 1966*).
9 "*Role of Teenagers and Children,*" Library Quarterly, 33 (*January 1963*).

the library falls off sharply at the school-leaving age. Berelson's study in 1949 discloses that almost one third of the total school-age group use the library during a given month, but only one tenth of the groups beyond school age attend a public library during a similar time period. Studies conducted by Kaplan, Berelson, Link and Hopf, Field and Peacock, and the Survey Research Center (SRC), reported by Berelson, support the assertion that library usage decreases with increases in age (Table 2B–1.2). A 1966 study of the metropolitan areas of Baltimore and Washington, D.C., reported on the age distribution of public library users, showing approximately 47 percent of the users to be between the ages of twelve and twenty-one (Table 2B–1.3).[10] In a one-day patron count at the Evansville Public Library in 1961, 75 percent of the 2,005 individuals who checked materials out of the library were observed to be juveniles or young adults.

It is evident from these studies that library users are to be found primarily among younger age groups and that library usage decreases as the age of patrons increases. This lack of use of libraries by older individuals may be due to a number of reasons, including physical disabilities, depleted energy, or a desire to avoid a new experience.

The age composition of the library clientele brings to consideration another characteristic of library users, their educational level. The increase in educational requirements today from compulsory eighth-grade education to compulsory high school education in many state school systems means that students (juveniles and young adults) are given more information and required to seek more information. Library usage among juveniles and young adults no doubt reflects this need.

Education

The proportion of people either registered or actively using the library rises sharply with their level of schooling. In 1949 Berelson reported that 10 to 15 percent of the adults having only a grade school education were public library users as compared with four times as many of the college graduates. It may be that this difference is attributable to the better reading habits of the more highly educated. Those with more formal education have had more reading training plus motivation to use the library as a source of information. A disproportionately large number of public library users are people drawn from groups with the most schooling. At the same time, however, the absolute library clientele is composed predominantly of persons with lesser education. The reason for this is that the lesser-educated proportion is greater than any other group in the population. Statistics from Berelson's study reveal that in 1940 about 60 percent of the population over twenty-five years of age had an elementary school education or less, 30 percent had a high school education, and 10 percent had a college education. For the most part, then, although people with little education use the library relatively much less than the well-educated, they exceed the latter in absolute numbers.

It is generally from the group with a high school education that the public library has drawn the greatest number of users, according to Berelson at the time of his study. Although the population is predominantly composed of people with only an elementary education, the library clientele is composed of those with at least a high school education. The 1966 study by the University of Maryland indicates that perhaps college-trained adults have now become the predominant group of public library users. In this study, of all the adults queried, 8.3 percent indicated that they had last attended an elementary school; 28.1 percent said that the last school attended was high school; 60.5 percent said that college was the last school attended. Thus, just as those with less education (elementary level) are underrepresented as library users (compared to the proportion of them in the total population), those with a college education are strongly overrepresented. Even when other factors are considered (sex, race, economic level), the educational level of library users emerges as the most important single factor affecting library behavior.

10 *M. L. Bundy, "Metropolitan Public Library Use,"* Wilson Library Bulletin, *41 (May 1967).*

Sex

Berelson's study indicates that women are by far the more frequent users of libraries (Table 2B–1.4). They constituted about one half to two thirds of the total number of registrants at the time his study was conducted. These percentages are dependent upon three factors. First, women use circulation services more than men. Second, men use reference services more than women. Third, the larger the city, the greater the number of men attending libraries.

Occupation

In the past students constituted the greatest proportion of the library's clientele, followed in frequency by housewives and white-collar workers, professional and managerial people, and wage earners. The student group represented about one fourth to one half of the total registrants or users of public libraries, according to Berelson's data; housewives and white-collar workers made up about one third, and professionals and wage earners, each, a tenth.

The 1966 Maryland study shows that the majority of users are professional people. In this study, engineers and scientists accounted for 25.4 percent of the professional group. Teachers comprised 27 percent of the professional users; community and government employees, 12.6 percent. The professional group also included a sprinkling of authors (53) and clergymen (50). In other occupational categories 50 or more individuals reported occupying positions as officials in public administration, managers, proprietors, secretaries, clerical workers, insurance agents, brokers, and salesmen.

How representative is the user-of-libraries population of the total population of the area served by the library? According to the Maryland study, although 15 percent of employed adults are professional people, 52.3 percent of employed library users are in the professions. Of the employed population 8 percent are managers, but 14.2 percent of the user group are managers. The most underrepresented group are operatives. They constitute 15 percent of the population but only 1.4 percent of the employed library users.

Several generalizations may be drawn from Berelson's materials and the Maryland data concerning the occupations of library users: (1) proportionately more professional and managerial groups, white-collar workers, and students use the library as compared to other occupational groups; (2) members of these three groups become actual users, or at least registrants, in greater numbers than either wage earners or unemployed housewives; (3) the public library attracts more individuals from higher occupational status groups than from lower occupational groups.

Economic Status

Very little current research is available on the use of the public library by different economic groups. The Berelson, *et al.*, data for 1948 indicate that libraries are used by the higher economic groups preponderantly. Berelson attributes this to the differential in education among higher and lower economic groups. However, despite this disproportion in relative use, the majority of users come from the middle class. Neither the wealthy nor the very poor use the library extensively. The wealthy appear to buy their own books, and they have access to many other kinds of media (films, cameras, TV). The poor have reading difficulties because of their educational level, and the recent influx of paperbacks into the book market has made printed information and literature more accessible at relatively inexpensive prices. The public library, as a consequence, is patronized by a disproportionately large segment of the middle class of the community (Table 2B–1.5).

Marital Status

Although little current information is available about the relationship between marital status and public library usage, some conclusions may be drawn from Berelson's

1949 report and the data on student and juvenile use of libraries. Berelson reports that single persons use the libraries more often than married persons. Such a claim is justifiable in light of the fact that other studies showed that juveniles (children and teen-agers) account for 50 to 70 percent of the public library clientele. The studies reported by Johnson, Kaplan, and Berelson indicate that from 35 to 38 percent of the samples interviewed as users of the library were single and that 25 to 29 percent were married.

This does not indicate that there are more single than married individuals using the library. The differential refers to the proportionate share of these groups in the libraries' clientele. Berelson lists three reasons for the differential:

> First, the single adults are younger than married adults and age, with its correlate education, is a major determinant of library use. Second, married people borrow books for spouses and thus represent more library use than is recorded or measured. Third, married adults are more involved in domestic duties and therefore have less time for leisure reading.[11]

Race

No surveys among those reviewed compared the use of libraries with particular ethnic or racial groups when both library facilities and education were controlled. However, it seems reasonable to assert that where library service is provided to Negroes of moderate or high education, they will make as full a use of the public library as their white counterparts. Although several studies have been conducted on the use of libraries by low-income groups in similar areas, other factors than race were analyzed. Such a study was conducted by Margaret Peil in 1963, entitled "Library Use by Low-Income Chicago Families."[12] Peil measured differences in age, increased ownership of books, and reading time of mothers of 180 children in three Catholic schools with library usage. It is unfortunate that the racial dimension was not considered as a variable and compared with library usage. It is evident that there is little or no information available on the effect of race on library usage.

[The national study of library usage conducted in 1967 for the National Advisory Commission on Libraries and reported later in this chapter does present a racial breakdown of usage.]

Residence and Accessibility

Berelson indicates that the correlation between library usage and changes in growth patterns of the community takes four forms. First, the wealthier and better-educated population centers use the library more than poorer and less-educated population centers. Berelson mentions a nationwide survey reported by SRC in 1948, which revealed that 21 percent of the inhabitants of the North used the public library during a given year as compared with 9 percent of the people in the South who used the library during the same period. Philip Ennis's more recent demographical analysis of the library consumer in 1964 indicates that the population on the Pacific Coast, with its high income level and high educational level, makes extensive use of the library.[13]

Second, the expansion of urban and suburban developments is a major factor affecting library usage. No recent studies have been done to compare the library usage of urban, suburban, and rural communities. Four studies reported by Berelson indicate that: (1) public library service is far less available in rural areas; (2) where library service is equally available in rural and urban communities, urbanites use libraries more often than do rural residents; and (3) the differential in use may be due to inequalities in educational levels and inequalities in the availability of library facilities.

11 *Berelson*, op. cit., *p. 39.*
12 *M. Peil, "Library Use by Low-Income Chicago Families,"* Library Quarterly, *33 (October 1963), pp. 329–33.*
13 *Philip Ennis, "The Library Consumer: Patterns and Trends,"* Library Quarterly, *34 (April 1964), pp. 163–78.*

Third, there is a relationship between the size of the city and library usage. Most of the population registers with a public library in the smaller cities, and a somewhat large circulation rate is maintained per capita. It may be asserted that the impact of the library is greater in the smaller cities. Although small communities below ten thousand have libraries, they are usually poorly stocked and inadequately staffed. Although there are exceptions, the curve of library use declines in small communities.

Fourth, there is a relationship between the use of the library and the distance separating the user from it. The closer people live to a library, the more they tend to use it. Proximity is a major factor in determining library usage.

Recent surveys have not provided information on the impact of distance from libraries and their use by patrons. Field and Peacock's survey in 1948 indicates that fully 76 percent of the respondents used a particular branch library because it was close to home, another 5 percent because it was close to work. About half of the major part of library registrants live within four to eight blocks of the library. Berelson indicates that there is some suggestion that the factor of distance is less important in a small town, where the single central building seems to attract people from a wide radius. The public library, like other community service centers, has a natural service area. Distance is an important factor in the use of the American public library. Berelson's assertions about library distances from home and work were corroborated by the 1966 Maryland study. Of a total of 16,019 library patrons studied, about 74.9 percent set out for the library from home, 11.9 percent came from school, and 7.5 percent from work. For 73.9 percent the library visited was the one closest to their home. The majority used this close-to-home library at least once a month.

The automobile was the principal mode of transportation used. Two thirds of the library patrons traveled by car (67.9 percent), as compared with 24.6 percent who made their trip by walking, and 4.9 percent who traveled by bus. The distance traveled ranged from less than a mile to 420 miles, but 80 percent traveled less than five miles. Of the users surveyed, 39.7 percent traveled less than one mile; 44.4 percent, between one and five miles; 9.1 percent, between five and ten miles; 3.5 percent, between ten and fifteen miles; and 1.8 percent, over fifteen miles.

This study, like Berelson's, indicates that library patrons use the closest library to their home or work. The study also confirms earlier conclusions that the shorter the distance to the library, the greater the library usage by greater numbers of people.

WHY PEOPLE USE THE PUBLIC LIBRARY

The patrons of the public library have been described above, but the type of use they make of the library has yet to be explored. The public library of course provides a number of services to its users. It lends books, provides reference information, offers reading and study facilities, maintains newspaper and magazine files, facilitates research, does group work in reading, administers discussion groups, tells stories to children. The list is endless. What use then does the public make of these services offered by the public library system? Or in other words, why do people choose to visit the library?

Berelson indicates that of all library activities the circulation of books for home use represents by far the major public service provided by the American public library. Most of the people who use the library use its circulation services. A comparison of circulation and reference services derived from three studies indicates that circulation predominates over reference in a ratio of at least two or three to one. In short, the circulation of books is the single most-utilized service of the public library. The Maryland study also supports this, although the table indicating the reasons for using the library (Table 2B–1.6) does not reveal as high a differentiation in the ratio of circulation to reference uses as did Berelson's data. The greatest use of the library appears to be book circulation, and the next appears to be reference.

Circulation

Fiction makes up about 60 to 65 percent of the total circulation of the modern public library. This figure varies with the size of the population served by the library. The smaller the library, the larger the proportion of fiction in the literature held. Berelson's 1949 report indicates that fully two thirds of the circulation in communities of 25,000 to 50,000 population is fiction. In metropolitan areas the figure for fiction is only one half of the circulation. This may be attributed to greater use of public libraries by professional people, the presence of more advanced students, more research needs, and a higher educational level in the metropolitan areas.

As a whole, the distribution of nonfiction accounts for the second-largest category for public libraries, regardless of size. All major classes of nonfiction books receive a rather consistent share of the total circulations across the board (Table 2B–1.7).

Berelson's data may be compared with that obtained in the 1966 Maryland study. By Dewey Decimal Classification, the distribution of subject interest is shown in Table 2B–1.8. When the subjects are grouped in the three broad divisions—humanities, social science, and science and technology—the proportions are social science, 45.2 percent; humanities, 30.6 percent; and science and technology, 24.2 percent.

The circulation of types of library books has been examined from the standpoint of currency. A common belief is that public libraries provide the "latest books" or "recent best-sellers." Not much information is available on the relationship between age of the book and the frequency with which the book is used. However, a number of observations suggest that there is a decline in circulation as books grow older.

Reference Information

A key question is how public libraries are related to the personal, job, or community life of the patrons. In the Maryland study an answer to this question was sought by asking patrons why they wanted the materials or information requested. The replies indicated that public libraries are used primarily for personal reading and school-related use. Public library use to support occupational or group activities is minimal. Respondents in the Maryland study cited these reasons for using the library: 49.3 percent used the library for personal interest, 41.7 percent used the library for schoolwork, 9.1 percent used the reference library on behalf of another person, 6.5 percent used the services for their work, 2.0 percent used the library for a club activity, and 2.6 percent for some other reason; 5.8 percent did not respond to the question asked.

The results of this recent study contrast sharply with the 1948 data from Berelson's study. Berelson found that 26 percent of total users of the main library in Detroit, Michigan (as opposed to the branch libraries), used reference information for schoolwork; 27 percent of the patrons used information and reference services for their jobs; 38 percent used these services for some other reason.

Unrecorded Use

Anyone may visit the public library and browse through the volumes, read some interesting titles, secure some piece of desired information—in short, make use of the library without appearing in the library's records as a user. Berelson indicated that the actual incidence of such unrecorded use of library material is not known. However, the Maryland study sheds some light on this aspect of library usage. The study found that only a small proportion of users avail themselves of library tools, guides, and staff help. Browsing through books on the shelves seems to be the major way materials are located. Twice as many patrons reported this activity as compared with those who used the catalogs. Most users are apparently on their own, since only 16 percent reported they sought help from a librarian. The approaches used to locate material are significant because a high percentage of patrons apparently come to the library without a specific book in mind a priori. (See Table 2B–1.9.)

Satisfaction with Library Service

Use of the public library is affected by the public's attitude toward the institution. By and large, there appears to be general satisfaction with the library. In Berelson's research about 75 percent of the patrons reported that they were able to get what they wanted from the library. Berelson also found that very few library users were unable to satisfy their reading or information demands at the public library (Table 2B–1.10).

The more recent Maryland study revealed a relatively lower "completely satisfied" group. Here 47 percent of users reported being completely satisfied, 28.5 percent indicated that they were partially satisfied, and 7 percent indicated complete dissatisfaction with the library's services. In short, on the basis of this study, of every two persons leaving the library at any given time, at least one appears to be completely satisfied with the service recieved.

When library patrons go away dissatisfied, it is because they cannot obtain the materials they require. Either the books they want are on loan, or the library does not have them at all. Of these dissatisfied users in the Maryland study, 47 percent wanted a book already checked out, 35 percent wanted a book not in the library, 14.4 percent could not locate material, 6.4 percent found material outdated, 6.1 percent found material was too elementary, and 2 percent found locating material too difficult.

Further insight into patron dissatisfaction with libraries is suggested by the response of the total group of users in the Maryland study; only 23.5 percent named one or more difficulties they had encountered in using the library. The difficulties included: 7 percent, getting parking space; 5.4 percent, library was too noisy; 4.7 percent hard to figure out library arrangements; 3 percent, library crowded; 2 percent, unfriendly library staff; 1 percent, librarian didn't know how to help; 1 percent, took too long to get magazines from stacks.

Of the 14,225 patrons arriving by automobile, 13.5 percent complained about parking problems. Of the 3,417 patrons who sought the help of a librarian, 12.5 percent found the librarian to be unfriendly, and 5.8 percent felt the librarian offering help to be incompetent.

Another key to identifying library inadequacies was sought by asking patrons why they chose to bypass the library closest their home in favor of another library located at a greater distance. Of the 5,234 patrons who did not use the closest library, 54.3 percent said that the library eventually used had more material; 3.9 percent said that their local library was closed; 3.8 percent said that the eventually used library had better parking facilities.

The Nelson Associates Study of the New York Public Library System also sheds some light on the bypass problem.[14] At least 33.3 percent of their sample used one other library than the one closest to the patron's residence or job, 21.3 percent used at least two other libraries, and 19.6 percent used three or more other libraries. In this study 48.6 percent of users of other libraries indicated that they were dissatisfied with collections in their local libraries, 6.6 percent used other libraries because they had better working conditions, 40.4 percent found other libraries more conveniently located for parking, and 5.2 percent found the hours more convenient in other libraries.

Nonusers

None of the studies in this survey of the literature specifically identified the non-user of public libraries. The 1967 study that was done for the National Advisory Commission on Libraries did attempt to do so; the results are reported later in this section. Historical information on nonusers must be guessed at from the reseach on users of libraries.

The foregoing discussion suggests that the public library nonuser category is composed primarily of the poorly educated, the racial minorities, males, and low-income,

14 *Nelson Associates,* Prospects for Library Cooperation in New York City (*New York: Nelson Associates, Inc., 1963*).

elderly, and rural groups. Adult use of the public library is largely a function of educational level. The more highly educated individuals use the library's circulation facilities, and in particular, the informational services of the library. Some scattered observations indicate that the racial minorities (Negroes, etc.) in the lower-income brackets and with fewer educational opportunities use the library in fewer numbers than do majority-group members. The relationship between race and library usage is probably more a function of socioeconomic factors than of skin color per se.

Studies indicate that women are by far the more frequent general circulation users, although males tend to use informational and reference services more than females. Lower-income groups may use the library less because they have access to fiction circulation through paperbacks that may be purchased at low prices. The lower-income groups appear to use the library less because they are generally less well educated. Wealthy individuals may not use the public libraries because they can afford to maintain their own personal libraries in any manner they might desire.

The age of the library user is a factor affecting library usage. The older a person grows, the less likely he is to use the library. This appears to be a function of his physical capabilities, distance from library, and interests. The studies indicate that children are the most frequent users of public libraries.

Distance from library services has been shown to be a significant factor affecting library usage. The farther one is from library services, the less use he is likely to make of those services. Farthest removed from library facilities are farmers and individuals residing in isolated rural communities.

This concludes the review of literature on public library use. Summary highlights are shown in Table 2B–1.1 The following section reports the results of a new study.

TABLE 2B–1.1

SUMMARY HIGHLIGHTS OF A REVIEW OF THE LITERATURE ON THE USE OF PUBLIC LIBRARIES

Summary highlights

1. The body of recorded knowledge concerning the use of public libraries is inadequate, fragmented, and noncomparable.
2. Broad-based trend data concerning the use of libraries are almost totally absent.
3. The literature is nearly void of studies identified with the nonusers of libraries.
4. The growth of the nation's libraries has not kept pace with the increase in population served by libraries, which has doubled since 1949, when Berelson's classic study, *The Library's Public,* was published.
5. The juvenile proportion of the public library clientele (at least 50 to 75 percent of the total) has probably increased slightly during the past two decades.
6. As people grow older they tend to use libraries less.
7. There is a direct relationship between how much education a person has and the extent to which he uses libraries.
8. Although literature is sparse on public library usage by different economic groups, Berelson's report indicated that in 1948 the majority of users came from the middle class; neither the wealthy nor the very poor used libraries to a great extent.
9. When the available literature does describe those who use libraries, data are meager about the specific uses made by the various categories of library users.
10. The kinds of reference services rendered by a public library are highly influenced by the employment characteristics of the community in which it is located.
11. Apparently the reasons stated for dissatisfaction with libraries have not changed radically since Berelson's study.

SOURCE: The Use of Libraries and the Conditions That Promote Their Use, *a study by The Academy for Educational Development, Inc., commissioned by the National Advisory Commission on Libraries in 1967.*

TABLE 2B–1.2

COMPARISON OF REPORTS FROM VARIOUS STUDIES ON DISTRIBUTION OF ADULT AGE GROUPS USING THE PUBLIC LIBRARY

	Percent reported by various investigators					
USER AGE GROUP	KAPLAN 1943	BERELSON 1945	LINK & HOPF 1946	FIELD & PEACOCK 1948	BERELSON 1948	SRC 1948
Young	37%	31%	31%	37%	30%	22%
Middle	24	22	27	34	29	14
Old	18	19	32	23	19	14

SOURCE: *B. Berelson,* The Library's Public (*New York: Columbia University Press, 1949*), *p. 23.*

TABLE 2B–1.3

THE AGE RANGE OF PUBLIC LIBRARY USERS IN THE BALTIMORE-WASHINGTON, D.C., METROPOLITAN AREAS
(1966)

AGE RANGE	PERCENT OF USERS
12–16 years	22.4%
17–21 years	24.9
23–34 years	18.1
35–50 years	25.0
50 years and over	8.3
No response	1.3

SOURCE: *M. L. Bundy, "Metropolitan Public Library Use,"* Wilson Library Bulletin, *41 (May 1967), p. 953.*

TABLE 2B–1.4

COMPARISON OF REPORTS FROM VARIOUS STUDIES ON PUBLIC LIBRARY REGISTRATION AND USE BY ADULT MEN AND WOMEN

Percentages of group registered

SEX	WAPLES 1933	WERT 1937	JOECKEL & CARNOVSKY 1940	NORC 1946	FIELD & PEACOCK 1948	SRC 1948
Men	5%	34%	5%	29%	24%	15%
Women	7	35	7	34	25	21

Percentages of group using the library

SEX	JOHNSON 1932	KAPLAN 1943	BERELSON 1945	FIELD & PEACOCK 1948	BERELSON 1948	SRC 1948
Men	29%	25%	20%	31%	23%	17%
Women	37	33	28	30	30	20

Total number of cases in each group

SEX	WAPLES 1933	WERT 1937	JOECKEL & CARNOVSKY 1940	NORC 1946	FIELD & PEACOCK 1948	SRC 1948	JOHNSON 1932	KAPLAN 1943	BERELSON 1945	FIELD & PEACOCK 1948	BERELSON 1948	SRC 1948
Men	(Not given)	(Not given)	(5,406)	(Not given)	(469)	(511)	(487)	(2,002)	(240)	(469)	(448)	(511)
Women	"	"	(4,578)	"	(531)	(640)	(279)	(2,999)	(261)	(531)	(573)	(640)

SOURCE: B. Berelson, The Library's Public (New York: Columbia University Press, 1949), p. 31.

TABLE 2B–1.5

COMPARISON OF REPORTS FROM VARIOUS STUDIES ON THE ECONOMIC LEVELS OF ADULT PUBLIC LIBRARY USERS

ECONOMIC LEVEL OF USERS	Percent reported by various investigators		
	FIELD & PEACOCK 1948	BERELSON 1948	SRC 1948
High	21%	12%	41%
Middle	62	76	52
Low	17	12	7
TOTAL N	(310)	(264)	(228)

SOURCE: *B. Berelson,* The Library's Public (*New York: Columbia University Press, 1949*), *p. 38.*

TABLE 2B–1.6

REASONS FOR ATTENDING A PUBLIC LIBRARY GIVEN BY USERS IN THE BALTIMORE-WASHINGTON, D.C., METROPOLITAN AREAS
(1966)

REASONS FOR ATTENDING A PUBLIC LIBRARY	PERCENT OF TOTAL USERS
Return books	43.4%
Obtain materials or information on a subject	33.5
Pick out general reading	33.5
Obtain specific books	22.1
Bring child	12.9
Study, using own material	7.4
Meet or consult with friends	3.6
Other reasons	5.7
No response	1.1

SOURCE: *M. L. Bundy, "Metropolitan Public Library Use,"* Wilson Library Bulletin, *41 (May 1967), p. 956.*

TABLE 2B–1.7

DISTRIBUTION OF ADULT FICTION AND NONFICTION CIRCULATION IN PUBLIC LIBRARIES OF DIFFERENT SIZES*

(1946)

CATEGORY OF BOOK	Circulation percentages reported by libraries serving four population groups			
	25,000 50,000	50,000 100,000	100,000 250,000	250,000 AND OVER
Fiction†	67%	65%	62%	54%
Nonfiction	33	35	38	46
Useful arts	4	4	4	5
Fine arts	4	4	4	5
Literature	4	4	4	5
Biography	3	4	4	4
Social science	3	3	3	4
History	3	3	3	3
Philosophy and religion	2	2	3	3
Travel	2	2	2	2
Natural science	2	2	2	2
Other	6	7	9	13
Total number of libraries supplying data	(31)	(18)	(13)	(20)

* Constructed from information supplied by selected public libraries during summer 1947.
† The percentage of fiction in the juvenile circulation is only slightly less than that in the adult cirtion.

SOURCE: B. Berelson, The Library's Public (New York: Columbia University Press, 1949), p. 57.

TABLE 2B–1.8

DISTRIBUTION OF NONFICTION CIRCULATION IN PUBLIC LIBRARIES OF THE BALTIMORE-WASHINGTON, D.C., METROPOLITAN AREAS

(1966)

CATEGORY OF BOOK	CIRCULATION PERCENTAGE
000 General works (library science, bibliography)	1.6%
100 Philosophy	1.1
200 Religion	2.0
300 Social science	23.0
400 Language	1.3
500 Science	11.1
600 Applied science	12.7
700 Fine arts	9.5
800 Literature	16.2
900 History and travel	20.5

SOURCE: M. L. Bundy, "Metropolitan Public Library Use," Wilson Library Bulletin, 41 (May 1967), p. 958.

TABLE 2B–1.9

METHODS OF LOCATING MATERIAL REPORTED BY USERS OF PUBLIC LIBRARIES IN THE BALTIMORE-WASHINGTON, D.C., METROPOLITAN AREAS

(1966)

METHOD OF LOCATING MATERIAL	PERCENT OF TOTAL USERS
Looked through books on shelves	43.1%
Reference books	22.1
Library catalogs	19.0
Sought help from a librarian	16.0
Consulted books or magazines	12.4
Read news magazines or news	8.7
Perodical indexes	5.7
Recordings	2.7
Films	0.9
Other use	2.0
No response	11.1

SOURCE: *M. L. Bundy, "Metropolitan Public Library Use," Wilson Library Bulletin, 41 (May 1967), p. 956.*

TABLE 2B–1.10

COMPARISON OF REPORTS FROM VARIOUS STUDIES ON SATISFACTION OF PUBLIC LIBRARY USERS

	Percent reported by various investigators				
DEGREE OF USER SATISFACTION	HAYGOOD 1938	JAMES 1941	NORC 1946	FIELD & PEACOCK 1948	SRC 1948
Completely satisfied	A little over half	75%	75%	80%	70%
Partially or occa- sionally satisfied	Over a third	8	25	16	14
Not satisfied	14%	17	—	—	5
No answer	—	—	—	4	11
TOTAL N	(Over 16,000)	(6,986)	(400)	(608)	(228)

SOURCE: *B. Berelson, The Library's Public (New York: Columbia University Press, 1949), p. 83.*

2. *INSIGHT INTO ADULT PUBLIC LIBRARY USE AND NONUSE AS SUGGESTED BY A SOCIAL SURVEY OF ATTITUDES*[15]

Realizing that very little is known, except on an impressionistic basis, about the public's image of and perceived need for its libraries, the National Advisory Commission on Libraries called for a special study of library use. The preceding discussion, the literature-review part of this study, reveals clearly the inadequacy of research in library use and nonuse. The following pages present new findings that are directly relevant to the Commission's charge to explore the role and adequacy of the nation's libraries. Highlights of this survey are presented in Table 2B–2.1.

METHODOLOGY OF THE SURVEY

A national sample of adults was interviewed personally to investigate the following:

1. Frequency of use of public libraries and, to some extent, of other kinds of libraries.
2. Factors that explain why some adults go to libraries while others do not.
3. Factors that might induce greater use of libraries.
4. The public's image of libraries.
5. The frequency of book-reading by adults as related to where the books are obtained.

Personal interviews were conducted with 1,549 adults during the period June 21–27, 1967, using a series of questions that were developed by Professor Harold Mendelsohn, Director of the Communication Arts Center of the University of Denver, the questions were pretested and administered by The Gallup Organization, Inc., of Princeton, New Jersey. The following questions were asked:

1a. On the whole, do the various libraries in this city (town) do an excellent, good, fair or poor job of serving people like yourself?
  b. In what ways are they excellent, good, fair or poor?
2. Would you think back over the last three months and tell me how many times, if any, during this period you have gone to a *public* library?
3. Why is it that you don't go to public libraries (more often)?

Those who have *not* gone to a public library were asked:

4. Is there anything that would make it easier for you to go to public libraries or make them more useful or attractive to you?

Those who have gone to a library one or more times were asked:

5a. What is the very best service a library has provided you?
  b. In what ways have the libraries failed to serve your particular needs?
  c. On this card are various reasons for going to libraries. Please tell me the reasons that best describe why you go to libraries. [Respondents were handed a card on which the following phrases appeared:]
To get help or information on special kinds of problems I must deal with.
To use reference books and periodicals for particular assignments.
To attend lectures, exhibits, or performances.

15 *From* The Use of Libraries and the Conditions That Promote Their Use *by The Academy for Educational Development, Inc., one of the special studies commissioned by the National Advisory Commission on Libraries during 1967. Harold Mendelsohn was Director of the study; Karen Wingerd was Research Assistant. The poll reported here was conducted by The Gallup Organization, Inc.*

To examine manuscripts, historical documents, or microfilms.
To listen to or to borrow phonograph records.
To relax and browse.
To help my children get their schoolwork assignments done.
To be in a quiet place where I can think and concentrate without interruption.
To borrow fiction books.
To borrow nonfiction books.
Others (specify).

Everyone was asked:

6. And would you think back over the last three months and tell me how many times, if any, during this period you have gone to some other type of library—such as a school or college library, a reference library, a state library, or a medical, law, or other special library?

7. Here are some words and phrases that people use to describe public libraries. Read me as many words and phrases as you want to that best describe the libraries you usually go to or know about. [Respondents were handed a card on which the following phrases appeared:]

Stimulating	Dull	Gloomy
Inconvenient	Not very helpful	Convenient
Helpful	Modern	Pleasant
Drab	Unfriendly	Fast service
Usually have	Cheerful	Inefficient
what I want	Frustrating	Satisfying
Serious	Old-fashioned	Efficient
Slow service	Usually do not	Discouraging
Fun	have what I want	Encouraging
	Friendly	

8. In your opinion, what improvements in facilities or services or new services should the libraries be offering? (Probe:) Whatever you think is needed.

9a. Now, thinking back over the past three months again, would you tell me just how many books, paperbacks or hard cover, you have had occasion to read during this period?

If any books were read, respondents were asked:

b. Are most of these books those which you got from a public library, those that you have bought and own yourself, or those which you have received as gifts?

The Sample

The design of the sample was that of a replicated probability sample, down to the block level in the case of urban areas, and to segments of townships in the case of rural areas. After stratifying the nation geographically and by size of community in order to insure conformity of the sample with the latest available estimate of the Census Bureau of the distribution of the adult population, sampling locations or areas were selected on a strictly random basis. The interviewers had no choice whatever concerning the part of the city or county in which they conducted their interviews.

Interviewers were given maps of the area to which they were assigned, with a starting point indicated, and were required to follow a specified direction. At each occupied dwelling unit interviewers were instructed to select respondents by following a prescribed systematic method and by a male-female assignment. This procedure was followed until the assigned number of interviews was completed.

Since this sampling procedure is designed to produce a sample that approximates the adult civilian population (twenty-one and older) living in private households in the United States (that is, excluding those in prisons and hospitals, hotels, religious and educational institutions, and on military reservations), the survey results can be applied to this population for the purpose of projecting percentages into number of people. The manner in which the sample is drawn also produces a sample that approximates the population of private households in the United States. Therefore, survey results can also be projected in terms of number of households when appropriate. For the composition of the sample see Table 2B–2.2

THE REPUTATION OF PUBLIC LIBRARIES

On the whole, members of the adult public of the United States—whether they use public libraries or not—currently exhibit neither highly positive nor highly negative assessments, totally, of their local public libraries (Table 2B–2.3). Here, four in ten (the largest single bloc) rate their local libraries as being good rather than excellent (the rating given by 26 percent) or fair or poor (the rating given by 12 percent). Worth noting is the high degree of indifference reflected by the fact that one in five cannot assess the performance of his local library in any direction (22 percent replied "Don't know").

It appears, then, that the public's evaluation of the performance of public libraries in filling local needs is generally tepid. Caucasians, women, middle-aged persons, people with college educations, and individuals who are separated, divorced, or widowed—a highly selective subpopulation—tend to rate their local public libraries as giving excellent service.

Of those who rate the job performance of local libraries as good, the effect of differentiations in social characteristics is not notable, except for marital status; proportionately more single people voice a good assessment. A similar situation prevails among the "fair or poor" raters. College-trained individuals are most critical of their communities' public libraries as compared to all individuals who are critical. Otherwise social characteristics do not influence the group that is generally displeased with local public library service.

As discussed later, Negroes and all adults with eighth-grade educations or less use libraries with the least frequency. Thus it is not surprising to find disproportionately large "don't know" or indifferent responses *vis-à-vis* evaluation of local public library services among these two particular groups, whose membership overlaps to a large extent.

Generally speaking, all adults, regardless of whether or not they use public libraries, tend to select far more positive than negative descriptive statements about their libraries (Table 2B–2.4). On the positive side, the predominant reputation that public libraries apparently enjoy relates to: (1) their helpfulness, (2) their convenience, and (3) the services performed and the manner in which those services are performed. Other positive attitudes, but less frequent, refer to the general atmospheres that prevail in public libraries. Of the adults sampled, 36 percent thought of libraries as pleasant, 36 percent as friendly, 24 percent as modern, 23 percent as stimulating, and 22 percent as cheerful; 6 percent described public libraries as being "fun" places.

The most frequent negative description of public libraries, voiced by a maximum of only 8 percent, referred to inconvenience. Other negative perceptions of public libraries focused mostly upon atmosphere (5 percent, old-fashioned; 4 percent, drab; 4 percent, dull; and 2 percent each, gloomy, unfriendly, discouraging).

For those who consider their communities' libraries to be excellent or good, the poll discovered four different major manifestations of positive performance (Table 2B–2.5). In rank order of frequency of mention they are:

1. The variety of books available. (Notably more "excellent" than "good" raters offer this.)

2. Personal services rendered. (Again notably more "excellent" than "good" raters offer this.)
3. Over-all positive performance and service.
4. Special services to and for children.

The three major manifestations of fair or poor service expressed by persons critical of their local libraries in rank order of frequency of mention are:

1. Poor selection of books.
2. Overcrowded, inadequate facilities.
3. Poor personnel and service.

It is clear from the data presented in Table 2B–2.5 that how people evaluate public libraries depends mainly on two overall factors: (1) the selections of books that are offered (this is by far the most important) and (2) the services that are rendered to individual users. It appears that if public libraries are to maintain and increase their favorable standings within their communities, concentration on these two elements above all other efforts would seem to portend the greatest ultimate payoff in overall community goodwill.

THE CURRENT STATUS OF BOOK-READING

Since the use of libraries is a function of reading—and reading books primarily—the poll included a very brief look into the current status of book-reading among America's adult population. Table 2B–2.6 shows that 55 percent of all the adults surveyed claimed to have read at least one book over the three-month period preceding the interviews. Since the limitations of the study prevented actual verification of these claims, this figure may be somewhat inflated; by way of comparison, Gallup Poll surveys over a number of years have shown that between 20 and 25 percent of adults can actually name a book they have read in the "past month."

Compared to the national adult sample as a whole, book-reading occurs proportionately more frequently among young adults (70 percent), among the college-educated (79 percent), among the unmarried (66 percent), and among women (58 percent).

Light book-readers (one book reported to be read in a three-month period) characteristically tend to be found proportionately more frequently among young adults and among those who are high school trained. Heavy book readers (nine or more books over a three-month period) are distributed disproportionately more frequently among young, single, and college-trained adults.

WHO USES PUBLIC LIBRARIES AND HOW OFTEN?

Nonusers

Some seven out of every ten American adults currently do not use public libraries, as indicated by the figures in Table 2B–2.7. The largest proportions of nonusers are to be found among the least-well-educated, among the least-well-off economically, among Negroes, among farm people, and in rural locales with populations of less than 2,500. In other words, the classical "unreachables" who are located on the peripheries of American society are scarcely being reached to any notable degree by our public libraries, a characteristic they share with many other of our public institutions.

In addition, relatively higher proportions of the following types of persons are to be found in the *nonuser* category:

1. Men.
2. Persons fifty years and older.
3. Separated, divorced, or widowed persons.
4. Childless individuals and families.

Users

For purposes of this study, *users* were defined as adults who claimed to have visited a public library at least once during the three-month period preceding the interviews.

Three out of every ten adults in the United States can be characterized as users of public libraries by this criterion

The data in Table 2B–2.7 afford the following profile of users. On a proportionate basis, users are:

1. More likely to be women.
2. More likely to be young (age 21–34).
3. Most likely to be college-educated.
4. More likely to be either single or married, as opposed to widowed or divorced, particularly to be parents of two children.
5. Most likely to be Caucasian.
6. Most likely to live in large urban centers (one million population) or in middle-sized cities (50,000–249,999).
7. Most likely to be in the professions or in white-collar occupations with annual earnings of $10,000 or more.

In short, public libraries now appear to serve mostly a minority of adult Americans, members of our upper middle class in the main. In effect, this clientele can be characterized as a highly self-selected elite rather than as a wide across-the-board public.

Respondents were asked how frequently they visited a public library during the three-month period prior to the interview. The following classifications were made according to the responses elicited (Table 2B–2.7):

1. *Light Users:* visited a public library one or two times in a three-month period (10 percent totally).
2. *Moderate Users:* visited a public library three to eight times in a three-month period (13 percent totally).
3. *Heavy Users:* visited a public library nine times or more in a three-month period (7 percent totally).

Light Users

One in every ten adult Americans visits a public library some one or two times during a given three-month period, based on the results of this survey. This light user is equally apt to be male or female. Evidently light usage of public libraries becomes even lighter as age increases, for twice as many light users (15 percent) are to be found among those aged 21–34 years as are to be found among those aged 50 years and more (7 percent); all library use seems to decline with age. Educational attainment is another characteristic that is closely related to library use in general, with the least-well-educated preponderantly in the nonuser group. Among the light users, four times as many persons with college backgrounds (16 percent) are to be found as persons with grade school educations (4 percent).

Marital status affects general patronage of public libraries, with the divorced, separated, and widowed least likely to be patrons, but marital status does not appear related to light library patronage. Race does not affect light usage either, although far more Caucasians than nonwhites use libraries generally.

Other social characteristics reported in Table 2B–2.7 appear to have a similar relationship to light usage as to usage in general. Relatively fewer light users reside in less-populated areas (areas with less than 50,000 residents), a situation holding true for users as a whole. Light users are concentrated in the professional and clerical occupations, which holds true for users generally. Farmers, the retired, and the unemployed are least apt to be either general users or light users. Proportionately more persons earning $7,000 or more are apt to be both general and light users, and persons earning under $7,000 are least apt to be either general or light users. Childless families and individuals are least likely to be either a general or light patron of public libraries.

The light user of libraries is equally likely to be either male or female, and most likely to be younger, better educated, a small community resident, in the professions or in a white-collar job, upper-income bracketed, and a parent.

Moderate Users

A total of 13 percent of all adult Americans attend some public library between three and eight times in any three-month period, thus qualifying as moderate users. There is a preponderance of females (half again more than males) in this group. In addition, moderate public library users are more apt to be:

1. Younger.
2. Better educated.
3. Single, predominantly.
4. Caucasian (ratio to non-Caucasian is 3.5 times to one).
5. Residents of small to middle-sized locales (2,500–249,999 population).
6. In professional and white-collar jobs.
7. In the upper-income categories.
8. Parents of three or more children.

Heavy Users

Seven percent of the adults in the population attend libraries relatively often (nine or more visits during a period of three months), and thus are classified as heavy users. Twice as many women as men are heavy users of public libraries. People aged 50 or over, as compared with younger persons, are least likely to be heavy users. Three times as many college-trained persons as high-school-educated individuals are heavy users. The ratio of college people who are heavy users to grade school people in this category is seventeen to one.

Heavy library usage is generally unaffected by either marital status or size of community. Four times as many whites as nonwhites are heavy users. Heavy usage is most frequent among professionals and white-collar people and among persons earning $7,000 and more. Parents with two children are twice as likely as all other individuals or parents to be heavy users of public libraries.

Summary

1. Only three in ten adult Americans now use public libraries.
2. Women are more likely to use public libraries than men. Men tend to be light or moderate users, and women tend to be moderate users. Proportionately more women than men are to be found in both the moderate and heavy usage categories.
3. As age increases, library usage decreases (among people aged 50 and over only two in ten ever visit a library). Younger people (age 21–34) are more likely to be light and moderate users, and on a proportionate basis middle-aged persons (age 35–49) tend to be heavy users.
4. As educational attainment decreases, library usage decreases. Thus where more than half of the college-educated adults use public libraries generally, only one in ten grade-school-educated individuals ever uses a public library. College-educated people are most likely to be moderate users. People with high school and grade school backgrounds are least likely to be heavy users.
5. Single people in general are most likely to use public libraries, and the widowed, divorced, and separated are least apt to make use of these institutions. Single people are most likely to make moderate usage of libraries, and married individuals are equally likely to fall in either the light or moderate patronage categories.
6. Childless individuals make the least general use of libraries, and parents with two children use libraries in the greatest proportions. Parents with one child or two children are equally distributed among light and moderate users. Parents of three or more children, as well as childless individuals, are more apt to be moderate users rather than either light or heavy users.

7. Small communities (under 2,500) contribute disproportionately to the non-user group. Persons in the larger urban centers tend to be either light or moderate users with almost equal frequency. Residents of communities with populations of 2,500–49,999 tend to be moderate users proportionately more than they tend to be either light or heavy users of libraries.

8. The major proportions of users of public libraries come from among the professional and white-collar groups. Both these groups tend to be moderate users, although professionals are to be found in the greatest proportion among heavy users.

9. As income level decreases, library usage decreases. This holds true for all three user categories.

10. Nonwhites are far more likely to be nonusers than are whites. This disparity is not apparent among light users of public libraries, however.

WHY ARE PUBLIC LIBRARIES USED OR NOT USED?

Some questions in this poll were designed to suggest reasons for public library use and nonuse as perceived by the adult public.

Use of Other Libraries

Other libraries (e.g., academic, professional, special) are used only by a minute proportion of the total adult population, 13 percent. Table 2B–2.8 shows that:

1. 5 percent of all adults can be classified as light users of other libraries (one or two times in a three-month period);

2. 3 percent can be classified as moderate users of other libraries (three to eight times in a three-month period);

3. 5 percent can be classified as heavy users of other libraries (nine or more times in a three-month period).

Libraries other than public cater primarily to the college-educated adults in all usage categories, particularly in the heavy usage one. Persons with grade school education rarely use special libraries, and when they do, they use them lightly or moderately. Persons in white-collar occupations (clerical, sales) are to be found most frequently among the light users. Moderate users are mostly professionals and white-collar persons, and professionals are predominant in the heavy-user category.

All in all, libraries other than public ones are used most often in all categories by professional people and white-collar employees with college educations.

Reasons for Nonuse

Disinterest in books (Table 2B–2.6 shows that 45 percent of the national sample reported not reading a book over a three-month period) and preoccupation with a miscellany of activities are the two primary reasons for either infrequent use or nonuse of public libraries by adults (Table 2B–2.9). For nonusers these reasons are of equal strength. Light users show a greater need for books but less time in which to indulge their needs.

A substantial proportion of the adult population (close to a fifth in all) simply have no need for public libraries, as presently constituted, because they acquire books by other means. This is particularly so among light users, where the proportion rises to a full fourth. At least one out of every four light users uses public libraries as a supplement to his own private acquisition of books.

Note should be taken of the fact that one in ten among the nonuser group gives flaws in library availability or service as a reason. Half as many light users cite this particular circumstance. Physical incapacities account for some 7 percent nonuse, but this factor influences light use in only 1 percent of the cases.

When the 1,058 (70 percent) nonusers in the sample were asked what public libraries might do to facilitate their use of libraries, a full six out of ten of this subgroup categorically replied, "Nothing." In other words, among nonusers there is a hard-core majority that simply believes nothing on earth can get them to use these particular facilities.

Thus, the results of this poll suggest that in the total adult population there is a tough public library "resister" group comprising at least some 41 percent of all adults in the country. From what they say, it would take the most imaginative techniques possible to lure these particular individuals beyond the thresholds of our public libraries.

There is a "softer" resister group. A variety of possible lures was suggested, each by relatively few nonusers (by no more than 11 percent of the 1,058 nonusers in any single instance):

More available free time to read: 11 percent.
More branch libraries closer to home: 7 percent.
Bookmobilies: 2 percent.
Better holdings and selections: 2 percent.
Open longer hours: 1 percent.
Better parking facilities: 1 percent.

These figures are interesting to the degree that they indicate the nation's public libraries could attract some 13 percent of the current nonusers (8 percent additional clients from among the total adult population) if they succeeded in raising what might be termed their current levels of service-convenience.

All in all, these figures substantiate the data reported in Table 2B–2.9.

Evaluation of Services

Table 2B–2.10 indicates that three public library services are the most frequently appreciated by adult library users. These services are the provision of a variety of good books and other reading materials (31 percent), the provision of satisfactory reference and research materials (31 percent), and helpful, courteous all-around personnel service (20 percent). Auxiliary special services and personalized services are also mentioned as desirable, but by no more than 8 percent of the users in any one instance.

Asked to express their gripes about public libraries, 63 percent of the current adult users sampled were loath to make any criticisms whatever. Expressed grievances among users were of this order:

Too few books; inadequate selections: 12 percent.
Poor reference and research facilities: 9 percent.
Newer, recent publications unavailable: 4 percent.
Not open at convenient hours: 1 percent.
Miscellaneous grievances: 4 percent.
No opinion: 8 percent.

Table 2B–2.11 reports suggestions for improved services. When the adult public as a whole is asked what might be done to improve public library services and facilities, half (49 percent) of them (the resisters) cannot offer any substantive suggestions at all—another indication that public libraries really have no salience for at least four to five of every ten adult Americans. For these individuals public libraries are remote, almost nonexistent institutions that do not appear to generate even an occasional thought or feeling.

Of the total sample, 17 percent believe that no improvements in public libraries are necessary; 34 percent do make suggestions for improvements. Their recommendations add up to more or less the same story: better book selections and reference materials, better housekeeping and personnel, increased convenience, and personalized and special services.

Reasons for Use

Not surprising is the finding shown in Table 2B–2.12 that the three most frequently mentioned reasons given by the user group for using the library are the following: to obtain information on special problems (52 percent), to borrow nonfiction books (50 percent), and to borrow fiction books (46 percent). Although the last two are mentioned frequently as reasons why people go to a public library, it is evident that circulation alone is not the only reason. Of equal importance is information-seeking, for the category "to get help or information on special problems" is mentioned more frequently, and "to use reference books and periodicals" is cited almost as frequently.

Add to this the 35 percent who report that they go to public libraries in order to aid their children with their schoolwork, the 15 percent who wish to examine documents, and the 10 percent who attend lectures, exhibits, or performances, and we readily see that contemporary libraries are no longer mere circulation sources. They have emerged as primary information sources. Thus today's public libraries are viewed by those who use them as multipurpose institutions that simultaneously afford both information and circulation.

That circulation is giving way to information as a primary function of public libraries is highlighted by an additional finding from the study. Fifty-five percent of the sample claimed to have read at least one book in the three-month period preceding the interviews (Table 2B–2.6). Asked to indicate how they had acquired the books they read, the following multiple response emerged:

Bought them on their own: 40 percent.
Borrowed them from a public library: 18 percent.
Borrowed them from friends: 1 percent.

In all, less than a fifth of the adult public who claim to read books report that they borrow these books from a public library.

Not to be overlooked are some of the auxiliary functions that public libraries offer the adults who use them. For some 22 percent public libraries offer the opportunity to relax and browse, for one in ten the public library is a place where one can work in quietude and without interruption, and for 8 percent public libraries are used for borrowing or listening to phonograph records. Thus, a number of the adults who visit public libraries view them at least to some extent as oases—quiet refuges that offer a pleasant haven where one can retreat temporarily from the daily hustle and bustle of life.

TABLE 2B–2.1

SUMMARY HIGHLIGHTS OF A POLL OF ATTITUDES
TOWARD PUBLIC LIBRARIES AND THE USE OF
THESE LIBRARIES

(National sample of 1,549 adults)

Summary highlights

---

1. Four out of ten of the adult population sample rated their local libraries good, 26 percent rated them excellent, and 12 percent rated them fair or poor.
2. One person out of five could not assess the performance of his local library.
3. College-trained persons were more critical of their publc libraries than others who were critical.
4. Two factors contributing to positive outlooks toward libraries were available selection of books (by far the most important) and the services offered.
5. Of the nation's adults sampled, 55 percent said they had read at least one book in the three months prior to the survey.
6. Of the nation's adults sampled, 70 percent had not visited a library in the three months prior to the survey, and fewer than 10 percent could be considered heavy users.
7. The users and nonusers of libraries fell mainly in the following categories:

Users (3 out of 10 adults)	*Nonusers*
Women	Men
Young adults (21 to 34 years old)	Persons 50 years of age and older
College-educated persons	Persons separated, divorced, or widowed
Parents of two children	Childless persons
Caucasians	
Residents of large cities	
Professional people and those engaged in white-collar occupations	

8. The adult clientele of public libraries can be characterized as being upper middle class rather than a wide general public.
9. In an affluent society libraries may be considered more as a supplement to other sources of books (private acquisitions for instance) than as a primary source.
10. Most nonusers of libraries could think of no way that libraries could get them to use their facilities. Only a very few felt that more branch libraries, bookmobiles, better books, longer open hours, or better parking would attract them to libraries.
11. Of adults who use libraries, 35 percent said they do so to help their children with school-work.
12. Less than one fifth of those who said they read books indicated that they borrowed these books from public libraries; four out of ten reported that they bought books on their own.
13. Book-borrowing and special informational needs are cited with almost equal frequency by public library users.
14. The potential available adult library clientele is about 60 percent of the adult population, or double the current actual range of 30 percent.

SOURCE: *Tables 2B–2.1 through 2B–2.12 are based on the poll conducted by The Gallup Organization, Inc., as part of the study entitled* The Use of Libraries and the Conditions That Promote Their Use. *This study by The Academy for Educational Development, Inc., was commissioned by the National Advisory Commission on Libraries in 1967.*

TABLE 2B–2.2

*COMPOSITION OF THE SAMPLE**

RESPONDENT CHARACTERISTICS	PERCENT
NATIONAL TOTAL	100.0%
SEX OF RESPONDENT	
Men	47.1
Women	52.9
AGE OF RESPONDENT	
21–34 years	24.2
35–49 years	31.8
50 years and older	41.8
Undesignated	2.2
OCCUPATION OF CHIEF WAGE-EARNER	
Professional and business: professional, technical, and kindred workers (e.g., engineers, accountants, nurses); executives (managers, officials, proprietors, public administrators)	24.6
Clerical and sales: clerical and kindred workers (e.g., mail carriers, telephone operators); sales and kindred workers (e.g., retail clerks, claims examiners)	10.7
Manual workers: foremen, craftsmen, and kindred workers (e.g., railroad engineers, machinists, linesmen, maintenance, painters); operatives and kindred workers (e.g., coal miners, truck drivers, butchers, apprentices); service workers; laborers	39.7
Farmers: farm owners, farm managers, farm foremen, farm laborers	6.1
Nonlabor force	17.8
Undesignated	1.1
ANNUAL FAMILY INCOME	
$10,000 and over	25.3
$7,000–$9,999	22.3
$5,000–$6,999	19.0
$3,000–$4,999	14.1
Under $3,000	16.3
Undesignated	3.0
SIZE OF COMMUNITY	
1,000,000 and over, including urban fringe	19.3
250,000–999,999, including urban fringe	21.2
50,000–249,999, including urban fringe	13.9
2,500–49,999	15.5
Under 2,500	30.1
REGION OF COUNTRY	
East: Maine, New Hampshire, Rhode Island, Connecticut, Vermont, Massachusetts, New York, New Jersey, Pennsylvania, West Virginia, Delaware, Maryland, District of Columbia	28.7
Midwest: Ohio, Indiana, Illinois, Michigan, Minnesota, Wisconsin, Iowa, North Dakota, South Dakota, Kansas, Nebraska, Missouri	29.1
South: Kentucky, Tennessee, Virginia, North Carolina, South Carolina, Georgia, Florida, Alabama, Mississippi, Texas, Arkansas, Oklahoma, Louisiana	26.3
West: Arizona, New Mexico, Colorado, Nevada, Montana, Idaho, Wyoming, Utah, California, Washington, Oregon, Alaska, Hawaii	15.9

* *Allowance for persons not at home was made by means of a times-at-home technique rather than by callbacks. Either procedure is a standard method for reducing the sample bias that would otherwise result from underrepresentation in the sample of persons who are difficult to find at home. All results reported, including the composition of the sample, are based on data in which a times-at-home weighting has been incorporated. The actual numbers of interviews made for various population groups are reported in the findings.*

TABLE 2B–2.3

OVERALL EVALUATION OF LIBRARY SERVICE

The Question: "On the whole, do the various libraries in this city (town) do an excellent, good, fair or poor job of serving people like yourself?"

RESPONDENT CHARACTERISTICS	EXCELLENT %	GOOD %	FAIR OR POOR %	DON'T KNOW %	TOTAL %	NUMBER OF INTERVIEWS
NATIONAL TOTAL	26%	40%	12%	22%	100%	(1,549)
SEX						
Men	22	41	14	23	100	(779)
Women	30	39	11	20	100	(770)
AGE						
21–34 years	26	40	14	20	100	(363)
35–49 years	30	40	12	18	100	(495)
50 years and over	24	38	12	26	100	(658)
EDUCATION						
College	33	37	20	10	100	(388)
High school	28	41	11	20	100	(816)
Grade school	16	38	10	36	100	(344)
MARITAL STATUS						
Single	20	49	13	18	100	(84)
Married	26	40	12	22	100	(1,283)
Other	29	35	12	24	100	(175)
RACE						
White	28	40	12	20	100	(1,419)
Nonwhite	10	35	15	40	100	(130)

TABLE 2B–2.4

CHARACTERISTICS OF THE GENERAL REPUTATION OF LIBRARY SERVICE

(Multiple response)

The Question: (*Hand respondent card.*) *"Here are some words and phrases that people use to describe public libraries. Read me as many words and phrases as you want to that best describe the libraries you usually go to or know about."*

WORDS OR PHRASES BEST DESCRIBING LIBRARY	PERCENT OF TOTAL NATIONAL SAMPLE
Positive	
Helpful	57%
Convenient	41
Usually have what I want	37
Pleasant	36
Friendly	36
Satisfying	30
Efficient	29
Encouraging	25
Modern	24
Fast service	24
Stimulating	23
Cheerful	22
Serious	10
Fun	6
Negative	
Inconvenient	8
Slow service	5
Old-fashioned	5
Usually do not have what I want	4
Drab	4
Dull	4
Inefficient	2
Frustrating	2
Gloomy	2
Not very helpful	2
Unfriendly	2
Discouraging	2
Could not select any phrases	15
Number of interviews	(1,549)

TABLE 2B–2.5

REASONS GIVEN FOR LIBRARY SERVICE RATINGS

(Multiple response)

The Question: "In what ways are [public libraries] excellent, good, fair or poor?"

	RESPONSES OF THOSE WHO SAID SERVICES ARE:		
COMMENTS ON LIBRARY SERVICE RATINGS	EXCELLENT %	GOOD %	FAIR OR POOR %
Positive comments:			
Wide variety of books available	55	43	7
Personal service	31	21	4
Good (general; e.g., "do a good job")	16	16	10
Good for children	12	12	4
Modern ("up-to-date facilities")	9	5	*
Special services ("lectures," "good reading programs")	5	1	—
Bookmobile service	3	5	1
Have branch libraries	2	2	1
Hours are convenient	2	2	1
Audiovisual aids ("records," "films")	1	1	*
Miscellaneous positive answers	*	*	—
Negative comments:			
Poor selection of books	*	*	33
Poor facilities ("overcrowded")	*	—	11
Adverse criticism of personnel and service	—	*	9
Poor (general)	—	—	6
Inconvenient hours	—	—	4
Miscellaneous negative answers	—	—	3
No library in area	—	—	6
Couldn't say what services are performed by by the library	4	12	12
Number of interviews	(415)	(608)	(197)

* *Less than one percent.*

TABLE 2B–2.6

REPORTS OF RECENT BOOK READERSHIP

The Question: "Now, thinking back over the past three months again, would you tell me just how many books, paperbacks or hard cover, you have had occasion to read during this period?"

RESPONDENT CHARACTERISTICS	NUMBER OF BOOKS READ IN PAST THREE MONTHS								VIEWS INTER- NO. OF
	1	2	3	4	5–8	9 OR MORE	CAN'T RECALL; NONE	TOTAL %	
NATIONAL TOTAL	5%	6%	9%	5%	11%	19%	45%	100%	(1,549)
SEX									
Men	5	5	9	4	9	18	50	100	(779)
Women	5	6	9	6	12	20	42	100	(770)
AGE									
21–34 years	7	8	10	5	15	25	30	100	(363)
35–49 years	4	6	10	5	12	20	43	100	(495)
50 years and over	4	5	8	4	7	15	57	100	(658)
MARITAL STATUS									
Single	5	7	7	6	10	31	34	100	(84)
Married	5	6	9	5	11	19	45	100	(1,283)
Other	4	6	11	4	6	16	53	100	(175)
EDUCATION									
College	4	4	10	4	19	38	21	100	(388)
High school	6	8	11	5	11	18	41	100	(816)
Grade school	3	4	5	4	3	5	76	100	(344)

TABLE 2B–2.7

FREQUENCY OF PUBLIC LIBRARY USE

The Question: "Would you think back over the last three months and tell me how many times, if any, during this period you have gone to a public library?"

RESPONDENT CHARACTERISTICS	VISITS TO PUBLIC LIBRARY IN PAST THREE MONTHS					
	LIGHT USERS (1 OR 2 TIMES) %	MODERATE USERS (3–8 TIMES) %	HEAVY USERS (9 OR MORE TIMES) %	NONE %	TOTAL %	NO. OF INTERVIEWS
NATIONAL TOTAL	10%	13%	7%	70%	100%	(1,549)
SEX						
Men	11	10	5	74	100	(779)
Women	11	15	9	65	100	(770)
AGE						
21–34 years	15	17	8	60	100	(363)
35–49 years	13	14	9	64	100	(495)
50 years and over	7	9	5	79	100	(658)
EDUCATION						
College	16	23	17	44	100	(388)
High school	12	13	6	69	100	(816)
Grade school	4	5	1	90	100	(344)
MARITAL STATUS						
Single	10	20	6	64	100	(84)
Married	11	13	7	69	100	(1,283)
Other	9	7	8	76	100	(175)
RACE						
White	10	14	8	68	100	(1,419)
Nonwhite	9	4	2	85	100	(130)
SIZE OF COMMUNITY						
1,000,000 persons and over	13	16	10	61	100	(296)
250,000–999,999	13	12	7	68	100	(333)
50,000–249,999	14	16	8	62	100	(214)
2,500–49,999	9	14	8	69	100	(247)
Under 2,500	7	8	5	80	100	(459)
OCCUPATION						
Professional and business	15	21	12	52	100	(399)
Clerical and sales	14	19	9	58	100	(178)
Manual labor	10	9	5	76	100	(577)
Farmers	5	2	1	92	100	(99)
Non-labor-force	6	8	7	79	100	(281)
INCOME						
$10,000 and over	15	18	12	55	100	(412)
$7,000–$9,999	11	16	9	64	100	(347)
$5,000–$6,999	12	10	5	73	100	(281)
$3,000–$4,999	7	10	5	78	100	(219)
Under $3,000	5	6	3	86	100	(244)
NUMBER OF CHILDREN						
One	13	13	7	67	100	(254)
Two	14	13	12	61	100	(249)
Three or more	13	18	6	63	100	(374)
None	7	10	6	77	100	(668)

TABLE 2B–2.8

FREQUENCY OF NONPUBLIC LIBRARY USE

The Question: "And would you think back over the last three months and tell me how many times, if any, during this period you have gone to some other type of library— such as a school or college library, a reference library, a state library, or a medical, law, or other special library?"

	VISITS TO LIBRARY OTHER THAN PUBLIC IN LAST THREE MONTHS					
RESPONDENT CHARACTERISTICS	LIGHT USERS (1 OR 2 TIMES)	MOD. USERS (3–8 TIMES)	HEAVY USERS (9 OR MORE TIMES)	NONE	TOTAL	NO. OF INTERVIEWS
NATIONAL TOTAL	5%	3%	5%	87%	100%	(1,549)
EDUCATION						
College	9	10	17	64	100	(388)
High school	4	2	3	91	100	(816)
Grade school	1	1	*	98	100	(344)
OCCUPATION						
Professional and business	5	7	13	75	100	(399)
Clerical and sales	12	6	3	79	100	(178)
Manual labor	3	3	2	92	100	(577)
Farmer	4	—	1	95	100	(99)
Nonlabor force	2	1	3	94	100	(281)

* Less than one percent.

TABLE 2B–2.9

REASONS GIVEN FOR NONUSE OF PUBLIC LIBRARIES
(Multiple response)

The Question: "Why is it that you don't go to public libraries (more often)?"

REASONS FOR NONUSE	TOTAL SAMPLE	NON-USERS	LIGHT USERS
Does not read too many books; prefers magazines, news-papers, TV	40%	39%	27%
Too busy; no time; general preoccupation	35	36	45
Does not have need of a library; has own library; acquires books from sources other than public libraries	18	19	25
Inadequacies in public library availability and service; no library in area; selections, service, distance, or hours are unsatisfactory	8	10	5
Physical incapacities; bad health	5	7	1
Miscellaneous	5	4	2

TABLE 2B–2.10

USER EVALUATION OF PUBLIC LIBRARY SERVICE
(Multiple response)

The Question: "What is the very best service a library has provided you?" (Ask of those who go to the library.)

BEST SERVICE PROVIDED BY LIBRARY	PERCENT OF LIBRARY USERS
Provides a variety of books ("good reading material")	31%
Provides good research and reference material	31
Helpful and courteous service	20
Provides books for children	8
Purchased specific books that were asked for	5
Book reservation service	2
Current novels available	2
Current events coverage	2
Audiovisual aids ("tapes, records, films")	2
Good in all respects ("can't pinpoint one alone")	2
Miscellaneous	1
Don't know	8
Number of interviews	(491)

TABLE 2B–2.11

SUGGESTIONS FOR IMPROVED PUBLIC LIBRARY SERVICES
(Multiple response)

The Question: "In your opinion, what improvements in facilities or services or new services should the libraries be offering?" (Probe:) "Whatever you think is needed."

COMMENT ON IMPROVING LIBRARY SERVICES	PERCENT OF NATIONAL SAMPLE
Satisfied; no improvement needed	17%
Suggested improvement in library services or facilities:	
Be better stocked ("have more, better variety books")	8
Building improvement needs ("make buildings more pleasant," "less crowded")	8
More nonfiction reference material	4
More up-to-date book list ("more of the newer books")	4
Bookmobile	3
Special programs ("language series department," "story hours for children")	3
Offer audiovisual instruction material ("teaching records," "film strips")	3
Branch libraries	3
Knowledgeable, qualified personnel	2
More convenient hours ("evening hours")	2
Library should inform public of services available and how to use them	2
Improve internal organization ("new card system," "computerized card catalog")	2
Miscellaneous	1
Couldn't say	49
Number of interviews	(1,549)

TABLE 2B–2.12

REASONS GIVEN FOR USE OF PUBLIC LIBRARIES

(Multiple response)

The Question: "On this card are various reasons for going to libraries.
Please tell me the reasons that best describe why you go
to libraries." (Asked of those who go to the library.)

REASONS FOR GOING TO LIBRARY	PERCENT OF LIBRARY USERS
To get help or information on special problems one must deal with	52%
To borrow nonfiction books	50
To borrow fiction books	46
To use reference books and periodicals for particular assignments	41
To help my children get their schoolwork assignments done	35
To relax and browse	22
To examine manuscripts, historical documents, or microfilms	15
To attend lectures, exhibits, or performances	10
To be in a quiet place where I can think and concentrate without interruption	10
To listen to or borrow phonograph records	8
Other	2
Don't know	4
Number of interviews	(491)

C. THE EDUCATIONAL USER

Except for the testimony of a few students who appeared at the regional hearings held by the National Advisory Commission on Libraries, most of the material available to the Commission on the library needs of elementary and secondary school students and undergraduate college students came from the literature or from librarians themselves.

Children and teen-agers may be thought of as captive clients of library services, more or less involuntary users who must be guided to multiple sources of intellectual content as part of the educational process. That modern educational trends are giving this guidance increasing importance is clear from the record. The sophisticated young people who will emerge from today's elementary and secondary schools will take for granted their right of access to multiple sources and will make new kinds of demands on the colleges where libraries are still too often thought of as study halls and where the collections are considered substandard. As adults pursuing a variety of careers, they will make new kinds of demands on all the nation's library and informational services.

The purpose of the two papers that follow is to describe some of the trends affecting educational use of library services at the elementary and secondary level and at the undergraduate level of higher education. There is encouraging evidence that many members of the library profession are aware of the social forces that will affect their work in the years ahead and that these leaders are anxious to induce their more parochial colleagues to a more active role.

1. THE FUNCTIONS OF ELEMENTARY AND SECONDARY SCHOOL LIBRARIES[16]

As seen in section A of this chapter, trends in education over the past decade have had the greatest impact of any social force acting on the public library. Elementary and secondary school libraries have of course been much closer to this impact—they have in fact been part of it. Today library materials and instructional materials, in the public school systems particularly, have become almost inseparable. And the school librarian today is not only a librarian but a creative teacher and a counselor of young people.

THE HISTORICAL DEVELOPMENT OF SCHOOL LIBRARY SERVICE

School libraries exist to serve students, teachers, and the educational goals of the schools. Their development has had a long history in the United States, one that has involved not only public schools but public libraries, state departments of education, state library agencies, the National Education Association (NEA), the American Library Association (ALA), and private foundations.

The first public support for public school libraries was given by New York State; the date has been given variously as 1835 and 1838. In that first law state funds were offered on a matching basis to school districts that agreed to use their own funds to buy books for district libraries. A number of other states followed New York's lead, and by 1875 some 20 states provided aid for school libraries. Interestingly enough, the early efforts in New York State proved unsuccessful. The law provided money for books but made no provision for supervision of school libraries or for book selection. Reports made in the early 1860's indicated that the school district libraries were little used, that the books selected were more suitable for adult readers than for pupils in school, and that the book collections were poorly maintained. The funds that had been used to establish these district libraries in New York were reassigned for teachers' salaries in 1864.

The problems that arose in New York were paralleled in other states, and by 1876 the total number of volumes in school libraries throughout the country was declining.[17]

While these developments were taking place, the question of library service to young people was under debate. For the most part, public libraries did not serve children below the ages of twelve to fourteen, a practice that was deplored in the United States Government report *Public Libraries in the United States of America* in 1876.[18] In the years following that report, a number of library leaders emphasized the importance of library service to young people, along with the principle of cooperation between public libraries and schools. In 1890 the public library in Brookline, Massachusetts, established a children's room and other cities soon followed suit.[19]

In 1897 the president of the American Library Association appointed a committee

16 *Unless otherwise specified, the material in this section, based largely on a review of the literature, is from* School Libraries in the United States, *a report prepared by Nelson Associates, Incorporated, and commissioned by the National Advisory Commission on Libraries in 1967.*

17 *It is worth noting that many of the states that made early provisions for school library service placed responsibility for that service in state education departments. Later some states placed the responsibility in state library agencies. In most states responsibility for school libraries is presently assigned to the state education department, but a few states still delegate the responsibility to the state library agency.*

18 *John Eaton*, Public Libraries in the United States of America, Their History, Condition and Management: A Special Report, *Bureau of Education, Department of Interior (Washington, D.C.: Goverment Printing Office, 1876).*

19 *The public library in Hartford, Connecticut, may actually have preceded Brookline in taking this step.*

to study the interrelationship between the ALA and the National Education Association. The report of that committee gave official support to the principle of cooperation between public schools and public libraries.[20] Even then, the principle of cooperation could not solve all problems. A heated controversy arose between those who favored independent school libraries and those who believed that the public libraries should provide services to schoolchildren.

The movement to establish independent school libraries, which had begun in the 1830's and 1840's, only to falter in the 1860's and 1870's, began to revive, especially in secondary schools. Between 1890 and 1895 the number of libraries in the nation's high schools increased from fewer than 2,500 to nearly 4,000. Some of these were independent of public libraries and some were not. By 1913 there were four types of libraries in high schools:

1. A separate library housed in the high school building, supported by school funds and administered by the board of education and supervised by a teacher or a trained librarian for the exclusive use of students and teachers.
2. A central public school library housed in a senior high school but organized for all of the schools in the city, usually under the supervision of a trained librarian, with a branch library in each of the public schools.
3. A public library branch housed in a high school—or a collection of books loaned by the public library to the school for a definite period of time—under the supervision of a teacher or a public library assistant.
4. A school library housed in a high school, supervised by a teacher and organized to serve the community as a public library after school hours.

Changes in attitudes toward instruction and a new appreciation of the importance of nontext materials were related to this growth in school library services. As the child-centered school became more popular, so did the school library. Available resources continued to be quite sparse, however, and book collections tended to be small and poor in quality. The placement of library resources within the schools sparked debate over the relative merits of classroom as opposed to central collections. Elementary schools tended to establish classroom collections, largely because the resources at their disposal were meager, while most high schools moved to establish central libraries. Rural schools usually lagged behind their urban counterparts in the provision of library services, even as they do today, and traveling book collections from public or county libraries were made available to rural schools in some parts of the country.

The cooperative study of library service to school children made by the ALA and the NEA in 1897 led to the establishment of school library sections within both organizations.[21] One of the first joint efforts of these units was the preparation of a list of recommended books for school libraries and a statement of school and public library objectives. This cooperative effort was, in part, a response to the administrative problems faced by public libraries serving the schools.

Studies and reports prepared by the ALA and the NEA had a strong influence on the improvement of school libraries, especially between 1915 and 1933. The development of standards for accreditation of schools, which began in 1933, has also stimulated the improvement of school libraries. Several private educational foundations, including the Carnegie Corporation, the General Education Board, the Rosenwald Fund, and the Rockefeller Fund, contributed to school library development in the 1920's and 1930's.

By 1927 forty-five of the forty-eight states had laws governing the establishment of school libraries. The Depression slowed the development of school libraries, however. The need to economize again perpetuated public library involvement in school library services. A common measure was the "single library system," involving the deposit of

[20] *Quoted in Dorothy M. Broderick, "Plus Ça Change: Classic Patterns in Public/School Library Relations," School Library Journal, May 15, 1967.*
[21] *Today the American Association of School Librarians is both a division of ALA and a department of NEA.*

books owned by a public library in the school or simply the housing in the public library of material intended for school students.

The establishment of school libraries increased after the end of the second World War. Nevertheless, in 1962 slightly more than 50 percent of all the school facilities in the fifty states and the District of Columbia were still without centralized school libraries. Approximately two thirds of all elementary schools had no centralized libraries, but they had been established in well over 90 percent of all secondary schools.

As of 1967 the latest publication of national statistics on public school libraries was for the 1962–63 school year.[22] Of 83,428 schools in school systems enrolling at least 150 pupils in 1962–63, 58.9 percent had centralized libraries. Over 97 percent of the 17,000 or so secondary schools and 89.6 percent of the nearly 7,000 combined elementary-secondary schools had centralized libraries. In the more than 59,000 elementary schools, however, only about 44 percent had centralized libraries. Thus, nearly 98 percent of approximately 12 million pupils enrolled in secondary schools, 92 percent of approximately 3 million pupils enrolled in combined elementary and secondary schools, and less than 58 percent of approximately 21 million pupils in elementary schools attended schools with centralized libraries in 1962–63.[23]

Throughout the 1960's school library service in the United States has continued to undergo intensive and rapid development. After more than a century of fitful and sporadic development which left more than half of all elementary schools without centralized libraries and which, for the most part, left existing school libraries under-staffed and short of resources of every kind, an upward movement has begun to take place. This has been brought about by many factors: by active leadership within the school library profession; by changes in methods of instruction and improvement in the quality, quantity, and variety of instructional materials available; by upward revision of school library standards; and by increased financial commitments on the parts of states, local school systems, and—most notably—the Federal Government.

The year 1965 was a milestone for Federal concern with education, and libraries have benefited. Titles I and II of the Elementary and Secondary Education Act of 1965 (ESEA) have enabled many school libraries to expand their collections and services. They have also served as a stimulus for the establishment of school libraries where none existed before. For example, the Maryland state plan for Title II provided special incentive grants to those schools which proposed to establish a centralized library.[24] Preliminary figures from the United States Office of Education indicated that nearly 62,000 elementary school libraries were expanded and over 3,500 centralized libraries were established in public elementary schools in 1966 as a result of Title II.[25] ESEA continued to produce dramatic results, but it is amply clear that many schools still do not have any, or do not have adequate, school libraries.

RESPONSIBILITIES AND STANDARDS FOR SCHOOL LIBRARIES

Public school library service, like all of public elementary and secondary education, continues to be the responsibility of state government:

> There are three major branches of government which usually have responsibility for state educational policy: the state governor, the state legislature, and state education boards. Each state has a state educational leadership agency—the state depart-

22 *Effective reporting and compilation of current statistical information is one of the most pressing problems facing school library service today. It is specifically referred to in the discussion of one of the recommendations of the National Advisory Commission on Libraries (see chapter 12, section D).*

23 *U.S. Office of Education,* Public School Library Statistics, 1962–63 *(Washington, D.C.: Government Printing Office, 1964).*

24 *Richard L. Darling, "Current Activities in School Libraries,"* Bowker Annual, *1967.*

25 *U.S. Office of Education, "Annual Reports of Title II, Elementary and Secondary Education Act for Fiscal Year 1966" (unpublished).*

ment of education—to head its common school system and to develop policy according to the authority vested in it by the state government. Certain legal responsibilities, such as establishing regulations and standards, promoting research and school programs, providing consultative services, accrediting institutions, and making reports, devolve on state departments of education. The school libraries are generally a constituent part of these responsibilities.[26]

The fact that the basic responsibility for public school library service lies at the state level has not meant that state departments of education have, in every case, been very active in organizing and promoting programs of library service in the schools. Every state department of education has, however, been involved to some degree in school library service. In recent years, especially since 1960, these involvements have increased markedly.

Library services in independent and parochial schools depend on the discretion of the governing body of each school. Whether or not there is a library, how it is operated, and the level of support it receives, have depended upon the priorities each school's administrators and teachers attach to various educational services and upon the resources at their disposal. Public provision of instructional materials for students and teachers in private as well as public schools has increased the levels of resources available to support library services in these institutions.

Traditionally, most of the support for public school library programs, like that for other services in elementary and secondary education, has come from revenues generated at the local level, principally through property taxation. Considered on a nationwide basis, this support has not been strong in past decades. In fact, ". . . the general public has frequently, even when it supported the schools, assigned a low priority to such 'frills' as school library programs or instructional materials."[27] The result was the 1962 situation in which "more than 10 million children go to public schools with no school libraries; more than half of all public schools have no library."[28] The immediate cause of this situation was no doubt the lack of financial support for school libraries, but the attitudes and priorities of many teachers and school administrators at all levels have also been underlying factors.

As discussed in the historical sketch above, the early 1960's saw the development of school library service gain impetus. This movement continued to gather momentum, and with the participation of the Federal Government through the Elementary and Secondary Education Act of 1965, it has assumed massive proportions. The Knapp School Libraries Project—a national school library demonstration effort—ranks as a major influence of the 1960's for improvement in school library service.[29] So does the School Library Development Project, which attempted in 1961–62 to encourage and assist state and local groups in implementing the 1960 national standards.[30]

Although many individual school teachers and administrators have contributed to changing attitudes about the importance of library services in elementary and secondary education, the American Association of School Librarians (AASL) assumed a leader-

26 Fred F. Beach and Robert F. Will, The State and Education (Washington, D.C.: U.S. Office of Education, 1958); quoted in Mary Helen Mahar, State Department of Education Responsibilities for School Libraries (Washington, D.C.: Office of Education, 1960).

27 Mary V. Gaver, "Crisis in School Library Manpower: Myth or Reality?" in School Activities and the Library (Chicago: American Library Association, 1967).

28 U.S. Office of Education Statistics for 1962, quoted in Nation's Schools, March 1966, p. 85.

29 This project was funded by a $1.1 million grant from the Knapp Foundation in late 1962; it was carried out under the sponsorship of the American Association of School Librarians. The Knapp Project had as one of its central aims the creation, in different parts of the country, of selected school library programs designed to meet national standards, so that a "complete" program of school library services could be observed and evaluated. See Peggy Sullivan, ed., Realization: The Final Report of the Knapp School Libraries Project (Chicago: American Library Association, 1968).

30 American Association of School Librarians, Standards for School Library Programs (Chicago: American Library Association, 1960).

ship role in communicating the need for rapid development of library programs in schools across the country. It was the AASL that published the revised set of standards for school libraries in 1960, setting high goals, both qualitatively and quantitatively, for school library programs. In general, very few, if any, school library programs in operation at the time could claim to meet the standards completely. This was possibly more a reflection of the low effectiveness of many school libraries than an indication that the national standards were "too high." State and regional standards for school libraries were revised upward in the years following the publication of the new standards.

This process was guided and accelerated by the School Library Development Project.[31] In a sense, too, the Knapp School Libraries Project was a direct outgrowth of the publication of these standards. Substantial achievements in research and demonstration, planning, and the formulation of standards have been achieved in recent years, and activity continues. It should be noted that the national standards for school library programs have recently been updated through a joint effort of the American Association of School Librarians and the Department of Audio-Visual Instruction of the National Education Association. These standards, published jointly by ALA and NEA in spring 1969 under the title *Standards for School Media Programs,* give even greater emphasis than did those of 1960 to the unity of materials concept (discussed below) and to other advanced ideas on the nature of school library service. Consequently, it is likely that the influence of standards revision on school library development will continue into the 1970's.

THE ROLE OF THE SCHOOL LIBRARY PROGRAM

The above discussion becomes more meaningful in relation to the trends in education that have given school libraries a more important role in the educational mission. The growing acceptance of independent study and of the individualization of instruction in the nation's schools has accounted for the increased importance of the school library program in school curricula.[32] The development of team teaching has also influenced the role of the school library in elementary and secondary education. Finally, it should be noted that curriculum revision in many areas—mathematics, chemistry, and biology among them—has stressed the continuing need for more and better learning materials as knowledge multiplies in so many areas.

School libraries affect their own importance to the educational function of the school by promoting a policy that makes more and better materials easily accessible to all students. Thus, the school library serves as a direct instrument of instruction when the instructional program is organized to include independent study. In these circumstances the school library program is able to make a maximum contribution to the instructional program.

A school librarian may participate directly in instruction as a member of a teaching team. In any event, he will have direct contact with groups of students when he gives instruction on library materials and their use, and he will have many opportunities to reach students through informal contacts in the library. The school librarian performs an instructional function just as other teachers do, although his teaching role is centered on the resources and services of the school library.

[31] *Mary Francis Kennon and Leila Ann Doyle,* Planning School Library Development *(Chicago: American Library Association, 1962).*

[32] *J. Lloyd Trump, Director of the Commission on the Experimental Study of the Staff in the Secondary School, has proposed a plan (widely known as the Trump Plan) for organizing instruction that would facilitate individualization of instruction through team teaching and a division of the student's time. According to this plan, the student would spend 40 percent of his time in large-group formal lectures, 20 percent in small-group discussions, and 40 percent in independent study. Since it is the responsibility of the school library to provide the learning resources students require in pursuing independent study, this division of student effort has major implications for school library programs. See J. Lloyd Trump and Dorsey Boynham,* Focus on Change: Guide to Better Schools *(Chicago: Rand McNally, 1961).*

Although a fully developed team-teaching system places great emphasis on independent study and takes maximum advantage of the library, it is by no means necessary that team teaching be present in a school in order to establish an effective library program. It is essential, however, that appropriate library resources and services, provided by a qualified library staff, be available in each school. Students' time should be scheduled so that they are able to make use of library services and resources, and teachers should plan their teaching in such a way that the use of instructional materials is an intergral part of the teaching-learning process.

The school library cannot perform its functions in the educational program by simply acquiring and processing materials and making them available for use. The library must create an active program of services for students and teachers if it is to function effectively. A wide variety of services can be performed, some of which are mentioned below.[33]

Important services provided by school library programs to students include increasing the accessibility of library materials by means of photoduplication; reserve-book and multiple-copy service; duplication of titles through provision of paperbacks; interlibrary loan; home use of reference and audiovisual materials; provision of equipment for the use of audiovisual materials; extended library hours; general instruction in library use and library orientation, as well as library instruction integrated with specific subject areas; reading guidance for individual students and groups of students; the provision of vocational materials, college catalogs, and other materials for assistance to students in planning their postgraduation careers; school newspaper publicity and book reviews; and school programs on libraries and books.

Important library services for teachers include assistance and coordination with the instructional materials aspects of curriculum and course planning, consultation with faculty members on resources and services, provision of materials for classroom collections and for classroom use of reference and audiovisual materials, orientation of new teachers on the materials and services the library program makes available, special releases on new acquisitions and services, and provision of collections of professional materials in individual school buildings and in district materials centers.

In addition to direct services to students and teachers, the library performs certain general services, such as consultation and coordination of its activities with other school libraries and with public libraries, library talks to parents and youth groups, publicity and book reviews through outside agencies, participation in book fairs, observation of book weeks and library weeks, and other special celebrations or observances.

In the past school libraries have tended to emphasize, because of their limitations in staff and resources, those services which could be made available to a maximum number of students and teachers at a minimum of time and expense. The situation is changing rapidly as greater resources of staff, materials, and equipment become available for use in school library programs.

The service role of elementary and secondary school libraries is expanding in other ways. Formerly the school library was a facility that was usually open and available to students during school hours only. Three recent developments have altered this pattern. First, school libraries increasingly are opening before classes begin and/or staying open for one or more hours in the afternoon after classes end. Second, there has been an increased interest in many areas in providing school library services for preschool children. Third, in some parts of the country school libraries are providing supervised night and weekend study sessions for students.

INSTRUCTIONAL MATERIALS AND THEIR USE

The library's basic resources—printed materials, personnel to make these accessible to users, and adequate physical facilities—are as vital to school libraries as they are to

33 *This material is based on Mary V. Gaver and Milbrey L. Jones, "Secondary Library Services: A Search for Essentials,"* Teachers College Record 68 (*December 1966*).

other kinds of libraries. In addition, school libraries are turning even more than other libraries to the provision of nonprint materials for students and teachers.

If instructional materials are to be brought to bear on instructional programs effectively, economically, and efficiently, a number of administrative arrangements and educational practices must be brought into play. Many teachers today still must be convinced of the importance of making extensive use of multiple library resources in their teaching, a factor perhaps more important than any other, and materials must be easily accessible to students.

The Unity of Materials Concept

One of the dominant themes in the development of school library service in the United States today is that the content of a piece of material is more important than the medium in which it is presented. One medium may be more appropriate than another for the presentation of a particular topic, but materials in virtually all media can appropriately be used in instruction, and all are within the province of the school library. This view has been referred to as the unity of materials concept. It is manifested in the growing use of the term "instructional materials center" or "media center" in place of the more conventional term "school library." Though the more conventional term is used throughout this report, it is used with the full range of materials and services offered by the modern school library in mind.

The Montgomery County, Maryland, Public School System offers one of the better examples in the nation of well-developed school library services on a systemwide basis. According to that system's handbook for teachers and librarians on review and evaluation procedures:

> Instructional materials are those items which are designed to impart information to the learner in the teaching-learning process. A wide variety of instructional materials is essential for the best instruction. Instructional materials may be consumable and expendable but are generally nonconsumable and fairly durable, such as:

BOOKS: Library, Texts,	NEWSPAPERS
Reference, Supplementary	PICTURES
CHARTS	RECORDINGS: Tape,
FILMS	Phonograph
FILMSTRIPS	PROGRAMMED MATERIAL
GLOBES	SLIDES
MAPS	SPECIMENS
MODELS	TRANSPARENCIES
MAGAZINES	WORKBOOKS[34]

In addition to these items, the Montgomery County System uses microfilmed materials and various specimens of real objects. For example, an elementary school library may have a lump of coal in its collection. Many instructional materials are produced within the system, either in the schools or in a separate facility known as the Instructional Materials Center (IMC). Transparencies, audiotape, and videotape programs are among the materials produced at the centralized IMC. Videotapes produced are broadcast on an educational television channel for reception in local schools.

The *Standards for School Media Programs,* recently published, mentions all of the above kinds of materials plus several others. Although quantitative standards will not be included in this document, standards for every type of material and the appropriateness of all kinds of materials to programs of instruction are being recognized and promoted.

It is generally agreed that it is important that both teachers and librarians be involved in selecting, reviewing, and evaluating materials. Librarians can contribute to the process from their knowledge of materials and of their sources. Teachers need to be involved because it is they who will make use of the materials in instruction. Materials are apt to be used in the instructional program if teachers participate in their acquisition.

[34] *Montgomery County (Md.) Public School System, "Review and Evaluation Procedures for Textbooks and Instructional Materials" (mimeographed, undated; in use during fall 1967).*

Special Equipment

Record players and still- and motion-picture projectors have been in use in schools for several decades, and their importance in instructional programs continues to grow. Now new techniques for the storage and presentation of materials of instruction are being employed. The use of audiotape equipment, which first became widespread in the 1950's, has increased greatly in the 1960's. The utilization of videotape equipment is only now beginning, but it is a development that will eventually have a major impact on the methods of instruction.

Audio- and videotape programs can be centrally stored to be made available to students using individual carrels equipped with dial access and audio- and video-receiving equipment. Similar dial-access techniques will soon be used on a larger scale to transmit taped materials from centralized storage to individual classrooms and, in time, to schools located at some distance from the central storage facility.

Teaching machines, including computerized instructional aids of many different kinds, are coming into use, and the availability of quality programmed materials is increasing rapidly.

Centralized Services

In the 1960's, to a greater extent than ever before, services intended to guide or to support school library programs in individual schools have been made available at the state level and the school system or district level. The increased employment of state school library supervisors has been part of the provision of guidance services for individual programs at the state level. In a few instances, centralized purchasing and processing services for school libraries have been provided at the state level, by state library agencies, or through other arrangements.

At the system level there are many examples of the development of centralized services, including the employment of school library supervisory personnel, the provision of purchasing and processing on a systemwide basis, the establishment of centralized facilities for the storage and cooperative use of expensive or infrequently used materials, the production of instructional materials, and the review and evaluation of new materials and equipment.

SCHOOL LIBRARY PERSONNEL

The school library must be staffed by adequate manpower, in terms of both quality and quantity, if it is to fulfill its responsibility for developing and implementing an active program of services for students and teachers.

Ideally, a school librarian should be state-certified as a teacher and librarian and should possess a fifth-year or master's degree. All school librarians by no means have such complete credentials. For decades school library programs have been hampered by shortages of qualified personnel. In recent years enrollments and the number of schools in the nation have risen sharply. Consequently, the number of school library personnel required throughout the country has increased substantially.

It has been estimated that 35,000 school librarians who had completed six or more semester hours of library science were available to serve over 100,000 secondary and elementary schools in the 1965–66 school year.[35] The ratio of librarians to school buildings has been about one librarian to every four buildings during each of the past three years. An earlier investigation showed, however, that 77 percent of all school librarians in 1962 were in secondary schools.[36] This proportion applied to 1965–66 would mean that nearly 27,000 of the estimated 35,000 available school librarians were in secondary schools, giving a ratio of librarians to school buildings for secondary

35 Henry T. Drennan and Sarah R. Reed, "Library Manpower," ALA Bulletin, September 1967.
36 Henry T. Drennan and Richard L. Darling, Library Manpower: Occupational Characteristics of Public and School Librarians (Washington, D.C.: U.S. Office of Education, 1966).

schools of nearly one to one. The other 8,000 or so librarians would be spread thinly over a much larger number of elementary schools, so that the ratio of librarians to schools at the elementary level would be about one to eleven.

Estimates of the number of school librarians needed have run into tens of thousands. "The gap between our present supply of school librarians and the number needed to implement school library programs meeting professional standards is indeed astronomical. . . . In fact, . . . *school* librarians invariably rank close to the top among the dozen or so school specialists who are in *critical* shortage."[37]

School librarianship is not a single-level occupation. The head librarian, who directs the library program in the individual school, is the pivotal individual in the school library program. However, other workers both above and below this level are needed if adequate school library programs are to be implemented effectively and efficiently. The numbers and kinds of supporting personnel required vary with school size and the scope and variety of services offered in the library program.[38]

Clearly, the staff that works under the head librarian in a large library program should include professional librarians as well as other workers. At the secondary level these assistants may be assigned duties in specific subject areas, such as physical sciences or foreign languages. The need for more than one librarian in large programs means, among other things, that the ratio of librarians to secondary schools ought to be greater than the aforementioned one to one, since the 1960 *Standards for School Library Programs* recommends "one librarian for each 300 students or major fraction thereof" for schools of up to 900 students.

There are jobs in school library programs that are best performed by school library clerks or secretaries, and other jobs that are best performed by school library technical aides or "instructional materials aides." Some of the duties of both library clerks and technical aides are often performed by student assistants. This practice is increasingly being called into question, however. "A growing number of librarians have dropped the student assistant program. They reason that the student needs to use his time in the library as student, not housekeeper or clerk, and that the library needs salaried full-time clerks."[39]

Although professional school librarians are in critically short supply, the crisis can be eased by better job definition and assignment of subprofessional duties to workers who are not in such short supply. A fundamental staffing problem of school libraries has been that many of the subprofessional tasks mentioned in this section have for years been performed by professional librarians.

Highly qualified professionals are needed not only to direct library programs in individual schools but also at the system and state levels to provide supervision and guidance for individual programs and to administer centralized services.

The need for competent manpower is, therefore, critical at all levels of school library service almost everywhere in the nation. More support is needed for the professional education of school librarians, and greater efforts to attract qualified persons are essential. Since supervisory personnel for school library programs in years to come must be drawn from the ranks of successful school librarians, it is apparent that those ranks must increase if they are to meet the demands placed upon them. More attention needs to be given to job definition in school libraries, and appropriate supporting personnel should be assigned nonprofessional duties where that has not already been done.

---

37 *Mary V. Gaver,* op. cit.
38 *The library staff at Oak Park and River Forest High School, one of the secondary schools that participated in the Knapp School Libraries Project, reached a total of eighteen persons in 1967, divided about equally between half-time and full-time personnel, but including six full-time librarians.*
39 *Margaret H. Grazier, "The Secondary School Library in Transition," in John P. Picco, ed.,* The Secondary School Library in Transition: A Report *(Portland, Ore.: Knapp School Libraries Project and the School of Education, Portland State College, March 1967).*

OPINIONS OF SCHOOL LIBRARIANS

The foregoing very brief descriptive sketch of the history of school libraries and their emerging status as true instructional materials centers will reveal nothing new to those who are knowledgeable about education and school librarianship. It is presented here to emphasize not only the results of the recent infusion of Federal funds, but also the inextricable relationship between learning and the library that is so clearly exemplified at the elementary and secondary levels of formal education. Understanding the relatively new, actively creative "media expert" working with the students and the teachers in our nation's school systems may suggest some lessons to other libraries and other levels of education.

There is a good deal of research of various kinds under way, much of it of the demonstration model variety. Only one of the studies commissioned by the National Advisory Commission on Libraries attempted to ferret out some of the attitudes and opinions of school librarians themselves. It may be of interest to readers of this book to see some of the write-in comments from this questionnaire survey, "Major Social Changes Affecting Library Service in the United States."[40] One senses that there are plenty of day-to-day discouragements and problems, but that the front-line school librarian is accepting the challenge of responsiveness to educational pressures—possibly more enthusiastically than some teachers.

The sample of school librarians is quite small. Of the 80 questionnaires sent out, 32 were returned. In selecting recipients, attention was given to geographical spread and urban-suburban-rural balance. Questionnaires were sent to school librarians functioning in individual school buildings rather than to school library supervisors at the state and local level, who would have had to answer for a variety of school situations. Since much of the long-range planning and broad-gauged thinking in the school library field is done at the supervisory level, the replies from school librarians reflect for the most part only the immediate concerns and viewpoints relevant to a single school. Most librarians chosen, however, have held positions of leadership in their state professional associations.

Since school librarians serve in a special context a segment of their total community, it is not surprising that many of their observations tally closely with those of the public librarians. All respondents agreed that population in their service area (the school) had increased; there are more lower-class and more low-ability students, many with reading level below grade. Almost all respondents said repeatedly that the library and all its materials are much more an integral part of the curriculum and the learning process than formerly. To almost all of these librarians the young people in general seem more purposeful in their use of the library and much more at home in it. The great majority of those replying feel that they have not responded fully enough to the needs of the disadvantaged children in their schools.

School librarians came on strong in their assertion that their philosophy of program and service has changed, and in a major way. "There has been a vast change in the school library, from an auxiliary service to a supporting agency for the entire instructional program." "Library involved in the total school curriculum." "Liberalized! More correlation with curricular needs; more media; more effort to attract users." "Now a learning center." "More focused on individual needs." "Librarians are now initiating programs and ideas." There is the implication, too, that administrators and teachers are

---

40 From Social Change and the Library: 1945–1980, a special study commissioned by the National Advisory Commission on Libraries and conducted by the National Book Committee in 1967. The text above is from the survey of school librarians by Virginia H. Mathews, Staff Associate, National Book Committee; it is the same questionnaire that was used in the survey of public librarians reported in section A.1 of this chapter.

changing their view of what the library's program and services should be, and that their expectations are far greater than they were.

More students are seeking reading guidance, and several librarians indicated that teachers are leaving the choice of collateral reading to students and counting on the assistance of librarians, rather than sticking to prescribed reading lists. Group and individual program activities that will help students to learn to use books, records, and films for personal value development are being offered by more than half the school librarians replying.

Factors affecting the type of materials bought now as compared with 1955? "Changes in the school curriculum" was the resounding consensus, followed by, "Changes in teaching methods"; "Greater stress on academic excellence, coupled with the attempt to meet needs at all levels of ability"; "Emphasis on resources other than textbooks in most subject fields"; "Availability of material." Also mentioned was Federal money produced by NDEA and ESEA legislation. The advent of new programs and courses is a major factor, too, on which at least fourteen respondents spent 20 to 50 percent of their materials budgets during the past year.

"What kinds of materials would you like to have that you cannot find?" Reading material of high-school-level interest with a fourth-to-sixth-grade vocabulary headed the list of the majority. Other requests include material on sex and drugs at varying levels of understanding, uncondescending materials for the alienated adolescent, career material on beauty culture, easy books on foreign countries, and better and more varied filmstrips and tapes and 8 mm film loops in more areas of study. Five just needed more money to "buy what we can find."

It is not surprising that most school librarians replying to the questionnaire indicated that population and educational stresses had been felt most keenly by the school libraries (22); 16 mentioned the impact of research and the knowledge explosion.

> Changes in curriculum have completely changed our pattern of service. More and more teachers are substituting a variety of learning experiences, print and nonprint, for their textbooks. Their demand for services and materials has forced us to duplicate many of our materials and radically to increase our involvement with classroom instruction.

> Mobility of population has brought the disadvantaged child into our library; reading guidance needs have been emphasized.

The increased enrollment without extra staff has been a burden and a strain. One librarian cited "the trend toward more independent learning without ascertaining that pupils have study skills to carry through. Faculty members themselves have not been trained in independent library use." Several librarians mentioned the frustrations of the shift from all-white to integrated and then, due to resegregation and the middle-class flight to the suburbs, to all-Negro schools.

"What one social phenomenon," school librarians were asked, "has given you the most worry and trouble in day-to-day operational terms?" A large proportion answered this completely open-ended question in the same way that so many public librarians had answered it: lessening respect for other people's property and for authority; "The rate of theft has increased many times over the past ten years." One librarian mentioned general indifference to responsibility and to learning. One mentioned censorship, or attempts at censorship; another, apathetic parents and teachers; another, the frustration of trying to find material on "minute topics."

As to philosophical concerns, a few individual school librarians have been worried about the failure of school libraries to satisfy the needs of slum children, the potential dropout, the early social maturing of children, problems engendered by integration, the too-conservative philosophies of many school administrators, the rigidity of the library profession itself, and the pressure from both rightists and leftists to inject materials reflecting only their own viewpoints. Almost all the concerns expressed were connected with school, some even more narrowly than those above, as: attempting to meet individual differences, the growth of new media and learning to "fit them into the library picture." Too many left the space blank, and one wrote that she has "no philosophical concerns."

School librarians apparently feel that they have been successful in meeting and implementing educational change, "in keeping the library a relatively relaxed and informal place in the midst of a highly structured program," "in developing an attitude toward lifetime learning," in withstanding pressure groups, and in meshing book and nonbook media. Still, a few individual librarians expressed discouragement with lack of success in attempts to instill a sense of responsibility and honesty in students; in upgrading personal values of students, in combating breakdown of the family unit, in orienting teachers to new patterns in communications, and in dealing with attempts at censorship.

"What do you think will be your most pressing problem in the years between now and 1975?" Many of the answers boil down to "money." Some fifteen mentioned getting sufficient help as the big hurdle; nine mentioned space, especially in outmoded buildings, as a problem. Individuals indicated some other major problems: cooperation with other area libraries in order to give the most service, the education of teachers in use of the library, and eliminating the "single-textbook approach to learning." The thoughtful school librarian who made this last entry feels that the multiple-resource approach, as opposed to the single resource, will promote lifetime reading after high school and the enduring respect for a variety of opinions and viewpoints.

Answers to "How are you going to tackle it?" ranged from a desperate duo: "Pray!" and "Get out of the school system," to practical first steps: "Preschool orientation for new faculty" and "By visiting other libraries and processing centers." Public relations and the involvement of others in library matters seemed to offer help to several: "Publicizing the facts to parents and community leaders and setting up a special committee"; "By sending monthly reports to administrators"; "Greater use of teachers in reference and research areas"; "By keeping administrators and Board of Education aware of needs." Three wanted to get more clerical help; two wanted to focus on an in-service training program for teachers, one to the extent of participating in teacher education at the state university. But two of those who bothered to reply to the query (about half of the total number of respondents) felt that these problems were "not for me to solve."

As to the future:

> Curricular area libraries near department classrooms; central bibliographic control and locator devices manned by administrators and specialists comparable to those who man the telephone system; magnetized shelving via sliding conveyors which respond to digital stimulus. Same magnetism will be used in detecting materials not charged out as user exits through turnstile.

In the words of one school librarian:

> The library of the future will be the central focal point of the instructional process. It will provide a means for the student to involve himself more actively in each learning stage and to progress at his own rate of speed in a carefully planned sequential program geared to his own interests and needs. As we experiment more and more with independent study for all students, the library may well become a laboratory, with programmed learning of information taking the place of much formal classroom procedure. The school librarian of the future will have to combine administrative and organizational skills with a deep understanding of children and the educational process.

All the crystal balls carried approximately the same vision.

2. THE FUNCTIONS OF ACADEMIC LIBRARIES IN UNDERGRADUATE EDUCATION

The uses made of the libraries that serve higher education are many and diverse. Service demands range all the way from those necessitated by the intimate involvement of library-based media in instructional programs, more characteristic of modern elementary and secondary education, to those of an individual prebaccalaureate student whose independent study has created needs more characteristic of the highly specialized demands being made on the same university library system by teaching and research faculty, graduate students, professional students, and even the outside world.

The academic library feels all the social force of the educational, research, and service pressures acting on the private or state-supported institution of which it is a part—these factors determine the library's response as a vital supporting service. However, many of the academic libraries continue to fulfill but have transcended this minimal role to become true national resources. These are the university libraries that share with some large municipal and highly specialized private libraries the designation "research libraries." These are the models of excellence, the libraries with the high-prestige image referred to in section A.2 of the present chapter. Chapter 3 discusses the scholarly and scientific research users and the professional users of library and informational services, so often utilizing the same libraries that also serve the undergraduate college student and even the vocational student. In the discussion immediately following, the focus is on the functions of the academic library in undergraduate education, with some emphasis on junior college and four-year college library service.

HISTORICAL DEVELOPMENT OF ACADEMIC LIBRARIES[41]

The historical development of academic libraries in the United States parallels the development of the colleges themselves. The first such American libraries were established in the nine Colonial colleges located along the Atlantic Seaboard. Early book collections were small, included many donated books, and stressed theology, since this study was a principal concern of the early colleges. Regulations concerning the use of books by students were extremely restrictive, and the care of the book collection and administration of its use was usually entrusted to a faculty member as a part-time addition to his teaching duties. College administrators sought gifts and bequests of books for their libraries for many decades in the late seventeenth century and in the eighteenth, though they were able to give little direct support from college funds. Harvard, the first of the Colonial colleges, had the first library and received the lion's share of early gifts of books. Harvard still owns more books than any other college or university in the country.

As colleges were established in the Ohio and Mississippi valleys during the second quarter of the nineteenth century, small libraries were founded on their campuses. These library collections, like those in the older colleges, consisted mainly of old books, reference works, and standard editions. Although specialized libraries in law, theology, and science had been founded at Harvard and other eastern schools early in the nineteenth century, most collections continued to be storage collections rather than working libraries. Students used a limited number of textbooks in the main, supplementing them in some instances with books owned by student literary society libraries. These collections were established by students in some colleges because of the small collections in the

41 *The historical sketch and the discussion of the role of the library in the college are from* Undergraduate and Junior College Libraries in the United States *a report prepared by Nelson Associates, Incorporated, and commissioned by the National Advisory Commission on Libraries in 1967.*

college's own libraries and the restrictions placed on their use. According to one writer on the subject, these student society libraries were sometimes superior to the official college libraries in point of usefulness and sometimes even in size.[42]

Despite the fact that the early college libraries had meager holdings and received comparatively little support from their parent colleges, most library historians have felt that they were important in setting the pattern for library service in the college.[43] Guy R. Lyle, for example, summarized the importance of early college library development by pointing to patterns definitely established before 1900: the idea that books were necessary, the emerging acceptance of the library as important to the educational work of the college, the groundwork for professional library education, and such procedures as reserved books, uniform classification, and rapid processing and distribution of books. The idea of free access to books grew out of the student literary society libraries.

Several developments of the latter half of the nineteenth century are important. The establishment of the land-grant colleges just after the Civil War led to the establishment in those colleges of specialized libraries in agriculture and engineering. At the same time, libraries in the older eastern colleges grew rapidly, sometimes overflowing the physical facilities available for them and leading to the establishment of departmental libraries. However, classification schemes were unwieldy, cataloging of these growing collections was often poor or nonexistent, and as a consequence, the collections were often little used. The development and promulgation in 1875 of the decimal system of classification by Melvil Dewey had a revolutionary effect on classification schemes.

Moreover, new approaches to teaching as well as greater faculty and student interest in research led to substantial increases in the size of collections and in their use. New library facilities were constructed in many colleges and the concept of the central collection reasserted itself over the departmental library. College (and university) book collections grew more or less steadily throughout the last quarter of the nineteenth century and the early decades of the twentieth, until 1938, when restrictions imposed by the World War II conflict slowed the rate of growth.

In 1941 Dr. Louis Round Wilson categorized the forces that had increased the educational effectiveness of the college library under three headings: (1) forces outside the college, (2) changes within the college, and (3) changes within the library.[44] Guy R. Lyle borrowed Wilson's framework for the discussion of influences on college library service contained in the first edition of his basic work, *The Administration of the College Library*. The forces outside the college that stimulated the development of college library service included the work of the Carnegie Corporation of New York (which in 1928 organized the Advisory Group on College Libraries to study the problems of college libraries) to support projects aimed at improved services and to award grants to selected institutions, the effect of the regional accrediting associations, the work of the graduate library schools, and the influence of Friends of the Library groups.

Changes within the college that affected college library service were the development of broad survey courses; the development of honors courses, independent study, and similar curricular innovations; the general education movement; and the trend (exemplified in small experimental colleges such as Bard, Bennington, Sarah Lawrence, and Stephens) toward giving each student instruction in the use of the library tailored to his needs as an individual.

Changes originating within the library itself that affected college library service

---

42 *Elmer D. Johnson*, A History of Libraries in the Western World (*Metuchen, N.J.: Scarecrow Press, 1965*), p. 298.
43 *For example: Louis Shores*, Origins of the American College Library 1638–1800 (*Nashville, Tenn.: George Peabody College, 1934*); *Guy R. Lyle*, The Administration of the College Library (*New York: The H. W. Wilson Company, 1945*); *the third edition of the Lyle book was published in 1961.*
44 *Louis R. Wilson, "The Use of the Library in Instruction,"* Proceedings of the Institute for Administrative Officers of Higher Institutions, *1941 (Chicago: University of Chicago Press, 1942). Quoted in Lyle, op. cit.*

included a trend toward higher academic and professional training for college librarians, the practice of critical analysis and self-survey on the part of college libraries, a movement toward coordination and cooperation among college libraries, and innovation in library building programs.

In a later edition (1961) of *The Administration of the College Library,* Lyle points out the influence of the large public library on college library development. Large public libraries led in the development of the divisional organization plan, in the introduction of audiovisual services as an accepted part of librarianship, in planning of library buildings, and in the use of various labor-saving devices in library operations.

Private foundations have continued to be involved in activities that promote the development of college library service. In 1956 the Ford Foundation established the Council on Library Resources, Inc., an organization that has since made many grants in support of library-related research. The Rockefeller Foundation has been noted for support of scholarly publication and the development of bibliographic tools.

The growing public interest in the importance of education and in the relationship of library service to it has culminated in the passage of the library-related legislation of the late 1950's and the 1960's to date. The Federal Government has contributed heavily to the construction of college library buildings through the Higher Education Facilities Act of 1963, and to the growth of college library collections through Title II-A of the Higher Education Act of 1965.

THE ROLE OF THE LIBRARY IN THE COLLEGE

It might be possible to operate a college with no library at all. Lectures, discussions, and examinations could be based on textbooks, copies of which would be owned by each student. Text materials could be supplemented through the use of paperbacks. Some courses are, in fact, conducted much this way, and some students operate in this manner even when a good college library is available to them. Such students visit the library in order to use it as a study hall.

Although many programs of higher education might be conducted in the absence of library services, there are few educators who would turn down good library services if given a choice. The library is a shared resource for all of the students and faculty of the college. The books and other materials it provides bring meaning and content to students' endeavors. The library is able to make available to any student or teacher resources that are vastly richer than he is likely to be able to provide for himself. Further, the library has been called the "great interdisciplinary synthesizer" and a source for the student of more than one point of view on any given topic.

There is tremendous variety within a single institution and certainly from one college to another in terms of educational philosophy, ranging from a vocational orientation to broad liberal arts to early preprofessional specialization, and of course these objectives affect the library. Conventionally the college library is expected to support the curriculum. It is supposed to make course materials available, as well as materials that supplement textbook readings, reference works, standard works, and general works. It may be expected to provide the student with an approach to self-education to "fill in the chinks" of the curriculum, or as an instrument for use in independent study. It is expected to support the research needs of faculty members in greater or lesser degree, depending on the extent to which faculty members in the college are inclined to do research or are expected to perform it, and depending on the availability of research library facilities outside the college. The library is usually expected to support the extracurricular reading of students and of faculty and to make a positive contribution to the formation of students' lifelong reading habits.

A word should be said about the Library College idea and some of the newer experimental approaches that are being advocated or implemented in some institutions. Because American colleges and universities face difficult problems, including the problem of size, in attempting to provide higher education for an increasing percentage of the college-age population, some have begun to adopt certain aspects of the British university, particularly the division into small colleges and the tutorial system. By providing a wide range of resources and by stressing integrated or interdisciplinary programs, they try to counter the drive toward the education of specialists. In many colleges specialized programs (called independent study, tutorial instruction, honors reading, or some similar name) attempt to free the student from the traditional pattern of passive attendance at large discussion sessions and lead him to independence in learning.

Proposals for the Library College appear in many variations, but common to them all is the presence of a quantity and quality of library resources that would be drawn on by a community of students and bibliographically expert teachers. The usual pattern of mandatory attendance at class meetings and lectures, mandatory textbook assignments, and voluntary additional reading in the library would, in a sense, be reversed. Library reading (or use of other library materials) would be the basic element in the student's independent pursuit of knowledge, and discussion meetings would be optional; that is, the student would be free to request a session with a tutor or preceptor when he felt his work required it. Each student would move at his own pace and, to some extent, in his own direction. Each student would face comprehensive examinations in different areas and would be required to produce papers at frequent intervals.

Elements of this idea can be found in the present or planned programs of instruction in a number of American colleges and universities. These developments point to increased emphasis on independent study centered around the library as the integrating core of the college.

The Monteith College library experiment is a good example of some of the newer thinking. In 1960 this college, one of the eleven colleges that compose Wayne State University, became the object of an experiment in developing a more vital relationship between the library and college teaching.[45] Monteith College was chosen for the experiment for several reasons. Its interdisciplinary program, planned and taught by the college staff, was aimed at giving the student growing responsibility for the formation of his own ideas over the four years of his college experience. The curriculum had, as one of its main objectives, the development of the student's capacity for independent study. These conditions afforded the opportunity for the project, which was conducted over four semesters and two summer sessions between fall 1960 and summer 1962. It dealt with three basic factors: (1) the relationship of the library staff to the teaching faculty, (2) the coordination of library instruction with the curriculum, and (3) the role of the library in the educational experience of the student.

The project was concerned with "ways of investigating" these general hypotheses:

If librarians participate with faculty in course planning, they can get student library use built into the courses planned, and *if* student library use is built into courses, students will use the library for these courses, and *if* students use the library for their courses, they will acquire understanding of the library and competence in its use.

Out of the Monteith experiment grew a program that consists of a sequence of library assignments extending through the four-year curriculum and covering the three subject areas (science of society, natural science, and humanistic studies) taught in the college. A theory was developed that views the library experience as a coherent unity, as the bibliographic organization of scholarship. The program is designed to enable the student to learn to use a system of "ways" to get information, to learn how to retrieve information and ideas from a highly complex system of stored records. The student learns to find a path, given his resources and his purpose; he has to use a method that is suitable to the library as a collection of organized subjects as well as to scholarship as an organization based on an academic discipline.

[45] *Patricia B. Knapp,* The Monteith College Library Experiment (*Metuchen, N.J.: Scarecrow Press, 1966*).

To lead the student to this knowledge and skill, a sequence of assignments was constructed around the library as a system of "ways" moving from one level of organization to another, from one subject field to another, always aiming at the growth of the student's capacity to study independently. The first assignment (the Independence Assignment) demonstrated the pluralism of "ways" to get answers to questions from the card catalog, the *Oxford English Dictionary,* the *International Index,* the *Reader's Guide,* the *Syntopicon.* A preliminary and rapid appraisal of ten books (the Book Evaluation Assignment) used the "way" of open shelves. A paper predicting economic growth of one country (the Economic Index Assignment) required the use of sources of data and social science materials. At the end of the four-year sequence the student was required to produce a bibliographic review of the literature on the topic of his senior essay.

The Monteith experiment represents a serious attempt, perhaps the most significant at any college to date, to integrate library use with the program of instruction. The sequence of library assignments in an integrated library program of this type is intended to support and complement the goals and theories of the college and of the curriculum. To faculty members and students alike, the library must be presented as a highly complex system of ways to find and use resources, related to a coherent framework, and calling for problem-solving behavior and critical thinking.

RESEARCH FINDINGS ON STUDENT CHARACTERISTICS AND LIBRARY USE[46]

Attempting to measure library use and the effects of library use on the academic performance of students has been a major concern of college librarians for many years. Some progress in the development of techniques for such investigations was made at the University of Chicago as early as the 1930's. However, the accurate measurement of the use of the college library still faces certain basic obstacles, and too often the units of measurement are books loaned, reference questions asked, and interlibrary loan requests. Different studies have sometimes produced contradictory findings. Furthermore, these studies are generally conducted in a single institution, and their findings are frequently not comparable because one college's particular teaching approaches may emphasize library use more than another's. Also, there are instances in which other library facilities or private book collections are used by students, and this fact affects the results of such inquiries.

Part of the survey of the literature on library use and nonuse done for the National Advisory Commission on Libraries (see section B.1 of the present chapter) included a section on the undergraduate student user. A summary of the findings appears below. Note that only studies for which the unit of measure was people have been included.

This review of the literature shows that the college and university undergraduate student library user has been examined from the standpoint of such socioeconomic factors as class of enrollment, sex, grade-point average, and course-work assignments. One study in this area was completed by H. Clayton.[47] The data were collected at "Southwest College" from a sample of 545 students. Four socioeconomic variables were explored: occupation of the students' parents, total income of family, amount of schooling of parents, and the population of students' high school.

Clayton found that there was a slight relationship between the number of books borrowed by students and the occupation of their parents. For example, 25 percent of

46 *The sections summarizing research findings on student characteristics and on reasons for library use are from* The Use of Libraries and the Conditions That Promote Their Use *by The Academy for Educational Development, Inc., one of the special studies commissioned by the National Advisory Commission on Libraries in 1967. Harold Mendelsohn was Director of the study; Karen Wingerd was Research Assistant.*

47 *H. Clayton, "An Investigation of Various Social and Economic Factors Influencing Student Use of the Library" (unpublished Ph.D. dissertation, University of Oklahoma, 1965).*

the student body studied hailed from farm communities; these students were observed to have used a total of 2,234 books. Students from families in the salaried occupations (comprising 25 percent of the sample) used 2,168 books. Individuals from labor and those from wage-labor backgrounds (22 percent of the sampled population) used 1,719 books. The students of business-oriented families used 1,228 books. Students from families in the professions (comprising 14 percent of the student body) used 1,084 books.

Clayton found that students from high-income families checked out fewer materials than did students whose parents had earnings under $8,000. Those students whose families had earnings of less than $4,000 checked out the greatest number of library materials per capita. The relatively high incidence of library usage by the lower-income students may result from their inability to purchase texts and required reading materials even in paperback form (see Table 2C–2.1).

Another of the socioeconomic factors affecting student use of the library is the educational level of the students' parents. An examination of Clayton's data reveals that 8 percent of the sample were students whose parents had less than a high school diploma; these students checked out 530 books. Twenty-nine percent of the sample had parents with a high school diploma; this group accounted for 2,581 books checked out of the library. Twenty-eight percent of the sample had parents with from 13 to 15 years of schooling and accounted for 2,302 books checked out. Thirty-five percent of the sample had parents with a college degree or better; this group accounted for 3,012 books checked out of the library. Clayton indicates that although the education of the parents affects the children's desire to attend college, the educational level of the parents does not seem to relate to the absolute numbers of books they withdraw.

The size of students' secondary school was correlated with the students' use of the library. The purpose of this comparison was to determine whether evidence could be found to support the notion that schools with large enrollments and sizable libraries produce students who make greater use of the college library. Clayton found that 16 percent of the sample were from high schools with small populations up to 125 pupils. About 23 percent came from schools with 126 to 300 students; 29 percent of the sample came from high schools with between 301 to 850 enrollment; 32 percent came from secondary schools with enrollments of over 850 students. A summary of the reserve and regular loans made to students from differing high school enrollments indicated that the 16 percent of smallest-school students in the sample used 1,377 books; the 23 percent of students from the next largest schools used 1,891 books; and the 29 percent of students from schools of 301 to 850 enrollment used 2,221 books. Students from schools with over 850 enrollments (32 percent of the sample) used 2,672 books. These data do not reveal any significant effect of the high school enrollment size on the college students' use of the college library.

Branscomb's study in 1940 indicated that the average number of withdrawals per student progressed evenly from 1.79 for freshmen to 4.97 for seniors.[48] Knapp's study discovered that "there was a total increase in the use of the library between the freshman and sophomore years and a total increase in the use of the library between the junior and senior years."[49] Barkey, in two studies conducted in 1962 and 1963, found that freshmen were using the library more than other students, however; 44 percent of the freshmen borrowed one or more books as compared with 35 percent for those enrolled in the remaining academic classes.[50]

[48] H. Branscomb, Teaching with Books: A Study of College Libraries (Chicago: Association of American Colleges, 1940).
[49] Patricia Knapp, "College Teaching and the Library," Illinois Library, 40 (December 1958), pp. 828–33.
[50] F. Barkey, "Patterns of Student Use of a College Library," College and Research Libraries, March 1965.

Several recent studies have also provided data on the use of the library as a function of the academic class level of the user. In 1962 Gorham Lane (University of Delaware) conducted four studies on the use of the library.[51] In May of 1962 a brief questionnaire was distributed by library personnel sixteen times during a five-day period at three different hours a day. From an undergraduate population of 3,000, less than 700 responses were obtained. In proportion to the total number of students in their class, more seniors (28 percent of their class) were using the library than members of any other class. Sophomores were next in frequency and freshmen were the fewest (approximately 18 percent).

Book withdrawal increased progressively from the freshman year through the junior year in the Lane study. During the freshman year the average withdrawal of books was between three and four, during the sophomore year between six and seven, during the junior year between eight and nine, and during the senior year between six and seven.[52] Seniors did not spend more hours in the library than members of other classes, but they were more frequently found there.

Barkey's study indicates that sex was notable only in the number of men or women using the general collection of books. More women withdrew books, but the average number of books withdrawn per male student showed very little difference from the average number withdrawn per female student. Lane found that the increase in the number of books withdrawn by upperclassmen was much more notable for women students than for men students. As second-semester seniors, women students' book use was at its peak (six to seven books), whereas the comparable number for men was one to two books, a figure quite typical of the men's withdrawals when freshmen and sophomores.

Knapp's study of 738 students at Knox College in Galesburg, Illinois, indicates that students who receive high grades use the library more than students with low grades. Barkey's study of 2,967 students at Eastern Illinois University also reveals that more of the better students use the library (Table 2C–2.2). The lower the grade-point average, the fewer library withdrawals there are on a proportionate basis. However, conclusions drawn from the comparison of grade-point averages and library withdrawals are not too reliable. For example, in the same study Barkey found that where the mean grade-point average of all students at the institution he studied was 2.45, the grade-point average of book borrowers was 2.50. In other words, a C grade or better could be earned with or without using the library; 56 percent of those earning a B or B— did *not* use the library. Of a total of 1,025 students achieving grades from A to B—, only 474 (or 46 percent) were reported to have withdrawn books from the general collection.

Branscomb, in describing a similar situation, writes: "From the student's standpoint one could say that these students neglected the library's resources, because they found they did not need to use them in order to do acceptable work."

RESEARCH FINDINGS ON REASONS FOR STUDENT LIBRARY USE

Current research on the uses made of the college library focuses on four factors: (1) the purpose of the library visit, (2) the subject matter of the materials used, (3) the reasons for the use of specific materials, and (4) areas where materials are used.

Johns Hopkins University conducted a study on library usage in order to construct

---

51 G. Lane, *"Assessing the Undergraduates' Use of the University Library,"* College and Research Libraries, *July 1966.*
52 *One recent study, exemplifying some "analytic by-products" of a relatively new automated circulation-control system in Oakland University Library, also showed low freshman and sophomore use of the library, and the authors challenged academic librarians to recruit users from these classes. The reference is Floyd Cammack and Donald Mann, "Institutional Implications of an Automated Circulation Study,"* College and Research Libraries, *March 1967, p. 129.*

a picture of the activities that make up a library day.[53] The survey was in operation for a few hours on each day during July 3 to August 7, 1964. Two hundred and twelve completed questionnaires were received. According to this study, about 10 percent of the patrons conducted personal business and 50 percent used their own materials while they were inside the college library.

Jain studied the use of library materials at Purdue from July 1 to August 4, 1964; he found that use of one's own materials and checkout of materials for home use were mentioned by 60 percent and 20 percent of the sample, respectively (Table 2C–2.3).[54] When asked, "If checking out items, now, did you intend—when you came—to borrow them, or did you get interested in them as a result of browsing?" "came to borrow," "result of browsing," and "both" were mentioned by 59 percent, 34 percent, and 7 percent, respectively, of those who replied to this question.

About 46 percent of library patrons preferred to use library material in the library, and 29 percent preferred to check materials out for home use. The reasons for preferring the library were: "better study atmosphere" (46 percent), "to avoid mislaying of material" (17 percent), "easier to refer to other sources" (12 percent), and "save the trouble of carrying it home" (8 percent). The reasons offered by those not preferring to work in the library were: "more comfortable at home" (40 percent), "need for longer period" (29 percent), "can use at leisure" (16 percent), and "use in conjunction with typewriter" (7 percent).

Jain's study revealed that university libraries were used both as a source of library materials and as a place where students study their own notes. Lane's study indicated that more than half of the freshmen were using their own books exclusively, but the number of students using the library as a place in which to work from their own books decreased steadily from the freshman through the senior class. Conversely, the number of students using library books only increased. For somewhat more than a third of the students, using both the library's books and their own increased as students progressed from their freshman to their sophomore years. Reserve books were used by more people than any other library materials. Microfilm and recordings were used least. An analysis by class showed that, except for the use of recordings, seniors used the library more than any other group. Only 4 percent of the freshmen in the library used library materials exclusively. The comparable figure for seniors was 19 percent. The percentage of freshmen using periodicals was 3.9. For seniors it was more than 8 percent.

In the Lane study it was found that books in the categories of literature and the social sciences were by far the most frequently used, constituting 50 percent of all withdrawals. Pamphlets and general works, books on religion, and books on languages were withdrawn the least (less than 8 percent of total withdrawals).[55] Freshmen withdrew more books in literature; next in frequency for freshmen were books in the social sciences. Freshmen withdrew more books in history than other students, and they withdrew books less frequently in the area of technology. These same students as sophomores withdrew less than half the history books that they had when they were freshmen. Sophomores withdrew material on social science or philosophy.

Although the area of literature was most heavily used by students in all classes, the

[53] *Johns Hopkins University, "Progress Report on an Operations Research and Systems Engineering Study of a University Library," April 1963. Reported in the paper by A. K. Jain cited in footnote 54.*
[54] *A. K. Jain, "Sampling and Short-Period Usage in the Purdue Library,"* College and Research Libraries, *May 1966. A 1961 study by Guy R. Lyle also showed evidence of heavy use of the library building as a study hall for students using their own textbooks; "Use and Misuse of the College Library,"* The President, *the Professor, and the College Library (New York: The H. W. Wilson Company, 1963), pp. 51–7.*
[55] *The Oakland University Library study reported by Cammack and Mann in 1967 showed that the most frequently used books were literature, history, philosophy, education, and economics, but that the people with the highest average number of charges per person were secondary education majors in foreign languages and English, followed by liberal arts majors in the same fields; history and philosophy majors also had high averages.*

number of such books withdrawn decreased steadily from the freshman through the senior year. The books in the social sciences were next in frequency of use.

Jain's data indicate that in a sample of 152 library users at Purdue, 45 percent used library materials for their own interest; 34 percent used library materials for course assignments; 34 percent needed the library materials for term papers, and 18 percent for course exams; 11 percent who answered gave miscellaneous (other) reasons. The implications of this study are that 86 percent of the respondents used the library for course work.

Jain's finding is supported by Knapp's study. Knapp indicates that 90 percent of circulation at a small Kansas college library is course-stimulated. Knapp also found that one fourth of the courses offered by the college accounted for 90 percent of the total college library circulation. This means that a very small proportion of courses stimulated the use of most of the library's material. This, coupled with the fact that over 80 percent of library usage is motivated by class requirements, raises questions about the present role of libraries on college campuses.

Lane's study indicates that few students use the library for recreational reading. If students do not use the library for recreation, and only a quarter of the courses stimulate the use of most library materials, the question might legitimately be asked whether or not the library really fulfills its classic role for the undergraduate public in the modern college setting.

The question might also be raised about other sources of the students' information. Where does the student get his material? The boom in paperbacks might be considered legitimately as a major source of information for students. The accelerated use of copying machines (Xerox, etc.) has also made checking out of materials from the library more or less obsolete behavior on the part of many users. Also, public library use by this age group is noteworthy.

A summary of the results of several studies showing nonuse of the academic library reveals that a consistently high percentage of the samples studied do not make use of their institution's library facilities (Table 2C–2.4).

In a two-year longitudinal study of student use of the library at the University of Delaware, Lane found that the general library collection was infrequently used by students. Surveying a 20 percent random sample of freshman and junior classes at the University of Delaware, he discovered that the majority of men students (63 percent) from the sample withdrew no books from the collection in any given semester during the period covered by the survey. It is somewhat comforting to note that the percentage of undergraduates withdrawing no books decreases from freshman year through junior year.

Although such total figures for nonusers are available, little information is available on specific socioeconomic characteristics of these nonusers. However, Lane's data disclose: (1) freshmen reveal the highest incidence of nonuse; (2) seniors have lowest incidence of nonuse; (3) men consistently are greater nonusers of the library than are women.

The studies examined in this review of the literature might be considered as representing pioneering attempts to assess the use of college and university libraries. As first attempts they have their limitations. A principal limitation is an inherent problem in attempting to define what constitutes a user. None of the criteria used so far appears to account adequately for the vast amount of unrecorded library use (browsing, Xeroxing, finding reference data). In addition, the mere checking out of materials does not automatically guarantee the use of the material any more than turning on the TV guarantees that the medium is being watched. The first limitation of studies such as those discussed above is the inability to determine what and who the users are.

A second problem with this research is that few of the studies have attempted to determine why people select the materials they do. The emphasis has been on the material (subject matter, type of material, etc.). Nothing has been studied regarding the personal motivational factors (gratification, etc.) inducing the use of the library.

Finally, the research is confusing because none of the researchers appear to be aware of what other researchers are studying. The consequence is unnecessary duplication of the same materials, using the same obsolete research techniques. Cooperation among those engaged in library research might aid considerably in producing some breakthroughs in the study of library use and nonuse.

Even so, the results of the present research are suggestive and may have several important implications for professional and academic librarians. That fewer than 30 percent of college students and fewer than 40 percent in any one class were found using the library facilities during a given week, and that the majority of men sampled withdrew no books or materials from the general collection during a given semester, have important implications for curriculum and library planning. That a university's general collection is not widely used by undergraduates, and that when it is used, such use does not seem to have any significant relationship to academic achievement, suggest that an evaluation of the usefulness of a university library in terms of its general collection alone would be in order.

The finding that few students use the library for recreational reading raises questions about continuing to maintain a relatively high proportion of literature and recreational reading collections. The fact that a large proportion of students using the library bring their own materials and use the library for study purposes suggests that perhaps the old central college library is antiquated. The needs of the modern college community are geared to study rooms in dorms, university classroom buildings, and the student unions. There is a need for a highly technical, in-depth research library service on the college campus. The advent of Xerox and information retrieval and storage on microfilm and computerized tapes has made the old concepts passé.

That these points are already perceived to some extent, and being used as bases for decision-making, is not enough. Further research efforts, coordinated in approach and sophisticated in methodology, can clarify the needs of any library's various publics and validate the means of meeting them.[56]

OPINIONS OF COLLEGE AND UNIVERSITY LIBRARIANS[57]

What do the academic librarians themselves think about the educational users and uses of libraries in a changing society? Some impressions of both the basic similarities and diversities within this very mixed group of librarians may be gleaned from a small survey that was part of the same project reported in section A.1 of the present chapter.

The informal account below is based on the response of 56 out of 110 librarians working in higher education who received questionnaires. The institutions used by these librarians as the basis for their observations ranged from small private colleges to state universities; private junior and public community colleges were included in the sample, as were several Ivy League institutions; 17 of those replying in this group are connected with graduate library schools.

College librarians, like other librarians, appear to be faced with a growth in

56 *In March 1968 the final report of a* Study to Develop a Research Program for the Design Development of Modern College Libraries, *by the Historical Evaluation and Research Organization, was submitted to the Bureau of Research of the United States Office of Education.*

It should be noted that another reason for difficulty with some kinds of research on academic libraries is the lack of adequate annual statistics. The Office of Education has sought to remedy this with its December 1967 publication, Preliminary Report on Academic Libraries, 1966–67. *It presents limited data on a cross-section of academic libraries, broken down by type of support and type of institution: university, four-year with graduate program, four-year without graduate program, and two-year.*

57 *This concluding section of section C.2 is from* Social Change and the Library: 1945–1980, *a special study commissioned by the National Advisory Commission on Libraries and conducted by the National Book Committee in 1967. The material herein is based on a survey of college librarians conducted by Virginia H. Mathews, Staff Associate, National Book Committee; the same questionnaire was used as in the surveys of public and school librarians reported elsewhere in this chapter.*

numbers, as well as a vortex of changing patterns. There were some interesting reasons given for the apparent changes in the character of clients served in the college library; changes were noted by 33 out of 40 replying to the query about the nature of change in clientele and included: more graduate and professional students, more serious students, and an increase in postgraduate research; more women now admitted on campus, especially more married women seeking careers; an increase in the number of off-campus users, especially high school students and business and industry personnel; more high-achievers because admission standards have been raised; more lower-class, low-income users who are not library-oriented and are inclined to be poor readers; more employed people seeking job advancement; and in junior and community colleges, more liberal arts emphasis and more students preparing to transfer to four-year institutions.

These academic librarians tend to be increasingly user-oriented. When asked if they felt they had made progress in making it easier for people to use the library and its facilities, all 45 who replied to the question said "Yes." The most frequently cited ways of making the library's materials and services more user-oriented were through longer open hours and more evening hours; 27 have "cut complex routines," and 13 are conscious of "taking resources and services where people are." The provision of photo-copying machines is mentioned by several librarians; others mention more duplicate copies and greater freedom in lending, daily bus service between campuses, and faculty book pick-up and delivery service. At one large university, residence halls have new reference libraries with direct telephone service to the college library.

Of 51 librarians responding, 42 felt that there had been a change in their (and their staff's) philosophy of program and service. "We are not as concerned with routines as with services," neatly summarizes the change as most of them saw it; also, "more responsive to users' needs, voiced and unvoiced." Greater cooperation with the teaching faculty and greater involvement in the educational program are mentioned; greater concern with a broad range of media other than books is noted as a change. Several college librarians cited a new awareness of the library's responsibility for establishing a lifetime habit of library use and for developing of cultural interests.

Several large universities mentioned the development of an undergraduate library and a broader range of general reader services as differentiated from straight research: Music concerts, sponsored literary and philosophic conversations with faculty, etc. "Ten years ago we felt that it was our responsibility to 'be available.' Our service philosophy today is much more aggressive; we feel constrained to market our services vigorously wherever we know that doing so would be in the interest of total human and social economy, whether our patrons realize it or not."

Most of the 42 responding to another question felt that they had maintained a balanced approach to programs and collections despite pressures, but 9 felt that they had indeed gone overboard on some aspect in response to pressures. The demand for library support of new programs being added to the curriculum, especially in area studies and other graduate-level programs, has evidently distorted and—especially serious—has de-emphasized services to undergraduate students. One junior-college librarian said, "I believe we are overemphasizing A-V [audiovisual materials]. Some instructors tend to rely so extensively on them that other media are neglected."

As for book selection, 33 college librarians spent more time this way than formerly; 10 spent less time; 25 characterized selection of nonprint materials as "competent," 18 as "uneasy," and 2 each as "innovative" and "nonexistent." Respondents were about evenly divided (22 to 21) on the question of whether or not nonlibrarians are more involved in selection of materials than formerly. Faculty is more involved in many cases, but growing complexity of materials and resources makes it sometimes difficult to involve them; subject specialists on library staffs were seen as the ideal by several thoughtful librarians.

The crucial fact is that staff specialists (bibliographers) have taken over the larger portion of book selection, and this trend will increase in amount and in specialization. Faculty nowadays expect librarians to be competent to select even in exotic fields and exotic languages. They expect books to be on hand rather than to advise the library to acquire. Field trips for selection and procurement to all parts of the world are now standard procedure.

Thirty-two respondents thought that the selection function would become more important in the years ahead. Most of those who explained gave as reasons: more money to spend wisely, more materials to choose from, more diversified clients to select for, and a broader curriculum to support in greater depth. However, the 6 who thought selection would become *less* important (all from large university libraries) and the 5 who thought it would be "different" gave interesting and compelling reasons too. Said one, "In our terms, perhaps less. Trend toward increased automatic acquisition through judicious blanket orders." Noted one, in replying that selection will be different, "More materials available on microforms or computer stored with ready access when needed." Said another, also in a large university, "More standing orders for total press output." And another, "Less important in large libraries because they will be more concerned with comprehensive collecting. More selection by library staff specialists."

Asked what percentage of the books and other materials in the library is used for reference or circulation more than ten times a year, 46 hazarded an educated judgment: 21 said 15 percent of the material; 13 said 25 percent; 8 said 40 to 50 percent; one said more than 50 percent; and 3, less than 15 percent. Of course the percentage is much lower for the large research libraries with highly specialized collections than for the undergraduate or junior college library, where a high proportion of the material is in frequent use.

Again and again various questions elicited replies that point up the widening gap between the highly specialized and the very general college library. There were 45 librarians who felt the need for more highly specialized materials in their collections, and only 5 who said they did not; only 17 felt the need for more very elementary material, and 27 said that they did not. There were 30 mentions of meeting the needs at both ends of the spectrum (highly specialized and very elementary) by cooperative arrangements with a wide range of other libraries (special, public, state); 20 said that they continue to provide for "average" or "middle-of-the-road" demands.

Asked to identify the single factor in their service area that has most affected the type of material bought, the great majority cited, in the words of one, "enormous extension of research interest into previously neglected fields," and development of advanced graduate programs, such as foreign area studies. Several others noted more intensive individual instruction, the proliferation of paperbacks that students buy and keep, the upgrading of the institution (from college to university), and the enrollment encompassing a wider cross-section of society. The most frequently mentioned hard-to-find materials were materials for African, Middle Eastern, and Far Eastern (especially Mainland China) studies; out-of-print materials, especially foreign ones and serial publications; better sources for foreign publications.

Automation was by far the most frequent answer to the query concerning the most significant changes to come about in the near future in the handling and processing of materials. "More organization and method studies," said one. "Bibliographic control by computer," said another. "Better management, including machine and automatic processes, but also clearer, tighter organization with specific objectives (some of which are beyond immediate operation)." Most seem to be pinning their hopes to cooperative acquisitions and processing programs and to full use and implementation of the MARC program and other Library of Congress assistance.

One of the questions that drew the most interesting answers from this group of college librarians, as well as from other types of librarians who received the same questionnaire, was: "Do you think that different types of libraries will need to define and perhaps limit their functions more sharply in relation to each other and the clients in their service area?" There were 36 who said "Yes"; 9 said "No." Said one "Yes" man: "An optimal compromise must be found between the views that (1) library books are part of our cultural inheritance and should be freely available to all men, and (2) books are the chattel of the institution purchasing them. Both views are true." And: "Development of regional reference centers may make possible better definition of services to business and industry, now proving burdensome to many university libraries."

"Define yes, limit no," said a couple; and "Shared acquisition," said another. "In our town"—this from a southeastern librarian—"we have five institutions of higher learning with libraries, a city-county library, school libraries, and many special business and industry libraries and information centers. Too much uneconomical overlapping." Said one library statesman: "They should, but will probably resist the idea. Also, there will have to be more cooperation and expansion of functions and relationships; people will demand it." "Libraries should define what their most important services are—based upon analysis of the community they are responsible for serving—and develop affiliations with other agencies in their service area to provide mutual support for specific area-wide programs."

Respondents were about equally divided (24 to 22) between those who had and those who had not, in the past year, entered into any kind of formal (legal) regional or local sharing or mutual-aid agreement with any other type of library or institution. These ranged in nature from an agreement with another university to develop an Asian studies program to a "Flying Books" interlibrary loan by air with national libraries in Washington, D.C., and a telefacsimile link with the National Agricultural Library network. Five regional university libraries have undertaken cooperative study with intent to become a network ERIC facility; several have helped to develop reference and research centers within the state library system.

The remainder of the questionnaire was devoted to social issues affecting the libraries that serve higher education. When asked which set or sets of societal stresses their library had felt most keenly and most directly, 39 said population stresses; 41 said educational stresses; 36 said research and knowledge stresses; 22 said communications and documentation stresses. Occupational, political, and philosophical and social stresses were felt keenly by only 11, 7, and 10 college library administrators, respectively.

Asked how a particular set of these stresses had affected the library in practical terms, the majority mentioned stress resulting from huge enrollment increases and the broadened range of the curriculum. Here are some comments:

The burgeoning enrollments are far beyond our capacity—building, resources, staff—to handle adequately. . . . They are directly related to the increase in population. We raise entrance requirements, the state adds more community colleges, but the young people still keep flooding the university's gates.

Heavy demands from high school students to use our collections and service hours, which far exceed those of the school libraries. School librarians have quite failed in this area, at least, to meet the more sophisticated needs of today's students. At the same time, our own undergraduates, particularly at the upper and more sophisticated levels, now require services and collections at a level once thought necessary for beginning graduate students. Thus ten-year-old concepts of "undergraduate libraries" are quite out of date.

For example: With 1,200 new freshmen, unable to provide reading space, instruction in use of library, materials (say, for 1,000 students in a first-year English reading course). Effect: Set up new "college" library for students in first two years to provide both seating and access to specially selected materials; paperback packages through bookstore; individual study tables in library to improve level of use; "continuing show" basis for instruction, using both lectures and automatic projectors.

Other comments included: "Need for wider array of materials, greater duplication." "This university has taken on three new colleges in the past decade and gone into doctoral-level programs in more than a dozen fields." "Users have increased 50 percent in number." "The increase in school population and the recent emphasis on research have caused almost a total transformation of the university within the past few years." "We are serving a population of young people most of whom would not have otherwise gone to college." "Pressures on libraries to produce primary and secondary data suddenly on all aspects of the emerging nations have been great."

The next query was, "What one social phenomenon of the past ten years or so, whether listed by us or not, has given you the most worry and trouble in day-to-day operational terms?" Here, again, in this category of college library responses, as in the public and school library questionnaires, the most-often-expressed trouble and worry on a day-to-day basis related to students' manifest disrespect for public property and the theft and mutilation of books and other library materials.

It should be emphasized that this particular problem was not mentioned or suggested in the material accompanying the questionnaire, yet this concern was the single one most frequently expressed in answer to this question by *all types* of librarians in the survey. "Lack of recognition of the rights of others," says one junior-college librarian, one of many who see it as a symptom of deeper social and moral malaise. "The impatience of the young people. . . . These kids want everything for nothing." And another: "Ingrained and inbred feeling that everything is disposable and replaceable, hence careless attitude in caring for library materials, theft, loss, mutilation of library materials as a result."

One other major problem expressed in reply to this query was the feeling of being overwhelmed by growth (in student body, of research programs) and inflation. The pressures of the new educational program and the pressures of student activists were also mentioned.

What social phenomenon has given worry and concern in philosophical terms? Replies were thoughtful, and included:

> The increasing demands for professional training and skills, and the emphasis on "practical" and "useful" materials are killing the aesthetic tastes of our students. They read for information, not for enrichment. Our society demands more and better training, greater skills, faster-paced living; and little attention is paid to the importance of reflection, meditation, appreciation, and the needs of the spirit.

> Rapidity of change in all areas of society doesn't give us time to catch our breath. . . . We cope, but perhaps inadequately.

> The inconsistency of the society which demands that all qualified persons be given a chance to pursue a higher education, and then, on the other hand, tries to finance this enterprise with a sparse population tax base which is grossly inadequate.

> Mistaken concepts of potentialities of automation applied to libraries.

And one problem, very much on the minds of university librarians these days:

> The failure of the humanities and social sciences to persuade Congress that their activities are essential and significant, as indicated by the fact that federal support for the natural sciences annually is $16 billion, compared to $250 million for the social sciences. The effects of this generally are: (1) overemphasis on the natural sciences and the rewards for choosing them as vocational fields, and (2) a further decline of the humanities and social sciences because of the lack of personnel and support for research.

Other replies to this question indicated a wide range of concerns: integration and race relations generally, lack of adequate financing for college libraries, intellectual freedom vs. pornography, the disintegration of cultural values and the easy resort to violence as a nation and as individuals, and the need for a clear distinction between education and manipulation. "That in rejecting old values, some young people are embracing others—for no sound reasons in most cases—which lead to socially unacceptable behavior and to damaged health." "One matter that has had serious effect on colleges and on young people has been the draft."

Said one articulate librarian from the mountain plains states:

The Negro social revolution. The threat this poses to our society, due either to inaction of the white community or by overaction of the Negro community, could be cataclysmic to life as we are accustomed to it. . . . The Library as a social institution must play a more active role in meeting the educational-recreational-informational needs of minority groups as well as its traditional users.

"To what social pressure, stress, or opportunity do you feel that your library has responded most successfully?" In general, librarians in the colleges felt they had done well in coping with the diversified demands thrust upon them by rapid changes in curriculum, in teaching methods, and in proliferation of materials and students. Several were especially pleased that they had been able to provide materials on a variety and on both sides of major social issues; others cited their response to new programs and provision of supporting material for them; others believed they had done well in implementing social change, helping their institutions to integrate successfully, etc.

Here are some of the comments on successful coping:

Getting the idea across that the world is like McLuhan says, a global village, and that we must learn to relate to people of diverse origins and cultures.

As more and more people become aware of and concerned about major social issues (war and peace, race, poverty, overpopulation, etc.), the demand to read and know about these issues has become *much* greater. Fortunately, excellent material on these issues is available, and we have been able to meet the need for knowledge and understanding adequately, we believe.

I feel we have done quite well in keeping pace with the technological changes that have made internal library automation possible.

The trend toward independent study on the part of undergraduates. We are now retrogressing for lack of adequate physical facilities.

There is no apparent complacency however. The questionnaire also asked: "What effects of social change do you feel you have grappled with least successfully?" Several of the college library respondents expressed concern about their inability to encourage leisure reading in students and their failure to make the library a more effective force in developing a value system among students. As, here: "Stupid misuse of leisure time. Haven't been able to lead many students into areas which could be useful and enjoyable leisure-time pursuits." Several felt that they had failed to meet adequately the special needs of the disadvantaged student, who comes to college with the handicap of many gaps in his background reading.

Others mentioned failures with respect to financial support, housing, and "taking advantage of the advanced technology which must lead us to ways and systems which will handle the mass of data which is so necessary in operating a complex organization called a university library." Failure to attract and hold able staff was cited; others were concerned about "fitting collection development to changes in teaching and research emphasis. Still too ad hoc." One outstanding junior-college librarian was dissatisfied with "the use of the library by students in our adult education or continuing courses. We are open four nights a week, Saturday mornings, and Sunday afternoons, but are used little by students in these noncredit courses." A university librarian said: "We haven't really grappled very much as a library in a university. We support as we can the university's attempt to grapple." Finally: "We have failed miserably in our attempts to improve the dissemination of information to the university community. In this regard, we are still occupying primarily a passive role."

A number of free-response comments mentioned progressive steps, innovations, or changes giving the individual librarian the most personal and/or professional satisfaction. Examples of response were: "Reduction or elimination of routines, more time with students and faculty, and introduction of nonprint materials in general use." "Planning two new departmental libraries . . . salary improvements." "Greater attention to under-graduate students' needs . . . long-range planning begun." "The fact that we have survived at all in reasonably satisfactory condition may be attributed to our training of nonprofessional staff to assume much work hitherto done by professionals."

The beginning, planning, or completion of a new building was given by many as a source of satisfaction. Also: machine-readable circulation system, a machine-produced book catalog, redesign of functional locations of all operations, development in progress toward remote-access videotape library, and "gaining confidence of administration, faculty, students, and staff." And: "Movement toward a personnel classification scheme that recognizes individual expertise and growth, more in the professional style than the civil service hierarchical style." And from a junior-college librarian: "From the first book and the first brick to a beautiful new learning resources center with an opening collection of 20,000 volumes—in less than two years!"

Question: "What do you think will be your most pressing problem in the years between now and 1975?" Lack of space and money head the list. "Convincing statewide budget officers that a first-rate university faculty demands and must have ready access to an extensive book collection that is open-ended and grows at an ever-increasing rate. Convincing them that automation will not change this requirement within the definable future." "Increased funding to . . . keep pace with the proliferation of graduate-degree programs; the trials and tribulations of converting to an automated system." "To keep up with new developments of materials, methods, and computer possibilities that will lead to greater efficiencies and better service." Staff availability is evidently a constantly haunting problem, as is increasing workload without corresponding increase in staff. And finally, "Everything needed to handle growth: people of greater competence, physical space, how to automate (*not* whether to or not), where to get the money."

Respondents were then asked: "How are you going to tackle it?" Some replies were hopeful, some despairing, all determined: "Establishment of planning office on the director's staff . . . conscious attempt to work at state, regional, and national levels to be involved in the establishment of networks." "By supporting national and regional efforts to experiment and innovate; in other words, by cooperating." Some comments were lengthy:

> Dramatize the need enough to convince the president, make salaries more competitive, and beat the bushes in search of promising staff members with or without library school training.

> Answered generally, by taking advantage of available knowledge and practice in librarianship and in the contributing disciplines of public administration, scientific management, sociology, political science, education, engineering, computer science, and other areas. More specifically, by establishing specific objectives centered upon the needs of users, making plans intended to achieve them, improving organization and management, developing existing staff competence and effectiveness, and adding some competent new people who can help maintain awareness of social and technological change and of new knowledge in essential fields. . . . It is intended to proceed along lines already known in 1967, but to increase awareness of the changing environment and means of reacting usefully to it through the use of whatever knowledge and skills are pertinent.

> We will avail ourselves of all technological advances in data transmission and automated methodology for storage and retrieval. We will work with other libraries to cooperatively work out machine applications to library technology; we will develop regional storage depots and cooperative purchasing agreements with like libraries in our area.

> I'm hoping that more sophisticated cost-benefit accounting may help.

Some commentators focused on broad planning: "Develop a long-range plan which is coordinated with programs being developed in other parts of the university." But, some were expedient: "Piecemeal; storage of materials that are little used; new construction where possible." To match one who writes simply, "I don't know," there is another who says, doggedly and without details, "Do it."

As to the look ahead into the future beyond 1975, some were visionary but many college librarians figuratively shrugged their shoulders, believing that college and university libraries, at least, will not be so terribly different—just have more of everything. Library users, it is thought, at least on the college campus, will be sophisticated in the use of all kinds of media. Buildings will probably be fairly well fixed in their present new forms for the next twenty years or so. As to staff, says one, "Managers, technicians, public relaters, promoters, and subject specialists will run the library."

It is clear from the responses of the college and university librarians reproduced here that at least some are articulate leaders of their profession—looking far beyond the service demands of undergraduate education and placing these in context with other educational and research demands by some highly specialized users of library and informational services.[58] Here are some of the future-oriented commentaries:

> More branch library development, more interdependence for special materials, more use of microforms.

> Libraries will be used by people who have need of their particular services, and these people will represent a larger share of the whole population.

> Academic libraries may not change so much in nature unless higher education changes. There will of course be increased use of communications media, extended use of closed-circuit TV, etc. . . . Public libraries may more and more move into government-sponsored adult education, poverty-rehabilitation programs calling for multipurpose centers of which the library function will be but one part or unit. . . . Personnel: There will be a larger proportion of technical, paraprofessional assistants, supervised and directed by fewer librarians percentagewise than now obtains. The library may also find itself becoming a unit for rehabilitation of persons released from correctional institutions, to be employed in capacities where they can be as effective as their potential allows.

> On the local scene, microreproduction may loom larger but not much—the book will continue to be the best reading machine.

> The resources required by our information needs transcend our present definitions of libraries. Our society must be able to tap, manipulate, and combine data bases such as the following: data files of insurance companies, medical case histories, criminal identification files, deed and mortgage records, Census Bureau, Department of Defense, National Institutes of Health. Libraries have a major role to play or libraries will decline as new information operations develop in response to need.

One respondent, Dr. Neal Harlow of the Graduate School of Library Service, Rutgers—the State University, commented at length:

> A variety of agencies will comprise the information system of the future, and individual libraries will serve as outlets and means of entry to it. All units will have direct access to data, many will store it, but individual stations will vary in the formats of information handled. Some will specialize in books, for it is unlikely that the kind of individual access which books provide to "linear" thought will be offered satisfactorily by other media. Some parts of the system will handle summaries of content and provide electronic access through automatic indexing and retrieval, probably building up patterns of individual use to improve accessibility. Some units will focus upon other areas of community need, providing, for example, a centralized information base (representing a variety of public services) so that individuals, however uninformed, can satisfy their major information needs in a single place.

> The objectives of such an over-all system will be to assist in decision-making at every level by providing reliable information rapidly wherever it is required. The

---

[58] *The specialized users and their needs, so often met by the university library, are the subject of chapter 3.*

many conflicting forces and pressures in a democratic society which beset individuals, groups, and public and private agencies (locally, nationally, and internationally), and calling for decisions, will increasingy require that such sources of information be available. They will be developed either sporadically, as at the present, wherever the need proves to be overwhelming, or the process can be carried out systematically through an orderly program of research and planning. Whether the system will in fact eventually embrace the majority of libraries, along with other data stores, information agencies, and research collections, will depend to some degree upon the readiness of librarians to recognize the lines of development and take initiative in participation; certainly the latent resources of libraries and the extensive physical base for the dissemination of information which they provide (with a built-in bias toward information) offer a setting and an opportunity which can be claimed by no other existing type of agency. Libraries must, however, grasp the significance of this opportunity—it will not fall automatically into their laps—or other possibly more inexperienced but highly motivated groups may capitalize upon it instead.

Obviously the staffs of libraries and information services will be exceedingly varied, depending upon their responsibilities in relation to information, the user, operations, and administration. There will be administrators with responsibility for objectives, for planning, and for organization; systems analysts and managers responsible for effective operations; librarians and information officers to select and develop the information base and to serve as intermediaries between the intellectual source and the user; information processors to handle the technical input of data (indexing, abstracting, reviewing, cataloging, programming); technicians to run machines; and clerical staff for the varied bibliographic and office routines. Administrators at several levels will require a good deal of knowledge about information sources and systems, the nature of the community served and requirements for satisfying user needs, and about public administration and public affairs. Analysts and managers will specialize in designing, engineering, and operating systems. Librarians and information personnel must be competent in the information-transfer process to deal with content, people, and the data-retrieval system. Information processors may be subject specialists engaged in preparing state-of-the-art reviews, indexers-abstracters-catalogers, and specialists in preparing programs for information storage and retrieval. Technicians and clerical personnel will serve in many paraprofessional and clerical areas. The librarian's competencies will find best expression in planning and administration and in selecting and evaluating data and interpreting it to users.

TABLE 2C–2.1

MATERIALS CHECKED OUT OF COLLEGE LIBRARY BY STUDENTS IN FIVE INCOME CATEGORIES

PARENTS' INCOME	PERCENT OF STUDENTS	MATERIALS CHECKED OUT
$ 4,000 or less	13%	1,346
$ 4,001–$ 8,000	50	4,372
$ 8,001–$12,000	25	1,811
$12,001–$16,000	6	508
Over $16,000	6	396

SOURCE: *H. Clayton, "An Investigation of Various Social and Economic Factors Influencing Student Use of the Library" (unpublished Ph.D. dissertation, University of Oklahoma, 1965), p. 64.*

TABLE 2C–2.2

COLLEGE STUDENT GRADE-POINT AVERAGES COMPARED WITH LIBRARY WITHDRAWALS

GRADE-POINT AVERAGE	Total students		Students borrowing at least one book	
	NUMBER	PERCENT	NUMBER	PERCENT
A 4.0 to A 3.5	118	4%	75	62%
B 3.0 to B 2.5	907	37	399	44
C 2.0 to C 1.5	1,344	55	529	39
D 1.0 to D 0.5	73	3	16	22
F 0.4 to 0.0	7	—	1	14
TOTAL	2,449	—	1,020	42%

SOURCE: F. Barkey, "Patterns of Student Use of a College Library," College and Research Libraries, March 1965, p. 117.

TABLE 2C–2.3

USER REPORTS OF PURPOSE FOR VISIT TO PURDUE UNIVERSITY LIBRARY

(July 1964)

Purpose for library visit	Persons	
	NUMBER	PERCENT
Use of own material only	69	33%
Use of library material only	44	21
Checkout for home use only	7	3
Other only	17	8
Use of library and own material	40	19
Use of library material and checkout	17	8
Use of own material and checkout	5	2
Use of library and own material and checkout	13	6
TOTAL	212	100
Use of own material	127	60%
Use of library material	114	54
Checkout for home use	42	20
Other	17	8

SOURCE: A. K. Jain, "Sampling and Short-Period Usage in the Purdue Library," College and Research Libraries, May 1966, p. 218.

TABLE 2C–2.4

SUMMARY OF VARIOUS STUDY RESULTS SHOWING NO USE OF COLLEGE AND UNIVERSITY LIBRARIES

N	GROUPS STUDIED	PERCENT WITHDRAWING NO BOOKS
2,292	Students in one university 2nd half spring semester	42.0%
2,438	Students in 5 colleges 9 months	10.8
836	Men students in "College B" one semester	36.6
486	Women students one semester	28.0
738	Students Knox College one quarter	48.51
2,967	Eastern Illinois University 30 days (1962)	63.0
3,847	Eastern Illinois University 30 days (1963)	62.0

SOURCE: *F. Barkey, "Patterns of Student Use of a College Library,"* College and Research Libraries, *March 1965, p. 116.*

CHAPTER III

THE SPECIALIST USER
OF LIBRARY AND
INFORMATIONAL SERVICES

The preceding chapters have discussed the broad social functions of libraries in meeting the needs of society at large—and, further, in actively developing a sense of need in some largely apathetic segments of the public. The foregoing chapters have also pointed up the close relationship between education and libraries in benefiting voluntary and involuntary users from preschool through elementary and secondary schools, through vocational training and undergraduate college—all this involving public libraries, the libraries of school systems and of individual school buildings, and the academic libraries.

The specialist user, in pursuing his highly developed needs, may make use of some of the same libraries that serve the nonspecialist and the prespecialist; e.g., the large public and university library systems. The specialist, however, thinks of the libraries he needs as information centers or research libraries, and these latter may range from the library of a small historical society to the Library of Congress itself, with many other institutions, some privately supported, in between, libraries that are awesomely esoteric and unattainable to the general public and the undergraduate student but essential to the graduate student and the scholar.

Section A of chapter 3 is concerned mostly with the scholarly user, who is usually a university faculty member in the humanities or the social sciences—such fields as English, history, language, fine arts, philosophy, political science, and many others, including some professional fields like law and theology, and perhaps even some aspects of library science itself. Research needs here are literature-based, requiring documentary materials and utilizing qualitative more often than quantitative techniques. Such scholarly needs are often not appreciated in this age of research emphasis in the natural and physical sciences and those social and behavioral sciences sharing with them a quantitative approach, laboratory and field experimentation, and a readily applicable discovery of knowledge for the more immediate benefit of society.

The particular, and increasingly important, informational needs of the scientific scholar and investigator are discussed in section B, and those of the professional, both scholar and practitioner, appear in section C. It is hoped that section A, in discussing the less appreciated scholarly needs for library and informational services, can suggest the commonalities of all search for knowledge and also the social and cultural benefit to be derived from the interactions of many disciplines.

A. THE SCHOLARLY USER:
THE LIBRARY AND INFORMATIONAL
SERVICE NEEDS OF SCHOLARS

The National Advisory Commission on Libraries drew heavily on one of its special studies in delineating its objectives for the support of all kinds of research and for the provision of adequate access, both to information about the availability of materials and to the physical materials themselves (see chapter 12, section C). Two of the papers from this valuable report, *On Research Libraries,* appear here to describe the needs and problems of the scholarly user of library and informational services.

1. THE DEMANDS ON UNIVERSITY
AND OTHER RESEARCH LIBRARIES[1]

If the peculiar trait of man among living creatures is his capacity for thought, the peculiar mark of civilized man is his habit of recording knowledge for communication to other men, whether near or far in place or in time. For this purpose he has invented and used a vast variety of instruments and materials, from clay, papyrus, ink, paper, and the printing press to phonodiscs, magnetic tapes bearing symbols rather than letters and words, and photochromic dyes that can fix thousands of miniaturized characters on a chip of film an inch or two square. But in whatever form individual men have chosen to put down their thoughts and observations, they have for a very long time now taken pains to put them in safe places to which other men, before and afterward, have committed theirs.

From the time we know anything of history such accumulations, known as archives and libraries, have enjoyed a kind of sanctity as embodying the best efforts of men's minds. A barbarian was one who would or did destroy records of gathered knowledge in an enemy's country. Thus the library, as it has evolved in the Western world from the archival rooms of palaces in old Mediterranean lands, has become the symbol as well as the actual center of men's aspiration to better themselves and their society.

This is nowhere more strikingly true than in the United States. In its Colonial era America inherited the ideas of Western Europe through the migration here of books as well as people. Since its birth as a nation it has helped reshape and give the best of those ideas substance by its commitment to the proposition that intellectual freedom is an essential ingredient of political freedom—or, as Jefferson put it, that error is dangerous only when we are not free to contradict it. Economic developments in the nineteenth century and political events in the twentieth have broadened and deepened this trend. The growing wealth of the United States, together with its comparative security from wars that have ravaged most other parts of the world, has brought more and more treasures for safekeeping to our libraries, provided training and facilities for several generations of American scholars who now match in eminence their counterparts in older centers of learning, and attracted to this country increasing numbers of experts in all fields of thought and investigation.

1 *From the introduction to* On Research Libraries *by the Committee on Research Libraries of the American Council of Learned Societies, submitted to the National Advisory Commission on Libraries November 1967. The complete study,* On Research Libraries, *was published by the M.I.T. Press in 1969.*

These developments and others familiar enough in the life of our time have placed libraries at the heart of most of the worthy enterprises that Americans conduct. They are an indispensable part of our enormous educational effort on all its levels. American business and industry today support thousands of specialized libraries because they are vital to their operations and progress; the quality of their library resources and services is a reliable index to the quality of many types of corporations. Modern science, which is rendering so much of the world obsolete so fast and which is profoundly impatient with libraries as men have customarily built and operated them, is just as profoundly dependent on them for access to and dissemination of the data and findings it feeds on.

Finally, government itself is one of the chief consumers, as it is one of the chief producers, of library goods and one of the chief operators of library services. In 1814, when Thomas Jefferson offered his library to the nation at a nominal price after the burning of the infant Library of Congress, some congressmen doubted the wisdom of purchasing such a collection. What need could officers of the United States have, they asked, for books written in foreign languages, including Greek, Latin, and Anglo-Saxon? Today, under the authority of recent legislation, the Library of Congress endeavors to acquire a copy of every book of substantial value published in *any* language. All of this is not only natural and proper but represents a trend that will grow stronger rather than decline—always provided that human wisdom succeeds in preserving human civilization.

The worth and importance of libraries in general, then, may be taken as virtually self-evident. We are concerned here, however, with one type of library, the research library, and the adequacy of its performance as the rising demands for its services coincide with a tidal wave of new publication the world over. The collections and services of the nation's research libraries undergird the whole library structure as well as higher education and scholarship in every area of human significance.

Research libraries may be defined as institutions whose collections are organized primarily to meet the needs of scholars and so to facilitate effective action on the frontier of every field of knowledge, traditional and novel. Most American research libraries are integral parts of universities. At their best they are notable for the variety and depth of their holdings and for the quality of research that they support. The collections of the seventy university libraries that are members of the Association of Research Libraries range in size from 500,000 to almost 8 million volumes. The present average is just over a million and a half; it will approach 3 million in less than twenty years.

These relatively well-stocked libraries make an indispensable contribution to higher education and research in every section of the country. Increasingly their collections are used by scholars from all parts of the world; each year their lending to other libraries and photocopying for research mount; and steadily their role in higher education expands, for the universities to which they belong account for 80 percent of the nation's doctorates. Any inadequacy in the range or depth of their research materials or their services will jeopardize American scholarship and limit its services both to ourselves and to the world. At the same time, the extraordinary needs of the numerous new or expanding universities should be given earnest attention. Their research collections must be built up almost overnight if they are to attract able faculty, offer graduate work worthy of the name, and contribute adequately to their communities, states, and regions.

In addition to university libraries, the Association of Research Libraries includes three Federal libraries, one of which—the Library of Congress—holds some of the world's greatest research collections; two public libraries with important resources for research; and several unaffiliated libraries. Outside the Association are institutions of the first rank, such as the Folger Shakespeare Library and the American Antiquarian Society, distinguished by priceless materials in history, literature, and other fields that are vital to scholarship and placed freely at its service. These unaffiliated libraries have no alumni; some lack adequate endowment and their very existence may be threatened as expenses rise. Yet if the premise is granted that the nation's resources for promoting knowledge are indivisible, it should be clear that no part of its network of research libraries can be impaired without impairing all.

PROBLEMS OF RESEARCH LIBRARIES

While there is diversity in the age, size, control, and clientele of American research libraries, they are all faced with refractory problems that impede their satisfactory performance. At first glance the dilemma of the research library appears to be simply the consequence of growth. It is axiomatic that American research libraries double in size every fifteen to twenty years, and it follows that they must be chronically short of space, staff, and funds. But just as challenging as these shortages are the accelerating demands that have been made upon American research libraries since World War II. Their services have been heavily taxed by the rising university population, a fourfold growth in graduate enrollment, and a sharp increase in postdoctoral research. The demand for information from the business and industrial world has multiplied, and the Government's massive investment in research and development has added substantially to library burdens without compensatory support. Even foundation grants for research, welcome as they are, have further taxed library resources without proportionate financial relief. At the same time, the national interest has necessitated knowledge of cultures and geographical areas we had previously ignored, and the widened angle of vision of American scholarship, as well as of education, industry, and government, has obliged libraries to seek out and acquire research materials in countries without bibliographical tools or a book trade and in languages totally unknown to their own catalogers.

These new demands and developments have called into question the research library's habitual pattern of acquisition and cataloging. When American scholarship staked out the whole world as its sphere of interest, it was no longer possible for research libraries to do all their foreign buying through a few reputable dealers in Western Europe, and when an Asian and African inflow began through other channels, much of it defied the skills of the local catalogers. Arrearages in cataloging mounted also at the Library of Congress, with serious consequences for other libraries. From the first of the century it had shared its cataloging skills with other libraries by selling them catalog cards, but in recent years it has been able to supply cards to other research libraries for no more than half of their foreign purchases. This has meant wasteful duplication of effort on a large scale and intense competition for a limited number of specialized catalogers. At many libraries research materials piled up that could not be cataloged or even fully identified, and to this degree the librarian was no longer in bibliographical control.

At the same time, the proliferation of publication here and abroad began to raise serious questions about the adequacy of the bibliographical apparatus on which scholars depend for notice of everything published that may be relevant to their research. What bibliographical information they were receiving on current research materials, whether American or foreign, was frequently out of date, and they were supplied with virtually no information about foreign books or periodicals that were not bought and cataloged by an American library.

While the librarian was adding more volumes to his collections than ever before, he was becoming increasingly aware of the impermanence of a substantial proportion of his institution's past acquisitions. Older books were surviving well, but most works published during the last hundred years were printed on paper whose acid content would bring about its disintegration in a matter of decades. In consequence, research libraries had to divert part of their budgets to photocopying books whose pages were too fragile for further use. And since there has been no general move to adopt acid-free papers on the part of the Government Printing Office or commercial publishers, expenditures for photocopying are likely to rise on a curve that parallels the graph of acquisitions a generation earlier.[2]

Research libraries could have faced these challenging developments with greater assurance had they been adequately staffed, but the demand for American librarians at home and abroad outstripped supply in the 1950's, and libraries of all types were henceforth understaffed, with persistent vacancies at every level of skill and authority. Research libraries had special staffing difficulties because their requirements for linguistic and subject-matter competence go far beyond standard library training, and catalogers were in especially short supply. The competitive bidding resulting from heightened demand has raised salary scales, but this and other persuasions to recruitment have not yet sufficed to interest as many able young men and women as are needed in library careers.

During these two decades, moreover, library costs were rising much more rapidly than the general price index, and in university budgets library needs were habitually underestimated. The financial needs of libraries are formidable today, and they are sure to become more formidable. Indeed, substantial new sources of income will have to be found if the nation's research libraries are to continue to perform their function satisfactorily. Libraries at new branches of state universities are immediately faced with the double cost of simultaneously acquiring retrospective and current material, and even established university libraries are confronted with sharply rising expenditures. According to a careful analysis and forecast, library costs at Harvard are expected to rise from $5.7 million in 1964–65 to $14.7 million in 1975–76.[3]

To these developments must be added another which is at once a problem and a promise. This is the automation of the library's operational and bibliographical functions. Its promise is so clear that it is already being widely applied to the manifold routine tasks that libraries have hitherto had to perform manually. At the same time encouraging experiments are being conducted in coding catalog data for central storage, fast access, and mechanical transmission to a geographically unlimited constituency. How satisfactorily the intellectual content of books, manuscripts, and other library materials—as distinct from bibliographical description and indexing of them—can be coded for these purposes is currently unknown and a matter of debate. One daily hears and reads predictions of a breakthrough to a new world of electronic ease for librarians and scholars. Such predictions are delusive, and by their false promise impede more than they help those working toward solutions of research library problems by means within, just beyond, or even well beyond our grasp.

As far ahead as can be foreseen, the computer and its accompaniments will supplement rather than replace the library materials we are familiar with, and even the most sophisticated electronic circuitry will remain an aid to, not a substitute for, men's minds in contact with books. But if wisdom cannot be extracted from machines, they are marvelously rapid and accurate processors and disseminators of information. They must therefore be developed to their fullest capacity in research libraries. Ambitious experiments are now in progress, and as more cost studies and performance reports become available, there is every prospect of steady and productive advance in this area.

Briefly stated, these are the major problems that face research libraries today in serving the needs of the scholarly user, and vast resources of money and manpower, to say nothing of imagination, planning, and cooperation, will be required to resolve them.

2 *American Council of Learned Societies initiative during the life of its Committee on Research Libraries directed attention to the problem of short-lived book papers, and progress toward its solution was noted. On August 25, 1967, the Government Printing Office agreed to use lasting paper in categories of publications the Librarian of Congress might designate as worthy of longevity. Early in 1968 a joint committee of the American Library Association and the American Book Publishers Council sent out a questionnaire on permanent/durable paper to both publishers and paper manufacturers. This should measure what is already a perceptible shift toward nonacid book papers.*
3 *Harvard University Library, 1966–76,* Report of a Planning Study *(Cambridge, 1966), p. 29.*

The future of our free society depends on our access to accumulated knowledge organized to facilitate learning and scholarship. Libraries are not inert repositories of artifacts and documents of the past or mere bits and pieces of information. They are living agencies for intellectual enrichment and progress, for public policy and social improvement through scholarship. They are at once man's memory and the embodiment of his faith that despite the tragic vicissitudes of our time, his creations, his ideas, and his spirit will live forever.

There is a final problem. "You have the ages for your guide," Edwin Arlington Robinson once told Americans, "but not the wisdom to be led." Libraries store wisdom, but they offer no guarantee that it will be effectively employed. Nevertheless, one can hope that the recommendations of the National Advisory Commission on Libraries will enable the libraries of the United States to possess vastly more knowledge in a far more usable form than has been available to any other country in mankind's history.

2. SCHOLARLY NEEDS FOR BIBLIOGRAPHICAL CONTROL AND PHYSICAL DISSEMINATION[4]

by *EDWIN E. WILLIAMS*
Associate University Librarian, Harvard University

Research can be defined as studious investigation directed toward the extension of knowledge. Obviously it must build on what is already known. It may require expeditions to unexplored regions of the earth or beyond, laboratory experimentation, or study of the collections in galleries and museums; the sources of knowledge are as varied as knowledge itself. Almost always, however, research depends in part (and often it depends almost wholly) on libraries. Almost always, likewise, the results of research are reported in written, printed, or other records that libraries collect, organize, and make available to scholars.

Research libraries have helped to create modern civilization; their strength and vigor directly affect the health of scholarship and hence of society as a whole. The rapidly growing abundance of knowledge, which would have been impossible without research libraries, now confronts them with far more difficult tasks than ever before.

This abundance is reflected by striking quantitative increases in publishing; the output in many fields is now doubling every seven to ten years. There are new forms of publication, many of them difficult to obtain and to organize, and they are now produced by every inhabited area of the earth. Traditional boundaries between subject fields are breaking down, so fewer scholars now find that highly specialized collections are adequate to meet most of their needs. Moreover, traditional methods of collecting and organizing research materials are too slow to satisfy these needs.

The demands upon research libraries are made by a rapidly growing clientele. In 1870, less than a century ago, there were 5,553 faculty members in American institutions of higher education; by 1964 there were 494,514. One Ph.D. was earned in 1870; there were 382 in 1900, 2,299 in 1930, 3,290 in 1940, 6,633 in 1950, 9,829 in 1960, 11,622 in 1962, 14,490 in 1964, and 16,467 in 1965. Scholars engaged in formal postdoctoral work are now more numerous than graduate students working for the

4 *From* On Research Libraries *by the Committee on Research Libraries of the American Council of Learned Societies, submitted to the National Advisory Commission on Libraries November 1967. This paper was written for the Committee, and the author is indebted to its members for valuable suggestions that have been incorporated in the text. The complete study,* On Research Libraries, *was published by the M.I.T. Press in 1969.*

doctorate were until a few years ago. A study made during 1960 indicated that there were then some 10,000 postdoctoral scholars (most of them in the sciences and in medicine, and most of them supported by Federal funds) in addition to perhaps 15,000 medical interns and residents, college teachers, and visiting faculty. It can be anticipated that the National Research Council's Study of Postdoctoral Education, which is now under way, will reveal a substantial increase in numbers during the past seven years, and the rate of increase should accelerate for years to come.

This is yet another result of the speed at which knowledge is growing; postdoctoral study is becoming essential for professional scholars and those in more and more callings that demand constant upgrading and updating of knowledge. Those who teach in colleges and universities are by no means the only scholars whose research is producing the new knowledge that will shape the future; research materials are as essential to the industrial as to the academic community, and research libraries are essential to economic as well as to cultural development.

Fortunately the increased demands of scholars come at a time when the opportunities are also unprecedented—most notably those opportunities that arise from automation and other technological advances and those that stem from increasing recognition of scholarship, and the libraries essential to it, as national resources that must be nationally supported. Needs must be assessed and plans must be made.

BIBLIOGRAPHY IN GENERAL

Collecting by libraries is essential, but it is equally essential that there be bibliographical apparatus by means of which the scholar can learn of the existence and location of materials that may be useful to him. The catalogs and classification systems of libraries, important as they are, meet only a fraction of scholarship's needs; research depends also upon periodical indexes and abstracting services, national and subject bibliographies, and a multitude of other records of what has been written.

The latest edition of Besterman's *World Bibliography of Bibliographies,* though it excludes general library catalogs and all bibliographies that are not separate publications, lists 117,187 volumes of bibliography under 15,829 headings. Four years ago the Library of Congress prepared a *Guide to the World's Abstracting and Indexing Services in Science and Technology* listing 1,855 works that were then currently appearing at regular intervals. It is not easy to enumerate even all the major kinds of bibliography. Some bibliographies, like the 1,855 just mentioned, are current serials that attempt to provide information as promptly as possible on recent publications; others are restricted to works prior to a given date. Some attempt to include everything in their field; others are selective and critical. Some list titles only; others include annotations or extensive abstracts. Some list works only under the names of their authors; others list them under subject headings or in classified arrangements. Some confine themselves to books; others are restricted to articles in periodicals. Despite the international character of scholarship, national bibliographies are among the most ambitious and most useful achievements in recording what has been published; it is unfortunate that such bibliographies are still lacking for many countries.

Many bibliographies give no indication of where the scholar may obtain copies of the works they list; but library catalogs are among the major species of bibliography, and some of the outstanding subject bibliographies are catalogs of single great collections. Union catalogs and lists also include some of the greatest achievements of bibliography. The *National Union Catalog* at the Library of Congress has demonstrated that a great unpublished bibliography existing in a single copy can be highly useful, but its contribution to research will be greatly increased when its publication in book form, which is now under way, has been completed and it can be consulted in libraries throughout the world. Finally, it should be observed that not all published bibliographies appear as books or periodicals; alternative forms include cards, microfilms, and now magnetic tapes and other machine-readable media.

No one nation is going to do all the world's bibliographical work; no one agency or type of agency is going to do all the bibliographical work of the United States. Government departments, libraries, professional societies, and commercial publishers will continue to produce bibliographies, and this diversity ought to serve the constantly changing needs of scholarship better than any monolithic system. Yet coordination is an obvious need; the field of bibliography has become so vast that it is difficult to obtain the information on which decisions and plans ought to be based. At present the Federal Government has no bibliographical policy, and no one is responsible even for a continuing survey of the growing bibliographical output of the Government itself, much of which fails to meet recognized bibliographical standards.

There is no comprehensive and systematic effort to collect, appraise, and disseminate information on current developments in the application of computers to bibliographical work, yet these developments seem to offer the best grounds that scholarship has for hopes that bibliography can after all succeed in keeping track of the rising output of recorded knowledge. As library catalogs, bibliographies, indexes, and abstracting services are automated, it is vital that their machine-readable stores of information be compatible. Lack of uniformity in present book-form bibliographies may do relatively little harm, but a great advantage of converting bibliographical information to machine-readable form is that it can be mechanically consolidated, manipulated, and rearranged to meet specific local needs. Only a vigorous and extremely well-informed effort can hope to assist and persuade the host of organizations that produce bibliographies to cooperate for the benefit of scholarship as a whole.

Consequently, a National Bibliographical Office should be created.[5] This, it should be emphasized, is not envisaged as a regulatory agency in any sense, but as a central source of information on which voluntary coordination can be based, an advisory body identifying needs and formulating bibliographical standards, a referral center for bibliographical inquiries, and possibly, under contract, an agency for making special searches and compiling bibliographies.

This office would have international as well as domestic responsibilities; it should work closely with UNESCO and other international agencies as well as with bibliographical centers in other countries. Here it should be kept in mind that assistance to foreign bibliographical undertakings directly aids American research and American libraries; when any other nation establishes a good national bibliography, for example, it benefits scholarship everywhere.

Domestically the office should supplement rather than supplant effective existing agencies such as the Office of Science Information Service of the National Science Foundation, which "is responsible for providing leadership among non-Federal science information services, and in developing appropriate relationships between Federal and non-Federal activities," its objective being "to supplement internal Federal information activities, and insure that scientists and other users have ready availability to the world's current and past output of significant scientific and technical literature."[6]

In medicine, with the National Library of Medicine, and in other scientific fields a great bibliographical advance is now under way. MEDLARS, the National Library of Medicine's Medical Literature Analysis and Retrieval System, stores citations to a portion of the world's biomedical literature on magnetic tapes and retrieves information

5 *The National Advisory Commission on Libraries does recommend that one of the functions of the Library of Congress as the formalized National Library of the United States would be to provide basic national bibliographical services (see chapter 12, also chapter 10). Consideration of the future establishment of another agency for overall bibliographical coordination would presumably be one of the many functions of the recommended permanent National Commission on Libraries and Information Science.*
6 Annual Report (*Washington: National Science Foundation, 1965*), p. xviii.

electronically, making individual demand searches, producing bibliographies, and printing the *Index Medicus* by means of a computer-driven phototypesetter. Decentralization has now begun with the establishment of regional search centers to which tapes are supplied. The National Science Foundation reported in 1965 that national science information systems now appear to be within reach, and the same report announced that the American Chemical Society had contracted for a two-year program for mechanized informational services; under this $2,043,600 contract, 800,000 chemical references are to be fed into the system. The Foundation suggested that this arrangement might well be a prototype for future Government–scientific society relationships. It has been observed that bibliographies are produced and supported by a wide variety of agencies, but it should be emphasized that the scholars in each field cannot expect to be well served bibliographically unless they determine and make known their needs; hence their own organizations, the professional and learned societies, have a clear responsibility for leadership here.

Bibliographically, the nonscientific fields of learning, with their different kind of literature, have lagged behind. However, the United States Office of Education has now inaugurated ERIC (Educational Research Information Center) with a center in Washington and twelve clearinghouses in universities and other institutions throughout the country, each with responsibility for covering a specific subdivision of research in problems of education, such as junior colleges, counseling and guidance, exceptional children, and educational administration. These clearinghouses acquire, select, abstract, and index relevant documents; the center stores full texts of documents on microfilm, announces all new acquisitions, and makes copies available at nominal cost. Important data-archive projects such as the Inter-University Consortium for Political Research at Michigan and the Roper Public Opinion Research Center at Williams College should also be noted.

The sciences, where pressure is greatest and where financial support has been relatively easier to obtain than in other fields, can be expected to lead the way in comprehensive and automated bibliography. Other areas of scholarship must be assisted to follow.

LIBRARY CATALOGING

Subject bibliography and informational systems involve analysis in depth of the content of publications, and it is evident that urgently needed improvements in present services will require continued efforts by learned societies and other organizations as well as by libraries. Library catalogs, since they deal for the most part with whole volumes, may seem less complex, but the listing and classification of millions of books in a great library—or in the libraries of the nation—is not a simple matter. Cataloging at present is often too slow to serve the needs of scholarship, and libraries can ill afford to waste their inadequate supply of trained manpower on the duplication of work that far too often is still required.

A great step forward in library cataloging should result from the Higher Education Act of 1965, which authorized a proposal by the Association of Research Libraries for expanding the foreign acquisition and shared cataloging programs of the Library of Congress. This legislation authorized sums of $5,000,000 for 1965–66, $6,315,000 for 1966–67, and $7,770,000 for 1967–68, but fully adequate appropriations were not or have not yet been voted. Under this legislation the Library of Congress is to acquire, as far as possible, all library materials of value to scholarship that are currently published throughout the world, and it is promptly to provide catalog information for these materials. This is by no means an easy task, but the efforts made thus far are already enabling American research libraries substantially to reduce their duplication of work, and hence to save money as well as to give better service to scholars by speeding up their cataloging.

Later in this section there is some discussion of developments that may grow out of the acquisitions part of this program; here it should be noted that the new program promises to contribute to bibliographical progress internationally and to library automation. The Library of Congress has been collaborating with foreign national libraries and national bibliographies in setting up its machinery for acquisition and cataloging. American libraries are beginning to use cataloging done abroad, and the result is to reduce duplication of effort internationally as well as within the United States.

In addition to the efforts in acquisition and cataloging that it is making under the Higher Education Act of 1965, the Library of Congress, in cooperation with a few research libraries, is experimenting in the dissemination and use of cataloging data in machine-readable form. Research library records, for acquisition and circulation functions as well as for cataloging, have long been based on cards; now, as the transformation to a computer-based record system gets under way, it is essential that compatible methods be adopted. In other words, computers in each research library must soon be prepared to incorporate into the local system information received from computers at the Library of Congress and elsewhere, just as in the past it has been possible to incorporate printed cards of standard format into card catalogs. It is to be hoped also that the new computer age will lead to more standardization internationally than has been achieved in library cataloging up to now.

Whatever else research libraries do in the immediate future, they can afford to let nothing take precedence over the effort to move ahead with the shared cataloging program that has been launched under the Higher Education Act of 1965. This is not to suggest, however, that all major problems of research library cataloging can be solved by this program or that other efforts are not required. It deals with current publications and hence must emphasize the speedy transmission of data, which makes it all the more desirable to automate procedures as soon as possible. But research library catalogs contain millions of cards listing publications of past years, and research libraries must continue to acquire and catalog such publications by the thousands. The largest libraries do this as they strengthen their great collections by filling in the gaps, but the multitude of new or relatively weak libraries must attempt to build up research collections adequate to meet the growing needs of their scholarly communities.

A major advance in the vast field of retrospective cataloging was assured recently when the American Library Association was able to announce the completion of arrangements for publication in more than six hundred volumes of the *National Union Catalog*'s record of books published prior to 1956. (The record for publications since that date has already been published, and is kept up to date by monthly supplements with annual and quinquennial cumulations.)

This colossal publishing project, the largest ever undertaken anywhere, has been planned and contracted for without Governmental or foundation subvention. It will disseminate a store of bibliographical data accumulated since 1901, when the Library of Congress began to print catalog cards and to exchange them for those printed by other libraries. A Rockefeller grant enabled the *Catalog* to add more than 6.3 million cards from the period between 1927 and 1932. Major American research libraries have been reporting their acquisitions for many years, and there are now some 16.5 million cards recording locations of books in eight hundred libraries of the United States and Canada.

Hitherto, this information has been available only in the single card file at the Library of Congress; its publication will enable scholars to locate books without directing inquiries there and will give catalogers in each subscribing library access to catalog information for more than 10 million publications. In selection and acquisition it will be of great value in identification of books, and more importantly, it will enable libraries to avoid needless duplication of books already held by other American collections. Costs of editing and publication will be paid by subscribing libraries.

The *National Union Catalog*'s record of American research library holdings is far from complete and far from impeccable. It has not yet been automated. Something better will be possible a few years from now, but postponement of publication would have meant that for some years to come scholarship and research libraries would have had to do without the incomplete and imperfect but highly useful catalog that can now be made available. It should be added that provision has been made for changing the "printer's copy" during the course of publication from the present cards to machine-produced output at any time when this becomes practicable; thus the present undertaking will not entail any delay in future automation. Eventually the American *National Union Catalog* should be consolidated with similar records of research library holdings in other countries.

Clearly it is now reasonable to expect that research library catalogs will eventually move from card files into computerized form, but it is unrealistic to suppose that this will come as a single step; the beginning, presumably, will be made with data for current publications. This might well be followed by putting the Library of Congress catalog on computer tapes (or their successors) and enabling other research libraries to draw from the tapes, for their own automated catalogs, data for those books of which they have copies. At the same time, they would add to the tapes data for those of their holdings that were not represented at the Library of Congress. This procedure would minimize duplication of effort in putting catalog data into machine-readable form; eventually it would also produce a completed, revised, and greatly improved *National Union Catalog*. This catalog, since it presumably could be consulted electronically from a distance or through duplicate local stores of machine-readable data, might never need to be reproduced and disseminated in book form.

Completion of the *National Union Catalog* would deserve a very high priority even if it could not be done with the help of computers, and even if it could not be regarded in part as a by-product of research on library automation; its value to the scholar who works with noncurrent publications can hardly be overestimated. The effort to complete it should not be confined to the incorporation of a record of holdings of large research libraries; many other collections, particularly those of historical societies, possess books of great value for the study of America's past that are to be found nowhere else.

An attempt to set up a timetable for this mechanization of research library catalogs would seem premature until present experiments in the transmission of data for current publications have led to an effective program for supplying machine-readable data in conjunction with the shared cataloging project. Valuable experience is also being accumulated as work continues on projects such as Harvard's shelflist automation, the University of Chicago's "integrated, computer-based, bibliographical data system," and Project INTREX at the Massachusetts Institute of Technology (M.I.T.).

Harvard is transferring its handwritten loose-leaf shelflist to machine-readable punched cards and publishing print-outs produced by the computer in three sequences: a classified arrangement, alphabetically by author, and chronologically by date of publication. The University of Chicago, with the help of a National Science Foundation grant, is attempting to combine into a computer-accessible permanent record all elements of information about each book or other bibliographical item added to the library; the stored information will be used for many purposes: to determine holdings, prepare orders, maintain acquisition files, generate acquisition lists, prepare charge cards and labels, and produce full sets of catalog cards. M.I.T. is experimenting with its 125,000-volume Engineering Library in providing scholars with remote access to a computer-controlled magnetic memory store of bibliographical information on books and other library materials; consultation is to be through consoles linked to a central computer by ordinary telephone lines.

Costs of installing automated systems may seem high, but costs of operating these systems compare favorably with those of operating the present manual systems, and the scholar can be expected to benefit greatly from the improvements and innovations in service that automation can produce. The 1963 study *Automation and the Library of Congress* estimated the costs of conversion to an automated system at $50 million to $70 million, but operating costs of the system in 1972 were forecast at $4.5 million, compared with $5 million for the present system and its substantially less satisfactory services.[7] Other libraries, incorporating into their systems machine-readable bibliographical data produced by the Library of Congress, should have relatively lower costs of conversion and operation, and the scholars who use them should benefit enormously from access to an automated national system as well as from the increased accessibility of local holdings.

Despite its magnitude, the *National Union Catalog* is by no means the only important source of information on the location of research library materials, and it must continue to be supplemented by publications such as the *Union List of Serials,* which contains more than 225,000 entries describing periodical and other serial holdings of 680 libraries in the United States and Canada. Its current supplement is *New Serial Titles,* and the Library of Congress, having completed publication of the *Union List*'s third edition, is now planning a *World Inventory of Serials in Machine-Readable Form,* as recommended by the Association of Research Libraries. When completed, such an inventory can be a tool of inestimable scope and utility. The next step would be a union list of serials in machine-readable form, the additional information being, of course, locations.

Further improvements in the system for reporting and disseminating the record of serial holdings are needed. Other important aids to the scholar in finding specialized types of material include *Newspapers on Microfilm,* the *Union List of Microfilms,* the *Guide to Archives and Manuscripts in the United States* (now seriously out of date), the *National Union Catalog of Manuscript Collections,* and services like the new Center for the Coordination of Foreign Manuscript Copying. The Library of Congress is also maintaining a National Register of Microcopy Masters and is disseminating lists based on this, but there is as yet only rudimentary machinery for the coordination of copying or for support of the massive program of copying both books and manuscripts that would be highly desirable.

Guides to the location of materials in American libraries such as those that have been mentioned have numerous foreign counterparts, and the development of microfilming facilities abroad is making it increasingly easy for American scholars to obtain copies of library holdings wherever they may be. The demand for copying rises sharply as information regarding manuscripts becomes more readily available.

It should not be forgotten that manuscripts are by no means the only important type of material omitted from both the *National Union Catalog* and the *Union List of Serials.* Union lists of African, Russian, and Latin American newspapers have appeared during the past fifteen years, but there is no source of information on holdings of most foreign newspapers, and Winifred Gregory's *American Newspapers, 1821–1936,* now thirty years old, has not been brought up to date. Neither has her *List of the Serial Publications of Foreign Governments, 1815–1931.* Publications of great importance in special fields—sheet music and art exhibition catalogs, for example—have largely escaped the bibliographical net, to say nothing of maps and nonwritten materials such as sound recordings and photographs of all kinds.

COLLECTING AND COLLECTIONS

It may seem illogical to have considered bibliography and library cataloging before dealing with library collections, on which many bibliographies and all catalogs must be based. The scholar, however, normally approaches research materials through bibliog-

---

[7] Automation and the Library of Congress (*Washington: Library of Congress, 1963*), pp. 2, 32.

raphies and catalogs. Moreover, the work of selection and acquisition that builds any research collection must depend in large measure on bibliographies and on catalogs of other research collections. This was the case even when libraries were more self-sufficient than they are today; as it is, the sharing of information and of physical materials is so fundamental to research library operation that one cannot intelligently discuss collections and collection-building without constantly keeping in mind the bibliographical apparatus that makes each individual research library part of a much larger—though as yet very imperfectly articulated—library organism that extends beyond local and even national boundaries.

The members that make up this organism have been called research libraries, but it needs to be kept in mind that this term covers a multitude of diverse institutions, many of which are not exclusively engaged in supporting research. The small college library serves research needs of its faculty to the extent that it can; the large university library is heavily used by undergraduate students as well as by graduate students and faculty. Some state and municipal public libraries have important research materials; there are still proprietary libraries like the Boston Athenaeum with outstanding collections, and a number of major libraries, including the American Antiquarian Society, Folger Shakespeare, Huntington, Library Company of Philadelphia, Linda Hall, Morgan, and Newberry, that depend largely if not wholly on endowments and gifts for their support but continue to make their resources available to an increasing number of scholars under increasing difficulties.

The Reference Department of the New York Public Library is among the largest and most significant institutions in the country. Its holdings (i.e., those of the Reference Department alone, which is not supported by taxation, as is the Circulation Department of the New York Public Library) are surpassed in extent only by those of the Library of Congress, Harvard, and Yale, and they are unequaled in many subjects. Yet funds available for services, current acquisitions, and preservation of the collections are becoming more and more inadequate; endowment is being used up in order to keep the library going.

The current *American Library Directory* lists more than 7,700 specialized libraries in the United States, some 2,000 of which form part of university or other library systems. The total includes 1,231 medical, 569 law, and 246 religious libraries, and collections on scores of other subjects, maintained by government agencies, private industry, and associations of all kinds. There are special libraries with more than one million volumes—the National Library of Medicine, National Agricultural Library, and Harvard Law School Library—but it should be emphasized that a relatively small, highly specialized collection may also contain important research materials. Notable examples, as previously suggested, are many historical society libraries possessing manuscripts and other unique documents of inestimable value for the study of history.

Research libraries, then, are of many kinds, and research materials are more varied still. Much has been written during the past few years about how difficult it is to collect and organize the rapidly growing abundance of scientific publications. The difficulties are indeed great, and they will not easily be overcome, but the difficulties of collecting and controlling research materials for history and other social and humanistic subjects are far greater.

At the risk of oversimplification, chemists may be contrasted with historians. The record of research done by other chemists and by scientists in related fields is what the chemist normally needs to consult. There are far more research chemists than there used to be, yet they form a relatively limited and identifiable group. Their writings are issued by publishers who intend to disseminate them to scientists and to the libraries used by scientists. These writings now appear in "near print" and in technical reports as well as in the books and journals published by academic institutions, laboratories, learned societies, governments, industrial corporations, and commercial publishers. As has been said, collection and control of this literature is no longer easy, yet the chemist's needs are of a strikingly different order from those of the historian.

Like the chemist, the historian needs access to all the relevant writings of his scholarly colleagues. But his method of adding to this body of knowledge is not laboratory experimentation like the chemist's; it is to search and sift materials of all kinds that were not produced by historians or, for the most part, issued for the use of historians. The latest and most up-to-date compilation of information in his field cannot provide all that he needs, for historical literature is noncumulative and older writings never become completely obsolete. He may find useful data in a newspaper or pamphlet, an advertising leaflet or a schoolbook, a dime novel or a sermon, a photograph, tape recording, correspondence file, or personal account-book. The memoranda or working papers prepared for use within a government department may be much more illuminating than its published reports. Perhaps it should be noted also that if the report of a chemical experiment is lost, it is possible to duplicate the experiment; but when the last copy of a printed book or the unique copy of a manuscript diary is destroyed, some portion of the record is erased forever.

Selection and acquisition of materials to serve research of this kind can never have been a simple matter, and the difficulties have multiplied as the interests of American scholarship have extended to all areas of the earth. When American research in the humanities and social sciences was largely focused on the United States and Western Europe (and when these areas also produced nearly all the world's scientific and scholarly literature), American libraries could identify much of what they needed in good bibliographies and obtain much of it from an established publishing industry and from dealers who specialized in supplying libraries. In many of the countries that are now of particular interest to American scholars, it is almost impossible to discover what has been printed or to obtain copies unless a library can send its representative to scan the shelves of bookshops and deal personally with officials of the government departments that issue useful publications.

The world's publishing output has not been listed nor, indeed, has it been counted; there are no reliable statistics even for books and journals. The Library of Congress was adding more than 300,000 volumes and pamphlets per year *before* expanded foreign acquisitions began under the Higher Education Act of 1965, and the largest university libraries, though some of them acquire 200,000 books per year at a cost of more than $1 million, find their collections less and less adequate to meet the current demands of teaching and research.

Hence American research libraries have sought Federal assistance. In 1962 appropriations authorized by an amendment (Section 104–n of 1958) to Public Law 480 (of 1954) enabled the Library of Congress to begin to use foreign currencies from the sale of surplus agricultural commodities for buying and distributing to American libraries current books, periodicals, and related materials. Though few countries have as yet been included in this program, it has clearly demonstrated the desirability of establishing acquisitions agencies in countries lacking a well-organized publishing industry and book trade. Now, as the Library of Congress augments its foreign acquisitions program under the Higher Education Act of 1965, it evidently should be enabled to make its acquisitions facilities available to other libraries. (Appropriate legislation is now before the Congress.)

Regardless of the assistance that it may be possible for them to obtain from the Library of Congress, research libraries will need to continue cooperative efforts in foreign purchasing. Publications that are unobtainable commercially can often be acquired by exchange, which also provides useful American books and periodicals for many foreign institutions that cannot get dollars for buying in the United States. It has often been recommended that each country establish a national exchange center, and the UNESCO *Bulletin for Libraries* already lists thirty-nine such national centers.

Though the Smithsonian Institution has long functioned as a shipping agency for international exchanges, the United States has no national center; and funds should be provided to enable the United States Book Exchange (USBE), a nonprofit clearinghouse sponsored by major American library associations, to serve as the American national center. As such, it would maintain up-to-date information on current American and foreign serial publications available for exchange from the libraries of universities and other institutions, assist in arranging direct exchanges between institutions, and extend its duplicate clearinghouse activities to foreign libraries, which cannot for the most part afford the service charges that are necessary since USBE is self-supporting. It is unfortunate that the Agency for International Development (AID) terminated, in 1963, the program under which USBE had supplied more than 2.5 million books and journals to 1,800 foreign libraries during the preceding nine years at a cost to AID of some $1.5 million for service charges. A revived and expanded program of this kind should be supported; in addition, the program for information and service as an exchange intermediary that has been recommended could be financed for some $150,000 per year.

It should be emphasized that the acquisition of new publications is not enough to build the research collections required by American scholarship. The largest and oldest libraries constantly discover gaps in their collections—even the best of their collections—that ought to be filled in, and as new programs develop in their institutions, they are frequently called upon to support research in fields that hitherto had been neglected. There are more new and rapidly developing universities than ever before, and all of these, if they are not to be seriously handicapped by inadequate libraries, must build up extensive retrospective collections in many subjects.

There are great differences here between the needs of one scholar and the next; many a scientist and many a specialist in such contemporary problems as economic development may rarely need to consult a publication that is more than five or ten years old. For such scholars, a library with a good program of current acquisitions may soon become adequate. In the case of many other scholars, regardless of all that can be obtained by borrowing or photocopying, no equally useful substitute is now in sight for the great retrospective collections that traditionally have required decades and even generations for libraries to assemble.

The oldest and largest American university library is at Harvard, where a recent planning study estimated that the University's library collection (7,791,538 volumes in 1967) would grow to more than 10 million volumes in 1976, and that annual expenditures for the library ($7,543,791 for 1966–67) would increase to $14,655,000 in 1975–76. These estimates were based upon surveys of student and faculty needs, and took account of substantial savings anticipated from automation and increasingly effective library cooperation; the actual rate of increase in expenditures for the past eleven years has been greater than was predicted for the next eleven. It has also recently been estimated that within ten to fifteen years there will be 60 to 70 universities in the United States with graduate programs of real quality. Each, presumably, will need to acquire current publications on a scale comparable to Harvard's, and some of them at least, in an effort to increase the relative strength of their retrospective collections, can be expected to spend more than Harvard does on the acquisition and organization of noncurrent publications.

It has been emphasized that research libraries are diverse and numerous, but it would be a mistake to overlook the particular significance of the libraries of major universities, both those now in existence and those that can be expected to reach maturity during the coming decade. It is these libraries in which most of the nation's scholars—most of those who teach the teachers and most of those who add to the store of human knowledge—receive their advanced training.

Even when funds are provided very generously, the new institutions find that it takes enormous effort and considerable time to build great collections. Some desirable books rarely come on the market, and the competition for all useful out-of-print books is increasing, which has its natural effect on their prices. This competition, incidentally, is both domestic and foreign, since new universities are by no means an exclusively American phenomenon. Theoretically it would be possible to argue that the new institutions have been born too late, should specialize in research that normally requires only recent publications, and ought to leave old books to their elders. However, if this theory had been adopted a century ago, all the great research libraries would be in Europe; if it had been adopted a generation later, it would have restricted American research libraries to the eastern seaboard.

The reasonable assumption, therefore, is that traditional library-collecting ought to continue and will continue. The problem is how best to supplement it: how to reduce as much as possible the disadvantage under which scholars in new institutions would labor for years to come if they had to depend entirely upon the slow traditional processes of collection-building. Plans for coordination and sharing of resources are discussed later in this section. First, however, substitutes for original books ought to be considered.

These substitutes are provided by photographic reproduction in all its forms. The market provided by hundreds of new colleges and universities has stimulated a vigorous republication industry, which is bringing back into print many important books. Obviously the works that are reprinted are those of which the most copies can be sold, so needs of the college library and of undergraduate instruction are more likely to be met in this way than the specialized needs of advanced research.

For small editions, particularly for small editions of voluminous sets or collections, microphotographic reproduction is evidently more likely to be practicable than full-size republication. Recognizing the fact that scholarship can no longer afford to depend almost wholly on commercial sources for reprints or for microform projects, the Association of Research Libraries has recently established a program to improve access to materials that currently can be obtained from mainland China only in unique copies or very small quantities. Supported by a grant of $500,000 from the Ford Foundation, this program will identify texts that are of interest to the scholarly community and make them available in a variety of formats, ranging from microforms available on loan to offset reprints. The Association is now investigating the possibility of extending its Scholarly Resources Development Program to other areas of the world, such as Africa and the Slavic nations.

With modern reader-printer machines that will immediately produce a full-size copy of pages selected by the scholar, the disadvantages of having to work with microreproductions can be considerably reduced. The lack of an integrated system of library copying has delayed and seriously limited the exploitation by scholarship of the potentialities of microreproduction. Essential features of such an integrated system include quick and automatic conversion apparatus for all forms of copying, microforms readily manipulable by hand and by machine, automatic conversion to microform of machine-readable information, and microforms that facilitate immediate access to each page of text as well as rapid scanning of many pages.

It should not be forgotten, however, that some scholars—notably those engaged in bibliographical investigations of how texts were printed and of their vicissitudes in successive editions—must examine originals, and that many others may be seriously impeded by the inconvenience of having to depend on microfilm reading machines and the impossibility of browsing through the shelves of a collection arranged according to a systematic subject classification. On the other hand, it should be observed also that the largest and strongest libraries are relying to an increasing degree on microreproduction, both to supplement their collections and to replace publications that have physically disintegrated.

No problem confronting major research libraries is more alarming than the deterioration of paper, and nothing short of a comprehensive national effort will suffice to deal with it. The oldest books, on the whole, are surviving much better than most recent publications; the paper that was used for more than four hundred years after the invention of printing was remarkably durable. About a century ago, however, there was a great change with the adoption of certain acid-sizing processes in the manufacture of paper and with the increasing use of wood pulp; as a result, a very large proportion of the books printed during the past hundred years are rapidly becoming too brittle to use and many are already crumbling into dust. In 1965 the Association of Research Libraries adopted in principle a plan based on investigations financed by the Council on Library Resources. This calls for a national center that would preserve, insofar as possible, the best example of each deteriorating book deposited with it, would maintain a collection of master microfilm negatives, and would disseminate photographic copies (both microphotographic and full size) to libraries. The total cost of the program during its first ten years was estimated at slightly less than $10 million.

A preliminary study of procedures for identification of materials is now under way at the Library of Congress. Establishment of the National Register of Microcopy Masters there was also an important development because it provides information that is essential if libraries are to minimize needless duplication of filming for preservation as well as for other purposes, but nothing has yet been done to insure the preservation of master negatives, which ought to be in the custody of a national center or of research libraries. These negatives must conform to high standards and must not be exposed to the hazards of use except for making positive microcopies; likewise it is essential that they be permanently available for this whenever a scholar may need such a copy.

An effective national center for preservation and dissemination of research library materials would seem to be the appropriate agency to coordinate copying projects of all kinds. The need for coordination and for support of such projects has been mentioned apropos of the National Register of Microcopy Masters and other bibliographical services, and it has been noted that the Association of Research Libraries has now launched a Scholarly Resources Development Program in order to supplement commercial copying. A national center, with the full cooperation of research libraries, could in effect bring back into print all books held by these libraries, and the benefit to scholarship throughout the nation—to scholars based in the old and large libraries as well as to those in new institutions—would be hard to overestimate.

Further steps should be taken as soon as possible to put the 1965 plan of the Association of Research Libraries into effect, and continued research is needed on several questions, including optimum storage conditions for the books that are to be preserved, practicable methods of deacidification that will retard the disintegration of books now on research library shelves, the durability of film copies, and the chemistry and thermodynamics of paper. Very preliminary reports of current research at the University of Chicago suggest that deacidification may soon be practicable on a large scale, which would be an enormous boon to individual libraries and would help to make the national program more effective.

Every effort should also be made to induce publishers to use permanent/durable paper for the books that libraries will be acquiring during the coming century, and organizations representing the scholarly community ought to launch a vigorous campaign.

COORDINATION AND SHARING OF RESOURCES

From bibliography to the proposed center for preservation and dissemination of research materials originally printed on disintegrating paper, repeated reference has been made to cooperative or centralized activities. In a sense all the research collections of the world form a single great library; certainly the holdings of American research libraries constitute a national collection that is more a functioning entity than an abstraction. Scholars depend on many of the same bibliographies regardless of which unit of the national collection they may be using. Each unit has on its shelves the catalogs of many others and can refer to union catalogs giving the locations of millions of volumes that are not in its own stacks. Each uses—and hopes in the future to use far more effectively—cataloging done elsewhere. There are joint acquisition projects, copies of whole collections in other library units are acquired on film, and there must be a joint attack on the menace of disintegrating paper. In addition, each major library lends thousands of volumes annually to others and borrows thousands for its own community. Microfilms and other photocopies are being produced in rapidly growing numbers as a substitute for loans. Finally, each major library attracts hundreds of visiting scholars each year.

There are many flaws in the present organization. It is expensive to obtain copies of books, photographic and interlibrary loan services are far too slow, and there are too many uncertainties. Even so, the scholar who knows that a book he needs is in a distant research library can usually obtain a copy, and the sources of information through which he can learn it is there are being improved. Most of the suggestions that have been made here for strengthening American research libraries would do so by improving the national system and taking advantage of the opportunities now offered by automation.

When resources are shared to the extent that they have been for many years, each research library benefits directly as their total increases. It does not gain much from those books in other libraries that duplicate its own holdings, but it can and does draw upon collections that supplement its own. This inevitably suggests the possibility of specialization in collecting, and some sixty American research libraries have now been participating for twenty years in the Farmington Plan, under which each has agreed to collect current foreign books intensively in certain fields. Each, in other words, has undertaken to acquire more in the areas for which it has accepted responsibility than would be selected if only the needs of its own institution were taken into account; in return, each has the assurance that a similarly inclusive collection in every other subject is being built up by one of the other participants, from whom it can borrow.

The time now seems to have come for considering changes in this plan in the light of another major cooperative achievement, the Center for Research Libraries in Chicago. This began as the Midwest Inter-Library Center, a regional organization for acquiring and housing infrequently used publications, but modern communications make collections of books and microfilms in Chicago almost as accessible to new members of the Center in Vancouver, Cambridge, and Los Angeles as to its original participants in Minneapolis and Columbus.

Now, as has been noted, it is hoped that the Library of Congress, under provisions of the Higher Education Act of 1965, will acquire current foreign publications comprehensively—more comprehensively, it is reasonable to expect, than individual Farmington Plan participants have been successful in doing. If the Library of Congress could acquire two copies of each new publication and forward one of these to the Center for Research Libraries, the Center might function as a national lending library, and individual responsibilities under the Farmington Plan could then be discontinued.

Would a centralized national collection be preferable to the decentralized one that is now being created by Farmington Plan specialization? An affirmative answer seems to be justified by the fact that it would no longer be necessary to guess how a book had been classified for purposes of Farmington Plan allocation or to consult the *National Union Catalog* to determine the location of recent foreign publications. Furthermore, centralization of responsibility should make possible better service (in cataloging, in interlibrary lending, and in filming) than can be expected from sixty individual libraries, each of which has primary obligations to its own community. (Indeed, a few of the participating libraries cannot lend publications and can only provide photocopies.) If centralization is desirable, should it be at the Center for Research Libraries rather than at the Library of Congress? Here it may be observed that the Center is an instrument of American research libraries and is responsible to them, but the Library of Congress naturally must continue to give priority to service to the Congress and to agencies of the Federal Government.

A certain measure of insurance would also be provided by having two collections rather than one. The United Kingdom, it may be noted, has supplemented the British Museum, its great noncirculating national research library, by establishing two separate institutions specifically for circulation and dissemination: the National Central Library and the National Lending Library for Science and Technology. The former has a relatively small collection (less than 400,000 volumes) of its own but maintains a large union catalog and is the center of the national interlibrary loan system. The latter, dealing primarily with periodicals, currently receives 30,000 serials; it undertakes to handle loan requests the day they are received and to send out photocopies the day after orders reach it.

The Farmington Plan has been the major national effort in specialization by American research libraries. Hence it might appear that disillusionment with specialization is implied by the proposal discussed here to include Farmington Plan collecting among the national services that the Center for Research Libraries should be assisted to develop. In fact, however, as has been indicated, this proposal for centralization is prompted by the desire to make the nation's comprehensive collection of current foreign publications as accessible as possible. It should be emphasized that even when maximum accessibility has been achieved, the existence of this national collection will not relieve each research library of the need to build a strong collection of its own to serve its own community.

There is evidence that specialization and cooperative effort are becoming increasingly desirable at the local and regional levels. One reason for this is that there are more universities. Few metropolitan areas have had more than a single genuine university or a single major research library. Soon, however, there will be few such areas without a number of institutions conducting substantial research programs. This suggests the possibility of local agreements to specialize in collecting as well as the development of central research collections to supplement the other academic libraries in a metropolitan area. Here, as in other programs for sharing and increasing resources, the special problem of the college (as distinguished from university) professor should be kept in mind; the undergraduate college cannot build up research collections, yet many members of college faculties need access to such collections for their own scholarly research.

Locally as well as nationally there are limits, of course, to the extent to which any institution can depend on central collections and on those of libraries with which it may share responsibility under agreements for specialization in collecting. Each university library must support the changing research programs of its own university, and no university can or should undertake to forgo certain specified subjects for all time and to continue forever to emphasize certain others; indeed, the individual scholar sometimes finds that his investigations have led him to areas in which he had not expected to require strong library resources. Each institution must plan but must also be prepared to modify decisions regarding what must be collected on its own shelves and what can properly be left to other collections, either national or local.

It seems evident that scholars will depend more and more upon microtexts and other photographic copies. The many new institutions must acquire photocopies of millions of volumes that are no longer available in any other form, and older research libraries have millions of volumes on their shelves that will soon—if they have not already—become too brittle for normal use. An increasing number of scholars will live at a distance from major research collections. The largest libraries can acquire only a constantly decreasing percentage of the total output of the world's presses, and consequently will rely to a growing degree upon other collections such as the national lending library that has been proposed. If much of the increased use of microcopies is inevitable, there are also many instances in which choices can be made between lending and filming, between storing immense collections of books and substituting microcopies plus, of course, the reading machines required for their use.

Investigation of both research needs and of economic factors must provide information on the basis of which intelligent choices can be made. Thus the Center for Research Libraries, under a grant from the National Science Foundation, is now studying the costs and service characteristics of alternative methods of making journal literature available to scientists. There must be further studies of this kind, and there must be periodic reexaminations of the problem in the light of technological developments, particularly in the area of high-reduction techniques, which promise to make it possible to reproduce multiple copies of large collections at relatively very low cost. Difficult copyright questions are involved. So are questions relating to fees for use and their effect on scholarship; libraries traditionally have absorbed the costs of interlibrary loan, but with a few exceptions—notably the National Library of Medicine—have charged for photographic copies supplied in lieu of loan.

Something has been said of the limitations of microphotographic reproductions as substitutes for original books, and it should be added that although everything practicable ought to be done to aid scholars in institutions that do not have great library collections, there is little prospect that any substitutes can serve the scholar in many fields quite as well as a great collection on his subject located where he is working. It is one thing to search bibliographies and catalogs and to request that books be supplied on loan or in film or other copies; it is another to live with a great collection, freely able to look into scores of books shelved next to the ones that have been identified through bibliographies and catalogs. We must not fail to support such collections. As barriers to access are reduced and a national network is perfected, it must be emphasized that the strength of the network depends on the strength of the outstanding collections that it links.

GENERAL OBSERVATIONS

As the problems of access to recorded knowledge are considered and as efforts are made to facilitate the scholar's access, it may be well to keep in mind certain general principles.

First, balance should be maintained, and progress is needed along more than a single line. New institutions must be assisted to build collections of their own and to draw readily upon the resources of older and larger libraries. Important as this is, however, it would be a mistake to concentrate all efforts upon helping the new and the weak; we must build upon strength and maintain the quality of existing great collections while creating the new ones that are now urgently needed. All libraries benefit from further strengthening of the outstanding research collections on which all depend to supplement their own holdings, just as all benefit from improvement of bibliographical apparatus, research in the application of automation to library operations, and cooperative projects in cataloging and acquisition.

It should be kept in mind that most research libraries are now hard pressed to maintain the collections and services required by their own particular constituencies; they cannot be expected to provide greatly increased regional or national services unless means can be found to reimburse them for the additional costs of these services. The nation's first great universities and great libraries were built by private benefactions; a few state governments have had the vision and the resources to emulate this example. Now, as the time has come when Federal funds must supplement private donations and state appropriations in supporting research and research libraries, the gravest mistake that could be made—yet, unfortunately, perhaps the most natural—would be to neglect the institutions that are strongest and seem relatively affluent.

Second, existing services and procedures must not be abandoned until better services and procedures are in operation. Scholars must be supplied with research materials today and tomorrow; service cannot be suspended while systems are installed that will provide much better service the year after next. Present libraries are sometimes described as obsolete; perhaps this is really praise, for there is a saying in technological circles, "If it works, it's obsolete." One can almost always assert that with the technology that may become available, a project might be done better next year than it can be done now, but to wait for this reason means never to do anything. Publication of the *National Union Catalog* is an example; rather than wait, it seemed preferable to do the imperfect job that can be done with present machinery, particularly since embarking on the project now did not preclude a change to better machinery during the course of publication.

Finally, without losing sight of the diversity of scholarship and of the materials it requires, all research libraries should be alert to opportunities for profiting from the advances that are being made by specialized scientific libraries. The National Library of Medicine is collecting comprehensively, producing the great bibliography in its field, sharing its resources with medical libraries throughout the nation, and pioneering in the development of automated procedures. The Medical Library Assistance Act of 1965 has made provision for a comprehensive program including assistance in library-building, instruction, special projects, research and development, improvement of basic library resources, publication, development of a national system, and establishment of regional search centers and possibly a branch of the National Library of Medicine. The authorization was for $23 million per year, and the budget of the National Library of Medicine is now approximately $6 million per year. These are not extravagant sums, it would seem, in view of the contributions that this program should make to teaching and research in the medical sciences.

National library service and national programs for development should be practicable in other subjects. It has been noted that the National Science Foundation has contracted with the American Chemical Society for mechanized informational services, and this suggests that services like those of the National Library of Medicine might sometimes be provided by contract between a Federal agency and an existing non-Federal library.

The President's Science Advisory Committee found in 1963 that "Since strong science and technology is a national necessity, and adequate communication is a prerequisite for strong science and technology, the health of the technical communication system must be a concern of Government."[8] It was good that science and technology led the way in 1963; recent establishment of the National Foundation on the Arts and the Humanities, modest as its resources are thus far, seems to demonstrate that the nation now realizes that scholarship and research as a whole are national necessities. It must likewise be recognized that research libraries are the indispensable basis for an adequate communication system in all fields of scholarship.

The increasing concern of Government is inevitable and it is welcome, but this must be accompanied by increasing concern also on the part of private organizations and individuals. The natural sciences and, to a lesser extent, the social sciences have been fortunate in having an industrial constituency to demand that bibliographical and library resources be provided and to help in financing these resources. The humanities must enlist private support on a comparable scale; equal opportunity for research in all fields of knowledge is essential for the healthy growth of scholarship and for the civilization that scholarship builds.

---

[8] Science, Government, and Information: A Report of the President's Science Advisory Committee (*Washington: U.S. Government Printing Office, 1963*), p. 1.

TABLE 3A–2.1

POSSIBLE APPROACHES TOWARD THE OBJECTIVES OF SCHOLARLY ACCESS FOR THE FURTHERANCE OF RESEARCH*

(With particular reference to university and other research libraries)

Continuing, innovative, and experimental approaches

---

1. *Much that is now being done must continue with increased support and at an accelerated rate:*
   a. Support of numerous useful current bibliographies, indexes, and abstracting services.
   b. Maintenance of the strength of existing strong libraries and rapid development of the additional strong collections that will be needed for a total of 60 to 70 universities with graduate programs of real quality.
   c. Strong emphasis on Library of Congress programs for shared cataloging, increased foreign acquisitions, and sharing of acquisition facilities with research libraries.
   d. A variety of experiments in library automation.
   e. Publication of the present *National Union Catalog* and improvement of supplementary guides to the location of research materials; there must be no delay in making information on serial holdings readily available through a machine-readable *Union List of Serials.*

2. *Several innovations are essential:*
   a. Creation of a National Bibliographical Office to promote coordination of effort in this vast area.
   b. Provision, for a number of other subjects, of bibliographical services and informational systems like those now being developed for a few scientific fields.
   c. Study of needs and bibliographical planning in all fields, with leadership from the professional and learned societies.
   d. Completion of the *National Union Catalog* by the incorporation in it of a record of all significant American research collections.
   e. Dissemination to research libraries in machine-readable form of the bibliographical information contained in the *National Union Catalog.*
   f. Automation of bibliographical systems and research library operations as rapidly as proves feasible.
   g. Extension of responsibilities of the Center for the Coordination of Foreign Manuscript Copying to include American as well as foreign materials.
   h. Development of a National Exchange Center at the United States Book Exchange.
   i. A program for preservation and dissemination of materials on deteriorating paper along the lines proposed by the Association of Research Libraries.
   j. Use of durable paper by publishers.
   k. Creation of a National Lending Library, supplemented by regional centers.

3. *Continuing study and experimentation is required throughout; two areas need particular attention:*
   a. Periodic reexamination of the bibliographical needs of each research field in the light of changes in the field and new developments in technology.
   b. The economics of microphotography and the use of microcopies, taking into account both the changing needs of scholarship and the changing state of the art.

---

* *This recapitulation from the paper by Edwin E. Williams is consistent with the spirit of the conclusions and recommendations of the National Advisory Commission on Libraries but should not be interpreted as a set of formal Commission recommendations.*

B. THE SCIENTIFIC USER:
THE LIBRARY AND INFORMATIONAL
SERVICE NEEDS OF SCIENTISTS

by LAUNOR F. CARTER
Vice President and Manager, Public Systems Division
System Development Corporation

INTRODUCTION

As has already been seen in the preceding papers, the library requirements of diverse users can differ radically. The research worker in the humanities or the arts is very dependent on highly specialized and extensive library services—indeed, for most researchers in the humanities the library is the one indispensable tool required for serious work. By contrast, the scientist has a more limited dependence on the centralized traditional library, though he requires information and document services for the effective development of theoretical positions and the undertaking of meaningful research. The traditional mode of communication among scientists is through the publication of research papers, the number of which has increased dramatically in the past and is expected to continue increasing as research expands in the future.

The dependence on documents and reports applies to all kinds of scientists, whether in the behavioral sciences or in the natural sciences. It has recently been stated:

> Today, the behavioral sciences focus strongly on the informational aspects of communication processes, and these are indeed a central consideration. Yet, the information problems of the behavioral sciences, however serious, cannot presently be described as desperate. Behavioral scientists are not about to drown in their output of information. Nor are they in a situation said to be typical of the natural sciences, in which, it has been calculated, a scientist who reads 3,000 characters a minute would be forced to read 13 hours a day if he wanted to keep up fully with the scholarly literature of his specialization.[9]

The above quotation might seem like an overstatement of the amount of material available to the research scientist. Yet a recent tabulation of the publications in various scientific areas (Table 3B–1) suggests that the number of articles published in the physical sciences is indeed extremely large and that any physicist or chemist trying to keep up with his field would be overwhelmed. However, William Koch, Director of the American Institute of Physics, says:

> In general, individual physicists have not been outwardly aware or concerned about the information expansion, a characteristic they share with their scientific colleagues. However, physicists as a group have been showing increasing evidences of an unconscious reaction to information problems. They have been reacting to the increasing difficulty of maintaining an overview of a given field of specialization because of the larger number of journals in that field that must be monitored. They have been reacting to the slowly increasing subscription costs, the time delays in publications, and the increasing number of simultaneous sessions at national meetings. Also, they have been reacting to the increasing availability of new information

[9] Communications Systems and Resources in the Behavioral Sciences, Publication 1575 (Washington, D.C.: National Academy of Sciences, 1967).

techniques represented by the facsimile-reproduction machine, the computer, and the jet airplane.

The reactions have taken the form of (1) an increasing use of preprints, laboratory visits, hallway conversations, and coffee breaks at meetings in order to maintain an overview of a given technical field before going into print; (2) decreasing relative individual subscriptions to journals and increasing development of private collections of separate documents accomplished by the use of library subscriptions to journals and the facsimile-reproduction machines; (3) greater use of multiple authors on papers and multiple speakers on talks; (4) increased interest in, and use of, information analysis centers for critical data evaluations and of review articles; (5) increased requests for new formats for information.[10]

A SCIENTIST'S REQUIREMENTS FOR
LIBRARY AND DOCUMENTATION SERVICE

In view of the large amount of material published in science and the fact that many scientists can successfully cope with this great volume of material, one must ask how scientists have been able to work out an adequate system of information transfer. There are several answers. In the first place, most scientists tend to become fairly specialized and are actively interested in only a small proportion of the articles published in a given field. Secondly, scientists are essentially forward-looking and are interested in new material rather than in historical material. Finally, they depend to a large extent on both informal means of communication and on various secondary sources to sharpen their awareness of the material directly germane to their interests.

Scientists differ a great deal in their dependence on documentation resources, depending on the particular nature of the work being undertaken. A theoretical physicist may be heavily dependent on published material or on preprints and informal memoranda regarding new experimental evidence. On the other hand, astronomers or geologists may be much more dependent on photographs and the analysis of physical specimens for the development of their theoretical understanding. The social scientist, although he is certainly interested in what other people write in his discipline, is to a large extent becoming more dependent on data banks and large collections of survey material than he is on more traditional document sources. Thus the particular informational requirements of a scientist depend largely on the nature of his discipline and whether his interests are oriented toward theoretical or experimental understanding and contributions. This has recently been stated by a committee of the National Research Council as follows:

> Perhaps the most important distinction is between those sciences in which an information system operates largely over the scientific literature of the field (for example, via abstracts and indexes) and those in which it operates extensively over files of descriptive data about the world. Theoretical physics is an example of the former, while meteorology with its large weather data series is an example of the latter. Except for psychology, most social sciences operate extensively on descriptive data files. It is, therefore, natural that one of the more significant trends in social science today is the development of data archives.[11]

Not only do the documentation and information requirements of scientists differ depending on their field of specialization, they also differ with the status and seniority of the scientist involved. The elite scientists—the members of the so-called invisible colleges—are less dependent for initial alerting and early exchange of ideas on library and document services than are the scientists who are on the periphery of the elite group or those engaged in teaching or the graduate students who are becoming steeped in the knowledge of a particular field. Indeed, one of the serious problems in designing infor-

10 H. W. Koch, "A National Information System for Physics" (talk given at the American Physical Society meeting, January 29, 1968).
11 Publication 1575, National Academy of Sciences, op. cit.

mational systems for scientists revolves around the fact that the requirements for such systems are very differently perceived, depending on where one stands in the hierarchy of the scientific community. Recently Dr. Philip Abelson, the editor of *Science,* wrote an editorial titled "The Custodians of Knowledge," in which he discussed the problem of the transmission of knowledge:

> This generation's major contribution to the human heritage is a great fund of new knowledge and the means of using scientific principles effectively. This knowledge was accumulated at a cost to society of billions of dollars, and scientists should consider how the facts that they discovered can continue to be made available. So long as books and archives are preserved, information can be retrieved if scholars are willing to spend enough time working on it. However, to many scientists the continuing increase in information is a source of worry. Some scientists look hopefully to electronic data processing as a means of meeting the problem. Others manage to cope with the information explosion. They keep current in their own fields through participation in invisible colleges. In a short time and after a few telephone calls the skilled scholar is in a position to tap much of the world's store of knowledge. Reliance on this human network provides more than the raw information. It provides judgment and suggestions of more feasible approaches to the problems being considered. In view of the many strengths of this information network, computer technology has far to go to match its effectiveness and especially in cost.[12]

It is hard to deny that for the lucky few who are members of the invisible college, Dr. Abelson's emphasis on reliance on the human information network as an information transfer system is hard to match. But one must wonder about the thousands of people in any given discipline who are not members of the invisible college or about the students and scholars who are unable to participate so directly with the elite few who make up the invisible college.

Though the elite scientist may venture infrequently beyond the four walls of his own study and laboratory in search of library materials, the beginning scientist or the graduate student is dependent on material stored in specialized science libraries. In many academic institutions each science department traditionally has its own library as a part of the building in which the department is housed. The library for a major science department may consist of a relatively small number of volumes but must contain the important serials in that field. In many areas there may be only twenty-five to fifty really significant serials that need to be available to graduate students and teachers. The elite may not even have these requirements, as pointed out in the recent study *Communication Systems and Resources in the Behavioral Sciences:*

> For the most part these systems, even those that are computer based, are document oriented. They take the published document as their basic unit for storage and retrieval and devise systems of classification based typically upon descriptors or key words. Indexes and abstracts are prepared and either distributed or made available on demand. All this activity is designed to enhance the communication of scientific information through increasing the accessibility of information concerning printed documents.
>
> There is some reason to believe, however, that, although these traditional formal communication aids are necessary, they are of limited utility to the research scientist. A large part of the significant transfer of information between behavioral scientists depends, as has been stressed, upon informal contacts. These contacts carry much of the information load in the process of communication among behavioral scientists who are engaged in research.
>
> In fact, in many fields the utility of published documents seems to be confined almost exclusively to the communication of research results to teachers, students, and practitioners. Thus, documents will often have relatively little use for com-

12 *P. H. Abelson, "Custodians of Knowledge," Science, 159 (1968), p. 582.*

munication among research scholars. As compared with communication by means of documents, informal information transfer provides some distinct advantages, three of which are outstanding: promptness, breadth of content, and adaptiveness.[13]

DISCIPLINE-ORIENTED INFORMATION SERVICES

Since the needs of scientific researchers tend to be specialized and focused on a limited set of documents, the general solution to the information problem among scientists has been to develop a set of discipline-oriented information services; that is, each major scientific discipline has developed those methods of scientific communication required for workers in that particular area. Traditionally, many of the professional societies grew up around this communication need: for many years the major activities of scientific societies consisted of publication of journals and annual meetings for communicating the latest research. This is still true for those professional societies where the membership is relatively small. However, in the larger societies, such as the American Chemical Society, the American Institute of Physics, and the American Psychological Association, the problem of communications and publication has greatly proliferated to include not only the holding of meetings and publishing of journals but the development and supplying of very sophisticated secondary services, such as indexes, abstracts, preprint distribution, and selective dissemination of information.

The policy of the Federal Government with regard to the information needs of scientists is oriented toward supplying these needs through the professional societies. The National Science Foundation (NSF) has played an essential role in supporting many of the professional societies by helping them to expand and refine their information services. Projections indicate that the National Science Foundation will support the communications services of the various discipline-oriented societies to the extent of over $100 million in the next eight to ten years. Until there is an overall national policy with regard to library and information services, this is probably a sound way to promote the scientific communication effort.

To present an idea of the extent and variety of information services offered by some of the larger organizations, several are described below. Perhaps the largest program being carried out by a professional society is in chemistry. The American Chemical Society sponsors the Chemical Abstracts Service (CAS) as a resource for the professional and research chemical community. Chemical Abstracts Service's Computer-Based Total Information System is to be in operation by 1971.[14] By mid-1970 CAS will produce all its publications and services through a computer system, and in 1971 CAS expects to provide routine on-line, remote-terminal service. This computer-based total information system will involve tie-ins with primary journals published outside the American Chemical Society.

In 1967 CAS started a Selective Dissemination of Information (SDI Experiment) program based on computer searching of magnetic versions as well as printed issues of SDI abstracts. This SDI Experiment was changed to *Chemical Abstracts (CA) Basic Journal Abstracts* in 1968 and was combined with *CA Condensates,* which includes titles, authors' names, journal and patent references, and *CA* issue index entries for each abstract published in *CA.* The combination provides access to the entire content of *CA* in machine-readable form.

Other significant parts of the CAS computer system are already in operation. Chemical Titles (CT), introduced in 1961, represented the first use of computers to produce a publication on a significant scale. In 1965 CAS inaugurated Chemical-Biological Activities (CBA), a more sophisticated computer-produced service. CAS has just

13 *Publication 1575, National Academy of Sciences,* op. cit.
14 Science Information Notes, 9 (*Washington, D.C.: National Science Foundation, February-March 1967*).

introduced a third computer-based service, Polymer Science and Technology (POST). All three services are produced and used both as printed publications and on magnetic tapes.

In 1969 computerization is to be extended to the *CA* subject and ring indexes, and in 1970 to *CA* itself, and 1971 should see a complete shift to a direct-access system, with a unified storage and search system in operation and complete registration of all compounds indexed in *CA* before 1965 as well as subsequently. On-line, remote-terminal service should become routine in 1971. NSF's Office of Science Information Service is supporting the research required for the development of these wholly computerized CAS information operations. To explain the status, plans, and systems approach of CAS, a full-day symposium was held in Washington, D.C., January 31, 1967, and was repeated February 1. Nearly three hundred people attended—two thirds from Government, representatives of several foreign embassies and foreign patent offices, and seventy others.

Those concerned with traditional library services must ponder how their operations can be modified to take advantage of advanced services such as those described.

The American Institute of Physics (AIP) was awarded the initial installment of a $1.1 million NSF grant effective January 1, 1968, and has begun a two-year study of physics information needs. AIP is a federation of the leading societies in the field of physics and currently has a membership of over 40,000 physicists, some 8,000 students, and 157 corporate associates. The purpose of the study is to develop a national physics information system. The study will concentrate on all aspects of the transfer of physics information from the producer to the ultimate user. It will identify the various factors that enhance or diminish the flow of this information and will also investigate the utility, complexity, and cost of the channels through which physics information flows.

Once these studies have been completed, the AIP will undertake the development of a system based on two considerations: the first is focused on the individuals, groups, and institutions that will be the producers and users of the physics information system; the second will focus on the physics information system itself. Here the AIP will attempt to develop a system that deals with all aspects of the acquisition of manuscripts and printed materials. It will then cope with the intellectual organization of physics information and concepts. Various new information retrieval techniques will be utilized and tested. These will include traditional methods such as journal indexes, abstracts, and classification methods, as well as new computer-based techniques.

The AIP recognizes that any major change in one of the principal science information services will interact with the services offered by the others. As a result, they are including a study of interface problems, both with other information components in the physics area (for example, the abstract activities of the British Institute of Electrical Engineers) and with services from other disciplines (such as the Chemical Abstracts Service, the American Metals Society, and the Institute of Electronic and Electrical Engineers, and their various publication services). Likewise, within the Government there are several mission-oriented systems that produce documents related to physics, such as those supported by the Atomic Energy Commission (AEC), the National Aeronautics and Space Administration (NASA), and to some extent the National Library of Medicine (NLM). Problems of compatibility, standards, formats for information exchange, and so forth become extremely important. Lacking any overall coordinating body, each of the societies assumes the individual responsibility to look to these interface problems. It has frequently been suggested that since much of the development in these areas is Federally funded, the Federal Government has a larger responsibility than it is currently exercising to assure that these interface requirements are given adequate attention and are solved.

In medicine the situation is quite different from the information services of the two scientific societies presented above. Although the various medical societies publish a large number of journals, the National Library of Medicine is responsible for most of the secondary publications in medicine and for the active dissemination of medical knowledge to practitioners, researchers, and scholars. It is worth noting that although the National Library of Medicine has been designated a major national library, and indeed has a 1.2 million-volume collection of medical publications, NLM is much more than a library in the traditional sense. Particularly is this true because NLM exercises the positive responsibility of informing potential users of the information available. It does this through the publication of *Index Medicus,* which is the major index service in the medical area. In addition, it furnishes bibliographical services for many research organizations, and has set up regional information centers so that material may be readily available to research personnel. Since the information services of NLM are relatively unique and are handled entirely by the Federal Government, it is instructive to examine the costs associated with such an effort. Recently the operational costs of the Medical Literature Analysis and Retrieval System (MEDLARS) were presented as follows:

> Cost data for the FY 1966 operation of MEDLARS have been presented by the NLM at a recent conference on Electronic Information Handling, showing a total of about $1.5 million, which is distributed over capital investment (pro-rated over five years) $557,000; equipment rental, maintenance and supplies $146,000; personnel costs (administration, operation, programming and input, indexing and searching) $692,000; and printing and distribution $73,000.[15]

Table 3B–2 shows the cost picture in terms of MEDLARS product categories and gives a good idea of the cost of various services available to one major professional and research specialty. If similar services were to be offered in all major scientific and applied areas, an annual cost of many millions would be incurred. Serious consideration should be given to the question of the extent of Federal Government responsibility for seeing that such services are available for all branches of science and applied technology.

As mentioned earlier, the social sciences have somewhat different requirements than the natural sciences. Some of the specialties in the social sciences have had extensive primary and secondary publication services, but other areas have been notably lacking in such services. The American Psychological Association, for example, has for many years published a number of primary journals, thirteen journals being currently published. The *Psychological Abstracts* has, since the mid-1920's, been a major source of bibliographical service in this area. In contrast, some of the other social sciences have had only a very limited number of primary outlets, and some disciplines still have no systematic abstract services. However, the requirements for traditional research library and documentation services are undergoing significant changes in the social sciences. A recent study in this area comments as follows:

> Some years ago it appeared plausible that maintenance of repositories of behavioral science research data would gradually be brought under the umbrella of the conventional research library in matters of personnel and financing, after the initial innovative phase. Such a possibility is not, of course, to be ruled out completely for the future, but it is already clear that such a future remains distant.
>
> Most data facilities for research are growing up outside conventional library institutions. Few research libraries are adequately subsidized or staffed even to keep up with current advances in bibliographic automation. Pressures to fulfill a new set of roles in the maintenance of archives of machine-readable behavioral science data are understandably greeted with indifference, if not horror, by research librarians. At this formative stage conventional libraries appear overwhelmed by information revolutions on other fronts. The differentiation between "book libraries" and "data libraries" is likely to persist for some time, and may even harden permanently.[16]

---

[15] *National Library of Medicine Staff, "Needs of the Health Sciences" (paper presented at the Conference on Electronic Information Handling, April 12–14, 1967, University of Pittsburgh).*
[16] *Publication 1575, National Academy of Sciences,* op. cit.

Finally, it should be noted that many information services are springing up outside of the tradition of the regular serial journals and their associated abstracts. Some of these are being developed by professional societies and others are commercial ventures. For some time a commercial company has offered a citation index and has more recently offered a title-listing of all current publications over a very wide variety of journals. This material is contained on magnetic tapes, and although its cost is quite high, its currency and breadth of coverage make it attractive to many industrial research organizations. Table 3B.1, showing the number of journals published by the several professional societies, includes a column for the publishing company McGraw-Hill, Inc. It can be seen that this commercial house publishes a large number of scientific and technical journals, as do many other publishing organizations. These facts are mentioned simply to indicate that although the professional societies play the major role in scientific publication, an important component is found in private industry.

Private industry has been among the leaders in developing new science information services. Recently the Academic Press announced a new information service titled *Communications in Behavioral Biology*. According to a letter in *Science,* the *Communications* is a computerized journal and consists of two primary sections: first, a section of abstracts and indexes and, second, the original articles.[17] All articles are published as singles but are prepunched so that they can be inserted in binders provided to subscribers. The *Communications in Behavioral Biology* was organized with funds from the National Science Foundation and from NASA and with technical assistance from the Academic Press and University Microfilms. The report states: "Readers will be able to subscribe to categories of information, preprint distributions will be available, magnetic and microform editions will be produced, separate articles and abstract index editions can be purchased, and finally, publication lag will be reduced to less than three months." Certainly the consequences of these new methods of publishing scientific and technical material will have an important impact on the library.

NATIONAL POLICY AND LIBRARY AND INFORMATION SERVICES IN SCIENCE

The Federal Government has assumed responsibility for library and information services in the areas of medicine and agriculture. The National Agricultural Library and the National Library of Medicine both play important roles in serving the information and library needs of practitioners and researchers in these two important areas. As mentioned earlier, it should be emphasized that these libraries are much more than libraries in the traditional sense of the word because they perform positive services by aggressively developing bibliographical publication services so that researchers in medicine and the agricultural field can depend on these major resources. It is sometimes suggested that a National Science Library be formed, perhaps as a part of the Library of Congress or as a new library that might utilize the very extensive holdings of the Library of Congress in the science area. Generally, scientists do not show enthusiasm for this recommendation, primarily because the requirements of research scientists do not revolve around massive and authoritative collections, nor are scientists usually dependent on the development of a long historical background; rather, they are oriented toward the current and developing state of knowledge.

However, scientists are greatly concerned about Federal policy with respect to many other aspects of national scientific information and document-handling activities. It is well recognized that since World War II the Federal Government has become the major source of support for scientific research in almost all fields. Associated with this support is the responsibility for making the results of research a matter of public record and

---

[17] *S. A. Weinstein, "Computerized Journal," Science, 159 (1968), p. 582.*

assuring their wide dissemination throughout the scientific community. For some time the Federal Government did not recognize this obligation, and the costs of publication were not borne as a part of research contracts. This led to an acute straining of the capabilities of professional societies to publish sufficient journal pages to accommodate the traditional free publication of scientific research.

In October 1961 the Federal Council for Science and Technology endorsed as Federal policy the payment of page charges to nonprofit publishers when the authors of the article had been funded by Federal agencies. Thus the costs of journal publication finally became a recognized obligation associated with Federal funding of research. This policy was very helpful in relieving the backlog of articles awaiting publication in professional journals. Another indirect result of this policy was the tacit recognition of the major role of the professional disciplines in the information dissemination process and the previously mentioned Governmental support of this role through the National Science Foundation. Thus *de facto* policy for scientific information has developed based on Federal support of the scientific and professional societies rather than through the more traditional library services.

Associated with the great growth of scientific research in the last twenty years has been a marked increase in the amount of scientific information entering the communication channels. Much has been said about the growth of scientific literature and the ever-deepening involvement of the Federal Government in funding scientific information services. Both Congress and the Executive Branch of Government have shown an interest in this problem. The Committee on Scientific and Technical Information (COSATI) of the Federal Council for Science and Technology has taken a focal position in trying to define long-range policy in the scientific and technical information and document area. COSATI and the National Science Foundation have both sponsored several significant studies directed toward the development of overall national policy.

In an attempt to rationalize this increased Federal responsibility, a major study was undertaken by a team from the System Development Corporation, which resulted in a book titled *National Document-Handling Systems for Science and Technology*.[18] The work includes an assessment of the current situation regarding scientific and technical documentation and information services and a description of the many Federal activities in this area. A set of propositions was developed regarding Federal responsibility in this domain, and a number of recommendations were made with respect to ways of organizing and fulfilling the Federal Government's responsibility for the adequate dissemination and support of document-handling services. Some people have questioned the wisdom of limiting the focus of this study to science and technology.[19] Although this limitation was a part of the charter of the study, this criticism expresses one of the most important problems regarding Federal involvement in all types of library and informational services, namely, the lack of a central authority within the Federal Government to deal with the total information and library problem.

Today many agencies are involved in supporting various aspects of library and documentation services. Until such time as an integrated national authority is achieved, it appears to this author that the study recommendations of the joint concepts of a "capping organization" and the delegation of operational responsibility to a set of "responsible agents" are the most reasonable way for the Federal Government to deal with the growing problem of scientific and technical information. The fact that the National Advisory Commission on Libraries did not develop a comprehensive scheme for the integration of over-all Federal activities in this area underlines the difficulty and seriousness of this continuing problem.

18 *L. F. Carter,* et al., National Document-Handling Systems for Science and Technology (*New York: John Wiley and Sons, 1967*).
19 *P. A. Richmond, "Utopia for Scientists,"* Library Journal, *August 1967, p. 2742.*

TABLE 3B–1

SCIENTIFIC SOCIETY MEMBERSHIP AND JOURNAL DATA

(1966)

	AMERICAN INSTITUTE OF PHYSICS	AMERICAN CHEMICAL SOCIETY	INSTITUTE OF ELECTRONIC AND ELECTRICAL ENGINEERS	MCGRAW-HILL*
Membership	40,900	100,000	160,000	—
Publications				
Primary journals	19	18	36	40
Translated journals	11	0	5	0
Editorial pages				
Primary journals	54,000	33,900	18,600	52,000
Translated journals	21,750	0	7,900	0

* *Exclusive of Buyer's Guides and Newsletters.*

SOURCE: *H. W. Koch, "A National Information System for Physics" (talk given at the American Physical Society meeting, January 29, 1968).*

TABLE 3B–2

MEDLARS COST DATA BY PRODUCT

PRODUCT	*Costs*		
	TOTAL ALLOCATED (× $1,000)	PER DELIVERED CITATION ($)	PER UNIT PUBLICATION ($)*
Index Medicus	$928	$.67	$ 5.77
Demand bibliographies	456	.71	150.00
Recurring bibliographies	83	.74	1,604.00

* *Per copy of* Index Medicus, *per average demand bibliography, per average issue of recurring bibliographies.*

SOURCE: *National Library of Medicine Staff, "Needs of the Health Sciences" (paper presented at the Conference on Electronic Information Handling, April 12–14, 1967, University of Pittsburgh).*

C. THE PROFESSIONAL USER:
THE LIBRARY AND INFORMATIONAL
SERVICE NEEDS OF PRACTITIONERS

by ESTELLE BRODMAN
Librarian and Professor of Medical History
Washington University School of Medicine

As was brought out over and over again to the National Advisory Commission on Libraries by the testimony at its hearings around the country (see Appendix C), for the average citizen the word *library* connotes the public library of his community, which provides him with an undifferentiated melange of recreational, educational, and inspirational material, but which has only peripheral relationship to the way he makes his living. This is understandable because the public library, as the middle-class American knows it today, is the outgrowth and descendant of an institution—developed widely in this country—based on a theory of the perfectability of citizens through self-study, which is found in the writings of the eighteenth century philosophers. This belief holds that citizens will make rational decisions for the commonweal if they are informed of the facts; indeed, that from such facts they will choose only the best and most logical actions.

The general practitioner, on the other hand, whether he is practicing business administration, law, medicine, engineering, theology, or any of the other disciplines that translate theories into actual practice in the community, hardly ever thinks of the public library as the source of data for his administrative and operating decisions. In some communities, of course, the public library has taken on the responsibility of providing some of this help; for example, the New York Public Library and the Newark Public Library are well-known for their business sections; the St. Louis Public Library is noted for its aid to chemical industries; the Library of Congress is outstanding in its law collections, among other things. But by and large, the practitioner expects to obtain his help from nonpublic libraries, especially from academic, special, and personal collections.

MULTIPLE NEEDS OF PROFESSIONAL USERS

The actual source used depends upon the traditions of the particular profession the practitioner represents and his relation to other segments of the scholarly community. In the field of law, for example, practitioners have traditionally banded together in bar associations to provide the necessary background material needed by lawyers; in addition, most of them expect to have smaller or larger collections in their own offices for their own and their partners' use. Similarly, physicians traditionally keep a few books and journals on hand for daily use and expect to find supporting material in a medical society library, the library of their community hospital, or (in the United States) in the National Library of Medicine. Architects and engineers expect to provide informational literature for themselves; ministers ordinarily have a smaller or larger theological collection of their own and depend upon their seminary libraries for additional help; business officials in large organizations look to the company to underwrite at least a basic library for their official needs.

A certain percentage of practitioners are also connected with academic institutions—perhaps more so in the field of medicine than in some of the other fields—and these people practice their profession in academic settings, often combining theory, practice, and research. Moreover, any one practitioner in most disciplines may act either as researcher, teacher, or translator of theory into daily practice at different times in his working life. The shadowy line between the places in which each of these groups finds its information and between the methods it uses to uncover this material thus becomes even more vague and uncertain, until it must be said that there is little or no difference between the use of informational sources by any of them. Since it is likely that any difference will become increasingly vague, any discussion of the future role and service of libraries to one group must include the needs and methods that would be applicable to all other groups.

This does not imply that all groups use the information stored in libraries and information banks for exactly the same purposes and with exactly the same methods. The practitioner is fundamentally interested in solving a particular problem with which he is faced in a particular real-life setting, under particular conditions, and usually he is faced with the necessity of solving it within a rather tight time-limit. For these reasons, he is more dependent upon compendiums, handbooks, digests, guides, and state-of-the-art reviews than is the research worker, whose goal is to diminish the unknown by building out from the cutting edge of the already known. To reach this goal, the research worker expects to study the small bits of knowledge reported by others and to synthesize this information himself. He is less likely to be interested in a specific datum than the practitioner, and he is also less likely to be as time-bounded in his need for the information. Where the practitioner uses a compendium and a digest, and almost never a complicated information system, the research worker is more interested in the complete bibliographic record.

It follows from what has been said that the researcher needs a larger array of literature and more detailed keys to it, but the practitioner needs more aid in finding the answers to his problems—both published aids and human intervention. Thus, one cannot say that either group needs more or less help than the other, but only that after the basic minimum has been passed, each needs a different kind of help. A good library for the researcher must necessarily contain almost all the tools needed by the practitioner, but it does not follow that a good library for a practitioner will cost less, since the tools and helps the practitioner requires are at least equally expensive as those required for the researcher. Moreover, as pointed out above, most individuals serve sometimes as research workers, sometimes as practitioners, and sometimes as students, so that no distinction can usually be made on class of user.

A further differentiation between the way a research worker and a practitioner use the literature is seen in the manner and purpose of the browsing done by each. The practitioner normally subscribes to a few periodicals on his own, which he scans for pragmatic solutions to problems he has encountered in the past or expects to encounter in the future. The research worker, on the other hand, tends to browse for general ideas, unifying concepts, and general insights not always connected with a particular problem; he needs a wider and often more catholic collection than the practitioner-technologist. The practitioner often browses at home or in the small collection, while the research worker prefers a larger and broader base.

Up to this point we have not discussed the matter of the professional student—the medical, pharmacy, law, theology, or engineering student, for example. As might be expected, the methods by which these students turn to the records of the past reflect the way in which they see faculty members and practitioners of their profession use these records, and these methods are modified only to the extent that immaturity in the subject field and the number of persons using the collection require. Professional students' use of a library is thus a mixture of the type of use by undergraduate and nonprofessional scholarly graduate students and the use of the literature by professional graduates. In general, therefore, a library meant for students in a professional school differs from one meant for the already-working professionals only by providing more space for readers, more copies of the same works, and more human aids to teach the students how to extract the most use out of the information available.

As pointed out above, the locus within which the professional user expects to find and use the pertinent information he needs to practice his profession effectively varies with the profession he represents. All start, however, with a small personal collection, which is used intensively and automatically, but almost all have to go beyond this to a collection maintained for them by some group: their school, professional colleagues and societies, or their company. One of the great difficulties this system brings in its train is that the cost of maintaining it is so great that few libraries are willing to take on the responsibility of providing for the library needs of any but the group for which they were established. Thus, a bar association library will serve the members of its bar, but rarely and only under special conditions will this collection be available to the physician needing legal materials; nor will the medical school ordinarily wish to become embroiled in helping bolster the cases of the lawyer. Libraries themselves cannot provide for all the needs of even their own core clientele, and in making use of the system of interlibrary loans, libraries of small commercial firms, research institutions, and hospitals often put large—sometimes intolerable—burdens on the nearest reservoir library.

Every large university library in the country has probably bemoaned the unhappy position it is placed in when its prime users and the library of a neighboring institution both wish the same item from its collection. The financial burden under which resource libraries suffer through attempting to meet the needs of the technologist and practitioner who are not part of their prime responsibility has led to many schemes for reducing the burden, none of which is really satisfactory.

The practitioners working in an institutional setting, such as a hospital, a law firm, a pharmaceutical concern, an architectural firm, or a business corporation, at least have some access to the information they need through the provision of institutional libraries and informational departments. The practitioner on his own—as many physicians and lawyers are today—is in an even less enviable position because his informational needs are the prime concern of nobody but himself and the society he ministers to. Yet if society believes that the work of these practitioners is so important to its members that the standards must be maintained through compulsory licensing to keep quacks and the untrained from harming the citizenry, then it follows that society as a whole ought to take a hand in providing some easy access to information for practitioners.

One thing society might do here is to give direct aid to the individual practitioner—say by paying for and giving widespread distribution to some publications, or by providing free courses of continuing education, perhaps with peripatetic lecturers. More economical, perhaps, is group aid, in the form of subventions to professional societies, to publications aimed at keeping the practitioner up-to-date, and to libraries to handle the needs of such practitioners. In the field of medicine two slightly different methods have recently been undertaken: (1) under the Regional Medical Programs information is brought to the practitioner through his local community hospital and through professional meetings, seminars, and publications; (2) under the Medical Library Assistance Act practitioners are being helped through aid to local and regional medical libraries, some already in existence and some especially set up for the task. Practitioners in fields other than medicine have not yet received as much attention, and the problem of the burden placed on resource libraries by commercial organizations has not even been seriously discussed in the essentially laissez-faire political-economic milieu of our time.

It must not be supposed that only great university or special libraries are concerned here. The New York Public Library is an example of a large group of libraries supported wholly or partly by tax funds, which are required to give service to all and are expected to serve the needs of the practitioners of their communities but are not given funds sufficient for their purpose because of the common idea of tax-paying citizens that public libraries contain mostly novels and books for schoolchildren.

Geographical factors confuse the picture further. Practitioners may reside in one community, to which they pay taxes, but use the facilities of another community, in which they practice. And because a reverse Gresham's law applies to libraries also, a good library in one community will attract users from other communities without such collections and staffs, thus transferring the burden but not the fiscal support needed. Where it is possible to consolidate—as in Metro in New York–New Jersey–Connecticut—some help can be found, but many libraries are founded on outmoded geographical bases and are legally unable to rise above their boundaries.

PUBLIC POLICY AND SOCIAL BENEFIT

What then is the Federal Government's responsibility in this area? Perhaps the best thing it can do is to underwrite several different approaches to solving the problems of the need of the professions for informational materials. It is unlikely that one monolithic, massive, and unyielding system will work equally well for lawyers, engineers, architects, businessmen, hospital administrators, and nurses. Indeed, there is some question whether the same methods are always necessary or desirable within a single profession. The Regional Medical Programs and the Medical Library Assistance Act take slightly different tacks in helping the practitioner of medicine, and it is likely that some elements of each one will be useful and appealing to some practitioners. Too rigid an insistence on uniformity is probably undesirable; instead, investigation of many different approaches should be made under Federal subventions. Here is one area in which the continuing Federal Institute of Library and Information Science, proposed in the Report of the National Advisory Commission on Libraries (see chapter 12), can be active.

Since it is obvious that information cannot be made available unless (1) the practitioner knows of its existence, (2) knows how to get hold of it, and (3) can get hold of it, the Federal Government should attempt to aid the various schemes already proposed (and some not yet considered) for calling new knowledge to the attention of the practitioner. The Government should also see to it that professional students are taught the entry points to the system of knowledge in their field, by requiring such knowledge for licensure wherever there is a national (not state) licensing system.

The Federal Government should also arrange a system whereby any practitioner anywhere can obtain the information he needs in his profession within a reasonable time and for a reasonable cost. This latter would include payment for such services to the already existing libraries and other resources that can or will answer the needs of such practitioners.

The provision of knowledge for different professions is based on different needs. The lawyer tends to look for precedents and therefore needs systems for retrieving retrospective knowledge; the physician is concerned with the latest information, which supersedes earlier data and is in turn superseded by new findings. The clergyman wants the theoretical discussion for the most part. The engineer needs the pragmatic methodology required to reach a certain goal. From the very diversity of aims comes the diversity of sources of information and usefulness of kinds of knowledge.

It must not be assumed, however, that all needs of the practitioner can or should be met by the literature, even when that literature is in the form of computer stores of hard data. Equally as important as recorded knowledge in the day-to-day study and practice of the physician, the lawyer, the engineer, and the businessman is the oral communication of information—and in some cases what is needed is not facts at all but advice and consultation. A library can act as a switching device, to use the phrase of the Weinberg

Report,[20] to bring in contact the practitioner who needs such consultation and the person who can become the consultant. Indeed, some such system is necessary because many practitioners do not wish to expose their ignorance to their peers or do not wish to tip their hands to their competitors by revealing the subjects on which they are working. A library can easily become the go-between for these people.

All of this implies the need for a staffing pattern for libraries serving practitioners that, by and large, is very far from the situation that presently prevails. Librarians in such situations need to be involved in the subject matter they are handling more than they are now if they are to serve the purposes and use the methods outlined above. Instead, it is currently the librarians of large research institutions who usually most nearly meet the requirements. By a vicious circle the librarians in institutions serving practitioners are paid less, have less education, and are given less money to acquire the expensive and necessary tools for the practitioner, who has no time to spend uncovering the information he needs by himself.

Moreover, at a time when newer technologies, such as single-purpose film programs, networks, and computer banks of information, give hope of providing data needed by the practitioner more speedily and more completely than in the past, the staffs of those libraries dedicated to serving practitioners in many fields are not only less knowledgeable than many other librarians in the use of these technologies, but their budgets are less able to encompass the costs of services offered by and through these methods. This is true whether one is talking about medicine, the chemical industries, law, or education. It is not only in criminal justice that wealth brings more protection and more "equality" than is found among the poor.

The task of the Federal Government is to take as its foundation policy the philosophic belief that it is vital to the well-being of the state that opportunities be made available equally to all citizens for acquiring information on which to base practice in the social professions. In the eighteenth century public health in England was taken over as a Governmental responsibility on the basis that the state would then have healthy citizens who would be able to produce more taxes for the Government than would be possible from a sickly population. A similar concept covering many other aspects of national life is necessary today.

But it is not only the Federal Government that has a responsibility here. It must not be forgotten that today's professional society is an outgrowth of the medieval guild, which had as one of its most important duties the education of its members and the standardization of their work in order to bring about a standardization of their wages and prices. The professional society today has an equally large responsibility in these fields; moreover, being closer to the practitioners themselves than the Governmental agencies, it can outline the needs and determine the results of attempts to provide help to its members. In many cases professional organizations can successfully prepare and distribute their aids, as, for example, the American Chemical Society and the American Nursing Association do for their members. More cooperation between the Federal Government and professional societies would be a desirable symbiotic relationship, with the citizen as ultimate consumer benefiting greatly.

Finally, the practitioner himself must be educated, as part of his formal education and by observation of his peers, to realize that he too has a responsibility for helping obtain the information he needs and for learning how he can do so most efficiently. The professional schools and the trade and professional organizations can work together here to present the practitioner with such information, and the Federal Government ought to help underwrite it by changes in the tax laws to encourage such endeavors by all groups. In a situation like this all groups are able to work together more easily than where deep

20 Science, Government, and Information: The Responsibilities of the Technical Community and the Government in the Transfer of Information, *a Report of the President's Science Advisory Committee (Washington, D.C.: Government Printing Office, 1963).*

differences of views on the advisability of the results exist. As with the virtues of motherhood and the evils of sin, there are few dissenting views on the values of obtaining information for use.[21]

---

21 EDITOR'S NOTE: *Perhaps more dramatically than any other "category" of user of library and informational services, the professional user—whose complex multiple needs cross the boundary lines of education, research, and service simply as a matter of normal functioning—illustrates the diversity of users and uses. Here it is perhaps easiest to see both the commonalities and the differences among those who seek and use information, and also to apply the criterion of social value that the National Advisory Commission on Libraries has proposed for decision-making in national library planning (see chapter 12, section A). "We should look at the value to our people and our culture that accrues from the activities of the user whose functions are to be enhanced by improved availability of library and information services. . . . The variety of . . . socially valuable functions determines the need for variety in kinds of libraries."*

PART II

Current & Emerging Problems in Meeting User Needs for Library & Informational Services

CHAPTER IV

AREAS OF INADEQUACY IN SERVING MULTIPLE NEEDS

by E. SHEPLEY NOURSE
Editor and Project Director, Duke University
Library and Information Science Publication Project

NATIONAL LIBRARY POLICY

The current inadequacies in meeting the nation's needs for library and informational services are both implicit and explicit throughout the preceding chapters of this book. There would be few advocates of the status quo; complex problems exist and are recognized not only as existing but as multiplying. This was the context which dictated the September 1966 establishment of the National Advisory Commission on Libraries in the first place. As the Commission addressed itself to its task, the diversity of user needs and the benefits to society as a whole were always uppermost in its thinking. The Report of the Commission, which documents the rationale for all of its conclusions and recommendations, appears in its entirety as chapter 12 of this book. It is appropriate here, by way of introduction to the problem analyses in chapters 5–7, to overview some of the Commission's findings.

Of all the Commission's recommendations, its first is truly basic and most important—the establishment of a National Library Policy:

RECOMMENDATION: That it be declared National Policy, enunciated by the President and enacted into law by the Congress, that the American people should be provided with library and informational services adequate to their needs, and that the Federal Government, in collaboration with state and local governments and private agencies, should exercise leadership in assuring the provision of such services.[1]

In the past there has been no formal policy statement to guide planning efforts. There has been Federal involvement to be sure, but there have been no mechanisms for the effective implementation of Federal leadership. Few user needs are being met with true adequacy.

The National Advisory Commission on Libraries did not favor the development of a single master plan for the fulfillment of the National Policy. Its administrative philosophy might be expressed as the coordination of multiple efforts through a system of interlocking bodies—a built-in flexibility and adaptability to continual change.[2] The

[1] *See chapter 12, section B, for the complete rationale as it appears in the Commission Report.*
[2] *The Commission's thinking is quite compatible with modern administrative theory. See, for example, Rensis Likert,* New Patterns of Management *(New York: McGraw-Hill Book Company, 1961), and Harold J. Leavitt,* Managerial Psychology *(Chicago: University of Chicago Press, 1958).*

recommended ongoing National Commission on Libraries and Information Science was conceived not as an authoritarian monolith but rather as an advisory agency for broad planning—a communications switching point, an essential structure in the coordination of diversity. The broad outlook is evolutionary rather than revolutionary; the goal is to foster evolving responsiveness to user needs, multiple dimensions in the national interest.

With this brief introduction to the broad policy conclusions developed by the National Advisory Commission on Libraries during more than a year and a half of deliberations and study, the purpose of this chapter is to overview some problem areas identified by the Commission in reaching its specific objectives. The ensuing chapters in Part II present detailed analyses, from varying viewpoints, of matters directly relevant to the understanding and eventual solution of some serious problems affecting the fulfillment of a National Library Policy. The potentials of Federal leadership and the realignment of some roles and relationships are the subject matter of Part III.

PERVASIVE PROBLEM AREAS

Men, money, and materials—and the waste of these basic resources through fragmentation and duplication of efforts—might be one way of stating the areas of dilemma confronting the recognition and development of library and informational services that truly meet the multiple needs of diverse citizens. A few observations on the identified and suspected inadequacies affecting each of these areas are given below.

MANPOWER

The old stereotype of the librarian as a stern but stupid dragon jealously protecting the precious volumes in her charge is of course passé. But old images die hard, and unfortunate vestiges remain at a time when it is generally accepted that effective library and informational services require both a personalization of service and an evaluation of intellectual content—on the one hand, the guidance of a sensitive librarian in a small public library serving an underprivileged community, and on the other, a sophisticated subject-matter expert choosing relevant content from an information store for a select clientele. Like other professionalized professions, librarianship today finds itself faced with outsiders: educators, scientists, engineers, social and behavioral scientists, and an array of varied technicians now mix with the traditional component of humanistically oriented scholars and threaten to enrich or destroy the profession as we know it.

The survival signs are hopeful, no doubt because manpower problems are so widely recognized and subject to so much discussion in the library world. There are apparent disagreements within the profession, but the National Advisory Commission on Libraries concluded that education for librarianship is a focal point for closing the gap between demand and supply—the many vacant library positions and the scarcity of qualified personnel. The graduate schools of librarianship have their own special manpower problem—a shortage of faculty—and they have financial weaknesses in supporting regular programs, not to mention special programs, continuing education, and experimentation. Financial aid for students is quite meager compared with some other fields.

Recruiting efforts on many fronts appear most desirable. As with other seemingly undifferentiated professions (e.g., law, medicine), the actual diversity of career possibilities within librarianship is not always appreciated by potential applicants. In the words of the Commission Report:

. . . Too few scientifically oriented young people understand that the profession of librarianship embraces all categories of specialists who mediate between the sources of recorded information and the people who need access to information in all subject fields and at all levels of sophistication.[3]

The profession itself could change in many ways also. Salary standards must improve for one thing, also promotional opportunities. The image of a "woman's field" is unfortunate; if more women were considered for the top jobs, and if more men in general were attracted into the field at all levels, this image could change. The intellectual stimulus that separates professional activity from simple occupational activity should characterize the work of the librarian, who is too often thought of as an unimaginative super-clerk.

The National Advisory Commission on Libraries approved the multidisciplinary trend, both in the curriculum of library education and as applied to the study of the changing profession itself and of education for it. One of the prime high-priority functions of the permanent Commission should be coordinating the study of manpower development in library and information science. There are many challenges to Federal leadership here, not all of which fall into the "more money" category.

FINANCING

The libraries of our nation, and the interrelationships between libraries of the same and different kinds, are as diverse as the uses to which they are put. Likewise, their patterns of financing are complex, for many libraries receive funds not only from both private and public sources but a variety of each. The National Advisory Commission on Libraries had no quarrel with the complexity, appearing in fact to favor the "healthy mix" of public and private. The Commission did, however, find difficulty in determining exactly what the costs of library and informational services really are.

There is an impediment to intelligent future planning for the development and utilization of financial resources. As the Commission Report points out, no one knows even with close approximation precisely what the nation's library expenditures are, far less what the Federal contributions to these expenditures are. The reasons for this situation include the lack of uniform accounting and reporting and the phenomenon of joint costs. What library statistics do exist are woefully inadequate either for decision-making or research, both important elements in planning. And the need for planning, in its broad sense, is a primary need identified by the Commission, which assigned this function to the ongoing permanent Commission.

The inadequacy of library statistics, particularly their incompleteness, tardiness, and lack of comparability, is dramatically illustrated in chapter 5, the study of the economics of library operation submitted to the Commission and reproduced in its entirety in this book. Some of the analyses attempted by this study group actually had to be discarded at the last minute when the shaky data base was identified!

The purposes for which some of the existing data can be used, however, are also illustrated in chapter 5, which concludes that library costs will continue to rise. This does not necessarily mean that cost minimization is an undesirable management goal, for it usually is primary in endeavors that are not characterized by the profit motive. It simply means that new "minimums" will be higher. The socially desirable prospect of more new publications, better preservation of older materials, more information in more formats, more uses and more users of library services, and more expert manpower prohibits any complacency about the absolute results of new operational efficiency.

Lack of sufficient funds to meet current demands, existing inequities, and lack of dependable bases for future planning are, then, some of the serious inadequacies in the financial area. More money will be needed from the Federal Government and other sources. How much more, and the when and where of its disbursal, were not within the

---

[3] *This quote from the Report appears in the context of the manpower discussion in chapter 12, section C.*

province of the original Advisory Commission, however much harried administrators may wish for even the false precision of a neat formula instead of the intellectual challenge of broad guidelines toward the inevitably changing future.

ACCESSIBILITY

As is clear in preceding chapters, the materials with which the library deals include not only conventional books and periodicals but also audiovisual materials—in great variety—manuscripts, assorted documents, and perhaps even an occasional cuneiform tablet. The paucity of materials available in some of the nation's libraries, an inadequacy not overcome by simple interlibrary cooperation, is one problem. The wasted wealth of little-used, perhaps not even cataloged, material available in other of the nation's libraries is another problem. These are but two of the factors contributing to the dilemma of accessibility.

The National Advisory Commission on Libraries differentiated between two kinds of access, (1) bibliographic, or what might be called access to information about sources of information, and (2) physical, or the acquisition of the desired content in a usable format.

There is no paucity of potential solutions to problems of access, and they range from the humble bookmobile to telefacsimile transmission—and on into the realm of science fiction. The haphazard development of solutions, however, presents a real difficulty, for a sophisticated bibliographic service developed for one subject area does not necessarily match another sophisticated service developed by others for a completely different user group. Effective multidisciplinary activity is obviously hampered by such a proliferation, and the development of anything approaching a national library network can encounter great difficulties without uniformity of standards. The need for coordination was an obvious conclusion of the Commission.

One of today's commonest ways of getting the desired information into the hands of the user is through copying by such reprographic devices as the familiar Xerox machine. Even some rather small public libraries are the proud owners of such equipment, and library copying is commonplace. Because at this particular time the status of library copying in relation to the law of copyright is receiving particular attention, chapter 6 presents three papers describing and analyzing various issues involving libraries and copyright. The relationship between copyright and published material and between published material and libraries is, of course, far more complex than the issue of library copying. It may well be, as one author suggests, that the views of copyright proprietors and librarians are very much the same in the final analysis. Both are vitally concerned with getting informational content to a consumer, which is in essence the only solution to problems of access.

FRAGMENTATION

One of the most currently fashionable words in today's lingo is fragmentation. Despite its triteness, it is still a very accurate word, for it describes with painful truth not only the administration of Federal efforts in the library and information area but also the administration of all efforts, public and private. The already evident phenomena of incompatible bibliographic services, developed independently, serve as a case in point. Another illustration is the variety of legislation, devoted to various objectives, that contains library components.[4] There are myriad examples of fragmentation.

The National Advisory Commission on Libraries looked on diversity as a source of basic strength while deploring the waste of duplicated and divergent independent efforts.

---

4 *For the Federal libraries alone it took an 862-page book to reproduce in one place, with appropriate commentary, all the laws and regulations affecting their operations. See* Guide to Laws and Regulations on Federal Libraries (*New York: R. R. Bowker Company, 1968*).

The keynote of all its recommendations is the maximization of diverse participation toward broad objectives through coordinating mechanisms.

The technological mystique surrounds us today. It seems clear that our existing potential far exceeds realization and that the very means of solving some problems of fragmentation are actually contributing to the difficulties. Hopefully the mechanisms recommended by the Commission—free from professional jealousies and industrial rivalries—can stimulate the kinds of administrative, social, technological, and educational research and development that can encourage both realistic application of existing technologies and experimental developments *de novo.*[5]

The time span here cannot be too short when one considers that some elementary schoolchildren today can stage recovery of a plastic space capsule in their own bathtubs and, with almost button-pushing simplicity, acquire further information on the subject from multiple sources at school. Tomorrow's young adults will not be very happy with the call slip that comes back "not on shelf" or with the "too-busy" attitude of professors and librarians.

Fragmentation of course is due to far more complex causes than multiple technology; it is in fact an administrative problem in the broadest sense and should be studied as such. But because our technological potential, so costly but often so rewarding, is such a dramatic example of the possible waste through uncoordinated efforts—the extremes of which are irresponsible cautious conservatism and irresponsible science fiction—one entire chapter of this book (the three-part chapter 7) is devoted to descriptive and analytical material on technology and libraries.

GOALS

Like the universities of which so many of the nation's finest libraries are a part, the libraries have interrelated goals that can be expressed as education, research, and service. The innumerable library inadequacies that exist hinder realization of these goals; they received considerable attention from the National Advisory Commission on Libraries.

EDUCATION

The educational goal is easy to identify with respect to the elementary and secondary school libraries of our public school systems. Libraries are becoming even more a built-in part of instructional functioning; the boundary lines between basic and supplementary instructional materials and library materials are often quite blurred, and sometimes the differences are slight between a school librarian and a teacher or counselor. Many districts are more fortunate than others, however, and in spite of the good that has been done by recent Federal legislation, too many schoolchildren badly in need of educational extras barely learn to read.

The educational goals of the public library are less obvious but more complex; furthermore, they are in a process of flux and should probably be encouraged to change even more rapidly in the future. The people's university is still that, supplying not only specific answers to specific questions (some quite technical), but also an unstructured intellectual browsing opportunity for any individual.

At the same time, many public libraries are becoming auxiliary study halls for urban college students. The demands being made on public libraries by even younger people far exceed what can be met by the library story hour. Formal education at elementary and secondary levels now seems to need the active participation of public librarians and new cooperative relationships between the people and the institutions

---

[5] *The Commission's recommendation is for a Federal Institute of Library and Information Science as a principal center for basic and applied research in all relevant areas.*

involved. Changing a few current attitudes may be the most difficult task in achieving some educational goals effectively.

College and university libraries assuredly exist for educational purposes. Here the competition of research and service goals can be clearly seen, as well as the ways all these goals can reinforce each other for the benefit of the clientele. It is difficult to think of an understocked two-year-college library as having much in common with a fully developed university library, yet both may be weak in serving the teaching and learning needs of faculty and students—for quite different reasons. The National Advisory Commission on Libraries identified many inequities and inconsistencies in this area, suggesting new patterns of financial support and new cooperative relationships as means of overcoming problems.

All libraries have educational goals in the broadest sense. Even the highly specialized libraries and informational services are involved here, for the continuing education of many professional and technical experts would be difficult without them. The acquisition of any bit of knowledge is education.

RESEARCH

As has been seen in preceding chapters, some libraries are specifically designated research libraries, and they have their own association. These libraries include primarily university libraries and libraries that are part of university library systems or are located on university campuses, as well as some private libraries. The Library of Congress is a research library, as are a few large public libraries.

The National Advisory Commission on Libraries was particularly interested in these libraries and their many problems, expressing concern that there was no program of Federal support for research libraries as such. They are true national resources, providing raw material ranging from rare documents for a scholarly historian to the latest scientific journal.

The commonalty of all search for knowledge appeared to be recognized by the Commission. All libraries have something in the way of a research goal: a school library provides material for a term paper (a future researcher's first exposure) as well as for some educational research; a business library can serve research in administration; a computer store can hold bibliographic clues and raw research data, but a journal usually holds the report and interpretation of results. Research is one of the means by which problems are solved, including the problems of library and information science.

The access problems referred to earlier are particularly troublesome in library attempts to serve research goals. In the words of the Commission Report:

> Research, basic or applied, requires source materials and itself produces new informational output—this is true of the arts and humanities as well as the natural and physical sciences, the social and behavioral sciences, and many technical areas. As society continues to demand both new knowledge and more rapid application of knowledge for its own betterment, the proliferation of information may defeat its own purpose unless it is adequately recorded, acquired, and available for use.[6]

SERVICE

Everything a library or librarian does is service. It is a most pervasive goal, exemplified by the simplest telephone answer to a reference question as well as by the most elaborate set of services to a profession. Most libraries serve a variety of users; many users require many services from different libraries. The nation's libraries and the people who use them are national resources as well as community resources. This thinking led the National Advisory Commission on Libraries to the identification of the criterion of social value in decision-making for future broad planning, specific planning, and immediate problem-solving.

---

[6] *This quote from the Commission Report appears in the context of discussion about the research objective in chapter 12, section C.*

The Commission suggested looking at the user of library and informational services. How, for example, would the improvement of a specific service affect the functions of the user of such a service? Would these functions be improved for the benefit of society as a whole? If a physician can function more effectively, if a teacher can teach more effectively, and if an underprivileged child can be encouraged to function at all—these are socially desirable results made possible as a result of, and often quite directly traceable to, the improved availability of library and informational services.

CONCLUSION

The potentials of planning and cooperation, with continual awareness of user needs and the social value of these needs, constitute the essential background for understanding the structural recommendations of the National Advisory Commission on Libraries. These appear, with their rationale and more detailed accounts of current inadequacies, in chapter 12 of this book, the Commission Report itself.

The purpose of this chapter has been to outline three pervasive library goals and four pervasive problem areas as they appeared to one who had the privilege of attending many Commission meetings and of working for the Commission while its members developed the Report.

It is appropriate to conclude this chapter with a summary of the six objectives identified by the Commission for fulfillment of a National Library Policy. The five specific Commission recommendations are directed toward achievement of these objectives.

OBJECTIVES FOR OVERCOMING CURRENT INADEQUACIES

1. Provide adequate library and informational services for formal education at all levels.
2. Provide adequate library and informational services for the public at large.
3. Provide materials to support research in all fields at all levels.
4. Provide adequate bibliographic access to the nation's research and informational resources.
5. Provide adequate physical access to required materials or their texts throughout the nation.
6. Provide adequate trained personnel for the varied and changing demands of librarianship.

CHAPTER V

THE COSTS OF LIBRARY AND INFORMATIONAL SERVICES[1]

There were those who expected the National Advisory Commission on Libraries to develop specific dollar-and-cents recommendations for private and public support of library and informational services in the years ahead. Such an expectation was unrealistic, for it turned out to be impossible even to identify with any accuracy the costs of current services. This is due largely to the inadequacy of library statistics—their lack of comparability and questionable bases. Improvement in this situation and the encouragement of sophisticated research are very much part of the job ahead.

One study commissioned by the Commission was particularly helpful to the members in understanding the economics of library operation, for even the inadequate data were sufficient for certain kinds of analyses in cost trends and relationships. This entire study is presented here in sections A–D of chapter 5.

One point emerges with special clarity: the nature of library costs is such that they will continue to rise overall, in spite of improved efficiency and cost-reduction efforts. This unavoidable phenomenon must be kept in mind in all future planning if the social value of the "product" is to be realized.

A. LIBRARY COSTS:
GENERAL DISCUSSION

INTRODUCTION

Libraries are currently beset by the effects of a number of developments that complicate their operation and require reexamination of some of their procedures. Above all, these developments have important implications concerning the nature of the financial problems libraries must face in the future. Some of the phenomena in question are:

    1. The "explosion of knowledge" has greatly increased the rate of publication of books and, therefore, has added substantially to the number of volumes a given

[1] From On the Economics of Library Operation, a MATHEMATICA report, one of the special studies commissioned by the National Advisory Commission on Libraries during 1967. William J. Baumol was the principal investigator; he was assisted in his work by Stanley W. Black, Margaret E. Stengel, and Linda A. Kime.

library must be prepared to carry if it is to continue, in some sense, to offer the same level of service as in the past.

2. A variety of innovations in technology, many of them related to the electronic computer and automation, have recently become available, and more are in prospect in the relatively near future. Librarians feel themselves under some obligation to examine the new alternatives opened for them by these innovations and to determine which, if any, will permit an improvement in the level of service they offer or enable them to reduce costs without any significant reductions of the utility of the library to those using its facilities.

3. The present and prospective shortage of librarians threatens to curtail the operations of libraries and causes some concern about the services they can offer in the future to scholars and readers.

4. Increasing costs of operation are a source of financial pressure that constantly gives rise to a need for greater funds. This in turn adds to the financial pressures that already beset the universities, the school boards, the municipalities, and the other sources of financing of the libraries.

This report, appearing here as chapter 5, has set itself several objectives in relation to the developments noted above. Primarily it seeks to supply an analysis of the sources of the cost trends that color the entire financial circumstances of our libraries and can have such important consequences for their operations. This discussion demonstrates that the rate of cost increase is perhaps greater than had generally been recognized and that there is no reason to expect this rate to diminish in the future; these rises in costs would have occurred even in the absence of the knowledge explosion. The reasons for the trends in cost arise not out of any inefficiencies in library operations but out of the very nature of their technology, the manner in which their product (service) must be produced. The prospective role of automation in library operations is also examined; this relates directly to the causes of the cost trends that were just mentioned, as well as to the predicted shortage of trained librarians.

Thus, all of the developments described at the beginning of this section will be seen to mesh, and together they will be shown to serve as portents of the future financial needs of our libraries and to act as a basis for a prescription of efficient modes of library operation in the future.

The authors urge that in reading this report, one should constantly keep in mind the haste with which it had to be prepared. Approximately three months was available for a study that should normally occupy one or two years. Consequently, no primary data collection was undertaken; existing data, although imperfect and sometimes highly limited, were considered ample for the purpose. In the course of the study some time series had to be discarded when found unusable, but fortunately the work reported here was primarily analytical in nature and for that the available data were sufficient.[2] Of course, further figures which could have provided additional confirmation of the results would have been highly desirable.

The preceding remarks are not intended in any way to constitute an apology for what has been accomplished. The results speak for themselves and can provide a variety of important insights into the economics of library operation that were previously unavailable. However, the gaps in the supporting data should not go unexplained; there

---

[2] Authors' Note: *Only toward the end of our work did it develop that there were serious errors in many of the figures and that they had been constructed in a manner which rendered many of them unusable. For example, many of our time series were completely discredited when we were informed, three weeks before the completion of the study, that the statistics were averages in which any cost figures that had not been reported were taken to be zero! Thus, a year in which a large number of libraries failed to report would be shown as a year of exceptionally low costs. By this time it was far too late to embark on any process of primary data collection. Had our assignment been the production of a compendium of reliable library statistics, this development would surely have proved fatal for the study.*

were good reasons for not providing individual sets of information for the many different classes of libraries: public libraries, university libraries, elementary school libraries, etc. In any event, the fundamental analysis and its policy implications are equally applicable to all of these classes of institutions (or rather, the variation in applicability is a relatively minor matter of degree). As a result, the absence of separate time series for each category of institution is, for our purposes, no serious loss.

BREAKDOWN OF COSTS

In discussing library costs it is convenient to break them into two major categories: capital (construction) costs and operating costs. The former are subject to much greater variation than the latter because building programs can usually be postponed and so their timing is highly dependent on the availability of funds.

In 1959 public libraries serving communities of 50,000 or more incurred operating costs of some $125 million (see Table 5A–1). Their capital outlays amounted to about $17.5 million, or about one seventh the costs of operation. In the same year (or rather, fiscal 1960) the operating costs of college and university libraries in the United States amounted to about $137 million (see Table 5A–4). We have no corresponding figures on their capital outlays. Public school libraries in schools with 150 pupils or more are estimated to have incurred operating costs of $210 million in 1960–61. The available data on library costs are presented in Table 5A–1 (public libraries, 1950–59), Table 5A–3 (our sample of 100 college and university libraries, 1951–66), and Table 5A–4 (figures for all college and university libraries, 1960–66).

The libraries' operating costs consist largely of two categories of outlay: staff salaries and book purchases (which might for some purposes also be interpreted as a capital expenditure). For example (see Figure 5A–1), of the $125 million of public library expenditures in 1959, $90 million, or slightly more than 70 percent, consisted of salaries and wages; $15 million, or about 12 percent, were devoted to the purchase of books, and about $1 million to periodicals. No other categories of expenditures amount to over $600,000 for the entire country!

In the college and university libraries our latest figures, those for 1966, show that of a total operating expenditure of $88 million by libraries in our sample, $44 million, or 50 percent, went to staff salaries; $6.6 million, or 7.5 percent, were devoted to payment for student assistance; and $28 million, or somewhat more than 30 percent, were expended on book purchases. Looking at the trends over time, we see that there has been some slight tendency for a relative decline in the proportion of current operating expenditure that is made up of staff salaries. In the decade of the fifties professional salaries constituted about 54 percent of the total operating costs, but during the sixties this figure declined fairly steadily toward its 1967 value of 50 percent. Meanwhile the relative magnitude of expenditures in new books grew from a little less than 20 percent of the total in 1951 to its recent 30 percent. All of this is illustrated in Table 5A–5, which shows the course of the percentage breakdown of the major categories of operating expenditures for our sample averaging 100 college and university libraries.[3]

---

[3] *Most of our discussion of costs in college and university libraries is based on our carefully constructed sample consisting, for the most part, of 100 institutions of higher education, selected from among universities, liberal arts colleges, junior colleges, and teachers colleges. In general, the sample seems very representative for the first two categories of institutions. For details on the construction of the sample see Appendix F–2.C.*

It will be noted that our analysis has attempted no breakdown of costs on the basis of library function; i.e, in terms of acquisition, cataloging, circulation, reference, etc. Obviously, we have not provided these data in part because the figures are simply unavailable. But there is a more fundamental reason which indicated that the data are unlikely to become available even if substantial effort is devoted to their acquisition. The librarian's work involves his going frequently from task to task; without elaborate records indicating hour by hour (and perhaps sometimes minute by minute) how he spends his time, one could not hope to get the information required. Moreover, some library costs

CAPITAL COSTS OF PUBLIC LIBRARIES

A small amount of information is available on capital needs of public libraries, mostly from a chapter on "State and Local Public Library Facility Needs" by Nathan Cohen of the Office of Education.[4] Table 5A–6 shows data on the age distribution of library facilities taken from the *Survey of Public Library Building Facilities, 1963–64*, reproduced in the 1966 report. These publicly owned buildings accounted for 89.4 percent of the estimated 56.5 million square feet of space occupied for public library purposes in 1965. The estimated replacement value of publicly owned facilities, including costs of land, site development, fees, and initial equipment, was $1,262.5 million in 1965. This figure was apparently arrived at by using estimated costs of new library facilities of $25 per square foot. Additions were estimated to cost $20 per square foot; remodeling averaged only $8 per square foot in 1965. These estimates were based on sample construction costs on projects completed in 1965. Table 5A–7 summarizes estimates of capital outlays for public library facilities derived from reports to the Office of Education in its periodic surveys. The Federal component in 1965 represents expenditures under the Library Services and Construction Act.

One may conclude from these figures that a substantial backlog of decrepit facilities exists, but its actual magnitude is open to doubt. Expenditures do appear to be rising rapidly, which should be alleviating the problem somewhat. The adequacy of the rate of expenditure cannot be judged on the basis of the statistics or economic considerations alone. In part, of course, the rising outlays on capital must be attributed also to increasing construction costs. Figure 5A–2 shows for the period 1950–66 the behavior of construction costs, indicating that construction cost per square foot has been rising almost without interruption at an annual rate exceeding 2.5 percent.

RATE OF INCREASE IN TOTAL OPERATING EXPENDITURES

The costs of operation of the nation's libraries have risen considerably in recent years. Tables 5A–1 and 5A–4 show paths of operating costs for public libraries and college and university libraries, respectively. Obviously they have been rising rapidly.

In our sample of 100 college and university libraries the annual operating cost per library has risen from approximately $295,000 in 1957 to about $880,000 in 1966. The figures represent nearly a trebling in outlays over the decade. As Figure 5A–3 shows, this rise in outlays has exceeded substantially even the very-well-publicized increase in college and university student bodies. Figure 5A–3 describes library operating expenditures per student from 1951 to 1966, and it is clear that even this ratio has gone up at an extremely rapid rate.

A similar result is indicated by the data for public libraries in cities with populations of 50,000 or more; Table 5A–1 shows that over the decade 1950 to 1959 operating outlays on the libraries in the sample increased from some $65 million in 1950 to $125 million in 1959. In part this represents a steady rise in number of volumes carried and number of volumes added annually as well as a steady rise in circulation. But as we shall see presently, there is more to the matter.

---

are joint costs that are inherently inseparable; lighting serves those who use the catalog and those who browse through nearby shelves. It is literally impossible to decide how much of the lighting cost should be assigned to each of these functions. In industry, attempts to obtain cost breakdowns of the sort under discussion have produced figures that are highly questionable and arbitrary, and which have been criticized by many economists.

In any event, it is difficult to see any important use to which such data can be put. If it were possible to show, for example, that circulation costs were surprisingly low relative to the cost per reference use, what modification in library operations would consequently recommend itself?

4 State and Local Public Facility Needs and Financing, *Vol. I, Public Facility Needs, Joint Economic Committee (Washington, D.C.: Government Printing Office, December 1966), chap. 36.*

In any event, a moment's consideration shows that these figures, if they represent any sort of portent for the future, are rather frightening. Over a period when the rate of inflation was relatively small, the cost of operation of a library was doubling or more every decade. It is difficult to overstate the long-run financing problems that are implied by such a figure.

BOOK PRICES AND LIBRARY SALARIES

We can go considerably further in our analysis of the components of the increasing operational costs of a library. Subsequent sections of chapter 5 are devoted to that subject.

Obviously, basic issues in the analysis of public library cost trends are the rates of increase in book prices and personnel salaries. Figures 5A–4 to 5A–8 show the figures on salaries and book prices that have been deduced from public library expenditure data.[5] Figure 5A–4, for example, gives the trend rate of increase of book prices for public libraries serving cities with a population of 100,000 and over as 3.2 percent per year over the 1953–62 period. Figure 5A–7 gives the rate of increase of salaries as 3.9 percent per year. The lines drawn on the charts suggest that absolute growth rates in book prices and salaries have been fairly steady. Results for public libraries in each size group are shown in Table 5A–8.

In 1966 some 4.4 million volumes were purchased by our sample of college and university libraries at an aggregate cost of $28 million, implying that they must have expended an average of a little more than six dollars per volume. This contrasts with an average acquisition cost of approximately four dollars per volume (1.8 million books for an outlay of $7 million) one decade earlier, suggesting an average annual rate of increase of 4 to 4.5 percent.

It has been estimated that the collections of major university libraries and scientific publications have both grown at about 6 percent per year.[6] We have already seen (Table 5A–1) that for public libraries the number of volumes and the number of volumes added per year have grown steadily. This, together with the growing cost per book, contributed materially to public library operating costs. Figure 5A–9 shows that similar trends hold for college and university libraries, with the total number of volumes over the period 1951–66 just about keeping up with the rapid rise in student population. The lower portion of the graph shows that the acquisition rate has, in fact, been going up far faster than the number of students.

Figure 5A–10 deals with expenditures on personnel per staff member in college and university libraries. It shows that these have been going up rather quickly, rising by more than 50 percent over the decade 1957–66. However, to see whether this implies that library staff salaries have risen at a fairly substantial rate, we must compare these figures with data on the behavior of other types of income.

Figure 5A–11 shows the behavior over the period 1951–66 of the salaries of library personnel in college and university libraries in relation to the cost of living, to per-capita personal income in the economy as a whole, and to the compensation of college and university professors. The graph shows that over the period reported, library salaries have increased at a surprisingly substantial rate of 4.8 percent per year. No doubt this represents in large part compensation for a lag in real incomes during the war and early postwar periods. But we note that over the period shown librarian incomes have gone up

---

[5] *These figures give, in the form of a scatter diagram, the average salary per employee and the average expenditure per book purchased for public libraries reporting in the United States Office of Education's annual surveys between 1954 and 1962, grouped by size of population area served. Trend lines were fitted by hand, so as to run through the point of means.*

[6] *J. P. Danton, Book Selection and Collections: A Comparison of German and American Universities (New York: Columbia University Press, 1963). Also E. A. Johnson, "The Crisis in Science and Technology and Its Effect on Military Development," Operations Research, Vol. I (1958), pp. 11–34.*

much more rapidly than the cost of living, thus representing a significant rise in purchasing power. Moreover, librarian incomes have risen far more rapidly than per-capita personal incomes in the economy, so that the relative economic position of the librarian has also improved. There is a slight distortion in the comparison resulting from the growth in population during the period, which tended to reduce the per-capita income figure. However, this does not affect our conclusion that librarian incomes have risen more quickly than incomes in the economy generally.

We note that over the entire period librarian incomes have exhibited trends very similar to those of professorial salaries. Indeed, during the earlier portion of the period shown, the beginning of the 1950's, the librarian's remuneration went up far more rapidly than that of the college professor. Since then, however, the two seem to have been rising at roughly the same rate. The figure shows a peculiar dip in the earnings of library staff members reported for 1964. This probably represents some change in composition of the sample and an addition in the number of junior staff members, which pulled down the over-all average salary figures.

A FINAL WORD

This, then, concludes the general discussion of library costs and the presentation of some of the data considered in this report. The text of section B proceeds to an economist's analysis of library cost trends.

TABLE 5A–1

CHARACTERISTICS OF PUBLIC LIBRARIES IN CITIES WITH POPULATIONS OF 50,000 OR MORE (1950–59)

CHARACTERISTICS	1950	1951	1952	1953	1954	1955	1956	1957	1958	1959
POPULATION SERVED	—	—	55,870,000	55,940,000	56,327,000	56,191,000	56,708,000	56,651,000	56,704,000	57,010,000
Public libraries reporting*	—	—	—	—	227	227	227	227	227	228
STAFF POSITIONS										
Total positions all staff	—	—	—	—	20,366	—	—	—	22,402	23,648
Professional positions	—	—	—	—	7,555	—	—	—	7,654	7,684
COLLECTION AND CIRCULATION (in volumes)										
Total at end of year	61,200,000	—	64,800,000	66,400,000	68,459,000	70,109,000	71,600,000	73,757,000	76,350,000	78,595,000
Volumes added during year	—	—	—	—	4,982,006	5,159,000	5,558,000	5,571,000	5,769,000	6,084,000
Total circulation	182,400,000	—	189,400,000	191,900,000	205,267,000	214,484,000	223,631,000	233,722,000	251,536,000	261,601,000
Juvenile circulation	—	—	—	—	89,463,000	95,932,000	95,715,000	101,611,000	110,108,000	—
OPERATING EXPENDITURES										
Total	$ 65,790,000	—	$ 78,830,000	$ 86,400,000	$ 90,118,000	$ 95,613,000	$103,260,000	$110,665,000	$118,730,000	$125,929,000
Salaries and wages (including building staff)	—	—	$ 55,070,000	$ 60,360,000	$ 65,060,000	$ 69,173,000	$ 74,017,000	$ 79,998,000	$ 85,130,000	$ 90,129,000
Books and periodicals	—	—	$ 10,190,000	$ 11,130,000	$ 11,610,000	$ 12,496,000	$ 13,099,000	$ 13,984,000	$ 14,674,000	$ 16,070,000
Audiovisual	—	—	—	—	—	—	—	$ 481,000	$ 489,000	$ 567,000
Binding	—	—	—	—	—	—	—	—	$ 2,398,000	$ 2,450,000
Other	—	—	—	—	—	—	—	—	$ 16,039,000	$ 16,712,000

* The New York Public Library Reference Department is not included in these public library data.

SOURCE: Public Library data were obtained from the following sources: U.S. Department of Health, Education, and Welfare, Office of Education, Statistics of Public Library Systems in Cities with Populations of 100,000 or more, annual; U.S. Department of Health, Education, and Welfare, Office of Education, Statistics of Public Library Systems in Cities with Populations of 50,000 to 99,999, annual. (Fiscal 1958 was not published as a separate circular; however, the relevant data did appear in the 1959 circular.)

TABLE 5A–2

RELATIVE SIZE CHARACTERISTICS OF THREE TYPES OF LIBRARIES

| TYPE OF LIBRARY | Number of | | | | OPERATING EXPENDITURES* |
	LIBRARIES	VOLUMES OWNED	VOLUMES CIRCULATED	REGISTERED BORROWERS	
College and university libraries (1966)	2,207	265,000,000	—	5,900,000	$320,000,000
College and university libraries (1962)	1,985	201,423,000	—	3,900,000	183,900,000
Public libraries (1962)†	864	163,000,000	524,000,000	—	253,000,000
Public school libraries (1961)					
Total all school libraries	102,500	—	—	35,952,000	210,000,000‡
With centralized libraries	47,500	143,540,000	—	25,300,000	—

* Excluding capital outlay.

† Figures are for public libraries (for city, county, and regional, and including the New York Public Library Reference Department) serving populations of 35,000 or more. The total number of public libraries in the United States (for 1962) serving all population groups is approximately 7,300, with almost half serving populations of less than 3,000.

‡ For public school districts enrolling 150 pupils and over.

SOURCES: American Library Association, Library Statistics of Colleges and Universities, 1965–66, Institutional Data, pp. 6–9. For public libraries, same as Table 5A–1. For public school libraries, see: U.S. Department of Health, Education, and Welfare, Office of Education, Statistics of Public School Libraries, 1960–61.

TABLE 5A–3

CHARACTERISTICS OF LIBRARIES OF INSTITUTIONS OF HIGHER LEARNING

(Special sample; 1951–66)*

CHARACTERISTICS	1951	1952	1953	1954	1955	1956	1957	1958
Undergraduates	460,000	370,000	320,000	350,000	425,000	490,000	515,000	510,000
Graduate students (total enrollment)	118,500 579,000	90,000 460,000	72,000 390,000	73,000 420,000	85,000 510,000	93,000 585,000	99,000 615,000	100,000 615,000
Book stock	40,020,000	33,930,000	31,855,000	35,825,000	43,610,000	46,990,000	49,000,000	49,680,000
Volumes added	1,620,000	1,400,000	1,280,000	1,435,000	1,680,000	1,800,000	1,790,000	1,950,000
Total full-time employee equivalent	4,225	3,630	3,175	3,400	4,050	4,385	4,570	4,745
Student hours	2,545,000	2,195,000	1,775,000	2,290,000	2,450,000	2,580,000	2,685,000	2,685,000
Total institutional expenditures	—	$527,675,000	$455,035,000	$519,480,000	$637,295,000	$754,100,000	$826,730,000	$927,070,000
Total operating cost	$20,080,000	$ 18,865,000	$ 17,565,000	$ 19,980,000	$ 24,070,000	$ 27,180,000	$ 29,570,000	$ 34,080,000
Staff salaries	$10,380,000	$ 10,280,000	$ 9,685,000	$ 10,205,000	$ 13,290,000	$ 14,990,000	$ 16,085,000	$ 18,290,000
Student pay	$ 1,810,000	$ 1,600,000	$ 1,345,000	$ 1,570,000	$ 2,085,000	$ 2,390,000	$ 2,795,000	$ 2,990,000
Book purchases	$ 3,965,000	$ 3,590,000	$ 3,720,000	$ 4,855,000	$ 5,785,000	$ 6,695,000	$ 7,240,000	$ 9,170,000
Number in sample	97	81	75	78	88	100	100	100

CHARACTERISTICS	1959	1960	1961	1962	1963	1964	1965	1966
Undergraduates	510,000	595,000	—	—	—	—	—	—
Graduate students (total enrollment)	110,000 620,000	135,000 730,000	775,000	830,000	890,000	930,000	—	1,020,000
Book stock	52,390,000	54,925,000	58,195,000	60,745,000	64,170,000	65,975,000	—	72,050,000
Volumes added	2,080,000	2,190,000	2,500,000	2,820,000	3,065,000	3,265,000	—	4,370,000
Total full-time employee equivalent	5,120	5,275	5,625	6,100	6,570	—	—	8,165
Student hours	2,800,000	2,900,000	3,350,000	3,415,000	3,640,000	3,685,000	—	4,390,000
Total institutional expenditures	$1,108,145,000	—	—	—	—	—	—	—
Total operating cost	$ 37,680,000	$41,295,000	$50,305,000	$52,980,000	$60,115,000	$68,005,000	—	$88,260,000
Staff salaries	$ 20,250,000	$22,310,000	$24,815,000	$27,805,000	$31,370,000	$34,725,000	—	$44,135,000
Student pay	$ 3,331,000	$ 3,670,000	$ 4,190,000	$ 4,486,000	$ 4,740,000	$ 5,085,000	—	$ 6,640,000
Book purchases	$ 9,930,000	$11,170,000	$14,190,000	$15,440,000	$18,455,000	$20,365,000	—	$27,860,000
Number in sample	100	100	100	100	100	100	—	100

* For details on the construction of the sample, see Appendix F-2.C. Since figures are reported only for a sample of libraries, the absolute totals are not of any particular significance. Only trends, cost proportions, and unit cost figures can validly be deduced from these statistics.

SOURCE: The college and university library sample for fiscal 1951 through fiscal 1959 was taken from: American Library Association, Statistics Committee of the Association of College and Research Libraries, College and Research Libraries, January issue, annual series. From fiscal 1960 to 1964 our data were extracted from the continuation of this statistical compilation by: U.S. Department of Health, Education, and Welfare, Office of Education, Library Statistics of Colleges and Universities, Part 1: Institutional Data, annual. In 1966 the American Library Association assumed responsibility for the series and published in 1967: Library Statistics of Colleges and Universities, 1965–66, Institutional Data.

TABLE 5A–4

SUMMARY OF COLLEGE AND UNIVERSITY LIBRARY STATISTICS

(Aggregate United States; 1959–60 to 1966)

ITEM	1959–60	1960–61	1961–62	1962–63	1963–64	1964–65	1966*
1. Number of libraries	1,951	1,975	1,985	2,075	2,140	2,168	2,207
2. Number of students served (enrollment)	3,402,000	3,610,000	3,900,000	4,345,000	4,800,000	5,300,000	5,900,000
COLLECTIONS							
3. Number of volumes at end of year	176,721,000	189,110,000	201,423,000	215,000,000	227,000,000	241,000,000	265,000,000†
4. Number of volumes per student	51.9	52.4	51.6	49.4	47.3	45.5	45.8
5. Number of volumes added during year	8,415,000	9,396,000	10,900,000	12,300,000	13,600,000	14,000,000	18,000,000
6. Number of volumes added per student	2.5	2.6	2.8	2.8	2.8	2.6	3.0
7. Number of periodicals received	1,271,000	1,399,000	1,505,000	1,600,000	1,760,000	1,800,000	2,700,000‡
8. Number of periodicals per student	0.4	0.4	0.4	0.4	0.4	0.3	0.4
PERSONNEL							
9. Total (in full-time equivalents)	18,000	19,500	21,100	23,300	25,200	27,000	29,000
10. Professional personnel	9,000	9,700	10,300	11,200	11,900	12,500	13,000
11. Professional staff as percentage of total staff	50%	50%	49%	48%	47%	46%	45%
12. Ratio of professional staff to students	1:378	1:372	1:378	1:388	1:401	1:402	1:454
13. Nonprofessional staff	9,000	9,800	10,800	12,100	13,300	14,500	16,000
14. Number of hours of student assistance	12,062,000	13,204,000	14,161,000	14,519,000	16,400,000	18,000,000	19,000,000

OPERATING EXPENDITURES

15. Total (excludes capital outlay)	$137,245,000	$158,904,000	$183,700,000	$213,000,000	$246,000,000	$275,000,000	$320,000,000
16. Expenditures per student	$40.34	$44.02	$47.13	$50.95	$51.25	$51.89	$54.23
17. Expenditures as percentage of total education and general expenditures	3.0%	3.1%	3.1%	3.2%	3.3%	3.3%	3.3%
18. Salaries (personnel not on hourly rate)	$ 72,495,000	$ 83,782,000	$ 95,900,000	$113,000,000	$126,000,000	$138,000,000	$155,000,000
19. Salaries as percentage of operating expenditures	52.8%	52.7%	52.2%	53.1%	51.2%	50.2%	49.0%
20. Wages (at hourly rates of pay)	$ 11,680,000	$ 13,889,000	$ 15,500,000	$ 17,000,000	$ 19,000,000	$ 21,000,000	$ 23,500,000
21. Wages as percentage of operating expenditures	8.5%	8.7%	8.5%	8.0%	7.7%	7.6%	7.3%
22. Books and other library materials expenditures	$ 40,760,000	$ 48,301,000	$ 56,400,000	$ 65,000,000	$ 79,000,000	$ 91,000,000	$111,000,000
23. Such expenditures percentage of operating expenditures	29.7%	30.4%	30.7%	30.5%	32.1%	33.1%	34.2%
24. Binding expenditures	$ 4,852,000	$ 5,000,000	$ 6,200,000	$ 7,000,000	$ 9,000,000	$ 11,000,000	—
25. Such expenditures percentage of operating expenditures	3.6%	3.2%	3.4%	3.3%	3.7%	4.0%	3.5%
26. Other operating expenditures	$ 7,458,000	$ 7,932,000	$ 9,700,000	$ 11,000,000	$ 13,000,000	$ 14,000,000	$ 19,000,000
27. Such expenditures percentage of operating expenditures	5.4%	5.0%	5.3%	4.2%	5.3%	5.1%	6.0%

* Estimated.

† Includes microtext.

‡ For 1965–66 the figures are for serials, which includes periodicals, annuals, proceedings, transactions, etc.

SOURCE: *U.S. Office of Education, Library Statistics of Colleges and Universities, 1959–60 to 1964–65. Institutional data compiled by Theodore Samore.*

TABLE 5A–5

PERCENTAGE BREAKDOWN FOR TOTAL LIBRARY OPERATING EXPENDITURES OF INSTITUTIONS OF HIGHER LEARNING

(Special sample, 1951–66)

YEAR	STAFF SALARIES	STUDENT PAY	BOOK PURCHASES
1951	51.7%	9.0%	19.8%
1952	54.5	8.5	19.0
1953	55.1	7.7	21.2
1954	51.1	7.9	24.3
1955	55.2	8.7	24.0
1956	55.2	8.8	24.6
1957	54.4	9.5	24.5
1958	53.7	8.8	26.9
1959	53.7	8.8	26.4
1960	54.0	8.9	27.0
1961	49.3	8.3	28.2
1962	52.5	8.5	29.1
1963	52.2	7.9	30.7
1964	51.1	7.5	30.0
1966	50.0	7.5	31.6

SOURCE: *See Table 5A–3.*

TABLE 5A–6

AGE OF PUBLICLY OWNED LIBRARY BUILDINGS

CONSTRUCTION PERIOD	PERCENT OF ALL BUILDINGS
Before 1905	16%
1905–24	22
1925–60	48
1961 or later	14

SOURCE: State and Local Public Facility Needs, *Vol. I.*

TABLE 5A–7

CAPITAL OUTLAYS OF PUBLIC LIBRARIES
(Million $)

YEAR	TOTAL	LOCAL	STATE	FEDERAL	OTHER
1965	$103.0	$70.9*	$0.5	$29.9	$1.7
1964	61.3	60.1	—	—	1.2
1962	27.7	26.8	—	—	0.9
1956	12.3	11.7	—	—	0.6
1950	4.4	4.1	—	—	0.3
1946	1.8	1.6*	—	—	0.2
1945	1.2	1.0	—	—	0.2

* *Estimated or extrapolated.*

SOURCE: State and Local Public Facility Needs, *Vol. I, p. 623.*

TABLE 5A–8

TREND RATE OF GROWTH OF COST PER UNIT OF INPUT FOR PUBLIC LIBRARIES

CITY SIZE	*Percent per year**	
	BOOKS	STAFF
100,000+	3.2%	3.9%
50,000–100,000	3.5	3.2
35,000– 50,000	3.0	—

* *The trend rates are computed as the ratio of the average annual increment given by the trend line to the mean value for the period. See Figures 5A–4 through 5A–8.*

FIGURE 5A-1

*BREAKDOWN OF OPERATING EXPENSES FOR PUBLIC
LIBRARIES IN CITIES WITH POPULATIONS OF 50,000 OR
MORE (1959)*

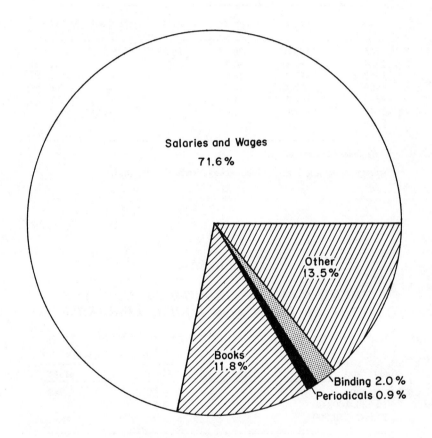

NOTE: *Details do not add to 100.0% because of rounding.*

SOURCE: *See Table 5A-1.*

FIGURE 5A–2

CONSTRUCTION COSTS INDEX (1957–59 = 100)

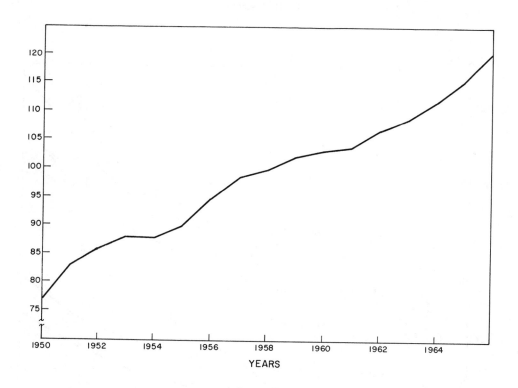

SOURCE: *For the years 1950–1964*
    U.S. Department of Commerce, Office of Business Economics, Business Statistics, *1965 Biennial Edition, p. 52.*

For the years 1965, 1966
    U.S. Department of Commerce, Business and Defense Services Administration, Construction Review, *April, 1967, p. 42.*

NOTE: *This is a Department of Commerce composite cost index: "an average, computed by the Bureau of the Census, of various cost indexes, largely privately compiled, weighted by the value in place estimates for the individual construction categories to which they are applied."*

FIGURE 5A–3

EXPENDITURES PER STUDENT
ENROLLED FOR LIBRARIES OF INSTITUTIONS OF
HIGHER LEARNING

(Special sample)

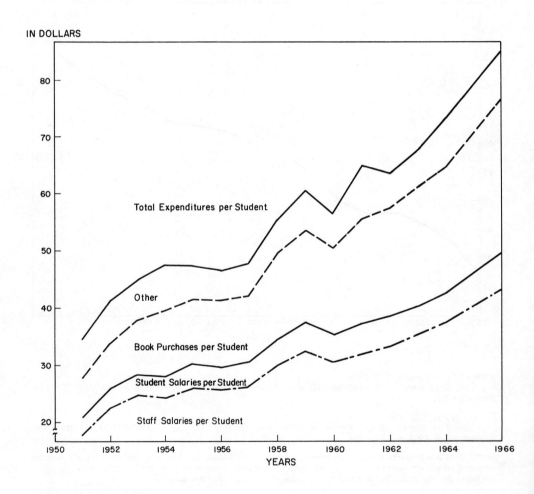

SOURCE: *See Table 5A–3.*

FIGURE 5A–4

TREND IN COST PER BOOK PURCHASED BY PUBLIC LIBRARIES IN CITIES WITH POPULATIONS OF 100,000 AND OVER

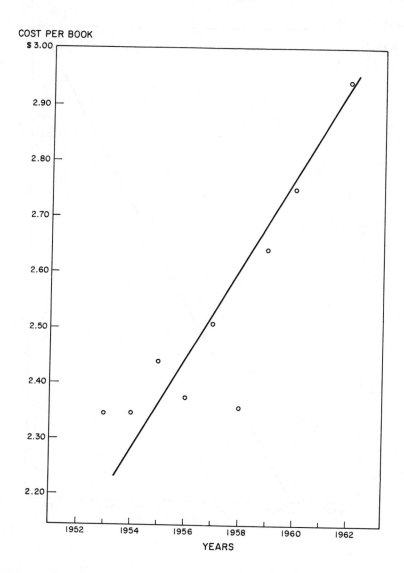

SOURCE: *See footnote 5.*

FIGURE 5A–5

TREND IN COST PER BOOK PURCHASED BY PUBLIC LIBRARIES IN CITIES WITH POPULATIONS OF 50,000–99,999

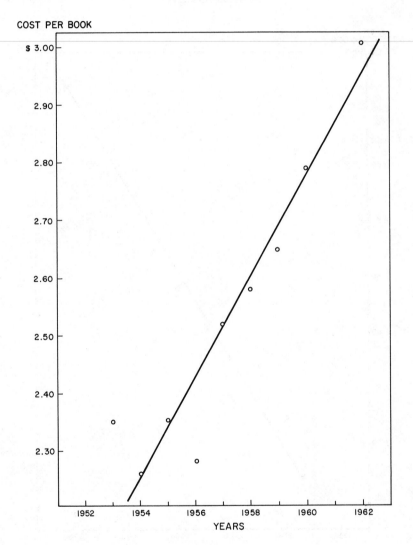

SOURCE: *See footnote 5.*

FIGURE 5A–6

TREND IN COST PER BOOK PURCHASED BY PUBLIC LIBRARIES IN CITIES WITH POPULATIONS OF 35,000–49,999

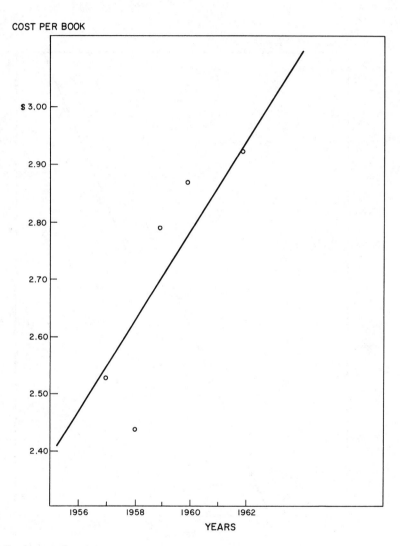

SOURCE: *See footnote 5.*

FIGURE 5A–7

TREND IN LIBRARY SALARIES OF PUBLIC LIBRARIES IN CITIES WITH POPULATIONS OF 100,000 AND OVER

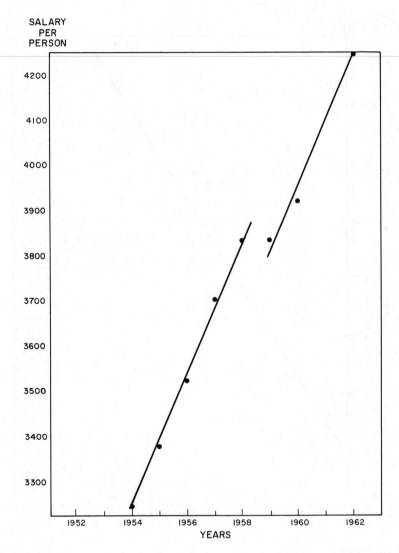

FIGURE 5A–8

*TREND IN LIBRARY SALARIES OF PUBLIC LIBRARIES
IN CITIES WITH POPULATIONS OF 50,000–99,999*

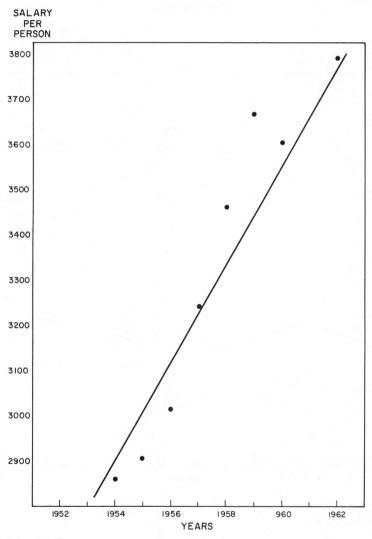

SOURCE: *See footnote 5.*

FIGURE 5A-9

TOTAL NUMBER OF VOLUMES AND NUMBER OF
VOLUMES ADDED PER STUDENT ENROLLED FOR
LIBRARIES OF INSTITUTIONS OF HIGHER LEARNING

(Special sample)

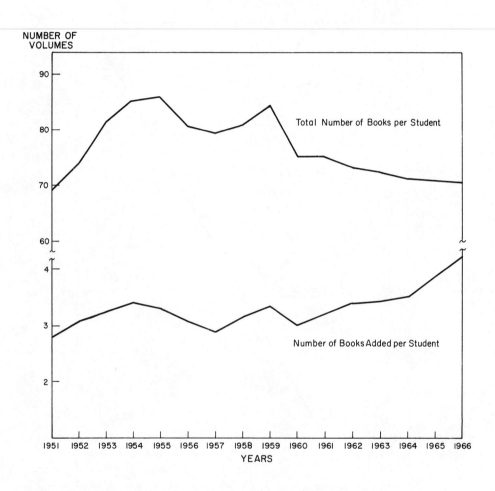

SOURCE: *See Table 5A-3.*

FIGURE 5A–10

AVERAGE SALARY PER FULL-TIME EQUIVALENT (EXCLUDING STUDENT HELP) FOR LIBRARIES OF INSTITUTIONS OF HIGHER LEARNING

(Special sample)

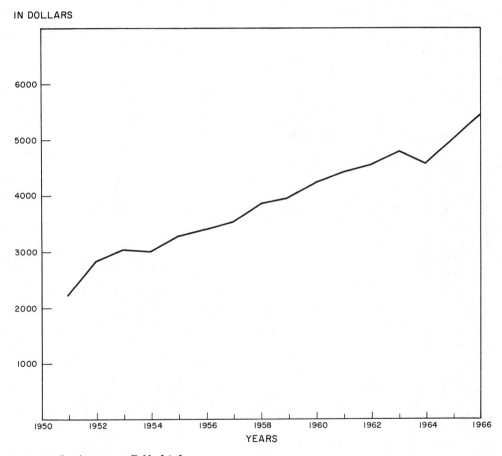

IN DOLLARS

SOURCE: *See footnote to Table 5A–3.*

FIGURE 5A–11

*AVERAGE SALARY PER FULL-TIME EQUIVALENT (EXCLUDING STUDENT HELP)
FOR LIBRARIES OF INSTITUTIONS OF HIGHER LEARNING, PROFESSORIAL SALARIES,
AVERAGE PER-CAPITA PERSONAL INCOME, AND COST OF LIVING INDEX*

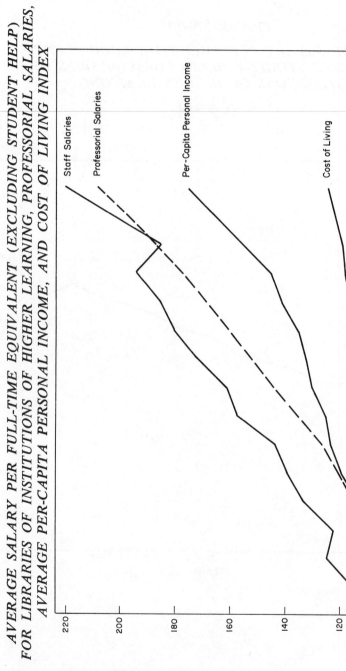

SOURCES:
(a) *Staff Salaries: see Table 5A–3.*
(b) *Professorial Salaries for Full Professors in 36 Universities: American Association of University Professors, as communicated by Mrs. Maryce Eymonerie.*
(c) *Per-capita Personal Income; Cost of Living: Economic Report of the President transmitted to the Congress January 1967, together with The Annual Report of the Council of Economic Advisers, U.S. Government Printing Office, 1967, pp. 232, 262.*

B. AN ANALYSIS OF
LIBRARY COST TRENDS

COST TRENDS AND THE NATURE OF
LIBRARY TECHNOLOGY

Before turning to an examination of more of the pertinent facts, it is desirable to provide an analysis that will bring them into focus. Parts of the discussion that follows are, unavoidably, somewhat abstract. The reader will soon see, however, that the implications are quite tangible and pertinent for the operation of libraries.

In analyzing library costs, the economist approaches the problem with no sentimental preconceptions. He considers a library to be, in effect, a workshop in which, with the aid of a number of productive processes, certain services are provided. It is only in the evaluation of these services and their social benefits (a subject discussed below) that he treats a library differently than he does any other productive process, such as the manufacture of shoes or the supply of engineering design services. By examining the technology of the library from such a matter-of-fact viewpoint, the economist is better able to arrive at the nature of its cost problems and the requirements for its efficient operation.

In many respects, as will be seen, the technology of a library has much in common with that of a college. The separate nature of the cost structure of the nation's colleges is epitomized in three factual observations—each of them straightforward but together constituting a paradox. These facts are the following: (1) *taking into consideration longer periods of time,* the compensations of college teachers have risen less rapidly than incomes in the population as a whole;[7] (2) in the budgets of liberal arts colleges, salaries constitute the largest single component in operating costs, excluding the cost of construction and the supply of other capital; (3) the cost per unit of service supplied, i.e., the cost of providing a student with one year of education, has risen far more rapidly than the average cost of all items supplied in the economy. None of these three facts, each of which is readily documented, is remarkable in itself. The lag in faculty salaries has been widely publicized; the relatively low nonsalary costs of the colleges are attributable to the fact that they use small quantities of fuel and raw materials (paper, pencils?) in comparison with most manufacturing processes; many parents have felt the effects of rising costs in the mounting tuition payments and the growing requests for contributions to which they have been subjected.

Yet the three observations together constitute a remarkable phenomenon; in effect, they state that college costs are largely composed of salaries, salaries in college have risen more slowly than elsewhere, and yet cost per unit of college service has risen more rapidly than those in the remainder of the economy! The explanation of this paradox is no mere *curiosum.* As pointed out later, it accounts for the essence of the financial pressures that beset the nation's colleges, and similarly it serves as the basis for the analysis of a substantial part of the economic problems of our libraries.

Before we turn to this explanation and its relevance to the circumstances of the libraries, one aspect of the preceding assertions bears some additional emphasis. The rising costs of colleges can be ascribed to a variety of sources: to the growth in population, to rising incomes (which lead a larger proportion of our population to demand a higher education), and to inflation (which causes increases in costs almost everywhere in the economy). However, these increases in college costs go beyond what

7 *"The Economic Status of the Academic Profession: Taking Stock, 1964–65,"* AAUP Bulletin, *51,* No. 3 *(Summer 1965), pp. 249–50.*

can be accounted for by any of these phenomena. We have been speaking of rising costs per student per semester, which means that the financial needs of our colleges would have increased even if there had been absolutely no growth in the size of the student body. These increases in cost go beyond anything that can be accounted for by inflation, for their magnitude is greater than the rate of cost increase elsewhere in the economy; i.e., they exceed in magnitude the rate of price rise that characterizes the inflationary process.

As we shall see, this all means by direct analogy that even if we were satisfied to offer no improvements in the services performed by libraries, no increase in number of persons served, and no growth in the number of volumes carried, the costs of library operation could be expected to rise. Moreover, it will be shown that these rises alone are, by their nature, progressive and cumulative. This suggests that those who supply the funds which support our libraries have not recognized the full extent of their obligation. They must learn that even with no improvement in library service, the amount which suffices to support our libraries today will prove inadequate tomorrow, and the amount which is enough for their maintenance tomorrow will be insufficient the day after that. This is no fortuitous manifestation of the current state of the economy but is rather a result inherent in the technology of library operation.

THE ROLE OF HUMAN EFFORT IN LIBRARY TECHNOLOGY

The similarity of the cost trends that characterize libraries and colleges is not a matter of accident. The production processes of both differ in at least one important way from those of a substantial segment of the economy. This difference consists of the central role of the direct services of trained personnel. In either activity any substantial reduction in the amount of labor time supplied by these persons per unit of output is likely to cause a deterioration of the product. In the case of colleges some reduction in the amount of faculty time per student may, in some circumstances, actually increase the quality of education. But, surely, after some point any further reduction in this amount, which generally means a further increase in the size of classes, must have serious educational consequences. There simply is a limit to the level of class size one is willing to tolerate—certainly, classes with 100 students and lectures with 2,000 attendees are not considered highly desirable.

Effective utilization of a library also requires at least minimal expenditures of labor time. In elementary school libraries pupils must be taught how to use the facilities, and even scholars who have had long practice in the use of library services frequently need help in locating the rare volume or the item alluded to in an incomplete reference. These services require substantial amounts of the time of skilled librarians, for whom there is no really satisfactory substitute.

Both of these activities represent a marked contrast with the circumstances of manufactured goods. In the production of washing machines, refrigerators, automobiles, or electricity the consumer neither knows nor cares about the quantity of labor that goes into the final product. As far as the consumer is concerned, anyone who discovers a way to reduce the amount of labor embodied in a kilowatt-hour of electricity is welcome to do so.

The historic result has been precisely what one might expect. In manufacturing, the product per man-hour of labor has gone up rapidly and steadily. At least since the beginning of the century productivity has risen at an average *compound* rate of 2.5 percent per year.[8] This means that the amount of labor per unit of manufactured goods has been reduced by about 50 percent approximately every twenty-eight years.

We do not know precisely what has happened to productivity per man-hour in the libraries; indeed, we will never know it precisely because the "number units of product" of a library has no unique definition—is it the number of books carried? the number of

8 *Victor R. Fuchs,* Productivity Trends in the Goods and Service Sectors, 1929–1961, *Occasional Paper 89 (New York: National Bureau of Economic Research, 1964).*

books borrowed? the number of readers served? and what constitutes a unit of reader service? However, there is every reason to believe that, as with most other services, the rate of growth of productivity per man-hour of the librarian has risen much more slowly than it has in manufacturing. Just as one cannot reduce without limit, year after year, the amount of faculty time in the educational process, the reduction of librarian time (the growth in librarian productivity) is also circumscribed by the nature of the activity.

RELATIVE PRODUCTIVITY AND COST TRENDS

We are now close to the climax of our analysis, the resolution of the paradox with which we began. As manufacturing productivity has risen relative to that in the libraries and the colleges, wages in industry have been rising. Manufacturing incomes have gone higher and higher, partly in response to the growth in productivity. Suppose that wages in manufacturing were to rise at an annual rate of 2.5 percent while librarian incomes trailed behind, increasing only at an annual rate of 2 percent. What would this mean for costs in the two activities?

In manufacturing, when wages rise 2.5 percent and productivity goes up 2.5 percent, the net effect on costs is zero. The rise in wage rate and the reduction in the labor content of the product offset one another precisely. Costs of manufacturing neither rise nor fall. On the other hand, in libraries, since there is virtually no offsetting growth in productivity, the 2 percent increase in salaries means that labor costs will increase at almost the same rate as salaries—2 percent a year compounded. This result does not depend on the particular illustrative wage figures chosen. It is easy to check that if the rate of increase in earnings were instead 5 percent in manufacturing and 4 percent in libraries, then labor costs would rise somewhat more than 2 percent per year in manufacturing and at 4 percent a year in libraries. In this case again we see library compensation figures going up more slowly than those in industry, and yet year after year, inexorably, library costs compound far more quickly than those in manufacturing.

The essence of the analysis, then, is that the technology of the library makes it very difficult to dispense with any considerable proportion of the librarians' services. Thus, it leaves little room for increases in productivity anywhere equal to those that have offset wage increases in manufacturing. As a result, if library incomes go any part of the way toward keeping up with the rise of incomes in the remainder of the economy, the costs of library operation will rise year after year in relation to the costs that characterize the economy as a whole.

One thing to be noted about this analysis is its implication about the effects of a speeding-up of the rate of increase of productivity in manufacturing. This indicates that the faster productivity grows elsewhere, the greater will be the resulting cost pressures that beset libraries. In effect, these library cost increases are part of the price of progress in the manufacturing process; thus, the greater the rate of that progress, the larger the magnitude of the price it will exact. This observation is particularly significant because preliminary evidence suggests strongly that the rate of productivity growth in manufacturing has itself been increasing. From its historic level of 2.5 percent it has gone up in the past few years to 3 percent or even higher. This suggests that the libraries have no reason to comfort themselves with the expectation of any reduction in cost pressures stemming from this quarter.

Before going on to consider the implications of this analysis for the future of the library, or to discuss the policy measures the analysis suggests, it is desirable to examine the empirical evidence—the facts relating to the longer-run trends in library costs and their components.

LIBRARY COSTS PER UNIT VERSUS COSTS IN THE ECONOMY

We turn, therefore, to the cost data which for the purpose of our central analysis are most crucial. We have recognized that rising circulation, a growing student body, and an increasing acquisition rate all play some role in increasing library costs. But we have suggested that these are but supplements to the basic cause of the increase—that even without them library costs would have risen, and risen far more rapidly than the price level.

This is confirmed dramatically by Figures 5B–1 through 5B–5, which show operating costs *per unit of output* and their breakdown into personnel and book purchase costs compared with the wholesale price index as a measure of costs in the remainder of the economy. These figures show that the pattern of behavior is essentially the same for public libraries, for college libraries, and for libraries at universities. The results do not change in essence when we take as the unit of output the number of students served, the number of volumes carried, or the amount of circulation.

Figure 5B–1, which depicts the *per-student* operating expenditures of college and university libraries, shows the typical pattern. This graph illustrates the behavior of costs per unit of service supplied; here we take the measure of service to be the number of students served. Subsequent figures in this set of graphs utilize alternative definitions of volume of service and report the results for some different classes of libraries to show the consistency of our findings for the various types of libraries.

Returning now to Figure 5B–1, we see that it depicts, for college and university libraries, total operating costs per student, staff salary costs per student, book purchase expenditures per student, and the wholesale price index, all shown on the same diagram. The data are all recalculated on an index basis (1951 = 100); i.e., they are all rescaled to start off from a common point, the left-hand end of the graph. If operating costs per unit had thereafter risen at the same rate as costs of commodities in the economy generally, as indicated by the wholesale price index, the three library cost lines would have coincided with the wholesale price index line. What we see is that, in fact, per-unit library operating costs rose far more rapidly than the price index. This is certainly true of staff salary expenditures per student, and new book purchase costs per student (uppermost line) have really risen phenomenally. The overall operating cost per student, which is a composite of staff and book costs, naturally rose at a rate intermediate between the two. This important graph leads to two significant conclusions: (1) although outlays on staff have risen, they have not gone up as rapidly as other operating costs, and hence they only account for part of the increase in unit costs, and (2) library costs per unit have indeed gone up at a substantially faster rate than those in the economy as a whole.

Figure 5B–2 shows the same results when costs are measured per volume carried; i.e., when the unit of service provided is defined in terms of the number of volumes available. Figures 5B–3, 5B–4, and 5B–5 show that completely similar results hold for the liberal arts college libraries separately, for the university libraries separately, and for the public libraries serving cities with populations over fifty thousand (for the earlier period for which data are available).

Our results are also confirmed in Tables 5B–1, 5B–2, and 5B–3, which show growth rates for library operating costs per unit of service and the comparable rates of increase in the wholesale price index. Table 5B–1 shows, for example, that while the wholesale price index has been rising at a rate less than 1 percent per annum, the operating cost per student in the college and university libraries has risen at the enormous compounded rate of 5.1 percent per year!

It will be noted that for the college and university libraries these unit-expenditure growth figures have all been of this substantial magnitude, ranging from 3 to 9 percent per year compounded. Table 5B–3 shows growth rates for college and university libraries for 1954–59, the same period as that for which we have data for the public libraries; these growth rates range from 5 to 7 percent per year. The public library growth figures (Table 5B–2) are somewhat lower, though still substantial, costs per volume carried rising at a little less than 4 percent. The sole exception is represented by cost per volume circulated, which, as a result of the rapid rise in circulation, went up at a rate a bit below 2 percent per annum, still not a totally negligible rise.

TABLE 5B-1

GROWTH RATES IN UNIT OPERATING COSTS IN COLLEGE AND UNIVERSITY LIBRARIES 1951–66*

ITEM	PER VOLUME OWNED	PER VOLUME ADDED	PER STUDENT ENROLLED
Total expenditures	5.8%	3.6%	5.1%
	(.948)	(.928)	(.949)
Staff salaries	5.3%	3.2%	4.7%
	(.959)	(.860)	(.931)
Student salaries	5.2%	3.0%	4.5%
	(.949)	(.860)	(.934)
Books purchased	9.0%	6.9%	8.3%
	(.986)	(.956)	(.966)

Wholesale Price Index = 0.7% (.759)

* The growth rates have all been calculated by fitting logarithmic least squares regressions. The figures in parentheses are standard errors serving as measures of significance. All the figures are significant at the one-percent level.

SOURCE: See Table 5A–3.

TABLE 5B-2

GROWTH RATES IN UNIT OPERATING COSTS IN PUBLIC LIBRARIES 1954–59*

ITEM	TOTAL EXPENDITURES	PER VOLUME CIRCULATED	PER VOLUME OWNED
Operating expenditures	6.7%	1.8%	3.9%
	(.998)	(.986)	(.985)
Salary and wage expenditures	6.6%	1.7%	3.8%
	(.998)	(.862)	(.985)
Book expenditures	6.2%	1.0%	3.4%
	(.992)	(.510)	(.977)

Wholesale Price Index = 1.9% (.934)

* See footnote to Table 5B–1.

SOURCE: See Table 5A–1.

TABLE 5B-3

GROWTH RATES IN UNIT OPERATING COSTS IN COLLEGE AND UNIVERSITY LIBRARIES 1954–59*

ITEM	PER VOLUME OWNED	PER VOLUME ADDED	PER STUDENT ENROLLED
Total expenditures	5.6%	5.7%	5.0%
	(.894)	(.978)	(.731)
Staff salaries	6.1%	6.1%	5.4%
	(.975)	(.971)	(.846)
Student salaries	7.6%	7.6%	6.9%
	(.991)	(.907)	(.967)
Books purchased	7.7%	7.8%	7.1%
	(.850)	(.948)	(.752)

Wholesale Price Index = 1.9% (.934)

* *See footnote to Table 5B–1.*

SOURCE: *See Table 5A–3.*

FIGURE 5B–1

OPERATING EXPENDITURES PER STUDENT ENROLLED FOR LIBRARIES OF INSTITUTIONS OF HIGHER LEARNING VS. WHOLESALE PRICE INDEX

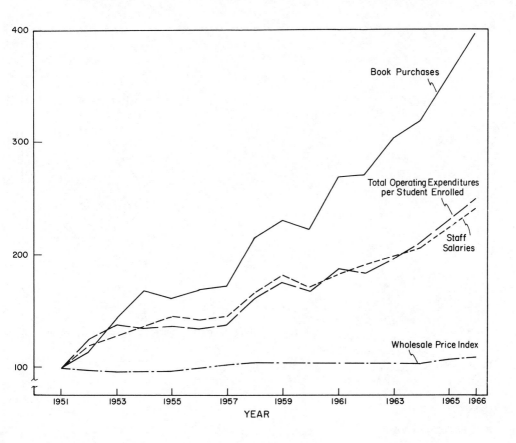

SOURCE: *See Table 5A–3.*

NOTE: *The Wholesale Price Index for Figures 5B–1 through 5B–5 was taken from* The Economic Report of the President, *transmitted to the Congress, January, 1967, together with* The Annual Report of the Council of Economic Advisers. *U.S. Government Printing Office, Washington, 1967, p. 264.*

FIGURE 5B–2

OPERATING EXPENDITURES PER VOLUME OWNED
BY LIBRARIES OF INSTITUTIONS OF
HIGHER LEARNING VS. WHOLESALE PRICE INDEX

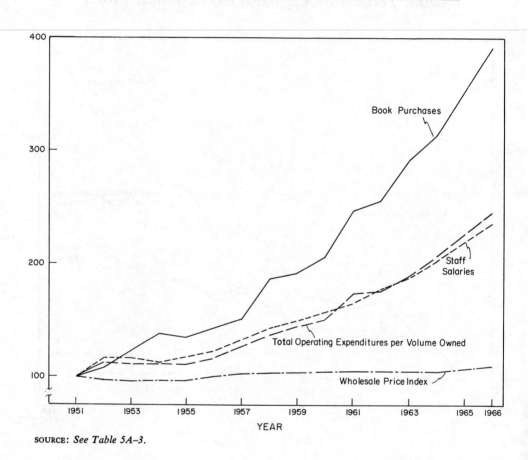

SOURCE: *See Table 5A–3.*

FIGURE 5B–3

OPERATING EXPENDITURES PER STUDENT
ENROLLED FOR LIBRARIES OF
LIBERAL ARTS COLLEGES VS. WHOLESALE PRICE INDEX

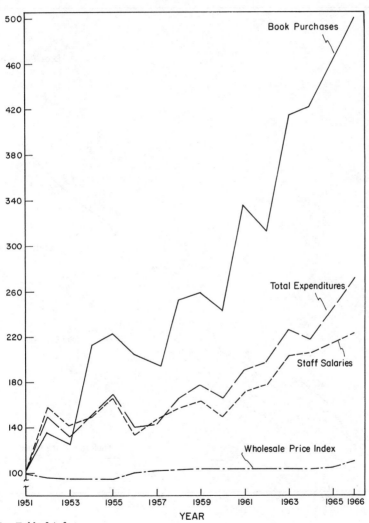

SOURCE: *See Table 5A–3.*

FIGURE 5B–4

OPERATING EXPENDITURES PER STUDENT ENROLLED FOR UNIVERSITY LIBRARIES VS. WHOLESALE PRICE INDEX

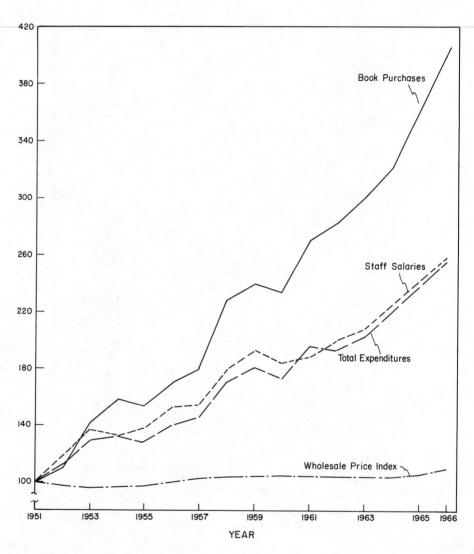

SOURCE: *See Table 5A–3.*

FIGURE 5B–5

OPERATING EXPENDITURES PER VOLUME OWNED FOR
PUBLIC LIBRARIES OF CITIES OF POPULATIONS OF
50,000 OR MORE VS. WHOLESALE PRICE INDEX

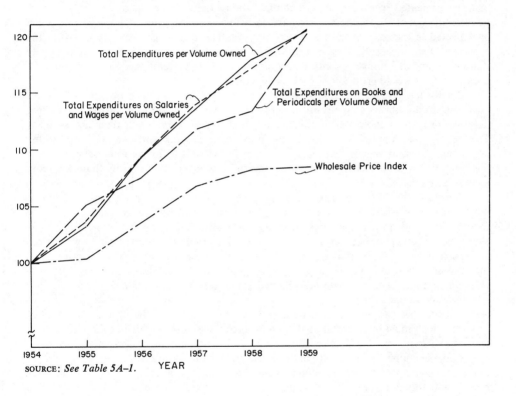

SOURCE: *See Table 5A–1.*

C. IMPLICATIONS FOR
LIBRARY FINANCING

POLICIES FOR GROWING COSTS: THE FINANCIAL
REQUIREMENTS

One of the most immediate implications of the factual evidence and the analytic material presented in section B is that the nation's libraries are going to require ever-increasing amounts of financing. We have seen that costs per unit of library service can be expected to increase, year in and year out, relative to average costs elsewhere in the economy. This means that even if prices in the economy were to remain completely stationary, and no improvements in library services and facilities were contemplated, library budgets would grow and grow ever higher.

But we live in an inflationary world, and rising prices in the economy will necessarily add to the library's cost problems. Moreover, the knowledge explosion means that libraries must stock more and more volumes and somehow maintain their accessibility. The rise in the number of college and university students and the increase in the population generally means that more and more individuals will have to be served. All of this implies that library costs can be expected to grow even more rapidly than our basic analysis suggests.

Somehow the funds to meet these rising demands will have to be found. If one is not to go from crisis to crisis, the financing of libraries will have to be placed on a new footing with the anticipated rises in costs built into future budget projections. The experience of other services suggests that those who supply the funds tend to grow tired of recurrent emergencies that occur when actual expenditures exceed, time after time, the amounts budgeted. Yet in an activity in which constantly rising costs are unavoidable, unless these cost increases are planned for in advance, such financial emergencies are almost certain to recur.

Our analysis can help to provide a basis for reeducation of the libraries' sources of support, which must be undertaken if such problems are to be avoided in the long run. It will not be easy, but legislators, college and university administrators, and others involved in the supply of library funds must be shown the nature of the long-run obligation they assume if they are unwilling to allow the nation's libraries to deteriorate. They must come to understand that cumulative rises in library costs are in the long run unavoidable, so that no fixed level of support, however generous, will do the job for any protracted period. They must be shown that these rising costs are not a matter of inflation or the consequence of mismanagement or inefficiency. This is precisely why the technological basis of these cost increases has been emphasized so heavily.

In the endeavor to get this point across at least one economic trend will facilitate the task of libraries. As we have seen, the cost increases can be ascribed ultimately to rising productivity of manufacturing, whose increasing efficiency renders the services ever more costly, at least in relative terms. It follows that the problem only arises as the economy as a whole grows more productive and hence wealthier. Thus, while the cost of maintaining libraries can be expected to rise, the means to pay this cost can be expected to increase as well, since the former is, effectively, a consequence of the latter. With a growing national income the community will surely prove more receptive to the rising financial needs of the library if the nature of these needs is explained effectively.

The statistical evidence on the prospects for support is described later in this report, along with the grounds on which public support can be defended in terms of the social contribution of libraries.

GROUNDS FOR INCREASING FINANCIAL SUPPORT

It is generally taken for granted that support of the nation's libraries is a public responsibility and that governments and individual contributors together are morally obligated to supply whatever financing is necessary for their effective operation. The evidence that library costs are growing relative to costs in the remainder of the economy and that they are likely to continue to do so forces us to reexamine this matter. In effect, rising costs imply that the public is to be asked to assume a cumulatively growing obligation. But this suggests in turn that at some point the sources of support may become reluctant to meet the increasing bill unless the issue is faced squarely. Someone will have to make an effective case indicating the grounds on which libraries merit this very demanding commitment.

This subject may seem a curious one for discussion in terms of economics. The contributions of libraries to learning, to the arts, to scholarship, and to research all obviously seem beyond the powers of the measuring rod of money. These virtues are intangible and their values may well be considered to go beyond price. Yet any activity that lays claim to public funds does automatically raise an issue that ultimately is economic. For this claim is a demand that resources be transferred from other uses to the activity in question—from the production of factories or hospitals or opera houses to the construction of libraries—and in principle such a choice is no different from that which confronts a housewife when she considers the transfer of funds from the purchase of one sort of vegetable to another. In each of these decisions rationality requires analysis in terms of the relative costs and the benefits that can be provided by the various alternatives.

It is a curious historical accident that libraries, museums, and elementary schools have so long received the bulk of their financing from governmental sources, while the nation's orchestras and many of its universities and hospitals have been expected to rely for their financing on a combination of user fees and voluntary contributions. One may well ask whether there is any good ground for this distinction, or more fundamentally, one may well inquire about the basis for the libraries' claim to any public support. Only by answering this basic question can one hope to make a really adequate case for the sort of commitment of public funds required by the rising costs of libraries.

Economists have, in fact, developed a very careful analysis of this sort of issue—the rationale of government support. They have shown quite clearly what sorts of activities merit public funds and have demonstrated that the choice is not simply a matter of relative merit. It may be highly desirable for the public to obtain good food, good shoes, and good soap as a means for personal sanitation, but no one suggests that the government should supply without cost all the food, the soap, and the shoes that are acquired by individuals. Rather, it is felt that the supply of such items, important though they may be, can safely be left to the market test; that is, to provision by private enterprise, which makes these commodities available only because their production yields a profit.

The reason the supply of such goods can be left to private firms is that the bulk of the benefits they provide is available directly to the purchaser. The food I consume offers little advantage to my neighbor. On the other hand, many other outputs are characterized by the very substantial benefits they provide to persons other than the one who consumes them, or else they impose heavy costs on other individuals. My use of an automobile imposes significant social costs by adding to air pollution and to road crowding; it contributes to the likely number of accidents involving others. On the other hand, education of the individual may provide benefits to society going well beyond those received by the student himself. Education is likely to increase his subsequent income, and thus provides him a very direct return. But, in addition, education may well reduce the crime rate and may make for better citizens in a variety of other ways. Above all, it may make possible those additions to knowledge that have contributed alike to the nation's culture and to its material standards of living.

The economist has coined the term "externalities" to describe such indirect costs and benefits of a product that go beyond the individual who consumes it. An item that produces deleterious effects on persons other than its consumer is said to impose "external costs," whereas a good or service whose utility extends beyond its immediate user is said to supply "external benefits." It has been shown by economists that it is precisely those goods and services which yield externalities whose provision cannot legitimately be left subject to the market test.

The reason is not difficult to see. A commodity that imposes external costs is likely to be supplied to its consumer at a price below its social cost. When the manufacturer pays for the labor and metal required for the production of an automobile, his outlays include no component corresponding to the pollution and the other social costs it will incur. He is, in effect, able to produce the car at bargain rates because he has shifted part of its costs to society. As a result, the profitability of automobile production to the manufacturer is no evidence of its profitability to society.

On the other hand, a service that yields external benefits, even if it clearly offers society good value for its money, may well be unable to pay its way. The reason is similar. If its consumer only receives a limited portion of the benefits that flow from the item, then the amount he is willing to pay for it can hardly serve as a measure of the social value of the commodity.

The preceding discussion at once provides the rationale for many types of current governmental activity. Pollution is an issue with which only governments can deal adequately because it is a manifestation of external costs, and its elimination therefore cannot be left to private enterprise. Similarly, the removal of slums has a legitimate claim on public funds, not merely as a charitable venture designed to rectify inequities in distribution, but also because by providing better, safer, and healthier neighborhoods, slum clearance offers (external) benefits to others in addition to their inhabitants.

It should be perfectly clear that libraries make available a variety of external benefits. Their claim to public support rests therefore not on the desirability of their service *per se,* but at least in part on the external character of the benefits they provide. If reading makes for better citizens, it is clear that the availability of libraries to the impecunious makes a social as well as an individual contribution. If libraries can help in the acquisition of skills that in turn contribute to the efficiency of the nation's productive process, then surely they provide yet another class of external benefit. Education has long been cited as a prime example of an activity that yields substantial external benefits, and the libraries, as a necessary instrument of the educational process, must therefore qualify correspondingly.

Although the external benefits libraries offer show conclusively that they merit financing beyond that offered by the marketplace, the argument does not by itself justify the full extent of the support that will be required by cumulatively rising costs. It is, however, not extremely difficult to deal with this issue in terms of material and tangible benefits alone. That is, one can argue that the economic external benefits alone may be adequate to justify public support of libraries, so that their cultural and intellectual contribution can for these purposes be considered as a bonus offered to society in addition to their economic yield.

The order of the economic contribution of libraries can be estimated by considering what would happen to productivity and technological progress in their absence. It is surely no exaggeration to say that without libraries, or some very similar institution, education and research would be severely hampered, if not substantially brought to a halt. In this sense it can be maintained that the existence of our libraries has been a necessary condition for the rising per-capita incomes that have occurred throughout our economic history.[9] Without library facilities national income would surely grow far more slowly than it has. Since, moreover, the total increase in library costs is a negligible proportion of the growth in national income, it would indeed appear to be a foolish economy to fail to provide libraries with the funds they will need to maintain the quality of their operations. These grounds then would seem to constitute full justification for providing libraries with the growing public support they will continue to require.

Before concluding this section, we may note one somewhat ironic result that follows from the analysis of this report. As we have just argued, libraries constitute an element essential for the long-run growth in productivity that characterizes our manufacturing sector. However, it has been seen that the rise in manufacturing productivity is itself the reason for the cumulative increase in library costs that constitutes the library's basic financial problem. It follows therefore that the external benefits that constitute the library's most tangible and material benefit to society bring with them the most pressing economic problem that besets the library.

PROSPECTS FOR FINANCIAL SUPPORT: THE ROLE OF VOLUNTARY CONTRIBUTIONS

As has already been indicated, libraries draw a relatively small portion of their financing from private contributors. This is obvious in the case of public school libraries, and for public libraries the situation is not much different. Table 5C–1 reports for a number of years the sources of funds utilized by public libraries located in the continental United States. The 1962 figures, which are probably the most reliable of these statistics, indicate that only some $5.5 million out of the $360 million received by libraries came from contributions and endowments together. That is, financing from private sources constituted less than 2 percent of the total. Not only is this percentage small, but if the earlier data are to be believed, it has been declining over time. It has fallen from about 5.5 percent in 1939 to a little over 4 percent in 1956 and then to its 1.5 percent value in 1962.[10]

Nevertheless, voluntary contributions are of some importance to libraries. They are of potential significance to public libraries because if these institutions find themselves under rising financial pressures as a result of cost increases, they may be forced to turn once again to the individual donor. Private libraries are, of course, heavily dependent on private contributions. But the primary significance of this source of funds is an indirect one. Since the nation's private colleges and universities are among the leading sponsors of library activity, the dependence of these institutions upon this type of financing automatically affects the libraries at second remove.

What then are the prospects for private philanthropy, and what trends have been observed in the recent past? It has been estimated that individual philanthropic contributions in the United States have risen from some 1.5 percent of Adjusted Gross Income in

9 *Here we refer of course to the basic research that has over the long run offered such a rich yield of benefits to the economy, but whose problematic outcome and distant payoff has rendered it unattractive as a subject for financing by private enterprise. Some rather specialized company or industry libraries do play an important role in research and development, but these can derive much or all of their funding from the firms and industries that benefit from them.*

10 *These trend observations should not be taken too seriously. The post-1960 figures were put together more carefully than the earlier data, and the sharp drop in the proportion of private contributions in 1962 may therefore simply reflect the change in statistical procedures rather than a variation on the underlying facts. There was also a temporary rise in this percentage from a little over 4 percent in 1945 to nearly 5 percent in 1950. However, the war years might well account for a drop in philanthropic contributions. In any event, the apparent decline in the proportion of funds from private sources may be ascribable in large part to the fact that endowment income is included in this category. The inflationary pressures of the postwar period have cut heavily into the purchasing power of many endowment funds, and so a number of organizations in other fields have drawn a smaller and smaller proportion of their total incomes from their endowments.*

the prewar period to nearly 2.5 percent after World War II.[11] The most striking increases in total philanthropic contributions occurred between 1950 and 1954, when the limit on tax deductions for contributions was increased (to 20 percent in 1952 and then, under certain conditions, to 30 percent in 1954). Their total amount has risen more than tenfold from an estimated $973 million in 1924 to over $9,800 million in 1962. Of course, inflation accounts for a considerable proportion of this increase, but even if one were to correct for changes in purchasing power of the dollar, the change would still be impressive. In terms of 1924 dollars the 1962 figure is $4,741 million, so that the real purchasing power of contributions increased nearly fivefold over the course of less than four decades.[12]

However, a very considerable proportion of these contributions (61 percent of all itemized contributions in 1962) went to religious activities. The bulk of the funds going to that class of recipient came from lower-income classes—over 60 percent of the gifts to religious institutions in 1960 were provided by donors reporting annual incomes under $10,000. The preponderant part of the funds provided to higher education—and hence, presumably, to libraries—came from higher-income groups. Thus in 1962, 23 percent of all contributions to educational institutions were provided by the relatively small class of persons whose family income was between $100,000 and $499,999, and about half the contributions to education came from the class of persons earning over $50,000 per annum.

In total, in recent years contributions by higher-income groups of individuals (which we arbitrarily define as the top 20 percent of the nation's families in terms of total personal income) have been rising at a compounded rate somewhere between 4 and 6 percent per annum. However, contributions to higher education have risen somewhat more rapidly as a result of the very carefully conceived and effectively executed fund-raising activities of the nation's educational institutions. One estimate suggests that, at least for several years, these contributions rose at a compound rate of 15 percent per annum, though subsequent investigation suggests that this figure is somewhat inflated.[13]

At any rate, it is clear that private contributions have been growing and growing rapidly. Certainly, if they were to continue to expand as rapidly as the postwar growth rate in giving to colleges and universities, this source of funds should, other things being equal, be able to help significantly toward meeting the rising costs of library operation.

Unfortunately, however, there is another side to the story. First of all, there is some evidence that total contributions and, in particular, the contributions of the upper-income groups have been leveling off. Estimated overall philanthropic contributions as a percent of adjusted gross income rose from 2.48 percent in 1956 to 2.50 in 1958 to 2.54 in 1960 and then fell to 2.51 in 1962. Over the period 1954–62 the top 20 percent of income earners increased their contributions at an average annual rate of 5.8 percent. But if we perform the same calculation for the slightly later period 1958–62, this figure falls to 3.8 percent per annum, a much slower rate of growth. In part this suggests that

[11] *The Adjusted Gross Income of all individuals is their total gross income less business deductions as reported for tax purposes. See Harry Kahn,* Personal Deductions in the Federal Income Tax *(Princeton: Princeton University Press, 1960), pp. 8–9, 17.*

These and a number of the figures that follow are taken from W. J. Baumol and W. G. Bowen, Performing Arts: The Economic Dilemma *(New York: Twentieth Century Fund, 1966), chap. XIII and XVII.*

[12] *The 1924 prices were calculated by dividing 1962 prices by the 1924 price deflator; i.e.:*

$$1924 \ price = \frac{1962 \ price}{1924 \ price \ deflator}$$

The 1924 price deflator was calculated from the GNP in 1958 dollars and the GNP in current dollars, as found in Long Term Economic Growth, *U.S. Department of Commerce, Bureau of the Census, p. 166.*

[13] *Council for Financial Aid to Education,* Guide Lines to Voluntary Support of America's Colleges and Universities *(New York), p. 22 (no date).*

there may simply be a limit to the proportion of their incomes that people are willing to give away. It may also reflect the fact that there have been no major recent increases in exemptions for charitable contributions. In any event, there is some evidence to suggest that current exemptions are so liberal that further increases might be of very little help.[14] Thus, although voluntary contributions to education and to other related activities may perhaps continue to increase as rapidly as they did in the past, one cannot count on it with any degree of assurance.

There is also a second caveat that is relevant in this connection. The availability of library funds from colleges and universities depends not only on the monies received by these institutions but is also affected materially by the competing demands of other college and university activities. Here there arises another problem. The costs of higher education have risen at a spectacular rate over the postwar period. A variety of reasons can be cited to account for this: the upsurge in the number of students, the increasing complexity of research equipment, etc. In addition, higher education obviously suffers from the limited opportunities for increases in productivity that also lie at the root of the financial pressures that beset libraries. Consequently, cost per student has been estimated to have increased after the postwar period at an annual rate of nearly 7 percent per annum. If we combine these influences, it is not difficult to show that outlays in higher education threaten to outrun significantly the growth in private contributions. This clearly means that libraries as claimants on the general budgets of private colleges and universities cannot anticipate an easy time in obtaining increasing amounts of money from this source.

REVENUES FROM MUNICIPAL SOURCES

Municipal and local governments play an extremely important role in the financing of library services. Since local governments provide so high a proportion of the financing of public schools, it is clear that public school libraries are highly dependent on them for funds. The public libraries, too, derive the bulk of their resources from them. As shown in Table 5C–1, over 85 percent of public library funds are derived from local appropriations and there is no discernible trend in this figure.

Yet although the municipalities loom large in the financing of libraries, the reverse is not true—the libraries constitute a minuscule proportion of the expenditures of local governments. For example, in 1962 a breakdown of public expenditures of United States standard metropolitan areas, which lists items constituting as little as 3 percent of the budget, leaves library expenditures over for the miscellaneous category.[15]

Since 1939, when the public libraries derived some $44 million from local appropriations, the amount received from this source increased nearly sevenfold to about $302 million in 1962, and it has almost certainly gone up further since that time. Again there is some question about the reliability of the earlier figures, but there is no reason to doubt their direction.

The critical issue, however, is whether the municipalities can be expected to continue to keep up with the needs of public libraries. Here there is little question about the good intentions of local governments, but as the reader is doubtless aware, in recent years the municipalities have encountered a variety of financial difficulties. On the revenue side, for a number of reasons, they have had some problem in increasing tax revenues. First, their revenues are limited by the fact that the taxes collected by local governments are characteristically not what the economist calls "highly income elastic." As local per-capita incomes rise, the tax receipts do not tend to increase correspondingly. With their heavy reliance on property and sales taxes, neither of which is progressive, municipal tax receipts are less responsive to income increases than is a straightforward

---

14 *See Kahn,* op. cit., *pp. 56–91.*
15 *See George F. Break,* Intergovernmental Fiscal Relations in the United States (*Washington: The Brookings Institution, 1967*), *p. 170.*

income tax under whose provisions tax payments usually go up, automatically, more than in proportion to rising incomes.

Second, with the exodus of the middle classes to the suburbs the urban municipalities have found that they have not shared fully in the rising incomes that have characterized the United States as a whole, and so their tax base—the source from which cities derive their tax funds—has tended to lag behind. Third, municipalities have been reluctant to raise their tax rates or to impose new taxes for fear of driving industry and wealthier residents into other locations. As a result, local governments have tended to compete with one another in their resistance to new revenue measures. Finally, the municipalities have found that where their proposed tax increases require authorization by the state, the state governments have often been niggardly in granting permission for such supplementary revenue measures. On all four counts, then, local governments have encountered difficulties in expanding the flow of revenues out of which their expenditures are financed.

While the municipalities have for these reasons run into trouble in trying to increase their revenues, their costs have refused to stand still. In large part this cost pattern can also be ascribed to the labor-intensive character of a considerable variety of urban services. Education, police protection, hospital care, and many other municipal services run into technological problems in increasing productivity of exactly the same variety as those that beset the library. For example, this is clearly true of education, which in 1962 took up 42 percent of the outlays of standard metropolitan areas in the United States.[16] Yet, as shown in Table 5C–2, costs per pupil-day rose nearly tenfold between 1920 and 1967. In the postwar period (1947–67) they increased at the astonishing rate of 6.7 percent per year, thus nearly doubling every decade, while the wholesale price index was rising at the rate of only 1.4 percent per year. The difference between an average of 28 students per class in 1947 and an average of 25.4 students per class in 1966 accounts for only a small proportion of the enormous rate of increase in cost per student-day. Add to this the postwar rise in student population and we can see why educational costs have constituted so rapidly increasing a burden on the municipalities.

Other municipal services can be shown to be subject to similar productivity problems and hence to have been characterized by the same sorts of cost increases. There is no point in providing any further illustrative documentation. The facts of the matter are clear—municipal costs have been rising at a phenomenal rate, and since technology accounts for a considerable proportion of these increases, there is no ground on which to expect any substantial decline in their rate of growth in the future.

The moral of all this is obvious. The municipalities are likely for the foreseeable future to continue to grow less and less generous in meeting the financial needs of the activities that in the past have been largely dependent upon them. Rapidly rising costs and inability to increase revenues at will are likely to continue to force local governments to be less generous in the financing of their services. Outlays will no doubt go up but perhaps not as rapidly as required to meet rising costs. Governments will find it ever more difficult to satisfy the ambitions of those who provide the services—their desire to offer ever better service in terms of the quality of the product and the number of persons who receive it. All of this does not bode well for the public libraries. Although up to this point, as we have seen, the share of local financing in library budgets has remained relatively constant, public libraries should begin to plan for the possibility that monies from this source will in the future not rise as rapidly as the amounts that may be considered necessary.

Perhaps the financial problems that this suggests will in fact never materialize. Particularly this may be so if the Federal Government implements on generous terms some of the proposals for revenue-sharing whereby some of the Federal revenues would

16 Ibid.

be returned to the states and through them to local governments. But revenue-sharing is still a long way from enactment, and in any event prudence requires that public libraries be prepared for the eventuality that municipal budgets will no longer prove adequate for their needs.

That being the case, one must look to the source whose ultimate prospects are most promising, the Federal Government, as a potential patron of the library.

FEDERAL FUNDING OF LIBRARIES

The following section on the federal funding of libraries is not meant to provide a penetrating look into the complexity of the relationship between the Federal Government and the nation's libraries. Its purpose is to provide a brief and superficial overview of the Federal Government's activities in this area, as they were in 1967 at the time this report was originally compiled, and to illustrate the point that the provision of resources to libraries by the Federal Government has increased considerably in the past few years. (For more recent information, see Appendix E.)

Federal funds are now available for the construction of facilities, the training of librarians, the acquisition of library materials, cataloging and bibliographical work, interlibrary arrangements, and aid for technological experimentation.

The Library Services and Construction Act[17]

Federal funding of libraries was not introduced in any significant amount until 1956. At that time the rural Library Services Act was passed and put into effect. The act, which applies only to public libraries, authorized a maximum annual appropriation of $7.5 million for five years to be used to stimulate the further development of public library services in rural areas with populations under ten thousand. Under its provisions funds were allotted to each state on the basis of its rural population and matched by the states on the basis of their per-capita income. Funds could be used for salaries, books and other library materials, library equipment, and other operating expenses, but they could not be used for the purchase of land or the purchase or erection of buildings. This act was the first aimed directly at the establishment, improvement, and extension of public library services.

The act was extended in 1960, and it has been estimated that as a result state expenditures in local libraries rose 135 percent and local funding rose about 115 percent from its 1956 level. In 1964:

> The Library Services and Construction Act amended the original rural program legislation to include authorization for grants for public library services to urban as well as rural areas and funds for public library construction. An appropriation of $55 million under the act was made by the Congress for each fiscal year, 1965 and 1966: $25 million for Title I, Services, and $30 million for Title II, Construction. To ensure that federal funds do not replace state and local funds, state and local expenditures for public library service cannot fall below those for the 1963 "floor" year.[18]

Subsequent authorization has provided $192 million for fiscal 1971. Thus, the amounts authorized have gone up to more than twenty-five times the original $7.5 million over the fifteen-year period, fiscal 1957–71.

For 1967, under this act the following amounts were authorized or appropriated for the purposes specified:

Title I: For general library services in areas without service or with inadequate service, $35 million was authorized and appropriated, with the Federal share of expenditures specified to constitute between 33 and 66 percent of the total.

---

17 *See John Frantz and Nathan Cohen, "The Federal Government and Public Libraries: A Ten-Year Partnership, Fiscal Years 1957–1966," (Washington: U.S. Department of Health, Education, and Welfare, Office of Education).*
18 Ibid., *pp. 2–3.*

Title II: For library construction in areas without library facilities to develop services, $40 million was authorized and appropriated, with the Federal share as in Title I.

Title III: For assistance in interlibrary cooperation $5 million was authorized but only $375,000 appropriated, without state or local matching funds required for the year.

Title IV: For library services to institutionalized persons and the physically handicapped, $8 million was authorized but only $625,000 appropriated, and no state or local matching was required.

The Library Services Act and Library Services and Construction Act have provided a great stimulus to the growth and improvement of public libraries during the past decade. A total of $159 million in Federal funds has been expended for both library services and construction during the ten-year program. About $600 million are currently being expended for public library services and construction from Federal, state, and local sources.[19]

The Elementary and Secondary Education Act[20]

Other pieces of legislation of significance for the library include the Elementary and Secondary Education Act of 1965 (which helps public school libraries primarily), the Higher Education Act of 1965 (which applies primarily to college and university libraries), and the National Defense Education Act of 1958.

The Elementary and Secondary Education Act of 1965 is oriented heavily toward assistance of educationally deprived children, and provides Federal help for the improvement in quality of education and educational opportunities in public and private elementary and secondary schools. Under Title I of the act assistance is offered to deprived children between the ages of five and seventeen years who are handicapped by poverty, neglect, delinquency, or cultural or linguistic isolation. With special provisions to assure the separation of church and state, some benefits are also extended to students in nonpublic schools. For school libraries in low-income areas Title I permits assistance for the purchase of books, periodicals, and equipment and for the hiring of staff.

During fiscal 1967, under this act $1,053 million was appropriated for the education of the disadvantaged. How much of this amount was devoted to libraries and related activities is not known. However, it has been suggested that the amount was substantial, improvement of library facilities being a fairly obvious and direct use of such funds.

Under Title II of the act, which provides funds for textbooks, school library resources, and miscellaneous instructional materials, $100 million was appropriated in fiscal 1966. For 1967, $105 million was appropriated, though only some $102 million was allocated. An allocation of $105 million is anticipated for fiscal 1968.

The Higher Education Act[21]

Title II of the Higher Education Act of 1965 was designed to provide assistance directly to college and university libraries. Title II consists of three parts.

Part A provides funds for basic grants, supplemental grants, and special-purpose grants to be used for the purpose of buying books, periodicals, and other library materials, and for necessary binding. Under Part A a total of $50 million was authorized for the fiscal years 1966–68: $10 million has been appropriated for fiscal 1966 and $25 million for fiscal 1967. There has been no appropriation for fiscal 1968. Basic grants are

19 Ibid., p. 13. *The source goes on to state:* "*Almost $2 billion more are needed to bring public libraries up to a minimal level of adequacy so that they may fulfill their vital role as 'The University of the People' for all Americans.*"
20 *The information concerning Title I of this act has been read and corrected by Mr. John Hughes, Administrator of Title I of the Elementary and Secondary Education Act. The information concerning Title II has been examined by Dr. Margery Johnson, Administrator of Title II of the Elementary and Secondary Education Act.*
21 *Paxton P. Price, Acting Chief of College Resources, Division of Library Services, U.S. Office of Education, has given his approval to the following discussion of the Higher Education Act.*

limited to $5,000 for each institution or branch of an institution, given only on condition that the institution does not decrease the amount theretofore expended for library purposes, and that it at least matches the amount of the grant. Special-purpose grants may be made to libraries showing special need.

Part B authorizes the Commissioner of Education to make grants to institutions of higher learning to cover the costs of training of librarians or for scholarships for library trainees. In addition, he may make grants for research and demonstration projects for the improvement of libraries or for training in librarianship. Under Part B $15 million was authorized for both library training and research and demonstration for 1966–68. In fiscal 1966, $1 million was appropriated for library training, but there was no appropriation for library research and demonstration. In fiscal 1966, $1 million was appropriated for library training, but there was no appropriation for library research and demonstration. In fiscal 1967, $3,750,000 has been appropriated for library training, and $3,550,-000 for library research and demonstration. As of July 10, 1967, there had been no appropriation for fiscal 1968.

Under Part C of Title II of the Higher Education Act the Commissioner is to "transfer funds" to the Library of Congress for acquiring library materials published throughout the world and for providing catalog information to libraries.

The National Defense Education Act[22]

The National Defense Education Act of 1958 was not specifically directed to the provision of increased library facilities. Nevertheless, three of its titles provide sources of funds for research libraries.

Title III, as revised in 1965, provides Federal matching grants to states to institute programs and to strengthen instruction in public elementary and secondary schools. Projects may include acquisition of laboratory and other special equipment, such as audiovisual materials and equipment, also printed and published materials (other than textbooks) suitable for use in providing education in the critical subjects. (For fiscal 1968 the act authorized an expenditure of $110 million for Title III, but the House-passed allowance for fiscal 1968 was $50 million.)

Title VII (A) grants the Commissioner of Education authority to further research and experimentation in the various media of communication. Under Title VII (B) he is authorized to "prepare and publish such materials as are generally useful in the encouragement and more effective use of those media."

Title IX provides the National Science Foundation with the right to establish a Science Information Service, which would aid in the dissemination of scientific information and would develop technological improvements in this area.

In addition to what has just been described, the Government has provided some indirect assistance which the legislation referring directly to libraries does not encompass. Through its general assistance to elementary and higher education the Federal Government has surely released school funds for use by the libraries, funds which might otherwise have been required for other purposes. There have also been some small unrestricted grants emanating from agencies such as the National Science Foundation that have been used in part to assist libraries.

A FINAL WORD

We conclude from the preceding discussion that from its modest beginning only a little more than a decade ago Federal aid to libraries has risen at an enormous rate. From an initial $7.5 million per annum in 1956, total Federal funds to libraries of all sorts rose to well over $100 million in 1966. This rate of increase obviously bodes well

---

22 *The following information on the National Defense Education Act has received the approval of Dr. Margery Johnson, Bureau of Elementary and Secondary Education.*

TABLE 5C–1

SOURCES OF FUNDS UTILIZED BY PUBLIC LIBRARIES OF THE CONTINENTAL UNITED STATES (1939–62)*

ITEM	1939	1945	1950	1956	1962
Total number of libraries reporting	5,798	6,026	6,105	6,375	—
Number of libraries reporting this item	—	—	5,685	6,190	—
Total receipts:	$50,485,000	$64,915,000	$117,065,000	$185,445,000	$359,345,000
Local appropriations	$43,755,000	$57,005,000	$102,350,000	$161,895,000	$301,540,000
	86.7%	87.8%	87.4%	87.3%	83.9%
State grants	$ 275,000	$ 955,000	$ 1,955,000	$ 4,975,000	$ 26,385,000
	0.5%	1.5%	1.7%	2.7%	7.3%
Income from endowments and gifts	$ 2,775,000	$ 2,645,000	$ 5,695,000	$ 7,910,000	$ 5,505,000
	5.5%	4.1%	4.9%	4.3%	1.5%
Contract service (school & other)	$ 480,000	—	—	—	$ 5,475,000
	0.9%				1.5%
Undistributed income	$ 290,000	$ 290,000	$ 59,000	—	—
	0.6%	0.4%	0.1%	—	—
All other receipts	$ 2,910,000	$ 4,025,000	$ 7,005,000	$ 10,665,000	$ 11,010,000
	5.8%	6.2%	6.0%	5.7%	3.1%
					$ 7,430,000
					2.1%
					(excluding fines & fees)

* Note the pre-1962 figures were not compiled on a sampling basis. Furthermore, when a library did not report a cost, zero was averaged into the aggregate cost figure!

SOURCE: U.S. Office of Education, Statistics of Public Libraries, issued approximately every five years.

for the future and suggests that the Federal Government has not shirked its responsibilities to libraries.

Political prospects for future funding by the Federal Government are always difficult to evaluate, particularly since they depend so heavily on political vicissitudes and on the nation's military commitments. But it is clear that in the long run libraries are likely to look more and more to Washington as a major source of financing. Without increasing Federal aid, libraries are likely to run into serious financial problems as a result of their rising costs and the financial pressures that beset their alternative sources of support. Because of their obvious importance for the nation's educational and research activity, and because of the relative modesty of their needs in comparison with those of many other claimants upon the resources of the Federal Government, it is difficult to believe that their requirements will not be met.

TABLE 5C–2

COSTS PER PUPIL-DAY IN UNITED STATES PUBLIC SCHOOLS

YEAR	$	YEAR	$
1900	$ .12	1952	$1.38
		1953	1.35
1910	.18	1954	1.48
		1955	1.51
1920	.33	1956	1.71
		1957	1.69
1930	.50	1958	1.85
		1959	1.94
1940	.50	1960	2.13
1946	.77	1961	2.20
1947	.86	1962	2.37
1948	1.02	1963	2.42
1949	1.09	1964	2.57
1950	1.18	1965	2.70
1951	1.26	1966	2.93
		1967	3.15

Annual rate of increase (compounded):
1900–67 = 5.0%; 1947–67 = 6.7%

SOURCE: *These figures were calculated by multiplying average daily school attendance for each year times the average number of days in the school year to give a number of pupil-days figure. This last number was then divided into the annual current expenditure on public elementary and secondary education to give the current cost per pupil-day. The sources of the data for these calculations are* Status and Trends: Vital Statistics, Education, and Public Finance, *Research Division, National Education Association, Report R13, August 1959, p. 22; also* Estimates of School Statistics, 1966–67, *Research Division, National Education Association, Report R20, 1966, pp. 11, 20. Data interpolations were used for some years.*

D. ALTERNATIVES FOR
LIBRARY OPERATION

ECONOMIES OF SCALE

The funding of libraries does not, of course, constitute the only economic issue that they face. Alternative modes of library operation are, in part, economic matters. If pressures on library funds do, in fact, increase materially, it may prove necessary to undertake new modes of operation that promise to be more economical. And in any event, where economies can be instituted without any significant deterioration in standards, they may release funds that the library can put to very good alternative uses. Economies then may constitute a prime candidate as the'source of financing for the library's future activity goals.

Consequently, we turn now to some of the alternative modes of library operation and seek to evaluate so far as possible, in light of the available data, their financial implications. The next few sections deal with the issues arising out of the possibilities for automation, describing some of the specific technological changes that are in prospect and suggesting the economist's view of their potential role.

Our attention will first be concentrated on the possibility of economies of large-scale operation in the library. In industry economies of scale have constituted a prime ingredient in technological progress. The assembly line, that ultimate exemplification of what the Englishman calls "industrial rationalization," is clearly made possible by large-scale operation. No minuscule firm could possibly specialize its manufacturing subactivities in a manner that renders feasible the assembly procedure. Many other economies have also proved to be available to industry only when the pertinent activity was carried out at a very substantial level. Small firms, for example, have found the opportunities for the use of computers to be far more limited than have the giants of industry.

In libraries economies of scale, if they exist, must clearly take a more subtle form. Happily no assembly line is in prospect for the operations of a library. Yet the issue of economies of scale is highly pertinent because it can play a critical role in the organization of library activity. In particular, it is important for matters relating to the choice between centralization and decentralization, for if economies of scale were to prove very substantial, it would mean that much could be saved by the operation of a few large central libraries as a substitute for a larger number of localized establishments. For a variety of reasons one might still prefer a considerable degree of localization; for example, the neighborhood public library may have no effective substitutes in impoverished areas—but at least one would have to recognize that such a decision incurs a very substantial cost.

The evidence on the subject is fairly clear-cut. It suggests quite categorically that larger libraries do operate more economically, though the differences in cost of operation are not enormous. That is to say, the evidence is all quite consistent, indicating beyond reasonable doubt that the larger library can serve a given reader's needs more economically. But although some money can be saved by increased centralization, the amount is apparently fairly modest.

Table 5D–1 presents one of the most convincing pieces of evidence on this matter. It is based on the experience of public libraries serving populations varying considerably in size. The table describes the variation in cost corresponding to libraries serving different populations ranging from less than ten thousand to over half a million inhabitants. This table seems to suggest not only that economies of scale are present, but that they are very considerable in magnitude. The cost per capita falls quite steadily from $15 for libraries serving populations under 10,000 to $6 for populations of half a million and over. These results may, however, reflect a relatively better provision of facilities for smaller populations and a higher level of activity in the smaller population units. Thus, for example, in the smaller communities the book stock per capita ranges from 3.5 to 5 and the square footage per capita runs from 0.7 to 0.8, but in the largest communities the corresponding figures are 1 to 1.25 volumes and 0.3 square feet per capita. One might argue, however, that this is an unavoidable concomitant of the operation of any sort of effective library. That is to say, even in a very small town a library with less than ten thousand volumes simply might not offer a reasonable level of selection on any criterion, and merely in order to provide effective library service, it must offer more volumes per capita than does a library in a larger metropolis.

Conclusive evidence that Table 5D–1 does somewhat exaggerate the scope for economies of scale is offered by the fourth column of the table, which shows that circulation per capita rises from 6.5 in the largest communities to 10 in the smallest. Whatever may be the reason, then, apparently circulation is significantly greater in small-town libraries than it is in large cities. As a result, although total library costs per capita are much larger in small communities, it is clear that the cost per unit of circulation falls much more slowly. As the last column of Table 5D–1 shows, cost per book circulated rises from a little under $1.00 in libraries serving populations of 500,000 and over to $1.50 per volume in libraries in communities of less than 10,000 persons.

Figures 5D–1 and 5D–2 show how the amount of labor employed and the number of volumes carried vary in relation to the library's total circulation.[23]

These graphs indicate that circulation requires just about proportionate increases in the amount of labor utilized and in the number of volumes carried. In other words, they suggest that if there are economies of scale, they are probably not very large. It should be emphasized that Figures 5D–1 and 5D–2 are not based on the data that underlie Table 5D–1. Table 5D–1 refers to the costs of libraries of different size in one given year, but Figures 5D–1 and 5D–2 report the costs of a given body of libraries as they expand their activities with the passage of time. As a result, they should not necessarily appear to suggest the same conclusions about economies. For example, it might transpire that a given library only learns slowly to take advantage of the best available technology for its size as the scale of its operation increases, so that a newly expanded library would then offer economies smaller in magnitude than those provided by one that has long been large. Nevertheless, further analysis suggests that these figures are not inconsistent with the results of Table 5D–1. We find, examining the intertemporal figures more carefully, that over the period 1954 to 1959 the average annual rate of increase of circulation in libraries serving populations of fifty thousand and over was 5 percent per year. Yet over the same period the number of books carried by these libraries grew at an average of only 2.8 percent per year (see Appendix F–2.B). Clearly, these results, which show that circulation can expand nearly twice as quickly as the number of volumes carried or as the amount of labor utilized, suggest that economies of scale are indeed a very real phenomenon.

All of this indicates that one large library can operate more inexpensively than two small ones. This observation is not meant to suggest that all small libraries should be abolished forthwith or that amalgamation should be the watchword of all future library

23 *These data are from the Office of Education's annual surveys of public libraries serving cities of varying populations. For each city-size grouping the graphs show total circulation for all libraries reporting in the group against total book stock and total number of employees. The years included are 1954 to 1962 for libraries serving cities of 100,000 and over, and fewer years for the smaller-size groupings. There is a change in the classifications in 1959.*

operation. The statement merely implies that if one chooses to expand the number of small libraries or even to retain their number, it must be recognized that this is not a costless decision, and so such a policy must be justified in terms of commensurate prospective benefits.

LABOR-BOOK RATIOS IN LIBRARY OPERATION

While discussing the relationship between scale of operation and cost, it is natural to inquire into the effect of level of activity on the ratio between inputs and outputs. This is essentially a digression at this point, and so this issue is dealt with only briefly. The brevity of our discussion should not be taken as an index of its potential importance, however, because on this sort of information one may be able to base an analysis making possible substantial efficiencies through improvement in the proportions of inputs utilized.

The two prime inputs to library operation are ultimately the efforts of the library staff and the books held by the library. Figure 5D–3 relates the number of books held by a library to the number of persons employed by it for libraries serving different sizes of population. Each dot represents the ratio for a given year for all libraries serving cities in one of the three population groupings.

It will be noted that the dots cluster rather closely about the straight line drawn through the origin. This means that the ratio of labor to number of books remains virtually fixed as libraries grow through time. It is possible that the effects of the use of computers in facilitating the work of the circulation desk and other time-consuming areas of operation may substantially reduce the labor component in the operation of larger libraries, because only the large institutions could afford to make full use of the expensive equipment required. However, as yet no significant change in the relative book-labor ratio seems to have occurred. There seems to be a slight curvature in the relationship for libraries serving populations of 100,000 and over, indicating some slight labor-saving in that range (books increase more than in proportion to labor), but this may also simply reflect a change in the composition of the sample that occurred in 1959.

Thus we see that, by and large, with current technology a doubling in the number of volumes carried by a library requires a doubling in the labor time required for its operation. This does not contradict the finding reported in the preceding section to the effect that there are economies of large scale in the operation of libraries. It means rather that these economies are achieved in larger libraries by more effective utilization of *both* books and labor. In larger libraries circulation per volume and circulation per labor-hour would then both have to be greater in the large library, with no significant change in their ratio.

RISING COSTS, PERSONNEL SHORTAGES, AND AUTOMATION

So far we have dealt with sheer scale of operation as a possible instrument of economy. In addition, one must consider the specific proposals for technological innovation in terms of their economic implications. Unfortunately, experience with most of these is extremely limited, so that they can only be dealt with descriptively because there are virtually no data permitting a reliable evaluation of their effects on library costs, let alone their consequences for the quality of library operation.

There is much that is inherently attractive about what might be described as handicraft modes of library operation. An open-shelf library through which the reader can browse can be of enormous help to the scholar and is pleasant for everyone. A microfilm is efficient to store and offers other advantages, but in many respects it is an imperfect substitute for a book. We have already discussed the importance of the librarian behind the desk, with whom one can discuss the sources one needs and who can expedite the user's request for them.

It is only natural, therefore, for everyone concerned to resist the innovations which threaten this state of affairs. Yet many libraries have long given up any attempt to operate on an open-shelf basis. Volumes that are infrequently used are sometimes stored where they can be obtained only after some delay, and many items are available only on microfilm. These innovations have met with relatively little opposition because they have not affected seriously the overall atmosphere of library operation. Some of the more Orwellian visions of what may be entailed by library automation may well give one pause. Pictures of volumes being available only on television screens where they are flashed in response to a volume identification code transmitted though push buttons may or may not be attractive depending on one's point of view. Obviously, automation can take far less drastic forms and encompass far less vital portions of a library's operation. For example, only routine and uninteresting labor would be replaced by an electronic device that scanned's one's library card when a volume was returned and automatically reported any fine that was due. The authors of this report can pretend to no expertise in library operation and therefore would not presume to judge the specific innovations that are possible. Our point is merely that their effects on the library would certainly not all be equally drastic.

What has all this to do with the anticipated shortage of librarians and the prospective increases in library costs? The relationship to the former is fairly obvious. If the number of librarians in prospect is inadequate, then something must be done to supplement their labor. In the more routine tasks of library operation the efforts of skilled individuals will simply have to be replaced either by the use of personnel less adequate in their training or by the use of technical devices—the equipment of automation. The object is, of course, to make the most effective use of such skilled persons as will be available. Hence, one must avoid, at all costs, a uniform reduction in their utilization in the various portions of a library's activity. Rather, their efforts should be transferred increasingly from the more-routine and less-demanding parts of the library's operation to those portions of its work in which specialized personnel would be missed most severely.

If, for example, one can routinize totally the borrowing and return of books by means of an automatic electronic device that senses both an identifying card for the borrower and another for the volume, the resulting reduction in labor should not decrease the usefulness of the library to the borrower. Similarly, if a standard and uniform cataloging procedure could be agreed upon, with a set of cards (including, perhaps, standardized descriptive computer-punched cards) and other requisite materials supplied by the publisher along with the book, a substantial reduction in labor time at the library might be effected. Indeed, in this case the change might perhaps even constitute an improvement in service. For if authors were, as a matter of course, to supply a standardized description of their works on which card or computer cataloging could be based, then the danger of misclassification might be reduced significantly, particularly in the case of works in more specialized and technical areas.

Automation is then an appropriate, indeed an unavoidable, response to a shortage of librarians. However, its introduction requires a great deal of thought and analysis of the nature of library operation in order to plan the use of automated equipment in a way that minimizes any resulting reduction in the quality of library services. Though such a desideratum smacks of the platitudinous, it is in fact a very serious matter, for in the absence of such planning it is likely that the course of technological development will simply follow the line of least resistance—the design of new equipment will be ordered in accord with the ease with which the technical problems can be solved; and as the shortage of skilled personnel becomes more acute, libraries will be forced willy-nilly to adopt the labor-saving equipment that happens to be available, without regard to its consequences for quality of service. Only early study of these matters can provide the designers of library equipment with adequate guidelines to the library's needs and can thereby avoid forced utilization of devices that meet only very inadequately the needs of effective service.

The rising costs of library service are also highly relevant to the issue of automation. As has been seen earlier, a critical component in the cost problem is the high labor-content of library operation and the difficulty besetting reduction in utilization of this input. Since an inability to decrease the use of labor per unit-of-output is tantamount to failure to increase productivity, the unit cost of library service must increase constantly in relation to those of the remainder of the economy in which rising productivity is commonplace.

Automation may well constitute an effective means to deal with this problem. Although it may not eliminate the difficulty, it may render it far less critical. Even if the costs of the equipment are such that its immediate cost advantage is not very great, its long-run contribution to the library's cost problem may well be substantial. For any activity, once it has been taken over by the machine, loses its characterization as a personal service. Consequently, its labor content is no longer correlated directly with the quality of its output. Thereafter it becomes eligible for exactly the same sorts of increases in efficiency and increases in productivity as those from which the remainder of the economy constantly benefits. Thus, every library suboperation that can be automated becomes one less contributor to the fundamental long-run cost problem of the libraries—the continuous and cumulative rises in costs that inevitably characterize the supply of every personnel service output.

These, then, are two compelling grounds for the library to undertake the utilization of mechanical and electronic substitutes for human effort wherever it can be done without substantial reduction in quality of service. The assertion that current quality of output is as good as that which the machines can provide is not an effective answer, for in the long run unless one takes advantage of opportunities to reduce the utilization of labor, shortages of trained librarians and cumulative rises in costs may well cause a very serious deterioration in service that earlier planning and greater flexibility in mode of operation might have been able to avoid.

WHEN DOES A PIECE OF EQUIPMENT BECOME ECONOMICAL?

As a piece of electronic library equipment or some other instrument of automation becomes relatively less expensive, there is likely to come a point where its introduction becomes economical for some particular library. However, to those who have not specialized in this type of decision it may not be entirely clear how one determines when that point has been reached. Suppose a piece of equipment costs $100,000 and that it can be used to do the work of three employees whose combined annual income is $20,000. Is the purchase of the machine a cost-saving decision? The two figures by themselves do not provide the answer, for the long-term capital expenditure of $100,000 on the machine is not directly comparable with an outlay of $20,000 per annum. It would, for example, be wrong to estimate that the machine is expected to last six years and is therefore economical because it saves $120,000 in salary payments. Such a crude comparison makes no allowance for uncertainty about the expected future life of the machine, which might unexpectedly break down or be rendered obsolete by a new invention before the six-year period is over. It also makes no provision for inconvenience caused by the tying up of so much money in the machine, funds which the library might otherwise have put to good use.

Rather sophisticated methods of calculation have been devised to deal with this sort of decision, methods that are described in books dealing with capital budgeting.[24] However, for those who have neither the time nor the inclination to go into this matter in detail, there is available a direct and simple approach to the matter. Most computers and many other pieces of equipment are available on a rental basis. Whether the library

24 *For a brief but somewhat mathematical discussion see W. J. Baumol,* Economic Theory and Operations Analysis *(2nd ed.; Englewood Cliffs, N.J.: Prentice-Hall, 1965), chap. 18, secs. 9, 11; chap. 19, secs. 2–8.*

considering the item wishes to rent or buy the item is not the issue. The point is that the annual rental cost of a machine is (if calculated correctly by its supplier) the annual equivalent of the item's total value. It is this annual rent which should, therefore, be compared with the potential saving promised by the item. If the machine described in our previous illustration rents for $15,000 per annum, its purchase would represent a net saving to the library because it avoids the annual outlay of $20,000 in salaries. On the other hand, if the annual rental were $30,000, the machine would represent no net financial gain (though it might perhaps still be worth purchasing on other grounds—if it represented a net addition to the services of the library valued at more than the $10,000 net increase in expenditures it incurred).

ALTERNATIVE INSTRUMENTS OF AUTOMATION: IMPROVED SERVICE

As yet the employment of automation by libraries has been relatively limited. A number of experiments involving particular portions of library operation have been reported, and apparently, only in a very few cases is a really major modification in operation even imminent.[25]

Some of the discussion, on the other hand, has been far less conservative. For example, some degree of attention has been attracted by the systems approach, in which the entire library operation is viewed as a sequential process and is subjected throughout to the ministrations of the computer. In the words of William Dix:

> It seems possible to have the computer play a major role in the entire process of adding a book to the collections, from the moment a decision is made to acquire the book until the book is on the shelf and the bibliographic record fully available in the on-line computer store. From the beginning of the process with the search to make sure that the book is not already in the library, a record can be fed into the computer and, taking advantage of the efficiency of the computer in accepting additions and revisions, this record can be perfected progressively. During this process the computer can prepare the order for the dealer, check on outstanding orders, keep the rather complex financial records, accumulate and organize the various elements of descriptive and subject cataloging and classification, prepare book labels and book cards, and produce various cards and lists as required, such as selective lists of new acquisitions. This enumeration is by no means complete.
>
> The computer cannot perform the intellectual operations of cataloging. It can, however, do a great many file-keeping and clerical operations for which it is increasingly difficult in all libraries to find competent personnel. It can do some of these internal library operations better than they are now being done. No one seems prepared at this time to say with certainty that the computer will perform these operations more inexpensively than they are now being done.
>
> It should be emphasized at this point that no large university library has a computer-based system of the sort which I have sketchily outlined now in full operation. Various elements of it are being tried on an experimental basis in individual libraries.[26]

The authors of the present report have no special competence for a detailed examination of the technology and its potential areas of application. Yet economics does provide the basis for a number of observations that may prove helpful to those involved in planning and decision-making. The following discussion is intended to confine itself to such areas. It is convenient for this purpose to divide the proposed innovations into two categories: those that promise reductions in cost and those that offer improvements in

---

25 *For an illuminating survey by a visitor from abroad see Harrison Brian, "American Automation in Action,"* Library Journal, *January 15, 1967. The article includes a brief discussion of the Florida Atlantic Experiment, the case where automation seems to have gone as far as it has anywhere, and discusses the plans and experiences of a considerable number of other institutions.*

26 *William S. Dix, "Annual Report of the Librarian, Year Ending June 30, 1966," (mimeographed, Princeton University Library, reissued with minor revisions November 1966). This report contains a very valuable survey and evaluation of the various aspects of automation in the library.*

the quality of library service. However, it should be recognized that the distinction between the two classes is somewhat artificial. A modification in technology that makes possible an increase in service, *ceteris paribus,* by definition will also normally permit a decrease in cost that requires no commensurate reduction in the quality of service provided. For example, a procedure that reduces the cost per circulation by 20 percent would permit either a 20 percent increase in level of operation without any expansion in outlays or, alternatively, a 20 percent reduction in the level of service.

Nevertheless, it is possible to list a number of proposed innovations, particularly those involving the use of computers, whose primary rationale is not reduction in cost but an improvement in the usefulness of library operations.

One promising application of computers of this variety is their use in interlibrary loans, though this is probably a development for the very distant future. If it becomes practicable to store a library's catalog information in some sort of computer memory, the linkages among the computers employed by different libraries could be utilized to determine quickly where some particular item is to be found. The computers could then automatically forward the request for the interlibrary loan, provide the requisite records, and handle all the other relevant details with no delay except that involved in the physical transportation of the requested volume.

The most characteristic of the types of innovations whose primary purpose is to increase quality of operation is the use of computers to find pertinent references in a particular area of research. Here a determined effort is under way to find methods not to replace relatively unskilled labor but to obtain substitutes for the efforts of the most highly skilled librarians.

Ideally, computer memories would be asked to store information on a vast variety of subjects, each of which would be characterized by a limited number of key phrases. The scholar searching for references in some particular area could simply punch out the key words that describe his area of interest, and the computer's memory storage would then regurgitate everything that appeared to be pertinent. If such a system were put into operation, it might be hoped that the computer would be more effective in helping the scholar in his researches than anyone but the most highly skilled and specialized librarian.

Unfortunately, the facts suggest that such a goal may never be achieved, or if it is, it will be a very long time in coming. In essence, electronic computers are not the giant intelligences that the literature of science fiction sometimes alleges them to be. Rather, they are more felicitously characterized as extremely quick idiots capable of doing no more than is required by the instructions that have been fed to them in excruciating detail. As a result, computer compilations of reference materials are likely to include the products of serious misunderstanding of what happens to be required. Just as computer-produced translations are hopelessly literal and lacking in insight, the programmed response to a scholar's request for information in any particular field is likely to produce large amounts of redundancy resulting from misunderstanding of alternative denotations of words and phrases utilized in the instructions. Moreover, the computer's response may well omit some crucial references simply because it is incapable of grasping the over-tones of the information request.

These comments are not meant to imply that the computer cannot supply effective assistance to the work of the scholar. On the contrary, the evidence suggests overwhelm-ingly that it has already done so. What the observations mean is that the computer constitutes no real threat of technological unemployment for the skilled librarian. Rather, these specialized personnel may in the future require even more training and a higher level of specialization as the sophistication and complexity of library technology increase; for if they have to learn how to communicate with the electronic computer, they will also have to understand fully the nature of its limitations and the ways in which one can compensate for them.

In short, where the new technology undertakes to provide service relating to the most demanding requirements of library users, it cannot be expected to yield any significant reduction in costs. The computer may perhaps render the library an instrument of research that is even more useful than it is today. But this is apt to call for even more effort and training on the part of skilled librarians than has been provided in the past.

COST-SAVING INNOVATIONS

As has often proved true elsewhere in the economy, if innovations are really to make possible significant reductions in cost, their primary focus should be the relatively unskilled operations of the library rather than those calling for the highest levels of specialization and training. Thus they would relate to comparatively routine operations such as the recording of a loan, or even the cataloging of a newly acquired book, rather than the search for the reference imperfectly identified by a scholar. An activity that requires no specialized training is by that very fact a prime candidate for mechanization.

Spotty evidence suggests that even those innovations that fall under this heading are by and large uneconomic for the moment. Electronic equipment in general and computer time, together with the preparation of the pertinent software (the required auxiliary instructions), are still usually more expensive than the corresponding human effort. But, as has already been indicated, this relationship is not likely to continue indefinitely. In real terms, the computer effort may be expected to become relatively cheaper and the human effort more expensive, so that planning based upon reasonable expectations must prepare for the substitution of equipment for comparatively unskilled labor wherever this seems a reasonable possibility.

From the point of view of the outsider who is not aware of their nuances, the most routine portions of library activity proper include check-out operations, calculation and billing of fines, shelving of returned volumes, and at least some aspects of cataloging. In addition, library operations include a variety of routine activities that are not peculiarly related to an area of specialization; e.g., budgeting, accounting, and building maintenance.

CONCLUDING COMMENT

The study reported here as sections A–D of chapter 5 has examined in considerable detail a number of aspects of the economic structure of the library. It has made no attempt to provide an exhaustive survey of all phases of library activity but has sought to focus instead on those matters relating to important current and prospective policy issues. The data have related almost exclusively to two important classes of libraries: the public libraries and the college and university libraries. The discussion has been confined to these institutions simply because virtually no information was available about other classes of libraries—indeed the data for the types of institutions the study group did examine proved extremely difficult to acquire.

Nevertheless, we were able to investigate a considerable variety of economic issues, among them considerations relating to automation, the role of economies of scale, the prospects for funding from various sources, the compensation of librarians, and above all, the nature of library costs. The last of these topics was examined in some detail and provided the subject of a more extensive analysis. It was shown that in the nature of library technology as currently constituted, cumulatively rising relative costs per unit-of-service are an unavoidable consequence. To some extent this can be offset in the long run by automation. But it means also that those who provide financial support to libraries—the governments, the institutions, and the individuals—must learn that this entails a dynamic responsibility, that as the wealth of the economy grows, the financial needs of libraries will unavoidably also increase. Unless this is generally recognized and understood, the nation's libraries are likely to find themselves plagued by financial pressures that might well have been avoided.

TABLE 5D-1

EXPERIENCE FORMULAS FOR PUBLIC LIBRARY SIZE AND COSTS*

CITY POPULATION	BOOK STOCK PER CAPITA	SEATS PER 1000 POP.	CIRCULATION PER CAPITA	TOTAL SQ. FT. PER CAPITA	DESIRABLE 1ST FLOOR SQ. FT. PER CAPITA	1961 EST. COST PER CAPITA	COST PER UNIT CIRCULATION
Under 10,000	3½–5	10	10	.7 –.8	.5 –.7	$15	$1.50
10,000–35,000	2¾–3	5	9½	.6 –.65	.4 –.45	12	1.30
35,000–100,000	2½–2¾	3	9	.5 –.6	.25–.3	10	1.10
100,000–200,000	1¾–2	2	8	.4 –.5	.15–.2	9	1.10
200,000–500,000	1½	1¼	7	.35–.4	.1 –.125	7	1.00
500,000 + over	1 –1¼	1	6½	.3	.06–.08	6	0.90

*Without furnishings (add 15 percent) or air-conditioning (add 10 percent). These figures originally based on 1940 conditions, now increased to reflect larger book stocks. Floor space reduced because of economies.

SOURCE: *Joseph L. Wheeler and Herbert Goldhor, Practical Administration of Public Libraries (New York: Harper and Row, 1962), p. 554.*

FIGURE 5D–1

CIRCULATION VS. LABOR USED IN PUBLIC LIBRARIES

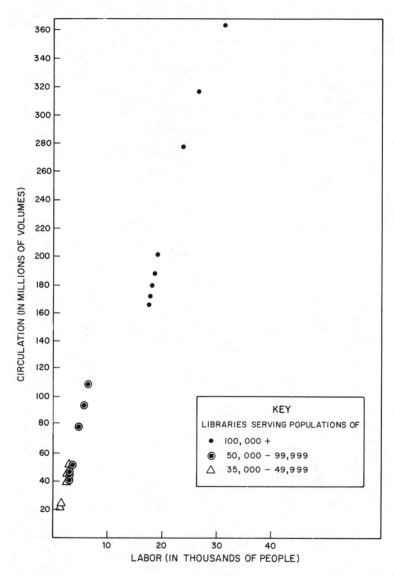

SOURCE: *See footnote 23.*

FIGURE 5D–2

CIRCULATION VS. TOTAL NUMBER OF BOOKS IN PUBLIC LIBRARIES

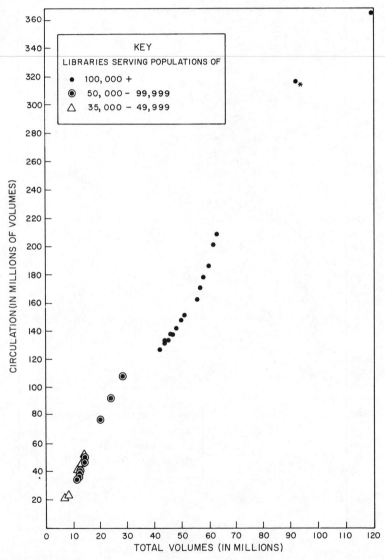

SOURCE: *See footnote 23.*

* Change in sample

FIGURE 5D–3

LABOR USED VS. TOTAL NUMBER OF BOOKS IN PUBLIC LIBRARIES

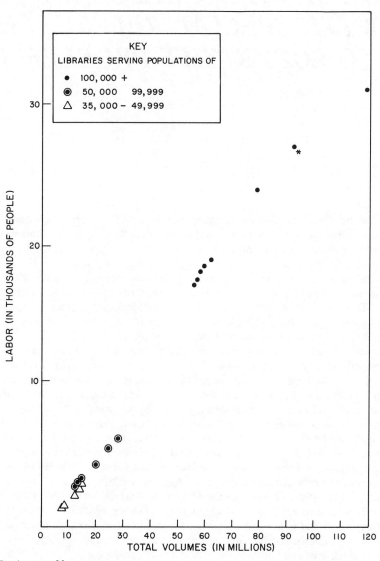

SOURCE: *See footnote 23.*

* Change in sample

CHAPTER VI

THE AVAILABILITY OF LIBRARY AND INFORMATIONAL SERVICES WITH SPECIAL REFERENCE TO COPYRIGHT PROBLEMS

As has been seen in chapter 4, many of the nation's current inadequacies in the provision of library and informational services manifest themselves as problems of access to information about the availability of materials and problems of access to the content itself in whatever physical form it may be stored. Getting the right material to the right place at the right time is a pervasive challenge to those serving all users of library and informational services—from the grass-roots private citizen to the most esoteric research scientist. This issue of access is basic to the national policy recommended by the National Advisory Commission on Libraries: ". . . that the American people should be provided with library and informational services adequate to their needs."

Current difficulties involving access to information and the present law of copyright and proposed revision thereof, particularly in view of new copying and storage and retrieval techniques, have occasioned so much discussion and attention that the National Advisory Commission on Libraries decided not to focus a major part of its effort on a constellation of problems that were being studied by so many others. Thus, outside of the statement that arrangements for the protection of copyright proprietors should not unreasonably hinder access to and use of information (see chapter 12, section C), the Commission's Report did not make any recommendations about copyright issues. For purposes of this book, however, it is important to state some of these issues and describe the current controversy and the nature of the ongoing problem.

Chapter 6 consists of three sections: section A is an overview of the copyright situation by a professor of law, which appeared in one of the Commission's special studies; sections B and C are papers written for this book by Commission members who are particularly knowledgeable and bring a rich background of experience to their analyses of proprietor and librarian views of copyright problems.

A. COPYRIGHT: AN OVERVIEW [1]

by RALPH S. BROWN, JR.
Simeon E. Baldwin Professor of Law
Yale Law School

Troublesome issues have developed because of the availability of cheap and easy reproduction of all kinds of documents, either by copying techniques that are already well advanced or by electronic storage and retrieval, the application of which to library collections may be imminent. Much of the copying that these technologies permit or require may call for clearance and payments in order to avoid copyright infringement. Clearance and payments, in the modern setting, are burdensome. What is to be done?

Some resolution of the differences between copyright owners and library users should emerge from the general revision of the copyright law long pending in the Congress. A bill passed the House in April 1967. Prompt hearings in the Senate created a further opportunity to express opposition to parts of the bill that are claimed to be immoderately restrictive of reprographic copying and computer services. Such opposition had been relatively tardy in making itself heard, when one considers that draft bills have been circulating since 1961. But now the complaints have reached senatorial ears. The first response of Senator John L. McClellan, chairman of the relevant Senate subcommittee, took the form of S. 2216, introduced on August 2, 1967, to create a National Commission on New Technological Uses of Copyrighted Works.

The statement of purpose of S. 2216 was close to the major copyright concerns of libraries, particularly research libraries:

The purpose of the Commission is to study and compile data on the reproduction and use of copyrighted works of authorship (1) in automatic systems capable of storing, processing, retrieving, and transferring information, and (2) by various forms of machine reproduction. The Commission shall make recommendations as to such changes in copyright law or procedures that may be necessary to assure for such purposes access to copyrighted works, and to provide recognition of the rights of copyright owners.

But nothing came of the proposal for a commission. And, when other opposition to the revision hardened, Senator McClellan in May 1968 decreed that the whole enterprise would have to go on to the new Congress in 1969.[2] The issues abide.

REPROGRAPHY

The legal status of reprography (photocopying plus other copying methods that do not technically involve photographic processes) and of computer use differ somewhat and should be separately summarized.

The extent of permissible copying of copyrighted documents for scholarly purposes is not a new problem. The concept of fair use of copyrighted materials has long been assumed to permit the hand copying of excerpts from copyrighted works by researchers. The arduous nature of manual copying tended to establish its own limits. If the researcher then, as an author, reproduced such excerpts in his own published work, with

---

1 *From* On Research Libraries *by the Committee on Research Libraries of the American Council of Learned Societies; submitted to the National Advisory Commission on Libraries November 1967. The complete study,* On Research Libraries, *was published by the M.I.T. Press in 1969.*
2 Congressional Record, *May 22, 1968, p. S6127.*

or without quotation or attribution, the notion of fair use again came into play. Although its contours were vague, judicial definition and agreements among publishers, such as the Resolution on Permissions of the Association of American University Presses, made the rules workable.

The development of photocopying, from beginnings more than half a century ago, brushed aside the constraints of hand copying. For libraries that furnish or use photocopies, appropriate limits have never been firmly resolved, despite such efforts as the Gentlemen's Agreement of 1935 and subsequent attempts by the American Library Association to gain recognition for the practice of furnishing single copies to scholars, either of parts of a work or of the entire work (with certain qualifications relating to its commercial availability). Libraries stated their position before the House Committee that shaped the present general revision bill. They all, I believe, favored wide leeway; some thought that there should be a statutory definition, others preferred the conclusion reached by the committee, which in its 1967 Report said that it "does not favor a specific provision dealing with library photocopying."[3]

Meanwhile, the photocopying flood was upon us. In libraries as well as in educational institutions generally, copying goes on that would not be legally permissible under conventional criteria of fair use. At the same time, some surveys that were made tended to show that the bulk of photocopying was from scholarly journals and that, up to the present time, such copying served the cause of increased dissemination of research work, especially in the sciences, and did not appear to be causing serious economic harm to the journals from which copies were being made.

But even if the surveys accurately reflected the situation in the early 1960's, it was rapidly changing as reprographic methods became ever better and cheaper. By 1966 the ineffable Marshall McLuhan had already proclaimed that "In the age of Xerox, the reader becomes a publisher." Professor Marke, who quotes this dictum, adds a pointed comment: "In essence, this is exactly what commercial publishers fear."[4] And it is not only the commercial publishers—university presses and other nonprofit publishers have a similar concern.

The general question then becomes: How should the moderately elastic doctrine of fair use, or even the principle of copyright itself, adjust to the reprographic explosion, one of the many explosions of our time? Before suggesting partial answers to this question, let us first consider the situation with respect to computers.

COMPUTERS

Any current problem that is not an explosion is a revolution. The potentialities of electronic storage and retrieval of information may indeed revolutionize publishing, libraries, and reading.

Copyright law has not yet taken on the computer. The Copyright Office is accepting computer programs (that is, instructions for getting data in and out of computers) as copyrightable material, but that practice rests on shaky support in the present law and has little significance until it is tested in the courts. For libraries, the recognition of exclusive rights in programs, whether by copyright or by patent, would also be troublesome; but I doubt that protection will extend beyond the detailed expression of particular programs. In any event, this subject will not be dealt with in this paper.[5]

The burning question is the status of computer inputs and outputs of copyrighted

---

3 H. R. Report No. 83, 90th Congress. 1st Session, p. 36.
4 J. Marke, Copyright and Intellectual Property (Fund for the Advancement of Education, 1967), p. 72.
5 Consult J. F. Banzhaf, "Copyright Protection for Computer Programs," 64 Columbia Law Review, 1274 (1964), also in ASCAP Copyright Law Symposium, No. 14 (1966), p. 118; A. Miller and B. Kaplan, "The Copyright Revision Bill in Relation to Computers," Interuniversity Communications Council (EDUCOM), 10 Communications of the ACM, No. 5 (May 1967), p. 318.

material, however they are programmed. Some legal conclusions can be baldly stated with respect to the present state of the law and the general revision in its current form.

A computer print-out of a copyrighted text or a substantial part of a text is an infringing copy unless it falls within the scope of fair use. There is no reason to think that fair use should be differently defined for computer "hard" copies, even though the computer is undiscriminating, tireless, and prolix. The revision bill does not alter this situation.

Suppose that a computer produces a rearrangement of significant parts of the copyrighted work (assuming that what is produced is from the "expression" of the author and not simply his "ideas" or "information"—terms that also embrace a large set of issues). For example, say the computer is directed to extract and rearrange all the references to marriage customs from a book on Polynesia. This will probably infringe the copyright owner's exclusive right to "translate the copyrighted work into other languages or dialects, or make any other version thereof, if it be a literary work. . . ." "Literary" in this setting does not have any esthetic content; it is simply a way of distinguishing musical works, works of art, etc. (sec. 1 [a]; cf. sec. 7). The general revision bill removes most definitional ambiguities by giving the author an exclusive right "to prepare derivative works based upon the copyrighted work," keyed to a generous definition of "derivative works," which embraces "any other form in which a work may be recast, transformed, or adapted" (secs. 106, 101). It has a marginally broader reach than the present law.

Suppose that a retrieval system, instead of making a print-out, shows the whole or a significant portion of the work on a screen, either in the library or in a researcher's office (for present purposes I am ignoring the more difficult questions of classroom and other like displays). Under the present law this is probably not an infringement. The act doesn't address itself specifically to transitory displays, only to exhibits or representations, which may not be the same thing. It could be argued that a projection is just a reading aid; it is the usual way of reading microfilm. But if the retrieval input had not been authorized, a court sympathetic to authors could declare that the display infringed, as a kind of ephemeral copying.

The revision bill is again clarifying, in that the copyright owner would indeed have the exclusive right "to display the copyrighted work publicly" (sec. 106).[6] "Display" is adequately defined. Discussion about the new display right has centered more on classroom and other student use of teaching materials than on the needs of research libraries. Discrimination is called for, to avoid any unintended restraints on transiently showing parts of the work, as by a research scanning technique, comparable to leafing through a book.

Practically, ephemeral projections from photocopies and from computers should be treated alike, with considerable scope for fair use and a library privilege of display to researchers if the work displayed is legitimately in the possession of the library. Sec. 109 (b) of the House bill partly—but only partly—meets this need. It exempts a display to a viewer "present at the place where the copy is located."[7]

This brings us to the status of computer inputs for storage (what is functionally first has been intentionally put last in this summary because it involves the sharpest controversy). In my opinion, under the present law input and storage, without more, are not infringement. Conventionally, to copy a visually perceptible work requires the production of a visually perceptible equivalent. A 1952 amendment to the statute did prohibit

---

6 *No comfort should be sought from the word "publicly." As defined (sec. 101), it would cover an on-demand scanning device. See H. R. Report No. 83, 90th Congress, 1st Session, pp. 28–29, 31 (1967).*
7 *Does the "place where" include the Widener Library? The Harvard campus? A faculty member's on-line study in Lexington? Probably only the first; see Report No. 83, p. 39. This seems unduly confining. The narrow exemption is influenced by the disputes about radio and television transmissions, and other classroom displays, which are very complicated. Ibid., pp. 40–46.*

the making of "any transcription or record" of a copyrighted work from which it could "by any method be exhibited, delivered, presented, produced, or reproduced" (sec. 1 [c]). But it is doubtful that this language, which is in a passage directed to the *oral* presentation of copyrighted work *for profit*, was intended to cover the invisible electrical imprints inside a computer.[8]

Whatever the uncertainties of the present law, there is little question that the House bill intends to make input a form of copying. This results from the otherwise commendable departure in the new bill from the old requirement that a copy be tangible and intelligible. The revision bill defines a copy as a "material object" (e.g., a magnetic tape) "from which the work can be perceived, reproduced, or otherwise communicated, either directly or with the aid of a machine or device" (sec. 101).

The interesting question is not what is proposed, but why. Although there has been little sustained discussion, copyright spokesmen are insistent that computer input should be controlled; computer spokesmen are equally insistent that it should not be. Why do publishers want to control what goes into the storage system if they can control what comes out? The answer lies partly in the "if." Publishers argue that they will not be able to police the output of computerized systems, just as they fear the present proliferation of photocopying machines. A partial rejoinder to this fear is that you cannot hide a complex storage and retrieval system in a closet. Further, it is hard to imagine how a price could be set on inputs, unless both parties had a fairly clear idea of what use was to be made of the stored work. To be sure, some value could be attached to the availability of the work in the system. This raises the possibility that copyright owners hope to exact a charge for what would otherwise be fair use of the work; for example, to search it for particular ideas or bits of data that would ordinarily be open to use without permission.

One may also speculate that publishers, faced with the great unknown of the effect of future systems on the market for conventional printed works, want to get control of the use of their works in the new technology at the earliest possible stage. By the same token, those who are engaged in fashioning the brave new world want to be free of such controls until they produce copies or displays that would fall within the scope of copyright as hitherto understood. And perhaps they want to have even greater freedom. This leads to consideration of the emerging clash of attitudes about copyright.

OPPOSED POSITIONS

Behind the skirmish lines, sniping away from one outpost or another, two main bodies of opinion may be forming. The martial analogy is closer to Vietnam than to Waterloo, but two main-force positions can be identified amidst the swirl of debate.

One position (stated here in extreme terms) views copyright as an obstruction on the path of progress. It may be a manageable system for recognizing rights in the entertainment industries, but it should not be permitted to slow down the magnificent advance of science, education, and research libraries. Research libraries exist to serve the scholarly community. They now have within their reach devices for finding and transmitting knowledge (by way of copies of documents) that are quite incompatible with the clumsy necessities of identifying a copyright holder and obtaining his permission. The cost of the permission, and even more the cost of obtaining it and the time it takes, threaten to block the free flow of information.

Therefore, copyright is obsolescent. The producers of knowledge have other sources of support anyhow. To the extent that a replacement for the rewards of copyright is needed, let the Government subsidize authorship as it is subsidizing education. We observe this happening on a large scale, first in natural science and now in educational

---

8 *It is also argued, I believe, that putting a written work into machine-readable form necessarily requires making a version of it. This is an ingenious contention, but it probably fails if the process results only in operations that are not visually readable. Thus, the distorted numbers on a bank check are readable, but card-punches or magnetic impressions are not.*

research itself. The policy of the Office of Education not to permit copyright in works supported by it is the right one, and should be extended.

If it is granted that this position cannot prevail, owing to the obstinate resistance of authors and publishers, then the system will be tolerable only if the publishers organize a system of clearances that will keep the use of copyrighted materials in reprography and computers speedy, cheap, and easy.

The contrary view—standing on hard-won and long-held high ground—sees copyright as a minimal expression of the natural right of an author to deal as he will with his own intellectual creation. It is a right that has constitutional recognition. A reasonable statutory framework permits creative authors through their agents, usually publishers, to control any reproduction of their work. A wise policy permits the free use of ideas; but the author's expression, mixed as it is with his labor, is his to exploit. Those who want copies must pay for them, just as they do for the hardware they use to make the copies.

As a concession, if the volume and variety of desired copying make it difficult to seek out the author, then it is up to the users to develop a scheme that will keep copying easy. Since they are probably destroying the normal sources of income for the author, there is no reason for users to expect that their machine copying will be cheap.

PARTIAL SOLUTIONS

It soon becomes apparent, when one attempts to use either of these polar positions as a basis for action, that neither can be uniformly applicable. That part of the copyright world which is of special concern to research libraries is only one of several continents. And within that continent there are subareas where varying considerations apply. I will give only two examples.

One is the status of scientific papers, ordinarily published in one of the thousands of specialized journals. There has been much talk and even some investigation of copyright as a hindrance to extensive machine copying. Assertions that authors of scientific papers have no expectations of commercial exploitation through copyright seem altogether plausible. If there is no strong copyright interest, there is a fairly simple solution. Instead of pushing legal measures to make copyright ineffective, why shouldn't we persuade scientific authors not to claim copyright? Fortunately, an effort to make copyright automatic (without any claim by notice or registration) has had no success in the revision efforts. While it is easy to get copyright, it is just as easy to put one's work in the public domain.

Librarians might well consider launching a campaign for abstention from copyright, or for limited copyright, in scholarly publications. An example of what I call limited copyright comes, appropriately enough, from the volume reporting a useful symposium on Reprography and Copyright Law. Its copyright notice reads as follows:

Copyright, 1964, by George P. Bush

George P. Bush will not enforce his copyright after January 1, 1970. Permission to copy the whole or part of this document is hereby granted to those who wish to use such copies in educational works, professional journals, as well as in an information handling storage or retrieval system. Permission to others to copy is governed by "Fair Use."[9]

This sort of limited claim to copyright could, through the efforts of librarians and others, be codified in two or three standard categories. These could then be identified by simple symbols. This is not the place to develop such a scheme, but it does illustrate that copyright need not be an all-or-nothing affair.

One difficulty with the abandonment of copyright is the lack of other adequate legal controls against fraudulent copying (taking and misrepresenting another's work as one's

[9] L. Hattery and G. Bush (eds.), Reprography and Copyright Law, American Institute of Biological Sciences, 1964 (papers from a 1963 symposium at American University).

own), and the similarly imperfect state of the law in respect to assigning proper credit when avowedly borrowing the work of others (one aspect of the notions embraced in "moral right"). If the statutory system were not so obsessed with perfecting and tightening copyright, it would pay more attention to these intermediate kinds of protection. But there is some possibility of achieving them through voluntary action if there does exist the claimed consensus within the scientific community about the free dissemination of scientific papers—a consensus, one might observe, that surely does not obtain with respect to texts and other works that can earn royalties.

What has just been said ignores the economics of journal publishing. Many journals are entirely supported by subscriptions, most of which come from libraries. Others are partly subsidized by sponsoring societies, etc. Although it may be that up until now machine copying has led to no decline in subscription revenues, when one looks further ahead, great changes are in prospect. The visions of an on-demand reproduction system can carry one to the point where only one copy of a work need be acquired for a regional system comprehending scores of libraries as we now know them. Looking even further ahead, we are asked to consider why even one copy, in any conventional format, is necessary. The thoughts of an author may be composed directly on microfilm or magnetic tape (exposing us all to the unedited outpourings of ubiquitous dictating units!).

As we approach these transformations, the whole institution of publishing will have to be reconstructed, and copyright along with it.

If scientific journals may be an example of a consensual solution, my second example clearly is not. Briefly, it concerns the Educational Research Information Center (ERIC) of the Office of Education. ERIC has doubtlessly laudable aims. But (this is from a partisan account, a publisher's) ERIC has been seeking blanket permissions to microfilm quantities of educational titles that are commercially published—without offering compensation.[10] If the publishers are cold to these requests, they may not be unreasonably so. The magic words "education," "research," and "microfilm" are no substitute for sales of the books. If ERIC is going to distribute fifty copies to state boards of education, why doesn't it buy fifty copies?

This episode is incomplete. Some accommodation may have been found, and one should withhold final judgment. It does seem to represent a fairly clear collision of interests. It could be resolved by legislation; it might be more easily resolved by compensation, that is, by simply paying for what is taken.

CLEARINGHOUSE PROPOSALS

A discussion of compensation for machine reproduction leads quickly to consideration of general licensing arrangements. Some kind of central clearinghouse is variously seen as a panacea or as a monstrosity which, in one publisher's words, spends "dollars to collect dimes."

Licensing and clearing arrangements need much more detailed examination than they have so far received. We already have long-standing and elaborate arrangements for the licensing of public performance of copyrighted music, through the American Society of Composers, Authors, and Publishers (ASCAP) and other performing-rights organizations, especially Broadcast Music, Inc. (BMI). These will serve as a guide but not as a model. ASCAP deals with something transient—a performance—but detectability is made less difficult because it is only *public* performances for profit that are to be licensed. The bulk of ASCAP's revenues come from a few large users, the broadcasting networks; large computer networks may turn out to be similarly visible. ASCAP also tries to police a tangled fringe of small users; this experience has some bearing on the photocopying market.

10 C. Benjamin, "Computers, Copyrights and Educators," *address June 19, 1967.*

At this stage, however, we have no data on which to begin to construct charges for blanket licensing of an entire repertory, as ASCAP does. A blanket license still requires a way to meter copying, either totally or through a good sample, in order to provide a basis for distribution among the copyright holders. It is the prospect of recording and reporting copying of all shapes and sizes that stimulates fears of costly obstructions to rational retrieval systems. Is it thinkable that the ingenuity that can produce computer systems cannot build into them copyright-metering devices? A copyright reference can permeate a computer input just as thoroughly as does the identity of the work. In reprography of parts of a copyrighted document identification of copyright claims may be more difficult. Still, microcopying must be similar to computer storage, in that the identity of the work presumably appears on each card or microfiche. Copyright data can go along with it.

Casual photocopying on the office Xerox may not be controllable. The proposal for a licensing scheme in which payment would be made through adhesive stamps seems curiously archaic in an electronic age.

Another major aspect of centralized licensing that has not been adequately explored is the probable need for some degree of public regulation. Again the ASCAP and BMI experience is illustrative. When there is a massive pooling of copyrights on the publishers' side, even if (indeed, especially if) the publishers are confronted with an alliance of users, the antitrust laws cannot be ignored. ASCAP, and to a lesser extent BMI, have been subject to regulation of their rates and practices since 1941. It is a curious form of regulation, with the Antitrust Division of the Department of Justice as the watchdog and the Federal courts as sometimes ill-equipped enforcers. Antitrust consent decrees are the source of standards for regulation. There are no statutory criteria at all, except the underlying sanctions of the antitrust laws, which are intended to maintain competition not to regulate monopolies.

WHERE NEXT?

For libraries, particularly research libraries, as they rethink their mission and calculate the resources needed for it, the new technologies loom large. They are going to be costly, and anything that adds to their cost is understandably disfavored. Clearing and paying for copyright permissions are so stigmatized.

It seems to me that compensation for authors and publishers, now underwritten by the institution of copyright, is not properly viewed as a parasitic charge. It has always been part of the cost of maintaining libraries in modern times, as part of the price of the book. To the extent that the new technologies make some of the functions of publishers redundant, for example the manufacture and distribution of books, publishers have no claim to continued payments. They will have to see if they can compete in the manufacture and distribution of microfiches and tapes. But machine authorship and editing are beyond present horizons. Those are the creative and ordering functions that have to be supported somehow. Increasing, preserving, and diffusing knowledge all have their costs that have to be faced and somehow fairly apportioned.

Legislative action can and does powerfully affect these apportionments. Thus, the present law, by protecting public performances of music and other nondramatic works only when they are "for profit," creates a sector of free use for educational institutions (but there is not and never has been a blanket exemption for nonprofit users). In the current enterprise there is considerable and justified irritation with the copyright interests, who appear to be chiefly concerned with enlarging their rights and to be giving very little constructive thought to the new era. (On their part, they complain that educational users particularly are simply demanding exemptions that cut down copyright, and likewise are not seeking ways of accommodation.) When one looks again at the copyright revision proposals, the impression does emerge that there is a lot in them for the authors and publishers, and not much for the consumer. The substantial extension in duration of copyrights (on the average, 50 percent) is the most conspicuous example.

But such irritants (or worse) should not obscure what seems to me the main consideration. The new technologies, with their speed and abundance, raise formidable challenges of convenience and efficiency to the copyright system. The costs of clearance, that is, of obtaining information about claims to copyright, must be brought down, and the costs of using copyright works bargained out. That is where the main effort is needed. I should, however, reiterate that these exhortations are not intended to imply that the legal posture is unimportant. Clearly, one interest or another can be powerfully preferred by the grant or denial of the revision enterprise (which, on technical grounds, is sorely needed). The Congress, in the troubled fields here reviewed, must for a while attempt the difficult feat of standing still on a tightrope.

B. COPYRIGHT:
A PROPRIETOR'S VIEW

by DAN LACY[11]
Senior Vice President
McGraw-Hill Book Company

The preceding section has outlined the general dimensions of the copyright dilemma in this era of social and technological change and this period of legislative review. The purpose of this paper, written from one proprietor's vantage point, is to illustrate some frequently obscured but genuinely basic commonalties in the objectives of authors and publishers on the one hand and librarians on the other, within the context of broad social responsibility rather than immediate controversy.

As has been seen in section A, the Congress for the past four years has had under consideration a bill that, if enacted, will provide the first comprehensive revision of the United States copyright law since 1909. However, many if not most of the principal changes proposed in this bill have little bearing on problems of library service, since they relate primarily to the recording and performance of music. Indeed, the bill proposes no changes in the law, or in the effect of the law, in most areas of principal importance to libraries. In areas that are relevant the response of proprietary groups is frequently consistent with that of library groups. Proprietary groups have joined with librarians to support the continuation of the present exemption of libraries from import restrictions in the bill; proprietors' groups have not sought the insertion in the bill of any public lending right, requiring the payment of a royalty on library circulation, such as appears in the copyright law of a number of European countries; proprietors' groups as well as librarians have supported the continued requirement of deposit of copies of copyrighted works in the Library of Congress.

On the crucial issue of library photocopying the position of the American Library Association and other library groups throughout the hearings in the House and Senate

---

11 AUTHOR'S NOTE: *Although I have had rather extensive opportunities to become familiar with the viewpoints of proprietors generally on copyright, this essay is entirely personal and does not profess to speak for proprietors generally, or for publishers generally, or for the American Book Publishers Council, or for the McGraw-Hill Book Company. Indeed, it is probable that no single statement could be made about copyright that would truly reflect the views of all book publishers, much less of all proprietors. This paper was specially written for this book in 1968.*

had been that they wished the new bill to deal with the subject only in terms of the doctrine of fair use. Proprietary groups made it clear that they desired in no way to reduce or constrict freedoms enjoyed by libraries under the present law, and joined with librarians and other user groups in supporting the language on fair use in the revision bill as it passed the House of Representatives. This language stated that the doctrine of fair use as developed over a century and a quarter by the courts was fully applicable to library photocopying, which had not been specifically dealt with by the courts.

In general, the record shows that the objectives of proprietary groups (authors, composers, and publishers) appear to be substantially identical with those of libraries and their users. Both want to achieve a maximum availability and use of copyrighted works; both want to minimize the burdens of red tape in connection with copyright clearances; both want to assure an equitable return to authors and composers for their work and to publishers for their investment and risk in order to provide an incentive for creation and publication. And, as the foregoing summary indicates, both groups—beneath a good deal of rhetoric on both sides—did support very similar concrete positions in the House and Senate hearings.

ISSUES OF CONTROVERSY

The matter was not altogether so simple however. Librarians expressed a considerable concern about, though not definite opposition to, the provisions of the revision bill with respect to the term of copyright. Under present law copyright in published works exists for a term of 28 years from first publication, subject to renewal for a second 28-year term. Unpublished works, on the other hand, remain permanently under common-law copyright, except that certain works intended to be performed (e.g., plays, music, and songs) can be registered for Federal statutory copyright without publication. Such works have two 28-year terms, like published works, but dating from registration, rather than from publication.

The revision bill, however, puts all works, published and unpublished, under a single term of copyright. For works created after the law comes into effect, that term would extend for 50 years from the death of the author, and in the case of anonymous and corporate works, 75 years from the date of publication. Works already under Federal copyright would have 19 years added to their second term. The term of copyright under the new bill would hence differ from the term under the present law in three ways: it would be a *single* term; it would usually, though not always, be a *longer* term; and it would run from the death of the author rather than from date of first publication.

Librarians have been unhappy about the single term in the belief that it would uselessly keep under copyright vast numbers of works that would otherwise come into the public domain. Librarians place emphasis on the often-quoted estimate that copyrights are not renewed for a second term for 85 percent of the works originally copyrighted. Proprietors would point out, however, that most of this unrenewed 85 percent consists of never-published songs, advertisements, photographs, games, and other ephemera whose copyright status is of no significance, and furthermore that one who is concerned about the copyright status of a work originally copyrighted more than 28 and less than 56 years ago must assume that its copyright has been renewed, unless he is willing to accept the delay and expense involved in having a search made in the records of the Copyright Office. Hence the proposed elimination of renewals in itself would not only save a vast amount of useless paperwork and protect authors against the inadvertent loss of their rights, but also would not really keep under copyright any large number of significant works that users would otherwise know were in the public domain.

Less controversy has been engendered by the lengthened-term aspect than by the elimination of renewals. As mentioned above, the proposed revision would keep future published works under copyright law for a longer period than at present, unless the author should die within six years of the publication of a work, in which case, of course, the period would be actually shortened. Existing published works would all enjoy a lengthened term. Librarians and other users have not vigorously objected to the longer term as such—except sometimes to allege that it is a windfall to publishers, in exchange for which they should agree to concessions in other parts of the bill. In point of fact, the longer term is of relatively little benefit to book publishers. Few literary works survive as major income-producing properties for so long a period, and in any event the benefit of the additional period of protection accrues entirely to the author and not to the publisher or any other licensee of rights. The longer period is of much greater importance in the field of music, where many more works are long-lived. In view of the severe legal disadvantages under which authors and composers labor in comparison with those who invest their talents and efforts in less creative ways, and in view of the fact that the United States now offers to authors and composers a shorter term of protection than does any other developed non-Communist country in the world, the lengthening of the term seems a matter of simple equity.

It should also be pointed out that for unpublished works, now enjoying a perpetual copyright under the common law, the bill would provide a definite term after which they would pass into the public domain. This would provide an important benefit to librarians, archivists, and historians.

More disturbing to librarians than length per se has been the proposed substitution of a term dating from the death of the author for the present system of dating from the first publication of the work; critics often refer to this as replacing a "fixed" term by one that is "indefinite" or "indeterminate." This is a misnomer: one term is obviously as fixed as the other. The confusion rather arises from a belief that one can now easily determine the date of first publication, and hence of expiration of the copyright of a work, by reading the copyright notice in the copy at hand; it may be very difficult to determine the date of death of an obscure writer. Neither assumption can be wholly sustained. Many published works, including those most often copied, have been published in varying formats and editions and versions: in newspapers, magazines, books, and anthologies. They may have been revised many times, and one particular paragraph may be in the public domain while others in the same work, added later, may still be under copyright. For such works, and for anthologies, encyclopedias, and the like, it is simply impossible to determine from the copyright notice the date of first publication of any particular passage. It is far easier to determine the date of a poet's death than the true date of first publication of any one of his poems. Moreover, not until 2019 at the earliest would it be necessary to know the date of death of an author in order to determine the date of expiration of a copyright; by that time computerized vital statistics data will surely have solved the problem. The inconvenience to libraries of the proposed term would appear to be minimal; indeed the new system would often be more convenient, providing the library with one clear-cut date on which *all* the works of an author passed into the public domain and before which they were all under copyright.

More significant than other differences between librarians and proprietors are those relating to the application of copyright to reprography and to the use of copyrighted material in computerized information storage and retrieval systems. Both sides have agreed with respect to reprography that the doctrine of fair use as hitherto defined by the courts should continue to prevail. However, proprietors have opposed one amendment to the revision bill that librarians have sought: it would relieve librarians of liability for photocopying of materials in their collection done for and at the order of another, and from which the library did not itself benefit. Both groups have agreed that the present law should continue to govern the input of material into computers pending a proposed extensive study of copyright and new information technology to be undertaken by a Federal commission that would be created by another pending bill supported by all groups.

But this broad agreement on statutory language is probably made possible in part by disagreement as to what the language means. Libraries, while wishing not to damage authors and publishers, have wanted to be free to do whatever photocopying their clients asked for without having to concern themselves one way or another about the copyright law; proprietors, while wishing not to restrict the service of libraries or impede the work of scholars, have wanted the protection of a law that could be invoked when their interests were in fact damaged. In actual practice it is likely that most proprietors and most librarians would usually agree with respect to the "fairness" or "unfairness" of most uses of reprography. Probably almost all librarians would agree, for example, that it is improper for a library to make and sell, or give, or add to its collection, an entire volume or a discrete item (e.g., a map, photograph, motion picture, or piece of sheet music) that can be separately bought from the author, composer, other proprietor, or his licensee. Probably most librarians would also agree that to reproduce, as from a Xerox master, several dozen or hundred copies of a copyrighted poem, essay, or story for distribution to a class of students is similarly improper. On the other hand, probably almost all authors and publishers would agree that the kind of note-taking formerly done by hand and now done by reproducing individual pages or excerpts is normally an entirely fair use.

The most crucial point of difference between librarian and proprietor views would probably relate to the systematic duplication of recent journal articles on a large scale, providing a service on which recipients may rely in lieu of subscribing to the journal. Many librarians, at least, appear to conceive this to be a fair use; few proprietors would do so. A legal action now pending may throw light on this issue.

Recently the American Library Association has proposed two amendments to the copyright revision bill that relate to copying. One is intended to provide a statutory license for the making of replacement copies of physically deteriorating materials in a library's collection. The other relates to the liability of libraries in making copies for users. It professes no purpose to provide any greater freedom to copy but only to relieve the library of any liability for infringement as a result of the copying it does for its users; it is based on the assumption that responsibility should rest on him for whom the copy is made. Proprietary groups have taken no formal position with respect to the former amendment; probably a few would object to the copying involved for replacement purposes, but most would consider it under most circumstances as a fair use. Indeed libraries might well consider this stand, for the enactment of such an amendment might establish the implication that the fair-use principle is too narrow to extend to such copying, which might in fact be adverse to their interests. Proprietary groups, however, have violently opposed the other amendment, relating to the liability of libraries.

The opposition is based on the narrow conception of the proposed amendment. It imposes no limits as to the nature or amount of the material copied or as to the number of copies, except to state that the material copied shall be in the library's collections and that the library shall not benefit financially. Also, since the proposed amendment does nothing to impose on recipients the legal responsibilities of which it seeks to relieve libraries, it could have the effect of legalizing wholesale copying up to and including the nonprofit republication by a library of copyrighted materials in its collection. Undoubtedly nothing like this is really intended by the proponents of the amendment. What apparently is intended, however, neglects important issues, for the amendment is addressed only to the self-protection of libraries and not to the establishment of proper limits of photocopying. Thus, proprietary groups believe that the present proposal would seem to contribute little to the resolution of the basic question. [Since this paper was originally written, subsequent consideration and discussion have brought the positions of proprietors and librarians much closer on this point.]

ISSUES OF BROADER CHALLENGE

It is now apparent that no general copyright legislation will be enacted by the Ninetieth Congress. If the succeeding Congress does enact a revision bill, it also seems clear that it will neither forbid all library photocopying nor permit all such copying.

Under both the present law and any future law we shall all have to live with a situation in which necessarily imprecise boundaries separate the permissible from the impermissible. We shall need to exercise the maximum mutual goodwill and common sense to devise a workable system under the general provisions of the statute. The coming months before the Ninety-first Congress addresses itself to copyright revision give a welcome opportunity to attempt to arrive at such a common understanding. The commission to study copyright in relation to computers and similar devices will give an even more ample opportunity to work out constructive solutions in that area.

It is probable that both proprietors and librarians have taken too narrow a view of the problem. Proprietors have looked to their investment of funds and labor in the existing, usually printed, form of copyrighted works and have seen the problem in large part as one of being recompensed for a possible loss of income or royalties from their sale. Librarians and other users have been concerned with freedom to use new reprographic and information-handling techniques primarily as ancillary means of disseminating already-existing printed materials. The broader implications should not be forgotten, for the new technology in fact makes it possible to achieve an effective dissemination of many kinds of information to meet demands much too small to justify conventional printing, and to package information in new forms custom-designed to meet the needs of individual users or small groups of users.

From the point of view of society's needs, and quite aside from issues involving the rights of proprietors of existing works in their existing forms, there is a most important need to erect an adequate legal framework to provide incentives for investment in the new techniques. Uncontrolled freedom of libraries or others to employ reprography, computer document storage, and similar techniques without payment not only may do an injustice to those who have invested their labor and funds in writing and publishing the originals, but may seriously injure users by denying an incentive for the centralized and more efficient use of the same techniques. Some illustrations of this point follow.

Because the authors of doctoral dissertations have a copyright in their work and are willing to license University Microfilms to reproduce them, that firm has an incentive to make a central collection of films of such dissertations, to publish catalogs of them, and to provide microfilm or paper-print copies at reasonable prices, to the great advantage of users. In the absence of such an incentive such a service might never have been created, and users might have had to canvass the hundreds of institutions giving the doctorate to learn of relevant dissertations and to negotiate with perhaps dozens of libraries to get their copies in varying format and at more expensive prices.

The fact that libraries have felt free to provide photocopies of back issues of journals on demand, in contrast, has meant that no central organization has had an incentive to provide this service. Now if a scholar wants a copy of an article from, say, a 1947 issue of a journal not available in his library, he must first make inquiry as to what institutions have that volume and which are equipped to provide photocopies of what physical specifications at what price; having ascertained this, he must place an order and then await delivery according to the schedule for filling orders at that institution.

There would be obvious advantages if some central organization were prepared to offer this service for all or nearly all journals, necessarily in cooperation with a group of major research libraries. The concentration of this service would provide a flow of business of at least several hundred million pages of copy a year, which might be expected to grow soon to billions. With this volume of business the central organization could afford to put on microfilm all the files serviced and to automate its services so that positive-roll microfilm, or microfiche, or enlargements could be supplied much more cheaply and quickly than by the photoduplication services of most libraries. A modest royalty could be paid to the original journals to help bear the increasingly heavy cost of original publication.

Somewhat similar considerations apply to current journal issues. It is probable that for most purposes the individual article is a more useful unit than the journal issue or volume, and the newer information technology makes it increasingly feasible to deal with the individual article as the unit both for bibliographical control and for physical dissemination. It appears to be the case that in many institutions, academic and corporate, in which a library serves a number of diversified scholars, it has increasingly become the practice for a single subscription to a journal to be made to serve the entire group through the multiple photoduplication of individual articles to meet the varying needs of the library's clients. The recent survey by the Committee to Investigate Copyright Problems indicates that this sort of service probably represents the majority of all reprography of copyrighted material.[12] It appears to have resulted not only in a failure to achieve expected increases in circulation, but also in some cases in a decline in circulation of scientific, medical, and scholarly journals—even, it is claimed, to the point that their continued publication without subsidy is seriously threatened.

No one would want to prevent or delay the transition to the individual article, in contrast to the journal issue, as the primary unit for the dissemination of information of the sort published in journals if the character of the demand and the resources of reprographic and bibliographical technology make that the more efficient method. But two things are important: (1) that the users of material produced for them in the form of individual articles bear an equitable share of the costs of creating, editing, producing, and disseminating the material, so that those processes can be sustained, and (2) that the journal publishers themselves have an incentive to provide their material in unit form capable of being separately ordered if that is the way many scholars and other users would prefer to have it. Under present practices publishers are actively *discouraged* from offering a service that might be very useful to the academic community and might relieve libraries of a burdensome nuisance.

Several of the new reprographic techniques greatly reduce the cost of making multiple copies of an existing work, so that it has become quite inexpensive to reproduce fifty or one hundred or more copies of a poem, story, essay, or journal article for classroom use. No library or educational group has asserted that it is or ought to be lawful to reproduce entire copyrighted works in these quantities, although some individual witnesses in Congressional copyright hearings did so, and the practice is in fact believed to be rather widespread. Most schools and libraries do still refuse to undertake large-scale multiple copying however, and so a powerful incentive exists for the private publication of anthologies and collections of readings. These have poured forth in enormous quantity, in far better format and at much lower cost than any school can produce for itself. Nor have the special needs of individual teachers been ignored. At least one large publisher has offered to produce for any teacher or school an anthology of the particular materials desired, gaining and paying for permission from the proprietor and producing the material again in better form and more cheaply than can any individual school. If the incentive were removed by a general practice of free multiple reproduction, the further development of an important new publishing service would be thwarted.

Similarly, the problem of reproducing deteriorating books, now divided among many research libraries and constituting an expensive burden, might quite possibly be handled centrally and more efficiently by a service that would invest its own funds in systematically making negative films from which it could supply prints or enlargements on demand at reasonable cost if there were assurance of a market.

Perhaps the most important issues of all relate to the use of the computer as an information storage and retrieval device and as an instrument in computer-assisted

[12] *Gerald J. Sophar and Laurence B. Heilprin,* The Determination of Legal Facts and Economic Guideposts with Respect to the Dissemination of Scientific and Educational Information as It Is Affected by Copyright: A Status Report *(Washington, D.C.: Committee to Investigate Copyright Problems Affecting Communication in Science and Education, Inc., December 1967).*

instruction. In these areas the development of machinery, of "hardware," has far exceeded the development of the necessary programs, techniques, and materials. The production of these materials requires great and highly speculative investment, and most major educational publishers and many electronics companies are investing millions of dollars in projects for the development of such materials. If the copyright law should be so amended as to abridge the proprietorship of the companies that are undertaking to develop such materials, their experimental work would be halted or sharply curtailed and their products withheld from the market until means for their protection could be found. Stable copyright protection, far from inhibiting the experimental development of uses of the computer in instruction, communication, and documentation, is in fact indispensable to the development.

These examples have been adduced to make the point that a principal—and too often ignored—consideration in the development of the copyright law should be the construction of an adequate legal framework to encourage the investment of time and money in the application of new technology to the needs of users.

As this review has indicated, the fundamental social objectives of proprietors of copyrighted material on the one hand and of libraries and their users on the other are substantially identical. Granted mutual confidence in each other's sincerity, there should be no really major barrier to their coming to agreement as to the desired content of any new copyright revision act and as to workable arrangements for the application of the present and any future law. Society as a whole will be the beneficiary.

C. COPYRIGHT:
A LIBRARIAN'S VIEW[13]

by VERNER W. CLAPP
Consultant
Council on Library Resources

This paper is organized in three major sections: (1) a survey of all library activities affected by copyright, including copying; (2) a more detailed analysis of issues involving library copying, including especially photocopying; and (3) a concluding section summarizing a librarian's view of the copyright dilemma.

LIBRARY ACTIVITIES AFFECTED BY COPYRIGHT

IMPEDIMENTS TO LIBRARY SERVICE CAUSED
BY COPYRIGHT: COPYING SERVICES

A principal purpose—in some senses the principal purpose—for which libraries exist is to facilitate the copying of relevant documents. Some historical observations are to the point.

In 1901 the Library of Congress went to considerable trouble, apparently unimpeded by considerations arising from copyright, to facilitate the copying of materials in its collections. Its regulations at that time stated that it not only stood "ready to

---

13 *This paper was specially written for this book;* © 1968 V. W. Clapp, Washington, D. C.

suggest . . . persons who will transcribe lengthy extracts where these are desired" but it "freely permitted" photocopying, including specifically the photocopying of "articles bearing claim of copyright," and even reserved a special room for persons who wished to engage in such copying. However, such persons were admonished that "in granting permission to photograph these [articles] the Library gives no assurance that the photograph may be reproduced or published or placed on sale. These are matters to be settled with the owner of the copyright."[14]

By 1912 the Library had acquired photocopying equipment and could render a public photocopying service.[15] Although the Copyright Act of 1909 had been enacted in the meantime, it apparently did not affect the Library's copying services, for these continued to be offered in terms substantially identical with those of 1901.[16]

In 1968, by contrast, although the Library of Congress offers probably as complete an assortment of photocopying services (exclusive of self-service) as any library in the world, it is a condition of these services that "[c]opyrighted material will ordinarily not be copied without the signed authorization of the copyright owner."[17] (It is true that an interesting provision is made for exceptions "in particular cases"; this will be the subject of comment in a later section of this paper.)

What accounts for the difference between 1901 and 1968? Under the copyright law in force in 1901 (as more fully explained later) the infringement of copyright in books and other works reproduced from type was specified, as it had been since the earliest copyright act, an Act of Parliament of 1710, as consisting in unauthorized printing, publishing, importing, or offering for sale of copies of the copyrighted work. Merely to copy did not infringe.

But this situation was changed by the Copyright Act of 1909, which, as Title 17 of the U.S. Code, is still in force. With a view to precision and economy of statutory expression, that act abandoned the traditional specification of actions constituting infringement, leaving infringement to be defined simply as any violation of the copyright. The copyright included, among other things, the exclusive right to copy—to all intents and purposes a new right. Merely to copy without authorization from a copy of a copyrighted work, no matter what its physical form, thus became for the first time an infringement, in literal terms at least.

There is, as pointed out later, good reason for believing that the verb "to copy" was brought to the Act of 1909 from usage in which, as the equivalent of the verb "to print," it referred to the mass production of works produced from plates, etc., as distinguished from the production of those produced from type, and that it only gradually lost that specialized primary meaning and took on the generalized meaning that it holds for us today. If this is so, it would, among other things, account for the fact that the creation of this wholly new right was so completely unremarked at the time and for a number of

---

14 *U.S. Librarian of Congress,* Annual Report (*Washington, D.C.: Library of Congress, 1901*), *p. 208.*

15 *U.S. Library of Congress: General Order No. 229* [availability of Photostat and Flexotype machines], *January 8, 1912. "Accompanying this order are copies of a memorandum of charges for the general public for photo-duplicates."*

16 *"Photographing is freely permitted. The permission extends to the building itself and any of its parts, including the mural decorations. It extends to articles bearing claim of copyright, but the Library gives no assurance that the photograph may be reproduced or republished or placed on sale. These are matters to be settled with the owner of the copyright."*—Rules and Practice Governing the Use and Issue of Books (*Washington, D.C.: Library of Congress, 1913*), *p. 6.*

"Photo-duplicates of books, newspapers, maps, etc., can be furnished at a reasonable rate by means of the photostat, installed in the Chief Clerk's office. Apply to the Chief Clerk for a schedule of charges."—Ibid.

The offer to provide names and addresses of copyists and the announcement regarding the photoduplication service are repeated in Information for Readers in the Main Reading Room (*Washington, D.C.: Library of Congress, 1914*), *p. 12.*

17 *Library of Congress. Photoduplication service:* Order for Photoduplication. [*Form*] 25–15 (*rev. 10/63*).

years later. It would account for the fact that the Librarian of Congress continued unchanged for at least five years after the enactment of the new act the copying services that the Library had offered in 1901, and even added to them. It is interesting to note that the Librarian was himself a member of the New York bar as well as a member of a well-known publishing family with a particular interest in copyright, and he was so much interested in copyright that he personally introduced the first draft of the Act of 1909 to a joint meeting of Congress; moreover, one of his principal colleagues and daily associates was the Register of Copyrights.

The exclusive right of copying, in the sense of making single copies, thus seems to have been created quite inadvertently, as the result of a nicety of legislative drafting, by the very public official who might have been supposed to be the last by whom this would have been done!

Since the exclusive right to copy has never been construed by the courts, no one knows exactly what it means. A literal construction of the law would make any unauthorized copying of a copyrighted work, in any amount, for any purpose and by any means, an infringement. The unauthorized penciled copy of a sentence by a schoolchild would be no less an infringement than a pirated facsimile edition for sale of the entire work.[18]

If he should accept this literal construction of the law, the prospective copyist of copyright materials would have three alternatives: (1) to secure authorization to copy in every case from the copyright proprietor, (2) to find some basis to justify copying without authorization, or (3) to desist absolutely from copying. There can be little doubt that no one—not even he who most fiercely claims exclusive rights of copying for copyright proprietors—adopts alternatives (1) or (3). In the absence of construction of the law by Congress or the courts, every user of copyright material is forced to be his own Blackstone and to follow alternative (2).

In regard to the copying services facilitated by libraries (whether performed by libraries themselves or by their users), a number of bases of justification have been suggested:

a. Asserted traditional institutional practice long antedating printing and copyright.[19]

b. The precedent of a publishers-scholars agreement made in 1935 between organizations no longer in existence (the "Gentlemen's Agreement").[20]

c. An asserted private right of copying.[21]

d. The judicial doctrine of fair use.[22]

e. The thesis of the present writer that the history of the verb "to copy" in the law shows that it does not refer to single copying at all but to the multiplication of copies associated with publishing in editions.

All of these justifications, which are discussed further later in this paper, assume that copying services provided by libraries are intended either for the preservation and

---

[18] A. W. Weil, American Copyright Law (*Chicago: Callaghan & Co., 1917*), pp. 69–70.
  M. B. Nimmer, Nimmer on Copyright (*Albany [etc]: Mathew Bender, 1967*), sec. 101.3.
[19] *Edward G. Freehafer, "Summary Statement of Policy of the Joint Libraries Committee on Fair Use in Photocopying,"* Special Libraries, 55 (*February 1964*), pp. 104–6. *This article cites the numerous publications involved in the reporting and adoption of the policy.*
[20] " 'Gentlemen's Agreement.' Copyright in Photographic Reproductions," Library Journal, 60 (*October 1, 1935*), pp. 763–4.
  "The Gentlemen's Agreement and the Problem of Copyright," Journal of Documentary Reproduction, 2 (*March 1939*), pp. 29–36.
[21] *Ralph R. Shaw,* Literary Property in the United States (*[Washington, D.C.]: Scarecrow Press, 1950*), pp. 149–50.
  Louis Charles Smith, "The Copying of Literary Property in Library Collections," Law Library Journal, 46 (*August 1953*), pp. 197–206; 47 (*August 1954*), pp. 204–8, especially p. 206.
[22] *Alan Latman,* Fair Use of Copyrighted Works (*Washington, D.C.: Copyright Office, Library of Congress, August 1958*), General Revision of the Copyright Law, Study No. 10.

security of the collections of the libraries themselves or to assist the study, investigation, or research of library users, and are limited to the making of a single copy per user.

However, the validity of these justifications, equally with the validity of the literal construction of the law, is quite speculative. Lacking clarifying legislation, the only method by which this validity can be tested is in a court action for infringement, and in the nearly sixty years in which the law has been in effect there has been no action for infringement involving a single copy, whether manuscript, typewritten, or photocopied, made through the copying services provided by a library.[23]

In this absence of precedent establishing the legality of library copying, every library that facilitates the unauthorized copying/photocopying of copyright materials exposes itself to litigation. The desire to avoid litigation is sufficient to lead even important libraries and service-minded librarians to withhold copying facilities from their users except under onerous conditions that destroy much of the usefulness of these facilities, such as identifying and locating the copyright proprietor and securing his "signed authorization" to copy.

Ironically, this restriction comes at a time when document-based research—if it is to be able to deal with the proliferating masses of material with which it is confronted—must be able to take advantage of every available device for improving its effectiveness through speeding up its procedures, increasing its accuracy, and releasing for useful intellectual work the energy and time spent in unnecessary and arduous clerical operations.

IMPEDIMENTS TO LIBRARY SERVICE CAUSED BY COPYRIGHT: OTHER SERVICES

The present restriction upon photocopying—discussed above and at some length later in this paper—is the best known and, at the moment, the most serious of the impediments that library-based research now suffers from copyright. However, the indications are plain that it is not likely to be the last. In fact, the pending Copyright Revision Bill (H. R. 2512, S. 597, 90th Congress) contains a number of such restrictions:

a. Libraries currently have an unqualified right to lend, sell, give away, or otherwise dispose of their copies of copyrighted works. The Bill would reduce this right to a "privilege," subordinate to the exclusive right of distribution which would be vested in the copyright proprietor.

b. Libraries currently have an unqualified right to exhibit materials in their collections, whether or not for profit, by various direct and indirect methods and transmissions. For copyrighted material the Bill would reduce this right to a "privilege" of publicly displaying a copy of a copyrighted work, either directly or by the projection of not more than one image at a time to viewers present at the place where the copy is located. Any further display, whether or not for profit, by optical or electronic projection, broadcast, telefacsimile or otherwise, could be performed only by license or permission.

c. Libraries currently have the right to broadcast nonprofit performances (e.g., readings or recitations) of copyrighted nondramatic literary works and nonprofit performances of copyrighted nondramatic musical compositions. The Bill would take these rights away.

d. Libraries currently have the right of nonprofit performance of nondramatic motion pictures. The Bill would take this right away by making it an infringe-

[23] Miles O. Price, *"Photocopying by Libraries and Copyright: A Précis,"* Library Trends, 8 (*January 1960*), pp. 432–47.

Borge Varmer, Photoduplication of Copyrighted Material by Libraries (*Washington, D.C.: Copyright Office, Library of Congress, September 1959*), *General Revision of the Copyright Law, Study No. 19.*

ment to perform any copyrighted motion picture without authorization in a place "open to the public."

e. The right of libraries to provide copying (including photocopying) services for copyrighted materials, though clouded by the wording of the copyright law and though never adjudicated (as described above), is nevertheless arguable. (Arguments are presented in a later section of this paper.) The Bill would injure the libraries' case in two ways. The first is probably unintentional: by substituting new for traditional terminology (specifically, the word "reproduce" for the word "copy" in the specification of copyright, sec. 106), the Bill would nullify the argument based on traditional meaning. The second is less fortuitous: the Bill presents criteria for determining whether or not a particular instance of copying would constitute fair use. (Since such a determination can be made only by the courts—the Bill does not state by whom it is made—this would continue the situation in which libraries must accept risk of suit if they are to attempt to make their collections serviceable through photocopying.) But meanwhile, in the report accompanying the Bill one of the criteria is defined so restrictively as to nullify the very doctrine that it claims to explicate, by a sort of *de minimis* rule in reverse, viz.:

> Where the unauthorized copying displaces what realistically might have been a sale, no matter how minor the amount of money involved, the interests of the copyright owner need protection.[24]

f. In addition, the report, explaining why the Bill does not make provision for library copying, urges an accommodation under which the "needs" of scholars and the "rights" of authors would both be respected (page 36). Instead of providing a legislative solution of a conflict between the public interest and the profit-seeking of a commercial interest, the Bill and the report thus tip the scales in favor of the latter.

Meanwhile the following additional restrictions impend, although they have not as yet reached the stage of legislative consideration:

g. The so-called public lending right. Under this "right" a royalty is charged for the private reading of public library books. The Register of Copyrights has concluded that "in this country, at the present time at least," the advantage to copyright proprietors of enforcing the "right" would be outweighed by the practical difficulties of working out a system without hampering library service.[25] However, since the copyright proprietors don't pay for working out the system, it is not surprising to find that they have not found the practical difficulties insuperable in Denmark and Sweden, where it is claimed that the small populations and the languages of restricted use require the additional subsidies to copyright proprietors resulting from implementation of the "right." But even without such justification the "right" is being actively promoted in the United Kingdom.[26] Accordingly, more may be expected to be heard of it in this country, and the threatened reduction of the present lending right of libraries to a "privilege" by the Copyright Revision Bill (see item "a" above) may be presumed to be a

24 *U.S. Congress, House of Representatives, Committee on the Judiciary,* Report No. 83, 90th Congress, 1st Session, Copyright Law Revision. Report to Accompany H. R. 2512, March 8, 1967, *p. 35.*
25 *Copyright Law Revision.* [Reports of the Register of Copyrights on the General Revision of the U.S. Copyright Law.] Printed for the House Committee on the Judiciary (*Washington, D.C.: Government Printing Office, 6 vols. 1961–5*), vol. 6, p. 31.
26 The Arts Council and Public Lending Right (*London: The Arts Council of Great Britain, January 1968*).

[*The Society of Authors*], Public Lending Right, a Short History (*London: The Society, September 1967*), *Bulletin 3.*

The Society of Authors, Public Lending Right: Outline of Proposals, 1968 (*London: The Society, 1968*).

harbinger of this. However, even if the public interest is found to require further subsidies to copyright proprietors, it may well be doubted that the best way to calculate them will be on the popularity-contest basis of library circulation.

h. A general lending right. Although this does not appear to be as yet claimed under copyright, a number of current publications contain the following notice:

> Conditions of sale: This book is sold subject to the condition that it shall not, by way of trade or otherwise, be lent, resold, hired out, or otherwise circulated without the publisher's prior consent, and without a similar condition including this condition being imposed on the subsequent purchaser.[27]

i. A binding right. A number of current publications contain the following notice:

> This book is sold subject to the condition that it shall not, by way of trade or otherwise, be lent, resold, hired out, or otherwise circulated without the publisher's prior consent in any form of binding or cover other than that in which it is published and without a similar condition including this condition being imposed on the subsequent purchaser[.][28]

The trend of all these restrictions is unmistakable—it is toward a situation in which libraries will be on a strictly payment-for-use basis with respect to the materials in their collections. They will be permitted, as now, to purchase copies of copyrighted works, but they will be required in addition to pay royalties for any use that is made of them. From the proprietor's point of view, of course, such an arrangement should prove very profitable, combining the advantages of sale and lease.

AUTHORS' RIGHTS VS. PUBLIC INTEREST

There is, of course, no cause for surprise in the trend described above. The whole purpose of a monopoly, from the proprietor's point of view, is to make money. In the words of the Register of Copyrights, "all of the author's exclusive rights translate into money."[29] At the present time he has only fifty-six years to do this. He should not, in consequence, neglect to take advantage of every opportunity for profit.

On the other hand, from the point of view of the Constitution, which authorizes Congress to create the monopoly, the purpose of copyright is to promote the public interest: "The Congress shall have power . . . To promote the progress of Science and useful Arts, by securing for limited Times to Authors and Inventors the exclusive Rights to their respective Writings and Discoveries."[30]

In the words of Chief Justice Hughes: "The sole interest of the United States and the primary object in conferring the monopoly lie in the general benefits derived by the public from the labors of authors."[31] And in those of Justice Douglas: "The copyright law, like the patent statutes, makes reward to the owner a secondary consideration."[32]

But the classic expression of the relationship was by the House of Representatives Committee on Patents of the Sixtieth Congress in its report accompanying the bill that became the Copyright Act of 1909. Since the Senate Committee adopted the House report verbatim, the following statement has the combined authority of both bodies:

> The enactment of copyright legislation by Congress under the terms of the Constitution is not based on any natural right that the author has in his writings, for the Supreme Court has held that such rights as he has are purely statutory rights, but upon the ground that the welfare of the public will be served and progress of science

27 E.g., Jean-Pierre Hallet, Congo Kitabu (Greenwich, Conn.: Fawcett Publications, Inc., January 1968), verso of title page.
28 E.g., Froissart, Chronicles, selected, translated, and edited by Geoffrey Brereton (Baltimore: Penguin Books, 1968), verso of title page.
29 Copyright Law Revision, op. cit. (see footnote 25), vol. 6, p. 13.
30 U.S. Constitution, Art. I, Sec. 8. United States Code, 1964 ed., vol. I, p. XLIII.
31 Fox Film Co. v. Doyal, 286 U.S. 123, 127 (1932).
32 United States v. Paramount Pictures, Inc., 334 U.S. 131, 158 (1948).

and useful arts will be promoted by securing to authors for limited periods the exclusive right to their writings. The Constitution does not establish copyright, but provides that Congress shall have the power to grant such rights if it thinks best. Not primarily for the benefit of the author, but primarily for the benefit of the public, such rights are given. Not that any particular class of citizens, however worthy, may benefit, but because the policy is believed to be for the benefit of the great body of the people, in that it will stimulate writing and invention, to give some bonus to authors and inventors.

In enacting a copyright law, Congress must consider two questions: First, how much will the legislation stimulate the producer and so benefit the public; and second, how much will the monopoly granted be detrimental to the public? The granting of such exclusive rights, under the proper terms and conditions, confers a benefit upon the public that outweighs the evils of the temporary monopoly.[33]

How is the public interest to be reconciled with the proprietor's natural desire for profits?

THE FOR-PROFIT PRINCIPLE

Until now, the for-profit principle has served as a principal device for mediating between proprietors' desire for profits and the public interest.

The basic right conveyed by copyright is the right of publication, typified by the right to multiply copies. But there are other ways of publishing a work profitably than by the sale of copies. A lecture can be published profitably by delivery, and a play by performance. In consequence, in order to assure to the copyright proprietor the profits resulting from these other ways of publishing his work, copyright in the United States has been progressively extended beyond the original "printing, reprinting, publishing, and vending" to include certain performances of plays (1856); music (1897); lectures, sermons and addresses (1909); motion pictures (1912); and nondramatic literary compositions (1952). And it is similarly proposed in the Copyright Revision Bill to extend protection to the "display" of all classes of copyrighted works.

Originally, the owner of a copy of a copyrighted work was free to use it in any manner he liked, short of reprinting it. If it were a book, he might read it silently or aloud, in public or in private. If it were music, he might perform it under any conditions. He could exhibit his copy, lend it, give it away, or otherwise dispose of it. With each statutory extension of copyright, however, such an owner's rights have diminished. He may no longer perform the work publicly if it is a play, read it aloud in public for profit if it is a book or lecture or sermon, or perform it publicly for profit if it is a musical composition.

If there has been no significant objection to these restrictions, it is because the general principle upon which they are based has been recognized and accepted as consonant with the public interest. This general principle is the for-profit principle; namely, that where the public use of a copyrighted work results in a profit, there can be no question as to the justice of the copyright proprietor's claim to it and the copyright should extend to that use; otherwise not.

With a signal exception (the jukebox exemption), copyright in the United States has exemplified the principle by being extended to profitable public uses of copyrighted works. With a signal exception, it has exemplified the principle by not being extended to nonprofit public uses of copyrighted works. This exception was the first enactment of the kind (1856), which extended copyright to public performance of dramatic compositions,

---

33 *U.S. Congress, House of Representatives, Committee on Patents,* House Report 2222, 60th Congress, 2nd Session, February 22, 1909, Accompanying H. R. 28192, a Bill to Amend and Consolidate the Acts Respecting Copyright, *pp. 6–7.*

U.S. Congress, Senate, Committee on Patents, Senate Report 1108, 60th Congress, 2nd Session, March 1, 1909. Report to Accompany S. 9440, a Bill to Amend and Consolidate the Acts Respecting Copyright, *pp. 6–7.*

not only those for profit but also those not for profit. This extension was continued by the Copyright Acts of 1870 and 1909, but the Committees on Patents in 1909 felt the need of justifying the continuation, and in the process of justifying an exception, implicitly recognized the general rule.

However, the 1909 Act made an even more important acknowledgment of the for-profit principle by applying it to public performances of music, which had been subjected to copyright without such a limitation in 1897.

But the for-profit principle received its most emphatic endorsement by Congress in 1952, when copyright was extended to public performances for profit of nondramatic literary works. The original bill (H. R. 3589, 82nd Congress) had provided for the extension of copyright to public performances of these works. The House Committee on the Judiciary, fearing the consequence "that a teacher reading excerpts from a copyrighted schoolbook in a schoolroom, a minister reading from text in a church, or a speaker at a civic meeting would be held to have infringed the copyright," added the words "for profit" to the phrase "public performance" wherever it occurred.[34]

And not only did the House of Representatives agree, but the Senate, to make doubly sure, inserted the word "pecuniary" each time before the word "profit"! In conference the House persuaded the Senate that this was unnecessary, but the incident serves to emphasize the extent of the commitment of Congress to the for-profit principle.[35]

THE FOR-PROFIT PRINCIPLE IN THE COPYRIGHT REVISION BILL

As recently as 1961 the Register of Copyrights was also to be found in the ranks of those who considered the "for-profit" principle an acceptable device for mediating between proprietors' desire for profits and the public interest:

> We believe that the principle of the "for-profit" limitation on the right of public performance in nondramatic literary and musical works, and the application given to that principle by the courts, strike a sound balance between the interests of copyright owners and those of the public.[36]

Four years later, however, the Register completely reversed his position:

> [W]e believe the day is past when any particular use of works should be exempted for the sole reason that it is "not for profit."[37]

The reasons given by the Register for this reversal include the possibility that technological developments may reduce the demand for copies. But the controlling consideration appears to have been the Register's view that the copyright proprietor should be able to profit from any use of his work, even though that use is itself nonprofit:

> It does not seem to be too much to ask that some of the money now going to support educational broadcasting be used to compensate authors and publishers whose works are essential to those activities.[38]

[34] *U.S. Congress, House of Representatives, Committee on the Judiciary,* House Report 1160, 82nd Congress, 1st Session, October 15, 1951, to Accompany H. R. 3589, Amending Title 17 of the United States Code, *p. 2.*
[35] *U.S. Congress, Senate, Committee on the Judiciary,* Senate Report 1778, 82nd Congress, 2nd Session, June 16, 1952, to Accompany H. R. 3589, Amending Title 17 of the United States Code.
   U.S. Congress, House of Representatives, Committee on the Judiciary, House Report 2470, 82nd Congress, 2nd Session, July 3, 1952, Conference Report to Accompany H. R. 3589, Recording and Performing Rights in Certain Literary Works.
   U.S. Congress, House of Representatives, Committee on the Judiciary, House Report 2486, 82nd Congress, 2nd Session, July 4, 1952, Conference Report to Accompany H. R. 3589, Recording and Performing Rights in Certain Literary Works.
[36] *Copyright Law Revision,* op. cit. (*see footnote 25*), *vol. 1, p. 27.*
[37] Ibid., *vol. 6,* p. 14.
[38] Ibid., *p. 35. See also House Report 83,* op. cit. (*see footnote 24*), *p. 42.*

Accordingly, the Register was led to devise the following principle for drafting copyright legislation:

> [W]e believe that the author's rights should be stated in the statute in broad terms, and that the specific limitations on them should not go any further than is shown to be necessary in the public interest.[39]

This principle—reversing the order of priority prescribed by the Constitution, deliberately asserted by the committees of both houses of Congress in 1909, restated by Chief Justice Hughes in 1932 and again by Justice Douglas in 1948—subordinates the public interest to the claims of copyright owners. It puts on the public interest, furthermore, the burden of proof. Whereas the Constitution and the 1909 committees would ask, "Why should the monopoly be extended?" the Register asks, "Why should it not be extended?"or even, "Why should it be withdrawn?"[40]

The Register's views regarding the for-profit limitation, as well as his principle of drafting, were both incorporated into the Copyright Revision Bill and are restated in its report on the Bill by the House of Representatives Committee on the Judiciary. Just as did the Register, the Committee has justified its elimination of the for-profit requirement by the argument that "many 'nonprofit' organizations are highly subsidized and capable of paying royalties," with specific mention of educational broadcasters.[41]

Thus, because some educational broadcasters are well-heeled, an established principle is to be overthrown, many tens of thousands of nonprofit users—including public agencies such as public libraries—are to be taxed for the use of materials for which they have already paid, and the public interest is to be permanently damaged; all in the interest of additional profit to an already highly protected industry, the sixth largest in the country in terms of income.[42]

Under the formula for drafting proposed by the Register and adopted by the Bill, the criterion for selecting the "broad terms" in which the author's rights are to be stated is simple—it is that of "providing compensation to the author for future as well as present uses of his work that may affect the value of his copyright."[43] This would include everything: the unforeseen uses equally with the foreseen, the private with the public, the nonprofit together with the for-profit; and this is exactly what the Copyright Revision Bill does.

By contrast, no criterion is offered by the Register whereby to recognize the public interest which, he states, may necessitate the limitation of the author's rights. He has specifically pushed aside the claims of nonprofit users such as teachers, librarians, and educational broadcasters "who seek to advance learning and culture by bringing the works of authors to students, scholars, and the general public" on the grounds that such use may result in loss of sales of copies.[44] From this it would appear that if a particular use, no matter how meritorious, results in loss of sales, no matter how conjectural, such use cannot be admitted to be "necessary in the public interest."

---

39 *Copyright Law Revision,* op. cit., *vol. 6, p. 14.*

40 *In June 1906 the Librarian of Congress introduced to a joint meeting of the Congressional Committees on Patents the first draft of the bill that was to eventuate in the Copyright Act of 1909. This bill had been drafted in the Copyright Office after a series of conferences that the Office had attempted to make as representative as possible. Of the draft, the Librarian stated to the Committees, "The bill has that purpose—that is, for the protection of the property. It comes before you for consideration on the ground that it goes too far."*

The Librarian's statement is quoted from pp. 16–17 of Arguments Before the Committees on Patents of the Senate and House of Representatives Conjointly on the Bills S. 6330 and H. R. 19853 to Amend and Consolidate the Acts Respecting Copyright. June 6, 7, 8, and 9, 1906 *(Washington, D.C.: Government Printing Office, 1906).*

41 *House Report 83,* op. cit. *(see footnote 24), p. 26.*

42 *W. M. Blaisdell,* Size of the Copyright Industries *(Washington, D.C.: Copyright Office, Library of Congress, May 1959),* General Revision of the Copyright Law, Preliminary Study B, p. 2.

43 *Copyright Law Revision,* op. cit. *(see footnote 25), vol. 6, p. 13.*

44 Ibid., *p. 14.*

It may be objected, however, that it is of the essence of the public interest in copyright that certain uses may result in loss of sales. If, for example, it were found contrary to the public interest to extend copyright to obscene publications, or to cookbooks, this would be expected to result in loss of sales. Similarly with nonprofit use.

In fact, with respect to loss of sales, it may be remarked that the effect of the public. interest is exactly the same as the effect of the fair-use doctrine, which may be said to represent the judicial interpretation of the public interest. When a court rules a quotation to be fair use, it states in effect that the public interest relieved the quoter of any obligation to seek a license or pay a fee for the privilege of quotation. But had he not supposed his use to be fair, the quoter might have been willing to pay a fee. Thus the doctrine of fair use resulted in loss of sales.

MASS DISSEMINATION VS. NORMAL USE

It has been shown above that as other methods than printing acquired importance for the publication of copyrighted works, control of profitable applications of these methods was extended to the copyright proprietors; but that so long as the principle upon which this extension was based was recognizably in the public interest, there was no significant resistance to it even though it simultaneously diminished the uses that the owner of a copy of a copyrighted work could make of that work. The principle so recognized is the for-profit principle.

By contrast, when a public body such as a library that has lawfully acquired a copy of a copyrighted work is prevented from making normal and traditional use of it, not because the use is profitable but merely in order that the copyright proprietor may make additional profits by charging for such use, the public interest is injured. It is injured the more if in the process of licensing the work of the public body is hampered. Both tendencies are found in several of the restrictions listed above.

In regard to copying, severe restrictions have already been invoked, to which even some important libraries have submitted. Meanwhile, the proposal for a clearinghouse to license photocopying, which the Register finds attractive as a "solution" to the problem, has been recognized even in sympathetic quarters as likely to "cost dimes to collect pennies."[45]

Similarly, a first step has been taken, as reported above, to deprive libraries of their right to lend. This may be expected to open the door to a tax on lending, burdened in addition by attendant record-keeping. Although the threatened loss of rights of display, performance, and broadcasting may be of minor importance, the situation would nevertheless reduce the number of techniques available to libraries for publicizing and putting to use the contents of their collections. It is, in addition, unlikely that the licensing of these uses by libraries will be more than a very minor source of revenue to copyright proprietors.

THE RIGHTS OF OWNERS OF COPIES OF COPYRIGHTED WORKS TO USE THEIR COPIES

During the drafting of the Copyright Act of 1909 a situation occurred similar to the one described above. Because of ambiguous wording in the drafts before them the responsible Congressional committees became concerned lest the rights of owners of copies of copyrighted works be endangered. In consequence, on two occasions they took action to protect these rights.

The first occasion was with respect to the right "to sell, distribute, exhibit, or let for hire, any copy of [the copyrighted] work," which had been included in the specification of copyright in the first draft of the Act. Of this the Committee on Patents of the House of Representatives said:

---

45 Ibid. *See also Curtis G. Benjamin, "Everything Is Not Coming Up Roses," Special Libraries, 56 (November 1965), pp. 637–41; see p. 640.*

It was insisted that this paragraph would prevent the purchaser of a copyrighted book from reselling it or lending it or giving it away or the letting for hire of any such book, thus putting an end to circulating libraries. Your committee believed that this section was susceptible of that construction and that under it a man might have only a qualified title in the copyrighted books in his library. This entire paragraph was eliminated, and in this bill the phraseology of the existing law has been substantially reproduced.[46]

The second occasion was with respect to the word "vend" as used in the specification of copyright in the final draft of the Act. In the then recent "Castaway" case, a price-cutting suit by the Bobbs-Merrill Company against Macy's, the Supreme Court had decided that the exclusive right of the copyright proprietor to control the sale of the copyrighted work did not go beyond the first sale.[47] The Committee wished to make it clear that it had no intention of disturbing this decision. Accordingly, remarking that it would be "most unwise to permit the copyright proprietors to exercise any control whatever over the article which is the subject of copyright after said proprietor has made the first sale," the Committee, joined by its Senate counterpart, added a final clarifying clause to what is sec. 27 of the present law:

[B]ut nothing in this title shall be deemed to forbid, prevent, or restrict the transfer of any copy of a copyrighted work the possession of which has been lawfully obtained.[48]

If such statutory assurance was needed in 1909 to confirm owners of copies in their title to such copies, it is much more urgently needed today. To libraries such an assurance would give nothing that they do not now possess and would only confirm them in their rights to make nonprofit use of copies of copyrighted works that they have lawfully obtained (usually by purchase) for the purposes for which such copies are normally used. The following wording is suggested for inclusion for this purpose in any copyright legislation that may hereafter be enacted:

Notwithstanding the provisions of section [106 of H. R. 2512, S. 597, 90th Congress], it is not an infringement of copyright for a library to use a copy or phonorecord of a copyrighted work, the possession of which it has lawfully obtained, in not-for-profit public exhibits, displays, performances, and transmissions, or to lend, sell, give, or otherwise transfer such copy or phonorecord to another person, or to make no more than one copy or phonorecord of such copy or phonorecord for any given user for purposes of study, investigation, research, preservation, or security, or to lend, sell, give, or otherwise transfer any copy or phonorecord so made to another person.

COPYRIGHT AND LIBRARY COPYING/PHOTOCOPYING

Up to this point library copying/photocopying has been briefly treated as but one of a number of library activities affected by copyright. Here it is given a closer view.

REASONS FOR LIBRARY COPYING

Library-based research has always been dependent upon copying. Unless it can offer copying facilities, a library cannot pretend to serve serious study, investigation, or research, but must restrict itself to recreational-type reading.

46 *U.S. Congress, House of Representatives, Committee on Patents,* House Report 7083, 59th Congress, 2nd Session, January 30, 1907. Report to Accompany H. R. 25133, a Bill to Amend and Consolidate the Acts Respecting Copyright, *pp. 8–9.*
47 *Bobbs-Merrill Co. v. Straus, 210 U.S. 339–351 (1908).*
    Richard Rogers Bowker, Copyright: Its History and Its Law (*Boston and New York: Houghton Mifflin Co., 1912), pp. 54–7.*
48 House Report 2222, op. cit. (*see footnote 33*), p. 19.
    Senate Report 1108, op. cit. (*see footnote 33*), p. 19.

The reason is simple. The original documents that are consulted in the course of library-based research cannot be assembled, held together for indefinite periods, studied, moved from place to place, compared, marked up, interfiled, sent through the mails (without risk of severe or irreplaceable loss), used as typist's or printer's copy, or be otherwise manipulated for the purpose of the research and be disposed of when the research is concluded. For such purposes transcripts and copies serve as substitutes or surrogates for the originals. The essential purpose of library copying is thus not to avoid the cost of additional copies of the original, as copyright proprietors are said to fear, but to serve purposes for which the original is for the most part unsuited.

Modern conditions increase the dependency of library-based research upon copying services. The modern investigator needs more copies, faster, more ample in extent, more accurate, and less expensive than did his predecessors in order to cope with the vaster number of documents with which he has to deal—documents often scattered in many parts of an enormous library or among many libraries, perhaps in many cities and even in many countries. Accordingly, every improvement in copying services contributes to the timeliness, thoroughness, accuracy, and economy of research (to the extent that it is based on library materials) as well as to the efficient use of investigator manpower.

Interlibrary exchanges have for millennia (at least since the days of the great libraries of Nineveh and Alexandria) been dependent upon copying services, and have become increasingly so during the last half-century. Regional and national arrangements for specialization of collections and sharing of resources depend upon such exchanges. And upon such arrangements, in turn, the ability of library users to call upon resources other than those in their immediate neighborhoods is dependent. The purpose of such arrangements is again not to reduce duplication in acquisition for its own sake, as is claimed to be feared by some copyright proprietors, but rather to use the available funds for a wider and more useful selection of research materials.

To mention one category of regional organization of collections, the willingness of "working" libraries (as contrasted with "libraries of record") to improve their efficiency by weeding their collections of less-used materials is dependent to a considerable degree upon their ability to count upon the availability of copies of such material from other collections when needed. The fear that copyright restrictions may interfere with such availability is currently discouraging many such libraries from taking action that is desirable not only from the individual institutional point-of-view but also from that of society as a whole.

Still another reason for photocopying by libraries is to replace deteriorated or mutilated originals in their collections.

LIBRARY COPYING SERVICES

Originally it was no doubt normal for a library user to make his own copies by hand, and the earliest library manual (1627) stresses the importance of providing copying facilities.[49] However, the employment of agents for this purpose relieved the investigator of burdensome work and even the necessity for foreign travel, while greatly increasing his productivity, and important books have been written with such assistance.

At a later stage libraries undertook to provide or arrange for copying services. As mentioned previously, the Library of Congress in 1901 stood "ready to suggest . . . persons who will transcribe lengthy extracts where they are desired." At that date transcription by typewriter was becoming general. At the same date, however, the Library permitted photocopying, including specifically the copying of copyrighted materials.[50]

Library copying services have increased since then by leaps and bounds through the introduction of the Photostat (1912), the development of the portable typewriter

---

49 *Gabriel Naudé,* Advis pour dresser une bibliothèque (*Paris: I. Lisieux, 1876*), *pp. 100, 105, 108–9.*
50 *U.S. Librarian of Congress,* loc. cit. (*see footnote 14*).

(1910–), microfilm (1930–), and office photocopying devices (1950–). Today the copying services offered by libraries typically take the following forms:

    a. Assisting users in the making of single copies by providing or permitting them the use of pens, typewriters, darkrooms, coin-operated photocopying equipment, etc.

    b. Making arrangements to enable users to procure single copies through agents; e.g., by furnishing the names of copyists or photographers.

    c. Employing the library's own staff and facilities to make and furnish single copies to users.

Attention is called to the use of the phrase "single copies," meaning one copy to a user. Although libraries, like other institutions, make multiple copies of documents for various administrative purposes, such activities are not comprehended here by the term "library copying." Whenever library copying is referred to in this report, single copies are intended.

Commercial vs. Library Copying Services

It has been suggested that library copying can be performed efficiently by commercial services. This should certainly be the case where the copy is wanted as additional to or in lieu of the original; i.e., when the service is that of a "reprint" service. Not only do commercial services exist for this purpose, but attention is called to them in the Single Copy Policy statement (see below), and they do an active business in spite of frequent dissatisfaction with the delays and sometimes other aspects of their service. But such services are of little or no value when copies are needed as research notes or transcripts. For such purposes the researcher cannot be dependent upon the possible later aid of a distant supplier. To be of adequate value to him, the copying service must be at hand— prompt, convenient, inexpensive. Otherwise he will do better (as he is still forced to do even in some of the greatest libraries when they do not provide adequate copying services) to transcribe laboriously and inaccurately by obsolete methods.

THE COPYRIGHT PROBLEM IN LIBRARY COPYING

The increasing inexpensiveness and convenience of photocopying services eventually provided occasion for the raising of copyright questions with respect to library copying that might otherwise have lain dormant.

In its opening section the copyright law (basically the Copyright Act of 1909 codified as Title 17 of the United States Code) reserves to the copyright proprietor an exclusive right to copy the copyrighted work. Accepting a literal construction of this provision, many even service-minded libraries withhold from their users copying services that are all but indispensable under modern conditions of library-based research. The contraction of the services of the Library of Congress between 1901–14 and 1968 has been previously cited.

But although the current rule of that library states, "Copyrighted material will ordinarily not be copied without the signed authorization of the copyright proprietor," this is accompanied by the statement, "Exceptions to this rule may be made in particular cases."[51] It appears, interestingly, that requests of copyright attorneys, in the conduct of their professional practice (presumably gainful), constitute such "particular cases."[52]

Of course, what the Library of Congress has done here under its regulatory powers with respect to copyright for one category of users is all that libraries generally desire or claim to do for intellectual workers generally, without regard to the gainful or nonprofit motivation of their requests.

However, lacking regulatory authority to impose their own construction upon the copyright law, libraries are confronted by the three alternatives previously mentioned:

[51] Order for Photoduplication, op. cit. (*see footnote 17*).
[52] *U.S. Copyright Office*, Regulations *201.2 (4) ii, "Request by Attorney."* See also Nimmer, op. cit. (*see footnote 18*), *p. 944.*

(1) to seek authorization of the copyright proprietor in every case of copying, (2) to find some theoretic basis with which to justify copying without authorization, or (3) to desist from copying absolutely. Since both (1) and (3) are absurd, all users of copyright materials resort to (2).

The principal bases used by libraries to justify copying copyright material without authorization are considered below. Since all libraries permit such copying (though not all libraries permit photocopying), it is probable that—where thought has been given to the matter—reliance would be placed upon a combination of these bases rather than upon any one of them. Following this discussion is a section that advances the present writer's thesis that the verb "to copy," as used in the copyright law, historically refers (as does the verb "to print" there used) to the making of editions and not to the making of single copies, and that the framers of the law had no intention of creating an exclusive right in the making of single copies.

BASES FOR JUSTIFYING COPYING WITHOUT AUTHORIZATION
The Gentlemen's Agreement, 1935

The first concerted attempt to find a principle to justify library photocopying was in the Gentlemen's Agreement into which the Joint Committee on Materials for Research of the American Council of Learned Societies and the Social Science Research Council entered with the National Association of Book Publishers in May 1935; in January 1939, after it had succeeded the Association, the Book Publishers Bureau confirmed the Agreement.[53]

The Agreement recalled (1) that "a student has always been free to 'copy' by hand"; (2) that "mechanical reproductions from copyrighted material are presumably intended to take the place of hand transcriptions, and to be governed by the same principles governing hand transcription"; and (3) that "the courts have recognized the right to a 'fair use' of book quotations." Citing these precedents, the Association granted an "exemption from liability" whereby a "library, archives office, museum, or similar institution owning books or periodical volumes in which copyright still subsists may make and deliver a single photographic reproduction or reduction of a part thereof to a scholar representing in writing that he desires such reproduction in lieu of loan of such publication or in place of manual transcription and solely for the purposes of research," with the further conditions that the recipient be warned in writing not to infringe copyright by misuse of the reproduction, and that the furnishing institution not derive a profit from the copying.

For many years the American library world leaned heavily on the Gentlemen's Agreement to justify its photocopying service. The Agreement was cited by the American Library Association's Reproduction of Materials Code 1940 and by the General Interlibrary Loan Code 1952 adopted by a number of library organizations.[54] However, by 1956 there was considerable dissatisfaction with the Agreement. It was objected that the "exemption from liability" granted by the Agreement implied an admission of wrongdoing that libraries were not prepared to concede. Furthermore, the organizations that made the Agreement in 1935 and confirmed it in 1939 had gone out of existence without leaving successors to their commitments; and even had this not been the case, it was very dubious what value the "exemption from liability" would possess at the later date. Accordingly, at that time the Association of Research Libraries appointed the committee that eventually produced the Single Copy Policy mentioned below. Most

53 *American Council of Learned Societies,* Bulletin, *23 (June 1935), p. 4; 25 (July 1936), pp. 4, 67–8. See also "Gentlemen's Agreement," op. cit. (see footnote 20).*
54 *"Reproduction of Materials Code," ALA Bulletin, 35 (February 1941), pp. 84–5; "Reproduction of Library Materials," ibid., p. 119.*
   "General Interlibrary Loan Code 1952," College & Research Libraries, 13 (October 1952), pp. 350–8.

regrettably, the validity of the "exemption" extended by the Gentlemen's Agreement has never been tested in a court of law.

The Private Right to Copy

Ralph R. Shaw in 1950 made the next major effort to find a principle that would meet the requirement mentioned above. He distinguished between the public use of copyrighted material (e.g., in a publication) and copying for private use (e.g., for purposes of study). The first, he asserted, is controlled by the copyright law and the Doctrine of Fair Use; the second "is outside any statute and requires no permission from anyone." In 1953–54 Louis C. Smith, without referring to Shaw's work, proposed an identical distinction as justifying library copying.[55] Unfortunately, the private right to copy has never met a court test.

The Single Copy Policy

In 1956 the Association of Research Libraries, dissatisfied with the legal basis of library photocopying, appointed a committee that soon became the Joint Libraries Committee on Fair Use in Photocopying, representing the American Association of Law Libraries, the American Library Association, the Association of Research Libraries, and the Special Libraries Association. This committee employed legal counsel under whose guidance a survey was made of actual photocopying practice in a number of principal American research libraries in order to determine what kinds of material were being photocopied and the likelihood of damage to copyright proprietors. In 1961 the Joint Libraries Committee reported four findings and a recommended policy for single-copy photocopying; these were approved by the four parent associations. In 1963 the Committee recommended, as an amendment to the policy statement, that libraries check for commercial availability before copying an entire work; this recommendation was also approved by the four associations. The final form of the findings and the statement of policy is in consequence as follows:

SINGLE COPY POLICY

Findings:

1. The making of a single copy by a library is a direct and natural extension of traditional library service.
2. Such service, employing modern copying methods, has become essential.
3. The present demand can be satisfied without inflicting measurable damage on publishers and copyright owners.
4. Improved copying processes will not materially affect the demand for single copy library duplication for research purposes.

Recommended policy:

The Committee recommends that it be library policy to fill an order for a single photocopy of any published work or any part thereof. Before making a copy of an entire work, a library should make an effort by consulting standard sources to determine whether or not a copy is available through normal trade channels.[56]

As with the foregoing bases for justifying copying, the Single Copy Policy has never met a court test.

The Doctrine of Fair Use

A principle selected with increasing frequency for the justification of library copying since its mention in the Gentlemen's Agreement of 1935 is the judicial Doctrine of Fair Use.[57] With the aid of this doctrine a court can find that under certain circumstances the unauthorized printing or publication of a copyrighted work does not justify

55 *Shaw,* loc. cit., *and Smith,* loc. cit. (*see footnote 21*).
56 *Freehafer,* op. cit. (*see footnote 19*).
57 *Copyright Law Revision,* op. cit. (*see footnote 25*), vol. 1, pp. 24–6.

the infliction of penalties for infringement, and it is presumed that the doctrine would also apply to the making of single copies by schoolchildren and others.[58] It is of course possible that a doctrine that can excuse book reviewers from infringement in quoting purple passages and preachers from copying extracts of consolatory verse may also be used to get librarians off the hook of library copying.[59] However, since only the courts can tell whether a particular instance of copying may or may not be excused as fair use, and since—just as with the other principles mentioned above—the fair use of library copying has not met a court test, certainty eludes us.[60]

Furthermore, it may well be doubted whether the Doctrine of Fair Use would apply to the copying services rendered by libraries to their users, since the libraries themselves are not in those cases the users of the copies.

THE MEANING OF THE VERB "TO COPY"

The thesis is here advanced that the verb "to copy," as used in sec. 1 (a) of the Copyright Law, was never intended to refer to the making of single copies. It was intended, by contrast, to refer, as does the word "print" in the same sentence, to the production of multicopy editions that make it possible to publish the work; i.e., to disseminate it to the public—an entity of which an essential characteristic is plurality.

The verb "to copy" was not applied to books in United States copyright law before 1870. The word had first appeared in a copyright law in an Act of Parliament of 1735 that extended copyright to prints.[61] There it was used to describe multiplication of copies of prints, just as the verb "to print" had been used with respect to books in the Statute of Anne 1710, which first provided for copyright in books.[62]

In its earliest copyright legislation the United States closely followed the British precedent. The Act of Congress of 1790, providing for copyright in books, maps, and charts, specified infringement as to print; and the Act of 1802, which provided for copyright in prints, specified infringement as to copy.[63]

In the first general revision of the United States copyright law (1831), music was added to the publications previously covered by copyright. But now, for purposes of specifying infringement, the classes of publications subject to copyright were divided into two categories, differentiated by method of multiplication of copies. One section of the law dealt with publications multiplied from type; namely, books; this specified infringement as to print. The other dealt with publications typically multiplied from plates; namely, maps, charts, prints, and music; this specified infringement as to copy.[64]

The second general revision of the United States copyright law took place in 1870.[65] This added paintings, drawings, chromos, statues, statuary, and other art works to the classes of material subject to copyright. Hitherto the basic right of copyright, that of multiplication of copies, had always been expressed through the use of the terms "print" and "reprint." It was obvious that these terms did not aptly describe the multiplication of copies of paintings and statues. In consequence, the verb "to copy" (in its participial form) was borrowed from the infringement section for prints and other plate-produced publications of the previous act and inserted in the specification-of-copyright section of the new act. This now read as follows:

[A]ny citizen of the United States, or resident therein, who shall be the author, inventor, designer, or proprietor of any book, map, chart, dramatic or musical com-

---

[58] *Latman*, op. cit. (*see footnote 22*), *and Nimmer*, loc. cit. (*see footnote 18*).
[59] *Varmer*, op. cit. (*see footnote 23*).
[60] *Price*, op. cit. (*see footnote 23*), *and Smith*, op. cit. (*see footnote 21*).
[61] *8 George II, c. 13 (1735). Enactments embodying similar provisions are found at 7 George III, c. 38 (1766), and 17 George III, c. 57 (1776).*
[62] *8 Anne, c. 19 (1710).*
[63] *1* U.S. Statutes at Large *124–6 (1790)*; 2 ibid., *171–2 (1802)*.
[64] *4* ibid., *436–9 (1831)*.
[65] *16* ibid., *198–217 (1870)*.

position, engraving, cut, print, or photograph or negative thereof, or of a painting, drawing, chromo, statue, statuary, and of models or designs intended to be perfected as works of the fine arts . . . shall have the sole liberty of printing, reprinting, publishing, completing, copying, executing, finishing, and vending the same. . . .

Here the verb "to copy" was for the first time associated with books. But it was clear that it did not apply to books, for the infringement sections of the act still separated the type-produced publications (books) from the others and still specified infringement for the former as to print and infringement for the latter as to copy. Any claim of exclusive right to copy a book based on the presence of this word in the specification-of-copyright section would have foundered on its exclusion in the infringement section.

This is the reason that, as previously mentioned, the Library of Congress could permit the photocopying of copyrighted material in 1901. Nevertheless, here was planted the well-intentioned seed that in 1909 produced mischievous fruit.

The Copyright Act of 1870 was codified and reenacted in 1873–74, as secs. 4948–71 of the Revised Statutes and, as amended, remained in force until superseded by the Copyright Act of 1909.

The third general revision of the United States copyright law resulted in the Act of 1909, which, amended and codified as Title 17 of the United States Code, is the law today.[66] Two major changes effected by this act created the ambiguity that infects library copying. Curiously enough, the important and potentially mischievous effect of these changes went wholly unnoticed at the time and received no comment in the hearings, the reports, or the debate on the bill.

These two changes were as follows: through one the Act elevated the verb "to copy" to a position of eminence (or even dominance) in the specification-of-copyright section; through the other it omitted from the specification-of-infringement section the traditional distinction between classes of materials based upon method of multiplication of copies, which would have controlled the application of the verb "to copy."

The original draft of the Act (S. 6330, H. R. 19853, 59th Congress) reduced from the seven terms quoted above from the Act of 1870 to one phrase the formula for the multiplication of copies in the specification-of-copyright section. This one phrase, intended to be "fully as broad" as the seven terms it replaced, was "to make any copy."[67] However, the second draft (S. 8190, H. R. 25133, 59th Congress) and the third (final) draft (S. 9440, H. R. 28192, 60th Congress) substituted the present formula, "To print, reprint, publish, copy, and vend" (the final comma did not appear until the third draft).

Committee comment on this substitution is incomplete, inaccurate, and unsatisfactory. The report on the second draft referred in passing to the elimination of words from the Revised Statutes "which seemed to serve no useful purpose."[68] The report on the third draft stated incorrectly that the draft reproduced without change the phraseology of the Revised Statutes, but stated correctly that "this, with the insertion of the word 'copy,' practically adopts the phraseology of the first copyright act Congress ever passed—that of 1790." It added: "Many amendments of this were suggested, but the committee felt that it was safer to retain without change the old phraseology which has been so often construed by the courts."[69]

Ironically, so far from "retain[ing] without change" the old phraseology, the committees (the House of Representatives and the Senate committees shared the same

66 35 ibid., 1075–88 (1909).
67 Arguments, op. cit. (see footnote 40), pp. 7–8.
68 House Report 7083, op. cit. (see footnote 46), p. 9.
69 House Report 2222, op. cit. (see footnote 33), p. 4; also Senate Report 1108, op. cit. (see footnote 33), p. 4.

report) were introducing a word that was new in the context and that nearly sixty years later has not yet been construed. Through it the copyright proprietors, without seeking it and apparently quite by accident, acquired at least the semblance of a right to an activity that was to have increasing importance in the new century.

In summary, the exclusive right to copy was created in 1909 as the result of two accidents of bill drafting. The first of these had occurred in 1870, when the verb "to copy" (in the participial form) was added to the specification of copyright in order to describe the multiplication of copies of works of art. The second occurred in 1909, when the application of the word was permitted to extend to books and other copyrightable works as a result of the dropping of the detailed specification of infringement that had until then restricted the application of the word to the multiplication of copies of publications printed from plates and of copies of works of art. The previous use of the word in copyright law (beginning in 1735) had been as the equivalent of "to print," i.e., to mass-produce copies for purposes of publication; and there is nothing in the legislative history of the Act of 1909 to suggest that its meaning was there being changed or that the framers of the law had any intention whatever of extending its meaning to single-copying. In consequence, it is incorrectly presumed to apply to the making of single copies.[70]

This reference of the word to mass-copying is confirmed by the history of copyright. Copyright developed from the need of publishers for protection of investments in expensive mass-copying systems. No such investment would ordinarily be needed to produce a single copy. However, as with the four principles for justifying copying discussed earlier, this thesis has not been judicially considered.

DAMAGE TO COPYRIGHT PROPRIETORS FROM LIBRARY COPYING

Copyright proprietors express fear of damage from library copying (specifically photocopying) through reduction of demand leading to loss of sales (including especially the loss of subscriptions to journals) and (in the case of journals) through reduction of advertising revenue due to the failure of photocopying to bring advertising to the users' attention.[71] Although facts of this kind are recognized to be difficult to establish, there have nevertheless been several studies that cast some light on the matter.

In 1958–60 the Joint Libraries Committee on Fair Use in Photocopying analyzed the photoduplication work performed by ten libraries of various types in periods of from one day to three months. On the basis of its findings the Committee concluded that "Any economic damage to publishers or copyright owners through library duplication appears to be theoretical in view of the number of pages, dates of publication, and variety of demand revealed by the studies."[72]

In 1961–62 George Fry & Associates, under contract to the National Science Foundation, made a study of the photocopying of the literature of science and technology. An extensive report was published. In it the "basic conclusion" was reached that

[70] *Four years after the enactment of the Copyright Act of 1909, R. R. Bowker, among those principally responsible for it, defined the right to copy as follows: "As to the right to copy, this word in the broad sense as interpreted by the courts covers the duplicating or multiplying of copies within the stated scope of the statute." From Bowker, op. cit. (see footnote 47), p. 53.*

[71] See, e.g., Herbert S. Bailey, "Book Publishing and the New Technologies," Saturday Review, June 11, 1966, pp. 41–2; William M. Passano, "Statement of William M. Passano, president, the Williams and Wilkins Co.," Copyright Law Revision; Hearings Before the Subcommittee on Patents, Trademarks and Copyrights of the Committee on the Judiciary, United States Senate, Ninetieth Congress, First Session, Pursuant to S. Res. 37 on S. 597 (*Washington, D.C.: Government Printing Office, 1967*), pp. 974–6.

[72] *Joint Libraries Committee on Fair Use in Photocopying, "Report on Single Copies," Special Libraries, 52 (May–June 1961), pp. 251–5; Bulletin of the Copyright Society of America, 9 (October 1966), pp. 79–84.*

"at the present time no significant damage occurs to the copyright holders in the scientific and technical fields although duplication of this material is widespread and is growing rapidly." Findings with respect to loss of subscriptions were similarly negative, with some indications that subscriptions might actually be stimulated. Findings with respect to loss of advertising revenue were negative.[73]

In 1966, in a study conducted for the American Textbook Publishers Institute and the American Book Publishers Council, it was reported that the average secondary school spends about $13,000 a year to buy textbooks and workbooks and about $100 a year to copy such works.[74] It may be conjectured that a similar disparity would be found between the expenditures for book purchasing and the payments for copying services of libraries with respect to copyrighted materials.

In 1967 the Committee to Investigate Copyright Problems conducted, under contract to the United States Office of Education, a study of photocopying in libraries. It concluded among other things that:

97 percent of library photocopying consists of single copies.

90 percent of the materials copied in United States libraries are less than ten years old.

54–59 percent of the material copied is copyrighted.

Over a billion copyrighted pages were copied in the United States in 1967.

The Committee did not particularly study the question of damage to publishers resulting from photocopying, but contrasted the cumulative effect of much copying with the not-measurable damage of a single copy.[75]

Publishers' claims that photocopying has led to loss of sales are hardly supported by statistics of sales during the period in which photocopying has become increasingly available, convenient, and inexpensive. Specifically, the circulation figures for periodical publications for 1967 show in general a marked increase over those for 1959.[76] No doubt the circulation of some periodicals declined and some even went out of business during the period, but the present writer is not aware of any evidence that this was due to photocopying. It may be remarked that copyright does not guarantee a market for the copyrighted work.

However, it may be suspected that it is not so much the loss of sales of copies that copyright proprietors object to as it is the loss of opportunity to realize an additional profit from the photocopying. But as pointed out earlier, (1) it is not the policy of the United States copyright law to extend copyright to nonprofit uses of copyrighted works where publication of the work is not involved; and (2) the subservience of the interest of the copyright proprietor to the public interest sometimes requires the forgoing of potential profit. This would appear to be one of those occasions.

In an interesting recent development the threat of penalties for infringement of copyright is used as a deterrent against the abuse of photocopying facilities; e.g., by members of an office staff. Here the loss which it is sought to avoid is not the conjectural loss of sales by the copyright proprietor but the cost of photocopying to the owner or lessor of the copying equipment.

73 *George Fry & Associates,* Survey of Copyrighted Material Reproduction Practices in Scientific and Technical Fields (*Chicago, 1962), pp. i, ii; VI, 4–7, 12.*

74 *Philip, Ennis and Frederick A. Schlipf, "Copying and Duplicating Practices in American Education,"* An Economic-Media Study of Book Publishing (*New York: American Textbook Publishers Institute and the American Book Publishers Council, 1966), pp. 169–283, p. 219.*

75 *Gerald J. Sophar and Laurence B. Heilprin,* The Determination of Legal Facts and Economic Guideposts with Respect to the Dissemination of Scientific and Educational Information as It Is Affected by Copyright: A Status Report (*Washington, D.C.: Bureau of Research, Office of Education, U.S. Department of Health, Education, and Welfare, 1967), pp. iii, iv, 71. (Final report, Project No. 7 0793, Contract No. OEC 1-7-070793-3559. Committee to Investigate Copyright Problems Affecting Communication in Science and Education, Inc.)*

76 *N. W. Ayer & Sons,* Directory: Newspapers and Periodicals, 1959 (1968) (*Philadelphia, 1959, 1968).*

TAXING LIBRARY COPYING: DISCRIMINATORY AND SELF-DEFEATING

The Register of Copyrights, on the assumption that copyright proprietors should profit from library copying, regards with favor the proposal for a clearinghouse to license photocopying.[77]

It may be pointed out, however, that many more copying devices exist in commercial, industrial, business, professional, and even in domestic establishments than in libraries. It would be impossible to police the use of the former. It would be discriminatory to extend copyright to the use of the latter merely because it is possible to police them.

By the same token, any attempt to extend copyright to library copying would be self-defeating. As has been cogently stated, "[I]t would cost dimes to collect pennies" from the copying devices in libraries.[78]

CONCLUSION

From this survey the following conclusions emerge:

a. Libraries exist for a (or even the) principal purpose of facilitating copying, and their arrangements to this end antedate statutory copyright by several millennia.

b. Copying is indispensable to library-based research. Modern conditions have progressively increased this indispensability of copying services for the efficient organization of library resources and the efficiency of library-based research. The public interest requires adequacy of copying services.

c. The literal meaning of the copyright law notwithstanding, no copyright proprietor has ever had an exclusive right to copy the copyrighted work. Such a "right" would be unenforceable.

d. The literal prohibition of unauthorized copying contained in the law was an accident of legislative drafting, unintended by the writers of the legislation and unnoticed at the time.

e. This prohibition has nevertheless deterred even some important libraries from providing adequate copying services. This is contrary to the public interest.

f. There are, however, a number of bases for justifying library copying services for copyrighted materials in spite of the wording of the law. One of these consists of the formal action of a principal organization of copyright proprietors in giving general permission to libraries to photocopy copyrighted materials under certain conditions.

g. However, neither the meaning of the law nor the validity of any of the suggested bases for justifying unauthorized library copying of copyrighted materials has ever been adjudicated. Until this happens, or until the matter is clarified by legislation, the meaning of the law will continue to be debatable.

h. Many libraries, justifying their action by one or more of the theories discussed above, offer not only traditional copying services but photocopying services for copyrighted materials. But in the absence of certainty regarding the meaning of the law, all such libraries expose themselves thereby to risk of litigation and penalty. This is contrary to the public interest.

i. In spite of fears asserted by copyright proprietors several studies have failed to demonstrate that library photocopying services lead to significant loss of sales of copies of the copyrighted works. (However, some copyright proprietors feel

---

[77] *Copyright Law Revision.* op. cit. (*see footnote 25*), *vol. 6, p. 14.*
[78] *Benjamin,* loc. cit. (*see footnote 45*).

sufficiently strongly on this point that it appears that some of the issues will receive a court test in a suit for infringement now pending.)[79]

j. Even if such loss were demonstrated, it might be justified in the public interest. It is of the essence of the public interest that it sometimes requires the proprietor of a monopoly to forgo the full exercise of his exclusive right. In the case of copyright the public interest is stipulated by the United States Constitution to have the superior claim.

k. It is proposed by copyright proprietors as well as by the Register of Copyrights that libraries should pay for authorization to photocopy copyrighted material. This (1) would be contrary to the traditional policy followed by Congress, which has hitherto with a single exception (involving publication by performance) exempted nonprofit uses from copyright; (2) would establish an ugly precedent by charging libraries for the normal use of material for which they have already paid; (3) would discriminate against libraries as contrasted with the much more numerous but much less easily policed profit-making establishments that operate photocopying equipment; (4) would burden libraries with unproductive and sterile record-keeping; and (5) would be self-defeating in that it would "cost dimes to collect pennies."

l. Libraries have no objection to copyright proprietors making an honest dollar (and indeed serve as the source of many such), but they do not cotton to the notion of paying a second (and a third and a fourth) time for the use of material that they have already bought and for which they have already paid.

m. The various attempts to develop the principles for justifying library copying have led to increased understanding by librarians and the research community of limitations which should go far toward preventing unjustifiable losses to copyright proprietors.

n. Meanwhile, the arrangement permitting the unauthorized copying of copyright material by attorneys for use in copyright litigation, which the Library of Congress has established under its regulatory authority, might create a helpful precedent toward a solution of the problem.

The cloud that the Copyright Act of 1909 placed on library copying, and especially photocopying, can be dispersed by legislation or litigation. In 1961 the Register of Copyrights recommended legislation:

> The statute should permit a library, whose collections are available to the public without charge, to supply a single photocopy of copyrighted material in its collections to any applicant under the following conditions:
>
> (a) A single photocopy of one article in any issue of a periodical, or of a reasonable part of any other publication, may be supplied when the applicant states in writing that he needs and will use such material solely for his own research.
>
> (b) A single photocopy of an entire publication may be supplied when the applicant also states in writing, and the library is not otherwise informed, that a copy is not available from the publisher.
>
> (c) Where the work bears a copyright notice, the library should be required to affix to the photocopy a warning that the material appears to be copyrighted.[80]

This proposal, which went far toward meeting the requirements of libraries and of their users under conditions that were certainly not formidable, was incorporated by the Register in the preliminary draft of a copyright revision bill, 1964. It was understandably

---

[79] *Williams and Wilkins v. U.S.*, Petition 73–68 *filed in U.S. Court of Claims, February 27, 1968, alleging infringement of petitioner's copyright by the National Library of Medicine and the library of the National Institutes of Health. Although not stated in the petition, it is understood that the alleged infringement involves photocopying.*

[80] *Copyright Law Revision, op. cit. (see footnote 25), vol. 1, p. 26.*

opposed by principal groups of copyright proprietors, such as the American Textbook Publishers Institute, and was omitted from the 1964 draft; but library groups do not appear to have contested this omission, for no comments appear to be reported.[81] In any event, the House of Representatives, in enacting the Copyright Revision Bill (H. R. 2512, 90th Congress), treated the matter not as one affecting the public interest but as one merely involving the opposing views of parties at interest. It accordingly rejected a legislative solution in favor of accommodation between the parties, while tipping the scales, as previously noted—whether intentionally or by inadvertence—in favor of the copyright proprietors.[82]

Although it is not impossible that library copying and photocopying might fare better at the hands of the courts than of Congress, the fact remains that the primary responsibility for decision in this area is laid by the Constitution upon Congress. It now appears that the studies of this subject heretofore commissioned by the Copyright Office, ground-breaking and valuable though they were, need to be renewed and carried further in order to provide Congress with the information needed in order to reach a wise decision—based to the fullest extent possible upon settled policy and unshaken by conjecture—in a matter so nearly concerning the public interest.

[81] Ibid., *vol. 3, pp. 6–7, 337–40;* ibid., *vol. 5, pp. 1–32.*
[82] *House Report 83,* op. cit. (*see footnote 24*), *p. 36.*

CHAPTER VII

SOME PROBLEMS AND POTENTIALS OF TECHNOLOGY AS APPLIED TO LIBRARY AND INFORMATIONAL SERVICES

Perhaps no other area has received as much attention in the library world today as the so-called new technology. Some idealistic visionaries would have it that books, library buildings, and librarians themselves as we have known them are so out of tune with the times that drastic action is required for total automation of the transfer and storage of knowledge. The other extreme is represented by a reactionary fear of the costly disruption of status quo.

The National Advisory Commission on Libraries found in favor of broadly conceived planning, based on careful research and experimentation, toward the application of existing technology and the development of new tools and new organizational relationships specifically geared to the needs of users of library and informational services. The Commission favored a diversity of efforts, at the same time deploring the proliferation of noncompatible special-interest services. It deplored the fact that one of the most promising means for solving problems was itself creating new problems.

What in fact the National Advisory Commission on Libraries did recommend was an evolving responsiveness to user needs, coordinated under Federal leadership. It recommended establishment of a Federal Institute of Library and Information Science as a principal center for basic and applied research in all relevant areas, to which would be assigned the system engineering and technical direction involved in the design and implementation of an integrated national library and information system. This institute would work closely with the permanent National Commission on Libraries and Information Science, the continuing Federal planning agency recommended in the Report.

Three of the special studies commissioned by the original National Advisory Commission contributed to its conclusions and recommendations with respect to the problems and potentials of technology. These reports appear here as sections A, B, and C of chapter 7.

A. RESEARCH LIBRARIES AND THE NEW TECHNOLOGY[1]

by MAX V. MATHEWS
Director, Behavioral Research Laboratory

and W. STANLEY BROWN
Head, Computing Mathematics Research Department
Bell Telephone Laboratories

INTRODUCTION

The nation's research libraries are threatened by the rising stream of publication, and they are not likely to save themselves without the help of technology and, in particular, varying degrees of automation. But automation of any existing process is a complex change, with many pitfalls, which must be approached with great care. The germane question is not how to automate libraries but rather what processes of libraries, if any, will be improved by automation.

The huge storehouses of material in libraries are hard to change and would themselves resist the sweeping restructuring that any attempt to achieve complete automation would entail. Research libraries are large and varied collections that we wish to preserve, and this puts an additional requirement on plans for automation. Except for a few special cases concerning new fields that have no body of retrospective literature, we must plot a viable evolutionary path along which present collections can be made more useful for research by means of automation technology. Desirable as certain ends may be, they will remain hypothetical utopias unless we can foresee a course of development. Hence, a legitimate and essential question, which must always be asked as part of any plan, is "How do we proceed from our present libraries?"

We must avoid errors of both overconservatism and overoptimism in applying new technology. Libraries are so important and expensive that we must overlook no possible savings in cost or increase in effectiveness that can be furthered by technology. On the other hand, we cannot afford the very expensive mistake of relying on technology that does not exist and may never be created. Neither can libraries themselves be expected to develop extensive new technology.

From this point of view it seems reasonable in this paper to discuss the next steps in library development that can be taken over the next ten years, and that use foreseeable modifications of existing technology. The considerations are organized into three aspects: computer technology and machine-readable information, microform technology and copying, and means for interactions between libraries. All aspects are interrelated and each will develop its full potential only if the others follow the course outlined.

Our concentration on relatively secure goals should in no sense be interpreted as a rejection of venture research of an advanced nature. Computer "understanding" of natural languages, automatic abstracting, optical readers capable of reading any book from the shelf, economical long-distance facsimile transmission of entire books, and other similar developments deserve attention when and if research and experiment solve their basic problems. Current and realistic library plans must not be based on the future success of these still-developing projects.

[1] *From* On Research Libraries *by the Committee on Research Libraries of the American Council of Learned Societies; submitted to the National Advisory Commission on Libraries November 1967. The complete study,* On Research Libraries, *was published by the M.I.T. Press in 1969.*

COMPUTER TECHNOLOGY

The impact of computer technology on libraries will be felt in two different directions: (1) improving bibliographic access or assisting the library user to obtain information, and (2) automating library operations. In the first area, machine-readable catalogs will assist research by making widely available multiple copies of the catalog, subcatalogs, and union catalogs. In the second area, the prime candidates for automation are acquisition, circulation, and inventory control.

A card catalog is a remarkable invention. It can be used to locate one document among millions. It is simultaneously accessible to many users. It can be edited and kept reasonably accurate. However, one cannot use it without going to the one place where it exists. This explains the current interest in catalogs in book form, on microfilm, and on magnetic tape, all of which can be made available wherever they are needed.

A magnetic-tape catalog is well within the capabilities of current technology, and it has striking advantages over the other types of catalogs. The original card catalog can be kept up-to-date. The catalogs in book form or on microfilm cannot be kept up-to-date, though supplements can be added, and they do not lend themselves to any but the simplest search. Magnetic tape has many advantages. It can be constantly updated; it can be restructured in several different ways to facilitate different search strategies; it can be used to make humanly readable microform catalogs, and two or more tapes can be automatically merged to produce a union catalog.

The magnetic-tape catalog does not allow either librarians or library users to search the complete catalog in real time because of the time necessary to mount and spin tapes. Real-time access may become possible with a large enough on-line storage device that may be available within a few years. The feasibility of using it depends on the cost and on the availability of an appropriate computing system. Fortunately, real-time access is not essential to any of our major purposes, since all needs for rapid access to the complete catalog can be fulfilled by the printed or microform version. Making the conservative assumption that the machine-readable catalog exists solely on magnetic tape, the following paragraphs discuss its uses, its construction, and the associated costs.

To the library user, a catalog is for searching. We distinguish between two fundamentally different types of searches. An easy search is one that requires the examination of only a very small portion of the catalog; for example, a search in the author catalog for a book whose author is known. A hard search is one that requires the examination of most or all of the catalog; for example, a search for all books whose titles contain a particular word. Easy searches must be rapid and need not involve a computer. Hard searches must involve a computer but need not be rapid. Because of their cost hard searches will be batched. It would be unreasonable to do them daily, but they could be carried out weekly or monthly, depending on the demand and the urgency.

Sometimes a hard search can be made easy by resorting and restructuring the catalog. For example, a search by title in an author catalog would be hard, but this catalog can be resorted and restructured into a title catalog, thereby making all subsequent title searches easy. Similarly, a search for titles containing a given word is hard in a conventional catalog but easy in a permuted index. (Unfortunately, the sheer bulk of a permuted catalog might be a serious obstacle to its construction and use.)

We turn now to the construction of the machine-readable catalog. Clearly we cannot ask that the old catalog be converted suddenly into machine-readable form. What we can do is to begin to automate the processes of acquisition and circulation, and to grow a machine-readable catalog as a by-product. If each item that is acquired, copied, or loaned is entered into the machine-readable catalog, then it will not be long before all items that are new or frequently used will be included.

This type of catalog will not meet the needs of all scholars. One of the characteristics of research, particularly in the humanities and social sciences, is its requirement for access to many library materials that are neither new nor frequently used. Knowledge advances by building on the accumulated data and wisdom of the past, and improved access to this body of literature is no less needed than improved access to what is being currently published. Attention must therefore be given to finding an economically viable method of making the old catalog, that is, the existing catalog of existing literature, widely available in machine-readable form. Few individual libraries can afford the capital cost of completely converting their own catalogs, and the duplication of holdings between libraries would make such individual effort wasteful. Still, the unique holdings of every research library should be listed on tape for the national benefit. This is a national problem for which a number of solutions have been proposed; one, of course, is completing and converting the *National Union Catalog,* even while it is in process of publication in 600 volumes.

How about the costs of a machine-readable catalog and the associated operations that we have been discussing? In order to get some feeling for magnitudes, take for example the library at the University of Chicago, which has almost 2.5 million volumes. The card catalog contains about 5 million cards of 300 characters each. Fuller description of each document would be as desirable in the machine-readable catalog as in the card version and would greatly increase its value to the scholar. In the listing of costs, conversion is omitted because the assumption is that this occurs as a by-product of automated processing and circulation. However, the cost of getting a single catalog card into a computer has been estimated at 35 to 42 cents; for the entire catalog this cost alone would have a highly deterrent effect. Some other cost estimates are:

1. The machine-readable catalog would occupy about 80 reels of magnetic tape, worth about $5,000 ($60 per reel).
2. One pass through the catalog would take about 5 hours of computer time (4 minutes per reel) and would cost about $1,000 ($12 per reel). During this pass one could edit the catalog, make several updated copies, and perform several exhaustive searches to assemble valuable subcatalogs.
3. A complete resorting of the catalog would take about 32 hours of computer time (24 minutes per reel) and would cost about $5,800 ($72 per reel). For a much smaller catalog (less than 10 reels) the time would be 20 minutes per reel and the cost would be $60 per reel. For a larger catalog (more than 100 reels) the time would be 28 minutes per reel and the cost would be $84 per reel.
4. A microfilm version of the catalog would occupy about 30,000 feet of 16mm film (or 10,000 4″ x 6″ microfiche), worth about $1,500.
5. A microfilm version of the catalog could be generated from the machine-readable version in about 10 hours at a cost of about $1,000 plus the cost of the film.
6. A microfilm version of the catalog could be copied photographically, and would therefore cost little more than the cost of the film.
7. A paper version of the catalog, with characters of the size found in a telephone directory, would occupy 100,000 pages. A crude estimate for generating a few copies is $3,000 per copy, based on a three-cents-per-page copying cost. This does not include binding costs.

These figures give an indication of both the possibilities and the limitations of a machine-readable catalog. It would be reasonable to revise such a catalog, make updated copies, and perform complete searches to assemble valuable subcatalogs, but this could only be done on a weekly or monthly basis. It would be possible to resort and restructure the catalog for major purposes, but this could not be undertaken lightly. A microfilm version could be published once or twice yearly. Supplements would be necessary.

From these estimates it seems to the authors that machine-readable catalogs will be very useful and will not flounder even in very large libraries. However, they will only make sense if they are used carefully in the proper ways.

Now let us consider the automating of library operations—acquisition, circulation, and inventory control. Manual methods for performing these operations are barely able to cope with existing-sized libraries. Automation is essential if the size of libraries continues to expand. Furthermore, highly effective programs appear feasible with present computers.

The most important point in the automation of acquisition is that one machine-readable description of a document, possibly prepared by the publisher, may be the major input to an over-all program that ends with the document available to library users, several entries for it in the main catalog (or more likely in the current supplement), and the bill checked and paid.

Circulation and inventory control are different aspects of the general problem of keeping track of library holdings. In principle the borrowing and returning of documents could be recorded directly in the machine-readable catalog if it were kept in on-line storage. Fortunately a separate small machine-readable catalog of currently borrowed items would serve equally well; this would, for example, permit the automatic generation of overdue notices.

How can a good set of computer programs be created for libraries? They must be built up gradually by experimental development in an existing library. With focused objectives and effort, progress should be clear in a period of perhaps five years. Some programming experts must be brought into libraries—but, more importantly, librarians must learn to use computers and must come to understand their strengths and limitations. This education process will take several years under the best conditions. From experience in other fields we can emphasize that there is no alternative to *having library experts learn computation.* Any other course will lead to inferior results with great waste of money and effort.

What kind of computation centers will be best for libraries? For acquisition, a little time on a local computer in batch-processing mode will suffice. For keeping track of circulation, a small amount of time-shared computing will be required. It may also be desirable to keep subcatalogs in on-line storage at a local computing center. For this, also, time-shared access will be essential. Fortunately, libraries will not need to have their own computers for any of these purposes.

For processes involving the entire machine-readable catalog or a major portion of it, we believe it will prove advantageous to establish special library computation centers. The normal computation facility serving a university community is not well suited to the economical processing of large catalogs. A regional library computation center could serve perhaps ten or twelve libraries. The computing system at one of these centers will have a large number of tape drives (perhaps 20) and a large but relatively slow memory. The tape catalogs will probably be kept at these centers since they will be safer there and they would be of little or no use elsewhere.

MICROFORM AND COPYING TECHNOLOGY

We believe microform and copying technology will be at least as important in libraries as computer technology. For example, in the instances where cost and copyright are not overriding factors, full-sized copying machines have already revolutionized circulation habits. Needless to say, copying technology will interact strongly with computer technology and will affect the entire structure of library automation.

The importance of this technology results from its impact on the storage, handling, cost, and circulation of library holdings. These factors will always be fundamental in libraries. Storage space will be reduced, handling by machine (as well as by people) will be made possible, cost of a document will be reduced, and circulation will be pushed in the direction of copying rather than borrowing.

As will be clear from subsequent details, microforms will supplement rather than replace conventional library holdings. Some materials cannot usefully be photographed.

All materials will be available as or convertible to conventional hard copy. Hence, the user who specifies conventional books, either for objective reasons or for subjective preference, will continue to be satisfied. It is usually too costly for individual libraries to convert extensive hard-copy holdings to microfilm form. However, there is a growing microfilm publication business. Many periodicals and a number of books can be purchased directly in microform; new libraries turn to microfilm for out-of-print books; crowded libraries save space by putting bulky materials on film.

In contrast to full-sized copying machines, why is the adoption of microforms so much slower? There is undoubtedly reader resistance, though there is some evidence that the established scholar is more insistent on the original than the graduate student, and high school students are the microfilm's warmest friends. But we believe that the answer is simply that no over-all system properly engineered for the reader has ever been assembled. Almost all the pieces of such a system already exist, however, and the over-all system could be created with a little well-directed encouragement of existing companies plus a little standardization. Listing a few requirements will clarify our concept of such a system; we envision three forms of information: full-sized hard copy, microforms, and machine-readable digital tapes.

1. Quick, automatic apparatus must be available for copying any of these forms and for converting from any one of them to any other.[2] There are three modes of copying and six modes of conversion, as illustrated in Table 7A–1. A full-sized, high-quality, dry sheet of paper should be produced from a microform in seconds. Further, a sequence of sheets should be generated automatically without manual intervention between pages. Immediate output is not as essential in converting from full size to microform, but the process should have a high speed to minimize costs. Microform copies of anything must be immediately available to customers in the library or for interlibrary loans. They should be automatically produced. The quality of images must be such that several generations of copies can be made without serious degradation. Methods for publishing machine-readable information are especially vital. Microform copies will often be preferred. Present microfilm recorders for computers come very close to meeting library requirements.

2. Microforms must be hand and machine manipulable. None should be so small or delicate that they cannot be hand carried. They must have a shape such that a simple and cheap machine can store, move, and look through any aggregate. Labels that can be read with the unaided human eye and by a simple machine must be an inherent part.

3. Some must be mailable. Much interlibrary communication will be by microform. These must be suitable for mailing—light, flat, and not brittle.

4. The microforms should be humanly readable in simple apparatus. Further, it should be possible to scan pages with as much facility as scanning a book. More specifically, we envision an entire book imaged onto a few "cards" that can be mass-produced, handled, and filed easily, reproduced easily, and read comfortably. Any page should be immediately accessible, and it should be possible to scan rapidly through many pages. The cards should be labeled for both people and machines.

What is the state of development of microform apparatus to satisfy the requirements posed above? Some version of all machines exists, except possibly for a microform camera processor to produce immediate microforms from hard copy, and this would not be hard to create. Excellent and rapid microfilm printers for computers exist (see appendix F–3 for an example). Additional "human engineering" is needed on many

---

2 *Reading by an optical scanner is possible only in special instances, and the free convertibility here described depends on the development of a satisfactory general-purpose optical scanner.*

components. Some "machine engineering" is needed to add machine-readable labels to all microforms.

The most pressing need is for standardization and completeness. By standardization we do not mean one huge machine that will do everything on one kind of microform. A multiplicity of smaller machines is preferable from all standpoints, and rolls, "cards," and aperture cards are probably a minimum number of different forms to handle different functions. However, machines should be obtainable to convert from one form to another.

How much time and money will be needed to make these machines available? We have not been able to get an estimate from companies in the microform business. One way to promote the development of this system is to create a small laboratory of four or five workers. About half their effort would be spent for their own research, the other half would be spent prodding the microform industry by means of contracts pointed at specific objectives. The laboratory costs would be about $300,000 per year and substantial progress should be clear in about five years. Much of the total development costs would and should come from the microform industry.

What about copyright? The system we have described depends utterly on the ability to make copies. Revision of the present copyright law is now before Congress, and it is vital to avoid prohibiting the flow of information for research by the wrong laws. (See the discussions of copyright in chapter 6.)

INTERACTIONS BETWEEN LIBRARIES AND SPECIAL-PURPOSE LIBRARIES

The most important changes in libraries will be (1) increasing interactions between them, which will reduce duplication of holdings, and (2) the growth of special-purpose collections dealing in depth with narrow fields. Effective interaction will be greatly facilitated through some of the automation procedures under discussion here.

Any interaction first requires some means for one library to know what is in the collection of another. Since it would be costly for one library to purchase and hold the individual catalogs of many other libraries, the best solution is a union catalog.

The appeal of a union catalog has long been felt, and indeed, the *National Union Catalog* is a notable response. In its card form at the Library of Congress it of course suffers from the lack of accessibility to the country's other research centers. The forthcoming published form will be widely available and its cost, between $8,000 and $9,000, will not be prohibitive. But it will be far from complete, its six hundred volumes will take ten years to print, and those volumes can never be changed.[3]

A machine-readable union catalog can be kept up-to-date, and it can be structured in several ways, in contrast to the *National Union Catalog* which is an author catalog only.

How can a machine-readable national union catalog be constructed? The card form of the *National Union Catalog* could be keypunched, but we think it preferable to grow the catalog by merging the machine-readable catalogs as they are developed by existing individual libraries. A union of several machine-readable catalogs (say, up to ten) could be constructed (see appendix F–3 for details) at a cost of $12 for each reel of the union catalog plus the cost of the tape. Unions of union catalogs would soon follow. We are assuming here that most of the decisions about whether two cards represent the same document can be made by a sophisticated computer program, so that expert human handling of the remaining difficult decisions would not be unduly burdensome.

Since the union would include only the machine-readable portions of each library's catalog, it would initially omit substantial parts of the library's holdings. However,

---

[3] *It should be added that provision has been made for changing the printer's copy of the* National Union Catalog *during the course of publication from cards to machine-produced output at any time when this becomes practicable. Also see chapter 10.*

within a few years the union catalog would include all recent acquisitions and all books in common use. Such a catalog would serve the clientele of a medical or science library where the value of a book often diminishes rapidly. It would be less useful in the general research library or to the scholar who requires seasoned material that is infrequently called for. For this reason it may be desirable, when financially possible, to supplement the current union catalogs with the *National Union Catalog* in machine-readable form.

Typically the catalog holdings of a moderate-sized library would include its own catalog, a union catalog, and perhaps a number of special-purpose catalogs. The dividing line between special-purpose catalogs and indexes will be very thin—one will blend into the other. By purchasing microfilm catalogs, the small library without a computer will obtain many of the advantages of machine-readable catalogs.

Unfortunately, access to a catalog is not the same as access to a collection, and there are limits to interlibrary lending in view of the prior claims of the local clientele. But photocopying has greatly broadened the possibility of sharing, particularly technical reports and journal articles, and most copying of this sort falls under the cover of fair use. In case of urgent need, a facsimile could be made within minutes, but the price would be much higher.

The publication of union catalogs in machine-readable form will stimulate strong pressures for uniformity of bibliographic reference. This is most desirable, particularly if it can be extended to foreign documents.

Many of the special-purpose libraries will be national libraries devoted to particular subject areas. Each will strive for completeness in its own area and will develop its own indexing system for that area. The subject areas will overlap very substantially, and their subject-indexing systems will reflect fundamentally different world-views in the regions of overlap.

Special-purpose libraries should be very broadly defined. Thus, for example, the abstracts and indexes published by the American Chemical Society will often be referred to for the same purposes as catalogs of other libraries.

Small new areas of knowledge have the great advantage that they can start a fresh body of information. Early progress in machine-readable text, machine retrieval of facts, and sophisticated machine-searching will likely come in these areas, where computers will provide access to highly refined bodies of information.

Handbooks of facts, formulas, and algorithms will be created and used. Here innovation is properly left to experts within the special fields, and the continuing function of libraries will be to make their results generally and uniformly available. An exception to this statement about innovation might be made regarding a research library with staff librarians who were themselves scholars and whose collaboration in such projects would be highly valuable.

CONCLUSIONS AND RECOMMENDATIONS

Recommendations must be weighed both with respect to their importance and to the certainty that they can be achieved. Accordingly, let us start with the most important and sure possibilities.

The best hope for dealing with the increased amount of material with which research libraries must cope is greatly to reduce multiple holdings of the same document in different libraries. This can be achieved by effective interactions between libraries, both existing libraries and special libraries that may be uniquely structured to handle remote business.

The key to such interactions is the machine-readable and, hence, reproducible catalog. With existing technology it is both possible and economical to keep catalogs of large libraries on many reels of magnetic computer tapes. These tape catalogs can be copied. They can be published via a computer-to-microfilm printer. They can be combined into union catalogs, searched to create subcatalogs, and restructured to facilitate different modes of referencing. They can be edited, corrected, and kept current. Thus any library can be accurately and currently informed on the holdings of a wide range of other institutions. Its users will be able to identify and order documents from other institutions.

Development of machine-readable catalogs, particularly union catalogs, is by far the most important and most certain recommendation that we can make. In addition, library interactions will be furthered by better copying facilities and microforms. The nature of these innovations is not as clear to us, despite the many possibilities that exist in the area of microforms. The major uncertainties arise from user acceptance and from copyright laws. Hence, a more timid and speculative development program must be undertaken here.

We have said nothing about communications. With adequate machine-readable catalogs a workable network of library interactions can be based on existing facilities— the mails, the teletype, and the telephone. These links are a good starting point. Needless to say, interactions will be improved by the better channels that will be developed. However, the cost of networks is so great that libraries must share them with other users; it is not reasonable for libraries to be prime movers in the development of new networks.

It is clear that automation can and should be applied to handle the internal operations of large libraries. Current manual operations are barely workable in present-sized libraries and threaten chaos in the larger institutions of the future. Fortunately, many library tasks are ideally suited to computer organization; we have no doubt that this will be effective. Moreover, some of the records used in internal operations will be useful in making catalogs.

To achieve these general ends, certain more specific suggestions are made below in the areas of microform technology and computer technology.

The microform technology had best be developed in industrial laboratories concerned with reproduction and photographic processes. Many places with great competence already exist. However, some central direction is necessary to establish standards and to see that problems unique to libraries are solved. The commercial value of microform equipment, as estimated by present market analysis, may be insufficient to support the development of the system we have outlined. But once the complete system is in operation, it will be the foundation of an entire new industry. The development will consist of a number of separate machines and microforms. Their value depends not on individual machines but on the over-all system. Central direction must make sure that a complete set of machines is created for making all the transformations discussed above, and central direction must see that the machines are compatible.

Computer technology for routine library functions and for a machine-readable catalog can best be developed in a large, existing, operating library. Only in this way can we guarantee that a useful system will be created and that the transition from existing manual procedures to automated procedures is viable. Funds for the development should be supplied outside the library's normal operating budget. However, the costs must continually be appraised so that the final system makes economic sense for libraries.

A fertile institution in which to develop library automation would include not only a library but also a strong computer-science department and a strong library school. The differing viewpoints and experiences of library users, computing specialists, and librarians must be reconciled and focused on the library's problems if these problems are to be solved.

Technology offers the librarian a variety of means by which his problems may be lightened or even solved, with consequent improvement in the library's service to research. At the same time technology offers an evolutionary advance toward a national library system that will realize the ideal of equal and rapid access to the nation's research treasures.

TABLE 7A–1

MODES OF COPYING AND CONVERSION

From \ To	paper	microform	machine-readable
paper	copy	photograph and reduce	read page
microform	enlarge	copy	read micropage
machine-readable	print	microprint	copy

B. THE IMPACT OF TECHNOLOGY ON THE LIBRARY BUILDING[4]

BACKGROUND

The image of the library has been as immutable as the shape of the steeple in a village landscape. Time has given these forms the stamp of authenticity. Within the past decade, however, cracks have been appearing in the library's facade—and they are growing wider.

Computer technology, microform technology, and developments in communications have created a potential for the storage, retrieval, and exchange of information beyond any means ever before attainable. Indeed, Sunday supplement writers, fired by the far-reaching visions of pioneers in these fields, declare that the book will become obsolete. It will be an artifact exhibited in museums, they tell us, its functions assumed by electronic circuitry. And libraries, as the institutions we have known them to be, will be things of the past.

This hypothesis, as Mark Twain reported on the news of his death, is greatly exaggerated. The book, which appears to have extraordinary survival power, has stood up thus far against the real and imagined threats of radio, film, and television. Witness its career since 1945, for example, when general television broadcasting began. The circulation of public library books in the United States has increased by more than 200 percent, and from 1960 through 1965 the numbers and titles of new books and new

---

4 *From a position paper of the same name prepared for Educational Facilities Laboratories; submitted to the National Advisory Commission on Libraries in 1967. Participants in the conference that developed this paper are listed in appendix F–3.*

editions of books produced in the United States increased by more than 90 percent.[5] *Publishers' Weekly* reports that 1965 and 1966 were banner years for book sales, continuing an upward trend in annual over-all book figures for more than a dozen years. In 1965 dollar volume ran to over $2 billion.[6] In 1966 how to meet the bottlenecks in production and delivery caused by the demand became a major industry issue.

The survival powers of the book notwithstanding, technological changes in the making *could*, one day, profoundly alter the traditional operations of libraries—and their buildings. And those within the profession, as well as college and university presidents, trustees, governing boards of public libraries—all those responsible for planning library buildings and committing large funds to their construction—are concerned.

This concern is by no means a matter of resistance to change. On the contrary, library professionals are acutely aware of the dire need for new solutions to mounting library problems. Major among these is the flood of new information. Most of the nation's libraries are hard pressed for money to buy, and space to house, the torrent of books and journals pouring off presses around the world. There are 400,000 books published annually worldwide, roughly twice that of a decade ago.[7] In the sciences alone, where old-fashioned physics, biology, and chemistry have bred new fields like biomagnetics, macromolecular physical chemistry, and cryogenics, to name only a few, there are 35,000 separate journals published annually with over 1.5 million articles in them. The journals themselves are estimated to be growing in number at the rate of 5 to 10 percent a year, the literature in them doubling every ten to fifteen years.[8]

The Library of Congress owns some 54 million items. Cornell University catalogs over 85,000 titles a year. And if one considers that academic and research libraries tend to double the size of their collections every sixteen to twenty years—then, in the words of mathematician J. G. Kemeny, "the cost of building, of purchasing volumes, of cataloging, and of servicing these gigantic libraries could eventually ruin our richest universities." This says nothing of the difficulties that lie in wait for the user as he approaches the card catalogs of awesome dimensions, or the reference librarian, who is estimated at the present time to walk an average of eight miles a day on the job.

How to cope with it all is by itself a subject of prolific literature in the library world. Librarians themselves are the first to recognize that the solution is not simply more books, more buildings, and more librarians. What they look forward to, and *need*, is a change in the very concept of what a library is; that is, beyond its function as a depository of books the library must become a source of active information transfer. The new technologies offer the long-range hope of realizing this concept, and librarians, above all, welcome it. Through computer storage and retrieval, microforms, long-distance transmission, and the like, it may yet be possible to multiply the usability of every information unit, to transcend the physical and geographic limitations of the library building, and ultimately, perhaps, to make one's home or office in Kimberly, Idaho, as fruitful a place for learning as the best public, academic, or research libraries in major centers.

But to what extent this will ever be a reality is the big question. Almost as important is the question of when.

The answers are urgent because well-planned, flexible buildings erected today can serve for a hundred years; because current construction costs per square foot for library building space range from $25 to $40 per square foot, depending on the region of the country and other variables, with total project costs running roughly a third more, including fees, furnishings, and the like; and finally, because we are in a period of intensified activity in library construction.

[5] Illinois Libraries, *48* (*September 1966*), *pp. 562–3, as quoted in R. J. Blakely, "The Wit to Win,"* ALA Bulletin, *61* (*February 1967*), *p. 168.*
[6] *"Statistics, News, and Trends in the Industry,"* Publishers' Weekly, *191* (*January 30, 1967*), *p. 46.*
[7] *Figures for 1964 from* Statistical Yearbook, 1965 (*Paris: UNESCO, 1965*).
[8] *"The Literature of Science and Technology,"* Encyclopedia of Science and Technology (*1960 ed. updated in 1966; New York: McGraw-Hill, 1966*), *vol. 7, p. 542.*

Increased population, greater numbers of young people going further in higher education, Federal assistance, the opening of new fields of employment, greater leisure time—and present library deficiencies, which are acute—are behind the building surge.

The United States Office of Education has reported that among public libraries, though capital outlay soared from $12.3 million in 1956 to $103 million in 1965, prospective capital expenditures to construct 68 million gross square feet of public library space by 1975 come to $1.9 billion.[9] Still, this will not satisfy the full needs, estimated to be more than 90 million square feet by 1970. For libraries in public and nonpublic schools estimates are that more than 3.4 billion square feet of space will be necessary by 1972. And in institutions of higher education the indications are that more than 135 million new square feet of space will be required by the same date.[10] Scheduled for construction in two- and four-year colleges are 1,200 buildings to go up between 1966 and 1970. Their anticipated cost, including furniture, comes to $2.17 billion.[11]

Given the magnitude of monies already committed and the additional sums likely to be so allocated, it is little wonder that librarians are deeply concerned. If it is indeed true that in the future the bulk of knowledge will be stored on magnetic tapes or greatly reduced microforms and fed into computers; that information transactions will be negotiated through terminals located at home, in the dormitory, the classroom, the office, or in service stations remote from where information is stored; and that information will be transmitted to users over long distances—then indeed it is imprudent if not illogical to plan costly structures to house nonexistent books and their readers.

The questions that hang over the heads of library planners are (a) the probability of these propositions; (b) whether they will be true for all types of information, in all types of libraries, in small ones as well as large; (c) whether they will be economically practical or prohibitively expensive; and (d) the speed of change.

Between the myths and the realities, between the oversimplifications of the space-age writers and the arcana of the new sciences, planners are caught in a web of dilemmas.

It is not uncommon to encounter representatives of small liberal arts colleges, influenced by the space-age prose, who are afraid they have fallen behind the times because their libraries lack automated information systems. In fact, such highly sophisticated operations are at present confined to a very few specialized national libraries such as the National Library of Medicine or the American Chemical Society. These deal mainly with bibliographical material, not text, and almost all of them are in some important aspects still experimental or developmental.

Similar misconceptions exist in relation to automated housekeeping processes such as circulation, acquisitions, serials control, and the like. Although these chores are in fact automated in many libraries, it is at present more economical in small ones to manage them in the traditional mode. There are still other situations where new library facilities are desperately needed, but planners are sitting tight, chary of committing sizable funds to structures that may turn out to be anachronisms.

Clearly there is a need for shared expertise and for common sense in its application. Those with responsibility for decision-making must be informed of the implications of the new technology and provided with guidelines so that they can proceed with the confidence that the buildings they plan today will be usable in the future. The present

9 *Nathan M. Cohen, "Public Libraries,"* Public Facility Needs (*"State and Local Public Facility Needs and Financing," vol. 1, study prepared for the Subcommittee on Economic Progress of the Joint Economic Committee, Congress of the United States [Washington, D.C.: Government Printing Office, 1966]), pp. 616–24.*

10 *Estimates of need in public, school, and college and university libraries were prepared by Henry Drennan, Acting Chief, Library Planning and Development Branch, U.S. Office of Education, 1967. For further discussion of estimates see section A, chapter 12.*

11 *Data from unpublished report, "Projected Construction and Financing of College and University Libraries, Fall 1966 to Fall 1970," prepared for EFL by Consultants to Industry, Inc., Stanford Professional Center, Palo Alto, California, in 1967.*

state of the art of library architecture, based on modular principles that allow for interior flexibility, has until now provided that confidence. We knew that such buildings, appropriately located, capable of expansion, and with provisions for the addition of electric and air-conditioning loads, could serve as well in the year 2067 as they do today. But in light of the unfolding possibilities for the management of information, do these principles remain sound and adequate?

To probe for viable answers, Educational Facilities Laboratories (EFL) arranged a symposium of experts from the relevant disciplines. Communications and information technologists, librarians, and architects (see list of participants in appendix F–3) met at EFL's offices in New York City on June 7 and 8, 1967. Broadly, they addressed themselves to the impact of technology on library buildings. Their task was to separate rhetoric from reality, fact from fancy. Specifically, they explored the wisdom of continuing to build libraries along traditional lines and plumbed available knowledge for cues on how to prepare buildings to adapt to the new era.

Two days of discussion explored four principal areas of relevance: computer technology, microform technology, communications technology, and the relationship of human beings to the possible changes ahead.

Other points dealt with, in addition to those noted earlier, were the cost of envisioned programs; patterns of library use; how the library may absorb particular innovations or be absorbed by them; centralization, decentralization, and networks; and the implications for space requirements, mechanical provisions, and the physical environments of buildings.

Every question could not be fully answered either for lack of time or because there are no answers at this point in time. The critical questions, however, were covered. What follows represents the consensus of views expressed concerning the impact of technology on library buildings over the next twenty years or so, beyond which period forecasts would take on aspects of pure speculation. It is EFL's hope that they will resolve for the present some of the uncertainties that beset the profession and will provide a guide to assist planners in the approach to their task.

COMPUTERS

The first substantial application of the computer to library processes began in 1959, propelled by the scarcity of librarians, the rapidly soaring costs of processing books, and the increasing flood of publications. Since that time there has been a great deal of pioneering work in most areas of library operations, usually in large libraries, and with varying degrees of success. These early attempts have been to a great extent random and unrelated to one another, even competitive, with programming developed for local operations only and with scant or immature reports of results.

Four areas of library activities have been repeatedly attempted: bookkeeping operations connected with the ordering and receiving departments (in many libraries); the handling of catalog data for books, sometimes accompanied by book catalogs printed by computer (such as that at the University of Toronto); circulation control (such as that at the University of California at Los Angeles); and information retrieval of technical data, law citations, bibliographical citations, and most ambitiously, the Medical Literature Analysis and Retrieval System (MEDLARS) program at the National Library of Medicine. The latter results in computer production of the *Index Medicus* and the searching of information contained in it on demand. The Library of Congress now has under way in Project MARC (Machine Readable Catalog) a series of ambitious experiments in computerized library processes, concentrated at present on the handling of catalog data. Since the Library of Congress is pivotal, to the degree that these experiments are successful they will affect the entire library world (see chapter 10).

Many of the results obtained to date are impressive, but conflicting claims have created confusion about the entire field of computerization in libraries. The questions facing any library interested in computerization today are: Should we computerize, when, and why? What should we computerize? What are the costs involved, and should we accept them? What relation will local computerization have to regional or national computer projects, such as those of the Library of Congress? What information about library computerization can we depend on?

The course of computer development and use within the library over the next twenty years is likely to proceed as follows:

Its first general impact will be in the area of housekeeping chores—order records and reports, fiscal control, circulation systems, etc. Application of the computer to bookkeeping operations, such as buying and receiving, is the easiest to accomplish. Moreover, it is the area in which considerable experience in many libraries to date indicates clear cost advantages in large operations.

The second field of general application—and impact—will be the computerization of the library card catalog. Some aspects of this are now technologically feasible. The promise is that this will extend greatly the usefulness of information contained in the present card catalog. Its advantages lie in its accessibility to users beyond the library, in permitting the interchange of catalog information between libraries, and in mobility within the library itself for checking holdings, changing location records, and the like. Although the conversion of any library operation to automation must be undertaken with the greatest care and planning because of the very large costs involved, this is especially so with regard to computerization of the card catalog.

Totally aside from costs there are technological and intellectual problems of the greatest magnitude to be overcome before computerized catalogs will be generally usable. Direct-access files of larger storage capacity than presently available in computer systems will be required to store the catalogs of great research libraries. The capability of simultaneous consultation of the catalog by very large numbers of users must be expanded (the present limit is about thirty). Problems of what terms and how many to use in describing catalog information must be resolved. Programs to retrieve only the materials specifically required by a user must be developed. But despite these problems, it is expected that within ten to twenty years the use of computerized catalogs will be widespread.

When dealing with the storage and retrieval of text, equally formidable problems exist. Data or factual evidence of small unit size are easily manipulable by the computer, but much more complex bodies of thought or of knowledge are not. As of the present it would appear that most of the literature in the humanities and social sciences will remain primarily useful in book form. There is no signal advantage in converting Plato's dialogues to machine-readable form and retrieving them or juxtaposing them by the computer. It is therefore economically senseless to attempt a massive conversion of existing library books to machine-readable form, since the advantages of doing so are minimal in many subject fields, and the costs enormous. The change to computer storage of full texts, when it comes, will be evolutionary not revolutionary, and it is unlikely that the library as a repository of books will be replaced in the near future by a computer in the basement consulted by remote consoles.

The first phase of development in information retrieval will use the computer to store and retrieve highly used specialized data, probably in nonalphabetical languages, in the physical and life sciences—as is now being done on a limited scale. Sometime later, perhaps within ten years, the texts of some highly used materials selected from current science and nonscience publications will be originally published in computerized form. But for the next twenty years or more the great bulk of publication will be in conventional print form, with a gradual increase in the production of microform texts. Retrospective conversion of texts to machine-readable form is not expected to any great degree for a very long time in the future. Therefore, the bulk of a scholar's negotiations in a library will be with books even thirty years from now.

MICROFORMS

The vision of carrying the Library of Congress around in miniaturized form in a shoebox has long been held—and in a smaller way, projected and abandoned at Wake Forest College.

The use of microfilm to preserve deteriorating material, to reduce the size of bulky materials such as newspapers, and to facilitate transfer of texts from one library to another dates back to about 1935. The microfilm was soon joined by the microcard, heralded as a great space-saver for research collections. For about twenty years the principal use of microforms in libraries was to store the texts of newspapers and periodicals to save space (and to preserve the text). With the proliferation of printed material, especially of technical reports, in the fifties, pressures for space generated many new types of microforms and experiments to reduce their size.

One of the latest of these is that recently announced by the National Cash Register Company, which has succeeded in writing a two-micron line width (a size equal to about half the width of a red blood cell) with a laser beam. In terms of storage this means that ten thousand pages could be recorded on an area the size of one page. The distribution by the Government of National Aeronautics and Space Administration (NASA) and Atomic Energy Commission (AEC) reports in microfiche added further impetus to the microform world. And recently there have been repeated attempts to adapt microforms to computer systems for automatic retrieval of documents.

At present the usefulness of microform technology is minimized by the fragmented nature of the industry. This has resulted in a lack of standardization in the production of microforms. The past few years have seen a rapid multiplication in the kinds and shapes of microforms, which are not compatible, have little or no relationship to each other, and are in fact mutually exclusive. Advances in use will depend on standardization of a reasonably restricted number of kinds of microforms and on the production of a system of machines interrelated so that their output can be automatically converted, quickly and cheaply, from one form to another. It must be possible to convert from micro to micro, micro to large, and large to large, producing retention copies of such quality that copies of the copies can be made with no deterioration of the image. In addition, and most important, there must be equipment for consulting microforms that is inexpensive and easy to use, and that has excellent legibility.

These developments do not seem likely to occur in the near future. Progress in the field is slow since there is no single firm in the industry that plays a dominant role in setting the pace for all of the others, as IBM did in the computer field.

In the view of the participants, the long-range effect of microfilm technology on the book and library building will be greater than that of the computer. In the short run, i.e., the next twenty years or so, while the use of microforms will gradually increase, they will not replace the book in a significant way.

COMMUNICATIONS

Facsimile transmission of text over long distances holds enormous implications for the library world. Contained within it is the potential solution to the problems of duplication, unmanageable growth, and rapid access.

Although it has been possible since the advent of television to transmit images of text over long distances, the impermanence of the image makes this unsatisfactory for library use. The recent development of machines for facsimile transmission that print out text at the receiving end has added a new dimension to communications technology. And there are now experimental projects under way that substitute the transmission of text for interlibrary loan: one between the campus of the University of California at Berkeley and the University's Davis campus, the other among libraries in New York State.

Facsimiles of text printed at the receiving end are transmitted by conventional telephone cables or microwave stations. Since this requires a broad-band transmission channel, the line costs are very high. The costs of microwave transmission are still higher. Even more restrictive is the lack, at present, of a national switching system that would allow rental of a broad-band channel for a few minutes of time to any geographic location, which interlibrary transmission requires. And even if educational communication satellites were available today to facilitate transmission, the lack of an adequate switching system on a national scale would prevent facsimile transmission of text from becoming a common means of information exchange for libraries.

Eventually, a common-carrier network, equipped with adequate switching, is likely to be set up to accommodate such developments as the picturephone and the transmission of data between computers. If this develops, the system would serve well for library needs. Such a common-carrier network is within the present technology, but the economic basis of the service has yet to be established. Initially the service may be too expensive for libraries. Also, such a network cannot be suddenly created but must grow over a period of years.

Regional, national, and special-purpose libraries will become increasingly important. To be effective, adequate communications must make these centralized facilities available over a wide geographic area. An initial arrangement, practical with present communications, consists of published or microform catalogs plus distribution of the documents by mail. (Witness MEDLARS, for example, the most sophisticated computerized retrieval system, which now sends the results of its bibliographic retrieval by mail.) The catalogs could be widely distributed and would enable remote users to locate documents that they would then receive in a day or two. As a broad-band network develops, fast electrical transmission of both bibliographical and textual material will gradually evolve to replace mail service. The time scale will depend very much on the particular region. Big cities like New York, Boston, Washington, Chicago, Denver, San Francisco, and Los Angeles may be firmly interconnected within five years, but it may take thirty to forty years to reach Peru, Nebraska.

When it materializes, the use of facsimile text transmission between libraries may be economically practical. It would be unwise, however, for the next generation of libraries to depend on its general availability. It would appear at present that while bibliographical citations will be exchanged electronically, in the face of competition from more conventional and vastly cheaper forms of haulage like trucking and mailing, facsimile transmission of books and documents will be restricted for a long time.

Pertinent, too, is the matter of copyright ownership of text and other intellectual products, as applied to electronically stored and transmitted materials as well as to all forms of photoduplication. Legislation pending in Congress acknowledges the need to extend copyright protection from the traditional to the new formats. The problem is not one that lends itself to easy solution, however, and until viable arrangements are evolved, this will pose a barrier to realizing the potential of the new technologies. (The discussion of copyright in chapter 6 touches on these considerations.)

With regard to the implications for buildings, since facsimile text transmission is simply a newer and better form of interlibrary loan, it would have no significant effect on the interiors of library buildings. It would, however, slow down the rate of expansion, since research materials easily obtainable from regional and national resource centers would not need to be bought for local storage.

IMPLICATIONS FOR BUILDINGS

Computers

Even if a library were completely computerized, there would be no necessity to locate the central computer equipment within the library building. If local considerations should make it desirable, however, a total of some 2,000 square feet apportioned as follows, along with the environmental conditions described, would provide the needs for a library of a million volumes.

1. The central processing room: This does not need to be large since the processing needs of even a large research library are well within the capacity of quite small computers (in terms both of physical size and of processing speed). A thousand square feet is adequate, but the space should be planned to accommodate a progression of facilities. (That is to say, a library might opt initially for a punch-card installation or a small-scale computer, and would use this facility for certain clerical functions for two or three years. At that time it might decide to employ a machine of larger capacity. Some years after that it might decide to incorporate on-line processing in the facility, and then, at a later date, to establish on-line connection to a much larger utility computer located elsewhere—such as in the computer center of the university or a commercial computer utility that may possibly be in existence by 1980.)

The central processing room should be located away from all reading areas and acoustically controlled to contain the noises produced by the machines. It should have a double floor, with a one-foot space below the standing floor to carry computer cables. Also, it should have a separate air-conditioning system to hold the temperature at 75° F. and the relative humidity at 50 percent. (This has particular significance for the magnetic tapes, which tend to change their operating characteristics under excessively low or high temperatures.) There should be a continuous recorder for both temperature and humidity, with an alarm set to indicate dangerous variations of either, and a cutoff for the air-conditioning system located within the room. The best possible filtration system should be provided to remove dust from the air, such as a pad filter backed by high-efficiency bag strainers rated at 95 percent. Dust control is necessary, again, primarily because of its effect upon the reliability of magnetic reading and recording systems.

Power requirements will depend on the machines used, but a typical load is 20 KVA at 175 amps. Because a stable power source is essential, surges must be controlled to within 5 to 10 percent. A continuous voltage recorder should be provided, again with an alarm set to indicate dangerous variations and a cutoff for the power located within the room.

For connection to peripheral terminal units throughout the building, there must be a flexible system of electrical conduits both vertically between floors and horizontally on each floor. Likely locations for terminals are the catalog, acquisitions, circulation, and serials departments, and the card catalog itself. Any terminals that involve card-handling or typewriter equipment will make noise, and provisions must be made to control it. There must also be provisions made for running cables out of the building from both the computer processing room and the peripheral terminals to reach a larger computer facility for special or rapid processing—or, in the remote future, to tie into computer networks.

2. Ancillary spaces required: Two offices convenient to the central processing room. One, for the computer director, operators, and programmers, should allow 150 square feet per person; the other, for key-punch operators, 75 square feet per person. Immediately adjacent to the processing room should be two additional rooms of 100 square feet each, one for mechanized storage forms such as punched cards, tapes, etc.; the other for spare parts and testing equipment. Finally, storage of cards, forms, and other supplies should be provided in still another room, of about 200 square feet, near the processing center. The entire complex of rooms should be provided with the same atmospheric conditions as the central processing room itself.[12]

Seating

The impact of technology on seating in academic libraries is likely to be slight. With an increase in the use of electronic carrels, dial retrieval, computerized retrieval of texts, and teaching machines, the formula for square footage allowed per reader will have to

12 *Architects recommend that computer manufacturers be consulted in the programming and planning of these spaces, as well as in the mechanical and electrical requirements necessary in each situation.*

increase. Even with a great increase in the ability to receive information from remote sources, the dormitory room is not likely to replace the library. The present surge of students to the library for concentrated, disciplined study, especially at times of academic pressure, is not likely to be rendered less by technology, and will probably increase. Demand for seating in the science sections may diminish, however, since that class of information will be most heavily computer-stored and retrievable in laboratories, offices, and points on the campus remote from the library. The more technology facilitates access to information, the more will information and libraries be used, which will tend to increase, not reduce, library workloads and the size of library facilities.

The Card Catalog

Changes in the card catalog will generate physical objects to take its place—multiple copies of book catalogs or many consoles. Great change in the form of the catalog would not involve much change in planning a library building at this time.

Shelving

Modification or redesign of shelving now provided for books will be necessary to hold forms of information of smaller unit size than books; i.e., microforms, magnetic tapes, etc. The smaller unit size will not reduce total space requirements, however. As microforms become easier to use—as they must if they are to replace books to any significant degree—the very ease of their use will then accelerate their purchase. Together with the installation of machines for their retrieval, the result will be a shift in space or even an expansion of space requirements. Since shelving will have to be moved, the preferred practice of using free-standing stacks will be even more important in the future.

Other

A library built today is not condemned to early obsolescence by the new technology, but the changes in store do place a greater premium than ever on planning buildings to be adaptable. The column system should be coordinated with the lighting layout and with stack and furniture modules, so that shifts between seating and shelving are easy to make and rearrangements of partitioning inexpensive. Perimeter and underfloor ducts should be provided large enough and in sufficient numbers to allow access to cables and electrical wiring at unpredictable locations on the floor and to run easily from one floor to another. Air-conditioning shafts throughout the building should be oversized to provide room for additions to the air-conditioning system.

It is also important to avoid illumination levels above 70–80 footcandles, maintained, for such levels tend to bleach out the image on computer display terminals, television screens, microfiche projectors, and other rear-screen projection equipment. Indeed, it will be necessary to lower the light intensities in areas of the library as they become occupied by these machines.

CONCLUSION

In sum, it is the consensus of those who participated in the conference that for at least the next twenty years the book will remain an irreplaceable medium of information. The bulk of library negotiations will continue to be with books, although the science and technology sections will gradually shrink. Remote retrieval of full texts in large amounts over long distances will not be generally feasible, and the continued use of a central library building will still be necessary.

It follows, therefore, that library planners can proceed at this time with confidence that technological developments in the foreseeable future will not alter radically the way libraries are used. In planning library buildings today, we should start with the library as the institution we now know it to be. Any departures in the future should be made from this firm base.

To be sure, technology will modify library buildings. But the changes will involve trade-offs in space and demands for additional space, rather than less. Thus, buildings planned now must be planned for expansion. At the same time, it is imperative that an added cost factor of 3 to 5 percent be allowed in order to assure adaptability, especially in the electrical and air-conditioning systems.

This should not invite complacency however. Predictions in a swiftly changing society are a risky business and must be hedged with caveats. All the fields of technology are swirling with action, and it is certain that in every individual library planners and administrators must be constantly alert to innovations, to local potential for assimilating developments, to the possibilities for interaction between libraries. On a broader scale, continued research, experimentation, and study must be carried on to help solve today's planning problems. Technological progress perforce will continue. But it is not break-throughs that are going to make a new world so much as the constant accumulation of new experiences over a considerable period of time.

Finally, we need much more consideration than has yet been given to the library user. Any applications of technology to library activities will have to be engineered to be humanly acceptable, since there will be resistance to them all—to the use of microforms in place of books, to console-typed texts instead of print, to engaging in complicated interaction with a machine, to reading in a fixed place without moving around. The machines will breed their own resistance to the extent that they place restrictions on people.

Now, more than ever, it is important to design library buildings so that they will be inviting and comfortable for people to use. The library building itself will gradually change, but people, who use libraries, are a constant factor.

C. TECHNOLOGY AND LIBRARIES[13]

1. INTRODUCTION AND SUMMARY

INTRODUCTION

The basic objective of this report was to assist the National Advisory Commission on Libraries—and, through it, other interested audiences—in examining the applicability of technology to libraries, possible library systems of the future, and problems of effecting a transition between the present and the future. In accordance with this basic purpose, the project team endeavored to present as objective and balanced a review of technology as possible, without either overemphasizing or minimizing its achievements or potential. The analyses and conclusions contributed notably to the deliberations of the Commission, which judged this report to be one of the most valuable of its studies. For this reason, the entire text appears here in somewhat revised and updated form.

The major types of libraries of concern here are public libraries, libraries in educational institutions, and special libraries. For purposes of this report, state libraries are treated together with public libraries, rather than as a special category. Some attention is also given to selected librarylike information facilities. The technology domain is considered to cover both equipment and techniques that presently have some impact on library systems.

---

13 *This section of chapter 7, consisting of six subsections, is from a special study of the same name commissioned by the National Advisory Commission on Libraries and performed by the System Development Corporation in 1967. Carlos A. Cuadra was the principal investigator; the entire study group is listed in appendix F–3.*

Statements and predictions in this report are based on findings reported in the literature, on interviews, or on System Development Corporation (SDC) staff studies. References are given wherever possible. A special word regarding statistics is necessary. It is acknowledged that statistics concerning libraries are not wholly satisfactory. Nevertheless, there is some agreement among librarians that the statistics are *relatively* accurate. The reader is cautioned to interpret any statistics offered in this report in their relative, not absolute, sense.

Some aspects of libraries and technology are given less attention than others in this report because they are the subject of other, more complete and detailed reports commissioned by the National Advisory Commission on Libraries (see appendix B). An effort was made to exchange outlines, drafts, and ideas with other study groups to minimize both omissions and unnecessary duplication.

This report consists of six sections and includes an analysis of present and projected library service requirements, a survey of potentially applicable technology, a description of current applications and trends in the use of technology, a prediction of future directions in library operations and services (including a discussion of the problem of planning for transition from the present to the future), and recommendations for a program of action. (See appendix F–3 for a description of three kinds of technology related to the library: computer technology, procedural technology, and related equipment and materials technology.) The following summary of major findings and recommendations of this study group highlights the content presented in the subsequent sections 2 through 5.

SUMMARY

Present and Projected Library Requirements

The purpose and general character of library services have not changed greatly over the past forty years. What have changed for most libraries are the range and volume of demand and use. The rapid and pervasive growth of specialization in new subject matters, together with an increasingly large and literate user population, has placed severe burdens on libraries of all kinds.

If the nation's libraries are to keep pace with the growing pressures of literature expansion and service requirements, the libraries will need to accelerate and expand some of the programs for library improvement that some of them have already undertaken; and if the libraries are to do *more* than keep pace—i.e., to provide better and broader service than they now do—a much more aggressive and integrated approach to improvement will be needed. To bring about a nationwide improvement in libraries, it will be necessary to think in terms of more interdependent modes of operation. It will also be necessary to take better advantage of the developing technology.

Technology Related to the Library

The domain of technology applicable to the library encompasses such areas as data processing by computers; procedural technologies such as document storage and retrieval, automated indexing and classification, machine translation, automated abstracting, and automated question-answering systems; and a variety of related equipment and materials technologies, including microform techniques, reprography, computer-assisted publication techniques, and materials handling and storage devices and procedures.

Computer technology has the greatest *potential* impact for library operations. Computer equipment is currently available in a number of configurations spanning a purchase range from $6,000 to $10 million. Although not adequate to meet all of the processing needs of very large libraries, it is quite adequate for a wider range of individual library automation tasks. Barriers that stand in the way of library applications include cost, lack of adequate library-oriented computer programs and associated procedural methodology, too little commputer memory capacity, and limitations in the input and output equipment.

The next five to ten years are likely to see at least a tenfold reduction in computer-system costs for a given level of performance, while computer speed and storage capabilities will increase severalfold. These changes will accelerate the library use of computers both for housekeeping tasks and for assistance to bibliographical tasks.

How much and what kind of computer capability libraries *should* have is impossible to determine now. Two quite different computer-support concepts present themselves: (1) a large number of geographically remote consoles, connected by data-transmission lines to very large, powerful, time-shared computers; and (2) individual use of separate computers of the smaller and less expensive kind now beginning to appear. Both concepts will probably be adopted: time-sharing by the smaller libraries and private computers by the larger, more affluent libraries.

As for procedural technology, a number of applications of computers to processing textual material offer promise to library operations. Many operating systems in business, industry, and the military currently store and retrieve data from files. These operations are similar, in some respects, to those required for the storage and retrieval of bibliographical information, and some of the techniques developed for data-retrieval work are applicable to types of library data that can be highly structured and formated. Automatic analysis of nonformated full-text materials is a more complex task, and accordingly, progress in fully automated retrieval of textual content lags behind that in formated data-handling systems.

Fully satisfactory programs for automatic indexing or subject-heading assignment are not yet available; still, some current systems provide a high degree of automation of other retrieval functions. One system permits users to pose requests directly to the computer system and to receive computer assistance in identifying document representations meeting prescribed criteria. Such systems are not yet within the economic range for use by library patrons but could be used to provide assistance to library personnel. With decreasing computer costs, more ready-made programs, and better-trained library staff, such services can eventually be extended directly to library users, particularly in special or experimental libraries.

Fully automated indexing, classification, abstracting, machine translation, and question-answering must still be considered to be in the research or development stage. However, substantial assistance to library processes is likely to come, in the very near future, from concepts of operation in which the machine serves as an aid to, not a replacement for, the librarian or information specialist. Computer-aided instruction is likely to play an important role in training library personnel for work in computer-based systems and in helping patrons learn to use such systems.

The third area of technology related to libraries encompasses related equipment and materials technologies. Microforms—previously valued for reasons of space-saving and materials preservation—are also used increasingly as a medium of communication. Inexpensive microform readers are currently available. During the next five to ten years we may expect the establishment of large-sized microfiche collections and significant improvements in microform technology, including stable color microfilm, sophisticated microform-handling equipment, direct information transfer between microimage and computer subsystems, and ultramicroform technology.[14] The current trends of lowering costs and increasing quality will continue for copying, offset printing, and the printing and reading of fiche.

The advent of photocomposition—computer-controlled preparation of reproduction masters with electro-optical techniques—is very important because it provides libraries with the option to abandon card catalogs in favor of book-form catalogs, up-to-date versions of which could be printed in multiple copies to be available in several locations

14 *In 1968 several commercial firms engaged in contract microfilming announced the availability of stable color microfilm. These firms now offer color microfilm service and processing.*

in the library. The availability of library materials—either text or catalog-type information—in machine-readable form will provide an opportunity to explore other computer applications economically.

Printed materials will be the primary carriers to be dealt with for some years, and few libraries will be able to use electronic means exclusively to manage their information. Texts will have to be stored and handled by humans, aided in some instances by mechanical devices. There are some promising materials-handling devices—conveyors, tubes, containers, lifters, stackers—some of which can be useful in future systems where materials-handling is largely computer-controlled. Most of these devices appear too expensive at present for widespread use.

Transmission of materials is becoming increasingly important to libraries, particularly in relation to possible network operations. Of the several means for the transmission of materials, mail is currently still the most practical. Efforts are under way to create working systems that employ advanced communications technology to support retrieval of material from a central store and its transmission to different places. Both the accuracy and the data-transmission rates of various kinds of telecommunications equipment can be expected to increase in the near future. It is not yet clear whether there will be sufficient equipment compatibility to serve the purposes of highly integrated library networks.

Current Applications and Trends

A number of libraries, primarily the larger academic libraries and special libraries, have begun to use data-processing equipment in their operations. All of the major library functions (acquisitions, cataloging, circulation control, serials management, reference work, etc.) are drawing attention in this connection. The emphasis is primarily on functions related to technical processes and circulation control, rather than reference services.

Certain aspects of the acquisitions process lend themselves particularly well to data processing, and some groups of libraries have even been exploring the idea of cooperative or centralized processing for some aspects of the acquisitions process.

The most popular application of technology in the cataloging process has been to reproduce catalog cards. Book catalogs, frequently used many years ago but abandoned in favor of card catalogs, are returning to favor with the help of the computer and computer-controlled typesetting procedures. In cataloging, as well as in acquisitions, the combination of interlibrary cooperation and new technology offers great potential for the reduction of costs and wasteful duplication of effort. The Library of Congress MARC Project, which is a prototype of a national network for the distribution of machine-readable catalog data, provides an example of this potential.

Data-processing technology is being used for a variety of tasks associated with circulation control, and a few institutions are beginning to work toward the development of on-line operations that will tie a circulation-control system directly into a computer at all times. Such a system will bring libraries a step closer to still another feasible approach, that of operating circulation-control systems on a network basis within a region.

A number of projects are under way to use data processing for serials records control. Few institutions, however, have operational systems, and those that exist do not perform all the necessary functions of serials management. The project at the Library of Congress to determine what elements of information should be put into machine-readable records for serial titles can provide a valuable framework on which individual libraries can build and through which they may eventually participate in regional or national serials projects.

In comparison with other library operations, the reference function shows very little in the way of applications of technology for most libraries. Very few libraries have automated their information- and document-retrieval functions. There are a few primitive automated-data-retrieval systems, but they are nearly all in information centers, not in libraries.

Technologies other than data processing are being put to use in libraries. Micro-forms are being used increasingly, but their vast potential still seems to be untapped. Materials-handling equipment, specialized communications equipment, storage equip-ment, etc., have all found some use in libraries, but such use has largely involved the *adaptation* of equipment and procedures developed for other purposes, rather than those especially tailored to meet library needs.

Many libraries have looked to technology to reduce costs or to hold them constant. Cost-consciousness sometimes has not been extended to consider the effect of changes on the users of libraries: some ostensible cost reductions may "cost" the users more than they save in time, effort, or even money.

Technology offers an opportunity to provide access to and services for nonmono-graphic materials of all kinds as good as those that have been furnished for printed monographs. There are also indications that use of technology may allow new services to develop in libraries to serve certain user groups better. Technology may also provide a means of improving the organization and management of libraries.

At present only about 3 percent of the approximately 24,000 libraries in the United States are using data-processing equipment. One can foresee that in the future many more libraries will seek to use such equipment, especially computers. Much of the effort is likely to be focused on particular problems in particular libraries. Much more coordination would be desirable to channel these disparate efforts into a national effort that would bring all aspects of our technology to bear on the problems of library operations.

Future Directions in Library Operations and Service

There are two different approaches toward prediction of the nature of the library of the future. One approach stresses the continuation or extrapolation of current trends. The other approach stresses what it is theoretically possible to achieve. Both approaches are useful: the first is useful in short-range planning because it takes adequate account of the problems of transition; the other takes note of distant goals, which helps to broaden the horizons of one's thinking.

An extrapolative view, which assumes no major acceleration of effort, sees the large majority of libraries operating much as they do today over the next ten years. In spite of continuing improvements undertaken by libraries, there will probably not be any *net* gain in service for the majority of individual libraries. Indeed, some deterioration of service is likely to occur because of the vast increases in published materials that must be dealt with. Large categories of nonbook materials will continue to be neglected to a large extent. Without some form of accelerated planning and support the majority of libraries are not likely to be able to participate in or benefit from emerging network-arrange-ments.

A conditional view of library activities, which assumes major acceleration of effort over the next ten years, sees libraries becoming elements of one or more integrated networks. Through connection with a network, libraries could provide their staff per-sonnel with better tools, with relief from some processing chores better handled through the network, and with network-supported facilities for handling reference problems. The library's users could also be provided with much more in the way of materials and services, such as outright distribution of certain kinds of materials replacing loans. The availability of nonbook materials could be increased in libraries of all kinds and sizes across the nation.

There are a number of problems of transition from the present to the future that are not entirely technological in nature. Libraries, already facing serious staff shortages, may find it very difficult to obtain staff with the broad training and experience necessary in both the requirements of library operations and those of technology. Too, library users will need better training in exploiting available library services and facilities. Here, technology itself offers some promise of providing useful tools.

Standards of operation, as well as standards necessary for the compatibility of bibliographical data, are still lacking in the library world. As new data files are created and old files are converted, this problem will become more serious. The several possible approaches to standardization need active consideration if the many separate and independent library organizations are to achieve adequate cooperation and communication using the newer technologies.

A Program of Action

Several approaches offer themselves for the improvement of the nation's libraries. One is to depend on the mechanisms already being used to improve library operations and service, without attempting to accelerate the rate of improvement. This approach requires no drastic change in present activities, concepts of service, funding, or patterns of involvement of the Federal Government. On the other hand, most libraries would almost certainly continue to lose ground through this approach in the face of increasing processing loads and demands for service.

A second approach would be to plan and attempt to develop a nationwide, highly integrated library system. Such an approach would permit certain kinds of systemwide operations that are not likely to evolve otherwise. It would also reduce duplication of effort by many individual libraries. On the other hand, this approach has some very stringent requirements—e.g., common, agreed-upon goals and strong top management— that might be difficult to meet at this point in time.

The third approach, which this report recommends, focuses on more limited goals and subsystems or networks, and attempts to identify and support *selected* high-impact projects. This approach recognizes the operational independence of most of the nation's libraries, while at the same time taking advantage of their willingness to participate in interdependencies that offer mutual benefits. This approach also has the advantage of not precluding the undertaking of other projects and programs.

Some high-impact projects could and should be aimed at the development of model subsystems that could later be incorporated into a more fully integrated nationwide system. Five such projects are recommended for consideration; undertaken together, these projects could lead to operational systems in from two to four years.

1. A Prototype of Regional Libraries.
2. An Expanded Computer-based *National Union Catalog.*
3. A National Bibliography.
4. A National Referral and Loan Network.
5. A National Library Storage and Microform Depository System.

Although these high-impact projects are dependent on technology, and although they involve subsystems that will eventually be important in extensive, technology-dependent national networks, they do not contribute directly to the exploitation of technology by individual libraries. It is recommended, therefore, that concurrent with the operations-oriented projects a comprehensive program of technology-oriented library research, development, and education and training be undertaken. It should encompass hardware specification and development, procedural (software) specification and development, direct supporting research, and education and training. Also recommended for consideration as part of this program is the establishment of a test bed for handling new forms of nonbook materials.

Before such activities can or should be undertaken, several things must be done. These are offered as the primary recommendations of this report:

1. The basic approach of using high-impact projects, together with supporting research, development, and education and training, should be examined and, if possible, endorsed as the means by which library improvement will be sought during the next five to ten years.

2. The particular high-impact projects and research and development requirements outlined in this report should be examined by the Commission and by other interested members of the library and information science community, in the light of other issues, requirements, and constraints, to determine what priorities these and other possible projects should be assigned at this time.

3. For those projects selected for implementation, arrangements should be made to develop more detailed objectives, together with preliminary cost appraisals and implementation schedules.

4. For those projects selected for implementation, arrangements should be made to identify all potential sources of support and, at the appropriate time, to obtain the funds necessary to carry out the projects and programs selected.

5. Responsibility for carrying out the activities indicated or implicit in the foregoing recommendations should be placed at a high administrative level in an existing or new agency of the Federal Government or in a public-private body created for this purpose.

The last recommendation is of particular importance. The need for assessment and planning for libraries does not diminish or disappear because the National Advisory Commission on Libraries has presented its Report. To ensure that effective planning and implementation continue, a permanent body is needed that can be responsible for: (1) keeping informed on the existing and prospective state of library service and operations, (2) planning for improved library service at both national and local levels, (3) developing legislative proposals, (4) coordinating various projects affecting library service, and (5) planning and coordinating financial support, from both the public and private sectors.

Of the several possibilities that suggest themselves for such a permanent body, the most attractive one involves extension of the life of the former National Advisory Commission. This would help to ensure continuity of thinking and planning and would take advantage of the interest, expertise, communication, and working arrangements developed by the Commission. The permanent Commission would need to be supported by a highly capable, full-time technical staff, some of whose members might be drawn from the Government or private sector for extended periods of time. This of course is quite similar to the first recommendation in the Commission's Report, the establishment of a National Commission on Libraries and Information Science as a continuing Federal planning agency.

Whatever the planning mechanism actually adopted, it is critically important not to lose momentum. A sizable and indeterminate time gap between the Commission's work and the development and implementation of an action program could itself foster a paralysis of planning on the part of libraries and might lead to yet other status surveys covering much the same ground as the present Commission has covered. Technology and the needs of library service are certainly changing, but the changes are not so rapid or erratic that they should encourage a succession of independent assessments. The need for library improvement is clear, and so is the potential contribution of advanced technology. Aggressive, concerted, and timely action should be taken now to effect a nationwide improvement of our libraries.

2. PRESENT AND PROJECTED LIBRARY REQUIREMENTS

KINDS OF REQUIREMENTS

It is widely accepted that people have needs for library services; i.e., access to books, serials, reports, and other library materials, and/or the information contained in them. Satisfying those needs imposes requirements for the design, construction, operation, and evolution of library systems. Requirements, in system-design terminology, are formal statements describing functions that need to be performed to allow a specific set of objectives to be met.

There are several categories of library users, whose needs differ greatly from one to another (see Part I of this book). These needs, in turn, imply several kinds of requirements for different kinds of library services. From the perspective of a given library serving a given public, it is useful to distinguish three related types of requirements: (1) requirements for direct service to users; (2) internal operational requirements, essential for rendering direct service in a library; (3) external operational requirements; i.e., requirements for interfacing with external systems of libraries and other information-handling organizations.

Table 7C–2.1 illustrates typical requirements for direct service to library users, and Table 7C–2.2 lists the major internal operational requirements or functions associated with the satisfaction of user service requirements. Both of these kinds of requirements appear much the same as have always pertained to library operations. This is because, at least in the United States, the purpose and character of library services have not greatly changed over the past forty years. What have changed for most libraries are the range and volume of demand and use, including the demand for faster and more accurate response.

Some of these needs cannot be met easily, if at all, by improvements in internal operating techniques. Rather, they require consideration of new and more complex forms of interlibrary dependency. Thus, increasing attention is now being paid to the external operational requirements of libraries. For a given library these requirements may involve a series of dependencies on the existence of several different kinds of networks; e.g., of libraries, publishers, and communications.

PRESSURES FOR LIBRARY IMPROVEMENT AND EXPANSION

Changes in demand and use have been particularly observable in the production and use of scientific and technical documentation. Since World War II a dozen new technologies have emerged, and a tremendous volume of invention, research, and discovery has been reported along the way. In the 1950's, thanks in part to changes in the nature of national and international political and economic interdependence, the character of scholarship in the social sciences began to change as well. There has been a shift in the character of demand and use of documents in the direction of far more comprehensive coverage of wide-ranging subject matter. These changes, of course have been accompanied by a large increase in the number and variety of specialist and general library users and in the variety, range, and volume of documents produced.

So pervasive have these changes been that it has become customary to speak of the information explosion or the information deluge, and any report on library problems that does not take notice of this phenomenon may be thought to be lacking in perspective. Although quotations can be found from learned and famous men of the distant past that also bemoan the condition of too much written material for men to cope with, it is clear that the proliferation of publication, the fragmentation of knowledge, and the synthesis of older fields of learning into new fields are placing increasingly severe burdens on libraries. This is particularly true for the larger research libraries. Their book budgets have needed to be enlarged to purchase materials from dozens of new countries as well as old, staff personnel must be sought who can catalog publications in dozens of exotic languages, and new research institutes have demanded specialized information services. What seems to be clear—information explosion or no—is that really good libraries can save their users a great deal of valuable time and effort in dealing with recorded knowledge.

It is important to recognize that there are hundreds of smaller libraries around the country that have not changed perceptibly for the last thirty years. The information explosion seems not to have had much effect on these libraries. We must then ask the question, "Should the larger libraries (most of which are part of academic institutions) receive the major part of the national attention, or is it also a national problem that so many smaller libraries have not felt great impact from the continuing increase in publication?"

PRESENT AND PROJECTED DEMAND FOR SERVICE

Public Libraries

It is estimated that in the year 1967 the more than 6,700 public libraries in the United States will have circulated 430 million volumes to some 55 million borrowers.[15] The holdings of only a small percentage of these libraries are represented in the *National Union Catalog* or the *Union List of Serials*. There are no comprehensive union catalogs available for any type of library for documents, reports, and many other categories of library materials.

Over the next ten years one may expect the number of potential public library users—i.e., those who might use a given library—to more than double, and the character of that user population to change in the direction of a much more literate and highly educated set of customers, whose needs and demands for library services will be much more specialized and varied than they now are.[16] If these demands are to be met, the public libraries must implement specific means to meet them. These libraries, as nodes in national networks, must also develop mechanisms both for internal operation and for interfacing with (i.e., participating in) the networks that alone can enable them to identify, locate, and obtain all the materials that can satisfy the needs of their publics.

The requirements for building and operating mechanisms capable of meeting these service demands include the development and operation of automated procedures for the support of acquisitions, cataloging, circulation, reference, and managerial functions that provide for effective internal operation and compatible communications with other library systems and networks. These imply, in turn, requirements for developing and maintaining standards for operations common to libraries, and for organizing the necessary planning and coordination.

Educational Libraries

For discussion purposes, educational libraries may be divided into elementary and secondary school libraries on the one hand, and college and university libraries on the other.

First, let us consider elementary and secondary school libraries. Total enrollment in the United States for 1966, for kindergarten through grade 12, has been estimated at just under 50 million students, with the ratio of elementary students to those in secondary schools being roughly three to one.[17] School libraries typically contain small general collections of books geared to minimum-to-moderate levels of literacy and knowledge, a few periodicals, sizable pamphlet collections, and other special library materials.

Although nearly all secondary schools and over 90 percent of the secondary school libraries are served by personnel having six or more hours of formal library science training, the number of libraries served by fully qualified librarians is much smaller. A great proportion of the library service demands of elementary and secondary school students continues to fall upon public libraries, either because of the lack of school libraries or the limited hours of service, limited size of collections, and limited capacity of personnel to meet reference, referral, and guidance needs.

---

15 Bowker Annual of Library and Book Trade Information (*New York: R. R. Bowker Co., 1967*).
16 *Kenneth E. Beasley, "Social anl Political Factors,"* ALA Bulletin, *60 (December 1966), pp. 1146, 1151–5.*
17 Bowker Annual, op. cit.

A great improvement in potential response to current student demands might be effected, particularly in the larger metropolitan areas, if technical processes were centralized and adequate communications for reference, referral, and sharing of literary resources were organized between all school districts in the area. This would require applications of data-processing and communications technologies as well as a reorganization of work. Applications of these technologies would also make it possible to improve the state of knowledge and skill of school librarians through various kinds of on-the-job training programs.

Development of a library service that is appropriately responsive to increasingly high standards of education will require a different kind of access to library resources than is now available to most school libraries, particularly access to library materials of many collections and to the knowledge and reference skills of a range of library personnel. This, in turn, requires going beyond the boundaries of the school system to share library resources with many libraries. Too, it may require—if only for reasons of cost—extensive use of microforms and other nonbook materials, which could help to broaden the school library's resources. Large collections, reduced to microform and adequately cataloged, could be reproduced relatively inexpensively if done in large quantity; i.e., several thousand sets.

What has been said above concerning public libraries frequently applies as well to college and university libraries. Current demands for college and university education imply requirements for library support that can be met fully by only a small minority of libraries in these institutions. Even these few libraries have had difficulty in serving their user populations adequately, particularly with the rapid expansion of demand in volume and variety that has occurred over the past ten years. Another feature in common between the public and college libraries is that while there is a steady increase in the annual number of volumes acquired and the number of serial titles subscribed to, there has been a steady drop in the number of library items available per library user.[18]

As of 1967 there were estimated to be some 7 million *students and faculty* in colleges and universities to be served by college libraries. New library buildings in these institutions until recently have been constructed at the rate of about 50 per year, but current plans call for some 1,200 buildings to be constructed by 1970 for two- and four-year colleges. In ten years one may expect some 14 million *students* (not counting faculty) in the institutions and a doubling of the current volume of library materials being acquired.[19]

There are additional pressures on those libraries of academic institutions that aspire to the title "research library." Library operations to support graduate programs, faculty research, and postdoctoral research are much more difficult and costly—perhaps twice as much—than operations to support undergraduate teaching. All of the foregoing implies that the ability of individual libraries to serve their customers will decline if the current trend continues. There is, even now, a need for making the wealth of library materials and services concentrated in relatively few institutions available to the nation's library users. This can be accomplished only through the further development and application of advanced information-handling and communication technology to individual libraries and to library networks.

Special Libraries

Special libraries are considered to be those libraries that concentrate upon highly specialized collections of materials and serve special groups, largely of highly educated and trained specialists in a subject area. It has been estimated that there are more than 6,000 special libraries in the United States, including government, society, business, and

---

[18] Ibid.
[19] *See section B of this chapter.*

industrial libraries (with some overlap with university libraries). As of 1965 it was estimated that these libraries account for expenditures of some $189 million per year, as compared with $267 million for public libraries and $229 million for college and university libraries.[20] In short, there are nearly as many special libraries as public libraries, and operational costs are about two thirds those of public libraries.

Because of the changes in the direction of research, development, and ancillary activities from subject-oriented work to mission-oriented work, which cuts across traditional disciplines, the special library has found it increasingly difficult to collect widely enough to gratify its user demands and, even more importantly, to serve its potential user population. Even today many special libraries have been able to satisfy their clientele only because they are able to fall back on the resources of nearby academic libraries. Such use constitutes a heavy burden to more than one academic library.

ACCESSIBILITY FOR USERS

The current state of copyright matters leads to a certain amount of uncertainty in projecting requirements for library systems and networks of the future (see chapter 6). The present copyright law was written before there were ready means of making copies in libraries other than by hand or by rather cumbersome photographic methods. Over the years, as copying devices appeared that were easy to use and relatively inexpensive, a doctrine of so-called fair use developed outside the copyright law. The doctrine of fair use has worked reasonably well, but many practicing librarians are well aware of abuses in the system, especially where copying machines are not monitored by the library itself.

Since this report addresses itself to technology, it is perhaps best to confine our comments to observations of the effect that an increasing number of copying devices will have on the libraries of the future. Such devices will become more common and will cost less to use, and the quality of copy will improve. Under pending legislation it would appear that future library systems and networks would have to provide for contracting, accounting, and compensating mechanisms to pay owners of copyrights. No one will predict how a new copyright law will affect such library operations as telefacsimile transmission and other rapid-copying methods. It seems likely, however, that there will be at least some categories of materials for which library systems and networks will have to provide compensation to the owners of copyrights for copying and other usage that would, without compensation, constitute infringement.

If it is a basic objective to satisfy the needs of all library users in the United States, present and future, a way must be found to ensure that the needed documents are available to them. Since there is no way, a priori, to judge the utility of documents to potential users, all potentially useful documents must be sought. The basic considerations for a system with this capability are:

1. The networks must be so constituted as to ensure that there exists within the United States at least one accessible copy of all the published documents produced in the world—past, present, and future.
2. The library systems and networks must provide appropriate mechanisms for acquiring, announcing, processing, searching, and making accessible the library holdings of the nation to library users throughout the country.
3. The library systems and networks must provide for contracting, accounting, and compensating mechanisms to pay the owners of copyrights for copying and other usages that would, without compensation, constitute infringement of copyrights.

[20] Bowker Annual, op. cit.

It is recognized that the goal stated in the first consideration can only be approximated because it certainly cannot be known what documents exist at any point in time. The notion of accessibility implies further techniques to ensure that the existence of documents be widely known and the documents themselves, or facsimiles thereof, be made available to users throughout the country in an economic and timely fashion.

The second consideration implies a great expansion in the creation, timely updating, and dissemination of union catalogs, union lists, special bibliographies, and indexes to library collections. It also implies a great increase in the availability of document facsimiles via microform, machine-readable files, or other reproduction facilities. Copying, in turn, implies a need to deal effectively with holders of copyrights, the third consideration.

It is true that many of the pioneering efforts in automation of library processes have occurred in special libraries and that many of the most highly automated libraries are in this category. These, however, constitute a very small minority of special libraries. As with projections for public and educational libraries, the increase in the volume and variety of materials, as well as the trend to more specialized use of materials, indicates that if current trends in library development and practice are continued without acceleration and without a concomitant development of viable national networks, special library users of the future will not be served as well as they are today.

IMPLICATIONS FOR INTEGRATED LIBRARY SYSTEMS

The foregoing discussion of present and projected demands for library service points to two primary conclusions: (1) if the nation's libraries are to keep pace with the growing pressures of literature expansion and service requirements, the libraries will need to accelerate and expand some of the programs for library improvement that some of them have already undertaken; and (2) if the libraries are to do *more* than keep pace, i.e., to provide better and broader service than they now do, a much more extensive and integrated approach to improvement will be needed.

The external requirements for all libraries, taken together, point to the need to develop networks, construed here as functional dependencies whose mechanisms provide for the transfer of messages and/or material within and between library systems and subsystems. In order to plan for and operate such networks, there must be agreement among the participants on certain desiderata of library services.

It appears very unlikely that the operational requirements implied by the foregoing desiderata can be met by the techniques in current use. More extensive application of advanced technology will certainly be required. There will also need to be a shift toward more interdependent modes of operations. If the transition from current practice toward more automated and interdependent operations is to be an orderly one, there will probably need to be an organized body or agency that exercises responsibility for planning and coordinating such transition and for seeing that the network operations are economical and effective in meeting the nation's requirements for library service. Without such coordination, wholly effective network operations will not come into being. (This problem is discussed in section C.6 of this chapter, "A Program of Action.")

In discussing requirements, it is important to keep in mind that many of society's requirements are created and not preexisting. Thus, current accepted requirements for such things as telephone service, air transportation, and computer support stem at least in part from the very availability of the services involved. In the same sense, requirements for library service should not be thought of as entirely preexisting and stable. The availability of better library service will necessarily reinforce and intensify the demands for higher standards in the nation's libraries. The important implication of this is that the requirements and desiderata for improved library service should not be too narrowly conceived or too closely tied to present limitations, lest the system or systems developed to meet them become obsolete almost as soon as they are completed.

TABLE 7C–2.1

TYPICAL REQUIREMENTS FOR DIRECT SERVICE TO LIBRARY USERS

User service requirements

---

1. Browsing access to library materials.
2. Searching access via catalogs, indexes, and other reference tools.
3. Question-answering service.
4. Directive service for reference or referral.
5. Reading guidance.
6. Instruction in use of catalogs, indexes, and other reference tools.
7. Reading, viewing, and listening facilities.
8. Bibliographic compilation.
9. Reproduction of materials (copying facilities).
10. Loan and interlibrary loan.
11. Discussion groups.
12. Storytelling and readings to users.
13. Paging and other delivery services (e.g., bookmobiles).

TABLE 7C–2.2

MAJOR INTERNAL OPERATIONAL FUNCTIONS FOR SATISFYING LIBRARY USER SERVICE REQUIREMENTS

Internal operational requirements

---

1. Acquisition of materials:
   a. Selection and bibliographic checking.
   b. Gifts and exchanges.
   c. Ordering and accounting.
   d. Receiving and disbursing.
   e. Transaction record-keeping and filing.
2. Cataloging:
   a. Bibliographic checking.
   b. Descriptive cataloging.
   c. Classification and subjecting cataloging.
   d. Marking and labeling.
   e. Card ordering, reproduction, and/or printing.
   f. Announcement and dissemination.
   g. Record-keeping and filing.
3. Storage:
   a. Shelving and other storage media.
   b. Preservation and protection.
   c. Locating and arranging.
   d. Retrieval and replacement.
   e. Inventory and record-keeping.
4. Management:
   a. Planning, organizing, supervising, delegating.
   b. Coordinating, reporting, budgeting.
   c. Personnel selection and training.
   d. Record-keeping and statistics.
   e. Maintenance of physical plant, facilities, and equipment.

---

3. *TECHNOLOGY RELATED TO THE LIBRARY*

The domain of technology related to the library is wide, encompassing not only data processing—perhaps the most obvious kind of technology—but also computer-assisted publication techniques, materials-handling and storage devices, microform techniques, and reprographic devices. It also includes a variety of procedural technologies such as document storage and retrieval, automated indexing and classification, machine translation, automated abstracting, and automated question-answering systems.

This subsection of chapter 7, section C, briefly reviews some of the more important technologies that are having, or are likely to have, an impact on library systems of the future. The same topics are covered in greater detail in the three appendices to this report, which appear in appendix F–3.

COMPUTER TECHNOLOGY

Of all equipment represented by modern technology, the kind with the greatest potential impact for library operations in the next five to ten years is electronic data-processing equipment, specifically, computers. These devices, together with associated equipment and procedures, offer the capability for relieving some of the serious technical processing problems of library systems and, eventually, for upgrading the range and quality of reference and retrieval service.

There is a wide range of computer equipment currently available, with various configurations spanning a purchase range from $6,000 to $10 million. These configurations can be thought of as consisting of five components: (1) central processing units (CPU), (2) main memories, (3) mass memories, (4) peripheral (input-output) devices, and (5) terminal devices.

Status of Computer Components

Most central processing units have been built for problems of scientific computation or business data processing, rather than for problems of library automation. Nevertheless, these units are more than adequate to handle most of the problems of library data processing. The barriers that stand in the way of library automation are not technical inadequacies of the CPU but price, lack of adequate software, too little peripheral memory capacity, or limitations in the input-output equipment.

Main memories—*internal* storage—are generally of adequate size to handle library problems, and their cost has decreased considerably in the past fifteen years, from $1.00 to $0.25 per bit.[21] Bulk storage devices have greater capacity and lower cost than main memory, and they provide external storage for large quantities of data that are read into the computer through the internal storage device. Magnetic tape has been widely used as a mass storage device but is being replaced by faster-access devices, such as drums and discs, and research is under way on even more sophisticated devices, as well as on "content-addressable" memories, all of which could see wide use in libraries.

Yet, because of its versatility, magnetic tape will probably be the main mass-storage device in the automated library of the near future. A typical 2,400-foot tape can hold the equivalent of over one million English words, and the present cost of tape for tape storage is only about $0.015 a word. Drums require less access time than tapes, though they also have a smaller capacity (up to 333,000 words) and cost is around $0.03 a word. A disadvantage is that the drum cannot be removed from the computer. About the same cost per word is estimated for disc storage, which has the advantage of now being available in a disc pack, thus giving nonserial accessibility of the disc. The disc pack will probably be used heavily for any changing data required in library operations.

---

21 *Used in connection with digital computing-devices, the word "bit" refers to a unit of memory corresponding to the ability to store the result of a choice between two alternatives.*

Developments in optical storage techniques, such as the photoscopic disc, continue to be promising. Such techniques, introduced several years ago, are expected to provide capacities of billions of words, at about $0.03 a word, and to permit updating of information by a photocopying operation. This will be relatively slow but may be well suited to fairly stable sets of library information such as dictionaries or authority files. And library retrieval will benefit greatly if economical associative memories are developed—memories in which retrieval will be based on coincidence of part of an input pattern with part of the stored reference pattern.

Input-output (I/O) equipment available includes cards, tapes, and the new scanning equipment. Cards are still the most widely used for input; they allow changes in a program to be made easily but are slow and limited to one type font. Paper tape is increasingly used for input because it transmits rapidly, but it is not used for output because there it is slow, difficult to search, and fragile. Magnetic tape is less fragile and can be used in high-speed typesetting. Optical readers scan pages of text and write it out on tape or card or directly into the main memory. Progress is being made in the development of these optical devices, and they hold great promise for use in libraries of the future. Some can read a variety of fonts, and they will probably see heavy use as a substitute for a key punch to handle the high volume of data in a library.

Terminal devices are used for man-machine interaction in real time, and fall into two classes: the relatively inexpensive typewriterlike device and the more expensive sophisticated console with a cathode-ray tube. They may be connected to a computer either by leased-line or by economical dial-up service.

The most commonly used terminals are keyboard devices, like typewriters, which are connected to telephone lines by a device called a modem (modulator-demodulator) or an audiocoupler. Pushbutton touch-tone telephones are also being used for input of data to a computer. A Model 33 teletype costs only about $470, requires little training in its operation, and can be located thousands of miles from a computer.

Cathode-ray tubes (CRTs) range from something that resembles a fourteen-inch television set with keyboard to the large sophisticated device that has graphic capabilities, a light pen that triggers displayed data or allows the user to write on the screen, and a number of other features. Both of these types of consoles are used at or near the computer; microwave links or video cables will probably be required before remote use is possible.

Other types of I/O equipment include a new device called an audio response unit and a set of equipment that permits converting pictures to digital data and transmitting them to the computer, and the reverse.

Future Developments and Computer Uses

Not all of the needs of very large libraries could be met with the equipment described above, which still features capacities and speeds that would be inadequate for some sophisticated automation efforts involving massive amounts of data. Yet most library automation tasks could be accommodated on the modern computers, and projected cost reduction and technological innovations (e.g., in optical readers) promise substantial use of automation in future libraries. In other words, there exists a wide range of computer systems and components that may be applied to library information processing.

The next five to ten years are likely to see at least a tenfold increase in computer capabilities, measured in speed and amount of data stored and processed. For a given level of performance, computer-system costs are likely to be only about one tenth of what they are today. These predictions do not depend on the assumption of spectacular technical breakthroughs.

In addition, more equipment specifically designed for handling textual data will probably be developed; e.g., CPUs for list processing, programming languages, or associative memories that increase the facility with which computers can handle information-retrieval-type work. As the cost of computer circuits continues to decrease and as production levels increase, it may still be more economical to use general-purpose computers of standard design than special-purpose computers.

Perhaps the most significant development for libraries will be the advent of very large memories. There is every reason to expect that one of the many forms of large memories—whether it be photographic, laser-written, or of electronic-beam technology—will be able to handle files of at least ten bits (333 billion words).[22] The advent of such files will provide the stimulus necessary to develop the software required to handle large files. If breakthroughs are necessary anywhere, it is in this area of software. Many expensive systems with sophisticated hardware are still operating as though they were faster versions of punched-card systems.

In line with other cost reductions, consoles should become much less expensive. In principle the console should not cost much more than a television screen and a keyboard. The advent of the small, powerful, and inexpensive computer will allow much of the circuitry presently housed in today's expensive consoles to be transferred to an intermediate computer.

Computers may be used in the library in two ways: (1) for clerical tasks (e.g., some portions of acquisitions, cataloging, circulation, and serials management), which will free librarians for other professional functions, and (2) to provide added capability in performing bibliographical tasks. This added capability, in turn, breaks down into two different categories. First, bibliographical material will be processed so that it can be more easily retrieved, as needed, by library or user personnel. Thus, it might include such activities as automatic indexing, automatic classification, and perhaps automatic abstracting. Second, the library user will be given tools for interacting directly with the information store and searching it for documents and data of interest.

How much and what kind of computer capability libraries *should* have is impossible to determine now, particularly since two quite different computer-support concepts present themselves. One concept involves a large number of geographically remote consoles, connected by data-transmission lines to very large, powerful time-shared computers. The other concept is that of using the small and inexpensive (but powerful) computers that are now beginning to appear. This school of thought forecasts that computers that would have sold for close to a million dollars in the past will—in the next few years—be available for only $25,000.

Both concepts will probably be adopted: time-sharing by libraries that cannot afford a $25,000 piece of equipment and the use of a small but powerful computer by the more affluent. Time-sharing will probably also be part of the really giant computers that will be used by very large and affluent organizations. From a library point of view one might expect to see small private computers in the medium-to-large libraries; large time-shared computers in information systems within the Federal Government; and large time-shared computers, with inexpensive consoles, serving a large number of libraries (the computer utility scheme mentioned above).

PROCEDURAL TECHNOLOGY

There are a number of applications of computers to textual material that either provide current capability or offer promise of support to library operations. These include document storage and retrieval, automated classification, automated indexing, machine translation and automated abstracting, and automated question-answering systems. A great deal of research and development work has been carried out on these

---

22 G. Bell and M. W. Pirtle, *"Time-Sharing Bibliography,"* Proc. IEEE, *54* (December 1966), pp. 1764–5.

techniques, and in some of them there has been substantial progress. A number of library-relevant techniques are available for use. (See appendix F–3 for greater detail.)

Storage and Retrieval Systems

Many systems are in operation in business, industry, and military operations for the storage and retrieval of data from very large files. Although these systems were not developed primarily with books in mind, the techniques used are similar, in many respects, to those required for the storage and retrieval of text. Current work in data systems centers not so much on the technical feasibility of large data-base operations as on the relative efficiency of various file organization and search techniques. The principles, techniques, and programs developed for data-retrieval work are applicable to those kinds of library data that can be highly structured and formated; e.g., authority files.

Document-retrieval systems—i.e., systems for handling textual information—presently lag far behind data-handling systems in the application of data-processing techniques. Most of these systems require that humans analyze material entering the system and prepare representations of it for computer storage. Some kinds of automatic indexing that are both technically and economically feasible—for example, permuted indexes of titles—have not yet proved adequate to meet the search needs in most document storage and retrieval systems. Given the need for human indexing, however, some current systems provide a high degree of automation thereafter. One system operated under the auspices of the Federal Government permits a large number of users, at widely dispersed locations, to pose requests directly and simultaneously to the computer system and to receive computer assistance in identifying document representations meeting prescribed criteria.

Such systems are not yet within the economic range for use by library patrons, but they could be used in connection with various kinds of special files to provide assistance to either technical processes or reference personnel. With decreasing computer costs, more ready-made programs, and better-trained library staff, such services are well within reach of extension directly to library users, particularly in some kinds of special and educational libraries.

In the next five to ten years we may expect to see the development and application of acceptably efficient computer aids to human indexing and classification using machine-readable inputs that are provided by optical readers or that are by-products of publication. Techniques of file organization and search, currently lagging behind equipment technology, will probably keep up reasonably well with the increasing demands placed on them by the very large files that new equipment techniques are providing. Too, the present somewhat embryonic techniques for direct interaction with the file—already accepted in the intelligence community and increasingly mentioned in libraries-of-the-future discussions—can be expected to become relatively commonplace in research-type libraries that can afford some degree of computer assistance.

Although many technical problems must be overcome to make substantial improvements in document storage and retrieval techniques, cost may be a more serious problem. The widespread applicability of document storage and retrieval techniques is heavily dependent on success in providing cheaper and more powerful computer equipment.

Component Techniques

Most of the specialized techniques associated with document storage and retrieval—automated indexing, classification, and abstracting; machine translation; and question-answering—must still be considered in the developmental stage. Within some of these areas, however, sufficient progress has been made to provide potentially effective tools for library use. The status and prospects in each area are summarized below.

As for automated classification, thus far studies have shown that computers can be used to generate classification categories that look reasonable and that one can achieve a moderate amount of agreement between human and computer sorting of documents into prescribed categories. Nevertheless, there are no fully automated systems available yet, and the relative merits of automated classification are still to be demonstrated.

The need for computer assistance to classification will undoubtedly continue to grow as collections grow and as more materials become available in machine-readable form. Yet, because of the fairly slow rate of progress in classification research, the most likely application of automated classification in the near future is likely to be for sensitizing machine-based systems periodically to changes in the character of the collection. By 1975 we may expect to see more extensive applications of automated classification; e.g., to "suggest" assignments to the human classifiers. This kind of joint man-machine document assignment holds considerable promise.

The term "automated indexing" refers to a variety of computer-based procedures, varying in complexity and potential utility to libraries. The simplest kind, which produces permuted indexes, has found widespread use, though more in connection with technical information systems than with libraries. On the other hand, the automatic selection or assignment of index terms from text, originally viewed with optimism some years ago, is increasingly recognized to be a difficult challenge. Fully automatic high-quality indexing does not yet appear to be within reach, a fact that has led to increasing interest in computer-aided indexing; i.e., man-machine cooperation. Capability to provide a number of useful aids to human indexing is already well within the state of the art. Exploitation of this capability will depend on evidence regarding its likely economic value.

Within three to five years one may expect to see widespread use of computer aids to indexing in most information facilities that have access to a computer. One may also expect to see, in many systems using text that is already in machine-readable form, index terms directly "suggested" through computer analysis of text. The quality of present-day automatic index-term extraction does not appear to compete with the best human indexing, nor does it seem likely to do so in the near future. Nevertheless, expected advancements in the understanding of language and of human indexing itself seem very likely to support a gradual increase in the acceptability of computer-selected index terms.

Both machine translation and automated abstracting involve processing of the full text of documents and the use of statistical, syntactic, and semantic tools to effect a conversion of the parent document into some other form—in one case a translated version and in the other a condensed representation of it. Although work in both these areas started out optimistically several years ago, the analysis of language has proved to be much more difficult and complex than was anticipated. Thus there is virtually no present applicability of either technique to libraries, except in a few special circumstances where there is ready availability of a machine-readable record and a willingness to use abstracts and translations as indicators of important information, rather than as conveyors of substantive information.

The future of both these areas is highly problematical since improvements are very dependent upon progress in other, more fundamental parts of language processing. Since, too, author-produced abstracts are increasingly being requested for submission with reports and articles, the need for automated abstracting may be diminishing. Given these considerations, there seems little likelihood that the use of these techniques will become attractive to most libraries.

Question-answering systems provide a rather direct analogy to the reference situation in which the user is provided with or directed to specific data. Automated question-answering systems may be considered an accomplished fact if one is dealing with highly structured data and if the questions asked can be confined to a simple and prescribed format. On the other hand, the answering of free-language inquiries against a file containing text is much more difficult, particularly if one expects to receive a well-formulated answer. Even today, however, question-answering systems could prove to be valuable to reference librarians (rather than users). They are cognizant of the file and could be trained to use acceptable question formats. The difficult problem is in deciding what kinds of reference materials would be worth the cost and effort to store and query in this fashion.

Although completely automated question-answering is many years away, we are very likely to see, in the next several years, some level of question-answering capability in a number of reference facilities, particularly large ones with special missions (e.g., intelligence) or those that are part of a network and can share not only computer costs but reference material.

Computer-aided instruction (CAI) techniques, originally developed in an educational context, are now being seen as having a broader applicability. They offer considerable promise to libraries and information centers both in the training of new library personnel and in the providing of service to users. The addition of an instructional element to an automated system—or to conventional systems, for that matter—can help library patrons learn how to use the particular library's resources or how to conduct some kinds of reference searches. The advanced study-carrels being developed by some colleges, as part of the library-college concept (see chapter 2, section C.2), may be the forerunners of new self-help ideas.

CAI techniques are not yet widely applicable in libraries because computers themselves are not widely used; also, no instructional materials have been prepared, either for the library staff or for users. With the increasing use of computers in libraries, however, and with the rapid progress being made in CAI, we are likely to see within a few years a number of CAI-type programs developed in connection with most operational programs for support to technical processes in libraries.

RELATED EQUIPMENT AND MATERIALS TECHNOLOGY

Another group of technologies that is particularly important for libraries includes microform technology, reprography, advanced publication-techniques, physical handling and storage devices, and information-transmission facilities.

Microfilm—previously considered valuable for space-saving and materials preservation—is seeing increasing use as a medium of communications as the Federal Government and others begin to view libraries as distributors of information, rather than merely circulators. Inexpensive (under $100) microform readers that could be installed in one's office are currently available, and during the next five to ten years one may expect to see a number of efforts to establish large-sized microfiche libraries that provide their users with either fiche or hard copy. As an example of the cost savings in microfilming, a $3.00 hardbound document can, when put on microfiche, be sold for only $0.65. We may expect to see many significant improvements in microform technology during the next ten years. These will include stable color microfilm, more sophisticated microform-handling equipment, and equipment for direct information transfer between microimage and computer subsystems.

Ultramicroform technology is now being developed that uses reductions of 150 or 200 to 1, rather than the usual ratio of 19 to 1, putting much more information on a single sheet. This ultrareduction allows for very inexpensive reproduction of a great number of copies, and has led to a proposal to create a thousand libraries of one million books in ultramicroform.

Reprography—reproduction by printing or copying—is of vital concern to libraries. With improvement of copying techniques, copying is competitive with offset printing techniques in cost and quality. Present reprographic techniques are efficient, rapid, and inexpensive and produce high quality copies, though costs and techniques vary widely (see appendix F–3).

It is clear that during the next few years the cost of copying will continue to drop, the simple types of offset printing will improve in quality, and fiche reader-printers will improve in quality and cost less. There will also be increasing use of color. Electrostatic printers will use fiche as the source document, and progress will also be seen in printing from optical storage devices, magnetic tape or holographic devices, and ultramicrofiche. Graphic material will also see an increasing amount of production under computer control.

The advent of photocomposition—computer-controlled preparation of reproduction masters with electro-optical techniques—is very important for the library. It provides a means for some libraries to abandon card catalogs in favor of book-form catalogs, up-to-date versions of which could be printed in multiple copies to be available in several locations in the library. Quite apart from the printing aspects of photocomposition, the availability of library materials (text or catalog-type information) in machine-readable form provides an opportunity to explore other computer applications economically.

With respect to physical handling and storage, it seems clear that printed materials will continue to be the primary carriers to be dealt with for some years, and that few libraries will be able to use electronic means exclusively to manage their information. The carriers will have to be stored and handled by humans, aided in some instances by mechanical devices. There are some promising materials-handling devices—conveyors, tubes, containers, lifters, stackers, etc.—some of which can be useful in future systems where materials-handling is largely computer-controlled. Most of these devices appear too expensive at present for widespread use.

Microfilm, magnetic tape, and magnetic discs pose less of a storage problem than books, though more sophisticated microfilm-handling devices will be needed, especially to support rapid and direct transfer between microimage and computer subsystems.

Transmission of materials is becoming an increasingly important area of interest to libraries, particularly in relation to possible network operations. The options include the mail and a variety of electronic means, such as television of facsimile transmission. The controlling factors in the selection of transmitting and receiving equipment include the material to be transmitted, the quality of transmission desired, the available interconnections between transmitting and receiving equipment, and the cost of the interconnections. Current interconnecting links are standard telephone circuits, private telephone voice lines, video circuits, and microwave relay.

Of the several means for the transmission of materials, mail is still the most practical. Fiche have the lowest mailing rates per page (five fiche for 6 cents, in contrast with books, at about 12 cents apiece). Video equipment, though it too provides low per-page costs, requires a high capital investment.

Efforts are under way to create working systems that employ advanced communications-technology to support retrieval of material from a central store, transmitting it to a different place, and viewing it there. In such systems libraries would have remote consoles with video displays; there would be video communication links between local and regional libraries. Thus, any document within the region could be viewed from any place in the region.

In general, it is expected that both the accuracy and the data-transmission rates of various kinds of telecommunications equipment will increase in the near future.[23] Communications satellites, which are currently in a development and testing phase, can also be expected to have some potential as a medium for transferring documentary information. What is not yet clear is whether there will be sufficient integration of the various kinds of transmission media and networks to serve the purposes of a more highly integrated library network.

23 *George W. Brown* et al., EDUNET (*New York: John Wiley and Sons, 1967*).

In the next few years communication among libraries may get a big boost from developments now under way in laser technology. The advent of laser technology promises a tremendous increase in what has been thought of as an already overcrowded communication capacity. Laser beams provide a wireless straight cable, on which it seems possible to impose signals. These signals can be carried along the surface of the earth or by repeat transmission from satellites. Though the results of laser research have been exciting and promising, the work is still experimental and the techniques are not yet useful for libraries.

The other aspect of laser technology that may be important to the library of the future is holography, which has several possible uses in libraries—e.g., for storing multiple images on one photographic plate or for storing color pictures of three-dimensional objects. This, too, is a technique whose perfection is still far in the future.

4. CURRENT APPLICATIONS AND TRENDS

INTRODUCTION

According to a fairly recent survey, 1,130 of the approximately 24,000 libraries in the United States in 1966 either had or planned to have within two years some aspect of their operations performed by data-processing equipment.[24] Of this number only 638 actually had some operational mechanized process; the others only had plans for mechanization. The majority of the 1,130 were libraries having over 50,000 volumes. Although there is some question whether the figures reported in the survey are entirely accurate, there can be little doubt that only a small percentage of the libraries in the country are actually using or working toward data-processing technology.

Table 7C–4.1, based on figures from the survey, gives some rough indications of how data processing is being applied. All of the major library functions are drawing attention, although the emphasis is primarily on functions related to technical-process requirements. For libraries that were currently using data-processing equipment in 1966, the function receiving the most attention (209 libraries) was probably that of serials management. The accounting function of the acquisitions process was also very popular, and logically so, since libraries are typically part of larger organizations whose functions in the accounting area may have been automated for some time. For other acquisitions functions, such as the production of purchase orders and accessions lists, the majority of libraries that were using data-processing equipment for these functions used electric accounting machinery rather than electronic computers.

Circulation control was also a popular mechanized function; 165 institutions in the study were using data-processing equipment for circulation control. Data-processing equipment was also used for the reference function; i.e., document retrieval; this was found in 131 installations, 76 of which were special libraries in industrial organizations. No public libraries, and only 18 colleges and universities, were undertaking this type of activity.

The following discussion describes, in somewhat simplified fashion, the major operations within libraries and reviews current applications of technology to these operations. Since specific procedures vary widely, even within libraries of the same size and type, the operational procedures described must be understood to be typical ones.

---

[24] *Creative Research Services, Inc.,* The Use of Data Processing Equipment by Libraries and Information Centers: A Survey Prepared for the Documentation Division, Special Libraries Association, and the Library Technology Program (*Chicago: American Library Association, 1966*). *Also, Eugene B. Jackson, "The Use of Data Processing by Libraries and Information Centers" (extracts), "An Interpretation of Creative Research Services, Inc., Report" (unpublished, 1967).*

ACQUISITIONS FUNCTIONS

Description

A logical starting point in discussing library operations is that of acquisitions, since materials must be selected and acquired before they can be used. The book trade is very specialized, and typical library practice is to carry out the purchasing functions within a specialized library department, rather than to use a purchasing department of the parent organization.

Contemporary United States publications from the larger trade and textbook publishers can be obtained anywhere in the country with a minimum of difficulty. The only problems likely to be encountered by a library dealing solely with such materials lie within the strictly clerical operations of handling the paperwork involved in the ordering process, and service from some suppliers is likely to be slow. Sometimes legal requirements of the parent organization add to the delay.

Research libraries, academic libraries, and some public and special libraries purchase materials in foreign languages and/or printed in every country of the world. The acquisitions process is complicated by the fact that not all countries have a well-established book trade. For this reason the Library of Congress, under recent legislation expanding the importation of foreign materials into the country, has found it necessary to establish and man field stations in certain countries.

Some libraries have additional problems with out-of-print materials such as items that are rare, old, fragile, and in exotic languages. Libraries are forced frequently to deal with particular vendors whose special requirements mean some kind of special paperwork or prepayment, which, under the rules of the particular library, may be very difficult, causing a great deal of extra effort. All of these factors have a bearing on the way that technology and automation may or may not be applicable.

Other types of acquisitions present special problems. For example, some libraries receive Federal, state, or local government publications automatically as designated depositories, and some acquire foreign government documents or the voluminous publications of the United Nations and its agencies. Depository libraries must claim materials that are due them but are not received for one reason or another, and must maintain records, even though there is no financial matter at stake.

Despite recent improvements in the distribution of Government documents, there are still large numbers of documents produced by various Federal agencies that do not find their way into the normal distribution channels through the United States Government Printing Office. For many of these documents it is not possible to achieve regular distribution and receipt by a particular library. Thus, a great deal of effort must be expended to discover and acquire such materials.

The acquisitions department also handles nonbook materials; for example, maps, phonograph records, tapes, slides, motion pictures, and microform versions of various standard publications. These all present special problems of acquisition.

A specialized aspect of acquisitions is the gift and exchange operation carried on by many libraries. Many gifts come to the libraries in poor physical condition and without a listing of the items included. To check such materials in order to determine which items to retain is time-consuming, and unless the gift is a particularly valuable one, it is probably more costly to the library in the long run to accept such materials than it would be to buy the relatively few items that it really wants.

The most critical problem connected with receiving large gift collections without a catalog is that the library must invest the time to produce a catalog of the collection if it wishes to derive any benefit from the gift. This is both a clerical and a professional operation, discussed in more detail under "Cataloging Functions" below.

Exchange is perhaps more peculiar to academic or certain governmental libraries than it is to most public or special libraries. Agreements for the exchange of materials free of charge conserve the book funds of the institution, and more importantly, they are the only way that some materials can be obtained at all from some foreign countries. For example, several United States academic institutions have been able to establish exchange agreements with academic institutions in Red China, and are thus able to acquire materials that cannot easily be obtained in any other manner. The same is true for the Soviet Union and certain other nations. Such agreements, however, require diplomacy on the part of the exchange librarian and maintenance of accurate and timely records of the exchanges, even though the volume of material received by exchange is generally small. There are a few libraries in the country (such as the Library of Congress) that have very large exchange programs.

Certain libraries also use blanket orders, a scheme for ordering on approval all materials published on a particular subject. Where the volume of materials received is large, these agreements with book vendors or publishers may involve considerable record-keeping, as well as very complicated financial arrangements with accounting departments; but the resulting speed of delivery and ease of selection are worth the additional paperwork, if any.

The final area of acquisitions to be discussed here is that of continuations, which can be defined as all materials outside of the one-time orders that bring in a complete item. They include serials, series, terminal sets, works issued in fascicles, anything issued in some numbered or ordered sequence, and other extended procurement. Regularity of issue is not a factor.

Serials are a form of continuation issued more or less periodically without a definite cutoff date. This contrasts with monographic series, which have no definite ending point but which do have a predictable end (e.g., the collected works of a given author, now deceased). Serials have a unique aspect that causes them to be handled, in most libraries, as a separate operation. For a given serial title an order once placed will result in the receipt of issues of that serial for years into the future, for most serials are published with the expectation that they will continue indefinitely.

The operational problem with continuations of any sort is not so much the placing of the original order but the maintenance of the records necessary to keep track of the continuing delivery of the items. Such continuations may extend over many years and over the employment period of several individuals. Serials are discussed in more detail later under "Serials Management Functions."

A useful starting-point for describing the operation of a typical library acquisitions section is the one at which requests are received. The library first searches to see whether the material is already owned by the library, has been ordered, or is being processed in the cataloging section. After this preliminary check is made, if the library decides to order the material, enough additional information about the item to establish a correct entry is sought, and an order is prepared and sent to a vendor or to the publisher. A record is kept of this order, notices are sent to any interested parties or departments, and a particular departmental book fund may be charged. When the item is received, copies of the order are pulled from the outstanding-order file and other files, and the book then moves into the cataloging process. Part of the acquisitions function may be the ordering of Library of Congress cards. Sometimes that function is carried out by the cataloging section. They receive a copy of the purchase order and, in turn, send a card order to the Library of Congress or to some other card service.

Applications of Technology

Certain aspects of the acquisitions process lend themselves particularly well to automation or to the use of other forms of technology. For example, the production of orders to vendors is very similar to the production of orders in any purchasing activity, and computers can do this very readily. The maintenance of purchasing records and the charging of funds against particular budgets are other activities that have been success-fully mechanized in the business world and that are being mechanized in some libraries.

As indicated in Table 7C–4.1, there were 102 libraries actually using some form of data processing in their acquisitions process as of October 1966. This survey reported that 419 institutions had plans for use of data processing in acquisitions, and that of these 419, 139 planned to begin such use by the end of 1968. These projects in acquisitions are endeavoring to do one or more of the following: (1) order library materials, (2) maintain financial records, (3) collect and record statistics on the order process, and (4) print lists in various arrangements of materials in process.

Financial reports may be arranged in a variety of ways; for example, on the basis of materials ordered, by fund, by subject categories that are not represented by funds, by accumulation of items ordered from particular vendors, by standing orders, etc. It is sometimes useful to know, for example, how many items have been ordered from particular vendors over a period of time, the amounts spent, the discounts received, how rapid the response to orders has been over a period of time, and the total number of orders placed within a particular calendar period.

Lists of materials in process are useful for a number of purposes, especially when items on order can be entered and located in a variety of ways. The typical method in the past has been to enter under a selected entry in an order file with no cross-references. This makes it exceedingly difficult, if one does not have precise information, to discover materials actually on order. Using lists that can be arranged in various manners, on-order and in-process materials can be controlled throughout the time from receipt of request within the division to mailing of the order to a vendor, to receipt of the materials, to cataloging, to the time they are ready for use.

Although there are some automated acquisitions systems operating, we know of none that include all of the possible products or operations listed above. A few institutions have either planned or are implementing systems that are as complete in concept as one could currently hope for. The literature describes several of the limited number of complete systems; none of these is operational yet.[25]

Aside from the use of data-processing equipment, and in some instances the use of related accounting machinery or bookkeeping machines, libraries have done little experimentation with available technologies. Very few libraries utilize materials-handling equipment, such as dumbwaiters and conveyor belts, in the acquisitions area. Some libraries have experimented with communications devices such as Deskfax, direct photocopying devices such as the Photoclerk, edge-notched cards, and automatic type-writers. In general, however, materials-handling devices and the use of photography in processing have not been given as much attention as "automation." Photography may not hold much long-range potential here, either for the reduction of costs or the improvement of output, but it is an area that is not receiving the research and develop-ment attention it deserves.

Since the acquisitions procedure seems to be so similar in libraries of comparable size and type, a number of cooperative projects have been started to develop processing centers for groups of libraries. Such cooperative processing centers have been in opera-tion for some time in northern California, Alabama, Michigan, Ohio, North Carolina, and Indiana; possibilities for centers are being studied in Colorado, New York State, Ohio, and other places. These centers perform all the typical functions—preparation of orders, selection of vendors, checking-in of materials, cataloging, and finally delivering the items, ready for the shelf, to the participating libraries. It is apparent, of course, that

25 *University of California, Santa Cruz,* Specification for an Automated Library System (*Santa Cruz, Calif., 1965*); *Robert D. Kozlow,* Library Automation Project: A Report on a Library Automation Project Conducted on the Chicago Campus of the University of Illinois, *supported by National Science Foundation, Grants 77 and 302, 1966, University of Illinois Report; Stanford University Library,* Bibliographic Automation of Large Library Operations Using a Time Sharing System (Project BALLOTS), *proposed to the United States Office of Education, 1967, Project No. 7–1145.*

such centers can operate in the same (manual) way that most library acquisitions departments have operated for many years. Yet the use of data-processing equipment makes the cooperative processing center a much more attractive proposition.

The potential savings of cooperative or centralized processing centers have not always been realized. For example, a recent study of a centralized processing center in Illinois showed that although personnel were relieved of the processing task and work-space pressure was relieved in some of the participating libraries, the actual cost of processing through the center was, for some of the participants, greater than that of doing the work themselves.[26]

Reported costs of existing cooperative centers vary widely. The reported costs are difficult to compare with previous costs since almost no one has obtained cost figures during a previous operational period and then studied the same operation after the processing center has been established. In addition, the services provided may differ from one center to another. For example, some centers use very simplified cataloging, whereas the center in Illinois, mentioned above, used a cataloging code that resulted in better quality but more expensive cataloging than had previously been the case in the individual libraries.

The Association of Research Libraries has been studying the possibilities of cooperation for many years. Under their Farmington Plan individual institutions under-take the purchase of foreign publications from a certain area or on a certain topic and then serve as a national center for such materials, thus relieving other institutions of the need to purchase in that particular field. Recent activity at the Library of Congress under Title II of the Higher Education Act has also served to further the cause of cooperative purchasing and processing. These cooperative activities could be the beginnings of true networks.

It is difficult to predict with accuracy the extent to which the trend toward central-ized and cooperative processing can be carried. The cooperative processing center or the centralized purchasing center tends to limit free enterprise within the book trade. It is conceivable that a cooperative or centralized purchasing activity could be large enough to dispense with the services of booksellers at the retail level, or even the wholesale level, and deal directly with publishers for all purchases. If extended over a large enough geographical area, this could adversely affect the fortunes of a number of booksellers. Also, there are numerous legal barriers in the way of widespread cooperative purchasing and processing if the members are located in different political jurisdictions (i.e., different counties, states, or countries) or if some members are publicly supported and others are privately supported.

CATALOGING FUNCTIONS

Description

Libraries have developed highly complex systems to categorize the materials they acquire to make them accessible to the library's clientele on the basis of subject matter, author, and title of the work. In the cataloging and classification process numerous categorizing schemes are used, the most widely used being the Dewey Decimal Classifi-cation and the Library of Congress Classification systems. Alphabetically arranged subject headings are also used, as well as the occasionally used newer techniques such as descriptors and key-word-in-context.

The amount of effort expended in the description of the item varies from library to library; some libraries expend a great deal of effort on a precise physical description of library materials, as well as on their subject categorization. Apart from the physical description of the item, there is the matter of assigning an entry to the material. Because of the nature of the so-called dictionary catalog (on small cards), the concept of main

26 *Donald D. Hendricks,* Comparative Cost of Book Processing in a Processing Center and in Five Individual Libraries, *Illinois State Library Research Series No. 8 (Springfield, Ill., 1966).*

entry has been important in cataloging work. Selecting the main entry, putting it into proper form, and selecting appropriate subject headings and classification numbers or coordinate indexing terms are time-consuming tasks.

In most libraries the descriptive cataloging and the subject classification are done by the same people; in others this work is separated; in still others catalog sections are operated in conjunction with the acquisitions activities. In many libraries the catalogers use Library of Congress printed catalogs for guidance, but they also maintain their own authority files, which give proper forms of names, series titles that are used or not used in that particular library's catalogs, proper forms of subject headings, and other information. Libraries typically maintain special catalogs known as shelflists, which are maintained in the same order as the books are shelved in within the library. It is an inventory record primarily but can sometimes be used as a classed catalog since the file is usually organized by the classification scheme in use in the library.

The end result of operations in a cataloging section is a series of codes assigned to a given item and a description of the item. Together these constitute the cataloging entry for that item. Typical library practice in the past has consisted of making catalog records on 7 1/2 × 12 1/2 cm. cards. Printed cards may be purchased from other organizations, e.g., the H. W. Wilson Company or the Library of Congress, or cards may be produced at the local library.

A particularly nagging problem for many libraries is that of "arrearage," which is the general term given to the large quantities of uncataloged materials so frequently found in catalog departments. Libraries often acquire large collections in one transaction, completely overloading the catalogers. More and more libraries have these unprocessed backlogs, for they are reluctant to pass up any chance to acquire materials that may later be unavailable or available only at greatly increased prices.

Applications of Technology

The most popular application of technology to the cataloging process has been to reproduce catalog cards. Although the cost of purchasing cards from the Library of Congress is relatively low, some libraries prefer to produce all of their own cards using copy provided by Library of Congress proofsheets (proof copy of new catalog cards) or Library of Congress printed catalogs. These libraries are sometimes able to reduce the costs below that of cards obtained from the Library of Congress. Techniques sometimes involve photocopying, but a few libraries rekeyboard the item on paper tape for production of the necessary cards by automatic typewriter or computer.

Book catalogs are catalogs in the form of a book (or codex) rather than individual cards. This form of catalog, frequently used many years ago but abandoned in favor of the card catalog, is returning to favor. With the new technology some of the disadvantages of the early book catalogs are no longer serious. The major objection to book catalogs of the past was that the cost of keeping them up-to-date was prohibitive. With present-day equipment, especially computer-controlled typesetting or computer printing in upper- and lower-case letters, the cost of reprinting catalogs on a regular basis has become much more competitive with the cost of maintaining large, complex card catalogs. A further advantage of the printed book catalog is that it can be produced in multiple copies for use at a large number of service points, including distant ones.

A few libraries are now producing catalogs by computer in a book form, with holdings arranged by author, title, and subject. These are produced on a regular basis and updated as necessary. One of the unresolved problems connected with the computer production of book catalogs is the filing sequence of entries within a particular catalog. Existing filing rules demand a high level of human intelligence for their accomplishment. The rules must be modified to some extent in order that a computer can follow them. There is not yet unanimous agreement within the library community on just what modifications should be made.

Some libraries are producing (or planning) cumulative monthly lists of currently cataloged items, authority lists of subject headings, and lists of currently cataloged items arranged by the special interests of the library or its clientele. In addition, some projects are seeking to gather by-product statistics for library administration; e.g., work-performance records by cataloger.

The combination of interlibrary cooperation and new technology offers great potential for the reduction of costs and wasteful duplication of effort in cataloging. There are already a number of smaller cooperative processing centers that combine acquisition and cataloging functions, presumably with economic advantage to the participating libraries. The Library of Congress also continues to play an increasingly important role in cataloging. Because it catalogs a significant percentage of books acquired by libraries in the United States, it has been—on economic considerations alone—an effective agency for the reduction of cataloging effort by a large number of libraries in the country. In fiscal 1966 over 72 million cards were distributed by the Card Division of the Library of Congress. With its expanded role in procuring materials abroad and cataloging them more promptly, even greater savings are possible. Project MARC, which is a prototype of a national network for the distribution of machine-readable catalog data, has great potential in this respect.[27]

There are other aspects of the cataloging process that could benefit from either centralization or mechanization. A cooperative centralized operation could consolidate authority files, or even official catalogs, and the consolidated authority file could become a part of a union catalog for the participating libraries.

Aspects of technology other than data processing are also beginning to contribute to the cataloging process. There has been some interest in camera equipment that a cataloger could use to copy data from available Library of Congress printed catalogs or other national bibliographical records. Only recently has a camera been introduced (by the Polaroid Company) that is especially intended for use by catalogers. Whether it is satisfactory is not yet known. Other efforts have recently been announced for development of a bibliographer's camera; the Council on Library Resources is sponsoring this work.

Materials-handling equipment also has potential, although this area has not been exploited to any large extent. A few libraries have installed large rotary shelves to offer better access to large reference sets, such as the Library of Congress printed catalogs. Some forms of compact storage have also been developed, but relatively little study has been made of possible improvements in materials handling to support the cataloging process.

Some equipment has been developed to aid in the placement of call numbers, letters, and numbers on book spines. This is a relatively unglamorous part of processing but one that is necessary in every library. The tool developed for this purpose by the American Library Association's Library Technology Program (LTP) works reasonably well and saves some amount of time and money, but it will not work with the most modern typewriters.

A few libraries have considered certain aspects of purchasing, receiving, and cataloging as a single process, and are attempting to establish systems that capture the bibliographical information concerning each item ordered at the time it is ordered, thus abolishing the need for rekeyboarding time and time again throughout the entire system. This is a promising approach, especially for handling currently published material for which full identifying information is available.

If consideration is limited to contemporary publication in English, by far the bulk of the acquisitions in libraries of the United States, there is no question that the single-process goal can be achieved. If there were library networks interconnected by com-

---

[27] *Library of Congress Information Systems Office,* A Preliminary Report on the MARC (MAchine-Readable Cataloging) Pilot Project (*Washington, D.C. 1966*).

munication links, keyboarding could be further reduced by storing the bibliographical information for each item in a machine-readable store. Any other library could then call out the complete record from the store by inputting only a small portion, sufficient to identify the entry. It might be possible to use only the Library of Congress catalog card number to retrieve the complete bibliographic record.

There are at least two current attempts being made to implement some of these ideas. Project MARC has already been mentioned. Another major effort is in New York State, where a network is being planned for a medical library system.[28] It is anticipated that there will be a centralized technical-processes center for the entire New York State University system, with communication lines linking all of the libraries.

In the near future the use of computers to produce book catalogs will undoubtedly become more widespread, particularly with the advent of devices that can transform computer output directly onto film. The Chemical Abstracts Service (see chapter 3, section B), which is preparing to print *Chemical Abstracts* entirely from computer output in a few years, has a device that will take computer output (using a character set of 1,452 separate characters) and place it on film, from which it can then be made into an offset printing plate. The same process could be used to produce library catalogs, either union or individual. In addition, microfilmed catalogs produced in this fashion could readily be copied and distributed in cartridge form, so that libraries could have union catalogs for their patrons at many points at a relatively low cost.

Communications technology could also be important in relation to uses of the catalog. One idea, which few libraries seem to have considered, is to establish direct communication from the public catalog area to the catalog department to help reference personnel or patrons obtain assistance in the use of the catalog. Communications technology may also prove very useful in relation to storage facilities. There have been some efforts to establish such facilities for a group of libraries in an area of low real-estate cost. The use of slow-scan television to send tables of contents, for example, to distant patrons over ordinary telephone lines, apparently not yet studied, is worth investigating.

The problems of arrearage might be eased by better exploitation of data-processing technology and, possibly, materials-handling technology. Various schemes have been devised by some large academic libraries to produce brief descriptions of these materials and then to store them away. None seem to have followed the lead of some special libraries that have used data processing to produce permuted indexes to their arrearages. The use of compact shelving of various types might enable libraries to handle their arrearages more effectively. Most libraries have not planned for such shelving, however, and its installation and use may be considered too expensive.

CIRCULATION FUNCTIONS

Description

Most libraries employ some kind of circulation-control system to keep track of the materials borrowed from the library. Such systems vary from the very simple to the extremely complex, in accordance with the type and importance of information needed. In England some libraries give their patrons a number of tokens, which are exchanged one-by-one for books that they take from the library. When a book is returned, the patron receives a token back, but no record whatsoever is kept to show what book the patron has or who has what book. The only apparent use of the tokens is to restrict the number of materials that a patron can have out of the library at one time. Libraries in the United States usually want much more information and control.

It is in the area of circulation that we find perhaps the greatest operational

28 *Barbara Evans Markuson, "Automation in Libraries and Information Centers,"* Annual Review of Information Science and Technology, 2 (1967), pp. 255–83.

differences among the three general types of libraries identified earlier. Although most public libraries do seem to have some sort of limit on the number of books that patrons may take out at one time, they generally attempt to maintain controls only with respect to the date of return. Thus, there is usually no way to discover what materials are out to what particular borrower.

Some academic libraries have special circulation problems, in that they have special collections of materials that are loaned for very short periods of time. These items may carry rather high fines for even short periods of overdue use, and record-keeping is a large operational problem for these libraries. Academic libraries, in general, feel it necessary to be able to determine who has a particular item when it is out and to control the length of time materials are out.

Special libraries generally try to keep some sort of inventory of materials out to each borrower, but they tend to be especially liberal regarding their loan periods. Some special libraries also need to maintain control of security-classified documents, not a typical problem in either academic or public libraries. For such documents the concept of accountability is paramount.

Another rather specialized aspect of circulation control involves nonbook materials, which have their own unique problems. For example, the circulation of motion-picture film involves not only circulation control but booking in advance. This requires specialized records as well as efficient routing and distribution. Other materials loaned by libraries also have specialized requirements. Phonograph records and audio tapes, for example, require special handling not typically afforded book material. Circulation of periodicals for limited periods and their inspection after each use present additional problems that seemingly demand human attention and have relatively little potential for mechanization. However, technology might have some answers if the proper efforts were made to discover them.

In recent years circulation control has received much attention, no doubt because many libraries have acute problems in this area. A number of studies have been made, evidently with somewhat questionable results, of circulation-control systems, under the sponsorship of the Library Technology Project of the American Library Association. Academic libraries, especially, have had their circulation systems very much in the public eye. Some have had operating problems that cause long queues to build up at charge-out points; waits of up to an hour for service are reported in the literature. Such conditions cause considerable dissatisfaction among the patrons. Thus, a number of libraries have selected circulation control as a first step toward automation. A case in point is Johns Hopkins University, which has devised what seems to be a fairly expensive system of circulation control, the design criteria for which emphasize the ease and speed of moving through the circulation-control point, from the patron's viewpoint.

Applications of Technology

According to the Creative Research Services survey, about 165 libraries are now using data-processing technology to support the circulation-control function.[29] Current projects in this area seek to do the following: produce lists of materials actually in use and identify their location; produce lists of materials in use by individual borrower; produce overdue notices automatically; and collect circulation statistics by borrower category, subject category, or any other particular category of interest to the library. Subfunctions of some of the foregoing processes are those of producing lists of materials having one or more requests outstanding (holds and recalls), so that management action could be taken; producing cumulative records of the use of particular items, with automatic notification of materials used so frequently that they are likely to need rebinding; and producing annual listings of materials out on long-term loans to certain categories of borrowers.

Some public libraries have had very comprehensive circulation-control systems for

[29] Bowker Annual of Library and Book Trade Information (*New York: R. R. Bowker Co., 1967*).

years. Perhaps the most outstanding is the Montclair (New Jersey) Public Library, which uses custom-built IBM equipment to keep track of the records by item, by borrower, and by due date. Only recently has comparable equipment become generally available.

A few academic libraries now have systems that permit an inventory of materials out to a particular borrower. Others can run an inventory for all materials out on long-term loans but cannot answer directly the question, "What materials are loaned to the borrower, Mr. Jones?" Most of the operating automatic or semiautomatic systems work on a batch basis. The concept of batch processing implies that data are fed to the computer all at one time, rather than being fed to it from time to time on line. A few institutions are beginning to work toward the development of actual on-line operations that will tie a circulation-control system directly into a computer at all times. Several are now operational.

Using data-collection equipment tied directly into a computer, libraries could handle one- or two-hour loans; this would demand considerable random-access memory, but the value of the use statistics that could not be gathered any other way might well justify the added cost. Within libraries of a size large enough to have branch operations, a limited network arrangement could be useful for circulation control. All the branches could participate in the one common system by the use of remote data-collection devices, thus placing in one central computer record the total circulation file. This would enable librarians to ascertain the current availability of particular titles within the system, much as airlines check for available seats. Public librarians have not felt that this was a necessary part of their service in the past, but they might well do so if the system permitted it.

Circulation control could also be operated on a network basis within a region, it would seem, quite efficiently. Many libraries banded together could afford equipment that no individual library, or even several libraries, could afford. This might allow effective on-line operations at a reasonable cost. Efforts along these lines will undoubtedly begin to take place; there is already some research under way along these lines by private organizations.

The concept of cost effectiveness has usually been absent from the discussion of circulation-control systems, especially in connection with existing manual systems. Cost effectiveness is not the same as cost per se, a distinction often misunderstood, for an all-too-common approach to circulation control considers only the lowest possible cost of the operation to the library. The idea that circulation statistics can also provide important management information over a period of time seems not to have taken hold yet, for few libraries have sought to devise circulation systems that would enable them to collect such management data at a reasonable cost. Future efforts undoubtedly will begin to see more attention paid to this. Cost to the user is also a topic that is beginning to attract attention.

After materials are used, they must be reshelved or replaced by the circulation section. Technology has had as little effect (in the United States) on this operation as it has had on the similar operation of paging books in libraries that do not allow their patrons access to the stacks. Although some use has been made of pneumatic tubes to transmit call slips and even books, these are point-to-point operations, and materials must be taken off shelves and replaced by hand.

Some interesting suggestions for materials handling have been made; for example, that the principle of the linotype could be used to position, deliver, and replace a book in a particular place within a collection.[30] Following this suggestion, another system was outlined using plastic boxes to contain and transport books in and out of the stacks.[31]

---

[30] *Stanley Humenuk,* Automatic Shelving and Book Retrieval: A Contribution Toward a Progressive Philosophy of Library Service for a Research Library *(thesis, University of Illinois, 1964).*
[31] *Robert T. Jordan,* The Jordan Plastic Book Box *(unpublished report, 1966).*

Remington-Rand has recently announced a system which is, in effect, an automatic stack and is intended primarily for automatic handling for storage and retrieval of materials kept in file folders. The manufacturer claims that the system will handle materials in codex form. The economics for library operations of this system are unknown since only a prototype of the equipment exists at the present time. (This equipment is also discussed in appendix F–3 under "Related Equipment and Materials Technology.")

REFERENCE AND REFERRAL FUNCTIONS

Description

Reference and referral is another aspect of the public-service side of all libraries. This includes helping the patrons find and identify materials of interest, making requests to other libraries if necessary, and helping patrons in the use of reference tools. Reference work also includes the production of specialized bibliographies. Public libraries also have a reader's advisory function, which is generally not considered important or necessary in special libraries or academic institutions, where the patrons are students, faculty, or research personnel.

Part of the help given patrons involves interpretation of the library's catalog. Thus, card catalogs are typically placed in a public area where they are handy to the reference and circulation sections, even though this may make them very unhandy for personnel in the technical-processes area. In some libraries greater use of library catalogs or library reference materials is made by the staff of the library itself than by patrons. However, the library's orientation toward service to its patrons usually dictates a location convenient for their use.

Some part of the public-services section of the library, usually the reference department, will handle requests to other libraries for materials the library does not have. In the area of interlibrary loans library cooperation has been truly remarkable. All libraries, public and private, can obtain interlibrary loans, not only throughout the United States but also overseas. Some of the larger libraries have used communication devices such as the teletype to handle their interlibrary loan requests. The Library of Congress, with its *National Union Catalog,* serves as a focal point for the activity in this country, although certain academic libraries may have local cooperative agreements within a region and therefore will make their requests within that local group before using the Library of Congress resources. For these reference and referral functions of interlibrary loans union catalogs are almost indispensable. Without them interlibrary loan activity would require circularizing a large number of libraries until one located a particular library that had the desired material.

Reference work frequently involves making copies of library materials for patrons. Sometimes these are copies of tables from reference works that cannot be removed from the library. Since circulation of periodicals is frequently restricted, there is also heavy traffic in photocopies of articles. There is also frequent demand for microform materials, especially the widely used roll microfilm in 35mm format.

Applications of Technology

Very little in the way of technology, with the exception of communication devices, can presently be found in most library reference departments. Very few libraries have automated their document-retrieval functions. In general, these systems work as follows: a variety of guides or indexes to document holdings are available, from which users select key words, subject headings, or uni-terms as search keys; the search produces lists of document numbers, sometimes including abstracts of material matching the subject criteria input.

There are also some primitive automated data-retrieval functions along the same lines, generally using some type of subject categorization for the construction of search requests. Most data-retrieval systems can do only such simple things as producing a series of sentences that contain some prescribed or desired words, or a listing of physical data that meet certain criteria. Most of the automated data-retrieval systems are in information centers; almost no conventional libraries have automated data-retrieval functions.

Project Intrex at Massachusetts Institute of Technology (M.I.T.) combines some aspects of document and data retrieval within a library function. Intrex (*in*formation *tra*nsfer *ex*periments) is a program of experimentation directed toward the functional design of new library services that might become operational at M.I.T. and elsewhere by 1970. The research program is addressed mainly to the broad problem of access—in particular, access to bibliographical material, documents, and data banks. The four areas of activity encompassed by the core program of Project Intrex are an augmented catalog (computer-stored), full-text access at stations that are remote from the store, fact retrieval, and network integration.[32]

Some current mechanization projects have implications for reference. For example, where libraries have mechanized their catalog records, using computers either to print catalog cards or to produce book-form catalogs, there is also the inherent capability to produce specialized listings of materials in a particular area. The computer can be used to retrieve references and tailor a bibliography specifically to the needs of the patron, within limits; for example, on date of publication, language of materials, and subject headings.

Some communication devices have been used in libraries for some time. The Electrowriter and similar systems have been used to transmit handwritten requests from one point in a library to another or from a branch library to another element of the system. Several recent projects have explored the use of telefacsimile processes to transmit needed materials from one library to another.

The promise is great, but so is the cost. Here, again, libraries are making use of equipment and technology developed for other uses and not especially suited to library problems. For example, the typical facsimile process is not usable with bound materials, except through the use of the television camera. With the typical commercial television equipment and common-carrier transmission systems, the cost for transmitting even a few pages is very great. No work has been done, so far as we are able to determine, with slow-scan TV processes for library purposes. Some studies have been made with closed-circuit TV, but these were made some years ago, prior to the advent of the slow-scan process. For ordinary TV use the costs are now too great because of band-width requirements.

Lecture demonstrations have been held at several places in the country where materials used by the lecturer at the transmitting end were displayed on a screen at the receiving end. Such equipment is said to work over voicegrade lines and does not involve too great a transmission time. On the other hand, it produces only a display, not hard copy, at the receiving end.

Typical library equipment for using microforms is far from satisfactory for long-duration usage. For some reason existing optical technology has not been exploited to the fullest. Microfilm equipment manufacturers seem to have planned microfilm readers and other types of microform readers that are always portable, and librarians have apparently accepted this position. Yet such machines are usually placed in a particular location, are used there, and are rarely taken from that location; they could just as well be built in. This would ease the normal restrictions on size and would allow the optical designer additional freedom to use long focal lengths to improve display on the screen. Existing standard optical techniques could be used to build a high-quality reader that

32 *Carl F. J. Overhage and Joyce Harman* (*eds.*), INTREX: Report of a Planning Conference on Information Transfer Experiments, September 3, 1965 (*Cambridge, Mass.: The M.I.T. Press, 1965*).

would be comfortable for a patron to use over a long period of time in a reasonably well-lighted area.

Evidently such equipment has not been built because the development cost seemed prohibitive without a guaranteed market. Not enough librarians have been actively concerned with utilization of microforms to demand the better products that could be made, and no efforts seem to be under way to improve the situation. Yet microforms will need to be used more extensively in libraries in the future. Large numbers of books printed over the past century are deteriorating, and some of these undoubtedly will be preserved only in microform. Most libraries that want them will be able to afford them only in microform. The possibility of large library collections (e.g., one million volumes) solely in microform is also very much on the horizon. The increasing amount of material available in this medium will undoubtedly help to accelerate efforts to improve the handling, storage, and use of microforms.

Some effort is being made to bring techniques of automated information-retrieval to reference work. A few libraries are already contemplating the use of computer equipment to make their catalog records available on line and are also considering placing computer display consoles in locations for use by patrons. Reference librarians may well be tied into the circuit, so that if the patron's own searching of the library catalog is unsuccessful, he can call a reference librarian who can interact with him and the computer to assist. Before this is an everyday occurrence, a great deal of experimentation must be carried on to determine what kind of retrieval system is needed for such interaction, and what kind of preparation and training are required of both the librarian and the patron.

The development and use of statistics regarding reference service has always been a shaky affair in libraries, largely because reference activity is very complex and because the personnel involved with reference functions do not have adequate time to record all of the daily transactions. This area will undoubtedly receive attention in the future as computers are called upon to interact with librarians and patrons.

Such devices could also allow the easy compilation of management information forms that could be very useful for library administration. For example, the use of statistics rapidly gathered from interlibrary loans and arranged for easy interpretation could enable the library administration to improve the library's collection systematically. Most libraries try to do this now, but without appropriate tools it often must remain a pious hope rather than an actuality.

SERIALS MANAGEMENT FUNCTIONS

Description

Serials were described earlier, in the section on acquisitions, as one form of continuation. It is difficult to say what constitutes a serial in a given library; most libraries have their own definitions. For purposes of discussion, we will consider as serials anything listed in *New Serial Titles* or the *Union List of Serials*.

Because they appear in such a wide variety of forms and because of the difficulty of maintaining records concerning them, serials have frequently been handled by a completely separate operating division within libraries, especially in libraries of medium to large size. Smaller libraries do not usually have the wide variety of serials that the larger public, academic, and special libraries have.

Although the more esoteric, foreign language, scholarly journals cause great difficulties in handling serial records, it is the sheer volume of details necessary in maintaining any serial that is the primary source of trouble. Also, serials have an additional problem that only infrequently is important in dealing with monographic works, namely binding. Periodicals have many separate discrete parts that must be gathered together and placed in some sort of hard cover for preservation. Most libraries either replace their unbound journals with microforms or bind them, which adds an additional aspect of record-keeping. (Records must be kept of what is at the bindery; separate records are needed of what is bound and what is not, because these materials may be shelved in separate locations.)

Large libraries with many branches have a tremendous record-keeping problem, since they try to record the exact items housed in any particular location. If an attempt is made to centralize such records manually, it can only be done economically in one place. Thus, branch locations may not have ready information on what materials may be in other branch locations.

An especially time- and manpower-consuming function is the claiming of serials that do not arrive on time, or at all. In order to carry on claiming, up-to-date information on serial receipts is necessary because some serials, if not claimed promptly, will be out-of-print and unavailable. Claiming is especially demanding of diligence and accurate record-keeping.

Union lists are another especially important aspect of serials management, since no library in the country has all of the journals ever published, even those of the United States. Every year literally thousands of new journals—scientific, technical, and others throughout the world—are born, and thousands die, seemingly with a gradual net gain of live titles.

Applications of Technology

There is an unknown but sizable number of projects under way to convert serial records and record-keeping to machine-readable forms so that they may be produced in a much more timely fashion. Some of the work on book catalogs holds promise for serials management. For example, book catalogs, extended to include periodical and serial holdings and reproduced in multiple copies, have been successful in alleviating the problem of providing ready information to branch libraries on serial holdings. Once there has been a sizable conversion of serials information to machine-readable form, it should be considerably easier to create and maintain union lists of serials. The monumental compilation of the third edition of the *Union List of Serials of Libraries in the United States and Canada* is a case in point; this final edition took literally decades to complete. If all the records had been machine-readable and computer programs had been available to manipulate them, new editions could have been produced on a yearly basis.

Communication devices and data-processing equipment offer tremendous potential for tying together the holdings of one library with that of another, within regions and nationally. With the addition of the capability of transmitting facsimile copy through communication links, it becomes possible to consider centralizing, on a regional or even national scale, serial holdings of lesser-used materials. There have been efforts along these lines—without advanced technology—by libraries in the past, a prime example being that of the Center for Research Libraries, located in Chicago.

The question of cost effectiveness becomes important in such considerations, and at present providing copies of journal articles for distant patrons is probably better carried out by common reproduction equipment and by mail than by costly telefacsimile processes. Initial efforts are already under way, in various regions of the country, to produce union lists of serial holdings for organizations with numerous branches. An example is the State University of New York, with its fifty-eight branches. Such efforts will undoubtedly accelerate in the near future.

A most encouraging development is the recent beginning of a project at the Library of Congress to determine precisely what elements of information should be put into a machine-readable record for a serial title. This is the groundwork on which a national serial-data project can be built; hopefully it will be undertaken at the Library of Congress in the near future. Both this effort and the recent known desire of the EDUCOM Network Task Force to convert the *Union List of Serials* to machine-readable form deserve greater support than they now have, since they offer tremendous potential for all libraries, not only in the United States but worldwide.

The semivoluntary efforts of the American Society for Testing Materials (ASTM) to establish a uniform code for serial titles were noteworthy; ASTM offered to assign a standard code (CODEN) to any serial title submitted to them in any field of knowledge. The Franklin Institute of Philadelphia has recently assumed responsibility for the CODEN effort. Standardization efforts of this kind, which help to establish codes for use in computer-based files, should have greater national and international support.

Despite several years of effort in the automation of serial records, relatively few institutions have operational systems, and those that exist do not perform all the necessary functions of serials management. Current projects undertake to produce the following types of records and control information: lists of currently received materials; cumulative lists of holdings, i.e., materials actually in the library; claim reports for issues that have not been received by a prescribed time; production of tags for bindery use; orders for new subscriptions and a renewal of the entire subscription list; financial records showing categories of expenditures by funds, by subject, by language, etc.; lists of materials not owned by the library that are needed to fill in gaps in holdings. Current efforts are aimed at producing all of the items above, but no one system does. Very few institutions have attempted to integrate work in this area with automation in other aspects of their operations.

SPECIAL COLLECTIONS AND MATERIALS

Description

Libraries handle a wide variety of materials in addition to books and magazines. Some libraries include the functions of museums, with collections of manuscripts, letters, and art objects, all of which demand special treatment. Some materials are given to libraries with restrictions on their use that the library must observe. Frequently the physical items are more important than their intellectual contents.

Some special collections are easier to categorize for subject use than book materials. For example, maps almost always refer to some geographic area that can be identified, if necessary, by precise coordinates of latitude and longitude. Art and architecture slides always refer to either a geographic location or a physical object. Although such materials may have a subject orientation that must be identified, subject use is much more limited than it is for book materials. The same is true for phonograph records.

Special collections usually impose special storage requirements upon libraries. Both manuscripts and some kinds of books must be kept under controlled environmental conditions or they will disintegrate. (Even ordinary books are not particularly long-lived, but they are usually more easily replaced.) Other materials do not necessarily need a special environment but must be protected from public access because of their rarity or fragility.

Applications of Technology

A great deal of specialized equipment is needed for the use of materials such as phonograph records, slides, and maps. Libraries typically use whatever equipment is commercially available, both for display and for storage. Better equipment than is currently available undoubtedly could be developed specifically for libraries.

A number of fairly new academic institutions—e.g., Oral Roberts University in Oklahoma and Oakland Community College in Michigan—are attempting to develop learning centers built around highly sophisticated and complex audiovisual equipment that has been especially designed to handle filmstrips, language tapes, videotapes, and programmed lesson materials. These institutions feel that if the library is to remain a significant part of the academic enterprise, it must involve itself in handling these materials and in processing traditional library materials into new forms that coordinate better with the audiovisual approach. There is some indication that there may be more interest by libraries in the use of these special forms of materials and equipment. This appears to be necessary to avoid competition between media personnel and librarians on the campus.

Libraries that handle special collections as their prime function are few in number, considering the total number of libraries in the country, and some persons have wondered whether such libraries need be considered in relation to the national problem. There are, in fact, some profitable lines of action that could be taken, with better application of technology, to improve the use of some of the special collections. For example, union catalogs have been produced for certain forms of rare materials, such as manuscript collections. It is now well within the state of the art to develop a truly comprehensive union catalog or national inventory of rare materials. Such a catalog would be widely useful and its maintenance relatively simple, since compared with regular library collections the growth of these special collections is not very rapid.

IMPLICATIONS FOR FUTURE APPLICATIONS OF TECHNOLOGY

It seems clear, from the foregoing examination of current applications of technology to libraries, that more and more libraries will soon be seeking to use data-processing equipment to support various aspects of their operations. Some will do so in the hope of saving money; others may do so primarily to improve their operations and service. The latter is probably a more realistic goal. Use of data processing has not saved money for many libraries yet.[33] However, it has enabled them to improve operations considered critical, to stabilize the number of employees, and sometimes to maintain certain operations that were ready to break down under continued manual operation and increasing workload. Machines may help to alleviate the recognized shortage of manpower in libraries long before recruiting and educational programs are able to meet the challenge. Too, despite some conspicuous failures, there is sufficient evidence to indicate that use of machines can improve service to library users, in ways that additional manpower cannot.

Judging by the Creative Research Services survey, many near-future applications of technology to libraries are likely to be largely on a hit-or-miss basis, with each library focusing on its most pressing current problem.[34] This is an understandable tendency, yet the greatest potentials of technology may have to do with functions or services that are not currently being performed by most libraries. For example, most libraries have tended to be concerned much more with the monograph than with any other physical carrier of information or data, in spite of the fact that the number of monographs published each year is relatively small compared to such other printed materials as periodical issues, report literature, and government publications. Although numerous local and regional union catalogs of monographs exist, and there is even a *National Union Catalog,* there are no union catalogs available for such materials as documents from the United States Government Printing Office. Use of existing technology could greatly enhance access to such documents. If the depository list of the Superintendent of Documents were to be published, using computer-controlled typesetting, as part of the *Monthly Catalog* issued by the Government Printing Office, depository libraries would no longer need to maintain their own catalogs (which consist largely of simple inventory files, rather than full-fledged catalogs, as are available for monographs). Technology could also improve access to other kinds of nonmonographic materials.

Technology can also be exploited for the extension of typical library activities to

---

[33] *John Harvey* (ed.), Data Processing in Public and University Libraries: Combined Proceedings of the Drexel Conference[s] on Data Processing in University Libraries and in Public Libraries (*Washington, D.C.: Spartan Books, 1966*).
[34] *Creative Research Services, Inc.,* op. cit.

serve certain user groups better. For example, Project Intrex at M.I.T. is examining (among other things) the expansion of the descriptive and subject cataloging of library materials, so that catalog data available to potential users will include evaluations as well as strict descriptive indications.[35] Undoubtedly other efforts will be undertaken to expand existing library operations into new areas that have not been feasible in the past because of limitations in the equipment and methods available.

This raises the question: Is it not possible that entirely new areas of service could be identified with subsequent creation of appropriate techniques and equipment? Without question, libraries of all types, as they are now constituted, are exceedingly valuable to our society. But how much more valuable they could be if their roles were seriously examined with a particular view to the development of new concepts of services, such as continuing education.[36]

Another aspect of libraries that one may not immediately associate with technology is their organizational structure. This structure has traditionally included operational and service functions, but might not current technology and that of the near future offer the possibility of changing the entire organizational concept of libraries? Do they need to continue operating in the traditional manner, with the traditional departments? Several libraries undertaking automation programs have found that existing divisions could be efficiently combined into larger operating units when data-processing equipment was put to work. If this aspect of library operation and management were given the attention it deserves and made the focus of design studies, could not significant improvements be expected in the total library system?

Just as computer technology provides the opportunity for individual libraries to think in terms of larger units of operation, so too does it provide the opportunity for groups of libraries to work together in ways that would be difficult, if not impossible, without the use of advanced technology. Although most of the current library automation efforts are oriented to the individual library, the time would appear to be ripe for many of these disparate efforts to be channeled into a better-focused national effort that would seek to bring all aspects of our technology—not just the techniques of data processing—to bear on the problems of library operations.

In this vein a reviewer of library automation efforts has written in the 1967 *Annual Review of Information Science and Technology:*

> In the past, much of the automation literature has consisted of reports of individual and quite isolated projects. This was perhaps necessarily so because the vision to see the relationship between the new technology and bibliographic processes was limited to a few individuals who often seemed to be "marching to the tune of a different drummer." This may be the classic pattern of technological advance, but this reviewer believes that to continue to regard automation as the plaything of an avant garde elite is dangerous. We have reached the point where further achievements will depend on the ability of a lot of us—librarians, computer specialists, system analysts, and information entrepreneurs of various ilk—to march at least occasionally in step.[37]

In her survey of recent progress this same reviewer gave primary attention to literature that described cooperative movements or literature that presented an honest attempt to discuss not so much an individual project, but the principles and concepts involved. She summarized things this way:

> To this reviewer the single most important facet of the literature of 1966 is that it clearly reveals that there is a vast and growing number of marchers, that national

---

35 *Massachusetts Institute of Technology Project Intrex,* Semiannual Activity Report, *period ending 15 September 1967 (Cambridge, Mass., 1967). Also Overhage and Harman,* op. cit.
36 *Leonard H. Freiser, "The Civilized Network . . . ,"* Library Journal, *92 (September 15, 1967), pp. 3001–3.*
37 *Markuson,* op. cit.

and international ventures are being planned and some are even under way, that there is an ongoing search for a *modus vivendi* between the library world and that of the specialized information center, and that at least minimum standards for machine-processable data are almost upon us.

It would appear that both the full exploitation of technology and the library needs of society will demand a reorientation of libraries from individual, isolated operating units into a cohesive national (or even international) structure capable of offering a given level of informational service at any point in the nation.

TABLE 7C–4.1

USE BY LIBRARIES IN THE UNITED STATES OF SOME FORM OF DATA-PROCESSING EQUIPMENT

(As of October 1966)

SELECTED FUNCTION	NUMBER OF LIBRARIES*
Acquisitions functions	
Acquisitions	102
Accessions lists	170
Accounting	235†
Cataloging functions	
Catalog cards	101
Book-form catalogs	125
KWIC indexes	135
Circulation control	165
Serials control	209
Union lists	133
Reference functions	131

* *It is not possible to add subgroups together, since some libraries are represented in each; e.g., a library may produce all three: catalog cards, book catalogs, and KWIC indexes. Total N=638.*

† *An unknown number of libraries have payroll operations included in this function.*

SOURCE: *Creative Research Services, Inc.* The Use of Data Processing Equipment by Libraries and Information Centers: A Survey Prepared for the Documentation Division, Special Libraries Association, and the Library Technology Program (*Chicago: American Library Association, 1966*). *Also, Eugene B. Jackson, "The Use of Data Processing by Libraries and Information Centers" (extracts), "An Interpretation of Creative Research Services, Inc., Report" (unpublished, 1967).*

5. FUTURE DIRECTIONS IN LIBRARY OPERATIONS AND SERVICES

INTRODUCTION

Many papers have been written on the libraries of the future. They vary greatly in their conception of library users, service requirements, desirable operational procedures, and applicable technology. They also vary greatly in their conception of the time scale on which such libraries can be developed, and in the depth of their grasp of the tremendous technical complexities involved in actually achieving highly advanced library applications that fully exploit the potentials in presently existing hardware and software technology.

Underlying many of the details in these conceptions are two fundamentally different approaches to prognostication. One approach stresses what it is theoretically possible to achieve, given massive infusions of effort and money and rapid acceleration of technological development. Projections along these lines have pictured a norm of large libraries making extensive use of computers for all their internal processing, with individual members of the using public seated at consoles conducting searches or otherwise interacting directly with massive files of computer-stored material.

The other, more realistic, approach toward prediction stresses a linear extrapolation of current trends. It charts the probable direction of future library operations and services as a straightforward extension or growth from the present, on the assumption that the purpose, organization, staffing, funding, and operations of libraries will not change radically within the next five to ten years.

Each kind of prediction has important uses. Glimpses of a possible future fire the imagination, help to widen one's horizons in thinking about library problems, and in many instances identify desirable paths for research exploration. Such glimpses also help to attract funding that might be more difficult to obtain for more pedestrian research or development. The critical weakness of this approach is that it often points to goals so distant and so demanding of social and technical changes that they are unlikely to be accomplished. In some instances all-encompassing plans can derail or forestall more modest but nevertheless important improvements of present circumstances. Some of the more visionary schemes may also create devices and techniques that are especially appropriate to a select class of library users—an elite, so to speak—but that afford little improvement for the vast majority of patrons.

Predictions based primarily on extrapolation of the present are useful aids to short-range planning because they are firmly rooted in present operations and thereby generally take more adequate account of problems of transition from the present to the future. Such predictions are more likely to be borne out than more far-reaching and visionary predictions because they demand less of society, the government, and technological innovation. The danger of the more conservative approach is that it may encourage preservation or mere mechanization of current procedures in some circumstances where only radical overhaul can make a significant and worthwhile change.

This section offers two views of the near future. One is primarily an extrapolation of current trends, intended to convey some picture of library operations over the next ten years if there is no massive infusion of energy, funds, and direction into the library picture. The other view is of a reasonably possible future, with the emphasis on operations and services that have some potential meaning to the main body of libraries, rather than the relatively few very specialized libraries that have ample funds for experimentation with advanced technology. Although it may appear that both views tend to err somewhat on the side of pessimism, the history of the application of technology to problems of information-handling suggests that undue optimism may be a more serious error and a greater source of disappointment.

Whatever approach one chooses to take toward prognostication, one must keep in mind that during the next ten years there will be an increasing demand for library services of all kinds, not only because of the population growth but because levels of education and needs for vocational training are increasing. One can foresee that over the next ten years a much larger proportion of the population of the country will be educated, either in an academic manner or in vocational or technical training, than has ever been previously. Many people will require a continuous regime of study to keep up with the changes and demands of their work. Thus, there will be great pressure for public libraries to acquire, represent, store, and make accessible to their publics new and varied materials, including magnetically recorded TV films, a wide range of microforms, and other media not commonly handled today.

AN EXTRAPOLATIVE VIEW OF THE FUTURE
The Demand for Services

Given only the extrapolative prediction, it is doubtful that more than a handful of public libraries—state, county, or city—will be able to respond to the pressures mentioned above. Many public libraries cannot now cope adequately with books and magazines; they cannot be expected to do better with the newer media. Too, the increasing workloads are likely to cause further deteriorations of the librarian's capacity to help readers in the selection of material. It is generally acknowledged that there is much out-of-date or erroneous material on library shelves. Many libraries have paid little attention to this problem, believing that their function is only to provide a collection of materials and a place to use them. Weak or nonexistent guidance is explained in terms of free access: if materials are available on all sides of a question, anyone can make a correct selection of materials to use. Since most libraries will not have the manpower to do anything more than attempt to keep up with increasing workloads, little change can be expected in this area.

To the extent that they can be, the demand for informational services will be met, if not by libraries, then by other agencies. The trends evident in serving specialized user groups will become manifest in the general populace in some of the more affluent areas. Specialized information centers may spring up to compete with the library not only in giving service, but more importantly in obtaining funds. At the Federal level the specialized information-analysis centers being established by the National Institute for Neurological Diseases and Blindness are indicative of this trend. These centers coexist, and perhaps actively compete, with established medical libraries.

One may project some of the same consequences for educational libraries of all types as for public libraries. The service loads on college and university libraries, however, are likely to be much heavier in the future, compared with the rise that might be foreseen for other types of libraries. Most of the fifty million or so students currently in primary and secondary schools will reach college age during the next decade, and an ever-rising percentage of the population will go to college. In addition to the sheer problem of numbers, emerging concepts of broader educational service—as embodied, for example, in the library-centered college concept now gaining favor—will add to the range of service demands.

There are whole categories of information, such as graphics, that cannot be adequately transferred by means of the printed word. If the library-centered college concept is to flourish, then the appropriate transfer media for such information must become an integral part of the library armamentarium. This is not likely to happen in more than a small number of well-financed institutions if the present competition for academic funds continues.

The increasing demands for service from public and educational libraries are likely to have an impact on special libraries. Special libraries have usually been able to draw upon the resources of other libraries—generally large academic libraries located nearby —but with these other libraries hard-pressed to meet the demands of their own users, assistance to special libraries may not be as readily available. In addition, of course, the special libraries will face ever-increasing demands for the highly specialized collection, description, and handling of information of many types and forms that are not characteristic of other types of libraries. (Specialized handling here refers to handling by specialists with a particular clientele in mind; e.g., chemical information handled by librarians with a chemistry background, for chemists.)

Considering the nation's libraries as a whole, and given a straight-line projection of current operational methods, it is not unreasonable to believe that the overall effectiveness of library services ten years hence will be considerably poorer than it is today.

Something more than straight-line improvement seems indicated if the present quality of service is not to deteriorate.

Available Technology

During the next ten years libraries will be able to choose from a very sizable array of equipment and procedural technologies to help them in acquiring, processing, and storing materials, and in providing reference and other services to their users. The most important class of equipment, from the standpoint of processing, is data-processing equipment, especially computers. Even without any acceleration of development, computer systems are increasing rapidly in speed and storage capacity and decreasing in cost, so that many more libraries may find some amount of computer support within their economic range. Some libraries may choose to rent computers or purchase them outright; others, particularly small libraries, may purchase shares in time-shared systems or use service bureaus.

From the standpoint of storage and distribution of materials, probably the most important kinds of equipment developed are those for microforms and reprography. Microforms are becoming increasingly inexpensive to produce and handle, and equipment for reading and reproducing microforms is steadily improving in quality.

During the next five to ten years, even without any acceleration of development effort, there may be very-well-developed techniques available for the use of computers or computer-supported systems for various aspects of technical processes and information retrieval in libraries. Fully automatic processing of language data still poses severe technical problems, but a variety of computer-aided language-handling procedures of quite general applicability may be available to libraries and other information facilities. The chief obstacles to widespread use of these will be the cost and the limited capabilities of library staffs to work with and take full advantage of computers. It would be necessary for libraries to have programmers and computer operators on their staffs.

Applications of Technology Within Individual Libraries[38]

Of the approximately 24,000 libraries in the United States, apparently only between 2 and 3 percent are presently applying data-processing procedures to some parts of their internal operations, as discussed in the preceding section, C.4. These applications are about evenly divided between punched-card operations and computer-based operations. During the next five to ten years we may expect to see a substantial increase in the percentage of operations using computers, particularly for educational and special libraries.

About 6 percent of educational libraries are using some form of data processing, and we may see well over 25 percent of them using data-processing equipment within the next five to ten years. Public libraries presently account for very little use of data processing—one half of 1 percent of them apparently use it—but it seems likely that the figure could rise to 10 percent within the next decade. Four percent of special libraries currently use data processing; this figure will also probably rise to about 10 percent.

Most of the libraries using some data processing have concentrated on technical processing of materials and hardly at all on service operations other than circulation; it is likely that this emphasis will persist.

The character of the use of data processing will differ from one type of library to another. Most of the larger public library systems will probably adopt computer techniques for some portion of technical processing operations and for such functions as circulation and materials control, binding, and records. This will be necessary because, thanks to the greatly increased support of the Federal Government through the higher education bills and other specialized legislation directed at improving library services, the

---

38 *All figures given in this section refer only to use of data-processing or related technology. No adequate projections were thought feasible on other uses of technology, such as microforms and copying devices.*

variety and comprehensiveness of public library collections can be expected to increase significantly in the next ten years.

The use of data-processing technology is also likely to be accompanied by a rather thoroughgoing integration of managerial record-keeping, payroll accounting, and the like, in support of the budgeting and recording process. Although various kinds of statistical and other record-keeping operations in public libraries will be increased, they are likely to be tied, as now, to internal operations for the accumulation of budgetary and administrative information, rather than for knowledge of and adaptation to the needs of library users. The larger public libraries (especially state libraries) are also likely to engage in a shift from card catalogs to book-form catalogs for some categories of materials. For smaller libraries we may expect to see only a relatively slow and gradual increase in the use of data-processing equipment.

Educational libraries will probably show the same general pattern of use of technology as the larger public libraries. The larger university libraries will adapt data processing to more of their technical processing work, and there will be an increased use of book catalogs and mechanized circulation control, but the effects on reference facilities and service will be relatively small. Secondary school and elementary school libraries will engage in cooperative ventures for purchasing, cataloging, and other routine record-keeping within the library, but the nature of services from the user standpoint will not be greatly different from those given today (but see chapter 2, section C).

Special libraries, particularly those that operate as information centers, will be able to draw on data processing and other technological advances to a much greater extent than will public and educational libraries. Because of their particular service goals, they emphasize the reference and retrieval aspects of their operations. In particular, they are likely to make use of the capabilities currently being developed for handling large databasis; i.e., large collections of relatively well-formated data. There is also likely to be an increasing use of selective dissemination or other selective alerting procedures.

Applications of Technology to Networks

It is widely recognized that the ability of individual libraries to acquire, process, and make available all of the materials demanded by their users is fairly limited. This recognition has spurred work on various kinds of cooperative systems and, more recently, on networks to interconnect libraries of various kinds. Although computer technology needs to play a role in these networks, the primary dependence is on communications and reproduction technology. Current work on networks has stemmed not as much from breakthroughs in these or other areas as from the availability of funds for experimentation. If funds continue to be available, we can expect to see much more in the way of network development.

The network currently being developed in New York State to link public, educational, and some special libraries is a prototype of one kind of network that we will certainly see within the next five to ten years in several of the wealthier states, such as California, Illinois, Indiana, Massachusetts, and Pennsylvania. Other types of networks that we can expect are subject-specialty networks, such as those for medicine (MEDLARS centers) or law, and educational networks of the sort being considered by EDUCOM. It is difficult to predict what proportion of the universities will be tied into an EDUCOM network in the next decade—perhaps no more than the twenty or twenty-five larger universities. At any rate, at the very maximum, no more than one third of the libraries in the United States will be tied into such networks. To put it another way, if network development continues at the present rate, it seems unlikely that 1977 will see an integrated nationwide system for announcing, finding, searching, and transmitting documents.

There are networklike operating arrangements, cooperative systems, already in operation, and it would be quite possible to implement more comprehensive ones, e.g., centralized processing-centers, within the next decade. More cooperation is likely to be realized, but not at a rate that promises full operational capabilities by 1977. The relatively slow rate of progress on networks and other cooperative systems does pose one danger. With increasing use of data-processing technology, particularly in the larger research and special libraries, we are likely to see a proliferation of specialized service centers, information and documentation centers, and the like, using a number of unique and incompatible practices and procedures and competing with libraries for personnel and funds. It seems likely that the consequences of such incompatibility can only be forestalled by greater movement than we presently have toward coordination and establishment of common standards.

Summary of the Extrapolative View

Projecting current trends into the next ten years, one may expect to see the large majority of libraries operating much as they do today. The number of libraries using advanced data-processing technology will certainly increase, possibly from the present 2 to 3 percent to 10 or 15 percent. Considering the growing demands for library service, this level of use of advanced technology will not result in any net improvement in library service for the majority of individual libraries. Instead, a deterioration of service is likely to occur because of increasing costs and competition for available manpower.

Large categories of informational materials will continue to be neglected to a great extent by libraries that are already coping inadequately with traditional printed materials. Thus the majority of libraries will not be able to contribute significantly to the improvement of information transfer. The truly significant improvements that could come from network or networklike arrangements seem very unlikely to come about by 1977 without some form of accelerated planning and support.

A CONDITIONAL VIEW OF THE FUTURE

Although an extrapolative view of future libraries sees most of them continuing to operate largely as independent entities, quite another view is possible. This view is conditional on aggressive planning, thorough exploitation of technology and significantly higher levels of financial support of libraries. Under such conditions, one could envision a tremendous improvement in library service throughout the United States. The conditional view of the future sees libraries as elements of one or more integrated networks. Each library would, as now, provide such services as its operating budget would allow, but its participation in the networks could enable that budget to go much further than would be possible in a largely independent operation.

Thus, each library could provide its own staff personnel with better information-finding tools, with relief from the burden of cataloging certain materials already appropriately cataloged through the network, and with computer-based, network-supported facilities for handling a greater number and variety of reference problems. The library's users would also be provided with better information-finding tools, with a much wider variety of materials (e.g., slides, microforms, and videotapes) than currently available, and in some instances with an opportunity to interact in a very direct way with the information store, including machine-stored data of a tabular or encyclopedic nature.

The Role of Books and Other Media

Although it is customary in some pictures of the library of the future to downgrade the role of books and other printed documents, realism demands recognition of their continuing central role, not because other information carriers are unavailable or too expensive, but because books are exceptionally efficient devices for holding sizable stores of information. Like the telephone directory, they provide a degree of access to information that would presently be difficult or impossible for machines to match on a cost-efficiency basis. The library of ten years hence will still be comprised largely of printed materials; however, it could take advantage of machine-stored data, microform representations, and other media to provide the kinds of service that cannot be provided as efficiently, economically, and satisfactorily through the printed word.

Future libraries are likely to make much heavier use of other media—such as audiotapes and phonograph records, slides and films, holograms, and videotape recordings—that carry certain types of information that the printed word cannot carry as well, if at all. Nearly all educational institutions have record and tape players and sound projectors, and some are acquiring videotape equipment. Although the latter equipment is not nearly as inexpensive as ordinary sound projectors, the expenses for producing videotape are much less than for film. Too, there is growing expectancy of a market for videotape units intended for use with home television sets. These could, of course, handle videotapes borrowed from the library.

Cooperation and Network Operations

The library of the future could find its selection, acquisition, and interlibrary loan processes for all media materially aided by the availability of such tools as a national bibliography and a current *National Union Catalog*. By current, we mean publication on the time scale of a weekly newspaper, rather than on the scale of several months, as is presently typical. With such tools—which it is certainly technically possible to develop —and the communication net, libraries could easily identify, locate, borrow, or purchase a copy of desired material. Appropriately accelerated developments along the general lines of the Library of Congress Project MARC could relieve libraries, in whole or in part, of what currently amounts to a greatly redundant cataloging effort. Individual libraries might not need or might not be able to afford direct computer assistance in processing, but they might well belong to and depend upon local or regional networks that, in turn, are part of larger networks.

The Library as a Distributing Agency

In the future some libraries, particularly educational and special libraries, are likely to shift from being primarily lending institutions to being more distributing agencies. We have already reached the stage where the cost per book of library circulation control is almost as large as the price of a paperback book.

Thus, with the prospect of replacing or copying full-sized or microform materials easily (the latter a rapidly developing capability), some libraries will prefer to give material away rather than to lend. Many more of them may also become sellers of microfilm copies. Some of the traditional antipathy to microfilm, based on low-quality images and the cost of viewing equipment, will certainly disappear as these problems are ameliorated and as libraries decide to grasp the opportunity to have much larger holdings without compensatory demands on their physical space or processing procedures.

Some record-keeping will undoubtedly be required in connection with appropriate compensation to copyright owners; this need not be a complex matter, particularly if the library is tied into a network supported by data processing for such routine accounting matters.

Automated Document Processing

Although relatively few libraries are likely to be engaged in automatic or machine-aided indexing, abstracting, classification, translation, and the like during the next ten years, many are likely to be beneficiaries of such processing by specialized elements in the network. There are significant technical problems in this area that are not likely to be completely resolved in the next ten years, but the more important barrier has been economic—the sheer cost of putting large amounts of text in machine-readable form. Expected improvements in optical readers will help to some extent, but even greater help will come from new publication techniques that use computers and provide a machine-readable version of the printed material.

Logical changes in the copyright law might give publishers an economic incentive for turning over such machine-readable material to indexing and abstracting agencies or the other organizations serving particular networks. Such agencies will have the equipment, trained personnel, and familiarity with the specialized subject matter necessary to make this kind of arrangement advantageous to all.

Expanded User Service

All of the improvements in acquisition, cataloging, and other aspects of technical processes that one can foresee in future libraries spell better service to users. The first kind of improvement will see computers used to provide services within the library that are provided today by intellectual effort. The second kind of improvement will allow libraries to offer new search and retrieval capabilities to certain classes of users and to the librarians, and to provide, particularly in educational and special libraries, a much higher order of access to reference materials, either in digital or photographic form.

Large systems for the retrieval of documents or specific data are already operational, some in versions that permit direct searching by the user sitting at a teletype anywhere in the United States. Such interactive devices, with output speeds at least twice that of current models, will be widely available and no longer a curiosity in some large libraries. More broadly useful consoles with rapid textual display capability will also be available in some special and educational libraries, although their cost will still be too high to have many such stations. Their primary use is likely to be for reference questions that are mediated by staff personnel.

Some kinds of information, such as census or election data, that are now available primarily in book form are likely to be made available to libraries in machine-readable form. With modest extensions of present capabilities for manipulating computer-readable data bases, a wide range of new information can be made accessible to library users. Certain kinds of tabular, dictionary, biographical, or encyclopedic data for which there are common and easily defined access paths might well be available, perhaps on line, in some research-oriented libraries. It is not out of the question to expect some modest amount of manipulation and/or statistical capability associated with such data stores; computer programs embodying such capability are already commonplace in many universities and research facilities.

Libraries of all types could change their role to a more active one by adding some of the features of the specialized information-analysis center. Libraries could actively disseminate factual political data; activities and plans of public and corporate institutions within their service area; and schedules of significant local, national, and international cultural and scientific events. Libraries could have more concern with information as a commodity rather than being concerned, as now, with the physical carrying of the information.

Libraries of the future may also provide dial-up reference service. Every telephone becomes, in effect, a receiving console connected to a library. Lessons by telephone have already been used by the educational community in Colorado and the medical community in Wisconsin, and there could be greatly increased use of this type of service within the next ten years. In the same class as telephone messages is the use of slow-scan TV to transmit information to individual homes. The advantage of slow-scan TV is the reduced requirement on the communication lines. It is quite likely that this type of transmission will come into demand when the videophone becomes a general item of telephone equipment. This will permit a much broader kind of library service to the public than most libraries currently envision.

Given continued growth of known pressures for change, three identifiable trends may well combine to augment the service concept of many libraries. One trend is the broadening needs for education and re-education brought on by accelerated technology. A second is the growing awareness of the need to prepackage information into maximally useful units. The third is the bandwagon effect that is created as an increasing number of people find the library very useful and easily accessible. Together these trends will create a massive pressure for libraries to put much more emphasis on educational materials, programs, and functions. Facilities may be modified to permit them to handle much larger volumes of course-sequenced materials, examinations, exercise stimuli, and self-diagnostic devices. These could serve such adult education objectives as correcting deficiencies, retraining, and supplementing education, which will become important for increasing numbers of citizens as our society undergoes changes wrought by science and technology.

Summary of the Conditional View

Assuming adequate planning support and aggressive exploitation of technology, the next ten years could see a very great improvement in library service throughout the United States. A most dramatic change could be in improved and expanded communication and cooperation among libraries. Communication networks could provide data-processing capabilities to smaller public, educational, and special libraries; reduce duplication and costs of purchasing and processing; and at the same time increase service to users through rapid interlibrary loans, improved reference support, and the outright distribution (rather than loan) of certain kinds of material. Active dissemination of certain types of information could be commonplace. Nonbook materials could be exploited by libraries of all sizes and types, and could be available virtually anywhere in the nation.

PROBLEMS OF TRANSITION

Both views of the future outlined above involve difficult problems of transition from the present to a desirable future. Some of the technical problems related to equipment and techniques have already been discussed (in sections C.3 and C.4). There are also a number of major problems that are not necessarily technological in nature. These have to do with training, the development of standards, and the development and implementation of government policy. Possible solutions to some aspects of these problems are discussed in section C.6 in the context of a larger program of action. The primary purpose here is to identify issues that must be given special consideration if the potentials of modern technology are to be exploited effectively.

Training of Library Users and Personnel

There are serious and persistent weaknesses in the knowledge and ability of today's library clientele to make effective use of library services and materials. Library customers are rarely equipped to make efficient use of the card catalog (or other indexes to the collections), reference materials such as bibliographies, periodical indexes, abstract services, and other aids to documentary research. Too, most library users do not fully appreciate that some skill and intellectual labor are required for effective searching with conventional library tools. The development and application of advanced technology to library operations not only changes but in several respects complicates and adds to the problems of bringing to the library user an adequate awareness of sources and devices and the skill to make them serve his increasingly wide-ranging needs for documentary access and service.

Perhaps a more serious obstacle to the application of advanced technology to library operations has been the lack of adequately skilled and trained staff, experienced both in the requirements of library operations and in those of technology, whether in computing, reprography, or communications. The education and training of professional librarians and other library personnel has ill-prepared them to appreciate or assimilate the capabilities and promise of the new technology. At the same time, persons skilled in the computing art and in other aspects of the changing technology are rarely equipped to deal with the specific and complex requirements of library operations.

If technology is to be exploited effectively for library operations, it will be necessary to give considerable attention to means of helping library users to understand and exploit library services and facilities, and to bring library personnel to a state of skill and preparedness for the new developments that technology will bring. Technology itself offers some promise of providing some of the tools to facilitate such training; e.g., demonstration via TV film, time-shared consoles, and computer-aided instruction. As the library systems of the future are developed, care needs to be taken to include devices and techniques for self-instruction and training of both library users and personnel.

Standards, Compatibility, and Convertibility of Data

New technology applicable to library operations is being developed at a rapid rate, particularly computer technology, which is increasingly being adopted by some of the larger libraries. In order for this technology to be maximally effective, especially for network operations, there must be some degree of compatibility in data descriptions and programs for processing computer-readable materials. Without some degree of standardization or provision for conversion, data files and programs developed at one installation are unlikely to be usable at another, and a great deal of material is likely to have to be keyboarded many times.

The desirability of some degree of standardization has long been recognized in the library field, and a number of standards have been created—a noteworthy example being the catalog-card format of the Library of Congress. There are a number of committees and subcommittees of the United States of America Standards Institute that are concerning themselves with standards on such topics as Reference Data and Arrangement of Periodicals, Basic Criteria for Indexes, Periodical Title Abbreviations, Basic Criteria for Filing, Basic Criteria for Abstracts, and Machine Input Records. Such committees represent one avenue for achieving the necessary standardization.

Another feasible approach is to accelerate the development of certain techniques in large and influential libraries and let the resulting products provide *de facto* standards. (A large number of libraries have voluntarily accepted the Library of Congress card as the standard catalog card because of the inconvenience and expense of using any other standard.) Both of these approaches to standardization may need active consideration if the many separate and independent library organizations are to achieve adequate cooperation and communication using the new technologies.

Legislation, Government Policy, and Continuity of Planning

A year or two ago it was estimated that about $900 million a year were being spent by various parts of the American public and private sectors for library service.[39] Taking into account recent and increasing support from the Federal Government, the current figure is probably about $1.3 billion. This rather massive investment has been made largely without a national program in mind. Thus the present legal, political, and jurisdictional structures are not ideal from the standpoint of integrated planning for library development.

If viable national networks responsive to the full range of library user needs are to come into existence, libraries in all of the states must have the capability of contributing to and interacting with those networks. For this to come about, Federal legislation will be needed to ensure adequate support for these libraries and to eliminate statutory, jurisdictional, and administrative obstacles to such participation. Legislation may also be needed to provide for development of a practical mechanism for the wide dissemination of document facsimiles and for compensating holders of copyrights to such documents. It may, in fact, be desirable to consider legislation that sets, as a matter of national policy, a minimum standard of library service at any place in the nation.

---

[39] Bowker Annual of Library and Book Trade Information (*New York: R. R. Bowker Co., 1967*); *Launor F. Carter* et al., National Document-Handling Systems for Science and Technology (*New York: John Wiley and Sons, 1967*).

On the Federal level there is a need for a thorough and continuing review of executive orders and statutes and coordination of proposed legislation, particularly laws that require matching funds and/or operational support from recipients of Federal monies. Ideally, Federal legislation should permit individual systems to operate more effectively, but it should not encourage abdication of any responsibilities they have already undertaken. Legislative efforts by the Federal Government should take advantage of the momentum and funding of present efforts and not simply supplant them. Otherwise, legislation intended to provide libraries with additional funds may merely find one source of tax support replacing other, already-existing funds.

In the discussion of present and projected library requirements (section C.2), it was pointed out that the development of networks, or other kinds of systems involving extensive interdependences, would very likely require some kind of coordinating influence or coordinating body. Such a body would need to be responsible for: (1) keeping informed on the existing and prospective state of library service, (2) planning for improved library service at both national and local levels, (3) developing legislative proposals, and (4) coordinating various Government projects affecting library service via grants and contracts.

From the standpoint of support, it seems evident that only the Federal Government has the position and resources to manage the coordination effort necessary to bring networks into existence on a large enough scale and in time to meet emergent requirements of the future, as well as present requirements not yet met adequately. As seen in chapter 12, the National Advisory Commission on Libraries recommended not only a National Commission on Libraries and Information Science as a continuing Federal planning agency, but also a Federal Institute of Library and Information Science as a principal center for basic and applied research in all relevant areas. This Institute should design a system of interconnected libraries, a prototype network as a model for information transfer by advanced techniques—this network was envisioned by the original Commission as the first step in the evolution of an integrated national library system.

6. A PROGRAM OF ACTION

INTRODUCTION

Previous sections have discussed present and prospective uses of technology in relation to library services and the operations that support them. The point was made, in those discussions, that there are a number of areas of library operation in which the potentials of various kinds of technology have not been fully exploited. The preceding section C.5 provided estimates of the likely role of technology in libraries some five to ten years hence, both with and without some kind of accelerating influence. Here in this section we outline a recommended program of action which could be undertaken if the decision were made to accelerate the improvement of our libraries and if adequate support were provided for that purpose. The program focuses on the entire complex of libraries, without particular emphasis on any one type of library.

CHOOSING A PHILOSOPHY OF PLANNING

A primary question confronting both individual libraries and organizations concerned with interlibrary activities is not only whether to use technology but what kinds to use and how to use them. As indicated earlier, there is no inherent requirement for the use of technology; technology is simply a means—and not the only one—to achieve certain ends derived from the broader goals of our society. Some library problems can be solved more effectively through changes in technical or administrative procedures than by the introduction of technology *per se*. On the other hand, some of the proposed new operations involving interlibrary cooperation are unthinkable without extensive use of technology.

The exploitation of technology to improve library operations and service can be approached in several ways. Three possibilities offer themselves: (1) to let things evolve, just as they have been evolving for many years; (2) to design and implement a highly integrated nationwide library system; or (3) to attack selected problems whose solution might have widespread beneficial impact. Each of these approaches has some commendable features; obviously some aspects of each approach could also be combined, and the combination might prove more fruitful than any single approach.

Letting Things Alone

The first approach (letting things alone) does not imply inactivity; rather it places reliance on the mechanisms already being used to improve library operations and service, without attempting to accelerate the rate of improvement. A major advantage of this approach is that it requires no drastic change in present activities, concepts of service, funding, or patterns of involvement of the Federal Government. It takes advantage of some of the benefits of the "squeaky-wheel" concept, permitting individual libraries or groups of libraries to apply remedies selectively at the point of greatest or most obvious trouble. It also avoids some of the waste that nearly always accompanies massive system design efforts in areas where goals are unclear, not universally shared, or subject to change.

The major disadvantage of this approach—and it is a very serious one—is that in spite of likely improvement, the nation's libraries as a whole would almost certainly lose ground, in the face of increasing processing loads and demands for service. Since this is not an acceptable prospect, letting things alone would not seem to be a satisfactory course of action.

Developing a Single Nationwide System

The second approach would plan and develop a nationwide, highly integrated library system. This approach implies a massive planning effort and a highly organized transition from the present situation to a more desirable one. The process ordinarily requires:

    a. Formulation of a clear, detailed, and specific statement of goals and requirements.
    b. Formulation of a set of criteria by which the existing system and any proposed changes can be evaluated.
    c. Evaluation of the present system in terms of the previously specified requirements and criteria.
    d. Design of a system to achieve the specified requirements.
    e. Design of the plan for transition to the specified new system.
    f. Implementation and evaluation of the new system.
    g. Modifications (if required) to the new system to assure that it meets the objectives.

The so-called system-development process, of which the foregoing elements are major steps, has proved to be a valuable tool for designing large complex systems to handle massive amounts of data. Because it is an orderly process, it helps to assure that major requirements are known and agreed upon, that the available resources (personnel, money, equipment, procedures, etc.) are known, and that various alternatives for meeting the requirements are not overlooked. This process does not guarantee that the correct decisions will always be made, but it helps to reduce the likelihood of making wrong ones.

The application of a system-development approach to the library problem might have two important benefits. One would be to permit certain kinds of operations that are not likely just to evolve, at least not rapidly. If such operations are to exist, or to exist as soon as they are economically and technically feasible, they must be planned for. A second major benefit of systematic and systemwide planning is the savings in cost and time by avoiding duplication of effort. Hundreds of libraries and information facilities are currently engaged in independent state-of-the-art appraisals and implementations of various automation technologies, and undoubtedly a significant number of these are, to some extent, redundant. Some groups of related libraries that are altering their operations to provide greater compatibility with each other are, at the same time, becoming less compatible with other libraries. There is, in short, a less-than-optimum use of funds, when one views the nation's libraries as a whole.

On the other hand, the system-development approach has some very stringent requirements that must be met before application to library system planning. The three most important requirements are: (1) formulation of a clear, detailed, and specific statement of goals or system requirements; (2) sizable and stable funding; and (3) effective management.

With respect to goals, it is clear that no common, agreed-upon goals of the nation's libraries have been formulated, at least not in terms that a designer could use to develop concepts for a desirable system or group of systems. It is indeed questionable whether one can develop such a set of goals for all libraries. At this point in time, agreement on common goals could probably be achieved only among particular subsets of libraries, such as public or research libraries.

A massive system-development effort also requires massive financial support. Whereas high and stable funding is provided for large military systems, such as, for example, the United States semiautomatic air defense system, it is not at all clear whether the improvement of the nation's libraries would have a sufficiently high priority over the next five to ten years to permit a full-scale program. A system-development effort without dependable funding might in some respects be worse than no systematic planning at all, because it could inhibit, postpone, or derail other potentially worthwhile efforts in library improvement.

The most crucial problem is that of management. There have been a number of notable failures or disappointments in system building, large and small. If there is a single most damaging factor in these instances, it has been the lack of top-level management understanding and control. Where responsibility has been abdicated to the system designers, consultants, equipment manufacturers, committees, or even to operating personnel, the results have sometimes been costly fiascos. Is there, or is there likely to be, the equivalent of an effective top management for the improvement of the nation's libraries? Considering the large numbers of sovereign entities that comprise the United States library community, one would have to say "no." Thus, in this domain, some of the advantages of the standard system-development approach are likely to be only illusory, and it might be better to aim for more limited goals and more limited systems, networks, or operating arrangements that can be developed effectively with foreseeable resources.

Supporting Selected High-Impact Projects

The third approach to improving the nation's libraries—and the one that this report strongly endorses—is to identify and support selected activities that are likely to have a beneficial impact on all or many of the nation's libraries. A major advantage of this approach is that it recognizes the operational independence of the majority of the nation's libraries while taking advantage of their willingness to participate in interdependencies—such as interlibrary loan systems—that offer mutual benefits. Another important advantage is that this approach does not in any way preclude undertaking other projects and programs.

Some high-impact projects could and should be aimed at the development of model subsystems that could later be incorporated into a more fully integrated nationwide system. Five such projects, briefly outlined below, are strongly recommended for consideration. None of them is an entirely novel idea; none of them involves technology for its own sake. Rather, each involves a recognized objective that technological progress has helped to bring within reach. Each of the projects is technically and economically feasible and the members of this study group believe that each could have a catalytic effect on the improvement of library service in the United States.

RECOMMENDED HIGH-IMPACT NETWORK AND SYSTEMS PROJECTS

In the past, libraries have had rather remarkable success in developing cooperative interlibrary loan and acquisition network enterprises, as well as such representation schemes as the *National Union Catalog* and *Union List of Serials*. Today, however, these fall short of what could be achieved, with full exploitation of technology, and short of what the nation requires even now, to say nothing of estimated future requirements. Described below are five projects that take advantage of current technology to provide important mechanisms that will ultimately be essential to an integrated network of library systems and services.

A Prototype Network of Regional Libraries

For national networks to operate efficiently, certain nodes in the system must function as major switching or referral points for communication between local libraries and national networks. A system of regional libraries could serve this function. Their responsibilities could include the maintenance of regional union catalogs and bibliographic lists of all kinds; the selective communication of portions of these lists to national union catalogs and lists; maintenance of accounting systems for reproducing copyrighted materials; and extensive reference, referral, lending, and copying services for local libraries. Because there are many organizational and technological unknowns in building networks, it is suggested that a prototype network be established as an operational experiment.

This project could be carried out within a four-year period, along these lines:

FIRST YEAR: Planning, staffing, contracting, design, and testing by means of simulation or pilot operations.

SECOND YEAR: Acquisition and installation of hardware, software, and communications equipment; system testing and initial operations between selected points. Equipment installed for this phase would tie together only the regional centers plus selected local service points.

THIRD YEAR: Procurement and installation of additional equipment to add a larger number of local service points to the network. All points actually tied in would become fully operational during this year.

FOURTH YEAR: Addition of more local libraries to the system, so that virtually all of the nation's libraries could participate in the network. All connected points would be fully operational and the network physically complete.

An Expanded, Computer-Based National Union Catalog

The system of regional libraries suggested above would maintain extensive and detailed union catalogs and union lists of all library materials held in local libraries. From these catalogs and lists, a selection could be made for the compilation of a broader-based *National Union Catalog* (NUC). For tasks of this magnitude to be done at all, it appears imperative that the catalogs and lists be produced in machine-readable form. If this were done, systems could be developed to exploit several important capabilities. The catalog could be interrogated directly through electronic communications (using the network described above); individual libraries could readily create special subsets of the catalog by subject or other kind of access for their own purposes; and, most importantly, the catalog could serve as a basic tool for libraries throughout the country to locate various kinds of materials for their users in a timely manner.

The developmental work for this project could be carried out within a three-year period, along these lines:

FIRST YEAR: Planning, staffing, contracting, design, and beginning of preparation of inputs in machine-readable form.

SECOND YEAR: Establishment of local union catalogs, through receipt of machine records from the Library of Congress, plus local input; communication of selected parts of Library of Congress to become part of the national record; and initiation of conversion of the post-1955 NUC to machine form.

THIRD YEAR: Completion of conversion of the post-1955 NUC and current additions thereto and initiation of distribution in machine-readable form on a regular basis to all parts of the nation. Complete geographical coverage would be achieved by having contributing libraries serve as NUC depositories in all parts of the United States. By the end of the year, NUC records would be maintained and distributed on a regular and timely basis. Union catalogs would exist in each region, and all would be interconnected to each other and to the NUC.

A National Bibliography

The Library of Congress card service does not cover all copyrighted materials, and the *Catalog of Copyright Entries* is not produced in a form that is satisfactory as a bibliography, nor does it include all publications. With appropriate use of computers, and particularly with use of computer-controlled typesetting or photocomposition devices, a comprehensive and timely national bibliography could be produced. This could relieve many libraries of most of their cataloging effort, provide a compatible input for the *National Union Catalog,* and serve the publishing and bookselling community as well as libraries. This service could also provide all of the advantages of flexibility and adaptability inherent in machine-readable files, and make the task of building responsive networks much easier.

The national bibliography could be put into operation in about two years, as follows:

FIRST YEAR: Planning, design, staffing, and preparation of pilot issues.

SECOND YEAR: Contracting, printing, and dissemination.

The short timetable implies that initial publication and distribution of the national bibliography could be expected to begin January 1, 1970, on a weekly basis. The bibliography would list all new publications, both copyrighted and noncopyrighted, that met agreed-upon specifications. There is a possibility that demand for the bibliography could make such an enterprise not only self-supporting but even profitable.

A National Referral and Loan Network

Building comprehensive and up-to-date reference tools such as a national bibliography, union catalogs, and lists, and organizing work through such entities as regional libraries would make it possible to go a step further and create a national referral and loan network.

A true network has not really been possible in the past, because of insufficient knowledge of the location of desired materials. With a machine-manipulated union catalog (or catalogs) and a properly designed communications network, requests could be routed automatically to the potential lenders. In addition, up-to-date corrections to the union catalog—possible because of the computer—could result in higher success ratios on interlibrary loan requests. With a sufficiently responsive configuration of equipment, procedures, and personnel, such a network would allow a library user anywhere in the country to obtain the materials he needs within a reasonable time.

The development of a national referral and loan network would require about four years:

FIRST YEAR: Staffing, planning, design, and coordination.

SECOND YEAR: Initial operations; begin use of communications links to expedite handling of reference questions and loan requests.

THIRD YEAR: Expanded operations, with initial, selective use of telefacsimile from region to region and full copying and mail or delivery service within regions.

FOURTH YEAR: Completion of network; telefacsimile would be available to all key points in the United States, with copying and delivery available to any library. There would be fullscale reference, referral, and interlibrary loan service available from any library in the network.

A National Library Storage and Microform Depository System

Physical deterioration of many kinds of library materials is recognized to be a nationwide problem. This project would establish a system of regional centers, supported by advanced technology, to house and preserve rarely used materials and provide loan copies or microform facsimiles to other libraries, as needed. The centers could also pursue research toward more effective preservation, with continuous study to determine what materials could be preserved and/or reproduced via microform. Such a program would diminish the storage requirements of local libraries and ensure that access to all documents is preserved.

The development of a national library storage and microform depository system would require about four years:

FIRST YEAR: Planning, staffing, and preliminary design; designation of the regional centers.

SECOND YEAR: Initial operations at the national center to preserve, restore, store, microfilm, reproduce, and loan selected printed materials.

THIRD YEAR: Beginning of operations at the regional centers. By this time the national center and the regional centers would be interchanging microforms, and a national inventory record would be maintained at the national center.

FOURTH YEAR: Extension of the system into full operations.

SUPPORTING RESEARCH, DEVELOPMENT, AND TRAINING

The five high-impact projects described above are oriented toward operations. Although they are dependent on technology and do involve subsystems that will eventually be important in more extensive, integrated, and technology-dependent national networks, they do not contribute directly to the exploitation of technology by individual libraries.

The major barriers to the more extensive use of advanced technology in individual libraries are lack of funds, lack of personnel with the experience necessary to select and use some of the new technology, and—not least of all—the limitations of some of the technology for library purposes. As noted earlier, much of the extant technology has been developed without any particular consideration for potential library applications. The library market as such has been regarded by many manufacturers and developers of equipment and techniques as small, compared to the market toward which they direct most of their efforts.

This has meant that libraries have often had to make do with what has been produced for very different purposes. Although there have been instances (e.g., in the MEDLARS system) in which special devices and techniques were developed for a library or library-like application, more devices, products, and techniques developed specifically for libraries are needed if future operational requirements of libraries, library systems, and library networks are to be met.

This report recommends that, concurrent with the operations-oriented projects outlined above, a program of technology-oriented library research, development, and training be undertaken. The identification of specific developments needed for library improvement should be based on a much more thorough study than this report attempts. However, examples are given below of areas where progress should undoubtedly be accelerated.

Hardware Specification and Development

The kinds of hardware of most potential interest to libraries include computers, communications equipment, microform-handling equipment, and other materials-handling equipment.

1. *Computer Equipment.* Several needs exist to make computer technology more compatible with library needs. Among these are:

   a. *Library-Oriented Input-Output Computer Equipment.* Present equipment is not capable of handling the large character sets needed by libraries, and lacks the speed to deal with the large amounts of input-output needed to process the very large files typical in libraries. Line printers having two hundred or more characters (about twice the currently available number), with little or no speed penalty, are needed. The need still continues, too, for optical scanners that are capable of reading a variety of fonts. Although an increasing number of publications will be produced by use of computer-driven printers, some new material, as well as the large mass of earlier material in the libraries, will not be available in machine-readable form.

   b. *Computer Consoles.* Most consoles available today for man-computer interaction were produced for other than library needs. Most of the more flexible consoles are too expensive for all but a few applications, and they cannot readily handle the character sets needed for libraries. Consoles are needed that are better tailored to library use.

   c. *Computer Memories.* The large computer stores presently available were developed for applications whose storage requirements are small and speed requirements large, compared to those of library applications. Continued work is needed to develop large (10 bits) storage capacity.[40] Further work is also needed toward the development of associative memories and other techniques to reduce the amount of time required for searches in main memory.

2. *Microform Equipment.* Good equipment for creating microforms has been available for some years, and reasonably good equipment is also available for reading some forms of microcopy. Yet no really superior equipment, particularly for reading, is available off the shelf. Some equipment, acknowledged to be superior to current equipment for library purposes, is no longer even available. An accelerated development effort is needed to build the best products possible, so that microforms of all types may be used with comfort over extended periods of time.

3. *Materials Handling.* One of the major tasks in the library is materials handling, i.e., routing, transporting, and delivering, books and other materials. Better and more economical devices are needed to improve the library's materials handling (i.e., shelving and distribution) capability, without seriously impairing the ability of library users to browse.

4. *Communications Equipment.* Equipment is needed to connect various libraries in such a way that, functionally, the user at any library can be provided with a catalog for the whole system and can obtain copies of material anywhere in the

40 G. Bell and M. W. Pirtle, "Time-Sharing Bibliography," Proc. IEEE, 54 (December 1966), pp. 1764–5.

system. The communication network must combine the low cost of operation suited to the individual library's budget with the high speed of operation suited to the user's attention span.

Although it may be appropriate to subsidize specific prototype hardware developments directly, another promising approach may be to attempt to focus the market by developing a consensus among libraries regarding their requirements and the kinds of devices that would meet them. With a clearer picture of desirable equipment specifications and of the market, a number of manufacturers could be expected to engage in developmental work without any need for direct subsidy.

Procedural (Software) Specification and Development

The identification of specific processing techniques worth developmental support should rest on a very careful analysis of projected library requirements in relation to the current state of the art. Some tools worth considering in such an analysis are listed below. Optimally, there should be concurrent hardware and software advances to achieve more effective processing techniques.

1. *Organization and Search of Large Files.* New approaches to computer organization and search in large memories are needed. Existing techniques are expensive, consume excessive amounts of time and memory, and cannot be easily adapted to library applications. Generalized retrieval systems suitable for libraries (i.e., capable of performing searches rapidly on a large volume of material) must be developed if the benefits of automated information systems are to filter down to the users. Such systems will need to be able to incorporate user feedback into the search process. This will require a combination of improved hardware and expanded software capabilities.

2. *Library-Oriented Filing and Sorting.* Today's computer sorting schemes are not capable of processing the large special-character sets required in libraries adequately, nor can they manipulate the large sort keys needed to sort library files effectively. Much more development along these lines is needed.

3. *Utilization of Publication Output for Automated Text Processing.* An ever-increasing amount of machine-readable information is becoming available as a by-product of publishing today's literature. Techniques need to be developed for the efficient capture, storage, and subsequent use of this information for libraries.

4. *Automated Subject Heading Assignment.* Textual materials require accurate assignment to subject categories such as are used in traditional library catalogs. Skilled catalogers are in short supply, and even the most skilled human does not do equally well with all materials. An effort should be made to develop inexpensive and reliable automated (or machine-aided) systems that would allow some of the cataloging load to be assumed by machine processes. Such items as authority files and special cataloging thesauri appear to be particularly suitable to machine manipulation, and certain subject heading assignments could also be performed by machine accurately, consistently, and economically.

5. *Time-Shared Processing Techniques.* Many medium- and large-sized libraries are currently using or planning automated techniques for selected aspects of their internal operations. The emergence of networks will demand even more attention to automated techniques and particularly to time sharing on computers. Many problems of scheduling, allocation, and communication need to be studied, preferably in operational contexts, if time sharing is to be used effectively in library networks. Special time-shared processing techniques suitable for smaller libraries are also needed so that these libraries will not be excluded from use of computer technology because of the high cost of developing and operating an individual system.

A Test Bed for Handling Nonbook Materials

The handling, representation, storage, and use of nonprinted materials have long presented problems to libraries, because practices appropriate to books have not been ideal for these other materials. With the continuing emergence of new media for information transfer, such as videotapes and magnetic recordings of several kinds, these problems will increase.

It would be desirable to establish a facility that could serve as a test bed for the development of new methods and techniques for storing and processing these materials and making them accessible and usable. The facility could also serve as a demonstration or model library and could thus play a role in disseminating information about the new techniques.

Direct Supporting Research

The history of library technology, and particularly the current history of projects introducing automation into library functions, has uncovered one point so repeatedly that it is almost a truism. This is that technological artifacts such as punched cards, computers, data-link lines, computer programs, consoles, character readers, programming languages, television channels, large core memories, and the like, do not in and of themselves represent the actual solution of information problems. Rather, they constitute a necessary technological framework through which the solution to information problems may be pursued.

Without the facilitating technology, no amount of understanding of information flow, transmission, and usage could result in sophisticated library or information systems. By the same token, no amount of sophistication, efficiency, and economy of hardware and software components will result in effective information systems unless the necessary knowledge is available to orient the activities of these tools to the actual processes and functions the system is intended to serve. The purpose of direct supporting research is to provide such knowledge as soon as possible.

By direct supporting research is meant studies displaying two characteristics: (1) the goals of the study can be clearly stated and are directly aimed at contributing to the solution of one or more of the immediate problem areas for library and information system design, and (2) the study is organized and conducted in such a way as to provide generalized knowledge rather than parochially oriented facts. There are at least three major areas of direct supporting research that should receive immediate and continuing attention:

1. *Information characterization.* The world of facts and ideas continues to change, accompanied by changes in man's responses to the facts and ideas, along with changes in his ways of characterizing or communicating about these things. Much more, for example, needs to be understood about the basic processes of analyzing and communicating information requirements, if the potentials of new equipment technology are to be exploited. Intensive studies are also needed of conceptual behaviors that form the bases of different classificatory schemes. A vast improvement needs to be achieved in our understanding of the manner in which situational and contextual constraints alter the conceptual and classificatory responses made to textual materials by librarians, information specialists, and users. A much better level of knowledge is required of the capacities and limitations for conceptual adaptability of a typical individual attempting to use an information characterization scheme that is somewhat foreign to him.

2. *Evaluation tools and methodologies.* The mechanism of progress consists of iteratively comparing two or more alternative paths or solutions and of selecting the better one. Therefore the method of comparison itself becomes of crucial importance in determining whether, in fact, progress will be made. Better, more

precise, economical, and meaningful tools are needed for comparing and diagnosing existing procedural options, systems, and services. More sensitive and subtle procedures are needed for uncovering the merits, defects, utilities, and penalties of various kinds of information media and channels, such as textual and audiovisual ones, so that each can be employed to its maximum advantage in libraries and library networks.

3. *Effects of information.* The services provided by libraries and other information facilities are based on a number of premises regarding the amount and kind of information their users want. Findings from some surveys that most of the material in libraries is not used much, if at all, raise questions about the adequacy of these premises and about the mechanisms libraries employ for staying attuned to the interests of their users. There is a need to develop a better understanding of the generation of new information and concepts, and applications to the world of action. Better understanding of these phenomena appears to be a prerequisite to the development of more effective and efficient library systems, particularly in the selection of materials and in determining what level of access they should have. It would also appear to be very important in learning how to design effective interfaces for the man-machine transactions that occur in request formulations made to automated retrieval systems.

Research in these and related areas is, of course, already going on, with the support of various agencies of the Federal Government and through private organizations such as the Council on Library Resources. However, both the amount and range of directly relevant library work supported by these agencies are limited and need to be expanded.

Education and Training

A limiting factor in the exploitation of technology is the ability and preparation of library personnel to appraise and use technology. The need to improve the readiness of library personnel to use applicable technologies effectively has been recognized in the library schools and has led to intensive studies for curriculum improvement. Agencies of the Federal Government have also concerned themselves with this problem. This report endorses such attention and encourages its continuation.

It is important that attention be given both to formal training and on-the-job training. On-the-job training is important because the administrative and technical personnel already on the job are the ones who will be confronted soon with decisions regarding new equipment, techniques, and approaches particularly relating to participation in network operations. However, remedial education and training will not be enough. It is hoped that current efforts to improve library science and information science curriculums, including postgraduate work, will continue to be encouraged and supported, not only by the Federal Government but by the library community itself.

Scholarships and fellowships have been made available in some subject fields to attract a wider variety of people into training. Librarianship has had relatively few students from scientific and technical subject majors. An expanded program of scholarships and fellowships would help to change this pattern.

Library schools themselves are not known for their affluent quarters and equipment. Vast improvement is needed in physical facilities, especially in terms of laboratory facilities for teaching and research with respect to technology. For example, remote-access consoles could be used to expose students to computer techniques; model installations of materials-handling equipment could demonstrate the problems of moving library materials by automated means.

A four-year program is recommended along these lines:

FIRST YEAR: Detailed planning for all aspects of training program; preparation of new curricular material; public announcements of scholarships, etc., and selection of first-year recipients.

SECOND YEAR: Awards to selected schools for improving physical plant and laboratory facilities; preliminary new curricular material available; expanded scholarship and fellowship programs.

THIRD YEAR: Physical plant and laboratory facilities improvement 90 percent accomplished; additional new curricular materials available; continued grant-in-aid programs.

FOURTH YEAR: Completed capital improvement program; fullscale evaluation study of new curriculum; other programs continued.

ORGANIZATION FOR ACTION

Basic Recommendations

The foregoing discussion has identified a number of activities that this study group believes would help to foster the effective use of technology in the service of United States libraries. Before such activities can be undertaken, several things must be done. They are listed here in the form of recommendations:

1. *Approach.* The basic approach of using high-impact projects, together with supporting research, development, education and training, should be examined and, if possible, endorsed as the means by which library improvement will be sought during the next five to ten years.

2. *Project Selection.* The particular high-impact projects and research and development requirements outlined in this report should be examined by the Commission and by other interested members of the library and information science community, in the light of other issues, requirements, and constraints, to determine what priorities these and other possible projects should be assigned at this time.

3. *Project Definition.* For those projects selected for implementation, arrangements should be made to develop more detailed objectives, together with preliminary cost appraisals and implementation schedules.

4. *Project Funding.* For those projects selected for implementation, arrangements should be made to identify all potential sources of support and, at the appropriate time, obtain the funds necessary to carry out the projects and programs selected.

5. *Program Management.* Responsibility for managing the conduct of the activities indicated or implicit in the foregoing recommendations should be placed at a high administrative level in an existing or new agency of the Federal Government or in a public-private body created for this purpose.

Recommendation 1 (Approach) is intended to assure that there is a common understanding of an agreement on the means by which the parties interested in library improvement intend to work toward it. It can provide a means for focusing the interests of the Federal Government, state and local governments, individual libraries, professional associations, manufacturers and suppliers of relevant equipment and services, and the public itself.

Recommendation 2 (Project Selection) is intended to assure that the parties whose operations and services will be influenced by high-impact projects will have an opportunity to comment on and influence the final selection of such projects. One cannot expect to find unanimity in such an appraisal; nevertheless, one will be able to proceed with greater assurance and a better sense of priorities after such an appraisal.

Recommendation 3 (Project Definition) takes cognizance of the fact that the projects recommended in this report are described at a rather general level and that it will be necessary to develop more detailed specifications of objectives, of facilities and resources, of equipment and personnel costs, and of the time schedule under which development should proceed.

The descriptions given earlier for the five network and systems projects and for the program of supporting research, development, and education and training may be used as points of departure for the detailed appraisal that must follow. Some very rough estimates of the costs for development and initial operations are offered in Table 7C–6.1 in order to provide an indication of the absolute and relative magnitudes of the projects as we envision them. The largest costs are for the library networks and systems projects, which are necessarily broad in scope and involve, in some instances, substantial expenditures for equipment and materials.

The cost figures are over and above present funding from all sources. Thus, the program could require $400 million to $500 million additional over the next five years for development and initial operations. No estimates are given for continuing costs, but they would presumably be less than those for the last year of each project's development and initial operations, particularly since the hardware required for some of those projects would already have been acquired.

Recommendation 4 (Project Funding) takes note of the obvious fact that any accelerated action program will require extensive funds. It is almost equally evident that the Federal Government will be expected to provide most of those funds. As indicated earlier, there are many parties with legitimate and continuing interests in the future of libraries. All do not have equal power to effect change. Thus, for example, although most of the support for the libraries in the nation comes from local (tax) funds, the leverage of local libraries to effect system change is exceedingly small compared to that of the Federal Government, because control of the funds is dispersed over so many localities. The difference in the power to effect change may help, in one sense, to ease the task of defining responsibilities for effecting change. What each party "ought" to do may become, in part, a function of what each party *can* do.

This does not mean that the Federal Government needs to carry the entire burden of funding, nor that it needs to bear the costs of continued operations, once the period of development and initial operations is over. Some of the programs, for example, the expanded *National Union Catalog,* could be self-supporting in a short time, perhaps almost from the outset.

Recommendation 5 (Program Management) recognizes that planning, starting, and managing the action program outlined above will require a high degree of coordination and the involvement and support of the Federal Government. The body responsible for the planning and administration of the library improvement program needs to have high-level status and support.

It is obvious that the need for assessment and planning for libraries does not diminish or disappear with completion of the work of the National Advisory Commission on Libraries. Changes will continue to occur and new technologies will need to be assessed for their impact on current and planned library programs. To assure that effective planning and implementation continue, a permanent body is needed. Such a body would need to be responsible or make provisions for (1) keeping informed on the existing and prospective state of library service; (2) planning for improved library service at both national and local levels; (3) developing legislative proposals; (4) coordinating various projects affecting library service; and (5) planning and coordinating financial support, from both the public and private sectors.

Such a body would require the participation of a variety of persons with diverse skills, experience, and points of view and should therefore include representation from Federal, state, and local governments, individual libraries, professional organizations, manufacturers and suppliers of relevant equipment and services, and the public itself. An organized group of this nature would be able to exercise the continued leadership needed for a concerted nationwide effort to improve library operations and services. This, of course, is quite consistent with the Commission's actual recommendation for a National Commission on Libraries and Information Science as a continuing Federal planning agency.

The Need for Momentum and Continuity

Whatever is done to implement the recommendations of the Commission, it is important not to lose the impetus provided by its work. Leaving sizable and indeterminate time gaps between the Commission's work and successive steps in the development and inplementation of an action program would run the risk of fostering a paralysis of the will and a resulting inactivity or delay in undertaking needed improvements. It would also run the risk, particularly if much time passes without action, of inviting another status-type survey covering much the same ground as the original Commission has already covered.

Both technology and the needs for library service are certainly changing, but not so rapidly or erratically that they should encourage an endless succession of independent assessments, discontinuous in time and concept. The need for library improvement is clear, and so is the potential contribution of advanced technology. Action is now needed to assure that the problems of libraries are not relegated to the background of happenstance. An aggressive, concerted, and timely effort, using modern technology and every other means that can be brought to bear, is needed to effect a nationwide improvement of our libraries.

TABLE 7C–6.1

ESTIMATED COSTS FOR DEVELOPMENT AND INITIAL OPERATION OF A LIBRARY IMPROVEMENT PROGRAM

PROJECT OR AREA	ADDITIONAL COST BY YEAR* (in millions of dollars)				
	FIRST YEAR	SECOND YEAR	THIRD YEAR	FOURTH YEAR	FIFTH YEAR
Networks and Systems					
Prototype network of regional libraries	$3.0	$36.0–44.0	$55.0–75.0	$80.0–120.0	$?†
Expanded, machine-based *National Union Catalog*	1.5	10.0	8.0–12.0	?	?
National bibliography	.5	2.5	?	?	?
National referral and loan network	.5	2.0	5.0	10.0	?
National library storage and microform depository system	1.8	18.0–22.0	40.0–50.0	50.0–60.0	?
Research and Development					
Hardware specification and development	3.0	6.0	8.0	8.0	5.0
Procedural (software) specification and development	3.0	4.0	5.0	4.0	4.0
Test bed for handling nonbook materials	.2	3.0	6.0	3.0	3.0
Direct supporting research	3.0	4.0	5.0	4.0	4.0
Education and training	1.5	5.0	2.0	3.0	?

* *These are costs over and above present funding from all sources.*

† *Continuing costs.*

Government Involvement in Library & Informational Services: Roles, Relationships, & Potentialities

CHAPTER VIII

THE ROLE
OF THE FEDERAL
GOVERNMENT

It is clear from the preceding chapters of this book that government at all levels is deeply involved with all the library affairs of the nation. This involvement is so complex that its outlines are difficult to delineate, and often a library benefit is "lost" in a governmental activity whose principal mission is elsewhere. As pointed out in chapter 5, it is impossible even to determine with any accuracy the exact amount of government support expended on behalf of libraries.

Because the National Advisory Commission on Libraries concluded that Federal leadership is vital to fulfillment of the National Library Policy on which all its basic recommendations rest, Part III of this book is devoted to the roles, relationships, and potentialities of all participants in the governmental involvement. Without clear understanding here, no workable national system can evolve. A chapter has been devoted to each of the primary Federal centers of activity—the Library of Congress and the United States Office of Education. Another chapter focuses on the role of local-state-regional cooperation.

Here in chapter 8, the subject is the Federal Government as a whole. The chapter is divided into three sections. Section A reproduces an updated version of one of the most comprehensive papers of all those in the Commission's series of special studies. Section B is a briefer and more informal view of some aspects of Government library organization; it is from the same Duke University study, "The Federal Government and Libraries," as section A. The final paper in chapter 8, designated section C, is from another study—it concentrates on the Federal Government *vis-à-vis* the research libraries, a class of libraries with a national resource role and special problems that were never far from the thinking of the majority of members of the National Advisory Commission on Libraries.

All of these papers represent the views of their authors, and these vary in some respects from the Commission's consensus—although all contributed to the deliberations, as indeed it is hoped they may contribute to the thinking and planning that can solve the still unresolved issues that lie ahead.

A. A BROAD LOOK AT THE FEDERAL GOVERNMENT AND LIBRARIES[1]

by RICHARD H. LEACH
Professor of Political Science
Duke University

The title of this paper may seem to imply two things: that the Federal Government has a clearly articulated policy regarding libraries and its relations with them and that the Federal Government is somehow monolithic, capable of acting with regard to libraries or anything else as a unit, with a single, across–the–board approach. It should be made clear at the outset that neither implication is correct. The Federal Government is active in many ways in connection with libraries, but there is no detailed, comprehensive Federal library policy to date. And with regard to libraries as to most of the other subjects with which it deals, the Federal Government speaks with many voices. There is no single spokesman for library interests in the Federal Government, and in many parts of the Federal establishment there is neither deep interest in nor fundamental concern about libraries. Nevertheless, the subject is a valid one for investigation, if only because of the large amount of Federal funds that has been and is being spent for library and library-related purposes and because, in this increasingly technical age, government itself, like every other aspect of American society, is increasingly dependent for the success of its mission upon the kind of services and functions libraries perform.

THE BACKGROUND

The Federal Government's involvement with libraries developed slowly and spottily. Although as early as 1800 Congress established the Library of Congress in the new capital city of Washington to remedy the deficiency in reference and other needed resources as far as legislative purposes were concerned, it was many years before any other action was taken in the library area. When it was taken, it was not the result of careful thought and study; rather, it resulted from the successful exertion of pressure by interested groups on the one hand and by default on the other, as library needs, not being met in any other way, gradually came to be included in departmental and agency planning. By 1968, in addition to the Library of Congress, a separate National Library of Medicine had been created, a National Agricultural Library had developed in the Department of Agriculture, and less well-known libraries had been established in most of the other Federal departments and in many independent agencies. Funds had been appropriated for libraries to serve residents of the District of Columbia and the terri-

[1] From The Federal Government and Libraries, *one of the special studies commissioned by the National Advisory Commission on Libraries in 1967. This paper is the most comprehensive of four comprising the entire study, which was conducted by a task force coordinated by R. Taylor Cole, Provost, Duke University. The author acknowledges that a good many people were generous of their time and suggestions during the preparation of the paper, among whom must be specially mentioned: J. Lee Westrate, Bureau of the Budget; Verner W. Clapp, formerly President, Council on Library Resources, Inc.; Paul Howard, Secretary, Federal Library Committee; Germaine Krettek, Associate Executive Director, American Library Association, and her staff in the Washington office; and James Skipper, Associate Librarian, Princeton University.*

tories, as well as for library units on military posts and bases and in Government institutions, thus bringing service to hundreds of thousands of members of the armed forces and residents in a large number of hospitals, penitentiaries, and reformatories.

Without exaggeration, it can be said that the Federal Government's library services, taken together, make the Government the largest library agency in the United States, if not in the world. As each library developed, it did so largely independently of any others, however, and to this day no single complete or detailed inventory of all Federal library facilities has ever been made. Paul Howard, Executive Secretary of the Federal Library Committee, estimates the number at between 2,000 and 2,500, broken down into the three national libraries, some 600 departmental and agency libraries, and possibly as many as 2,000 libraries scattered around United States Government posts and outposts throughout the world.

Prior to World War II, the Federal Government did not go much beyond establishing libraries of its own (or permitting them to be established without specific authorization therefor). The Smithsonian Institution early emphasized the development of a library collection. The Office of Education, which had been created in 1862, evinced some concern about libraries in 1876, when it published a comprehensive library survey. It continued to collect library statistics from that time on, but it did not do much more than that about libraries until 1938, when, on the basis of a 1936 Congressional authorization to do so, it created a small Library Services Division within its organization. For some time before the creation of that division, the Office of Education had employed a school libraries specialist (who was not a professional librarian) and later on other specialists were added. Even so, the Library Services Division continued to be oriented toward public libraries. It functioned largely as a study and investigatory unit, and it remained small (about four professional people) and was concerned largely with the collection of statistics.

It was not until 1956 that a combination of pressures resulted in the passage by Congress of the Library Services Act of 1956, which inaugurated, at a very low level to be sure, Federal aid to states for the development and expansion of public libraries in rural areas. That Act was subsequently renewed and in 1964 expanded to include urban libraries as well as construction. In 1966, it was expanded to include interlibrary coordination and library services to institutions and to the visually handicapped. The law is currently in force until 1971 and at a considerably expanded level of support.

Once the avenue of Federal aid to libraries began to be developed, it was probably inevitable that attempts should be made to broaden it further. Library legislation was popular in Congress. Educators, civic leaders, members of the general public, librarians under the leadership of the American Library Association, and other book interests were able not only to secure the passage by Congress of the Library Services and Construction Act, but also to get Congress to include libraries in the provisions of the Higher Education Facilities Act, the Higher Education Act of 1965, and the Elementary and Secondary Education Act of 1965, and to pass a number of other acts wholly or in part concerned with providing assistance to libraries and librarians. (See the list later in this paper under the heading "Recent Library-Aid Legislation." Also see appendix E.)

By 1968, Federal interest in libraries had come to be twofold. There were a great many Federal libraries in operation, among them the immensely prestigious Library of Congress, the National Agricultural Library, and the National Library of Medicine, and there was an extensive Federal aid to libraries program, which it seems likely will be continued into the indefinite future, as more and more studies indicate gaps in personnel, facilities, and holdings which still have to be bridged if American libraries are to provide the kind of help to the nation they ought to furnish.

In response to a growing awareness of the unrelated kinds of Federal activities which had developed in the library field, and concerned about the economics of the situation, President Lyndon B. Johnson appointed the National Advisory Commission on

Libraries in September 1966 and asked it, among other things, to look into whether the Federal Government's actions in the library field were as well coordinated as they might be and whether the taxpayers were getting the most that could be obtained for each Federal dollar spent in the library field. The President's action was the first concrete evidence of the desirability of the development of an overall Federal library policy.[2] It thus marked the beginning of a new—and third—kind of Federal activity in the library field.

The purpose of this paper is to inquire into the three areas of Federal concern with libraries: (1) the Federal Government's own libraries and related activities, (2) Federal aid to libraries outside the Federal establishment, and (3) the factors involved in the development of a Federal library policy—with an eye to providing the essential facts of the situation in all three areas and to suggesting possible areas of action in the years ahead. As far as this writer can discern, this is the first such attempt to have been made.[3]

Although the title of this section of chapter 8 is "A Broad Look at the Federal Government and Libraries," it is primarily concerned with the Federal library picture from the Executive side of the fence. Other papers in the four-part study commissioned by the National Advisory Commission on Libraries are devoted to some organizational alternatives in the Government's involvement with libraries (see section B of this chapter), to the international dimension of the problem (see appendix F–1), and to the impact of the total Federal library program on the states (see chapter 9, section B). The partial omission of these areas from this paper should thus not be regarded as a failure on the author's part to recognize the central importance of other aspects to a full understanding of the picture.[4] Table 8A–1, which appears here, summarizes the task force consensus on the basis of all the component studies.

FEDERAL LIBRARIES: THE NATIONAL LIBRARIES

THE LIBRARY OF CONGRESS (LC)

By an act of Congress approved April 24, 1800, an appropriation of $5,000 was made "for the purchase of such books as may be necessary for the use of Congress." Two years later a Librarian was authorized to take charge of the Library. Subsequently, a law library was required to be established within the Library of Congress, and much later a Legislative Reference Service was created to give direct and specific aid to members of Congress in the performance of their legislative duties. In 1866 the library of the Smithsonian Institution was transferred to the Library of Congress, and in 1870, the administration of the Copyright Act was entrusted to the Library. In 1897, upon the

---

2 *The President's action was the culmination of some three years of development involving a good many different people and agencies. It is hard to assign responsibility therefor, but the American Library Association, the Bureau of the Budget, the Office of Science and Technology, and the Office of Education all made contributions to it. The idea was discussed in the White House in 1963.*
3 *Reference should be made, however, to Carleton B. Joeckel, Library Services. Prepared for the President's Advisory Commission on Education. Staff Study No. 11. (Washington, D. C.: 1938); Study Committee on Federal Responsibility in the Field of Education, Commission on Intergovernmental Relations, Federal Responsibility in the Field of Education (Washington, D. C.: 1955); Winifred Ladley, ed., Allenton Park Institute Number 13, Federal Legislation for Libraries, paper presented at an Institute conducted by the University of Illinois Graduate School of Library Science, November 6–9, 1966 (Champaign, Illinois: 1967); and U. S. Office of Education, Federal Education Agency for the Future: Report of the Committee on Mission and Organization of the U. S. Office of Education (Washington, D. C.: 1961).*
4 *These areas have been the subject of little prior study. The story of the impact on state and local governments of the Library Services Act is told in part in the final chapters of Hawthorne Daniel, Public Libraries for Everyone (Garden City, New York: 1961), and in Mary Helen Mahar, "The Role of the Federal Government in School-Library Development," in Sara Innis Fenwick, ed., New Definitions of School-Library Service (Chicago: 1960), pp. 54–62.*

occupation of the then new main building of the Library of Congress, the basic law providing for the Library was rewritten to provide (1) that the Librarian be appointed not by the President solely, as had been the case up to then, but by the President with the advice and consent of the Senate, and (2) that the Librarian have the power both to appoint staff members on the basis of merit and to make all "rules and regulations for the government of the Library" which he felt to be necessary.

There are only a few other statutory requirements regarding the Library,[5] the most important of which are probably the numerous declarations by Congress that the facilities for study and research offered by the Library should be accessible to all duly qualified investigators, individuals, and students and graduates of colleges and universities, subject only to the rules and regulations set down by the Librarian. By and large, the Library is free to operate as it wishes, within the possibilities of appropriations to it and other funding it receives, and quite independently of other units of the Government and of other libraries as well. To be sure, Congress created at almost the same time it established the Library itself the Joint Committee on the Library, thus making it the oldest Congressional committee in continuous use, and over the years the Committee has exerted considerable influence on the Library. But for the most part, the Library has not been unduly restricted or subjected to the limitations of bureaucracy and red tape which are so often alleged to be the inevitable accompaniments of Governmental activity. Rather, the Library early developed a profound sense of professionalism and became recognized as the most important and the leading library in the country.

Only a few statistics need be mentioned to demonstrate its central position in the American library scene. As of June 30, 1968, its collection numbered 58,463,358 pieces, as compared to the total in 1962 of 41,879,900 items and the 1950 total of 27,382,000 items, making it the world's largest library. During fiscal 1968, over 2,453,440 items were brought from the shelves for the use of readers in the Library; 96,743 pieces were lent for Congressional use (except for members of Congress and for interlibrary loan, books in the collection of the Library of Congress are not made available for outside use); 974,777 reference inquiries were received by the Library; 78,767,377 catalog cards were sold; 303,451 copyrights were registered; and the Legislative Reference Service handled 131,558 requests from members of Congress and Congressional committees.

But more than the magnitude of its operations gives the Library its national standing, for that derives primarily from the fact that the Library has undertaken to perform many of the services and functions which are normally performed by a country's national library. Perhaps the most succinct description of the functions of national libraries is given in the study by K. W. Humphreys, Librarian of the University of Birmingham, in the *UNESCO Bulletin for Libraries*, July–August, 1966.[6] Mr. Humphreys listed the following:

Fundamental functions of a national library
  Provides the outstanding general collection of the nation's literature, broadly defined to include books, manuscripts, memorabilia, maps, music scores, periodicals, films, etc.

---

5 *Among the statutory requirements: a Library of Congress Trust Fund Board was created to accept, receive, hold, invest and administer gifts and bequests to the Library; unexpended balances of funds appropriated for the Library are to be "laid out" under the direction of the Joint Committee on the Library; books for the law library are to be purchased "under the direction of and pursuant to the catalogue furnished [the Librarian] by the Chief Justice of the Supreme Court"; the law library is to be open every day while Congress is in session; the Librarian of Congress is to give a $20,000 bond as a surety upon assuming office. The most generally worded statement among the declarations by Congress was contained in Joint Resolution No. 8, 52nd Congress, 1st Session, 27 Stat. 395.*

6 *Vol. 20, No. 4, pp. 158–69. For a longer and more particularized list of national functions as performed by the Library of Congress, see the list compiled by the Librarian of Congress, L. Quincy Mumford, in Annual Report of the Librarian of Congress for the Fiscal Year Ending June 30, 1962 (Washington, D.C.: 1963), Appendix I, p. 97. See also chapter 10 in the present volume.*

Serves as the central dépôt legal of the nation to ensure systematic collections of all published material in that nation

Provides as full coverage of foreign literature as possible through some sysmatic method of acquisition

Publishes a current national bibliography and a union list of periodical holdings

Serves as a national bibliographical information center

Publishes catalogues of the contents of the library

Exhibits its collections for the information and benefit of the people as a whole

Desirable functions of a national library

Maintains a system of interlibrary loans

Maintains a manuscript section

Conducts research into library techniques

Functions of national library service not essentially functions of the national library

Conducts an international book exchange service

Provides special library services for the blind

Offers opportunities for training in library service

Provides assistance to other libraries in services and techniques

Although this is not the place to match each of these functions with a description of what the Library of Congress does in that area, it is clear that the Library does in fact perform most of them and that it has done so over a considerable period of time. Indeed, Mr. Humphreys uses the Library of Congress as an example of a national library in describing the kinds of activities undertaken under several of the headings, and the general understanding in the nation is that it is *the* National Library. The Library refers to and conceives of itself that way, and it is increasingly customary for others to do so as well. (The Library of Congress speaks for itself on its potentialities for service in chapter 10.)

Problems and Limitations

Even so, the Library of Congress does not in fact occupy the national library position. It does not for two main reasons: (1) certain limitations in its own operations hold it back from full occupancy of the position, and (2) the Library of Congress must share the role with two other libraries designated as national libraries. With regard to the first point, Mr. Humphreys, whose work was referred to earlier, concludes his essay with a paragraph on library planning, in which he declares that "The national library should be the prime mover in library matters and should be expected to be the leading library in all fields."

> The national librarian, too, should play a central role in all systematic planning of a country's library services . . . [and should] see the country's library system as a whole and the relationship of the national library to it, thus ensuring that the various strands in the organization continue to form a golden chain of responsibility for service, from the smallest to the largest library and from the richest to the poorest.

Although for 30 years between 1899 and 1930 under Librarian Herbert Putnam and again for a short while between 1939 and 1945 under Archibald MacLeish, there was no doubt of the Library's leadership in American library affairs, there was an unfortunate hiatus in leadership immediately after the war which the present Librarian has only recently been able to bridge over. The full story is too long to tell here, but there is no doubt that when the present Librarian took over in 1954, the Library was in relatively difficult straits. The previous Librarian had become interested in activities outside the Library, some of them of a controversial nature, and by his actions had alienated Congress. As a result, Congress had severely cut the Library's budget, thus producing a greater than usual personnel shortage; there were a number of "serious backlogs of years' standing, in some of the basic but behind–the–scenes operations of the institution"; the deficiencies in acquisitions occasioned by World War II had not yet been fully made up, and at the very same time the production of books and library materials had begun to increase in geometrical proportions.[7] The Librarian recognized the problem in his 1962 annual report:[8]

> The Library of Congress has not abrogated its leadership in the library world. It has been necessary, however, for it to concentrate on strengthening its own collections and services during the past several years—to put its own house in better order. To have neglected to do this would be a great disservice to the library and scholarly communities, because so central is the Library of Congress to the library economy and research efforts of the country that, to the extent that the institution is weak, the whole fabric of library service is weakened. Every institution must go through such periods of catching up, of shoring up its operations.

Not only has the Library thus been faced in recent years with the primary necessity of shoring up its operations, detracting from the possibilities of national library leadership, it has also had to rebuild relations with Congress. Reference to the hearings on the Library's 1953 and 1954 appropriations is enough to demonstrate how much Congressional distrust of the Library of Congress had been built up. The new Librarian's achievements in overcoming that distrust have been outstanding, but the result of this forced attention to Congress was to hinder him for a good while from even thinking of extending his activities beyond the Library itself.

Even though Congress no longer is alienated from the Library, it does not support it at a level to permit the full exercise of national library leadership. Although it has been willing to increase appropriations to the Library over the years—thus the appropriations for FY 1967 amounted to $31,471,000; FY 1968, $37,141,400; and FY 1969, $40,638,-800—it has not responded with either the amounts requested by the Librarian (his request for FY 1969, for example, was $43,147,000) or needed to permit the Library to move as rapidly as it might to meet the range of demands placed upon it. Given the economic situation in recent years, some increase in appropriations is necessary to permit the Library—or any Governmental activity—merely to maintain current levels of service. Though it cannot be argued successfully that Congress discriminates against the Library of Congress in its appropriations procedures, it being widely understood that Congress generally fails to award an agency its full budgetary request, a strong case can be made not only for increases in the Library's budget to sustain current programs, but also for increases to support new and experimental programs in automation and preservation which are essential if the Library is to offer the nation the kind of leadership Mr. Humphreys describes.

Moreover, as the Librarian has pointed out time after time in hearings on the Library's budget and in his annual reports, the Library is severely cramped for space. In the Librarian's words, the Library's mission has for too long been subject to "the unfortunate circumscribing effects [of] lack of space."[9] Although Congress has been willing to appropriate funds for rental space, a permanent solution to the space problem will not be found until the James Madison Annex is built and occupied. It is high time Congress moves to action on the space needs of the Library.

In addition, there is a general shortage of trained library personnel throughout the nation, and the Library of Congress has not been immune from its effects. Once again, Congress has not done all it could toward alleviating that shortage. Recruiting efforts by the Library of Congress staff, and the overall salary increases authorized by Congress, have helped relieve the situation somewhat, but a pressing need for foreign-language-trained catalogers remains an inhibiting factor in the Library's national leadership potential.

---

[7] Annual Report of the Librarian of Congress for the Fiscal Year Ending June 30, 1962 (*Washington, D. C.: 1963*), p. 96–7.
[8] Ibid., p. 110.
[9] Ibid., p. 95.

Finally, it is the conviction of many that the Library has been restricted in fulfilling the role of national library by its position in the Legislative Branch, a position that Congress probably maintains for historical reasons and perhaps out of its sense of pride in "possessing" the greatest library in the world. In some ways, Congress seems to consider the Library of Congress as a club library and to overlook its larger role of national service. It may also be that Congress fears that if it permits the Library to broaden the scope of its activities, Congress will suffer a cut in service. Perhaps because of Congress' attitude, the Library has held back from exercising the full leadership role in national library affairs it might otherwise have, or sufficiently to satisfy the Humphreys requirement for a national library. Although the Library has recently taken the initiative in asserting leadership in such matters as book and library resource preservation, automation and cataloging, bibliographical services, and technical processes research, there is evidence to demonstrate that in other areas, it has hesitated to do so without specific Congressional authorization. If this is understandable, and even correct, it is nevertheless unfortunate that it must be so.

In any case, Congress is content to let the Library remain in the Legislative Branch, and thus, if the Library wishes to exert leadership over the broad range of library affairs, it must do so as a Legislative agency, which would introduce obvious difficulties in working with the Executive Branch. The Library's budget is not handled officially by the Bureau of the Budget, and so there is no regular opportunity for its activities to be coordinated with those of the Executive agencies. And no other formal method has been developed to relate either the Library of Congress to the Executive Branch or the Executive agencies to the Library. Despite the fact that a great deal of communication has developed between them on an informal basis, the Library of Congress has not sought to push the development further toward a leadership position within the Federal Government in behalf of libraries and library problems.

Even with all these caveats, there have recently been a number of signs that the Library is closer to achieving a national leadership status than ever before, partly in response to the demands for leadership made upon it. As Albert P. Marshall observed in 1966:[10]

> In deference to the internal as well as the external problems with which the Librarian of Congress is faced, there is a feeling among some librarians that in spite of actions to provide leadership in this "Age of Libraries," a more forceful type of direction is necessary. With the growing problems of research faced largely in university libraries, and the inability of these agencies to cope with them, the profession expects and is demanding vigorous leadership in finding solutions. . . . As librarians over the nation become increasingly concerned with the "knowledge explosion," and look . . . for leadership in the solution of acquisition, research, bibliographical, and processing problems, the Library of Congress must fill the need and do it energetically.

The American Library Association expressed the same demand when in its 1967 statement on Federal legislative policy it declared that the Library should not only improve and extend its present services, but that it should undertake "additional research programs . . . in library techniques and services" and should exert "even greater leadership in making library materials and services available in cooperation with other libraries." To this end, the American Library Association recommends that Congress specifically authorize the Library to "exercise these leadership functions."[11]

In response to such demands, the Librarian of Congress in his 1964 Annual Report promised that not only would the Library lead in automation as applied to libraries, but that it would provide leadership both in centralized cataloging and in the development of

---

10 The Library Quarterly 36 *(January 1966)*, *p. 72, in a review of the 1964 Annual Report of the Librarian of Congress.*
11 *American Library Association,* Federal Legislative Policy, *(January 12, 1967)*, *p. 10.*

a "cooperative complex of research libraries, constituting a national information system."[12] If provided with the funds with which to experiment, investigate, and innovate, the position of the Library in national library affairs may well soon be significantly altered. What Thomas P. Brockway concluded in 1966 rings even truer in 1968:[13]

> At the moment . . . the Library of Congress is looking and acting like a National Library. None of its intractable problems have been solved, but it is on the move with the active cooperation of ARL [Association of Research Libraries], and its future has new lustre. First, it will, in due course, have the third building it has long needed and pleaded for year after year; and when it is built as a memorial to James Madison the Library of Congress will, for a time at least, have room in which to perform its multifarious duties swiftly and well. Second, as already noted, the Library has accepted responsibility for a national preservation program and for greatly expanded cataloguing operations which will benefit everyone.

Another reason why the Library of Congress may not have moved as rapidly as it might to assume overall library leadership in the United States is because it is not the only entry in the field. There are two other national libraries which between them constitute an important proportion of the total Federal library effort and which in effect, if not in intent, compete with the Library of Congress for leadership in national library affairs. Indeed, the other two libraries conceive of themselves as independent and coequal national libraries. In the words of a report on the National Agricultural Library, "The Library was established by the first Commissioner of Agriculture, and with the Library of Congress and the National Library of Medicine, fulfills the traditional functions of a national library."[14]

In the same way, although the American Library Association notes that the Library of Congress "performs more national library functions than does any other library in the world . . . functions [which] are vital to the library and research communities of the United States," it goes on to observe that the Library, "together with the other United States national libraries, forms the keystone upon which any program of national library service must rest."[15] It is thus a triple keystone, not a single one, and there is very little likelihood that anything will be done to alter that basic fact.

THE NATIONAL LIBRARY OF MEDICINE (NLM)

The National Library of Medicine, which was made the successor in 1956 of the original Library of the Surgeon General's Office, United States Army, founded in 1836 and later known as the Army Medical Library and the Armed Forces Medical Library, has the most extensive holdings in the area of medical literature in the world. This Library serves as the ultimate source of biomedical materials in the United States with its collection of approximately 1.3 million books, journals, theses, photographs, and other records relating to the health sciences. Direct access to the NLM collection is available to all researchers, practitioners, educators, and the public. Biomedical libraries and specialized information centers of all types throughout the nation are serviced through interlibrary loan of materials not in their collections and through provision of centralized cataloging and bibliographic services. The Library's use of computerized indexing, cataloging, and reference retrieval services enable it to let others know what has been published throughout the world, and its use of a rapid photocopy technique makes efficient delivery of this information possible.

[12] Annual Report of the Librarian of Congress for the Fiscal Year Ending June 30, 1964 (*Washington, D. C.: 1965*), pp. xxxix-x.
[13] *Thomas P. Brockway, "Library Problems and the Scholar,"* ACLS Newsletter *17, (March 1966),* p. 6.
[14] The National Agricultural Library and Its Activities. *Compiled by Charles W. Mehring. (Washington, D. C.: 1967), mimeo, p. 1.*
[15] *American Library Association, Federal Legislative Policy, op. cit., p. 10.*

Plans are under way for the establishment of the Lister Hill National Biomedical Communications Center, the Secretary of Health, Education, and Welfare and the Director of the National Institutes of Health having recently appointed Dr. Ruth M. Davis as its first director. Legislation in the 89th Congress authorized the Library to establish regional libraries, thus further strengthening its ability to fulfill its purpose.

In fiscal 1968, $19,912,000 in Federal funds were appropriated to NLM, plus a transfer of $1,762,000, for a total new obligational authority of $21,674,000. Of that total, extramural program grants and contracts amount to $11,250,000.

Verner W. Clapp has declared that the National Library of Medicine is without an equal in the United States, at least in meeting service needs in its area of holdings. That library, Clapp has written, "is not only preeminent in its holdings, approaching comprehensiveness in a particular subject, but [it] also publishes a principal current bibliography of that subject and . . . has certain obligations for nationwide service." In sum, "the National Library of Medicine offers the most conspicuous example of a national backstop to local library resources in a specific subject" in existence today:[16]

> [NLM's] assigned [statutory] responsibility contemplates not a local but—at the very least—a national clientele. . . . This library provides a service for the literature of medicine complementing but not supplanting that of other libraries. Because of the comprehensiveness of the collections of this library, it is only occasionally necessary to turn to any other library in the United States for material on this subject, once the local resources have been exhausted. . . . The services of [NLM] . . . are additional services provided by the national government to reinforce the resources of local institutions. Whereas in most libraries the interlibrary services are subordinated to the needs of the local constituencies, in the case of [NLM] the interlibrary services have a primary claim.

Housed for administrative purposes in the Public Health Service of the Department of Health, Education, and Welfare, and located physically in Bethesda, Maryland, NLM operates entirely independently of the Library of Congress under the aegis of its own Board of Regents, consisting of ten members appointed by the President with the approval of the Senate, and seven *ex officio* members (one of whom is the Librarian of Congress), which advises it on policy, acquisitions, and services. No one can find fault with the quality or extent of the services NLM makes to the advancement of medical science in the United States, nor can any criticism be leveled at the way the Library has been operated. In its own particular field, it is probably as advanced in every respect as any library in the world.

As the result of a number of circumstances, not the least important of which was the nature of the bibliographic problem involved, NLM, not the Library of Congress, has taken the lead among American libraries in applying the possibilities of automation to its functions. By 1958, the *Current List of Medical Literature,* published by NLM, had become the largest indexing service of the literature of a special subject anywhere in the world. Even so, only about half the published material in medicine was being indexed, and there was a considerable time lag in publication. With the aid of a grant of $73,800 from the Council on Library Resources, an automation project was launched to overcome both deficiencies. By the end of 1959, the project was completed. The *Current List* was converted to *Index Medicus* by making use of an integrated series of mechanisms for the production of the new publication, including tape-operated typewriters, punched-card-entry machines, and automatic cameras for correcting the printer's copy.

Subsequently NLM went beyond the automation devised for its *Index Medicus* and, this time with funding from official sources, began to investigate via the MEDLARS (Medical Literature Analysis and Retrieval System) project the possibilities of bringing a computer into its operation—at least to use it to make searches and special lists based on

16 *Verner W. Clapp,* The Future of the Research Library (*Urbana, Illinois: 1964*), *pp. 42–3 and pp. 74–5.*

the bibliographic record as accumulated. As the seventh Annual Report of the Council on Library Resources put it:[17]

> The significance of the development consists in this—that the computer can now speak in the cultivated language of bibliography . . . the immediate consequence [of which] is to open up the possibilities of dissemination, in machine-readable form, of bibliographic information which individual libraries will be able to apply to local uses for the printing of accession-lists, catalogs and catalog cards, for the preparation of their many other records which are based on bibliographic information . . . and eventually perhaps for mechanized bibliographic searching.

Throughout the whole process, NLM undertook to report on its automation experience to others so that they might benefit therefrom.

If the National Library of Medicine has been at the forefront of library activity in one area, it has not, however, acted so as to facilitate the Library of Congress' role as *the* national library, and in fact it has only begun to cooperate to any degree at all with the Library of Congress. Obviously, there had been contacts between the two libraries prior to 1966, if for no other reason than that the Librarian of Congress is one of the *ex officio* regents of the National Library of Medicine. LC had been giving NLM second copies of United States copyrighted medical publications and all foreign clinical publications for decades and had been printing NLM's catalog cards and book catalog. But this did not result in integration of procedures, records, or collections. Indeed, it was not until 1966 that anything more was set in train. As the 1966 Annual Report of the National Library of Medicine put it:[18]

> There has been an unprecedented effort during the past year to increase and strengthen . . . cooperation [with the Library of Congress]. Staff members of the . . . libraries met to discuss shared cataloging and cooperative acquisition programs, with the hope of eliminating some duplication. . . . Arrangements were made for NLM to assist the Library of Congress in its national program for acquisitions and cataloging (Title II C of the Higher Education Act, 1965) by forwarding card catalog copy for each publication cataloged [by NLM]. When libraries request cataloging information pertaining to those titles which LC records indicate are in the NLM collection, LC will request the publication through interlibrary loan, and thus preclude the purchase of that item for its own collection.

And more recently, LC and NLM have initiated an experimental project to print NLM classification numbers and subject headings in brackets on LC catalog cards for medical titles that NLM is purchasing in Great Britain.[19] As Verner W. Clapp notes, "If this is occurring in the face of prospective automation of LC's records, it is probably because NLM has now carved out for itself a solid sphere of influence in national medical library assistance, and can afford to be less self-protective on details."[20]

If these arrangements are carried out over a sufficient length of time, and if other relationships, described later in this paper, develop as hoped between the two libraries, a greater degree of cooperation and collaboration will result. There is nothing to indicate, however, that NLM has indicated any willingness to give up its sovereignty in its area of interest, even if it could do so under the law, or that Congress will see fit to alter its designation as a national library. Thus the Library of Congress, for the foreseeable future at least, will not be able to assume full leadership in national library affairs, as Mr. Humphreys suggests to be necessary if it is to meet the ultimate requirements of a national library.

[17] Seventh Annual Report of the Council on Library Resources for the period ending June 30, 1963 (*Washington, D. C.: 1963*), *p. 11.*
[18] Annual Report, 1966 (*Bethesda, Maryland: National Library of Medicine, 1966*), *pp. 38–9.*
[19] *For a detailed description of the experiment, see* Library of Congress Information Bulletin, *Vol. 26, No. 20 (May 18, 1967), p. 322.*
[20] *Verner W. Clapp to author, personal correspondence (July 24, 1967).*

THE NATIONAL AGRICULTURAL LIBRARY (NAL)

The picture is further complicated by the existence of the National Agricultural Library, a unit of the Department of Agriculture. Established originally as the library of the Department of Agriculture, it was given its present title in 1962. Dedicated by the Act creating it to the acquisition and diffusion "among the people of the United States of useful information on subjects connected with agriculture in the most general and comprehensive sense of the word," and with current holdings of 1,300,000 bound volumes, it serves a broad public, both within the Government and without.

> The Library makes available to the research workers of the Department, agricultural colleges and universities, research installations, other government agencies, agricultural associations, industry, individual scientists, farmers, and the general public, the agricultural knowledge of the world contained in literature. It collects current and historical published material and organizes it for maximum use through reference services, loans of publications or photo-reproduction, and bibliographical services. The Library issues a monthly *Bibliography of Agriculture* in which is listed the agricultural literature of the world, and a biweekly *Pesticides Documentation Bulletin,* a computer-produced index to the world's pesticides-related literature. The Library also provides cataloging information to a commercial publisher for inclusion in the monthly *National Agricultural Library Catalog,* a listing of currently acquired titles. The National Agricultural Library collection . . . [includes] publications in 50 languages currently acquired from over 155 governments and jurisdictional entities.[21]

Currently housed on Independence Avenue, S.W., in Washington, it was scheduled to move into a new building at Beltsville, Maryland, in 1969. Its annual operating budget is around $2 million.

Like the National Library of Medicine, NAL has deep roots of its own, a well developed sense of pride in its own accomplishments and position, and a sense of independence in its operations that coincides exactly with its new location. Like NLM too, the National Agricultural Library operated in a national capacity long before the term became part of its name. The Library's policies, procedures, and programs are all oriented to national service. This is exemplified by the printing and distributing of catalog cards upon request to agency, field, and branch libraries; by the extensive development of special and general bibliographies which it makes easily available; by pioneering activities in the use of photocopy for interlibrary loans; and by assistance in the development of agricultural libraries. In 1963, to foster and maintain effective formalized cooperation between the NAL and the libraries of land-grant institutions, the Secretary of Agriculture appointed an Advisory Committee on Library Services to consider matters of mutual concern and to conduct studies and projects leading to the establishment of an agricultural library network.

Indeed, the National Agricultural Library has made a major contribution to the development of library processes. It pioneered in printing catalog cards in 1899, made the first use of photographic copies for interlibrary loan in 1911, and established the first major United States documentation center, Bibliofilm, in cooperation with the American Documentation Institute and Science Service in 1934. It performed the first library experimentation with automated storage and retrieval of information, and developed the first photographic devices for library service, including a traveling camera for use in stacks. The report of its Task Force ABLE (Agricultural-Biological Literature Exploitation) will probably stand for a long time as a model feasibility study in the field of automation. The NAL recently undertook by contract with a private research organization an extensive study of systems analysis and design with the goal of designing a computer program for the more effective and expeditious handling of the Library's scientific information. The goal of the project is to have a fully operational computer system serving the Library's patrons by 1971.

NAL has recently adopted the Library of Congress shelf classification scheme (which NLM has not), has engaged in informal discussions with Library of Congress personnel about their joint interests, with particular emphasis on shared cataloging, and maintains continual liaison with the Library of Congress with regard to acquisitions and services. But it can only go so far toward coordination. By statute it is required to serve as the national library in the area of agriculture, even as NLM is in medicine, and it is unlikely that Congress will alter either designation in favor of the Library of Congress. Indeed, the tone of the Committee on Agriculture of the House of Representatives in discussing the appropriation for FY 1968 gives every indication that that Committee at least, and very likely all of Congress, intends for NAL to continue on its independent way. The Committee noted that it was "aware of the importance of the work of the library" and the desirability of adding considerably to the size of its staff as soon as it moves into its new quarters, and while it was not willing to push it along faster than the research and other programs of the Department itself, it expects to continue to support its growth and development.[22]

RELATIONSHIPS BETWEEN THE THREE NATIONAL LIBRARIES

The three national libraries, as has already been indicated in part, are not wholly without relation and contact. Despite the broader nature of the Library of Congress, it is a great scientific library itself; some 25 percent of the volumes in its collections are in scientific and technical fields, and the Science and Technology Division is one of the largest reference and bibliographical units in the Library. Moreover, the Library operates the National Referral Center for Science and Technology, which it began at the behest of the National Science Foundation. Thus the three libraries have a great deal in common in terms of their interests and direction.

More than that ties them together, however. They have cooperated in cataloging for two years or more. The staffs of all three libraries are active in the Association of Research Libraries, and since October 1965 the three have been involved together in the Federal Library Committee, described later in this paper. Moreover, there is an opportunity for an exchange of views and some formalized cooperation with regard to efforts in scientific and technical fields between the three, and between them and the Office of Education and the National Science Foundation, through COSATI (the Committee on Scientific and Technical Information of the Federal Council for Science and Technology in the Executive Office of the President), also discussed in the ensuing pages. NLM has instituted specific talks with NAL directed toward the cooperative development of a thesaurus of veterinary medicine. The first step has been to organize a committee with representatives of NAL and NLM and outside consultants. NAL also is attempting to coordinate its cataloging and card reproduction processes with those of LC and NLM.

Formalized and regular cooperation between LC, NAL, and NLM has been a fact only since the spring of 1967, however. An organizational meeting of representatives of the three libraries was held in May, and plans for a coordinated effort in the automation field were developed. A statement describing those plans was made at the American Library Association meeting in June 1967 in San Francisco.[23] A National Libraries Task Force on Automation and Other Cooperative Services has been appointed and ten work groups have already begun work identifying the problems involved in developing

22 Congressional Record *113: H6663*, (*June 6, 1967*).
23 *See* Library of Congress Information Bulletin, *Vol. 26, No. 26,* (*June 29, 1967*), pp. 407–8; National Library of Medicine News, (*July 1967*), pp. 2–3. *The principal goals agreed upon by the three libraries were (1) the development of a national data bank of machine-readable information to be located in and serviced to other libraries by the Library of Congress and (2) a national data bank of machine-readable titles held by American research libraries.*

the area. In February 1968 the first two recommendations of the Task Force were accepted by the three libraries.

But for the most part the three libraries—the Library of Congress, the National Library of Medicine, and the National Agricultural Library—function as separate institutions. Certainly NAL and NLM have no desire to do otherwise. The fact that they do operate independently not only militates against the Library of Congress' taking full possession of the national library functions, but also produces a situation involving a good deal of overlap and duplication in scope and coverage, as well as in processes and procedures, on the one hand, and some competition between the three on the other. Some duplication is probably inevitable, inasmuch as the two specialized libraries have a more limited clientele than the Library of Congress, and a certain degree of competition is generally regarded to be healthy. Even so, a useful area of research might be a study of the validity of maintaining three independent national libraries and of the feasibility of alternatives to the existing situation.

OTHER FEDERAL LIBRARIES

DEPARTMENTAL AND AGENCY LIBRARIES

Just as the other two national libraries challenge the Library of Congress's supremacy in the Federal library field, so does the existence of a whole array of other Federal libraries. For the most effective fulfillment of the missions of a number of Federal Executive agencies, easily accessible and specialized library and information resources came to be recognized as essential, and thus departmental and agency libraries have been created throughout the Executive Branch.

Departmental libraries are not new. In his Annual Report to the Congress for the fiscal year ending June 30, 1898, Librarian of Congress John Russell Young spoke of the libraries in the Executive departments:[24]

> That of the State Department, with its manuscripts and works on history, diplomacy, and international law, is important. The War and Navy Departments have general libraries of value, and special libraries in their several divisions. The Department of Agriculture has a useful, well-administered, and progressive collection of books. The Department of Justice, the Bureau of Education, the Department of Labor, and, in fact, every department or bureau, has gradually accumulated a series of books more or less adapted to its needs.

The rate of establishing such libraries, however, was stimulated by World War II and subsequent events, particularly the launching of Sputnik and the inauguration of the rocket age. Almost half the libraries on which data are available were established within the last twenty-five years. By 1968, Federal libraries taken together had come to constitute a resource of national importance, some of them being the only library providing coverage in depth in a particular field of knowledge in the nation.

As might be expected, the departmental and agency libraries differ a great deal among themselves. Some of them are very advanced in terms of facilities (the new National Institutes of Health Library will be as modern and sophisticated as any library facility in the nation); processes (the Department of Defense, through Booz-Allen Applied Research, Inc., has made plans for the mechanization of its libraries, which, if implemented, will make its processing services virtually unique among libraries); and holdings (departmental libraries must be acknowledged as the bases on which great national libraries are built, as the National Agricultural Library and the National

Library of Medicine, originally established for the use of an agency and now regarded as principal national resources, attest).

Rosters of Federal libraries, compiled by the Federal Library Committee and distributed in December 1967 and January 1968, included more than 1,500 libraries in the Executive Branch of the Government. It was believed at that time that the rosters contained the names of approximately two thirds of the existing libraries in the Executive Branch. The libraries on the list range from the Library of the Southwest Archaeological Center, National Park Service, to the Library of the Air University; from Mare Island Naval Shipyard Technical Library to the library in the Veterans Hospital in West Haven, Connecticut; and from the Law Library of the General Accounting Office to the Base Library at McDill Air Force Base. The Civil Service Commission reports that Federal libraries employed approximately 3,500 professional librarians as of January 1, 1968.

Because there is, as already pointed out, no accurate count of how many departmental and agency libraries there are, nor of the extent and quality of their holdings, generalizations have been about all it has been possible to make about Federal libraries. As Robert D. Calkins observed in 1963:[25]

> The libraries of executive departments and agencies have received little concentrated attention either from government policy-making officials or from students of government. No general policy regarding their functions has been enunciated; no standing body of administrators or librarians is concerned with their problems; and no current and comprehensive statistics have been available on the magnitude of their holdings, the cost of their operations, or the range of their services.

The lack of information about Federal libraries in general, combined with the fact that each Federal library is a service organization attached to and oriented toward a particular governmental function and the fact that they are decentralized, makes it difficult for Federal libraries to work in concert with one another on common problems, to say nothing of finding ways to overcome duplication and take joint action to solve problems. Proposals for introducing a measure of system into the Federal library situation have been made regularly at least since Melvil Dewey proposed it to the Congressional Joint Committee on the Library in 1896. But the basis of fact-finding and planning for such an improvement, although sought on several occasions—e.g., in the David S. Hill, Carleton B. Joeckel, and Library of Congress Planning Committee reports of 1936, 1938, and 1947—has been hitherto insufficient. The principal obstacles to the further development of the idea were the unequal status of the several libraries and the lack of a clear identification of interests among them.

The prospective application of information-storage and communication devices (such as electronic memories, teletype, and telefacsimile) to library work and the belief that such devices might profitably be employed among the Federal libraries led to a renewal of the proposals. An informal committee, representing the principal library groups in the District of Columbia, proposed to the Council on Library Resources an inquiry into every aspect of Federal libraries, including their basis of establishment, operation, staffing, services, and their intra- and interagency and public relations. The Council responded with a grant to enable the Brookings Institution to conduct a study of Federal libraries, which it did under the general supervision of Luther Evans, formerly the Librarian of Congress.

The study was based largely on 1959 and earlier data and achieved only partial coverage. Slightly more than 200 libraries responded to the Brookings survey, and some information was gathered from about 279 libraries at military posts. No data, however, were gathered about Federal academic and judicial libraries, about nondepartmental libraries in general, nor about the operations of the information services of such agencies

---

25 *Robert D. Calkins, "Foreword" in Luther H. Evans,* et. al., Federal Departmental Libraries: A Summary Report of a Survey and a Conference (*Washington, D.C.: 1963*), *p. v.*

as the Atomic Energy Commission, National Aeronautics and Space Administration, the Department of Defense, and the Department of Commerce. However, it served to point out a number of facts about Federal departmental and agency libraries in general, and these are summarized below. For convenience's sake, much more recent findings of the Federal Library Committee, appointed in 1965, about which more will be said later, have been incorporated in the same summary. For the most part, the later findings only served to corroborate the findings of the Brookings study.

1. Most departmental libraries were of relatively recent origin.
2. Departmental libraries varied in size and quality; the average holding was 55,000 volumes; some of the libraries had become recognized as distinguished in their field, but the holdings of most of them were not outstanding.
3. With few exceptions, the departmental libraries were maintained at a relatively low level of support.
4. Departmental libraries were concentrated in the Washington area, but many were distributed across the nation and overseas; many of them were on military bases.
5. Departmental libraries had for the most part been created as an exertion of departmental authority and had no specific statutory base.
6. Departmental libraries had often developed without specific planning, either as to goals and purposes or acquisitions and operation.
7. Total holdings of these libraries constituted a national resource of considerable importance. Their collections of great depth in narrow subject areas often exceed those of major university libraries.
8. Agencies had often hidden their library budgets to protect them from Congressional budget-cutting.
9. Medical and medical-related personnel were the chief users of departmental libraries, with engineering personnel second.
10. Policy-making officers at the departmental level had not seriously concerned themselves with library development; this was particularly noticeable in the budgetary process.
11. A large part of the holdings of many of the libraries was in non-book materials, many of which were unique and added to the richness of the total collection.
12. A limited amount of interlibrary cooperation and exchange had developed, but the possibilities had only been scratched. Interlibrary loans, however, were common and frequent.
13. Departmental libraries were developed for the most part because for reasons of time and efficiency it seemed preferable to have immediate access to books and other material rather than to rely on other Federal libraries (particularly the Library of Congress) to supply them.
14. The purchase of books was often slowed up and made cumbersome by having to follow departmental regulations with regard to competitive bidding; only a small portion of the total number of libraries reporting in the survey actually placed their own orders for books.
15. A variety of different classification and cataloging systems were employed; many libraries manufactured their own catalog cards, ignoring the availability of Library of Congress cards altogether; full use of the *National Union Catalog* had not been made.
16. The problem of secret or classified material had been a severe one.
17. The issuance of bibliographies and indexes had been erratic and incomplete.
18. No careful system of cost accounting had been employed.
19. Reader services had been less than adequate.

20. No complete and accurate statistics on use or volume of loans were available.
21. The reference function was perhaps the major function expected of these libraries; for the most part, however, reference resources were inadequate.
22. Hiring and retention of qualified library personnel had been a problem; to a large extent no personnel policy had been articulated.
23. A great deal more research was needed to fill out the details of the Federal departmental library future.

The purpose of the grant from the Council on Library Resources and of the Brookings study was not only to provide more information than had been available, and so to meet the last point on the list, but to identify problem areas and recommend solutions therefor. The findings of the study were used as the basis for a conference of library experts, which was held in 1963 in Washington. If nothing else, the study and the conference demonstrated that, despite great diversities in size, quality, and purpose, departmental libraries had enough in common to warrant common consideration of many of their problems.

Federal Library Committee

The most significant recommendations emanating from that conference were that there was an urgent need for the development of a clear policy concerning Federal libraries as a whole and that a Federal library council should be established to advise on the development of such a policy and to assist in coordinating the work of the many Federal libraries. Specifically, the conference recommended that the Library of Congress, with the advice and assistance of the Bureau of the Budget, should invite appropriate departments and agencies to meet to discuss the establishment of such a group.

The Bureau of the Budget took the initiative in the matter, and at its behest, the Librarian of Congress called together a group of interested persons without particular regard to their departmental or agency representation to discuss the creation of a committee. From this group the Federal Library Committee was formed on March 23, 1965.[26] The Committee as designated by the Librarian of Congress (to date it has no other basis than his appointment) has permanent and rotating members. The fourteen permanent members are the Librarian of Congress himself, who serves as chairman, the directors of the National Agricultural Library and the National Library of Medicine, and a representative of each of the Executive departments except the Department of Agriculture. Six other members, representing the independent agencies, are chosen for two-year terms on a rotating basis. For the period ending June 30, 1969, the agencies represented were the Smithsonian Institution, the United States Information Agency, the Veterans Administration, the General Services Administration, the National Science Foundation, and the Civil Service Commission. A representative of the Bureau of the Budget has sat with the Committee at the invitation of the chairman since the beginning as an observer, as have representatives of the Office of Education and the Office of Science and Technology. At first, under a grant of $10,000 from the Council on Library Resources, the Library of Congress made staff available to the Committee on a part-time basis, but in April 1966, the Council on Library Resources granted $87,650 to the Library to support the Committee's secretariat on a full-time basis for the ensuing three years. In fiscal 1969 Congress appropriated funds for the continuation of the Committee, thus placing it on a firm continuing basis. The Committee is housed in the Library of Congress.

The terms of reference (drafted in the Bureau of the Budget) that were adopted by the Committee for its guidance are as follows:

The Committee shall on a Government-wide basis (1) consider policies and problems relating to Federal libraries, (2) evaluate existing Federal library pro-

26 *For a detailed discussion of the beginnings of the Committee, see L. Quincy Mumford, J. Lee Westrate, and Paul Howard, "The Establishment of the Federal Library Committee, A Symposium," D. C. Libraries, Vol. 36, No. 3 (Summer 1965), pp. 40–50.*

grams and resources, (3) determine priorities among library issues requiring attention, (4) examine the organization and policies for acquiring, preserving, and making information available (in use by Federal libraries), (5) study the need for and potential of technological innovation in library practices, and (6) study library budgeting and staffing problems, including the recruiting, education, training and remuneration of librarians.

Within these areas, the Committee resolved to concentrate on Governmental *research* libraries and to exclude temporarily from its major effort Federal academic libraries, public libraries (e.g., those providing public library service to servicemen and dependents and to hospital patients), school libraries under Federal jurisdiction, and special libraries having less than one full-time employee or less than $10,000 in expenditures per annum. Lately, however, the Committee has been showing increasing interest in these other types of Federal libraries. With these purposes and limitations in mind:[27]

> . . . the Committee shall recommend policies and other measures (1) to achieve better utilization of Federal library resources and facilities; (2) to provide more effective planning, development, and operation of Federal libraries, (3) to promote optimum exchange of experience, skill, and resources among Federal libraries, and as a consequence (4) to promote more effective service to the nation at large.

Since its establishment, the Committee has developed a program involving both the policy and operation aspects of Federal library work and has created nine task forces to investigate specific areas and report back to the Committee as a whole. The task forces are in the following areas:

1. Acquisition of library materials and correlation of Federal library resources.
2. Automation of library operation.
3. Interlibrary loan arrangements for Federal libraries.
4. Mission of Federal libraries and standards for Federal library service.
5. Procurement procedures in Federal libraries.
6. Recruitment of personnel in Federal libraries.
7. Public relations for Federal libraries.
8. Physical facilities of Federal libraries.
9. Role of libraries in information systems.

Through the task forces, and through frequent meetings of the Committee itself, a great deal was accomplished in the first year of the Committee's existence.[28] A clearinghouse on certain Federal library problems was established, as was a channel of communication between Federal libraries through the Committee's *Newsletters*.

A statement and guidelines on the Federal library mission was accepted in principle by most of the Federal libraries.[29] On May 19, 1967, it was distributed to Cabinet officers and heads of independent agencies for their information and comments, and forty-one of the forty-four heads of agencies contacted replied concurring in it. Indications are that it will come into general use as a standard for the organization and management of Federal libraries.

The Committee approved a *Federal Interlibrary Loan Code*. This was tested for one year on an experimental basis and then formally adopted. The code enunciates basic policies and responsibilities of Federal libraries in relation to each other and to the nation's libraries generally. It is an important step in opening up Federal library resources to qualified researchers. A research program, resulting directly from project proposals made by the Committee and amounting to approximately $300,000, is being funded by the United States Office of Education. Additional research funds amounting to more than $20,000 have also been made available to the Committee by other agencies and organizations. The compilation of a *Guide to Laws and Regulations on Federal*

27 *Federal Library Committee*, Newsletter, *No. 1 (October 20, 1965)*, p. 10.
28 *For a succinct summary, see Federal Library Committee*, Newsletter, *No. 24 (September 1968)*.
29 *See* The Federal Library Mission. A Statement of Principles and Guidelines (*Washington, D.C.: The Federal Library Committee, 1966*).

Libraries was completed and was published by the R. R. Bowker Company in 1968. A handbook on the procurement of library materials in the Federal Government was drafted. With regard to recruitment, the Committee consulted with the Civil Service Commission and approved a guide to the civil service standards for librarians issued by the Commission. It developed and publishes regularly a Library Vacancy Roster to assist Federal libraries in their recruiting efforts.

In its program to develop the basic information and data necessary for realistic analysis and planning for a viable and useful Federal library program, the Committee secured the cooperation of the National Center for Educational Statistics in the Office of Education in a pilot statistical survey of special libraries serving the Federal Government. The resulting publication is perhaps the most comprehensive collection of Federal library management data ever made. The fact that this collection covers less than one fourth of Federal libraries emphasizes the paucity of information available to library planners and the need for a comprehensive program to obtain library management and research data which is essential in developing a dynamic library and information service responsive to the needs of Government.

Not all the Committee's task forces have reported, but already the work of the Committee has created a new feeling of purpose, determination, and hope among Federal librarians that, in time, a Federal library service will develop which is dynamic and flexible and not only responsive to but anticipatory of the Government's and the nation's needs for information.

Thus there are now emerging the framework and substance of a potential coordinating agency for Federal libraries. As yet, it has no statutory basis. And, it must be emphasized, the Committee is solely an advisory body. However, as Paul Howard, the Committee's Executive Secretary, put it: "The Federal Government spends approximately $150 million annually on its library services. If the Federal Library Committee can bring about closer COORDINATION between Federal libraries and if it can secure widespread adoption of modern and more effective library techniques and programs throughout the Federal Government," it will have helped those libraries use the Federal investment in them in the most efficient manner and so exert a most beneficial influence on "the growth and development of library service throughout the nation."[30]

Perhaps as a result of the work of the Federal Library Committee, the Library of Congress has recently begun to take more interest in departmental libraries. It had not previously ignored them, of course. As implied in the summary above, many departmental libraries make use of Library of Congress catalog cards, and interlibrary lending of materials among the Federal libraries has a long history. In 1968 the Library of Congress loaned some 85,000 volumes to other Federal libraries in the District of Columbia and several thousand volumes to Federal libraries outside the District (lending between the other Federal libraries in the District was estimated to have attained about the same volume). Moreover, the Library of Congress is supplying facsimile copies of its materials at an increasing rate. The Library also is used by other Federal libraries for the deposit of their surpluses and little-used materials and so in a sense has become a central depository for the entire Federal library establishment. Finally, the Library has made its bibliographical and reference services available to other Federal libraries: a great deal of cataloging, abstracting, and indexing are done on a regular basis for other Federal libraries and agencies.

By 1968, in addition to the support in terms of personnel and space the Library was giving the Federal Library Committee, it had introduced an orientation series for professional personnel in Federal libraries, both in the District of Columbia and outside it, the purpose of which was to increase communication and the exchange of information between Federal librarians in the hope that better coordination and use of facilities would develop as a by-product. Thus the Library of Congress has for the first time

30 Ibid., *p. 12. Capitals in original.*

formally recognized its relationship to other Federal libraries and has acted to convert that recognition into fact.

PRESIDENTIAL LIBRARIES

There are other Federal libraries in addition to those developed in the departments and agencies of the Executive Branch. There are the Presidential Libraries, which are under the jurisdiction of the Office of Presidential Libraries in the National Archives and Records Service. That Office is charged with establishing and coordinating policies with regard to the four existing Presidential Libraries—the Herbert Hoover Presidential Library at West Branch, Iowa; the Franklin D. Roosevelt Library at Hyde Park, New York; the Harry S Truman Library at Independence, Missouri; and the Dwight D. Eisenhower Library at Abilene, Kansas—and with planning for the construction and development of the John F. Kennedy and Lyndon B. Johnson libraries. After President Franklin D. Roosevelt's death, the decision was made to develop individual libraries to house Presidential papers and collections, rather than to continue to have them placed in the custody of the Library of Congress, which already housed the papers of twenty-three Presidents. The decision was based on the desire to honor living and deceased Presidents, rather than library considerations, a fact which many deplore. Thus Walter Brahm, State Librarian of Connecticut, comments that the:[31]

> . . . trend of establishing a separate library for each President . . . means a multiplicity of presidential libraries scattered across the country, guaranteeing inefficiency as far as access is concerned. They soon begin to acquire materials unrelated to their purpose. Establishing and locating such libraries for memorial purposes is in conflict with what a library strives to be: a living, dynamic, conveniently accessible service agency.

The trend is by now probably irreversible, however, and in any case the Presidential libraries serve other purposes as well. But the fact that they are lodged where they are, under the National Archives, places them out of the range of effective leadership by either the Library of Congress or the Federal Library Committee.

JUDICIAL LIBRARIES

Finally, there are a good many judicial libraries (the Federal Library Committee places the number at thirty-seven), including the eminent Library of the Supreme Court of the United States, which serve members of the bar and the Federal judiciary, attorneys for Executive departments and agencies, and to some extent members of Congress. Nothing further is generally known about these judicial libraries, since neither the Brookings study nor the Federal Library Committee's survey included them within their purview. The Federal Library Committee attempted to include them, but many of the librarians involved had doubts about the legality of responding in the face of the separation of powers doctrine, and so did not comply with the Committee's request.

Thus the Federal Government's libraries are numerous, largely independent of each other, and operate under a variety of jurisdictions. Some of them are just coming into a cooperative relationship with each other, and the knowledge gap about Federal departmental libraries is beginning to be filled. There is still much to do, however, before the Federal libraries can operate under a general framework of policy with cooperative and coordinated methods of procedure.

COMMITTEE ON SCIENTIFIC AND TECHNICAL INFORMATION (COSATI)

The Federal library picture is further complicated by the fact there are some two dozen agencies of the Federal Government in scientific and technical areas that are concerned with providing special bibliographical services within their own fields of

---

[31] Library Journal 92 (May 1, 1967), p. 1805.

interest. Responding to the leadership of the Office of Science and Technology in the Executive Office of the President, these agencies have come together in a Committee on Scientific and Technical Information (COSATI). Although not a library in the technical sense of the word, COSATI has nevertheless concerned itself with matters ordinarily considered to lie within the range of library interest, and it has taken a number of actions that one might expect a regularly constituted Federal library to take.

The reason for the Committee's creation in the first place was a general concern in the Government about the information problem and the need for the development of an information system to store and dispense scientific and technical information for those who need it. Since 1962, when COSATI was established, it has identified as its continuing functions the following as they are concerned with scientific and technical information:

1. Identification of problems and requirements;
2. Review of the adequacy and scope of present programs;
3. Development or review of new programs and other measures to meet the requirements and solve the problems;
4. Recommending standards, methodology, and systems for uniform adoption by the Executive agencies;
5. Identification and recommendation of assignments of responsibility among the Executive agencies;
6. Review and recommendation concerning the resources assigned to the programs of the Executive agencies;
7. Recommendation of management policies to improve the quality and vigor of the information activities;
8. General facilitation and interagency coordination at management levels.

By giving agency representatives involved in these matters an opportunity to come together and discuss methods of approach to common problems of information handling and dissemination, COSATI has moved to an action position on national informational systems for science and technology and, by example, for other areas of knowledge as well. More than that, through COSATI discussions the agencies involved have begun to find ways to make their cataloging compatible, so that the materials held by each might be made better known and more useful to all the others. More generally, they have begun to devise ways of acquiring and storing scientific and technical information for the more effective use of all. The standard of descriptive cataloging it has issued, however, deviates from the standard used by the rest of the American library world, which means that most libraries will be unable to incorporate the cataloging product of COSATI automatically into their catalogs.

In a report released by the Committee based on an earlier background study prepared by the System Development Corporation in 1965, the problems in creating a network of information and document handling in science and technology were considered.[32] Although the report visualized that such a network would be developed in collaboration with the Bureau of the Budget and the Federal departments and agencies concerned, no mention of the role in all this of the Library of Congress or of the other national libraries was made. Indeed, both the System Development Corporation's basic study and the COSATI report developed from it rejected the Library of Congress as the manager of a centralized facility for handling significant scientific and technical documents and offered the Office of Science and Technology instead.

Moreover, both reports contemplated the establishment of one or more additional

---

[32] *COSATI, Federal Council for Science and Technology,* Recommendations for National Document-Handling Systems in Science and Technology *(Washington: 1965); System Development Corporation: Launor F. Carter, et al.* National Document-Handling Systems for Science and Technology *(New York: John Wiley & Sons, Inc., 1967).*

national libraries "under the aegis of appropriate Federal departments and agencies . . . as elements of the integrated national network," thereby suggesting a further complication in the development of national library leadership.[33] Indeed, to date COSATI has operated in the service of its "customers" and has shown little interest in the broader national library picture. It should be noted that COSATI is concerned with devising ways to aid Executive officials to make decisions in the information area, whereas the libraries in the Federal Government are concerned with libraries and with making library decisions. The interests of the latter are understandably far broader than those of COSATI. Hopefully, with the broadening of representation on its subcommittees, the gap between COSATI and the other Federal library interests may begin to be narrowed.

OTHER FEDERAL AGENCY INVOLVEMENT

It also ought to be noted that the proliferation of Federal agencies performing one or more library functions does not stop there. A number of agencies maintain data centers and information-analysis centers and information-distribution centers in their own area of operation. The Department of Commerce, for example, maintains a clearinghouse for the dissemination of Government-generated unclassified information on the physical sciences and engineering, and the Department of Defense operates the Defense Documentation Center for Scientific and Technical Information for the distribution of classified information.[34]

In another way, the General Services Administration is involved in libraries through the procurement regulations it sets as they affect the procurement of library materials by Federal libraries. The possibility of giving special consideration to procurement of library materials in the Federal Procurement Regulations, the lack of which up to now has made the work of Federal libraries both more difficult and more costly, has been under study, and, as mentioned earlier, a procurement guide is in the process of being published. Both the Atomic Energy Commission and the National Aeronautics and Space Administration established depository library systems, although the Atomic Energy Commission no longer maintains its system. Other examples of Federal agency involvement could be cited, but the above is sufficient for the present discussion.

FEDERAL AID TO LIBRARIES

As indicated earlier, the development of libraries within the Federal Government itself was the first step of Federal involvement with libraries. The second step, which was taken a great deal later, was the extension of Federal aid to libraries, at first almost indirectly and in dollops, later specifically and in large amounts:

By the outbreak of World War II it had become obvious, at least to those most closely associated with the library field in the United States, that the unmet library needs of the American people were so staggering that "it was all but hopeless to attempt to solve so gigantic and widespread a problem by merely local means."[35] However, no concrete proposal for Federal aid to alleviate the situation had yet been advanced. During the Depression a number of Federal relief projects had been concerned with libraries, in particular the Works Progress Administration state library projects, which

---

33 *COSATI*, Recommendations, op. cit., *p. 17.*
34 *The Defense Documentation Center, previously Army Scientific and Technical Information Agency (ASTIA) started as the Navy Research Section in the Library of Congress, but the activity became too large, physically, for LC to retain. This operation, it should be noted, is an example of LC leadership and of its concern for uniformity in Federal operations which ought to be related to the discussion of the Library of Congress earlier in this paper.*
35 *Daniel, Public Libraries for Everyone, op. cit., pp. 34–5.*

helped establish statewide library planning and gave impetus to later planning efforts in the states.[36] Partially as a result of these activities, a Division of Library Services had been established in the Federal Office of Education in 1938, and during World War II a library information section was established within the Office of War Information. The services these units offered acquainted "government officials with the functions of libraries" and also provided an opportunity for "libraries and librarians . . . to work with the Federal Government."[37]

At about the same time, the idea of developing a Federal aid to libraries program crystallized after nearly twenty years of planning, much of it by the American Library Association (ALA). By 1944, Carl Milam, then the Executive Secretary of the Association, had decided that the time was ripe to begin to explore the possibilities of Federal aid. In a series of informal discussions beginning that year, Milam found a good many receptive ears, and working chiefly through the ALA's Federal Relations Committee, was able to get the first Public Library Demonstration Bill introduced in both houses of Congress in March 1946. It had been agreed:[38]

> . . . that the greatest need was for library services in rural areas, and that po-litically, this was the point that offered the most favorable opening. It seemed apparent that a program aimed at progress in this particular area would be likely not only to rally most support, but also to show the most striking results.

That bill, although reported favorably by the Senate Committee on Labor and Public Welfare, died on the consent calendar in the Senate and was never reported out of committee in the House. The same bill was introduced into successive Congresses, each time meeting the same end (though not always in the same way), until finally in 1956 a somewhat altered version was enacted into law. The credit for the passage of the bill goes in large part to the American Library Association and its hard-working Washington representatives, who assiduously cultivated members of both houses of Congress until the sponsors of the ultimately successful bill included some of the most eminent members of both houses. That bill stood alone until 1964, when it was amended and recast as the Library Services and Construction Act.

RECENT LIBRARY-AID LEGISLATION

Currently extended through 1971, the Library Services and Construction Act now applies to public libraries irrespective of location (the rural restriction was removed from the old act) and Federal aid is provided by its terms, as the title of the act implies, for services, broadly defined (books and other library materials, staff salaries, equipment, and other activities and purchases relating to public libraries that are included in a state plan and approved by the Office of Education), construction of library facilities, inter-library cooperation, and fuller public library service to institutions and to the visually handicapped.

In addition to the basic act, libraries have been specifically singled out for Federal aid in recent years in a number of other acts, and they have been included by interpreta-tion or implication in still others. A list of the legislation relating to libraries would include the following major pieces of legislation, as of 1968 (see also appendix E) :

Library Services and Construction Act
      Title I   Public Library Services
      Title II   Public Library Construction
      Title III   Interlibrary Cooperation
      Title IVA   State Institutional Library Services
      Title IVB   Library Services to the Physically Handicapped

---

36 *See Edward B. Stanford,* Library Extension Under WPA (*Chicago: 1944*).
37 *Daniel, op. cit., p. 38.*
38 Ibid., *p. 39.*

Elementary and Secondary Education Act
    Title II   School Library Resources and Materials
    Title III   Supplementary Educational Services and Centers
    Title IV   Cooperative Research
Higher Education Act of 1965
    Title IIA   College Library Resources
       IIB   Library Training and Research
       IIC   Library of Congress Acquisition and Cataloging
    Title VIB Workshops and Institutes
Higher Education Facilities Act
    Construction of Academic Facilities, including libraries
    Title I   Undergraduate
    Title II   Graduate
    Title III   Loans
Medical Library Assistance Act of 1965
    Construction, training, special scientific projects, research and development, resources, regional medical libraries, publications
Depository Library Act of 1962
National Defense Education Act
    Title III   Instructional assistance
    Title XI   Institutes
National Foundation on the Arts and Humanities Act of 1965
    Sec. 12   Instructional Assistance
    Sec. 13   Institutes
Appalachian Regional Development Act of 1965
Public Works and Economic Development Act of 1965
State Technical Services Act of 1965
International Education Act of 1966
Economic Opportunity Act
Vocational Education Act
Mental Retardation Facilities and
    Community Mental Health Centers Construction Act

In addition to these acts, the Federal Government further aids libraries through its provision of special postal rates for library materials, of duty-free entry of imported library materials, and of exemptions from taxation for libraries. The depository library program is also of real aid to participating libraries, despite the fact that the receiving libraries themselves have to bear all the expense of housing and maintaining the books received thereby. The Government also makes surplus property available to libraries.

In addition to the foregoing, the National Academy of Sciences-National Research Council offered aid to libraries through the Conference on Scientific Information it held in collaboration with the Council on Library Resources in 1958. The Office of Science Information Service of the National Science Foundation (NSF) has for a number of years included library-based projects in its program of support. These projects have some relevance to the Office's overall concern for the improved transfer of scientific information. The Office shares the concern of such other Federal agencies as the Office of Education in the development of a nationwide information network and has supported activities contributing to that end in a number of universities and other institutions.

For several years, NSF and the Council on Library Resources joined in supporting the work of the U.S.A. Standards Institute Standards Committee Z39 on standards in library work and documentation leading to the preparation of United States standards for a format for the communication of bibliographical information in digital form, for library statistics (referred to later in this chapter), for the abbreviation of periodical titles, and for abstracts, proofreading, and transliteration of certain other alphabets to English.

In 1963, NSF suggested a Conference on Libraries and Automation, which was held at Airlie House, Warrenton, Virginia, May 26–29, 1963, under the joint sponsorship of the Library of Congress, the NSF, and the Council on Library Resources. The Library of Congress organized the meeting and subsequently published the working papers and proceedings. The National Bureau of Standards recently did a state-of-the-art survey of mechanized information selection and facsimile retrieval systems and published a report on its findings. And the National Archives of the United States sponsored, again with the financial assistance of the Council on Library Resources, an Extraordinary Congress of Archivists in Washington in May 1966 to consider ways to encourage greater ease of access to archives for scholarly uses.

All of these legislative programs and other actions amount to a virtual revolution in the relation between the Federal Government and libraries other than its own. Indeed, the Federal Government has moved from giving a minimal amount of support for libraries through the original Library Services Division in the Office of Education to the authorization and appropriation of millions of dollars of aid to libraries within thirty years. There is no indication at all that it has given all the aid it intends to. Quite the contrary. The very appointment of the National Advisory Commission on Libraries suggests that the Government's role in this regard may well be expanded and strengthened in the years ahead.

Some Generalizations on Legislation

It is not as important to list all the Federal legislation providing aid to libraries as it is to generalize about it. A number of points are discussed below.

First, library-aid legislation has come about chiefly at the initiative of Congress, or perhaps better put, at the initiative of lobbyists active in behalf of libraries, rather than as part of any Executive program or drive. To be sure, the Eisenhower Administration finally gave its support to the Library Services Act when its extension came up in 1960, and President Kennedy discussed libraries with some of his aides and had a definite interest in libraries in general and in the Library of Congress in particular.[39] Moreover, he is known to have considered the appointment of a library commission, but for a combination of reasons it did not come into being during his Administration. President Johnson began to lend his support to library legislation as soon as he assumed the Presidency.[40] Other concerns in the areas of national defense and foreign affairs, economic stability and development, and social welfare, however, have loomed so large ever since World War II that the Presidents were prevented from devoting much time and attention to libraries.

The lack of Presidential pressure for library-aid legislation might have been partially remedied by the advocacy of a library program by key members of the Administration, but by and large there have been no persuasive library-aid advocates in evidence in the Executive Branch in recent Administrations. Although both the former Secretary of Health, Education, and Welfare John W. Gardner and the former Commissioner of Education Harold Howe II testified in behalf of passage of the 1966 amendments to the Library Services and Construction Act, their support was confined to an endorsement of the objectives and need for the legislation and to a reminder about keeping expenditures down in the face of heavy domestic and international commitments. In any case, both

39 *See, for example, President Kennedy's statement in the 1962 National Library Week Report* (ALA Bulletin, *Vol. 57, No. 1, January 1963, cover) and his special education message to Congress of January 29, 1963.*

40 *See especially President Johnson's statements upon signing the Higher Education Facilities Act of 1963 and his State of the Union message, January 8, 1964, his message to Congress on education in 1964, his statements on National Library Week, 1964 and 1966, and his messages to the 1966 and 1967 annual meetings of the American Library Association.*

Gardner and Howe were concerned with education in general rather than with libraries in particular.[41] No other Administration spokesmen for libraries have stepped forward.

When President Johnson by Executive Order (September 2, 1966), established the President's Committee on Libraries, to which the National Advisory Commission on Libraries reported, he appointed to it the Secretary of Health, Education, and Welfare, the Secretary of Agriculture, the Director of the Office of Science and Technology, the Director of the National Science Foundation, and the Librarian of Congress. The last named cannot be considered by any stretch of the imagination as an Administration spokesman; the Secretary of Agriculture has at best only secondary interests in libraries in general (though his interest in the National Agricultural Library is understandably keen); and although the two science men have indeed demonstrated an interest in library matters, it has been primarily through COSATI and has represented a one-sided concern emphasizing science and technology and has not covered the broad spectrum of library responsibilities.

Another point that should be mentioned about legislative efforts in general is that, although it is obvious that Congress has responded generously to the demands made upon it for library aid, the response has not been based on recognition of the importance of libraries to the achievement of the nation's overall objectives. There has been no broadly based conception of how best to promote the growth and development of the nation's libraries toward that end. Rather, as it does in many areas, Congress acted in the library area in an essentially *ad hoc* manner and without taking time to evolve a fundamental policy to guide it in its actions. Thus, much of the library-aid legislation has been passed as an adjunct to aid to education rather than as a program having intrinsic value of its own. And since what has been asked for by those seeking to move Congress to act has largely been money, Federal legislation to date has been primarily limited to financial aid. Other provisions calculated to solve other aspects of the national library problem have not been included. Even in its appropriation of money, Congress has not followed a single set of precepts; it has often authorized more than it has actually appropriated, as if saying that, though the need is great and we are going to do something about it, we will not do quite as much as we indeed know we should.

Another point that should be mentioned is that the purposes for which Federal aid to libraries may be expended have been directed much more to the provision of books and buildings than to helping libraries meet the need they themselves have declared to be the most critical, namely, the shortage of trained manpower. The Council on Library Resources pointed out in its Second Annual Report in 1958 (and that was not the first time the proposition had been advanced) that the outstanding problem of library work as viewed by librarians themselves arose from difficulties in recruiting adequately trained staffs. However, Federal aid programs only began to provide assistance in that area in 1964, and with any degree of coverage only in 1965–66, and this in the face of evidence that there was by the mid-sixties an overall shortage of professional librarians amounting to about 5,000 actually budgeted positions and that, by 1975, when all the libraries now under or planned for construction are completed, an estimated 20,000 budgeted positions for librarians would be vacant. If enough librarians were hired to meet the generally recognized standards for library service, some 100,000 librarians would be needed by 1975. Perhaps the greatest need, indeed, is not even for trained personnel but for faculty members to staff library training programs.

Federal-aid legislation, in concentrating on money for physical things, has not only neglected library personnel but perhaps even more importantly, research into library problems. For years, virtually every discussion of library needs in the United States has given heavy emphasis to the need for research into a wide variety of library problems to

41 The Library Journal 92 (*May 15, 1967*), *pp. 1896–7, carries an article by John W. Gardner that portrays his interest in libraries.*

yield the knowledge necessary to plan adequately for library development. As Keith Doms, Director of the Carnegie Library of Pittsburgh, put it:[42]

> While there is much that can be done and should be done right now, librarians and their governing bodies . . . are severely handicapped in planning for the future. They need to know more about many things. As a specific example, why do some people use libraries while others do not? . . . [H]ow much is really known about [the] market? In other words, library planners have an urgent need for more information about users, manpower requirements, the suitability of library materials, interlibrary relationships and other areas which bear directly and indirectly on the question of access.

Yet for the most part Congress has neglected library research. From 1959 to 1964 library-related research received some $8.7 million, mostly from non-Federal sources. Only in 1966, when Title II-B of the Higher Education Act of 1965 was amended to include a library research program, was cognizance taken of its importance. There is still a vast deficiency to be made up.

Library-aid legislation to date has not provided equally for all types of libraries. Instead, it gives priority to public libraries, school libraries (broadly defined to include both elementary and secondary schools and colleges and universities), and medical libraries, leaving special libraries (other than medical libraries) and independent private research libraries virtually cut off from Federal support. Some of the most important library collections, however, are held by these libraries.[43]

Library-aid legislation to date, as Walter Brahm, State Librarian of Connecticut asserts, serves only to reinforce the present pattern of proliferation of library resources. Brahm points out:[44]

> Under the present federal program a state university, a city university, a new medical school, a community college, a private university, school libraries, and the public libraries in the same metropolitan area could all be receiving federal aid without any attempt being made to study the possibility of some coordination or to bring it about in actuality.

Present legislation for Federal aid to libraries channels funds mostly through the states, on the assumption that state library agencies are strong and that the states are uniform in their desire to promote library service. These assumptions have never been tested and in fact may not be valid. (See chapter 9.)

Library-aid legislation has neither been drafted nor administered with adequate consideration given to the other library involvements of the Federal Government. To a large extent, each piece of legislation has been conceived and implemented in isolation, without taking the related programs of such agencies as the National Science Foundation into account. By and large, Federal libraries receive no help under library-aid legislation. To be sure, the Library of Congress was granted $4 million for the shared cataloging program under Title II of the Higher Education Act, the Smithsonian Institution has been appropriated funds for cataloging biological specimens, the Department of Defense has been given funds in support of library studies through the Army Technical Library Information Services, and Army Special Services has been appropriated funds to supplement book collections in camp and post libraries. But these are the exceptions that prove the rule that Federal libraries do not receive aid under the library-aid legislation.

As helpful as Federal aid to libraries has been, it has not enabled libraries to keep up with the knowledge explosion in the United States. So much is being added every year to the informational resources of the nation that libraries everywhere and of every kind

---

42 *Keith Doms,* Access to Library Service, *a paper prepared for the April 16, 1967, meeting of the National Advisory Commission on Libraries, p. 19.*
43 *Many special libraries are maintained by private business organizations; these would probably not be encompassed by any Federal-aid program.*
44 *Walter Brahm,* Library Journal 92 *(May 1, 1967), p. 1805.*

are falling steadily behind in acquisitions, storage, and availability of materials to users. The situation is one of geometric increase in knowledge and materials to be handled with only an arithmetic increase—if that—in the ability of libraries to handle it. The National Inventory of Library Needs, made by the American Library Association in 1965, showed that the immediate needs for the country's school, academic, and public libraries *alone* amounted to $4 billion—this to meet cost of materials, staff, and operation only. Neither construction and equipment costs nor the costs of inflation were included in the estimate. If this figure is accepted as a minimum, it is obvious that Federal aid so far has not even dented the surface of library needs. Indeed, there is unanimous agreement that library service in 1968 is grossly inadequate and is falling behind steadily, despite Federal aid.

Perhaps the great deficiency of present Federal-aid legislation involving libraries lies in its administration. Library legislation has been considered originally by a number of separate committees and subcommittees in Congress, and so it has never been seen as a whole. Thus the legislative product has been a series of separate packages that have been assigned for administration to a variety of units within the Executive Branch. There also the approach is fragmented, and nowhere is library legislation dealt with as a single whole. Conceived of by Congress as a side issue to education, most library programs have been entrusted for their implementation to the Office of Education, where, if they have not quite been sent to the chimney corner, they have even so been handled at the fringes of the Office's concern.

Congress has not required the Office of Education to organize so as to deal with library programs in a coordinated manner, and lacking legislative mandate, it has not done so. Nowhere in the Office are all the library programs brought together for consideration and planning. As of 1968, responsibility within the Office of Education for the administration of library programs and the conduct of library-related activities were divided between the Bureau of Adult, Vocational, and Library Programs (Division of Library Services and Educational Facilities), the Bureau of Educational Personnel Development, the Bureau of Elementary and Secondary Education (Division of Plans and Supplementary Centers), the Bureau of Higher Education (Division of College Facilities), the National Center for Educational Statistics, and the Bureau of Research (Division of Information Technology and Dissemination, Educational Research Information Center (ERIC), and Library and Information Sciences Research Branch). This division of responsibility not only fragments the Office's concern with libraries, but results in a different center for decision-making for the several different aspects of Federal library activity. Moreover, not all of the units have even one trained librarian to give professional assistance. Nor have any formal arrangements been established for coordination of the work of the other units with the Division of Library Services and Educational Facilities.

The Library Services Division itself has operated under several handicaps. For quite a while its staff was too small in numbers and not specialized enough in many aspects of librarianship to fulfill adequately the functions required of it—for instance, there were no specialists in library construction, in library service to state institutions, or in service to the blind and physically handicapped. Even the position of director was vacant for over a year.

The Division of Library Services was reorganized in pursuance of Secretary Gardner's directive to decentralize to nine regional offices in Boston, New York, Charlottesville, Atlanta, Chicago, Kansas City, Dallas, Denver, and San Francisco. (For some recent trends in the Office of Education, see chapter 11.) Under the arrangement, program guidance comes from the Washington office; librarians at the regional offices handle day-to-day operations under the supervision of the Office of Education Regional Bureau Director. Thus the same person deals with all library problems—a person who must necessarily be a generalist. Also Congressional reluctance to appropriate funds could create a problem for the effective coordination of the regional offices; telephone communication achieves only partial coordination. The *Library Journal* worried in an editorial about whether it would result in the creation of:[45]

> . . . nine little semi-independent Library Service Branches. The dangers inherent [in this result from the fact that] [f]ar from having outgrown its essentially rural and suburban orientation, the administration of the Library Services and Construction Act to date shows that the thinking out in the field—at the state library agencies—is at best evolving slowly. With some notable exceptions, state library officials have not been coming to grips with . . . metropolitan problems, and indeed have shown an inability to work constructively with either big city governments or library officials. Whether this situation will improve or deteriorate when the decisions are being made on a regional basis is impossible to predict at this point; almost surely the danger will exist of weakening of standards and the adaptation of guidelines to the predilections of the regions. The program has been marked by weaknesses at the state level and in an inability of metropolitan and state library officials to work together; if the proposed regionalization of the Office of Education can solve these failures in the administration of the national program, it may well justify the inflation of staff expenses that will be necessary to duplicate the functions of the Washington office in nine separate locations.

AGENCY PROBLEMS IN ADMINISTRATION OF LIBRARY LEGISLATION

Office of Education

The Office of Education itself is plagued with problems, which inevitably affect the conduct of library programs as well as all of the other functions the Office performs. It has become almost exclusively oriented toward the administration of grant programs, and in the last few years has been so plagued by the continual addition of new programs that it has been hard put to get any of them well launched in terms of procedures and personnel before a new rival for attention comes along. In addition, the Office of Education is plagued by a degree of "bureaucratism" as are most Government agencies. Oriented as it is toward classroom teaching, it lacks an articulated, overall library policy to guide library program officers. The civil service procedures and red tape that it must follow are not yet oriented toward professional people and so have a particularly restrictive effect on library personnel in the agency. The lack of professional librarians on the staff has not been made up for in other ways.

The library staffing problems of the Office of Education are not entirely due to civil service restrictions, however. Part of the problem may be in the classification office of what is now called the Bureau of Adult, Vocational, and Library Programs. And part of it lies within the general climate of attitude within the Office of Education. An interview with some of the staff who have resigned in the last two years would reveal unbearable frustrations and profound discouragement over the future of the library program of the Office of Education and its chances of surviving as a dynamic force. The new Director of the Division of Library Services and Educational Facilities was faced with an extremely difficult recruiting problem because of the deterioration of the image of the Office and its program.[46]

Title II of the Higher Education Act of 1965 provided for the establishment of an Advisory Council on College Library Resources in the Office of Education, to consist of the Commissioner as chairman and eight members appointed by the Commissioner with the approval of the Secretary of Health, Education, and Welfare, and the Commissioner has made limited use of this, but there has not been utilization nearly to the degree there

45 Library Journal *92 (January 15, 1967), p. 175.*
46 *Comments of Paul Howard, Executive Secretary, Federal Library Committee, to author, July 20, 1967.*

might have been at all stages in the program process. Similar councils have not been required for other aspects of the library program administered by the Office. Without the specific requirement of establishing such councils, the Office has not gone about doing so and so has lacked the consultation and advice it might have profited from. As the *Library Journal* pointed out editorially:[47]

> . . . the library profession has had little to say about the contemplated changes [in the organization of its affairs]; they have been imposed by fiat from above essentially, in the name of "creative federalism," and rather than reflecting any thinking or influence by the library world, seem to be carrying library concerns along in a general panic reaction to outcries of indignation both from North and South against the occasionally stern rulings of the Office of Education on the use of federal funds.

Nor has the profession's advice been sought as it might have been on other matters, in particular on the development of guidelines for the implementation of the aid program. There is some feeling that in making guidelines, the Office introduced variations from what seemed to be the Congressional intent. Thus OE did not allow school libraries to buy workbooks or other expendable materials, although it was not prohibited in the statute. Again, the wording of the law permitted states to make a choice between textbooks and library books; the regulation set by the Office of Education forced primary attention to be on library books.

The Office of Education professes to have the following objectives regarding libraries:

1. The development of methods and standards for planning and evaluating library service programs.
2. The stimulation of new ideas and experimentation re libraries.
3. The promotion of a national network of libraries and information centers.
4. The promotion of library research.
5. The strengthening of state libraries.
6. Helping to relieve the library manpower shortage.
7. Fostering of public understanding and support of library needs and services.
8. The promotion of correlation and coordination of Federal library programs.
9. The encouragement of coordination between Federal, state, local, and private library efforts.
10. The promotion of library development in metropolitan areas and through interstate cooperation.

In fact, however, the way OE is organized to handle libraries and the overall problems they face places a severe handicap on the accomplishment of many of these objectives. It should, of course, be emphasized that organization is only part of the problem. Experience elsewhere in the Government makes it clear that organizational handicaps can be circumvented by imagination and leadership. Given these, an intra-Office effort might well have got around the organizational difficulty without involving any reorganization to accommodate libraries at all. Indeed, it is still quite possible to do so. (The Office of Education speaks for itself in the previously mentioned specially prepared paper for this book; see chapter 11.)

Obviously the administration of the various library acts has had an impact on all levels of government below the Federal level, particularly on the states. One of the primary problem areas in the Office of Education, indeed, is that of intergovernmental relations, a problem which has only begun to be grappled with there. But since this subject is being dealt with in other studies prepared for the National Advisory Commission on Libraries, it will not be treated here (see chapter 9).

47 Library Journal *92 (January 18, 1967), p. 175.*

Superintendent of Documents

The Office of Education is not the only Federal agency involved in the administration of library legislation. The Superintendent of Documents is also involved in library policy through the implementation of the Depository Library Act of 1962, which he administers. The Act of 1962 attempted to correct the situation growing out of the limited number of depositories by raising the permitted number of designations in each Congressional district from one to two and Senatorial designations from one to two. It provided for better distribution of publications and for preparation of an annotated list by the Superintendent of Documents. An important additional advance was the provision for a system of regional depositories (two in each state), which would be required to maintain *all* Government publications distributed through the depository system. Today there are thirty-seven regional depositories.

A final very significant change was a provision bringing into the depository distribution system not only the Federal publications produced by the Government Printing Office, but also those produced in Government departments and field plants throughout the world. Although the system established by the act was intended to make Federal documents more widely available to more libraries, and to users of libraries, implementation of the act has not lived up to the expectations of some. Although the number of libraries has increased to 963, so far it has only been possible to include four agencies (the Department of the Interior, the Department of Labor, the Department of State, and the Bureau of the Census) in the program of non-GPO distribution. The undertaking is so huge, involving as it does the printing and distribution of an avalanche of materials, that more rapid inclusion of other agencies has so far not been feasible. The Superintendent of Documents has neither the budget, staff, nor space to handle much more than has already been included.

The inspection of depository libraries provided for in section six of the act has been implemented only by questionnaires every two years and by personal inspection supplemental to the questionnaires only when serious difficulties are revealed to exist. Otherwise problems are handled by mail. The advisory committee of librarians that was appointed by the Public Printer to aid in the development of the depository program has had very little referred to it, although ways to tie it in better with the program are being explored.

There has been some response to state efforts to establish statewide planning for depository programs, but leadership has not been exerted in developing state or national programs. In effect, the act has been implemented so slowly that it has not produced the results hoped for when it was enacted.

Civil Service Commission

The Civil Service Commission is also involved in the administration of library programs through its control over personnel practices. Like most other units of the Government, the Office of Education in its employment of librarians is confined within the restrictions set by the Civil Service Commission. Although the Commission has recently worked with the Federal Library Committee to provide better publicity and consideration of personnel for Federal libraries, going so far as to create wholly new classifications and registers for them, the Office of Education's need for library specialists has so far not been given special attention. Thus the director of the Library Services Division had to spend the bulk of his time immediately after assuming office on January 1, 1967, in negotiating with the Commission with regard to filling the vacant positions in his unit with suitable personnel. Pay scales and job classifications have so far not been adjusted to meet the special needs of professional librarians, and the library program of the Office of Education has suffered as a result.

In this, of course, library programs are not significantly worse off than a number of other critical manpower areas in the Government. Thus there is a shortage of scientists, lawyers, and other professional people in many Government agencies. When the overall problem is attacked on a Government-wide basis, relief in the library sector may be expected.

Bureau of the Budget

Although it is not charged with particular responsibility for the administration of library programs, the Bureau of the Budget must be mentioned as another unit in the Executive Branch with an important impact on library legislation. Over the years, fiscal planning and management research and analysis have become major activities of the Bureau in most of the areas of Government activity and policy. In recent years, the Bureau has extended these activities to the Government's library programs, for it had early recognized the importance of the library function to the successful operation of Government and has been instrumental in focusing Presidential attention on libraries.

Although the Bureau works with libraries as it does with other areas of Government activity, largely behind the scenes, it is evident that it played a large part in bringing both the Federal Library Committee and the National Advisory Commission on Libraries into being, and that it has continued to provide assistance to both groups. Moreover, the Bureau of the Budget has taken an active role with regard to the aid-to-libraries program. Thus a Bureau staff member was assigned in 1963 to work on library legislation currently before Congress. Again in 1964 the Bureau worked on library legislation, this time to get included in the Library Services and Construction Act a provision for coordination between school and public libraries with the purpose of stimulating the use of public libraries by school children. A section was actually written into the draft law but was subsequently taken out by Congress (the section title, "Section 4, Development of Library Services for All Students," was left in the body of the act as it was passed but the rest of the section was deleted). The Education Program Evaluation unit gives regular analysis to all education bills, and on the basis of this, the Bureau has made several suggestions concerning library programs, including the proposal for the several different kinds of grants that was made part of the Library Services and Construction Act in 1964.

Although the Bureau of the Budget has taken no official position in regard to the administration of library legislation via the instrumentality of a circular or bulletin, a number of members of the Bureau's staff maintain continuing interest in library matters and speak for libraries when the occasion demands. One member of the Bureau staff, J. Lee Westrate, has been especially concerned with the Government's library programs. The Bureau, however, operates under an extremely heavy workload, and it cannot be expected always to take the initiative in library matters. Rather, it tends to feel that the operating agencies—the national libraries, the Federal Library Committee, and particularly the Office of Education—have been given the ball and that they should run with it, without looking to the Bureau of the Budget or to Congress for specific authorization for each play they make. Bureau staff are available for advice and consultation on both substantive and procedural matters, but their role necessarily stops short of assumption of the larger planning and operating functions, which must remain with the individual agency.[48]

[48] *A prominent Federal librarian dissents strongly from this view. Paul Howard, Executive Secretary of the Federal Library Committee, feels that the Bureau of the Budget (BOB) reflects "the general indifference which management has for libraries. Librarians have not been able to establish their programs as contributing materially and measurably to operations. No cost benefit ratios have been established partly because mangement is not willing to accept intangible benefits or any measures except time and money. BOB also seems to be willing to sit as a bystander while opponents grapple over issues, then to support the winner. In this situation new developments often have rough going." Comment of Paul Howard to author, July 20, 1967.*

SIGNS OF PROGRESS

There is no doubt that the rapid burgeoning of Federal aid to libraries in recent years has had a major impact on library needs and on the solution of the nation's library problems. Indeed, it would appear that the battle for library aid has been largely won. The Government has recognized libraries as a vital part of the total education complex and has made a definite and long-range commitment to aid libraries in fulfilling their role. Generally, Frederick H. Wagman, Director of Libraries at the University of Michigan, has observed, "Federal legislation in recent years in support of libraries has been enlightened and well directed."[49]

In terms of money alone, the Library Services Act and its successor, the Library Services and Construction Act (LSCA), had resulted in the expenditure of $108.2 million in Federal funds for books and library materials by the end of the 1966 fiscal year. In FY 1968 alone, through the LSCA, the Federal Government expended $18,185,000 on the construction of new public libraries in the United States, $34,934,-538 on extending public library services to areas in need of improved services or services for the first time, and $578,830 on state institutional services and services to the physically handicapped. Furthermore, a dent on the accumulated research needs was made by the appropriations in FY 1968 of $3,550,000 for library research efforts. As for manpower, a good many librarians have been able to participate in a workshop or institute, and many students have been able to begin library training under the several Federal programs for library education.

Millions of citizens now have access to books and library facilities for the first time in their lives, and millions more have access to better facilities and larger collections of books. What is more, Federal aid legislation has been eminently successful in stimulating state and local support for libraries as a result of the matching feature common to most of it.

A NATIONAL LIBRARY POLICY

By the middle of 1968, the Federal Government was deeply involved in the American library scene. With its own libraries, it was the proprietor of far and away the world's largest library system, encompassing libraries of all kinds. Through its numerous programs of Federal aid to libraries, it was a partner in library developments in most of the areas of library operation and development beyond its own walls. In the process, many parts of the Federal Government had become involved: Congress, through its original action in creating Federal libraries and adopting aid legislation and through the continuing need for appropriations; the President and many agencies in the Executive Branch, some operating their own libraries, others responsible for administering aid legislation; and even the Judicial Branch, to the extent that it housed a number of Federal libraries.

Yet the Government had come to its deep commitment and involvement almost by chance, willy-nilly, without having planned to do so in the first place and not following any carefully enunciated policy as to how to proceed in the second place. No one, inside the Government or outside it, knew whether the overall program was soundly conceived or whether it was being operated in the most efficient and effective way possible. Not until the National Advisory Commission on Libraries was appointed and began to function was a concerted effort made to find out.

49 *Frederick H. Wagman*, A Federal Government Structure to Deal with National Library Needs. A Paper Prepared for the April 18, 1967, Meeting of the National Advisory Commission on Libraries. *Mimeo. p. 4.*

Under the American system of distribution of powers, it is likely that most would agree that power to create and promote libraries lies primarily in the area of power generally held to be reserved to the states, and further that the states have chiefly concerned themselves with passing enabling legislation permitting local units of government to establish and maintain libraries. Boston led the way in establishing local public libraries by requesting the state legislature to permit it to tax to do so. Massachusetts responded affirmatively to Boston and to several other towns and finally passed general enabling legislation in 1851. Since then, all the states have done so, and since the enactment of the Library Services Act of 1956, in particular, have gone on to create state library boards and become involved in statewide library planning. But like the area of education, which has also been generally held to be within the power purview of the states, libraries fall within the range of subjects which the Federal Government can reach through its power to spend money to promote the general welfare of the United States, specifically through the grant-in-aid device.

Of course, there are no restrictions, implied or otherwise, on the Federal Government's power to enact library legislation applicable to Federal territories or affecting Federal institutions or the Federal Government itself. Thus the library field, like so many others, is one in which power is shared by all three levels of government in the United States. Increasingly, library activity has become cooperative and interrelated; in recent years, as has been noted, library legislation has made specific provision for interlibrary cooperation. With little or no difficulty, libraries could be made an excellent case study of intergovernmental cooperation, of cooperative Federalism at work.

Today it appears that the President and those concerned with library matters generally are acting on the assumption that the Federal Government has a responsibility for ensuring that the information and knowledge in the nation's libraries is made available to the American people and that it must act so as to convert that responsibility into fact. Within recent years a general understanding has developed that a number of library problems can no longer be solved locally or even regionally if the solution is to be the most economical and effective one that could be derived. Cataloging, automation, preservation, research, the development of a national network, all seem to require an exertion of national leadership and national power. No one, however, wishes to see a monolithic approach taken by the Federal Government. Local and private libraries must continue to have a large role to play in the achievement of overall library objectives. The kind of solution being suggested more and more frequently for the library problem involves bringing all the parties involved in library service together under Federal leadership and with Federal support for the most effective operation of each.

To bring this about, and particularly to identify the proportions of the role the Federal Government will be required to play in bringing it about, it is necessary first to conduct a great deal more research and study before an adequate amount about the Federal Government and libraries is known. At the most, this study has only laid out the general terrain and provided a few directions to exploring it. A well-conceived and amply supported research program is a basic need.

More important even than acquiring accurate and up-to-date knowledge about the Federal Government's relation to libraries is the development of some sort of comprehensive policy to guide future actions and to base judgments on what changes in present policies must be made. The development of such a comprehensive policy becomes steadily more imperative as the amount of Federal financial investment in library activities grows. Even without having all the information available to guide them, a number of people have given thought to what kind of general library policy might be developed within the context of current Federal Government policy to enable the Government to make the greatest contribution it can to accommodating the knowledge explosion about which so much is written. The final part of this paper is concerned with presenting some conclusions with regard to a national library policy that seem to represent the consensus of current thought on the subject. The National Advisory Commission on Libraries did recommend a broad and basic National Library Policy (chapter 12, section B), but the ongoing development of detailed policy is very much part of the job ahead.

GENERAL CONCLUSIONS

It is axiomatic that before it will be possible to frame a Federal library policy, agreement will have to be reached among those concerned with libraries as to what that policy should be. There is no doubt but that the failure to have developed such an agreement on policy to date reflects the lack of consensus, even among librarians, as to what a national library policy should be. Even on the basis of a cursory acquaintance with the library profession, it is possible to ascertain that it is not a solid phalanx but that instead it represents within it a good many divergent points of view on the ideal national policy as well as on other questions. The interests and concerns of school librarians are thus understandably quite different than those of research librarians, and even the prestigious American Library Association has not been able to bring these divergent points of view together. Within the Government, the same differing points of view as to library emphases and development are present and have yet to be reconciled.

Furthermore, no such policy declaration can be pronounced in final form as long as there is as great a void of information about libraries as there is at present. Although library statistics were originally collected by the Smithsonian Institution in 1850 and other compilations have been made from time to time since then, and although between 1936 and 1965 statistics were collected by the Library Services Division of the Office of Education, there is not today a single source of totally reliable and complete library statistics available upon which to base the thinking and discussion on which a national declaration of policy might be based. It might be noted in this connection that the split of interest and concern among librarians is reflected in what statistics about libraries it is desirable to collect. There is a notable lack of agreement among the different kinds of libraries, and between libraries of the same kind for that matter, on standards of measurement. As the Council on Library Resources points out:[50]

> Do ten pamphlets bound into one volume count as one or ten? Does a university law library count as a separate library or a branch? How is a collection of originals equated with one composed of microcopies? How are reference services measured—by the number of questions answered or the time spent in answering them? What is the common measure of cataloging in a small public library and in a specialized scholarly library?

Until these basic differences are resolved, a satisfactory set of library statistics will remain elusive. Fortunately, the possibility of arriving at such a set has recently been vastly improved by the work of Standards Committee Z39 referred to earlier.[51] Agreement on statistical standards alone is not enough. The Office of Education's National Center for Educational Statistics, which was created in 1965 and was to have included library statistics, needs to be improved operationally to the end that more complete library statistics are gathered and made widely available for use.

Experience with other areas of Government activity points out the desirability of having a focal point for attention to the problem at hand before a policy for working on it can be evolved. Thus, the basic premise of the Full Employment Act is that the Government, under the Congressional mandate to maintain economic stability set forth in the wording of the act, is to be guided in achieving it by policy recommendations emanating from the Council of Economic Advisers, which was created by the act itself. As the present paper has shown, concern for library matters is divided in the Government; though there are two agencies with major library responsibilities (the Library of

---

50 *Council on Library Resources,* 7th Annual Report, op. cit., *p. 31.*
51 *Standards Committee Z39 is discussed under the heading "Recent Library-Aid Legislation."*

Congress and the Office of Education), neither of them is specifically charged with broad responsibilities for libraries, and there are several other Governmental units with varying degrees of library interest and responsibility as well. Nor is Congress structured to deal with libraries per se. The result is that, with no one responsible for comprehensive policy formulation, it has not been developed.

Even the designation or creation of a responsible agency, however, will not automatically result in the development of a stable and comprehensive library policy. Even with a responsible agency in existence, the development of a library policy, as of any other kind of governmental program, will require leadership. The American governmental system has come in recent years to respond chiefly to Presidential leadership, so that what is required is Presidential interest in and concern about libraries.

Former President Lyndon B. Johnson early demonstrated the depth of his interest in libraries and, what is more, in their role in the attainment of the aims of the Great Society to which he pledged his Administration. However, even his interest was affected by the competing pressures and needs of the time. What will be the case with President Nixon remains to be seen. Obviously, the priority of library needs is low compared to those of our forces in Vietnam, the space program, civil rights, urban renewal, and the attack on poverty. But only the President can decide where development of a library policy fits into the list of priorities for the White House.

SPECIFIC POSSIBILITIES

Assuming that all the foregoing requisites for the evolution of a national library policy are met, what might that policy contain?

Society's Expectations of the Federal Government

There is agreement, first of all, that a national policy should make clear just what the nation and particularly the library community has a right to expect of the Federal Government as far as libraries are concerned. Those expectations might include:

1. Government action based on purposeful library planning which includes all kinds of libraries in its scope.
2. Library statistical and research services of a broad and comprehensive nature.
3. Continued and increased Federal financial aid to meet the mounting costs of library development.
4. Consideration of the role of libraries in bringing about the development of a national network of information services.
5. Usable by-products of the activities of the Federal libraries for the entire library and academic community.
6. Fair, rapid, and understanding administration of Federal library programs, including the establishment of harmony between Legislative intent and Executive interpretation.
7. Recognition of the role of state, local, and private libraries in the full development of library resources in the United States.

In general, as has been said:[52]

Federal legislation can lead the way by giving priority to larger units of service, cooperation among various types of libraries, [and] centralization of such functions as cataloging, technical processing, data processing, acquisition, retention, special indexing, circulation control, binding, interlibrary loans and hard-to-answer reference questions.

Focus on Realistic Library Goals

Next, the policy should be cast in terms of attainable objectives rather than in terms of an ideal situation. As Frederick H. Wagman, Librarian of the University of Michigan,

52 *Guenther A. Jansen,* Library Journal *92 (May 15, 1967), p. 1905.*

commented in the previously mentioned paper prepared for the National Advisory Commission on Libraries, increased Federal activity in behalf of libraries in recent years:

> . . . has led in some quarters to the rather holistic and wishful thought that, given intelligent planning, the stimulus of extra financial support for cooperative interlibrary undertakings, and the imaginative employment of modern technology, it may be possible to design a "national library system" which will reduce redundancy in library work, fill the still enormous gaps in availability of library service, and provide us with a national library network whose capabilities will correspond to the rapidly growing national need for highly improved information services of all varieties.

Obviously such a single integrated system is a long-range ideal which is difficult to define today in other than the vaguest terms. Too much attention to microfiche, informational retrieval, and photoscanning, while of long-range importance to be sure, may serve to alienate local librarians whose concern is to supply simple books to basic readers. Given the "enormous gaps in the availability of library service" Wagman refers to, basic library needs must be met before sophisticated additions can be introduced. Thus attention must first be paid to more immediately attainable library goals.

Appropriations up to Amounts Authorized

Recognizing that, basically, present library-aid legislation is in itself good, the immediate need is for appropriations up to the amounts authorized by the various legislative acts providing aid to libraries on the one hand and for increased appropriations to the Library of Congress on the other. The handicap that space deficiencies in particular impose on the Library's overall efforts must be removed at the earliest possible moment.

Reorganization and Coordination

Furthermore, a structural reorganization of the Office of Education is necessary to bring the library programs administered there under one administrative unit, and some provision for the coordination of all other library activities of the Federal Government with those under the jurisdiction of any new unit should be made. The Civil Service Commission should give special consideration to the personnel needs of Federal libraries and of personnel for administering library-aid programs.

At the same time steps should be taken to bring about closer coordination between the three national libraries themselves, between them and the other Federal libraries, between all the Federal libraries and the other agencies in the Federal Government concerned with information retrieval and storage, and lastly between the library-and-information-oriented activities of the Federal Government and those elsewhere in the nation, leading eventually to the establishment of some sort of cooperative network of American libraries.

Research Toward an Eventual Network

The Library of Congress might be assigned responsibility for coordinating the research in this latter area and for planning at the same time an expansion of the National Referral Center.[53] Perhaps it can bring to bear on these problems the same kind of imagination and enterprise it has demonstrated in connection with Title II-C. Simultaneously with all the foregoing actions, research should be undertaken to permit the gaps in knowledge about libraries and library needs and possibilities to be filled, and as knowledge and statistics are accumulated, program and policy plans should be made

---

[53] *Although much of the present paper contributed to the National Advisory Commission on Libraries' deliberations, resulting in specific recommendations for immediate action and further study by continuing bodies, the Library of Congress was specifically excluded from responsibility for "the development, administration, or coordination of a national library system." Research and development toward a prototype network as first step in a national system was recommended as a function of a new Federal Institute of Library and Information Science. See Chapter 12, Section D.*

to meet those needs and realize those possibilities. The Library of Congress should be doing much more research than it now can on library technology for all the libraries in the United States. The success of the MARC project shows what can happen if enough research funds are appropriated.

Creation of a New Agency

To spearhead the drive for the accomplishment of all these actions and particularly to perform planning, coordination, research, clearinghouse, and recommendatory functions, it may be necessary to create a special library agency within the Federal Government and perhaps to create a special library subcommittee of the Congressional committees on education and labor to provide the proper kind of attention to library needs in the Congress.

Creation of Public Understanding

Ultimately, library needs will not be met until widespread understanding of the vital importance of libraries to American society is achieved. The achievement of that understanding will require the combined efforts of the Federal library agency, the library profession, and inevitably of the mass media and the nation's educational facilities.

FURTHER DISCUSSION OF ALTERNATIVES

In considering any structural reorganization of the Office of Education, it might be noted that the American Library Association, as perhaps might be expected of a specialized professional group, has recommended that "all library activities in the Office of Education should be concentrated at a high level under one Commissioner, and that fragmentation of programs involving libraries should be stopped."[54] Moreover, the Association has also recommended the development within the Office of Education of "a strong staff to review all library activities . . . and to maintain leadership not only within the limits of current legislation but in terms of an ongoing program."[55] Finally, the Association is convinced that "it is essential that each of the [regional offices] be staffed adequately with professionally trained librarians to administer the [several] programs" so as to realize their full potential.[56]

In considering rationalization of the Federal library situation, it should be noted that no one has suggested requiring complete uniformity in the operations of the many Federal libraries. It must be accepted as axiomatic that Federal libraries are service units, existing to advance the programs of their parent agencies, and as such, subject to a variety of standards and procedures that are integral to the functioning of the agencies of which they are a part; thus a great deal of diversity must be expected and permitted among the libraries. What can be achieved hopefully is to bring about specific statutory and budgetary recognition of Federal libraries and to give them sufficient support so that they can be developed as models in both service and processes. Taken as a whole, opportunity should be provided for consultation and coordination, a reduction of overlap and duplication, and the development of joint procedures that will advance and improve the service extended by all the libraries, to the end that the Federal Government has a total library service that is fully commensurate with its research and information needs.

As for the development of a central unit as the focal point for library matters in the Federal Government, a number of alternatives has been suggested, but there appears to be consensus that some sort of unit will be necessary if national library policy is to be developed and implemented. Some of these alternatives are:

1. Continue the original National Advisory Commission on Libraries in being until its report has been studied by the President, Congress, and the public and

54 *"Statement of the American Library Association on Relations of the U. S. Office of Education to the Libraries of the Nation" for the National Advisory Commission on Libraries, April 13, 1967, p. 3. The National Advisory Commission on Libraries did recommend an Associate Commissioner for Libraries, specifying only an overall leadership function.*
55 *American Library Association,* Federal Legislative Policy, op. cit., *p. 11.*
56 *"Statement of the American Library Association," op. cit., p. 5.*

there has been ample time for its recommendations to have been given wide publicity—perhaps for two more years.

2. Continue the original National Advisory Commission on Libraries, placing it in the Department of Health, Education, and Welfare as a staff agency responsible to the Secretary, and create within the Office of Education a Bureau of Libraries to serve as the granting and operating unit.

3. Convert the original National Advisory Commission on Libraries to the National Library Commission as an independent agency in the Executive Branch.

4. Endow the Library of Congress with overall national library responsibilities, leaving it where it is in the structure of the Federal Government.

5. Pull the Library of Congress out of the Legislative Branch, make it independent, specifically designate it as *the* national library, and endow it with overall national responsibilities.

6. Make use of COSATI, or another horizontally organized agency, bringing together all the important information-oriented elements in the Federal Government.

7. So reorient the Library Services Division of the Office of Education that it could perform the function.

Those who favor the first stress that what is needed is the articulation of a national library policy and its acceptance by Congress and the Executive departments and agencies as a *commitment*. No permanent agency is required to bring this about; indeed, it is argued, a permanent agency would be superfluous, once a Government position in regard to libraries has been defined and accepted. Leadership and coordination to this end can be supplied within the existing structure of the Government, both in the Executive Office of the President and in Congress, where there are already a number of good friends of libraries.

Those favoring the second argue that the dynamics of the library situation in the United States will make necessary a continuous re-evaluation of the national library policy, and thus that an agency specifically charged with that responsibility remains a necessity. But rather than giving such an agency both staff and line functions, they would place the operating functions where most of them are now, in a strengthened and broadened unit within the Office of Education.

None of the other alternatives have won many adherents. The third alternative is generally held as administratively infeasible and so as unlikely of adoption. The fourth and fifth alternatives are generally regarded as unlikely to appeal to Congress and thus as politically impossible. The sixth alternative is generally held to be impractical in that an agency so structured would lack an effective power position *vis-à-vis* other Executive agencies on the same level, and the seventh alternative seems on the face of it to lack reality.

It is obvious that no national library policy can be implemented without the participation of the Library of Congress, and one of the problems of creating a permanent Commission would be in working out its relation to LC. Most observers agree that Congress is not likely to let the Library of Congress go, so that it will probably remain restricted and unable to assume the role itself. COSATI has already damned itself in the eyes of a good many by the independent course it has taken, and in so doing it has damned other units of its type. And there seems general agreement that the possibility of developing a satisfactory unit within the Office of Education is remote. Thus on balance it would appear that the first alternative might be the best.[57]

As for the Library of Congress, the evidence seems to be conclusive that the American pattern of national library service is too well established to permit a basic

---

[57] *The National Advisory Commission on Libraries lost its formal existence on completion of its Report. It did in fact recommend a permanent National Commission on Libraries and Information Science, leaving the question of its placement in the Federal structure for future decision, but suggesting the Office of the Secretary of Health, Education, and Welfare. See chapter 12, section D.*

change in organization now. The Library of Congress is a national library, as are the National Agricultural Library and the National Library of Medicine. When the three national libraries have been more closely related to the other Federal libraries, as they will be when they all begin to follow the general guidelines laid down in the Federal Library Mission, the library services of the Federal Government will very likely have reached the maximum amount of consolidation possible. The Library of Congress may well develop its leadership potential in a number of fields where it has so far not been active, especially in the area of research, and it may come to be *primus inter pares*. But it appears to be doubtful that there is any real likelihood of any more formal recognition coming about.

The possibility and utility of appointing a Board of Regents for the Library of Congress has also been raised.[58] The suggestion, in fact, is an old one, and the precedent has been used in the case of the NLM. Perhaps feeling that the Joint Committee on the Library serves in that capacity, or perhaps because no satisfactory way of composing such a body has ever been worked out, it has not been acted upon as far as the Library of Congress is concerned. The argument for it stresses that it would strengthen the hand of the Library in arguing its own case and that of libraries in general before Congress; that it would provide a way to bring the needs of the scholarly community clearly, and in a coherent and coordinated manner, before the Library and the Congress (now any group—and there are a great many—must approach both independently); and that it would assure that the Library's programs and interests took into account all aspects of the national library picture. By and large, however, the consensus seems to be that Congress is not likely to act on the suggestion, but that it might well reconsider the possibility.

The Library does make use of a variety of advisory committees as a sort of substitute for the kind of service a Board of Regents could offer it, but they do not in any sense perform the necessary function of linking the Library to the broad constituency the Library serves on the one hand or to Congress on the other. The present advisory committees are appointed by the Librarian; they have no statutory basis; they are not supported out of Congressional appropriations; and their advice is solicited only on items suggested by the Librarian, and when offered, may be accepted or disregarded as he sees fit. Careful study of the utility of the Board of Regents of the National Library of Medicine to the effective functioning of that library might produce evidence that would serve to remove Congressional hesitation to provide the Library of Congress with a similar body.

In considering the depository library program, it should be noted that one weakness of the program is to be found at its very center. To date, Federal agencies have not complied wholeheartedly with either the statutory requirement that they supply the Library of Congress with multiple copies of all their publications—book and nonbook, whether published by the Government Printing Office or not—or the statement in the 1967 Bureau of the Budget Bulletin (No. 67–10, June 5, 1967) requesting compliance therewith by supplying four copies of each publication. This situation should be rectified. Simultaneously, a thorough study of the total depository program is needed. A broadly conceived depository program, set in the context of a total documents service, involving not only the Federal Government but state and local governments as well, and related to the nation's total library program, needs to be considered for development. Consideration must be given to how the problems of sheer mass can be overcome, and decisions must be made on what proportion of the material would provide useful reader service.

As for the role of the Bureau of the Budget in connection with libraries, the Bureau might well group library programs together for consideration and study, on grounds of the amount of money involved and the intrinsic importance of the programs themselves.

---

[58] *The National Advisory Commission on Libraries did recommend a Board of Advisers and did recommend the formal designation of "The Library of Congress: The National Library of the United States."*

A change in that direction may be in the making, inasmuch as the 1968 and 1969 budgets submitted to Congress did single out and list certain library programs under the heading "Libraries and Community Services." The Library of Congress was, of course, included in the Legislative Budget, and the budgets of the other two national libraries were carried under their respective departments. The depository library program and the books for the blind and handicapped were not singled out. Until *all* the library concerns of the Federal Government are considered together, the full advantages of consolidation will not be realized.

Consideration might well be given to the problems encountered by Federal agencies in hiring professional librarians. Fundamental to improvement of the Federal library situation in general is the development of a strong, flexible civil service system, emphasizing professional qualifications and an aggressive recruiting program for librarians. The establishment of a single register of librarians, national in scope rather than decentralized as at present, might go far toward meeting these objectives.[59]

The following paragraphs, quoted in their entirety from the *Federal Library Newsletter,* suggest a method of procedure that the Civil Service Commission might adopt to remedy the situation:[60]

Federal librarians have complained loud and long about the difficulty of recruiting for professional positions. They are almost unanimous in their opinion that librarians should be placed in a shortage category so they may be brought into the service at salaries above the minimum for the grade.

In order to attain this objective, one or more Federal agencies will have to request action from the Civil Service Commission and support their requests with the following types of evidence:
1. Beginning salaries for librarians are above that which the Government is paying.
2. This seriously handicaps the Federal recruiting effort for librarians.
3. Government efficiency and operations are being seriously affected as a result.

Acceptable evidence would be statistics concerning the number of vacancies, length of vacancies, and the high cost of recruiting. This should be accompanied by evidence to show that other types of employees cannot perform the necessary work, and that agency programs are suffering through lack of qualified librarians. Such evidence should be factual and well documented; it should indicate that the problem is nation-wide.

Department of Defense and Veterans Administration libraries representing the two largest employing agencies might take leadership in compiling such evidence and requesting agency assistance.

A FINAL WORD

As indicated at the outset, the focus of this paper has been inward, on the Federal Government itself and on what actions it takes and might take to improve its own handling of library problems and programs. It should be remembered that the library field is not a Federal preserve, and that continued and enhanced attention to their roles must be paid by both state and local governments and private agencies concerned with library matters, if the achievement of a set of national library goals is to be realized. The Federal Government may lead by example, however, and it should do so before a problem becomes too difficult to solve. Thus the time for the Federal Government to act with regard to libraries is now; hopefully, as a result of the recommendations of the National Advisory Commission on Libraries, the way for it to do so will be made clear. If so, it will have accomplished its purpose.

The consensus of the task force on The Federal Government and Libraries, of which this paper was a part, appears in Table 8A–1. Not all the points covered in this

---

59 *Such an action was recommended in a letter from Paul Howard, Executive Secretary, Federal Library Committee, to. Z. W. Ramez, Chief, Program Development Division, Interagency Board of Examiners, U. S. Civil Service Commission, July 7, 1967.*
60 *Federal Library Committee,* Newsletter, No. 6 *(November 1966), pp. 3–4.*

paper are included, and not all the consensus points were adopted by the National Advisory Commission on Libraries in their broad and flexible recommendations. Because the Commission did act in favor of breadth, with emphasis on the ongoing activity of new and revised structures, the material in a study of this kind has more relevance than mere back-up for the development of the recommendations. Hopefully, all of the unresolved issues touched on here will receive future attention in the continuing context recommended by the Commission.

TABLE 8A–1

TASK FORCE CONSENSUS ON THE ROLE OF
THE FEDERAL GOVERNMENT

(Recommendations to the National Advisory Commission on Libraries, Fall 1967)

Suggested recommendations

I. National Library Policy.*
   To overcome a gap causing uncertainties with regard to libraries and the public interest, there should be an officially formulated statement—brief, challenging, and inclusive— directed toward national responsibility for library services adequate to the people's needs.

II. The Library of Congress.*
   A. Appointment of a Board of Regents (or Advisers).
   B. Designation of the Library of Congress as the National Library of the United States (but not as the administrative head of a hierarchically organized national library system).
   C. Retain Library of Congress in present relationship to the Congress (at least omit reference to an immediate switch to the Executive Branch, as frequently proposed).

III. Coordination of Federal Library and Information Policy.
   A. The role of the Federal Library Committee (FLC) and the Committee on Scientific and Technical Information (COSATI) deserve special encouragement with the hope that these organizations might be strengthened, their interrelationships deepened, and collaborative research activities assisted through financial support and reference to a common source to which both might eventually report.
   B. The development of fruitful working relationships between the Library of Congress, the National Agricultural Library, and the National Library of Medicine might be accelerated by forms of assistance, outside of the usual channels for their fiscal support.
   C. Study of the coordination of Federal libraries and programs with nongovernmental libraries and programs deserves continued attention.
   D. The effects of coordination of Federal libraries and programs upon libraries and programs at both the international and state and local levels merit more examination than they are correctly receiving.

IV. A Continuing National Advisory Commission on Library and Information Policy (Science).*

V. Matters Deserving Early Examination by the Continuing National Commission.
   A. Office of Education: strengthening through improvements and adjustments within present organization.
   B. Statistics: development of dependable current library statistics.
   C. The International Dimension: development of understanding international interrelationships affecting library and information science.
   D. State and Local Government: research attention to the impact of Federal library legislation on state and local governments and libraries.

Items that became actual formal recommendations of the National Advisory Commission on Libraries, July 1968. Other items were either not mentioned or embodied in other recommendations; future consideration was implied if not actually specified in the report.

SOURCE: *From the summary of recommendations compiled by R. Taylor Cole from the four component papers and other materials made available to the task force for* The Federal Government and Libraries, *one of the special studies commissioned by the National Advisory Commission on Libraries in 1967.*

B. OBSERVATIONS ON GOVERNMENT LIBRARY ORGANIZATION AND POLICY[61]

by HAROLD ORLANS
The Brookings Institution

This paper briefly analyzes three main areas of concern to the National Advisory Commission on Libraries: (1) the Library of Congress and various alternatives for its more effective functioning; (2) the United States Office of Education; and (3) the coordination of Government library programs and policies and the possible functions of a permanent National Commission.

THE LIBRARY OF CONGRESS

"Few in this country, and none abroad, would take issue with the assertion that the Library of Congress is the *de facto,* if not the *de jure,* national library of the United States," Librarian of Congress Quincy Mumford wrote a few years ago. "The Library of Congress," he declared, "today performs more national library functions than any other national library in the world"; and he proceeded to list sixteen of these functions.[62] However, excelling other national libraries is not so important to this nation as serving the needs of our own people, and the discontent of the research library fraternity at the performance of the Library of Congress (LC) must, unfortunately, be recorded.

In fairness, it should be said that this discontent has abated during the last few years. Some who were stern critics of LC only four years ago are now less critical and commend the Library for the position it has taken on Title II-C appropriations, on cooperation with the two other national libraries in developing compatible automated services, and on other matters. Nonetheless (rightly or wrongly) LC remains a target of criticism in noticeable contrast to the National Library of Medicine, which seems to represent the prototype of an alert, modern library, responsive to its diverse national clientele as well as its Congressional masters, and anticipating the needs of the future while meeting those of the day.

If one asks what specific functions LC should perform that it is either not doing or not doing as well as it should, various answers are given, such as: the issuance of complete (preferably automated) bibliographies of all of the nation's publications; the provision of certain indexing and/or abstracting services; more rapid lending and photocopying services; the establishment of one or more regional branch libraries; and so on. But overlaying and underlying these responses is a more fundamental criticism: the most important function that LC is not performing is leadership. LC responds rather than initiates; somehow our most indispensable library seems politically and administra-

---

61 *From* The Federal Government and Libraries, *one of the special studies commissioned by the National Advisory Commission on Libraries in 1967. This is one of four papers comprising the entire study conducted by a task force coordinated by R. Taylor Cole, Provost, Duke University. This paper is based upon discussions in Washington, D.C., with some twenty government and private authorities. The views expressed are those of the writer, and not of other staff members or officers of The Brookings Institution, nor of the entire National Advisory Commission on Libraries, with which they differ in some respects. This paper appears here to illustrate some of the alternatives considered by the Commission and some still unresolved elements that are part of the job ahead.*
62 *See L. Quincy Mumford, Memorandum of September 28, 1962, to members of the Joint Committee on the Library, in* Congressional Record *(October 2, 1962), Senate, pp. 21684–5.*

tively isolated from other major libraries within or outside of government. It is an empire unto itself, benevolent and hospitable, perhaps, but an empire nonetheless, rather than an agency involved in all of the normal processes of responsible, and responsive, democratic government.

And the reason is clear: the Librarian of Congress has only four significant masters: the Chairman and Vice Chairman of the Joint Committee on the Library and the Chairman of his appropriations committee in each house of Congress. The President and the Director of the Bureau of the Budget "invite," they do not "appoint" or "designate" his participation in Executive affairs (including his participation in the President's Committee on Libraries that was set up to review the report of the National Advisory Commission on Libraries). LC legislative proposals need not be submitted via the Bureau of the Budget to the normal review and comment by interested and equal parties in the Executive (who may, in turn, reflect the views of their national constituencies); LC programs need not be coordinated with those of other Government agencies; and LC budgets need not receive Budget Bureau approval. The fact that LC's authorizing committee is a joint committee further reduces the amount of public scrutiny its programs undergo (as the Joint Committee on Atomic Energy walls off the Atomic Energy Commission from more open bicameral political processes). And LC noticeably lacks the kind of influential advisory bodies that are so common in Executive agencies, providing both expert counsel and continuing communication with their clientele; the closest counterparts at LC are "liaison" committees, a term as neutral as their functions or, according to several commentators, their accomplishments.

There is surprising agreement among many about what should be done to correct this situation; some of these suggestions are discussed below.

Transfer to the Executive

Transfer LC to the Executive, while leaving the Legislative Reference Service in the Legislative Branch. Most analysts of the Federal library scene will accept this move as desirable, if unfeasible. At one stroke, it would remove all of the difficulties of formulating concerted Federal library and information policies which are attributable to the separation of powers. The President and the Director of the Budget Bureau could then issue common directives to the Library as well as to Executive departments and agencies. Free of the restraints imposed by its location, the Library could, in turn, exercise a markedly greater influence over relevant Government programs, and serve more frequently as staff or Executive agent for coordinating these programs. The normal difficulties of coordinating equal departmental powers would, of course, persist, as anyone familiar with the mouselike product of elephantine interagency committees will know.

Where should LC be lodged in the Executive? LC staff, and most librarians, are certain to prefer, and the Bureau of the Budget is equally certain to oppose, the status of an independent agency. Luther Evans once suggested that LC be housed in the General Services Administration, from which archivists are now striving to escape.[63] My own preference would be to return the Library to the Smithsonian whence it originally came. The Smithsonian has a suitable cultural aura, a loose "holding company" organization that would give LC the fullest possible degree of freedom, and a public-private character that would facilitate the private funding of special and experimental work. Most important, as the Smithsonian contains legislative representatives on its Board of Regents, it constitutes a halfway house between the two branches of Government that should be more readily acceptable to the Congress. A special group of regents or board

63 See Luther H. Evans, Federal Departmental Libraries (Washington: Brookings Institution, 1963), p. 48. General Services Administration (GSA) would be a more natural location for a single Federal library administration, were one ever organized to serve the library needs of all Government agencies, as GSA serves their needs for office space and equipment. But it does not follow that LC or the two other national libraries should be included in such a hypothetical administration.

of trustees for the LC could also be established on the model of the existing boards for the National Gallery of Art or the John F. Kennedy Center for the Performing Arts.

From the standpoint of the Congress, moving LC would have the advantage of reducing the legislative budget while gaining ample latitude for expanding the Legislative Reference Service; statutory provisos could ensure that Congressmen continue to receive the same special services from the Library to which they are now accustomed.[64] Any enlargement of the Library's importance following the transfer would also enlarge the importance of LC's Congressional committees; and, should Joint Committee members wish, they could continue to handle LC authorizations.

All told, the desirability of transferring LC is so clear that I believe that the Commission should have included such a recommendation in its report, after discussions with the Chairman and Vice Chairman of the Joint Committee to put it in a form that would be as acceptable as possible to them.

I share the general opinion that the Congress will probably not consent to a transfer at this time, regardless of how the pill may be sweetened. And the main reason is not rational, but simply a feeling that, "It is ours, and we won't give it up; the ruddy Executive has everything else."

Nonetheless, I think that a transfer should be pressed to the point at which sympathetic members of each House file a bill and hearings are held. For only then will responsible, and not hypothetical, judgments be entered on the record. Only good would come from the resultant public discussion of LC's national responsibilities.

Assuming that LC remains in the Legislative Branch, at least for a period of years, much can still be done to render it more responsive to the national interest.

A Board of Regents

At least some of the Executive can be moved into the Legislative side by creating a board of regents for the Library to which such officials as the Secretary of Health, Education, and Welfare, the Secretary of Commerce, the Director of the Office of Science and Technology, and the Director of the National Science Foundation could be appointed. They, in turn, could constitute the core of a new Governmental committee to oversee library and information policies.

Quincy Mumford has remarked, "The present Library administration has always regarded the Joint Committee on the Library . . . as a kind of board of trustees or board of regents." But neither that lay Congressional body, which "has not undertaken to review or support the Library's budget requests," nor the Library's powerless professional "liaison" committees can be deemed an adequate substitute for an influential board capable of reviewing the entire range of LC activities (other than those conducted explicitly for the Congress).[65] Many favor the formation of such a board, and, as it would in no way detract from the authority of the Joint Committee, it should encounter less Congressional opposition than a proposal to transfer LC to the Executive.

Two-Part Budget

It has been suggested that the LC budget should be presented in two parts, as a Legislative budget and a national budget. The idea is of sufficient merit to be preserved but not, I believe, to be adopted at present. For the most expensive and critical elements

---

64 *However, so far as I can judge from six months' recent residence in the Rayburn House Office Building, House staff receive little better service from the Library than do the staff of Executive agencies (or, for that matter, the Brookings Institution) via interlibrary loan. The Legislative Reference Service is another matter, and decidedly more responsive, even to the quick provision of photo-duplication services.*

65 *The September 28, 1962, Memorandum* op. cit. *Executive officials would be placed in a conflict of interest if given any power to review the operations of the Legislative Reference Service (LRS). The problem can be dealt with either by assigning LRS to the exclusive purview of Congressional members of a board composed of Congressional, Executive, and public members, or by exempting it from review by the board.*

which render the Library indispensable both to the Congress and to the nation—its past collections and current acquisitions, and the systems and staff affording access to them— could not reasonably be assigned to either budget alone.

New Staff Position

Unlike the Joint Committee on Atomic Energy, which has a large permanent staff, the Joint Committee on the Library receives only part of the time of a single professional staff member who alternates each year as the committee chairmanship alternates between the two Houses. The continuity and quality of Congressional review would be enhanced if a staff position were established to serve the Joint Committee on a full-time and permanent, rather than rotating, basis.[66]

The National Library

Finally, all parties seem agreed that the designation of LC as "The National Library" by formal action of the Congress is long overdue. Such a designation, which might take the form of a Joint Resolution or, better yet, be incorporated in new legislation establishing the board of regents and a permanent library commission, should add a subtitle such as "The National Library of the United States of America" and define the responsibilities inherent in that designation.[67]

THE OFFICE OF EDUCATION

No one is happy with the present organization and quality of the United States Office of Education's library programs. The kindest thing that can be said is that the Office of Education (OE) is a convenient and mindless conduit for channeling tax funds to public, school, and college libraries. Its methodical calculation of grants by arithmetical criteria keeps the system clean of politics—and intelligence.

From the standpoint of librarians, OE library programs are a shambles. Close outside observers know more about them than anyone inside the Office, because of internal fractionation and the departure of the many able staff members.

A radical solution advocated by some is to regroup all OE library programs, now broken into five major fragments (dealing, respectively, with the libraries of higher educational institutions, public libraries, school libraries, library research, and library statistics) into a single bureau. I have not looked closely enough at the programs to form an opinion about the wisdom of such a reorganization. In principle (but, in government as elsewhere, practice can be more important than principle), the present organization could be quite satisfactory, since the needs of different kinds of libraries differ, and the quality of library statistics and research is likely, ultimately, to be raised if it must pass the scrutiny of professional statisticians and research personnel. OE has suffered so much from repeated recent reorganizations (good as each reorganization may have been, in principle) that an additional reorganization should not be lightly undertaken. Accordingly, a serious effort should first be made to see what improvements can be made in the present organization:

1. The recruitment of qualified senior staff should receive the first priority. (This situation has improved since this paper was first written.)

[66] A similar recommendation was made by the Joint Committee on the Organization of the Congress (see Final Report, Joint Committee on the Organization of the Congress, 89 Cong. 2 sess. 1966, p. 42).
[67] Douglas Bryant has suggested the following illustrative language: "The mission of the National Library is to collect, preserve, and disseminate the world's recorded knowledge for the benefit of mankind. It should inform the American people of its holdings and facilitate their use. It should supplement the collections and further the work of other libraries in the United States, taking the lead in efforts to provide American scholarship with library services of the high quality that it deserves and that the national interest requires. It should stimulate and enrich the cultural life of America and its cultural interchanges with other nations." (Memorandum on The Library of Congress, from Douglas W. Bryant to the Honorable Claiborne Pell, May 1, 1962, p. 10.)

2. The staff responsible for the several library programs should meet together regularly (which they apparently do not now do) to keep each other better informed and to make better use of staff resources and outside consultants to solve common problems.

3. An official in the Office of the Commissioner should participate in these meetings and should be responsible for overseeing all OE library programs, for developing such common policies and plans as may be warranted, and for helping the Commissioner to resolve any internal conflicts. He should also serve as the principal OE representative in Governmental and private discussions on issues of library and information policy.

4. A general advisory committee should be established to review all OE library programs and to make periodic recommendations to improve their effectiveness.

5. OE intends to set up a library planning and development branch to work on the present and future needs of public, school, college, and research libraries. This staff should conduct more sophisticated and comprehensive analyses of OE library programs and should sponsor independent private evaluations of their effectiveness.

6. In general, and so far as the Congress will permit, OE grants should be directed toward more discriminating national goals, and more grants should be awarded not by formula, but by the best available professional judgment.

7. In due course, the desirability of any further reorganization should be examined by a special *ad hoc* committee reporting to the Commissioner.

COORDINATING EXECUTIVE PROGRAMS AND POLICIES

The main formal machinery for coordinating Government library and information policies is the Federal Library Committee (FLC) and the Committee on Scientific and Technical Information (COSATI). FLC is a voluntary committee of Government librarians established in 1965 at the invitation of the Librarian of Congress and with the approval of the Deputy Director of the Bureau of the Budget. COSATI, a subcommittee of the Federal Council for Science and Technology (established by Presidential order in 1959), was set up in its present form in 1964.

The proposal to establish the FLC encountered opposition from some of the information specialists represented on COSATI and, at the time, relationships between the downtrodden librarians and the prospering information specialists were strained. Although relations have since improved, there is substantial room for further improvement. The very existence of the two independent committees testifies more to the opportunism than to the rationality of Government, since the combined efforts of both are plainly essential to the solution of the nation's problems of obtaining, preserving, transmitting, and utilizing knowledge. Occasional joint meetings between FLC and COSATI, and regular meetings between their chairmen and staff, would be helpful; in principle, both committees should report to a single, higher-level body. This is more feasible, as well as more desirable, today—when the Government is allocating large sums to libraries, schools, higher educational institutions, and other educational, vocational, and cultural objectives—than it was a few years ago, when expenditures for intellectual objectives were confined predominantly to science and engineering.

If FLC is worth preserving (and I believe it is, for its work has been, if unspectacular, useful both morally and practically), it should be put on a more solid basis. The salary of its staff should be paid by the Government and not, as at present, by a grant from a private source. Full-time staff should more frequently be provided by participating agencies, to speed the work of task forces. The committee should receive a renewed and stronger form of endorsement from the Bureau of the Budget, when its three-year experimental period expires, than the approval of the Librarian of Congress's invitation under which it was launched. Such an endorsement might follow discussions (in which

FLC, COSATI, Bureau of the Budget, and Executive Office representatives should participate) outlining a set of new and more significant tasks for FLC, to be performed with the assistance of the best available talent.

Two additional interagency committees might well be established: one, to deal with the policies and objectives of Government-sponsored research into library and information systems; and the other, with the policies and consequences of the innumerable programs that directly or indirectly affect the nation's public, research, and specialized libraries. Both committees might best report directly to a new national commission on library and information policy which has been widely advocated (or, in the version I will suggest, to a standing committee of agency heads).

A Permanent Commission[68]

What should be the composition and function of this commission? Most informed opinion apparently favors a permanent commission, with both Government and private members, located (in order of preference) in the Executive Office of the President, as an independent Executive agency, or (most realistically) attached to the Office of the Secretary of Health, Education, and Welfare; were LC firmly in the Executive, it would be a most natural home. Ideally, commission members might be the same as the private and Executive (but not the Congressional) members of the proposed LC regents: they would serve on a part-time basis, assisted by a full-time professional staff.

Such a mixed commission with Government and private members might work, but I have some doubts. Its functions could only be advisory to the President and the heads of Executive agencies. But why should agency heads advise themselves, or commit themselves in advance to accept the advice of private spokesmen for one of the many special interests they must constantly consider? And if the commission is to be advisory, why should its recommendations be tempered at the outset by all of the compromises and expediencies to which they will in any event later be subjected? Would it not, in short, be better for the commission to retain that freedom of speech and action that private citizens enjoy more than public officials who must heed existing Government policies and lines of authority?

On this line of thought, an Advisory Commission on Library and Information Policy should be composed exclusively of private citizens (including the private members of the LC regents and, perhaps, one or more members drawn from such bodies as the National Academy of Sciences, the Defense Science Board, and the American Council on Education), with a full-time staff attached, let us say, to the Office of the Secretary of Health, Education, and Welfare. It should, I believe, have three primary functions. First, it should issue an annual or biannual report documenting and analyzing the status of the nation's library and information systems and services, highlighting major problems, deficiencies, successes, and lines of progress. Second, whenever necessary, it should advise on measures that should be taken to improve Government library and information policies and programs. The third function, which should be assigned to the staff with policy guidance from the commission, would be the sponsorship of research by private scholars into the relative effectiveness of various library and information systems and of various Federal library and information programs.

Clearly, advice is most effective when rendered directly to someone who has authority to implement any or all of it. But, equally clearly, no such person exists with regard to the Government's library and information activities, which are so integral a part of so many diverse programs that neither the President nor the Budget Director (who come as close as anyone to being such a person) is likely to act on any advice

---

[68] *The continuing Federal planning agency that the National Advisory Commission on Libraries did in fact recommend is entitled the National Commission on Libraries and Information Science (see chapter 12).*

without first consulting all the agency heads involved. Indeed, one major objective of any commission should be continually to demonstrate the need for consistent and farsighted national policies with regard to the accumulation and transmission of knowledge. The demonstration of the need for such policies with regard to scientific research and development has been one of the political triumphs of the scientific community during the last two decades, and that demonstration has been recognized by massive appropriations and the inclusion of scientists and engineers in the high policy-making apparatus of Government. Until a comparable case is made for library affairs, they will neither receive nor merit comparable attention from the Government.

Aside from programs of scientific and technical information, library affairs are, of course, most naturally allied to the Government's manifold educational and cultural programs. In principle, a Commission on Library and Information Policy should advise the head of a Department of Education, Science, and Culture or a National Foundation for Science, Education, and Culture (embracing the Office of Education, the National Science Foundation, and the National Foundation on the Arts and the Humanities, and, if possible, the National Institutes of Health, the Smithsonian Institution, and the Library of Congress). The closest present approximation would be for the commission, through one means or another, to advise the heads of essentially the same agencies. (If the commission did not itself do so, these agencies would be consulted in any case by the Bureau of the Budget before the Administration reached any decision on a commission recommendation.) This might be done either by requiring the Secretary of Health, Education, and Welfare to consult these agencies and take their views into account before transmitting any recommendation to the President, or by constituting a standing committee, composed of these agency heads or, essentially, of executive members of the LC regents, to review commission recommendations and transmit them, with its marks of approval or disapproval, to the President.

Some prominent national library spokesmen seem to look to the Bureau of the Budget for the ultimate solution of their Governmental problems. The Bureau is the right hand of the President; convince the Bureau that library programs should be better coordinated, should receive more money and provide better services to the Government and to the public—convince some high Bureau official and he will draft an Executive Order which the overburdened President will automatically sign, dutiful departments will obey, and the problem will be solved. So their thinking goes. Sadly, or happily, things are not that simple. Such power as the Bureau has (which is decidedly less than this image suggests) is not maintained by being squandered. It might be said that the Bureau does not so much attempt to order as to orchestrate, if any semblance of harmony can be detected in the cacophony of government. The Bureau will not issue an order unless an order is necessary to enforce the will of the President; it will not issue an order if voluntary compliance will do; and its orders may or may not be obeyed. The Bureau responds to the demands made upon it in accordance with its own estimate of their importance, reasonableness, and feasibility; and, more often than not, that estimate is deflationary.

Thus, the Bureau evidently felt that, at the outset, Federal libraries were worth the status of Federal library "committee" but not a "council." It is probably fair to summarize the Bureau's attitude toward the requests of librarians as sympathetic, even commiserative, but skeptical. The Bureau's second question to supplicants is: "Why don't you do this yourself?" Its third is: "Why don't you suggest something specific and realistic?" And its first and last questions are: "How much of our time and the time of the President, and the time and money of the public—how much attention in the United States Government budget and organization—does this claim really deserve as against a hundred thousand other legitimate claims?"

The nation's libraries need to answer these questions not once but repeatedly, and their answers need to become more and more thoughtful and convincing.

C. RESEARCH LIBRARIES
AND THE FEDERAL GOVERNMENT [69]

by CHARLES BLITZER
Assistant Secretary for History and Art
Smithsonian Institution
and REUBEN CLARK, *Attorney*
Wilmer, Cutler and Pickering

This paper from a report on university and other research libraries presents evidence that was taken into consideration by the National Advisory Commission on Libraries. The reader should note that, as with much of the Commission's study material, the rather specific recommendations of the authors differ from the Commission's consensus and formal recommendations (see chapter 12) in many details and in some more basic aspects—e.g., the Commission did not recommend a grants-making function for the Library of Congress or a new division on research library matters in the Office of Education. However, this paper appears here as it was submitted to the Commission in order to illustrate not only some of the alternatives that were considered, but also some of the unsettled issues that will be future grist for the mills of the continuing bodies that the Commission did in fact recommend. Reference is made, for example, to an integrated national system to serve the nation's future scholarly research needs; the thoughtful planning of such a system is only one of the many tasks that lie ahead.

THE PROBLEMS

America's university and other research libraries and archives are a precious and irreplaceable national resource. Their collections, buildings, equipment, and trained staffs, which represent a public and private investment of untold millions of dollars, are indispensable to the pursuit of scholarship and research in the humanities and the social and physical sciences. They serve industry and government as well as the world of learning. They are truly the foundation upon which the edifice of knowledge is built.

Historically, America's research libraries, archives, and manuscript collections were created and have been supported largely by private and state institutions, chiefly universities and research establishments of all kinds. Originally they were intended primarily to serve the faculties, students, and staffs of these institutions. They are now, however, also national institutions in a very real sense and undergird the entire national research effort. A government that has recognized the importance of basic research, and has accepted responsibility for supporting it, cannot afford to ignore the needs of research libraries and the opportunities inherent in the meeting of that need.

Today, demands upon America's research libraries and archives outrun their traditional sources of support. The accelerated pace of research in all disciplines, the opening up of new fields of knowledge, the vastly increased quantity of all types of publications throughout the world, and the sheer increase of the cost of books and other materials have confronted research libraries with staggering financial burdens. So, too,

[69] From On Research Libraries *by the* Committee on Research Libraries *of the* American Council of Learned Societies; *submitted to the National Advisory Commission on Libraries November 1967. The complete study,* On Research Libraries, *was published by the M.I.T. Press in 1969.*

has the vastly expanded national effort in graduate and postdoctoral education. The ever-increasing complexity of the materials that scholars need requires of librarians new language and subject-matter skills. Libraries are called upon to bear the cost of new types of sophisticated equipment which will permit them to fulfill their obligations more effectively.

Above all, the pressing need to incorporate existing research libraries into a national system for the dissemination of information about the location of materials and for providing access to them is clearly beyond the present resources of the nation's research libraries themselves.

TOWARD SOLUTION

If the current situation of research libraries argues for increased Federal support, it also suggests some things about the form that such support should take. If research libraries are to be supported not as adjuncts to particular institutions but as crucially important, integrated national resources, then this support must be provided in ways calculated to make these resources as widely and easily available as possible. The establishment of a rational, coherent Federal program of support to research libraries offers a great opportunity to move toward the creation of a truly national system of research libraries.

The research libraries themselves have shown a laudable willingness to cooperate in order to meet the needs of the nation, notwithstanding the inherent difficulties that must arise when diverse independent institutions seek to meet national requirements. Through such undertakings as the Farmington Plan, the Center for Research Libraries, the *National Union Catalog,* the Association of Research Libraries, and a number of less formal arrangements, such as the distribution of Library of Congress catalog cards, the country's research libraries have attempted, within limits set by available funds, to work toward the creation of a comprehensive library system in which ideally the resources of each library can be made more easily accessible to scholars, wherever located, and in which costly duplication of services and materials can be significantly reduced. It is now apparent that only with substantial Federal support and guidance can we hope for the realization of this goal.

Through such a system, every book would be cataloged only once—either by the National Library or by another research library nationally funded—and the result would be made rapidly available to every research library. Through such a system, every physically endangered book would be preserved, with micro- or photocopies being made available on demand to all libraries through Federal support.

Through such a system, research and development in library technology would be performed, both by the National Library and by other libraries nationally funded, and the results made available to all libraries.

The beneficiaries of a national library system would include all scholars and scientists, all educational institutions, all libraries, industry, and government itself—indeed, all those in need of research materals. The Library of Congress, already the beneficiary of wise counsel and substantial appropriations from the Congress, has contributed signally to the beginnings of such a system. Partial systems have already been created in agriculture and medicine, through the National Agricultural Library and the National Library of Medicine. Such precedents should be extended to all other fields, building upon the great resources that now exist. The active and enlightened participation of the Federal Government, dealing directly with the research libraries themselves, is required for the success of this enterprise.

A Federal program for research libraries, then, should serve two major purposes: (1) the support of research libraries themselves, and hence of all research and scholarship, and (2) the creation of a coherent national system of research libraries, minimizing unnecessary duplication, fostering cooperative efforts, and ensuring the freest possible access, consistent with local needs, to the resources of all libraries and archives embraced by the system. A Federal contribution, modest in comparison with both the vast sums already invested in America's research libraries and the current scale of private contributions being made to their support, can serve, in effect, to "nationalize" this precious resource by making the collections of our research libraries accessible to scholars across the nation.[70]

Specifically, research libraries and their far-flung constituencies look to the Federal Government for assistance of three related sorts. The first is direct financial support to research libraries. The second is a vigorous National Library able and willing to undertake, starting within the limits of existing technology, a broad range of programs of research and service to the entire community of research libraries and those they serve. The third is the effective articulation and implementation of national policies and plans for research libraries, particularly taking into account the fact of rapid technological change in the areas of communication and information storage, location, and retrieval. Of these, only the third entails a new departure for the Federal Government; the other two already exist in embryonic form.

Research libraries currently receive, or are eligible to receive, Federal funds under a number of programs administered by a number of agencies and bureaus. Notwithstanding the current substantial level of support for research libraries, Federal funding is, in terms of need, grossly inadequate. In addition, Federal activities in this area are presently fragmented and are generally associated (often at a low administrative level) with agencies whose primary missions lie elsewhere.

Similarly, the Library of Congress is already in effect the National Library of the United States. As such, it has for many years performed a wide range of services beneficial to the entire community of research libraries and those they serve. In the absence of an official mandate to perform such services, and in view of its formal designation as a legislative library, the Library of Congress has been unable to move forward boldly with programs of national service to all research libraries. In particular, it has been reluctant to seek, as part of its own appropriation, the funds necessary to enable it to serve as a true National Library and has tended instead to rely upon funds from other Federal agencies and from private sources for this purpose.

Nevertheless, both in the case of direct financial support to research libraries and in the case of the Library of Congress, clear precedents have been established upon which a truly comprehensive and effective Federal program can be built. What must be added is a coordinating and stimulating intelligence—a body that will be sensitive to the qualities and needs of research libraries and those they serve, that will take cognizance of all Federal programs affecting research libraries, and that will serve as a force both of coordination and of innovation.

A single agency of the Federal Government should be given responsibility and authority for all Federal programs directly related to research libraries. Since the Library of Congress (acting as National Library) will inevitably continue to play a major role in this sphere, such a solution would necessarily involve a change in its status.

Following the precedent of the National Museum Act of 1966, a National Library Act could transform the Library of Congress into a true National Library. It could then be explicitly authorized to continue and expand its programs of research and national service to research libraries, to receive both appropriated and private funds for the purpose of making grants to research libraries, and to bear major responsibility for the coordination of all Federal programs affecting libraries. Of course the Library of

---

70 *The extremely uneven geographical distribution of the nation's research libraries is a result of historical accident rather than of design. The deliberate creation of one or more great new research libraries, in addition to support of existing ones, has been advocated as a corrective to the present uneven distribution. Such an undertaking would itself necessarily draw upon existing research library resources, without which it would be unthinkable.*

Congress must, in any event, continue to serve as the legislative library of the United States. To this end, its Legislative Reference Service (perhaps restyled the Legislative Research Service) should build upon its already impressive strength and expertness, guided by the Joint Congressional Committee on the Library of Congress. In performing its national services, the National Library—which might be known as "The Library of Congress: The National Library of the United States"—should be guided by a strong and distinguished Board of Trustees, composed of both public and private members. The Board of Regents of the Smithsonian Institution, which represents the private sector as well as the three branches of the Federal Government, is a possible model for this Board.

Under this scheme, operating funds for the Legislative Reference Service would remain within the Legislative section of the Federal budget. Funds for national programs, whether performed directly by the National Library or by grants to other libraries, could be appropriated to the Library of Congress in the Executive Branch section of the Federal budget, either as an appropriation to an independent agency or under the category of Appropriations to the President of the United States.

Ideally, "The Library of Congress: The National Library" would embrace the existing National Library of Medicine and the National Agricultural Library. Failing this, every effort should be made to assure the greatest possible degree of cooperation among the three national libraries in order that duplication might be minimized and that cooperative efforts and compatible systems might be encouraged.

Such a structure, designed to associate as closely as possible National Library services and Federal grants to research libraries, would offer the best assurance that Federal programs in this field would be carried on with the greatest possible efficiency and the most beneficial results. The authors are aware, however, that the location of the Library of Congress within the Legislative Branch of the Federal Government, and its official status as a legislative library, pose serious questions as to the feasibility of moving immediately to a solution that combines in a single institution an operating National Library and a program of Federal grants to libraries. Even so, certain steps can and should be taken now to improve the effectiveness of Federal programs relating to research libraries and to bring us closer to the realization of the ultimate goal. We propose, then, three immediate steps for better organizing, in the national interest, the three functions stated above: direct financial assistance, National Library service, and planning and research.

First, we propose that there be created within the Department of Health, Education, and Welfare, and reporting to the Secretary, a permanent Commission on Libraries and Archives, the members to be appointed by the President of the United States. The members of this permanent Commission should represent education, scholarship in the humanities, research in the natural and social sciences, the library and archival professions, and the public interest generally. Affected Federal agencies—including the Library of Congress, the National Archives, the National Agricultural Library, and the National Library of Medicine—should be required to send observers regularly to the Commission's meetings. The Commission should have a competent staff and adequate funds for long-range planning and research.

The permanent Commission should, among other functions, have continuing responsibility for advising the Federal Government on the nation's library needs and for assessing the continued efficacy of existing library legislation, the impact upon libraries of all Federal legislation, and the implications for libraries of technological change; it could serve also as an advisory board for the Library of Congress, the other national libraries, and the National Archives; and it should bear a special responsibility for advising the Secretary of Health, Education, and Welfare and the Commissioner of Education about library programs of the Department. The Commission should be required by law to report each year to the Congress and the President, making such recommendations as seem to it desirable concerning Federal activities affecting libraries and archives.

This Commission would provide an essential overview of all Federal library programs and legislation. Since our specific concern in this paper is with research libraries, we propose, second, that all present programs of the Office of Education affecting research libraries be brought together in a single division within that Office. The administration of new Federal programs affecting research libraries should also be placed within this division. This would mean, for example, that funds presently available for construction of research library facilities, training of research librarians, acquisition of materials, performing bibliographical services, and research and development would all be administered by a single Division of Research Libraries and Archives.

This new division within the Office of Education, acting under the policy direction of the proposed Commission, should have as its mission the improvement of research library and archival services throughout the nation. It should administer Federal grant programs in these areas, building upon existing resources, both public and private. It should be authorized explicitly to make grants to such public institutions as the Library of Congress, as well as to other public and private research libraries, for the performance of national library services, including acquisition, preservation, and dissemination of library materials, cataloging and other bibliographical services, and research and development aimed at technological improvement of library and archival services.

The authors would recommend to the Secretary of Health, Education, and Welfare and the Commissioner of Education that this Division of Research Libraries and Archives be placed within the Bureau of Higher Education of the United States Office of Education. Although we are aware of the arguments in favor of a consolidation of all library programs—public, school, college, and research—we are persuaded that the special character of research libraries and of those they serve makes the Bureau of Higher Education a more suitable location for programs affecting research libraries than the Bureau of Adult, Vocational, and Library Programs or any other existing Bureau of the Office of Education. Furthermore, we believe that necessary coordination of all library programs can be accomplished through the efforts of the permanent Commission on Libraries and Archives.

Third, we propose that the Congress of the United States declare that the Library of Congress is, in addition to its role as legislative library, the National Library of the United States, with responsibility and authority to undertake programs of acquisition, cataloging, preservation, dissemination, training, and research and development, and to perform related services, either directly or by contract with other institutions, in the national interest.

CHAPTER IX

THE ROLE OF LOCAL-STATE-REGIONAL COOPERATION

It has already emerged clearly from the foregoing chapter that Federal involvement in the total picture of library and information services, often in combination with education and research, is not only firmly established, but productive of commendable results. Furthermore, it is clear that the very success of Federal efforts has led to the rapid proliferation of activity—and hence to the problems of fragmentation, duplication of effort, and lack of communication among participants.

That at least some agencies of Government are enthusiastic about their potentialities for service, within the broad framework of the objectives and recommendations of the National Advisory Commission on Libraries, is evident in the succeeding chapters 10 and 11. The present chapter is concerned with the fact that Federal leadership cannot be effective in meeting the needs of all the people without participative planning and strong cooperative activity at the local-state-regional level, particularly in view of the trend toward multistate regionalization in many areas.

Two papers available to the National Advisory Commission on Libraries discussed some very relevant issues at the local-state-regional level. These appear in the following pages. Section A highlights some glaring deficiencies of the state library agencies, whose role at the point of implementation of Federal legislation is distinctly hampered. Section B is a case-history sketch of the library situation in a single state. Both papers plead for future attention to what might be called the potentialities for service emergent from a thorough understanding of cooperative activity at the local-state-regional level in the years ahead. Section C highlights some of the Commission's findings from its regional hearings held throughout the nation during 1967.

A. AMERICAN STATE LIBRARIES AND STATE LIBRARY AGENCIES[1]

ROLE OF THE STATE LIBRARY

The role of the state in library functions has been defined as follows:[2]

States *provide* library service directly, *promote* service through other agencies, *coordinate* the various library resources, *aid* libraries financially, and *require* service through Standards and Regulations.

The report on state libraries that appears in the following pages rests squarely on a belief in the validity of this definition of the state's responsibility for library service. The several states accept this responsibility with varying degrees of enthusiasm and commitment. Differences in the extent to which state governments acknowledge their role in providing adequate library services for all partially account for the many dissimilarities in the manner in which each of the fifty states has chosen to execute its library functions.

In a few instances, the state government has embodied the bulk of the responsibilities implicit in the above definition into a single, integrated governmental unit. More commonly, however, the states fragment their library services among several agencies of government. It is not uncommon, for example, to find the law library administered by the state supreme court, legislative reference by a legislative service bureau, history and archives by an historical commission, public libraries by a separate extension agency, school libraries by a department of public instruction, and institution libraries by correction or mental health departments. Under such circumstances, it is impossible to identify any one agency in each of the fifty states as the "State Library" and mean the same thing in even a majority of cases.

How, then, does one specify the dimensions of the state library? In this report, the term "state library" refers to that agency or group of coordinated agencies charged with the task of implementing the library functions of the state. In this view, that agency or combination of agencies is appropriately identified as the *comprehensive state library*. Clearly, the role of the comprehensive state library is not very adequately simulated by collective references to the present activities of the fifty states' "State Libraries." Its role is best derived from the definition of the library functions of the state with which we began.

Accordingly, the comprehensive state library provides:

1. Leadership in the development and coordination of all library resources and services within the state, including those in school, public, academic, and special libraries and in the establishment of regional library networks, which often will be part of existing and emerging national information systems.

1 This "overview with recommendations" is from the report of the same name commissioned by the National Advisory Commission on Libraries and compiled by Nelson Associates, Incorporated, in 1967. It is based on the literature; conferences with a special advisory committee, with staff of the United States Office of Education, and with staff of the Washington Office of the American Library Association; and responses to a letter of inquiry from 33 out of 54 state library or state library agency officials. The authors, Nelson Associates, Incorporated, wish to cite particularly the wise counsel and advice they received throughout the study from Miss Genevieve Casey and Mr. S. Gilbert Prentiss, former state librarians of Michigan and New York respectively. The reader is reminded that this report is based on material prepared in 1967 and reflects the situation as of that date.
2 American Association of State Libraries, Surveys and Standards Committee, Standards for Library Functions at the State Level (Chicago: American Library Association, 1963).

2. Resources of statewide value, both for direct use by state government and as a backstop for local libraries of all types, in subject fields and to depths that have been predetermined by a careful appraisal of statewide needs and available library resources.

3. Special information services for state government officials, agencies, and institutions.

4. Consultant and promotion services for those libraries that bring facilities close to readers, particularly public and school libraries, but including college, university, reference, and research libraries.

5. Administration and regulation of state and Federal categorical aid to local libraries, as well as aid for cooperative projects among libraries.

6. Administration of standards for libraries, certification of school and public librarians, and workshops for the advancement of librarianship.

7. Programs for library trustees aimed at advancing recognition and understanding of trustee responsibilities.

8. Research and planning leadership, including work with citizen groups, to stimulate steady improvement in state-wide library resources and their utilization.

9. Leadership in establishing a body of state law congenial to the development of total library services of the highest caliber.

Since it is more difficult to capture the spirit of the comprehensive state library in a multiagency environment, there is some temptation to believe that the library responsibilities of the state are best executed through a single, all-encompassing agency. And although there is not, admittedly, empirical data to support this contention, the weight of the circumstantial evidence is substantial. Nevertheless, the means are less important than the goals; if a state can meet the full measure of its responsibilities for adequate, coordinated library services with several agencies working cooperatively, then it is doing no less than it might accomplish through a single governmental unit.[3]

However effected, coordination between various types of libraries within a state—public, school, academic, and special—and coordination of each state's library resources with those in surrounding states and with libraries at the national level becomes an increasingly important role of the state library as the informational needs of people become more complex and published resources become more voluminous.

Furthermore, as information networks proliferate outside library auspices—such as statewide educational television systems, interuniversity computer networks, and technical information facilities such as the Educational Research Information Center (ERIC) —the state library is faced with a new dimension of coordination. It is important that the resources in libraries and the professional competence of librarians in the intellectual organization of materials be utilized in the electronic systems being developed, and that the wealth of precise information available through these networks be opened to all citizens who need it.

Finally, economy and efficiency require that compatibility be built into the various information systems being developed on a state, regional, and national level. Although the latter is essentially a problem for the Federal Government, each state library must put its own house in order and be prepared to cooperate with, and contribute to, nationwide networks.

Since the passage of the Library Services Act (LSA) in 1956, the Library Services and Construction Act (LSCA), greatly enlarged in 1964 and 1966, as well as Title II of the Elementary and Secondary Education Act (ESEA) in 1966, state libraries have played an increasing role in the local-Federal partnership for library services. Additional

---

[3] *For those states where the library functions are so scattered that there is no recognizable comprehensive state library, the recommendations in this report are understood to apply to that agency which has been designated by the governor or state attorney general to administer interlibrary cooperative projects under Title III of the Library Services and Construction Act.*

efforts at the Federal level to improve all kinds of libraries will further underscore the necessity for effective planning and administration by the comprehensive state library.

In addition to acting as an intermediary between the Federal Government and local libraries by administering aid to public and school libraries, state libraries should also provide state government with reliable, timely, and intelligently organized information. The importance of upgrading the quality of state government has been recognized, and state government has serious need for sophisticated information services. Unless state government has full access to needed resources, it cannot effectively serve its people or interpret their needs to the Federal Government.

With their many faceted responsibilities for service to state government; for administering the partnership between Federal, state, and local government in the improvement of libraries; and for participating in the development and operation of information networks within a state and region, comprehensive state libraries are basic segments of a national plan for library and information services. It is appropriate, therefore, to determine how well equipped existing state libraries are and what should be done from the Federal level to strengthen them.

ADEQUACY AND NEEDS OF STATE LIBRARIES

Cognizant of the responsibilities facing the state libraries, the Association of State Libraries of the American Library Association announced in 1960 a survey of these agencies, financed by the Carnegie Corporation. The findings, based upon detailed questionnaires and careful field work in every state during 1961–62, were summarized and commented upon in the Monypenny Report published in 1966. This survey established the fact that the organizational patterns of state libraries differed widely from state to state, as did their level of competence. The areas that emerged as the most urgent for future attention were:[4]

1. Improvement of information services to state government, with emphasis upon staffing rather than more extensive resources.
2. Greatly enriched reference and research services in the entire state by a linking of present strong collections. ("Before such a linking can be accomplished," say the researchers . . . "a staff must be recruited . . . with a considerable knowledge of specialized materials, bibliographical tools and the needs of higher specialized users.")
3. Access by the whole population of the state to a competent and professionally trained library staff. (The surveyors speculate that state-paid librarians, strategically located at major libraries and supported by superior bibliographical tools might make significant improvement in service without necessitating reorganization of library units.)
4. School, community, and junior college libraries equipped with staff and materials appropriate to their educational programs.
5. Coordination and cooperation between all types of libraries, especially school and public libraries.
6. Plans for the adequate organization of service in metropolitan areas. This planning should be concerned not only with relationships between urban and suburban libraries, but also with nongovernmental institutions and autonomous colleges and universities.
7. Service to the disadvantaged, including the blind, the partially sighted, and patients, inmates, and staff at therapeutic, protective, and correctional institutions within the state.

The overall conclusion of Dr. Monypenny and his associates was that state libraries, in order to meet their present and anticipated responsibilities, require a level of staffing—

4 *Phillip Monypenny*, The Library Functions of the States (*Chicago: American Library Association, 1966*), p. 52.

both in size and quality—which far exceeds the present experience. "The most pervasive and subtle obstacle to the achievement of the stated purpose of state libraries is the shortage of staff," he writes. "This outweighs and is reflected in other obstacles—the inadequacy of public support, the existence of divisions within the ranks of librarians in a given state, executive or legislative indifference, limitations imposed by state and local revenue."[5]

This concern about increasing and improving staff in state libraries was underscored by nearly every state librarian queried in the course of the present study. To say that state libraries must greatly expand their staffs is of course to assume substantially increased revenues from some source.

Out of the survey of library functions of the states, standards for state libraries were evolved and adopted by the American Library Association in 1963. These were conceived as *minimum* standards essential if state libraries were to meet obvious responsibilities. After the American Library Association and the United States Conference of Governors had adopted these minimum standards, each state library was asked to conduct a self-survey to measure its own performance. Not one state met all the standards. Even the larger and more advanced of the country's state libraries found themselves lacking in the important areas of service to state government; coordination of public, school, academic, and special libraries; service to inmates and staff of correctional and mental institutions; development of centralized technical processing services; and the collection, analysis, and dissemination of pertinent library statistics. Salary levels for state library administrative staff, which frequently did not compare with those for positions of comparable responsibility elsewhere in the state, were cited as a major handicap to more effective state libraries.

The obstacles faced by the nation's state libraries in attempting to meet the library responsibilities of their states fall into four basic categories: organizational, structural, statutory, and financial. Each of these is discussed below.

Organization

Recognizing the diversity among the states in their provision for library functions, the American Library Association proposed these three standards for organization of state libraries:

1. Every state should make administrative provision for the three broad areas of state library service—building and servicing of subject and reference resources, direct service to state government, and consultation service over the state—and should have qualified personnel assigned to each.
2. The several agencies dealing with the three broad areas of state library responsibility should be unified as one department or division of government to the extent possible and advisable under state law and traditions.
3. To the extent that separate library agencies remain at the state level, they should be coordinated in a clear-cut plan which provides for consultation and cooperation and which specifies division of responsibility.

The degree to which any particular state endorses the comprehensive state library concept can be assessed by applying these three guidelines to the organizational pattern of the agency or agencies that have been assigned responsibilities for library services within its boundaries.

Structure Within State Government

As state government becomes larger, more complex, and more mechanized, it becomes attractive to reorganize into fewer, larger departments in order to effect

[5] Ibid., *p. 164.*

economies by centralized purchasing, record keeping, data processing, etc., and to narrow and tighten the executive span of control. Since 1960, extensive study leading toward executive reorganization and/or constitutional revision was reported in California, Florida, Georgia, Iowa, Kentucky, Maine, Michigan, Missouri, Nevada, New Hampshire, New Mexico, New York, Oregon, Pennsylvania, Utah, Vermont, Washington, West Virginia, and Wisconsin.

Being relatively small departments of state government, state libraries tend inevitably to be absorbed in reorganization into larger agencies. Although most state libraries still function as relatively independent agencies, there does seem to be a trend toward grouping them with departments of education.

If there is such a trend, is it desirable? To the extent that state government reorganization creates a department of education that has responsibility for the coordination of all levels of education, including higher education and adult education, then this department can be viewed as *one* of the logical units within which to locate the comprehensive state library.[6] This point is somewhat academic, however, since the states do not appear to be moving toward more comprehensive departments of education. In fact, the movement is often in quite the opposite direction. Consequently, if there is a trend toward grouping state libraries with departments of education, these agencies are more likely to become identified with departments concerned only with public instruction, kindergarten through twelfth grade, and this jeopardizes the wider, coordinative mission of the state libraries.

The important basic principle, then, is that the agency or agencies providing state library services should be so placed in the structure of state government that they have the authority and status that enables them to discharge the full scope of their responsibilities effectively.

In view of the continuing interest in state government reorganization, the question of the best position within the governmental structure for a comprehensive state library deserves a good deal of further study. Reaching objective positions is difficult, not only because of the diversity in the states themselves but also because, in practice, intelligent people of good will can work together within any organizational structure and transcend some of its limitations. Nevertheless, structure and organization can be decisive factors in a good state library program.

Statutory Authority

The agency or agencies providing state library services should rest upon clear statutory provisions that define the functions to be performed, provide authority for these activities, and insure the legal basis for a flexible program to meet the needs of the state.

Because the idea, or perhaps one should say the ideal, of coordinating all library resources and services within the state into a single network or system is comparatively recent, many state libraries, whether general libraries or extension agencies, lack the statutory administrative framework to assume this leadership function. State libraries have traditionally worked in their extension activities principally with public libraries and, to a lesser extent, with school libraries. Consequently, most of these agencies need a firmer statutory base for coordinating all types of libraries in their states. It would not be inappropriate if the states were, in the future, to go even further by formulating coordinating councils that would encompass responsibility for the whole range of library and information services.

---

[6] *Even within a broadly conceived education department, a high degree of independence for library functions must be maintained to assure that library needs are not submerged by the pressing non-library demands of schools and colleges. Alternatives to incorporation into a comprehensive department of education would include grouping the state library with a cultural affairs department or with an information processing agency.*

Fiscal Support

Faulty structure, lack of statutory authority, and inadequate support often form a vicious circle. On the other hand, no structural or legal base can guarantee that the state library will be provided with sufficient fiscal support to enable it to acquire personnel and resources of quality and quantity.

There is a critical personnel problem in state libraries—in 1965–66, state libraries reported a 16 percent professional vacancy rate, in comparison to a 10.2 percent average vacancy rate for all types of libraries in the country. This related very directly to a lack of state support, as does the common failure of state libraries to provide quality information services to state government, even minimal library service to inmates of institutions, or really adequate backstopping of the library collections of the state.

In the pilot gathering of statistics on state libraries, undertaken in September 1966 by the State Library Statistics Committee of the American Library Association, only 20 state libraries, out of 35 responding, reported that they had added over 10,000 volumes in the previous year. Most of the agencies reported collections in the 200,000 to 500,000 range, a slender resource to supplement the library collections of any state. Yet another indication of the lack of state support of state libraries is their inferior housing, often in rented, warehouse-type quarters.

There is ample evidence throughout the nation that while the Federal programs have placed new burdens on state libraries, they frequently have not resulted in significant improvement of state support of the state library per se. State librarians are concerned about the increasing tendency on the part of state administrations and legislatures to let the Federal Government support the state library. It is regrettable that such a large portion of the expenditures under LSCA Title I has had to go into strengthening state libraries themselves, rather than into the direct improvement of local public library systems.

SUMMARY OF PROBLEMS

If one accepts the views detailed above—in particular, that state libraries play a key role in the partnership between local communities, the states, and the Federal Government in the improvement of libraries and in the coordination of a wide variety of essential information services—then one must also face the fact that state libraries, on the whole, are not really adequate to their responsibilities. As of 1967 no state library in the nation fully met the minimum standards adopted by the American Library Association. Although many state libraries have grown in competence and prestige since the Library Services Act was first passed in 1956, most of these agencies are still plagued by the following limitations:

1. Service to state government has not grown in proportion to the growth in public library extension services, which has been accelerated by categorical Federal aid.
2. State support for local library service is, with few exceptions, pitifully inadequate. It is true that local support of public libraries has increased substantially since 1956, and there is evidence that the Library Services and Construction Act has stimulated increases in state aid to local public libraries and that it has resulted in the establishment of state aid in nine states. But whereas these increases in state aid to public libraries are often large percentagewise, only a few states appropriate significant *per capita amounts* of state aid for public libraries. School libraries across the nation are, in turn, at a stage of development where public libraries were in 1956, striving not so much for excellence as for coverage. Community college libraries almost universally fall below standard. As inadequate as state support of all types of local libraries is, however, the lack of state support of state library agencies is even more striking and does not appear to

have been influenced thus far by Federal library legislation. Equitable means for stimulating states to assume the full measure of their financial responsibilities for library and information services need to be ascertained and implemented.

3. Clear statutory authorization for the coordination of all kinds of library service is lacking in many states. Official coordinating councils on library and information services, encompassing all types of libraries, do not exist in any state.

4. The rural orientation of most state libraries, reflecting the prereapportionment rural imbalance in state legislatures themselves, was intensified by the Library Services Act. Despite the fact that the population restriction was removed from the Library Services and Construction Act in 1964, many state libraries do not yet work effectively with metropolitan libraries. One reason may be that the state libraries' weaknesses in personnel and resources have prevented these agencies from developing meaningful partnerships with urban libraries—whose interests frequently center on the middle-class suburban reader—that would result in programs focusing on the problems of the inner-city resident.

5. State libraries generally are not conducting research into the library problems of their states and are simply not tooled to gather, interpret, and disseminate statistics for all kinds of libraries with sufficient speed and depth. Finding reliable and meaningful library statistics less than two years old, especially for other than public libraries, is virtually impossible in most states.

6. An evident symptom, and at the same time a cause, of the above five problems is the critical lack, in both quantitative and qualitative terms, of professional manpower in state libraries. This condition reflects the general shortage in this country of competent manpower. It also stems, however, from low budgets and the noncompetitive salary schedules prevalent in these agencies. According to salary data collected in June 1967, ten state librarians were paid less than $10,000 and only five received over $18,000. Probably in no state is the salary of the state librarian on a level with that of the director of the principal public or academic library in the state.

7. Most state libraries fail to use modern communications technology, although the scope of their operation demands it.

In summary, state libraries too often are still low in the esteem of state government and low in the hierarchy of libraries within their state.

SUGGESTED APPROACHES TO PROBLEM-SOLVING

In order to improve state libraries, it was suggested that the National Advisory Commission on Libraries might recommend one or several of the following alternatives for public policy. In general, these suggestions are listed according to their relative priorities.

1. A title should be added to the Library Services and Construction Act to strengthen the state library agencies, somewhat in the pattern of ESEA Title V. This might provide to the states, distributed according to the formula used in LSCA, funds for such activities as:

   a. expanding the depth and range of state library collections to facilitate back-stopping of local library services;

   b. providing program leadership;

   c. coordinating library planning on a statewide basis;

   d. conducting periodic and continuing evaluation of state and local library problems;

   e. collecting, processing, recording, analyzing, interpreting, and reporting state and local library data;

   f. disseminating information on conditions, needs, and the current status of libraries;

g. publishing and distributing bibliographies and indexes;

h. conducting studies or providing support for studies concerning the financing of libraries;

i. providing local libraries with consultant and technical assistance; and

j. conducting workshops and other programs for librarians and library trustees.

The two years' experience with ESEA Title V would seem to document that direct categorical aid to strengthen a state agency is productive. Most state education departments have, in fact, moved to evaluate their programs and activities, identify their strengths and weaknesses and establish priorities for program improvement. It is significant that progress has been particularly evident in the strengthening of professional staff—the one area where state libraries are most in need of assistance.

As in Title V, the clear purpose of this title in the Library Services and Construction Act might be to secure more encouragement and support for the comprehensive state libraries from the state legislature and executive branch. Funds should be free for at least three years with strict provision for maintenance of effort by the states. The theory that categorical aid acts as a primer to state and local effort seems to be borne out in improved public library support and would suggest that a "Title V," Library Services and Construction Act, might also lead to improved support of state libraries by the states.

2. Deal directly with the staff problem by providing state libraries with funds for salary reimbursement for a position of research and development specialist, either on the state library staff or at a selected library school. Appropriations might be used for sabbaticals, further education, exchanges for key state library staff, or institutes at colleges and universities to upgrade state library staff. It should be pointed out, however, that such institutes could now be funded under Title II-B of the Higher Education Act.

3. Provide categorical aid to state libraries to coordinate and improve special information services to state government. This should be contingent on a state plan for the coordination and development of these services; it should be a free grant for a period of about three years (with assurance of maintenance of effort by the states), after which it could be either on a matching basis or be phased out to the states completely. One argument for the latter alternative is that such information services will be broadly utilized by the people in state government only if the state government itself has a direct responsibility for the cost of these services.

Strengthening state libraries generally with an LSCA Title V could also lead to improved services to state government, but the need for this service is so serious and so generally perceived that categorical aid seems justified. A plan for the development of services to state government might have the fringe benefit of integrating library services in those states where fragmentation remains a problem.

4. Add a Title I-A to the Library Services and Construction Act for library services to the disadvantaged. Libraries, like other social agencies, have on the whole failed to organize the record of human civilization so as to make its values meaningful to the disadvantaged. State libraries should supply leadership by in-service training of librarians working in inner cities and rural Appalachias; by encouraging innovative programs; by channeling funds and ideas; and by serving as catalysts to bring together community leaders, representatives from the group to be served, volunteers, persons from other disciplines (educators, social workers, clergy, etc.), and librarians to plan an all-out assault on this most urgent and difficult problem. Funds might be used for

staff, materials, equipment and/or rent, and should channel to the large cities, the Appalachias, Ozarks, and to the Indian, Eskimo, Mexican, and migrant worker enclaves.

An alternative suggestion would be to encourage the use of LSCA Title I-A funds for library services in metropolitan areas with priority given to innovative projects to serve the disadvantaged, since LSCA Title III should be providing monies for the other major aspect of the metropolitan library problem—the sharing of research resources. However, this alternative might be too inflexible for easy administration and it would exclude assistance to the disadvantaged on Indian reservations, etc.

5. The riots of the summer of 1967 and spring of 1968 have taught us that the focal point of the social problems of the disadvantaged lies in the great cities— the 59 major metropolitan areas. An alternative to suggestion 4 would be to amend the Demonstration Cities and Metropolitan Development Act of 1966 to provide funds directly to large metropolitan libraries for innovative projects with the disadvantaged. There is some reason to believe that unless Federal aid is direct, metropolitan libraries will not get the amounts they need to support programs of meaningful scope. The legislation might be flexible, with state libraries, metropolitan libraries, and universities eligible to apply for grants. This would recognize the diversity within states and enable the best talent, wherever it is, to attend to this crucial need.

If such legislation is attached to the Demonstration Cities and Metropolitan Development Act rather than to the Library Services and Construction Act, grants should clear through state libraries to insure integration with the total state plan for library development. In the interest of coordination and economy, administration of such a library title should probably be transferred from Housing and Urban Development to the Division of Library Services of the Department of Health, Education, and Welfare.

Although emphasis in both alternatives 4 and 5 should be on *action* programs involving cooperation between the library, other agencies, and lay personnel, funds should be provided to encourage wide dissemination of the insights and ideas that result from these efforts.

6. Research geared to practical action is urgently needed in several areas.

a. What is the "fair share" formula—Federal-state-local—to support libraries of all kinds? Some guesses have been made for public library service based on a formula first proposed to a Presidential Advisory Committee on Education by Carleton Joeckel in 1938. In 1948, with Amy Winslow, Joeckel proposed a formula for public library support of 60 percent local, 25 percent state, and 15 percent Federal. At an Allerton Park Institute in 1961, Hannis Smith proposed a support formula of 40 percent local, 40 percent state, and 20 percent Federal. In 1964, Lowell Martin proposed as a reasonable ratio 50 percent local, 30 percent state, and 20 percent Federal. All of these proposals are in striking contrast to the actual pattern of support in 1964, which was 81.1 percent local, 8.6 percent state, 2.1 percent Federal, and 7.5 percent from library fines and endowments.

Of course, an investigation of a fair-share formula immediately leads to the thorny problem of equalization. But if the source of *public library* support is based on very slender investigation, the problem of a fair-share ratio for support of school, academic, and state libraries has not been faced at all. There is, in addition, the very practical question of what proportion of the total public purse should be invested in each kind of library and in all libraries. In directing the agency charged with statewide planning for library development, state librarians need dependable guidelines. Indeed, the library profession itself requires more than educated guesses to impress legislative or Congressional appropriation bodies.

b. In the coordination of all library resources and services, what needs to be duplicated and what should be shared? Some guidelines based on solid investigation are urgently needed.

c. Are there new ways to organize for integrated library service which overlook the traditional barriers between types of library—school, public, academic, and special?

d. In the planning for library systems, does current technology suggest an organization of materials based on the subject boundaries of the library users' needs rather than along geographic boundaries?

e. Research is required to determine precisely what effect the provision of library service has on the well-being of the community. What is the appropriate role of the school, public, academic, research, and/or special library in the community's endeavors to meet its informational requirements? Given a particular set of community characteristics, what kinds of programs for library service involving which types of libraries represent the soundest community investment?

Every state library is confronted with such long-range, serious questions. Most lack the funds to pursue any of them. Federal monies to add a research consultant to each state library, as per suggestion 2, might get the job started. Substantially increased appropriations for library research in Title II-B of the Higher Education Act would also be a channel. Research at the Federal level by the Division of Library Services should be promoted, since many of the required inquiries need to be coordinated at the Federal level. At the very least, the Division of Library Services should be geared to collect and disseminate current library statistics on a national level, a capacity which seems to have been lost in the last reorganization of the Department of Health, Education, and Welfare.

7. Every state has a book gap—a variation from nationally accepted standards—in all kinds of libraries. When budgets are tight, as they perennially are, the book funds are inevitably curtailed as the only substantial part of a library budget with flexibility. Substantial grants, based upon a *coordinated plan,* might be made to the states to close the book gap in state, public, school, academic, and special libraries. Such action should encourage statewide planning and would represent an appealing supplement to Title III of LSCA, Title II of HEA, and Title II of ESEA. It should have immediately felt results. Such a program might be free of matching provisions for about three years, then either put on a matching basis or phased out entirely. It would need to be safeguarded by stringent provision for maintenance of state and local effort. Funds should be included for staff and equipment to support the acquisition and processing of material as well as for its purchase. Unless a program of this nature is undertaken, the chance of closing the gap between the standards and reality seems remote.

8. One of the problems of the library profession which a "book gap program" would intensify is the question of the validity of the so-called "national standards" for materials in all kinds of libraries. Anyone who has tried to justify these standards to appropriating bodies knows how difficult they are to document. Furthermore, it is impossible to specify the kind and level of gaps—if any—that would exist if users actually had access to all the library resources in their area. The National Advisory Commission on Libraries might, there-

fore, underscore the need for scientific research into the nature and application of meaningful standards for assessing the adequacy of materials in all kinds and sizes of libraries in a particular region.

9. It must be emphasized that full authorized funding for LSCA Title III would probably do more to improve library service across the nation than any proliferation of titles as recommended in suggestion 7 above.

10. A simple alternative to most of the previous suggestions would be substantially increased appropriations in Title I and Title III of LSCA. Since many states are not themselves supporting state libraries adequately, however, it would at least appear desirable to limit to specific percentages the amounts of such increases which may be used by the states for administration of each of the titles, and to add categorical titles to LSCA to strengthen the state library and to strengthen information service to state government.

 At any rate, an intensive re-examination of the matching formulas used in LSCA seems in order, to make sure that proper provision is being made for reasonable state and local support of libraries.

11. Even strengthened state libraries will continue to face the problem of their legal and administrative structure within the state government. Because the state library is a vital link in the partnership between local, state, and Federal governments, research should be encouraged on the relationship of state libraries to departments of education and on the best organization for a state library within the framework of fewer and larger units of state government.

12. Since so many states are, or shortly will be, in the throes of constitutional revision and executive reorganization, research on a model statute for state libraries could serve a very useful purpose. The recently completed report on *The Library Functions of the States* and the *Standards for Library Functions at the State Level* would be invaluable source documents for such a study.

 Although it has been argued that a model statute would be meaningless because states vary so radically in their organization and in the level of their development of library activities, research could be aimed at the development of several models for application to certain basic structures of state government organization.

13. To enable all state libraries to discharge their responsibility in the partnership between the states and the Federal Government, an up-to-the-hour index to all Federal programs funding libraries should be maintained and disseminated, perhaps by the Division of Library Services of the Department of Health, Education, and Welfare.

14. The Division of Library Services should be given capacity to provide leadership to the states, to assist them in the full utilization of all relevant Federal programs, and to assure that library components are written into the regulations for the wide spectrum of Federal legislation relating to health, education, welfare, technical information, etc.

 Furthermore, the scope of this agency's responsibilities should be broadened and strengthened to include experimentation in interstate, regional library projects. Some of the library problems of the states must be approached in a manner that necessitates interstate relations and agreements. Such large-scale programs for library service require and should receive planning attention and coordination at the national level.

15. The Library of Congress' automated cataloging program should be accelerated to include all books published. Plans should be developed for partnerships between the Library of Congress and state libraries—either singly or in regional combinations—for the latter to receive catalog copy in machine-readable form and to provide catalog cards or book-form catalogs to all libraries of every type within the state. The cost of multiple cataloging of the same book, some-

times thousands of times across the nation, represents a waste of public funds which ought not to be tolerated.

16. Federal legislation providing grants to support library services should, to the extent feasible, unify such services and strengthen the position of state libraries as coordinators of all kinds of library programs within their states.

The manner in which some Federal legislation affecting libraries has been written has encouraged inefficiencies insofar as the designation of an administering agency was left entirely to the individual states. Frequently this has resulted in further fragmentation of library services at the state level. For example, no provision was made for placing administration of ESEA Title II in any existing agency with responsibility for school libraries. Consequently, some states developed separate Title II units and now have two parallel agencies responsible for school library service.

17. Finally, since it is essential to the operations of the comprehensive state library that the Federal Government itself have a strong and well coordinated library effort, the National Advisory Commission on Libraries ought to take a strong stand on the need for a review of the organization and programs of agencies of the Federal Government engaged in providing library and information services.

EDITORIAL NOTE

The National Advisory Commission on Libraries, recognizing the problems at the state level in implementing Federal legislative efforts affecting libraries and education, did recommend very specifically the strengthening of state library agencies through the amendment of the Library Services and Construction Act to authorize aid to these agencies (see chapter 12). The need for research, so strongly emphasized in the foregoing suggestions, was also officially recognized by the Commission, as was the need for dependable annual statistics on libraries.

In its Report, the Commission did not comment on many of the recommended actions suggested to it; these omissions constitute material for future study by the continuing bodies the Commission did, in fact, recommend. Thus the several alternatives presented in the above study, and in a number of other studies, are included in this book. It is clear that the Commission recognized effective cooperation of the Federal Government with local-state-regional efforts as one of the important means of achieving its broad objectives stated in chapter 12, section C.

B. RECENT FEDERAL LIBRARY
LEGISLATION AND THE STATES:
NORTH CAROLINA AS A CASE IN POINT[7]

by THAD L. BEYLE
Assistant Professor of Political Science
University of North Carolina at Chapel Hill

In order to shed further light on the question of fragmentation of Federal efforts and weaknesses in their implementation and their coordination with regional, state, and local efforts, this brief case history sketching the library situation in one state was done

---

7 *From one of the papers comprising a report on* The Federal Government and Libraries *commissioned by the National Advisory Commission on Libraries in 1967 and conducted by a task force coordinated by R. Taylor Cole, Provost, Duke University.*

for the National Advisory Commission on Libraries. It discusses public libraries first, then school libraries, and then libraries for higher education. It concludes with a summary of trends and some possible approaches for the future.

PUBLIC LIBRARIES

FEDERAL AID AND ITS IMPACT IN NORTH CAROLINA

In 1955 North Carolina reorganized its public library program creating an active State Library. This was most propitiously, if inadvertently, timed, for the following year funds became available under the Library Services Act of 1956 (LSA) which were the responsibility of the State Library to allocate. As of 1961, these additional funds had "enabled the new agency to take on its added responsibilities in a shorter time than would otherwise have been possible. In both the State Library program and that of the (local) public libraries, the Library Services Act has made possible in five years what might have required ten years without it."[8] Some funds were used to provide additional resources and services at the State Library, but for the most part these funds have been used to stimulate and facilitate the growth of public library systems serving North Carolina's predominantly rural population.[9] This can be seen in the breakdown in Table 9B–1.

These figures indicate that the LSA program built on top of the 15-year-old state grant-in-aid program, which itself was granting $425,000 annually and which has been increased to a budgeted $794,579 in 1969. LSA made the financial "carrots" available to the State Library that are most impressive to the local public libraries.

Although it is impossible to isolate specific causes, per capita revenue for public libraries increased from 57 cents in 1956 to $1.31 in 1966. "Municipal government support has almost doubled. County support is up by over 200%. Nongovernment local contributions to libraries are also almost doubled. Thus total local support of libraries has increased from 47 cents per capita to $1.07. State grants-in-aid have increased from 10 cents to 14 cents per capita with Federal funds raising this 10 cents to 24 cents per capita."[10] These are impressive gains and represent a notable change in financing public libraries at all levels.

By other indexes there were significant gains, too. "In spite of sharply rising book costs from 1956–1966, the total volumes owned by public libraries rose more than 62 percent or from three-fourths of a book per capita in 1956 to approximately one book per capita in 1966. . . . In the meantime, circulation rose 42 percent. . . . Population without access to public library service was reduced 45 percent in the decade."[11] Of course one must be wary of figures based on "with access," because we just do not have figures on who actually does use this access. The general feeling is that such access is selective.

The figures on the first two years of activity under the Library Services and Construction Act of 1964 (LSCA) are equally impressive. In fiscal 1965, the State Library was able to plan for and allocate the state's allotment of $726,111, plus a reallocation of $132,455 from funds other states were unable to use, in aiding the construction of 12 public libraries in the state. These funds were applied on an individual library construction project basis running from a 35 percent to 60 percent Federal share, the actual

8 *State of North Carolina State Library, "North Carolina's Library Services Act Program, Five-year Summary, 1957–1961" (Raleigh: 1961), mimeo, p. 3.*
9 Ibid., *p. 1.*
10 *State of North Carolina, State Library, Fifth Biennial Report, July 1, 1964–June 30, 1966 (Raleigh: 1966), p. 33.*
11 Ibid.

percent based on an index of county wealth. In fiscal year 1966 the State Library used its full allotment ($726,111) plus a reallocation of $60,268 from other states, in aiding eleven construction projects.[12] Overall, since the passage of the 1964 Act, "29 new libraries and several major additions have been built or were under construction with Federal Aid" by the end of the summer, 1967.[13]

In 1966, the Appalachian Regional Development Program began financing some construction projects and holding promise for others in that portion of the state. The processing of these projects is through the Governor's representative to the Appalachian Regional Commission, whose staff is the State Planning Task Force in the Department of Administration. One such project was approved in 1966, and several others are under consideration at the present time.[14] Similar funding will become available under the Eastern Coastal Plain Development Region (North Carolina, South Carolina, and Georgia coastal areas) and the Economic Development Act regions currently being established.

The 1964 Governor's Commission summed it up this way: "The amount of federal aid received did not bulk large proportionately, but it has a stimulating affect on library progress in general and made possible valuable programs which otherwise could not or probably would not have been undertaken."[15] An example of this is the development in 1960 of the highly successful State Library Processing Center, with LSA funds, which orders, receives, catalogs and prepares books for circulation for 53 North Carolina library units covering 71 of the state's counties. Any public library in the state can contract with the Center for this service and thereby attain a highly professional service for minimal cost, a service which normally would not be available to the average local library or small library system.[16]

Another example is the establishment of library school scholarships "to qualified college graduates who are accepted by graduate library schools," the only obligation being that the grant is in the form of a loan that can be repaid by two years of service. Other grants are available "to public libraries to enable them to release staff members for a single semester to start or continue a graduate library science program." These funds are also provided under the Federal program.[17] In fiscal years 1965 and 1966 over $23,000 was spent for these scholarships.[18] The Library has also developed a system of personnel grants combining state and Federal money to upgrade salaries in local public libraries when certain conditions are met.

Therefore, the use of these Federal funds has been for construction of facilities, expansion of materials, increased state services to local units, and personnel upgrading. In an intriguing aside, the assistant state librarian has suggested that the building program may be the most important of these improvements as it represents a physical symbol of an improved library service and also heightens the need to upgrade materials and service.

THE STATE LIBRARY PROGRAM IN NORTH CAROLINA

At the state level in North Carolina several trends are apparent in the role that the State Library is playing. First, it can be asserted that the State Library's position has been enhanced by the newly available funds from the Federal programs. The State

12 Ibid., p. 25.
13 Elaine von Oesen, "The Growth and Development of North Carolina Public Libraries, 1942–1967," North Carolina Libraries, Vol. 25 (Fall 1967), p. 107.
14 State Library, Fifth Biennial Report, op. cit., p. 25.
15 State of North Carolina Governor's Commission on Library Resources, Resources of North Carolina Libraries, edited by Robert B. Downs (Raleigh: 1965), p. 55.
16 State Library, Fifth Biennial Report, op. cit., pp. 13–14.
17 State of North Carolina, State Library, "State Plan for Library Programs Under Library Services and Construction Act, As Amended," submitted to the U. S. Office of Education (March 9, 1967), mimeo, Plan Section Number 1.42.
18 State Library, Fifth Biennial Report, op. cit., p. 9.

Library is firmly established as the vehicle through which these funds must be funneled, and it is the Library that does the planning for their allocation. The experience of the earlier State Library Commission in the state grant-in-aid program carried out from 1941 to 1955 was instrumental in having the State Library ready to carry out the necessary planning requirements, and this had instilled in the public libraries across the state the understanding that the State Library was indeed the agency for dispensing these funds.

Second, the State Library has taken an activist stance in its relations with other state-level agencies and programs. It is no longer content to be seen as a repository of books. For example, the Library has taken an active and positive interest in working with the Governor's Office and the State Planning Task Force in the development of the Appalachian Regional Development Program. They responded early and quickly to a call for information and projects, and have succeeded in placing public libraries into the development scheme for Appalachia. The Library extension staff has also been active in various workshops connected with the Appalachia program to make sure the word gets out that the libraries are an integral part of the development effort.

In the same vein, the Library staff was active in the new state planning program, begun in 1964, and cooperated very closely during each of the stages of development. As a result of this and the Appalachia program, there have been some close relationships created between the State Library and the State Planning Task Force in the Department of Administration. This is important since it gives the Library access to the strong Department of Administration, the Governor's fiscal and management arm, in another form (programs and planning), rather than just through the normal budgetary process. The Library has also been working closely, again in a program and planning sense, with such state agencies as Juvenile Corrections, Mental Health, Prisons, Community Colleges, and the North Carolina Fund, which is the private, state-wide anti-poverty program established in 1963.

A third broad trend evident from this cursory glance is the rise in importance of adequate planning at all levels. Although the state had an allocation formula for its grant-in-aid program prior to 1956, it was only with the advent of the Library Services Act activities that planning became an integral part of the library process in the state. This has taken the form of individual project planning at the local level. "Careful planning prior to designing a building for even the smallest library is a fairly recent trend. It has not been too long ago that the appearance of a benefactor with funds, or the legacy of them, was the signal to call in the architect to build the 'best building possible' for the funds at hand. Only larger library buildings were professionally planned. . . . Since the program for LSCA projects must be approved by the State Library, the community has a further safeguard against an inadequate building."[19] As a particular requirement for the LSA and LSCA, the State Library has been called on to evaluate and relate local plans to the goals set under these acts. This means, at a minimum, a broader focus than architectural design has been established under these acts. Further, the realization that all the library resources in the state should be considered as part of an overall system brought to the fore the need to take such an overview, fostering the Governor's Commission on Library Resources, which reported its findings in 1965, and the current legislative commission studying public library financing across the state.

In addition, planning is going on in collateral activities that have a great bearing on library activities. All the new Federal grant-in-aid programs, such as the Elementary and Secondary Education Act of 1965, the Higher Education Act of 1965, and the Appalachia program, noted earlier, involve an active planning process. Local planning studies under the Department of Housing and Urban Development's "701" local planning assistance program also have an impact on libraries—not always positive. "Sometimes

19 *Elaine von Oesen, "Trends in Recent Public Library Buildings,"* North Carolina Libraries, *Vol. 25 (Spring 1967), pp. 39–40.*

such studies are inclined to put public libraries in a 'cultural complex' rather than in the preferred foot traffic area. It is important that the librarian be involved when these studies are being made."[20]

The final trend to be set out has been explicit throughout the discussion and need only be reiterated briefly. Since 1956, there has been a rapid increase in funds available for public libraries in the state from all levels of government. Who caused what is impossible to tell, but it has happened, and happened dramatically. Whether it is enough is another question outside the author's ability to answer except as follows.

If there have been weaknesses throughout this recent history of State Library activity, one can certainly be found in the basic state support given to the Library itself. The total appropriations that sustain the activities of the Library have risen nearly threefold in the decade, from $82,000 in 1956 to $235,000 in 1966.[21] And they will be increased to $264,000 in fiscal year 1968.[22] This is still not enough for the Library to carry out the services it could with adequate staff. Closely allied to this is the fact that the state merit system has classified library positions at such a level that even if the budget does open up more positions, the salary scales are too low to attract the needed people.

Additionally, the State Library in North Carolina for years has needed additional space and more up-to-date facilities. In 1963, the General Assembly allocated the funds to build a joint State Library and Department of Archives and History building in an attempt to solve the space and facility problems of both agencies. After several years of delay the building was begun and will be finished within the next year, but it will not sufficiently meet the needs of both agencies. One agency had to bend in the plans and it was the State Library: "the State Library was to occupy only 40 percent of the proposed building . . . which would not appreciably relieve its space needs. . . . As a matter of fact, there was no possibility of squeezing all of the Divisions of the State Library into the allotted space, and it was feared that rising construction costs might further limit space or equipment or both."[23]

So in terms of money, personnel, and facilities, there is a serious question of the overall state commitment to the concept of a total, comprehensive State Library. Therefore, Federal funds that can be used to support, in part or in whole, the necessary functions of the State Library (planning, processing center, grants-in-aid, construction money) are even more important to the overall operation of the State Library program than Federal grants to most other areas of government concern. Although there is no real proof, these funds seem to go further than other Federal program dollars—if for no other reason, because they have much further to go since the base is so low.

Another weakness in the State Library program lies in the planning and allocation process itself. Some observers have been critical of the tightness with which the plans are drawn and how the money is allocated—especially with respect to the smaller, non-regional library unit areas which are not as likely to receive funds under the planning criteria, which are biased toward regional or multicounty efforts. The planning criteria are quite specific on the priorities for construction grants since: "Federal funds available will not be sufficient for all pending approvable applications." The priorities are listed in this order: statewide service buildings; regional or multicounty headquarters; county headquarters; county and regional branches; and, finally "if funds remain available," municipal libraries not participating in a county or regional system.[24] It could be argued

---

[20] Ibid., p. 41.
[21] S. Janice Kee, "Library Services and Legislation," Book of the States, 1956–57 (Chicago: Council of State Governments, 1957), p. 272.
[22] Information provided by the State Librarian.
[23] State Library, Fifth Biennial Report, op. cit., p. 9.
[24] State Library, "State Plan for Library Programs . . . ," op. cit., Plan Section Number 3.1

that there is need for such pinpointing of investment, otherwise the limited funds could be frittered away across the landscape of the state.

What may be an even more significant criticism in the long run in the planning and allocation process is the lack of construction funds that have found their way into the urban areas of North Carolina to date. Considering the 23 construction grants made in fiscal 1965 and 1966, only two of the state's ten largest urban areas received direct construction grants, the Greensboro and Raleigh branch libraries. These were for only $138,279 out of a total of $1,658,193 Federal construction funds available, or slightly over 8 percent of the funds. Although there may be disagreement about this situation (e.g., the major urban areas having built their facilities earlier), state and Federal per capita support figures, for the various library systems across the state, show the urban systems toward the lower end of the stick consistently.[25] This bias is maintained by the allocation of the state grant-in-aid program and the library services portion of the Federal funds on a basic county or multicounty formula, and one can see that there remains a rural bias in the allocation of all these funds. Furthermore, there is no specific urban focus, and North Carolina is a state that is rapidly urbanizing. There are many factors at work here, among them the very structure of the Federal programs themselves plus the old-time rural bias in the state.

PATTERNS IN OTHER STATES

It is sometimes hard to develop comparable data across states, but there is some evidence that the trends and the criticisms cited above are not unique to North Carolina but to the states in general in the public library area. First, in terms of public dollars spent on public libraries, between 1956 and 1966 total expenditures rose significantly under the plans filed by the states for the Library Services and Construction Act. During the eight years, 1956 to 1964, when the LSA was rural in orientation, there was an increase of 119 percent in public funds spent, with the states increasing their appropriations by 135 percent. In the first two years of the amended program under LSCA, there has been an increase of 6.3 percent in public funds spent, with the states increasing by 10.9 percent. "Total expenditures for services under State plans for fiscal years 1957–1966 were $412.2 million. Of this amount, $167.9 million (41 percent) were local funds; $145.2 million (35 percent), state funds; and $99.1 million (24 percent), Federal funds. . . . But as a group, the states overmatched the amount of state and local funds required to obtain Federal funds."[26] A similar pattern is seen from the preliminary figures under the construction portion of the program. During fiscal 1965 a total of $99.6 billion was spent or obligated, $29.9 million federal and $69.8 state and local.[27] These figures do not include the amounts spent that were not part of the LSA or LSCA plans at the state and local level, which would show even further increases in effort.

In terms of grants-in-aid to local units, in 1956 there was only one state with a program of greater proportion than that of North Carolina, and that was New York with a program estimated at $2.34 million.[28] And there were at least 26 states without any grant-in-aid program at all in 1957–1958.[29] By fiscal 1965, this was reduced to 20 states without a program, and there were nine states with larger grant-in-aid programs than North Carolina—starting with New York at $9.7 million and Pennsylvania at $2.6 million, with Georgia, Maryland, New Jersey, Massachusetts, California, Kentucky, and

25 *State Library*, Fifth Biennial Report, op. cit., *pp. 25–28 and information supplied by the State Library.*
26 *John C. Frantz, and Nathan M. Cohen*, "The Federal Government and Public Libraries: A Ten-Year Partnership, 1957–1966," Health, Education, and Welfare Indicators (*Washington: Government Printing Office, July 1966*), *pp. 4–5.*
27 Ibid., *pp. 18–19.*
28 *Kee.* op. cit., *p. 272.*
29 *Eleanor A. Ferguson*, "Library Services and Legislation," Book of the States, 1958–59 (*Chicago: Council of State Governments, 1959*), p. 285.

Michigan following in order of magnitude.[30] However, although there was a total of $23.5 million allocated to state grant-in-aid programs to local units in fiscal year 1965, more than $18 million of this was from six states, another $3.2 million was from the next six states, for $21.5 million of the $23.5 million total. Hawaii has a totally integrated system, with all public library and state library support included in the 1965 agency appropriation of $2.3 million.[31]

Thus, at least on the basis of reading the written records, there is a distinctly varied pattern, running from 20 states without any program of state aid at all, to 17 with total programs amounting to $2 million, to 6 with total programs amounting to $3.2 million, to 6 with programs amounting to $18.3 million. But the direction is upwards, and more states are initiating programs and increasing their expenditures.

There can be little doubt that the LSA program had a stimulative effect on these state grant programs. Phillip Monypenny observed in his report for the American Association of State Libraries, "The available evidence does not suggest that Federal aid diminished the extent of support from state funds, but rather that it tended to increase it. Federal aid seems even to have added to the status of library agencies and hence made it possible for them to get increased state support. The data show that state appropriations increased sharply for agencies receiving federal grants once those grants became available."[32]

Across the states and in the local units, the Federal funds were spent in varying patterns, each state differing according to the priorities established in its state plan, and reflecting the varying needs. The pattern through 1966 indicates that the money has been spread to cover many different needs (Table 9B–2). By any index, the library services available to the people have increased.

There have also been many new programs and techniques developed with the LSA funds. As Monypenny indicated, LSA "has provided money for experiment and innovation which would not ordinarily have been available from state sources. . . . federal grant money is relatively free."[33] He also found that the LSA money had led to the expansion of library consultant staffs for local units, to surveys and proposals for regional development, to increased book collections and other library materials, to more equipment such as bookmobiles, and to a myriad of library demonstrations.[34]

The picture seems to show clearly that much new activity has been going on while traditional functions have also been buttressed. Money is obviously the catalyst, and although the total of Federal funds may not have been great, Federal aid is most often seen as the direct agent of change throughout the country.

There also appears to have been some upgrading of the state agencies. Roger H. McDonough, Director of the New Jersey State Library, talked to this point in 1961: ". . . the improvement in our state library agencies is one of the principal accomplishments of the Library Services Act. . . . State after state reported strengthened state library agencies in all parts of the country."[35] Unfortunately, the evidence available does not allow one to relate the change noted in North Carolina to a more activist orientation.

30 Eleanor A. Ferguson, "Library Services and Legislation," Book of the States, 1966–67 (Chicago: Council of State Governments, 1967), p. 306.
31 Ibid.
32 Phillip Monypenny, The Library Functions of the States (Chicago: American Library Association, 1966), p. 91.
33 Phillip Monypenny, "LSA: A Political Scientist's View," in Donald E. Strout, (ed.), The Impact of the Library Services Act: Progress and Potential (Champaign: The Illini Union Bookstore, 1962), p. 108. See also a listing of such experiments and innovations in Frantz and Cohen, op. cit., pp. 10–11. The American Library Association also obtained similar information in a 1966 survey, see S. Janice Kee, "The Impact of Federal Legislation on Public Libraries," in Winifred Ladley, (ed.), Federal Legislation for Libraries (Champaign: The Illini Union Bookstore, 1967), pp. 13–14.
34 Monypenny, The Library Functions of the States, op. cit., pp. 92–93.
35 Roger H. McDonough, "LSA and State Library Agencies," in Strout, op. cit., p. 40.

The trend toward more planning is also a nationwide phenomenon. From the 1940's to the mid-1950's there were about four published statewide plans or surveys each year. After the introduction of Federal aid, this figure rose to five per year; in 1962, it was eight; and in 1963, it was nine. These are over and above the LSA plans submitted by law to the United States Office of Education. Overall, "twenty-four of the forty-one plans and surveys (conducted since 1956) have been or are being financed out of federal funds."[36] There would seem to be no denying that Federal funds have come hand-in-hand with state efforts to re-evaluate goals and means to these goals. This is a most important factor in any system's ability to provide adequate and more effective service.

But by no means has this planning of services and facilities been uniform throughout the country. "Money alone could not make good the deficiencies in planning resulting from earlier neglect of state responsibility, or overcome the inherent difficulties of providing local service in states with vast areas, small populations, and low levels of taxable resources. The difficulties some states faced meant that in those states in the early years of the Act Federal funds were largely passed on to existing local units with no effective requirements of improved conditions of service. Planning improved during these years but still leaves much to be desired."[37] But, as an aside, this sort of comment could and should be made about many other areas of governmental action that are priding themselves on how well planned their activities are. Planning as an art or profession still has some distance to go—and above all it is no panacea if it isn't translated into effective action.

Evidence throughout the country on appropriations for the basic state library service is not clear. As of 1955, three quarters of those in charge of state agencies did not consider their appropriations adequate. Appropriations were, however, increasing in size. Four states showed an increase in 1952; there were 27 with increases in the 1953 legislative sessions; and in 1955, 34 legislatures increased their appropriations for state library services.[38] So even prior to the enactment of LSA, there appeared to be substantial upward movement in these budgets. By 1961, the estimated appropriation for these state agencies was $13.2 million, and the figure rose to $16.2 million by fiscal year 1965.[39]

Still, Phillip Monypenny noted in 1961: ". . . that small as the total sum (LSA) to be distributed was, limited as the purposes were which could be directly supported by the grants made available, these small grants, nevertheless, have virtually doubled the appropriation of a good many state library agencies in the United States, a fact which only underlines how thoroughly inadequate the state support of these activities has been and still is." Thus, like North Carolina, the states in general have been increasing their appropriations for state library services, but probably at a lesser level than is really needed.[40]

Finally, it should be noted that there are no real hard data on just where all these funds have been expended throughout the nation. But there is much talk on how the rural orientation of the first eight years of the Library Services Act has focused money on the rural areas, and that the amendment of 1964, which opened up aid to the urban areas, was much needed. A good guess is that by and large the rural orientation of the Act built on the rural bias that still resides in too many state governments. How quickly and well the 1964 Act reverses this is unknown.

36 Charles A. Bunge, "Statewide Library Surveys and Plans: Development of the Concept and Some Recent Patterns," The Library Quarterly 36 (January 1966), pp. 28, 33.
37 Monypenny, The Library Functions of the States, op. cit., p. 102.
38 S. Janice Kee, "Library Services and Legislation," Book of the States, 1954–55 (Chicago: The Council of State Governments, 1955), p. 260; also the 1956–57 edition, p. 269.
39 Eleanor A. Ferguson, "Library Services and Legislation," Book of the States, 1962–63, p. 333, and Eleanor A. Ferguson, "Library Services and Legislation," Book of the States, 1966–67, p. 306.
40 Monypenny, "LSA: A Political Scientist's View," op. cit., p. 99.

SCHOOL LIBRARIES

FEDERAL AID AND ITS IMPACT IN NORTH CAROLINA

A discussion of just what has happened in North Carolina and the other states under the programs of aid to elementary and secondary school libraries cannot be as extensive or complete as that of public libraries. Most of the programs are new and, although the money has been out there at work, it is still too early to get any reading on the full implications of its impact. Yet there are several things which are beginning to become evident in North Carolina, and possibly from what limited comments there are, in other states also.

Title III of the National Defense Education Act of 1958 (NDEA) has been providing funds to the state for eight fiscal years of record. Title III grants are made to acquire equipment and materials that will strengthen instruction in science, mathematics, history, civics, geography, modern foreign languages, English, reading, and economics. The North Carolina state agency, the Department of Public Instruction, through the division of Federal-State Relations, developed the state plan which had to be approved by the United States Office of Education and which contains the criteria of allocation and priority of action. But Title III program development in North Carolina has been done largely by the staffs of the local school administrative units.[41]

During this period of time there has been a total expenditure of $29.1 million at the local level, of which $14.5 million has been Federal funds. There have been 18,662 different projects approved for over 170 separate units—which included schools under the direction of the State School for Blind and Deaf, the State Board of Juvenile Correction, the North Carolina School of the Arts, the State Board of Mental Health, and the Governor's School. In fiscal 1966 alone, this title bought 438,000 volumes for 172 participating units.[42]

The local school superintendents were asked after fiscal 1965 what the effects of this program were in their view. Most of the comments had to do with instruction in particular course areas, but most indicated improvement in other areas, including libraries, through the increased purchasing power under the NDEA project grants. The North Carolina data on library expenditures and library volumes per pupil bear this out. In 1957–58 there were 5.5 volumes per pupil and expenditure of $1.50 per pupil for all library materials and supplies. By fiscal 1965 the year before the Elementary and Secondary Education Act (ESEA) went into effect, there were 7.97 volumes per pupil and an expenditure of $4.70 per pupil for all library materials and supplies.[43]

In 1965, the Elementary and Secondary Education Act became the first Federal general-aid program to the schools. Of interest to this paper are Titles I and II. Title I funds are the so-called "poverty-index" monies which are available to aid schools with certain levels of low-income families. The money can be used for additional staff, facilities, and equipment, based generally on the overall state plan and specifically on the project application for funds from the local unit. State supervision of the program in North Carolina is again in the Federal-State Relations Division of the Department of Public Instruction. But the key for any library component lies at the local level, for such a component must come up as part of local unit projects. Evidently there has been an

41 *State of North Carolina, Department of Public Instruction,* National Defense Education Act, Summary Report, 1965–66 *(Raleigh: 1966), p. 1.*
42 *State of North Carolina, Department of Public Instruction,* National Defense Education Act *(Raleigh: 1966), mimeo, p. 3; also Cora Paul Bomar, "The Impact of Federal Legislation on School Libraries," in Ladley, op. cit., p. 29.*
43 *State of North Carolina, Department of Public Instruction,* "State School Facts," North Carolina Public School Bulletin, *31 (March 1967), pp. 8–9.*

active articulation of this at the local level in this state, for under Title I in fiscal 1966 "over 700 positions were funded for library or instructional material supervisors, school librarians, and library aides."[44] This is in addition to the recent increases of school librarians the state itself has provided by state funds—474 in 1961 rising to 782 by 1965. Also, these data indicate the relatively low level of priority that library facilities and support must have had prior to these Federal grant programs.

There were also some library materials acquired throughout the state under this title. The budget "includes funds for instructional and professional materials administered through the Education Information Library and through the Center for Learning Resources," under the supervision of the Educational Media Section of The Department of Public Instruction.[45]

Title II of ESEA provides funds for the acquisition of instructional materials, school library resources, textbooks, etc. None of these funds may be used for personnel, equipment, or facilities. State supervision of this program in North Carolina is in the Educational Media Section of the Department of Public Instruction. As we noted above, this section has some responsibility for funds under Title I, but has the major responsibility for Title II funds. These funds were allocated in: "(1) an initial allotment of $1.00 per child for the acquisition of library books; (2) a special supplemental allotment for a few school administrative units for the acquisition of a full complement of school library resources for a limited number of demonstration school libraries; and (3) a relative need allotment based on a relative need index which took into consideration quantity of school library resources, textbooks, and other printed and published instructional materials available in relation to quantity needed and the recent local effort made to supply the needed materials."[46]

The plan for allocating the funds was drawn deliberately in a flexible manner so that local units had the opportunity to make several choices.[47] In fiscal year 1966, $1.2 million was allocated on the per-pupil basis; $75,000 for the Demonstration School projects; and, $1.1 million for the Relative Need Allotment.[48] Under this, the Department of Public Instruction estimates that 536,058 volumes were added to the school libraries in the state.[49]

The program with the least funds is the one for Demonstration School Library projects. In this program, funds are placed in already "good schools for the acquisition of a wide variety of library materials so that these schools can then serve as demonstration centers." This year (fiscal year 1968) there will be 26 demonstration school libraries in operation.[50] Of course this program's impact is a good distance away, but generally this indicates that the Federal funds can be used for new ideas, experiments, and demonstrations—and ones which would not normally receive state support.

In the short period that ESEA has been operating there have been some notable changes as measured by expenditures and resources per pupil. The expenditures per pupil in North Carolina jumped from $.71 in 1964 to $5.41 at the end of fiscal year 1966 and the number of volumes per pupil increased from 7.97 to 8.64 at the same time. Overall, in fiscal year 1966 it was estimated that $8 million was spent in the acquisition of library resources and materials—$2 million local funds; $2 million state funds; and, $4 million Federal funds—so that 50 percent of the total expenditure was Federal in origin.[51]

44 *State of North Carolina, Department of Public Instruction*, Annual Report, Fiscal 1966, Title II, P.L. 89–10, Elementary and Secondary Education Act *(Raleigh: 1966), p. 13.*
45 *Bomar, "The Impact of Federal Legislation on School Libraries,"* op. cit., *p. 28.*
46 Ibid., *p. 9.*
47 *Information provided by the Department of Public Instruction.*
48 *Department of Public Instruction,* Educational Media Bulletin *I (Fall 1966), p. 9.*
49 *Department of Public Instruction,* Annual Report, Fiscal 1966, Title II. . . . op. cit.
50 *Bomar, "Public School Libraries: Two and a Half. . . ."* op. cit., *p 8*
51 *Department of Public Instruction,* "State School Facts," loc. cit.

As with the public libraries, this increase in funds seems to have led to a strengthening of the state agency responsible for planning and allocating the Federal funds. For example, there has been a reorganization within North Carolina's Department of Public Instruction to consolidate some similar activities into the Educational Media Section. And several services have been established with the use of Federal funds which will aid the department in carrying out its activities and be of specific service to local units.

Expenditures for library materials, resources, and personnel from all sources are rapidly increasing. The figures over the last few years indicate that there have been significant increases in North Carolina, and one can only project a continuation of this. Certainly the Federal role here has been the most significant; witness its 50 percent portion of expenditures for library resources and materials in 1966. As with the public library area, the observer senses that a large amount of planning is under way at the state and local level. So far it may be that it is mainly project and program oriented.

COORDINATION OF PROGRAMS AT STATE AND LOCAL LEVELS IN NORTH CAROLINA

Evidence on how these programs are coordinated at the state and local level are not readily available—and possibly for a reason. First, there is some confusion in the state's Department of Public Instruction, at least from the outsider's point of view, as to just who is in charge of what. An example of how such confusion can be raised is contained in the following quote from a report on coordination of Federal programs at the state level:[52]

(1) NDEA. Staff served on planning committees to develop State Plan for ESEA Title II, using to advantage experience gained through participation in NDEA Titles III and V State Level activities. Later the NDEA Title III Accountant and the NDEA Title III Instructional Materials Supervisor transferred to ESEA Title II. NDEA Title III and EDEA Title II staffs work cooperatively on procedures, project approval, and evaluation of both programs. NDEA funds help support two offices directly integrated with ESEA Title II. . . .

(2) ESEA Titles I, III, and V. . . . The Title I Auditor supervises the work of the Title II Auditor. ESEA Title II staff members serve on Titles I and II State Committees. . . .

(3) The newly created Educational Media Section . . . is funded through eight separate budgets: regular State budget, three NDEA Title III budgets, ESEA Title I budget, ESEA Title II budget, and two ESEA Title V budgets.

It is no wonder that the first item listed in the same report as to what the local education units must do is:

(1) The usual pattern in North Carolina is for the *local educational agency to coordinate* ESEA Title II with ESEA Title I and NDEA Title III. The few school systems that have ESEA Title III projects and the school systems participating in the EOA Neighborhood Youth Programs coordinate these programs with ESEA Title II. [Emphasis supplied.]

There is no common plan, and for that matter there is no common staff. So it falls to the local level to develop all these plans and to seek the correct staff at the state level. Although the Department of Public Instruction may be in part to blame for this confusion, some of the rigidity in these confusing lines flows from the Federal programs themselves, and therefore can hardly be righted at the state or local levels alone without some correction at the Federal level.

A second reason for confusion in understanding the situation is that there is evidence both ways as to the coordination of Department of Public Instruction activities with other North Carolina state agencies in these Federal programs. It was noted above that NDEA Title III grants were made to units of other agencies of state government,

---

52 Bomar, "*The Impact of Federal Legislation on School Libraries,*" op. cit., p. 28.

which does indicate some sort of coordination and cooperation. Yet, the State Library and the Educational Media Section, both of which conduct Federal aid programs to libraries, held their first meeting to plan and coordinate their mutual interests as late as August 21, 1967. The Library staff reported that they have long suggested such an effort, but it was only under the compulsion of ESEA Title II, which calls specifically for a relationship, that the joint effort is under way. The assistant state librarian is responsible for part of the ESEA plan for the Department of Public Instruction, "The Purposes of a Public Library."[53] There are several other areas of planning and coordination in which the state's Department of Public Instruction has not been an active participant—although it could and should be a key participant.

Therefore, although coordination may be a key word within the Department of Public Instruction, there isn't overwhelming evidence this is so outside the Department. It may be that new planning constraints set down by the Federal programs may force some check-point procedures and joint work with other agencies. But it may be that the major problem lies at the Federal level, with the several different programs—aimed at a similar problem and goal—each calling for its own planning and allocation procedures and its own agency in the states.

"The expenditures of the federal government in all the fields of education are impressive. They run to some billions, but, taking them apart, one finds that always there is a specific purpose which is being supported to the exclusion of more general purposes and a more general program."[54] This was written in 1961 in conjunction with a conference on the Library Services Act. At this point one wonders just how far we have moved from this description with the general aid provision of the ESEA of 1965?

PATTERNS IN OTHER STATES

It is too early to tell just what is happening in the other states. Some general comments have been made. "ESEA has made school administrators more aware of the need to make more adequate provision for school library resources and services. There is also an increasing awareness of the need to strengthen state, regional, and national standards for school libraries. Local education agencies are becoming increasingly aware of the need for qualified school librarians and adequate library facilities. . . ."[55] In other words, the advent of general Federal aid to education has apparently caused a change in attitude toward re-evaluation of just what they have, where they are going, and how they can best get there.

The trends of increased funds, more planning, and stronger stature for the state agency are also evident, and there can be no doubt that coordination problems abound, witness this list of "weaknesses of Federal programs offering assistance to school libraries . . . :

(1) The maze of red tape with separate guidelines, procedures and offices for each segment of a Federal program.
(2) Duplication of efforts for similar Federal programs . . . .
(3) Lack of adequate Federal assistance for increasing personnel through recruitment, training, and employment.
(4) Lack of coordination with the Library Services and Construction Act.
(5) Diversity of regulations for each specific piece of legislation necessitating duplication of administrative personnel and administrative costs."[56]

But some of this critical commentary could be part of the growing pains in an area that has seen so much growth in the past several years, Federal aid to all types of

---

53 *Information provided by the State Library and the Department of Public Instruction.*
54 *Monypenny, "LSA: A Political Scientist's View," op. cit., p. 102.*
55 *Bomar, "The Impact of Federal Legislation on School Libraries," op. cit., p. 29.*
56 *Ibid., p. 30.*

education. This is especially true when most of the Federal responsibility for implementing the legislation falls to one agency, the United States Office of Education. More time is needed before any extensive evaluation of nationwide trends is possible.

LIBRARIES FOR HIGHER EDUCATION

FEDERAL AID AND ITS IMPACT IN NORTH CAROLINA

The final area of Federal aid affecting libraries that this paper will consider is aid to higher education. The major program of concern here is the Higher Education Facilities Act of 1963 (HEFA). North Carolina's state plan for the construction of facilities was developed by the Higher Education Facilities Commission established just for the purpose of planning and allocating the funds. The Commission has since added Title VI, Part A, of the Higher Education Act of 1965 (HEA) to its responsibilities. A separate agency was needed in these cases since other state agencies in the higher education area work only with public institutions, and this act specifies that grants must be made to both private and public institutions. By this state's plan for HEFA, the Federal funds can range up to 40 percent for public community or public technical institutes, and up to 33 1/3 percent for other institutions, not to exceed $1 million on any one project.[57] The state plan also ranks the various project applications by a point system, which seems to be at least mildly biased toward libraries. Table 9B–3 indicates that nearly one quarter of the $35.5 million spent in North Carolina under HEFA in fiscal years 1965, 1966, and 1967 was for libraries.

The individual grants for libraries have been made to 36 separate institutions: 11 community colleges, 9 public institutions, and 16 private institutions. The grants ranged from as low as $45,000 for Livingstone College in Salisbury to $926,143 for Duke University in Durham.[58] The state plan calls for a maximum of 33 1/3 percent for other institutions of higher education—the record shows 25 percent overall (including Duke), 33 percent for other public institutions, and 33.1 percent for private institutions if the skewing effect of the 10.4 percent Duke University grant is removed. In other words, more than one third of the total cost of construction on these higher education libraries in the state over the last three years (except Duke) has come from HEFA funds. This obviously represents a tremendous boost to the higher education system in the state.

There is no way to measure this, but it is generally thought that these additional funds made the difference between building or not building for many of these institutions. Certainly the growth of the Community College system has been greatly aided by the $8.5 million in HEFA funds spent on eleven Community Colleges, $2 million of this for libraries.

And we should not overlook the impact HEFA funds have had on the private institutions, whose sources of funds are always a problem. There were three grants less than $100,000 and five less than $200,000, but at close to the full 33 1/3 grant ratio. The Executive Director of the Higher Education Facilities Commission indicates that not the least of effects of these Federal monies to higher education institutions is the stimulative effect they have on private fund raising, both in private and public institutions.

There is every reason to see that this program has been quite successful in North Carolina in various respects, including the process of planning the allocation of funds,

57 *State of North Carolina, Commission on Higher Education Facilities, "State Plan for the Higher Education Facilities Act of 1963," submitted to the Office of Education, September 22, 1964 (Raleigh: 1966 revision), Sections 8.1 and 8.2, mimeo, p. 16.*
58 *It should be noted that the Duke Library project also received a $1,372,170 grant under Title II of HEFA, which is a direct Office of Education to individual institution program.*

the spread of funds that has ensued, and the obvious impact it is having on the public and private systems of higher education in the state.

But all this success has not been without its problems. The most obvious problem concerns the very structure of governing higher education in North Carolina, with a Board of Higher Education, a Board of Education (Community Colleges), and now the Higher Education Facilities Commission (HEFC) all being involved. And it is the existence of the third of these three which is the concern, for the HEFC only plans and allocates Federal grant funds and is able to duck many of the sticky questions of overall coordination and control of activities. It is not surprising that the Board of Higher Education looks longingly at the functions of HEFC which would provide that Board with a much needed set of rewards to bring recalcitrant institutions around to the plans and coordinating activities of the Board. Put another way, the existence of these Federal programs served to continue the fragmented control over higher education especially as seen by the particular agency established to play the controlling role. And there is some evidence that the individual institutions actually prefer such fragmented control as allowing them more leeway.

Other programs of aid from the Federal Government are also under way in North Carolina—some are almost too new to evaluate, and others bypass the state in their operation. For example, Title II of the Higher Education Act of 1965 provides direct United States Office of Education grants to institutions for library purposes—a flat grant of $5,000 to every institution, supplemental grants of up to $10 per full-time-equivalent student (this requires an institution plan for spending the funds), and some special-purpose grants for national, regional, or university group needs. However, in fiscal 1966 the modest appropriation allowed only the flat grants to be spent. It is obvious that most of the larger institutions would have little or no problem in spending these modest grants—but at least one small institution in North Carolina has complained of the problems in spending wisely these limited funds in the short time involved. This type of problem will undoubtedly disappear as the program and institutional sophistication develop.

With respect to Federal aid to higher education as it affects North Carolina, and probably the other states as well, the trends seem clear—increasing funds for facilities and resources, more planning going on in the states and institutions concerned, and the selective increase in a state agency role. The problems seem to flow from within the state government structure over just who should dispense these funds, and also from some aspects of direct Federal-institutional relationships where planning, if it occurs, will tend to be more project-oriented than comprehensive. Also, there is just the barest hint of coordination problems as these programs vary their approach from the Federal-state-institution path to the Federal-institution path. With such variation it would behoove the institutions to plan carefully their use of funds for matching purposes. They could be adding so much money by "grantsmanship" that they severely restrict their mobility in nongrant areas. But there is no doubting the fact that, for college and university libraries, the mid-1960's are opening the door to more affluence than ever before.

CONCLUSION

TRENDS AND PROBLEMS

There is no need to reiterate the various trends noted in this study at any length. They are restated here briefly and then some suggestions are made which may aid in considering ways to channel these trends to more effective service.

1. In the area of library services, at all levels and for all types of libraries, the key word is "more"—more of everything—money, facilities, resources, personnel—and, by inference, users. But there is the question if more is enough.

2. The agencies at the state level, which have responsibility for the direction of Federal grant-in-aid programs in terms of planning and allocating funds, have been enhanced in their stature in the governmental system.

3. The Federal grant-in-aid programs allow enough flexibility for some demonstrations, experiments, innovations, and even for the provision of needed state-based services under these funds.

4. The recent rise in the number of programs at the Federal level for aid to libraries has continued, and in some cases extended, the fragmentation of agencies and effort at all levels of government.

5. There has been a rapid rise in planning at all levels under the urging of, and most often under the direction of, the Federal grant-in-aid programs. Too often this planning has been too project-oriented, too restricted to a particular program rather than seeking a more comprehensive view.

6. There appears to have been a rise in professionalism in the development of these grant-in-aid programs, especially as measured by increased scholarships and grants for personnel, by state provision of basic professional services to local units, and by the planning of allocations and activities.

7. If there was any doubt before, there should be none now—the library function has moved out of any limited role and position into the world of politics and governmental grant-in-aid support. Libraries are in the political and government marketplace for general support funds and are not looking for bits and pieces of funding.

8. There is no evidence that commitments to library development will decrease in the future. In fact, there is more evidence that commitments will increase and thereby continue and extend most of the trends mentioned above.

SOME APPROACHES FOR THE FUTURE

The following suggestions, gathered from many sources, might better channel and direct these trends.

First, there should be more meaningful surveys of users of library facilities to ascertain just who uses which facility. Are they really as special purpose as so many suggest and maintain? Is the community college library used as much as the public library downtown—where all too few community colleges are located? Just how many purposes does the public library serve, and what other types of aid should be made available to support these other services? Is the school library tied to school hours by its location within a school building or from its image of being just a school library? The questions are endless, and each suggests some different types of demonstrations and innovations which might be made—if we had more adequate information on just who the users are or might be.

Second, and closely tied to the first, is to reduce the bias so often implicit in these programs. This bias is antiurban, or prorural, and is often maintained when state plans of action key to county or other traditional units of area government. I am not advocating a series of newer units of government, for this would be probably even more deleterious since it would be likely to cause serious political and governmental repercussions. Every effort should be made to focus the spending of funds where the people are, the urban areas. Plans and criteria for spending funds should be reviewed with an eye to making sure the needs of the urban areas are met.

Third, the trend of strength in the administrating agencies in the states should be explicitly recognized and furthered. Like the ESEA grants to help strengthen state departments of education, there should be similar grants to state library agencies for the same purpose. When one views our governmental processes as an interrelated system rather than some sort of adversary process between the various levels and departments, then it becomes evident that the Federal Government should aid if the states cannot, or do not, provide the necessary level of support. A weakness at the state agency level weakens the whole system in general and the provision of service in particular. Further, Federal funds should be as free of restrictions as possible so that state agencies can innovate and experiment with these funds, or can stimulate similar efforts by the local units. Likewise, state funds to local units should be made equally flexible so that local units are not placed in fiscal and programmatic straitjackets.

Fourth, although there is no indication that success is in the offing, all efforts should be continued to consolidate grant-in-aid programs where goals are similar. This is especially needed in the various education programs, where so many are focused within the same basic agency at all levels of government. Similarly, efforts should be taken to rationalize the various planning requirements and project application procedures where so much duplication is apparent.

Fifth, current expenditure levels for library facilities should be increased selectively. Not all programs have equal promise, nor do the funds in each go as far in providing service. The results of a users survey would help in determining just which programs should have larger funding—and at what level of government. This sort of selective increase of funds and the consolidation of some grant programs will help alleviate the fiscal bind of the states and of the local units. It is far wiser to take this course of action than to work for some sort of returned, unearmarked funds to the states from Federal income tax resources—this is still too distant to count on at all.

Sixth, we need to experiment and innovate on a grander scale than we have been willing to in the past. For example, the piles of paper attendant with plans, projects, and reports in any program often threaten the existence of a lively program. Surely the new techniques used by the communications, computer, aerospace, and electronics industries might be brought to bear to develop new procedures for the "rational" and most effective spending of funds for services. We need to change the stereotyped paper-passing that stultifies too many of our personnel; we should allow them to get away from the desk and go to the people and the provision of service.

Seventh, structural overhaul of many parts of our system is badly needed—but the effort to obtain it is often so great as to detract from the services to be provided. Therefore, new efforts must be made to coordinate activities—from planning, to project development, to the provision of service. Doors must open that have previously been closed, and the walls of various "establishments" must be broken down. Each agency must take a more comprehensive view of what libraries can do, and the best methods available for fulfilling that potential. Relationships with the other functions and agencies of the general government must become part of any library agency's priorities. Cooperative planning is an important vehicle to aid in any such effort, besides being a necessary ingredient in any agency's program.

Eighth, the concept of planning and what it means must be broadened from the project-only or program-only planning which is so often the sum of activities in any program area. Planning must be seen as part of a process of decision-making throughout the system rather than a discrete form of activity to be performed at a particular time. Budgetary decisions must be broadened to include the inputs that a planning process can provide, and priorities must be decided more on a need-and-service basis rather than on the available-funds basis.

Ninth, steps must be taken to alleviate personnel problems of various nature. Scholarships, grants, and aid to schools of library science are part of the answer to attracting more students, but salary scales must be upgraded so these people can be retained. This means that state civil service systems should be challenged and changed where library personnel are placed in too-low categories. Also, there is evidence that a new breed of person is needed in library service, the professional administrator of programs and larger agencies. It may be that specific training in a library school need not be a necessary condition for such a position, but merely a preferred one. This would open the door to the ranks of the professional administrators and other types who can assimilate agency function and service while carrying out the burdensome job of administration. Also, new types of personnel are needed in the complex areas of intergovernmental relations and public relations. Criteria for selection of these people should be carefully reviewed so that selection can come from the broadest range of people and talents. Such changes in personnel selection could free professionally trained librarians to provide the library service for the agency.

A FINAL WORD

This paper was one of the series considered by the task force for the study on the Federal Government and Libraries, whose summary of recommendations to the National Advisory Commission on Libraries is shown in Table 8A–1 in the preceding chapter. The Commission's concern with the fragmentation and other problems of Federal-state-local-regional cooperation are reflected in the recommendations for strengthening state library agencies and for strengthening the United States Office of Education (see chapter 12, section D). Clearly this is an area for continuing future research and planning in its broadest sense.

TABLE 9B–1

USE OF FEDERAL FUNDS IN NORTH CAROLINA UNDER THE LIBRARY SERVICES ACT

(1957–1964)

FISCAL YEAR ENDING 6/30	NORTH CAROLINA ALLOTMENT UNDER LSA	PAYMENTS TO NORTH CAROLINA COUNTIES
1957	$ 40,000	$ 14,031
1958	181,775	137,436
1959	229,997	204,159
1960	302,331	195,159
1961	302,331	179,371
1962	310,305	214,887
1963	310,305	223,944
1964	309,703	236,132

SOURCE: *State of North Carolina Governor's Commission on Library Resources,* Resources of North Carolina Libraries, *edited by Robert B. Downs (Raleigh: 1965), p. 55.*

TABLE 9B–2

COMPARISON OF SPENDING PATTERNS OF FOUR STATES UNDER THE LIBRARY SERVICES ACT

(Through 1966)

	WAGES & SALARIES	BOOKS & MATERIALS	EQUIPMENT	OPERATING EXPENSES
National	51%	27%	4%	18%
North Carolina	42	42	4	11
Georgia	12	71	2	16
Hawaii	73	16	4	9
Pennsylvania	24	14	3	59

SOURCE: *John C. Frantz and Nathan M. Cohen, "The Federal Government and Public Libraries: A Ten-Year Partnership, 1957–1966," Health, Education, and Welfare Indicators (Washington: Government Printing Office, July 1966), p. 7.*

TABLE 9B–3

TOTAL GRANTS IN NORTH CAROLINA UNDER HIGHER EDUCATION FACILITIES ACT, TITLE I

(Fiscal years 1965, 1966, 1967)

	LIBRARIES	OTHER FACILITIES	TOTAL
Community colleges	$2,007,243 (23.6%)	$ 6,512,444 (76.4%)	$ 8,519,687 (100%)
Other institutions (public and private)	6,683,770 (24.7%)	20,342,222 (75.2%)	27,025,992 (100%)
Total expenditures	8,691,013 (24.5%)	26,854,666 (75.5%)	35,545,679 (100%)

SOURCE: *Most of the above information on the Higher Education Facilities program was provided by the North Carolina Higher Education Facilities Commission. Although there are no comparable figures from other states or nationally, it would appear that the bias in the plan criteria have in fact biased the allocation of the funds, for one would not normally anticipate as high a percentage of the funds going to library construction.*

C. HIGHLIGHTS FROM THE REGIONAL HEARINGS

As documented in appendix C of this book, the National Advisory Commission on Libraries undertook a series of regional hearings throughout the United States in order to gather evidence that would bear on development of the Commission's conclusions and recommendations. The wealth of raw material so gathered is now part of the public domain, and it is hoped many future publications will appear that draw on this wealth of evidence.

Each of these 12 hearings had its own individuality, adding up to a combination of local difference and global commonality that defies documentation within the scope of the present report. It is important to note here that the "grass roots" are in some respects far more sophisticated than some pseudo-intellectuals would deign to credit. The demands of small industry and burgeoning universities are as compelling in the growing medium-sized communities as are those of their counterparts in our huge, overburdened, metropolitan communities. This emerged clearly in the regional hearings.

Perhaps, however, one of the most dramatic outcomes of the regional hearings of the National Advisory Commission on Libraries is exemplified by the one held in Pikeville, Kentucky, on October 20, 1967. In areas adjacent thereto, the bookmobile is still a magic caravan. The development of a permanent public library is a community project involving sweat, tears, and subsequent pride. In these days of sophisticated technological potential, it is important to be reminded that a simple need does not have to be answered by immediate and elaborate mechanization. Nationwide, a multiplicity of varipaced innovation is indicated—the individual citizen, whoever and wherever, is the key.

A report of the Pikeville hearing appeared in the *Wilson Library Bulletin*—it is reproduced here, certainly not as an example of the results of all the regional hearings, but as a statement of what transpired at one of them.

A REPORT FROM PIKEVILLE, KENTUCKY[59]

. . . It could have been any church auditorium in any small American town, sturdy, unpretentious, and spotlessly clean. In such a room one might expect to hear Bible readings or a biblical story hour, but on October 20, 1967, the testimony offered was not to one book, but to all books, for here in Pikeville, Kentucky, the . . . National Advisory Commission on Libraries held its public hearing.

The county seat of Pike County, Pikeville houses less than six thousand residents. Like other communities in the Eastern Highlands of Kentucky, its terrain has been lavishly endowed by nature: woods, mountains, and lakes are, to use Burke's distinction, at least picturesque if not sublime. But to those residents in the area the abundance of natural beauty cannot conceal the pockets of poverty, both economic and intellectual, which lie buried in the counties forming the eastern part of the state.

The day was but one in a series of public hearings arranged by two of the Commission's members, Carl Elliott, Alabama attorney and former Congressional representative from that state, and Mrs. Bessie B. Moore, a native Kentuckian who has been a member of the Arkansas Library Commission since 1942 and state supervisor of elementary education, Arkansas Department of Education, since 1958. Communities in which other public hearings were held include Tucson, Tampa, Bismarck, Austin, Wilkes-Barre, Great Falls, Portland, Baton Rouge, and Anchorage, Alaska.

Mrs. Moore, a fresh-complexioned woman with a tornado-like store of energy, conducted the meeting, secure in her reception by these sons and daughters of her native state. In fact, she discovered several kinfolk among the seventy-odd witnesses, and the pleasantries in which she engaged with them alleviated some of the embarrassment they might otherwise have felt in being called upon to give a speech. Also present were

59 *By Kathleen Molz. Reprinted by permission from the December 1967 issue of the* Wilson Library Bulletin. *Copyright © 1967 by The H. W. Wilson Company. The views are the author's own and do not necessarily reflect the opinions of the National Advisory Commission on Libraries as a whole or of its individual members.*

three of her fellow Commissioners: Mr. Elliott, a great hulk of a man gifted with the sonorous voice characteristic of the clergyman or the statesman; Caryl P. Haskins, a slender academician who serves as president of the Carnegie Institution in Washington, D.C., and Emerson Greenaway, the director of the Free Library of Philadelphia.

The sessions began promptly at 9:30 A.M. By then almost every seat in the room was filled. The list of witnesses was put before the members of the Commission, and they settled back to listen to the day-long testimony. For the most part, the selection of the witnesses was made by the staff of the State Department of Libraries, which has its headquarters in Frankfort, Kentucky, in consultation with local and regional librarians throughout the state.

The witnesses were highly diversified: finishing-school accents blended with mountain speech; fashionably turned-out costumes rubbed elbows with drabber dress; and occupations ranged in the economic and social scale from banker to housewife. Two things they had in common: their age, since they all were over thirty-five, and the common heritage of their Anglo-Saxon forebears, represented by the surnames which filled the roster: Boone, Winstead, Dobbs, Giles, Jesse, Grigsby, Gorsuch, Carter, and Clark. For the most part, the witnesses were all library users; very few librarians testified.

To understand more fully the account of the testimony which follows, the reader of this report should realize that of Kentucky's 120 counties only ten are more than five hundred square miles in area and only eleven contain a population larger than 60,000. In 1952, the per capita expenditure for public libraries in Kentucky was the lowest in the country; since that time, largely with the aid of federal funds, Kentucky has witnessed the growth of nineteen regional library systems serving eighty-five of the state's counties. The sparsity of population and the related inability of local residents to support public library service make the federal appropriation even more meaningful, and it was to the continuation and increase of this appropriation that the witnesses primarily addressed themselves.

The first major witness to testify during the morning session was the Mayor of Pikeville, Dr. W. C. Hambley. A surgeon, Dr. Hambley had obviously been exposed to new trends in thinking about library service. Believing that the present-day librarian spends too much time at "chores," he thought that the community library should find ways to mechanize its procedures. Pikeville needs some 250,000 volumes for circulation; its present holdings of 40,000 volumes are inadequate for county-wide service. In addition, he hoped that films and audiovisual materials might be added to the local collection. Most innovative of his proposals was a recommendation that an interstate library authority be formed so that Pikeville could cooperate more fully with neighboring libraries in West Virginia, situated just thirty-five miles away. When asked if he would cite the proportion of support to be funded by federal, state, and local government, the Mayor replied that he would like "maximal" local support. Unfortunately, he added, statutory limitations restrict the levying of municipal taxes in Pikeville to only a small percentage of the amount needed for library supports. The Mayor believed that the federal government would have to compensate for inadequate local support, supplying 50 percent of the library's appropriation; the state and local governments would then contribute the remaining 50 percent.

George Street Boone, who described himself as "a country lawyer" from Elkton, Kentucky, followed Dr. Hambley. A resident of Todd County, just north of the Tennessee border, Mr. Boone must journey sixty miles to Nashville in order to consult last week's newspaper. With no library service and no book store in the entire county, Mr. Boone and his fellow attorneys maintain their own law libraries. Aware that no major industry will seek a plant site in communities without adequate schools and libraries, Mr. Boone was particularly hopeful that a demonstartion library project be established in Todd County. Like Mayor Hambley, he pointed out the statutory restrictions which delimit the amounts that can be raised through local taxation: as he said, "1892 tax rates just can't encompass library service." At this point, Mrs. Moore interjected the comment that other hearings held throughout the country had also revealed the hopelessly antiquated status of many local and state laws regarding library service, a factor which contributes heavily to hampering the development of libraries everywhere.

Another self-described "country boy" was Max Hurt, a retired insurance executive who resides in Kirksey, Kentucky, on the farm where he was born. A slight, balding man dressed in a conservative dark blue suit, Mr. Hurt quite obviously charmed the Commission members. In a quietly rendered speech resonant with the echoes of the King James version of the Bible, he argued for federal support of public library service on a national scale. The taxpayers have come, he noted, to expect rural free delivery of mail; why should the government not provide a similar service for the distribution of books throughout the country? In this uneasy world "where all you read about is rancor," he said, "the library could come to be a handmaiden of the church," standing out like a lily on the pond, empowered "to heal and cure the minds of people." Mr. Hurt's idealism was streaked by a strong practical sense. Like attorney Boone, he too commented that new businesses and industries would not enter his county unless the families of their executives and staff could be guaranteed good library service.

An equally moving witness was a personable young woman, Mrs. Carol Hunt of Fortville, Kentucky. A registered nurse, Mrs. Hunt operates an old people's home in her community. Her wish for editions of Grace Livingston Hill in large-print type might fall on deaf ears among professional librarians, but her plea was genuine. The old people in her home can afford nothing more than their room and board; she relies on the public library to furnish films for their entertainment. She pictured for the Commission one elderly resident who repetitively beat his leg wth an old battered leather hat in the sheer pleasure of seeing a film. Although the Department of Health requires strict compliance with its regulations concerning the physical well-being of her clients, she concluded, no stipulations are made as to their recreation or diversion. Everything must be done in that regard voluntarily; hence, her dependence on such public agencies as the library. Shy and a little uneasy, Mrs. Hunt nonetheless greatly moved the members of the Commission, Dr. Haskins going so far as to comment that her story should be published.

A spare, pioneer woman straight out of the pages of one of her own novels was Mrs. Janice Holt Giles of Knifely, Kentucky, who came to testify on behalf of the continuance of the inter-library loan service provided by the Adair County Library. Regarding libraries as her "personal crusade," Mrs. Giles described for the Commission the help given her by this small library in gathering the information she needs for her books. Calling herself a "graduate of the people's university," Mrs. Giles obviously regards the public library as the greatest source of her own education, which in its formal sense never went beyond the high school level. Another well-known author, Rebecca Caudill, presented so moving an account of the success of one small Kentucky library that we wrote to her and asked her for the transcript of her testimony. When it came, we believed that printing it in its entirety would convey the spirit and fervor of the day far better, no doubt, than our recapitulation. What follows is Miss Caudill's statement:

A SUCCESS STORY

I want briefly to tell you a success story of one Kentucky mountain library.

People in the Kentucky mountains, particularly those in the field of education, have long been concerned with the quality of education in the mountains, which is definitely below standard, and the need for adequate free libraries. For several years the Kentucky State Department of Libraries has received annually from the federal government funds for developing regional libraries. In the beginning, a policy was adopted

—a wise one, I believe—that any county, no matter how poor, in order to receive aid from federal funds, must tax itself for a library and thus carry a part of the load.

In the fall of 1964, I was in Harlan County just before election day. There I met some of the people in Cumberland who were working day and night to persuade the voters of Harlan County of the desirability of passing a library tax of seven cents on each one hundred dollars of assessed property valuation. (Following a reassessment of property values, the tax is now 2.2 cents, but the yield of revenue is the same.)

Among the hardest of the workers was Dean Cadle, at that time librarian of the newly established Southeast Community College in Cumberland. In his work with Southeast's students, the majority of them from Harlan County, Mr. Cadle had soon discovered their inadequate reading ability. He found that in 80 percent of the homes represented by the student body not a single newspaper entered the home, and few books were on the shelves. One remedy for this he believed lay in a free public library in the county. With such a library, future students of the College might grow up on good books and so come to college better equipped to absorb a college education.

The first chapter of my story ends with the November, 1964, election, when Harlan Countians voted by a majority of almost three to one to tax themselves for a public library. It was a foregone conclusion that the library would be situated in the county seat town of Harlan in the lower end of the county. But in the area of Cumberland, Benham, and Lynch, in the upper end of the county, live some sixteen thousand of the fifty-one thousand inhabitants of Harlan County. These people, remote from Harlan, needed and wanted their own library.

The tax voted in 1964 yielded no revenue until December, 1965. The people of the Cumberland area, however, felt the need for a library was immediate. No sooner had the tax been voted than they announced to the Department of State Libraries that they were ready to begin. The State Library itself became infected with the enthusiasm generated by the Cumberland area people and decided to cooperate with them in getting their library started. If the people of the area would find a building suitable for a library, the state librarian told them, the Department of State Libraries, using federal funds available for the purpose, would set the library up in business as fast as the wheels could turn.

A building was quickly found—a store, next door to the Cumberland postoffice, which could be had for rent at seventy dollars per month. The business of turning the store into a library became a community project. Some people worked during the day, some at night, all donating their labor.

On a Saturday afternoon on the sixth of March, 1965, the library opened. There it stood—an example of volunteer local work and cooperation between citizens and their local, state, and federal governments. The long, large room glistened with fresh paint brushed on by the men of Cumberland. It was lighted with fluorescent lights installed at cost by the local office of the utilities company. The local florist had sent bouquets of spring flowers for the opening. The women's clubs of Cumberland, Benham, and Lynch served refreshments donated by local grocery stores. On the shelves were arranged 3,500 new books, publishers' samples, which were all the State Library had on hand. A case held two hundred classical records. On the tops of the bookshelves stood fourteen reproductions of famous paintings attractively framed. Prominent among the fixtures was a children's reading table with two benches painted a soft rose, the donated work of a local carpenter. And sitting at the librarian's desk was a librarian with only the training the regional librarian could give her in a few hectic days.

March 6, 1965, in the Kentucky mountains was a raw, cold day with snow blowing down the mountains and through the hollows. All afternoon people traipsed through the snow—adults and children, Negroes and whites, townspeople, and whole families from up the creeks—come to see, to rejoice, to carry away books. In the first five days more than one thousand items were checked out.

At the end of the library year, 1966, the Cumberland library had cataloged a total of 6,020 items. Its adult circulation for the year was 12,718; its juvenile circulation was 9,783, making a total circulation of 22,501. These figures, however, do not reveal the pride of the people of upper Harlan County in their library, nor the enthusiasm with which they use it. In 1967, not fewer than one new application for a library card has been received every day, and sometimes the requests are many per day.

The figures do not reveal the young Negro boy who came into the library quietly, browsed awhile among its books, and went away clutching a volume of the collected poems of Louis Untermeyer.

They do not reveal the dry cleaner who longed to make kitchen cabinets and who, through books and magazines supplied by a sympathetic librarian, has now gone into business as a cabinet maker.

They do not reveal the people of the little community of Partridge in Letcher County who had made some pottery of inferior quality, and who through books supplied by the Cumberland library and through interlibrary loan are now successfully marketing their products.

They do not reveal the father of whom his young son reported: "All the time my dad's got his nose stuck in a book that come from the public library."

They do not reveal the town whittler who was inspired by the librarian through books to perfect his art, nor do they reveal the lively display in the library window of the whittler's art and the books that inspired him.

They do not reveal the woman from up the mountain who recently checked out a novel of extraordinary length and explained to the librarian: "I may not get this one back on time. I have four neighbors, and every one of us reads every word of every book I check out."

They do not reveal the mother of whom her child reported: "She checked out a library book last week, and she carries it around the house with her, all over the house, and every once in a while she says, 'This *is* the best book I ever read.'"

They do not reveal the woman from Lynch who said: "I used to hate to drive to Cumberland. Now I love to go because I know I can bring back books."

They do not reveal the story hours for children held in the library; the local literary society and writers' club that was organized under the impetus of the library and holds its meetings there; the autographing parties held in the library for authors visiting the College; the avid checking out of books by children; the high school students that congregate in the library every day after three o'clock, when the school library is closed, to use the reference books; the much better prepared high school and college students; and the greatly enlarged enrollment at the College, mainly from Harlan County.

And they do not reveal the enthusiasm and dedication of the present librarian. Although her training consists of one course in library science at Southeast Community College and one session in a summer institute, her performance leads one to believe that librarians can be born as well as trained. She has transformed the former store into an attractive, welcoming library where all—the poor and the uneducated as well as the elite—know they have a place.

The pockets of poverty are deep in Harlan County. When the librarian discovered that many people on relief were not using the library because they thought they had to pay for the books, she used extraordinary means to convince them the library was their own, free. Overdue books were an excuse for the librarian to go into the homes of the poor, sometimes walking up the mountains where no car could go, to collect the books, of course, but primarily to encourage the people to come for other books, because the library was theirs, free. And she serves forty-five hours a week at a salary that persons serving on this Commission would consider outrageously inadequate.

The income from Harlan County's library tax, divided among two libraries and a bookmobile, is approximately eighteen thousand dollars annually. Without state and federal aid the libraries of Harlan County cannot function adequately, nor can they be adequately housed. Already the little store that serves as the Cumberland library is filled to capacity and is being used to capacity.

According to the Senate Republican Policy Committee Report on *The War in Vietnam,* our federal government is "spending over $300,000 to kill each enemy soldier." I dream of the transformation that would take place among the fifty-one thousand people of Harlan County if the federal government spent one quarter of that amount each year on free public libraries in the area.

FURTHER IMPRESSIONS FROM PIKEVILLE

There were other impressions from that day in Pikeville: the two blind readers, one of whom listened to some eight or ten talking books and read four or five braille books every month; the seventy-year-old veteran of World War I who was raised on McGuffey's Readers and read all of Jack London before he was nine years old; the middle-aged housewife who received books for her arthritic mother from a bookmobile which stopped at the family farm; and the minister's wife who admitted to having been married for some thirty years to "a half man/half book."

To say that much of the testimony was simple is not to imply that it was simplistic. For the most part, the Kentuckians who spoke were shaped in a tradition of American Gothicism: earnest, God-fearing, and intent on speaking their minds. In some cases, their wants were unrealistic; many of them, for instance, desire a separate library building for their localities, although it would be frankly impossible to subsidize separate library structures in every little town or hamlet in the state. Yet they seemed genuinely knowledgeable about the principle of cooperation and library systems and grateful to the State Department of Libraries; high praise was often given to Margaret Willis, the state librarian, and her staff.

Aside from its enormous cathartic value, what did the Pikeville hearing really accomplish? In the main, its worth was frankly political: the local press coverage, the involvement of political leaders from several levels of government, the very presence of a national commission in the town of Pikeville itself—all will contribute in the months to come to a furtherance of pubic understanding about Kentucky's library situation. To those of us, city-born, urban-reared, the day was a revelation, encompassing elements of the town meeting, the old-fashioned revival, and the chautauqua. One was disturbed mainly by the absence of the young people[60]; will the next generation of Kentuckians, not raised on the Readers of McGuffey or the King James version of the Bible, be so eager to spread the gospel of the book? Or will they find the public libraries in which their elders put such faith vestigial remnants of another age, just as the public hearing of Pikeville seemed to us part of another world, another era?

---

[60] *Actually more young people arrived later in the day at the Pikeville hearing. Student testimony was frequently a highlight at all of the regional hearings of the National Advisory Commission on Libraries (see appendix C).—Editor's Note*

CHAPTER X

THE LIBRARY OF CONGRESS AS THE NATIONAL LIBRARY: POTENTIALITIES FOR SERVICE[1]

by the Staff of the Library of Congress

NATIONAL LIBRARY AND INFORMATION SYSTEMS

During the past ten or fifteen years, the Library of Congress (LC) has been acutely aware—as have many others in different spheres of activity—of two great new forces that are bringing about rapid and startling changes in virtually every segment of our national life. The first of these is the vastly expanded role of the Federal Government and Federal policy in science, industry, education, health, welfare, and many other fields. The second is the advance in electronics, which provides new data-processing technologies and new methods of handling information.

The implications of these developments for the future of library and information services in all fields of knowledge and endeavor have been of great concern to us at the Library of Congress. At the same time, we have felt it incumbent upon us, in view of the present broad and far-reaching responsibilities of the Library of Congress as the *de facto* National Library of the United States, to move with due regard for the foreseeable consequences of whatever new responsibilities we might undertake or new techniques we might employ.

It may seem to some that we have not moved fast enough. To others it may appear that we have remained aloof when we should have become involved. Be that as it may, we are now moving on as broad a front as available resources and advances in technology permit. The Library of Congress, within the framework of its responsibilities to the Congress, to the library community at large, and to all the many publics that it serves, is not merely willing and ready but *committed* to play an appropriately central role in the planning and operation of the emerging national library and information network.

---

[1] *At the conclusion of the meeting of the National Advisory Commission on Libraries at the Library of Congress on May 22, 1967, the Chairman of the Commission requested that the Librarian of Congress give the Commission this statement of the Library's view of itself as the National Library of the United States, summarizing some of the points made to the Commission and looking into the future. This account is not intended by the authors as a review of the state of the art of librarianship. It considers possibilities for the future natonal library and informaon service network, but it does not pretend to be a blueprint for action. It is a vision and not necessarily a prediction of the role of the Library of Congress as the National Library.*

No copyright is claimed for chapter 10.

SOME RECENT BACKGROUND

When we attempt to define the relationship of the Library of Congress to the efforts that have been made to develop a plan for the national library and information network, we are confronted with a welter of studies and reports dating back a decade. The impetus for most of them has come from the Federal Government, notably from those elements of the Government concerned with science and technology. It is perhaps instructive to recall some of the principal proposals.

Early in 1958, the Stanford Research Institute produced *A Draft Program for a National Technical Information Center.* In 1962, there was the Crawford Report, *Scientific and Technological Communication in the Government.* Also in 1962, we had the Cahn Plan, *Bureau of Information for Technology and Science Proposed as "Key Station" of Federal "Network" of Information Services to the U.S. Free Enterprise System.* In January 1963, Dr. Alvin Weinberg of the President's Science Advisory Committee issued his famous report, *Science, Government, and Information.* Later that year, Management Technology, Inc., did a study called *A National Scientific and Technological Information System.* At about the same time, Robert Heller and Associates prepared *A National Plan for Science Abstracting and Indexing Services.* In July 1963, Dr. Mortimer Taube of Documentation, Inc., wrote his *Proposal for the Establishment of a Government Corporation to Create and Provide Services from an Integrated Store of Scientific and Technical Information.* In November of that year, Dr. J. H. Kelley of the Office of Science and Technology addressed to Dr. Jerome Wiesner his memorandum on the subject, *Government Science Package,* emphasizing regional decentralization. That same month, G. S. Simpson, Jr., of the Battelle Memorial Institute proposed *A Pentagon of U.S. Scientific and Technical Information and Data Services.* In February 1964, Dr. Stafford Warren addressed to President John F. Kennedy a *Memorandum on a National Library of Science System.* The Jonker Plan of May 1964, *A Model Information Retrieval Network for Government, Science, and Industry,* proposed the organization of a National Scientific and Technical Information Center; in January 1965 the Air Force Office of Aerospace Research issued a proposal entitled *Toward a National Technical Information System.*

It should be noted that many of these studies were carried out for, and all were reviewed by, the Office of Science and Technology in the Executive Office of the President. It was natural, then, that the Office of Science and Technology, through the Committee on Scientific and Technical Information (COSATI), a subordinate group under the Federal Council for Science and Technology, should have commissioned the System Development Corporation (SDC), with funding from the National Science Foundation, to undertake a synthetical review of the situation regarding the problem of planning and developing a national library and information system and to recommend one of the several alternatives which seemed to be open.

The result, published in September 1965, was the well-known SDC report entitled *Recommendations for National Document Handling Systems in Science and Technology.* The assumptions on which it was based and at least the general thrust of its recommendations have been widely publicized and commented upon. It was certainly the most ambitious of the national-plan documents. As a distillation and rationalization of many past proposals in the troublesome area of scientific and technical information service, it was a very useful report. Although there were in it elements with which to disagree, it served to crystallize the thinking of many individuals and organizations about the basic requirements of national system planning for library and information work. The report was disturbing to us at the Library of Congress mainly because we felt that both the philosophy by which we live and the role that we play were either largely ignored or misunderstood.

Despite the reputable sponsorship that many of the proposals referred to in the preceding paragraphs have enjoyed, we believe that few of the study groups have been characterized by a sufficient degree of competence for the task at hand; the studies have not been based upon the depth of experience nor the breadth of authority that one might expect for recommendations of such profound and far-reaching effect. There have been, nevertheless, sufficient weight, influence, and funding behind at least some of these thrusts to raise apprehension that one plan or the other might be rushed prematurely into being.

The establishment of the National Advisory Commission on Libraries by the President of the United States in September 1966 was, incidentally, a timely measure for the prevention of such an untoward result. The work of the Commission assures that the many complex problems associated with, as well as the variety of needs for, the creation of a national library and information system will receive mature consideration at every level of the Government and of the private sector where the national interest is engaged.

NEW TECHNOLOGIES AND SERVICES

The fears and frustrations that have brought on this rash of proposed solutions are understandable. Much of this striving arises from an honest concern for the better management of the rapidly proliferating information and information packages of the scientific and technological age. Libraries have been severely taxed by the problems of acquiring, housing, processing, and servicing the flood of new materials in such ways that this accumulation will meet the needs of tomorrow as well as of today. However, most of the proposed document-handling and so-called information systems simply have as an underlying objective the reduction, if not of the rising tide itself, then at least of the bulk of the accretions. There is much discussion nowadays of the compaction of information, the reduction of data, by a variety of possible means—physical (e.g., microforms, electronic processing) and intellectual (e.g., abstracting, evaluation, analysis).

There is merit in many of the schemes advanced. When bulky materials can be rendered less bulky, a diminution of the space required for storage is manifest. When cumbersome or time-consuming procedures can be simplified or performed by machines, savings in precious manpower, lead-time, and dollar costs are indicated. If unnecessary duplication and redundancy can be eliminated, efficiency is obviously improved. Where relevance and specificity can be increased, the opportunities for effective utilization are enhanced. Nevertheless, it is too often overlooked that a reduction in the physical bulk of information materials does not achieve a reduction in the number of units which must be handled and controlled in library and information systems.

On the contrary, every surrogate established for an original informational item becomes itself a new, additional informational item, and librarians are only too aware of the many surrogates that may be created for each original informational item if merely traditional control techniques (e.g., cataloging, classification, indexing, abstracting) are applied by traditional manual and visual methods. The application of new technologies to the creation, manipulation, and servicing of bibliographical records will no doubt yield many advantages to library and information-service work, but a reduction in the number of surrogates, quite apart from the original informational items themselves, will assuredly not be one of them.

It seems evident that the new technologies, coupled with the new types of information services they make possible, will in fact bring about an increase in the number of both original and secondary information items. This prospect, if recognized at all, does not disturb the proposers of new and supposedly sophisticated information systems.

The basis for many of the newer information service configurations is the desire to help the user by making it possible for him to look into the fewest number of sources and in those few, possibly only one, to find the precise information or data he needs, stated as tersely as the subject permits. It assumes that the researcher neither needs nor wants his information in the document, or the context, or the form in which the original researcher recorded it, but rather will welcome receiving it condensed by an intermediary, or series of intermediaries, provided the distillation is authenticated by a peer researcher, scientist, or engineer.

To accomplish this purpose, there have been created both within and outside the Federal Government numerous new information centers called analysis or evaluation centers, and the eventual need for many more in this country and abroad is actively contemplated. The System Development Corporation report mentioned earlier, which discussed the services of these centers at some length, ascribed their rise to "the apparent inability of conventional library systems to service the needs of the user group." One estimate suggests that 2,000 such centers strategically located around the world could systematically cover all significant existing literature at a possible annual cost of $200 million, or $100,000 each. Another calculates that an individual center could process as many as 1,000 articles a year at a unit cost of under $300.

Although a variety of operating patterns is foreseen for these centers, all have in common the concept of repackaging, condensing, and synthesizing the information contained in technical articles, reports, books, and patents in a particular, limited subject area, and of providing rapid—and therefore machine-aided—tailor-made service on this information. Various "compression factors" have also been discussed, some estimates running as high as 100 to 1. Yet, at the same time, nearly every analysis and evaluation center plan also provides for making available the full text of the evaluated and compressed information, both in printed and in machine-readable form, and for supporting the condensed material by machine-readable bibliographies of the original informational items.

How broad or how limited the user group proposed as the beneficiary of these services might be is not clear. From the general nature of the suggested systems, however, one is led to suppose that unrestricted public service is not considered either desirable or necessary and that dissemination would be to a selected or elite clientele. All the same, the "evaluated and compressed" new literature produced under these systems would become a part of the world literature of science and technology and would therefore fall within the purview of the national, or international, library and information network. This being the case, the new types of information services would leave us with all our present informational packages and their surrogates, together with the problems of controlling and communicating them, and would add several new kinds of packages and surrogates and the burden of handling them.

Here we see clearly illustrated what librarians have long realized: that each form or generation of literature and literature service produces additional forms and succeeding generations of literature and literature service, and that the accumulation must continue to infinity. For with knowledge and the literature in which its discovery is recorded, there is no death; whatever dies—that is, is superseded or appears to be superseded by new knowledge—remains. The dead, or seeming dead, is intermingled with the living, and no man can tell whether or at what moment it will spring to life again and to new meaning.

THE LIBRARY OF CONGRESS POSITION

It is the position of the Library of Congress that information, data, learning, and knowledge, however acquired or recorded, are a continuum. For the purposes of its management or handling, as well as for its use, information is inseparable from the media in which it is found. We have noted that the ferment for a national, even international, library and information network plan has come from the scientific and technical community. No one denies the importance, even the crucial importance, of scientific and technical information. Science and technology, however, do not, to our thinking, constitute a definable and viable field in which, or for which, a national library and information network can be constructed. Nor do we believe that a truly national library and information network, whether limited to science and technology or extended to embrace all knowledge, can be constructed solely by or solely within the Federal Government. The Federal Government, admittedly, has a huge stake—and in terms of national goals and policies possibly the preponderant stake—in scientific and technical information, both as a producer and user. But it has no monopoly of it and, in the last analysis, no suzerainty over it. And if, as we prefer, one takes a long view of life and culture, science and technology, though they may advance, sustain, and complement, cannot supplant or overbear the other great branches of learning and activity—education, the law, the arts, the social sciences, and the humanities.

From these considerations we think it follows that the attempt of the writers of proposals for national plans to dichotomize the community of learning or knowledge into libraries and library systems, on the one hand, and evaluation and retrieval systems, on the other, must be labeled arbitrary and artificial. We do not think that the facts will support a description of library activities, at whatever level of the community, as document-oriented. Both types of activity—and the activities themselves are often of a mixed nature—are concerned with documents *and* information. We would question the wisdom and the economics of attempts to separate them.

A cognate tendency of new-wave thinking that is disturbing to librarians, and particularly to a universal library like the Library of Congress, is its insistence on the ever-finer fragmentation of the fragments of knowledge. The parallel tendency is, of course, to design the components of the national library and information system in such a way that the area of responsibility of each component would be delimited to one of the finely fragmented fields. We believe that the ultimate effect of such a system would be to confine the scholar—the scientist, if you will—at the end of an uncomfortably and stultifyingly short tether.

The SDC Report of 1965 gave strong support to the so-called responsible agency concept. Since the concept was not fully spelled out, it is difficult to assess its full implication. Inherent in the idea, however, is the dubious assumption that science and technology (or any broad subject area, for that matter) can be subdivided arbitrarily into meaningful, or at least manageable, compartments—"subsets of the spectrum of science and technology"—which correspond, or can be made to correspond, to the functions or missions of the Executive Branch departments and agencies of the Federal Government.

In more recent planning documents emanating from Federal scientific and technical information sources there is a new and encouraging note that recognizes the desirability of achieving a harmonious array among information systems, whether they be in the Government or the private sector and despite their orientation toward specialized missions, or functions, or disciplines. Whether or not harmony could be achieved would depend, we believe, in large measure upon the pattern and the content of the array.

Since every important reference and research library is, by definition and inherent nature, a considerably more comprehensive information center than any of the activities—already in existence or proposed—to which this term is usually applied in the planning documents we have been discussing, the Library of Congress already stands at the focus of a large national information network. We maintain that the network is not something arbitrarily established by Federal fiat but has been developed over a period of many years in response to very real and important cultural and sociological needs. The network is dynamic and organic and cannot be ignored or supplanted in the paper plans for a new network, whether the purview be limited to science and technology or extended to all knowledge.

The basis of the existing network is the vast collections of informational materials that the components of the network collectively hold and on which they offer an impressive variety of services to many kinds of publics in this country and around the world. Many of the services are general and benefit large numbers of clients; other services are highly specialized, tailor-made to the needs of a few specialists.

One assumption underlying several of the recent proposals for a national system is that the Federal Government has a responsibility to ensure that there exists within the United States at least one accessible copy of every significant publication of the world-wide literature of science and technology. Semantics aside, this is a desideratum that is difficult to quarrel with. At the same time, however, it must be recognized that the library community—with the Library of Congress and the other two national libraries, the National Library of Medicine and the National Agricultural Library, in the van—has done, and continues to do, more than any other group to assure that a sizable portion of the world output of significant literature, including an exceedingly high percentage of the scientific and technical literature, is acquired, cataloged, and made available throughout the country. Under Title II-C of the Higher Education Act of 1965, the Library of Congress, as is well known, was given the mandate and, through subsequent legislation, the funds for a far broader acquisitions and cataloging activity in all subject fields, not merely in science and technology, than anything the library community has been capable of in the past—a larger effort, we believe, than that envisioned in the studies set forth by the scientific and technical community.

Leadership by the Federal Government has been another theme running through most of the planning documents. The Library of Congress certainly agrees that the Government must take a leading part in the evolution of the national library and information network for the future. We also feel that effective and enlightened leadership is best achieved without resort to compulsion. Moreover, we believe that, through many encouraging developments already unfolding, there is evidence that leadership is being provided.

In the library community, for example, through the activities of the American Library Association, the Association of Research Libraries, the regional library associations, the Council on Library Resources, Inc., the interagency Federal Library Committee,[2] and especially the formalization of closer cooperation among the three national libraries—not to mention the work of other groups—there is now taking place an impressive marshaling of resources, brainpower, and experience. We are gratified also that the Committee on Scientific and Technical Information (COSATI), in continuing its efforts in national network planning, and more recently the Committee on Scientific and Technical Communication (SATCOM) of the National Academy of Sciences are not only working with the Federal departments but are giving considerable attention and a large active role to the academic community and the professional societies.

The Library of Congress would like to go on record with an opinion we believe expresses the fundamental requirement for success in establishing an effective national library and information network for the future. Quite simply, the basic need is to develop a responsive, flexible, communications medium that will serve as the means for moving the information record throughout the system. Solution of the communications problem is more important than administration, or organizational structure, or areas of responsibility for subject coverage or for handling categories of documents. The network problem is an access problem, and the access problem is essentially a file problem. It is a problem, therefore, of what librarians, in their old-fashioned terminology, call bibliographical control—control of the record surrogate for the actual informational piece, the original informational package.

---

2 *In March 1965, a Federal Library Committee was established under the auspices of the Bureau of the Budget and the Library of Congress. Membership includes the Librarian of Congress as Chairman, the directors of the National Agricultural Library and the National Library of Medicine, representatives of the Executive departments of the Government and six representatives of independent agencies, selected on a rotating basis by the permanent members. The Committee gives consideration to the problems and policies of Federal libraries as well as to comparative undertakings that may be possible.*

For the ultimate national network, which of course must be envisioned as an automated system with fast response-time, even real-time capability, there is, then, an overriding need to develop a standard record, with a full range of appropriate codes, as the *lingua franca* of the entire system. The standard record should be modular in format, open-ended, multipurpose, highly manipulable, and responsive to the need for a wide variety of products and services that the system must be capable of providing.

THE LIBRARY OF CONGRESS AUTOMATION PROGRAM

It is from this, the technical end, that we in the Library are now approaching the network problem. The automation program was effectively launched with the release, early in 1964, of the 88-page report *Automation and the Library of Congress,* which was compiled by a team of experts under the direction of Gilbert W. King and was supported with funds made available by the Council on Library Resources. This survey team declared that the automation of the Library's central bibliographic record was technically and economically feasible and that automation would enhance the adaptability of libraries to changes in the national research environment and would facilitate the development of a national library system.

The Library's automation program has at present two parts. The first is a system-development program directed toward automation of the central bibliographic system; it is being carried out in seven phases: (1) survey of the present manual system, (2) system requirements analysis, (3) functional description of a recommended system, (4) system specifications for equipment and procedures, (5) system design, (6) implementation of a new system, and (7) operation of the new system. The third phase produced a functional description of the central bibliographic apparatus and also a first approximation of an automated system. The report, accepted by the Library in June 1968, contains broader analysis than had been anticipated and can now be used for making decisions in other areas as well as in regard to automation. Tasks (4), (5), and (6) are closely related, leading to an operating system in task (7). Because large expenditures for equipment and programming will not be available immediately at the end of task (4), a complete system specification will not be undertaken during fiscal year 1969. System specification will be advanced to a point where it can take advantage of new computer developments as they appear.

The second part of the current automation program is the MARC (*MA*chine *R*eadable *C*atalog) Pilot Project to test the feasibility and desirability of distributing cataloging data in machine-readable form. It began in November 1966 with weekly tape distribution to sixteen libraries in the United States which, in turn, have supplied the tapes and/or MARC print programs to twenty-four secondary MARC participants. The Pilot Project has been limited to cataloging data for current English-language monographs but, as an extension, it is planned that coverage will include several other languages. A new tape format (MARC II), based on reports from and visits with the participating libraries and on the Library's own experience with the MARC I format, has been devised and was published by the Government Printing Office in May 1968.

The MARC II format emphasizes the transmission of bibliographic data rather than the local computer-processing requirements of the recipients. It thus aims at convertibility rather than compatibility. This means that a library receiving a MARC II tape will probably have to convert to its own tape format. The conversion will be made without human intervention, however, and will be required only once. The new MARC format is universal enough to accommodate a large variety of material. Until the extensions and modifications are completed, Project MARC will continue to be an experiment. By October 1968, the Library expects to be ready to sell, through its Card Division, machine-readable records, as well as catalog cards, to all interested libraries. At that time, it is also expected that MARC coverage will be extended to monographs in French and German.

This statement of the main outlines of the Library's automation program is necessarily brief and may convey an impression that our objectives are too limited. On the contrary, our goals are very broad. For that reason, with all the technical problems that await solution, the time when they can be achieved may be more distant than we would like.

Perhaps the most immediate dividends, beyond those just described, may be expected in the more efficient performances of essentially managerial operations, such as extending and expediting the Library's vast card distribution service. The keeping of interlibrary loan records and internal charge files can certainly be improved, perhaps to a revolutionary extent. When a significant body of pertinent information becomes available through electronic devices, the compilation of specialized subject bibliographies will be facilitated in terms both of number and depth of coverage. Already, through the interest shown in the MARC Pilot Project in British library circles, there is opening up the prospect of the exchange between countries of nationally compiled bibliographic data in machine-readable form, with all that such a possibility implies for the improvement and greater effectiveness of bibliography and cataloging around the globe.

We would stress, therefore, that current developments are only a part of the Library's continuing interest in research and planning for better library and information services. The time frame for the future is difficult to predict, but the target date for the operation of the Library's automated central bibliographic system is 1972. Whether that precise deadline can be met or not may be a moot question. When that step has been achieved, however, we are confident that it will be a major contribution not only toward national but toward worldwide control of bibliographic information.

As we all look, then, toward the development of an automated national and eventually international, library and information system network, we must squarely face the fact that there is only a limited amount of money, time, and people to be devoted to the problem. If the hundreds of thousands of dollars and the thousands of man-years that have already been spent for so-called national system planning teach us anything, it is that nobody yet knows enough to be able to draw up effective national system plans. If we would seriously hasten the time when the gap between the *now* and the *then* can be closed, we must turn our energies and our intelligence toward the solution of the considerable range of technical problems that require attention. The Library of Congress makes no pretense to omniscience; it could not alone solve all the problems even if it desired to do so. Progress, we believe, will be made most rapidly and effectively through cooperative efforts to carry through a well-ordered program of research—the first step in the evolutionary process leading to a national system.

When we turn for illumination to a prophet of automation, we find that he views the phenomenon others have called an explosion as something exactly opposite. In his much discussed book, *Understanding Media,* Marshall McLuhan writes: "After three thousand years of explosion, by means of fragmentary and mechanical technologies, the Western World is imploding. . . . Electric speed in bringing all social and political functions together in a sudden implosion has heightened human awareness of responsibility to an intense degree. . . ." The implication of the compressing force of electronic technology, applied to the realm of information, is not merely that the old "mechanical" patterns of performing operations in lineal sequence become outmoded, but that the very definitions that divided knowledge and knowledge-based activities, such as teaching or scientific research, into disciplines and subjects are swept away. The movement is toward integration rather than separation, toward total participation and total commitment rather than fragmentation and disunity.

What is already happening in the library and information community as it goes forward into the electronic age would seem to bear out this forecast of the nature of things to come. Cooperation, integration, total participation, and commitment are, we believe, already unfolding realities.

THE NATIONAL LIBRARY CONCEPT
ORGANIZATION OF THE LIBRARY OF CONGRESS

The Library of Congress, like all human institutions, is the product of its past. As Federal agencies go, it has already had a very long history, having been established on April 24, 1800, in the act for the removal of the seat of Government to Washington. As its name implies, the Library of Congress was at first a parliamentary library, but after the destruction of the original small collection in the War of 1812, when the British burnt the Capitol (1814), and the subsequent purchase by the Congress of Thomas Jefferson's personal library of some 6,000 volumes, the merely parliamentary character was forever altered. Jefferson's library and the classification scheme he had devised for its organization embraced all fields of learning and determined that henceforth the collections of the Library of Congress would be universal in scope. Universality remains a fundamental principle of the Library's philosophy and of its services and activities. Any attempt to alter that principle or to fragment the collection would be viewed not only by the Library, but also, we are convinced, by the Congress and the American people, as destructive of one of the nation's most precious heritages.

During the nineteenth century, the collections were opened to the public and were greatly augmented by means that still form the basic pattern for acquisition. Materials were acquired not only through annual Congressional appropriations, but also by copyright deposit, international exchange, special purchase (the Peter Force Collection), gift (the Joseph Meredith Toner Collection), and official transfer from other Government departments. So great was the influx of material that by 1871 the Library was overflowing its quarters in the Capitol and was obliged to seek authorization for a separate building. Although the first appropriations for this purpose were granted in 1886, it was not until 1897 that the present Main Building was ready for occupancy. A second building, known as the Annex, came into service in 1939, a good many years after the Main Building had passed the saturation point in terms of housing collections and staff. Now both buildings are overflowing. It has been necessary to utilize rented space to afford temporary relief from the congestion, and recently preliminary plans for a third Library building, to cost $75 million and to be erected on a large vacant plot just south of the Main Building, have been approved. This structure, authorized by P.L. 89–260 and to be known as the Library of Congress James Madison Memorial Building, will more than equal the space in the Library's present two buildings. If funds are made available as needed and there are no further delays, present expectation is that the Madison Building will be ready for occupancy in 1972.

In a limited way, the functions of the Library of Congress are reflected in its present organization. In addition to the Office of the Librarian, there are six departments:

1. The Administrative Department is responsible for the Library's central fiscal and personnel administration, the preservation of library materials, the photoduplication service, and the general housekeeping operations of the Library.

2. The Copyright Office is responsible for administering the Copyright Law, examining and registering claims to copyright, recording assignments and related documents, furnishing copyright data and other information about copyright to the public, indexing and cataloging all registrations and printing catalogs of copyright entries, and making studies of copyright problems and recommendations to the Congress for the general revision of the Copyright Law, which is now before the Congress.

3. The Law Library has custody of legal collections numbering some 1,250,000 volumes and gives a reference service to the Congress, other Government agencies, the bench and the bar, and the public. It is the largest law library in

the country and the Government's only general law library. It is strong in American and British law, but its collections also contain legal literature of all foreign countries. At the present time, the newly developed subject classification for law (Class K)[3] is being applied to the Library's legal materials.

4. The Legislative Reference Service (LRS) is the department of the Library devoted exclusively to providing information, reference materials, and research studies for Members and Committees of Congress and their staffs to assist them in their legislative responsibilities. Although the first duty of the entire Library is to serve Congress, LRS is a relatively small department of about 300 persons —backed up, of course, by the total resources of the Library. Although its services are not directly available to the public, it should be pointed out that LRS, through the Congress, performs a national service and much of the research done for the Congress is embodied in published, publicly available Congressional documents.[4]

5. The Processing Department is responsible for acquiring books and other library materials from almost every country and in every written language through purchase, exchange arrangements, transfer from other United States government agencies, gift, and copyright deposit; cataloging, classifying, and otherwise preparing materials for use by Congress, Federal agencies, and the public; and preparing hundreds of volumes of book catalogs comprising the national bibliography and other lists that make known the availability and location of essential research material; and distributing over 74 million printed catalog cards annually to libraries and other institutions.

6. The Reference Department has custody of all the collections except law, is responsible for services on this material to readers in 13 reading rooms and 325 study facilities, and replies to inquiries in person, by telephone, and through correspondence. This department also prepares for publication a variety of abstracts, bibliographies, indexes, and lists to make the collections more readily accessible to the research community. In addition, it organizes for use materials in special form, including maps, manuscripts, prints, photographs, microfilms, and motion pictures.

PRESENT FUNCTIONS AS NATIONAL LIBRARY

At the outset of this paper, the statement was made that the Library of Congress is the *de facto* National Library of the United States. There can be no question that the foundation of this claim is the Library's already vast and vastly increasing collections of every type and kind of material in which human knowledge and experience can be recorded—from books and manuscripts to kinescopic and magnetic tapes. But collections alone cannot create a dynamic national library. The national-library concept implies the performance of a broad range of services and activities that sustain the library community of the nation and benefit, directly and indirectly, the national community of library users—from the world of scholarship to the general public. Although it is not in name the national library, the Library of Congress performs more typical national-library functions than any other national library.

It is instructive to review the list of national-library functions which the Library of Congress is already carrying out. In its national role, the Library:

1. Collects comprehensively, having collections that reflect the national heritage and are universal in scope, and serves as a national center for research.

---

[3] *Class K is the definitive Library of Congress Classification schedule being developed for the subject classification of legal materials.*
[4] *The National Advisory Commission on Libraries considered that the Library's services to Congress were not within its purview and therefore, LC, in preparing its report to the Commission, did not go into this important national function.*

2. Benefits from intergovernmental exchange, copyright, and legal deposits.
3. Receives gifts to the nation (personal papers, rare books, gift and trust funds).
4. Administers worldwide acquisitions programs, such as the Public Law 480 Program to acquire foreign materials for other libraries, as well as for LC, and the National Program for Acquisitions and Cataloging, authorized by the Higher Education Act of 1965.
5. Devises and keeps up to date classification and subject-heading systems that serve as national standards.
6. Serves as the national center for cataloging.
7. Has a national catalog-card distribution service, now to include also the distribution of catalog information on magnetic tape.
8. Publishes in book form the national bibliography, the *National Union Catalog,* issued in the early 1950's, with its supplements, including the *National Union Catalog of Manuscript Collections,* which was begun in the early 1960's.
9. Maintains other union catalogs on cards; the *National Union Catalog* on cards describing pre-1956 imprints is now being published in 600 volumes of 700 pages each.
10. Gives reference services, in house and by mail, and operates such information "switchboards" as the National Referral Center for Science and Technology.
11. Extends services by participating in interlibrary loan and national and international photoduplication service.
12. Has an active bibliographic and publications program, producing the *Quarterly Journal,* guides, subject directories, area bibliographies, materials relating to children's literature, etc.
13. Administers the National Books-for-the-Blind Program, expanded in 1966 to include library services to all physically handicapped persons unable to use or read conventionally printed material.
14. Presents concerts, exhibits, and literary programs, including extension concerts and loan exhibits, which enrich the cultural life of the nation.
15. Experiments and conducts research in library technology; presently the major program is directed toward the automation of the Library's central bibliographic apparatus, with the aim of developing a national information-transfer system in which libraries all over the country may participate.
16. Conducts a program for the preservation of library materials, planned as the nucleus of a national program to attack the problem of deteriorating paper faced by all libraries.
17. Engages in national and international cooperative programs, such as the development of the Anglo-American Code for descriptive cataloging, in order to promote standardization and to increase accessibility to the materials of knowledge.

Without a charter spelling out its responsibilities, but with broad powers and Congressional support, the Library of Congress has been able to undertake all the above national-library functions. There are many other activities the National Library of the United States might well perform, but we have not been able to undertake them. There is a real question whether or not a detailed charter, which so many urge, would have been, or would in the future be, more help than hindrance. If areas of responsibility and relationships within and outside the Government were defined in precise detail, we in the Library of Congress are convinced that a charter would quickly become outdated and would consequently become a serious handicap.

Much the same may be said of the Library's position as an agency of the Legislative, rather than the Executive, Branch of the Federal Government. Looking back over the 169 years of the Library's history, it would be difficult to argue that its freedom of action, its ability to respond whenever a need was strongly felt, would have been any greater, if as great, in the Executive than it has been in the Legislative Branch. The Library of Congress has grown to its present size and eminence not because of where it was placed in the structure of Government, but because it has been free to respond to changing times and to needs as they developed and were expressed by the American people through their elected representatives in the Congress.

NEED FOR A FORMALLY RECOGNIZED NATIONAL LIBRARY

Looking forward, the Library *does* feel that it would be highly beneficial if the Congress gave formal recognition to its dual role as the Library *of Congress* and as the National Library of the United States, to which for so many years the Congress has given its tacit consent and material support. If such recognition is to be fruitful, however, it must go beyond a mere Congressional resolution. There needs to be a felt demand from the country strong enough to convince the Congress to vote, not just for the addition of a subtitle, "The Library of Congress: The National Library of the United States," but for the funds required for the full support of national-library as well as of LC functions. Basically, it is *fiscal support* that the Library needs if it is to sustain and expand its role as the National Library of the United States. If we had the necessary money, now that adequate space is in prospect to take care of the physical needs of the next two decades, there is probably little in the way of expanded services and activities that we could not undertake.

The National Advisory Commission on Libraries has focused attention upon the central role of the Library of Congress in the Nation's library and information service economy, and on the need for formal recognition of, and adequate funding for, its national-library functions. If a pattern of organization and of Congressional bookkeeping can now be found that will not necessarily superimpose the whole burden of national-library funding upon the cost of running the Legislative Branch, we believe that the nation can have, and the Library of Congress can effectively be, the National Library. This objective—a basic step in the evolution of the national library and information service network for which there is so much agitation—requires the serious consideration and continuing attention of a *permanent* National Commission on Libraries, the creation of which the Librarian of Congress advocated as early as 1962, for library problems are continuing yet ever-changing.

Indeed, it is difficult to see how a national library and information system could operate effectively without a permanent advisory body on a national program. There is, of course, ample precedent from other spheres of endeavor and national interest, from interstate commerce, to finance, communications, etc. Such a permanent Commission should in our view and as the Commission recommended, enlarge its purview to include information science. It should work with all elements of the library and information community and with the Library of Congress, notably and particularly in its role as the National Library. The permanent Commission could be the chief instrumentality for bringing the much-talked-of system into being; it could formulate the system, identifying the members, the nodes or interconnections, and the channels of communication. It could propose legislation when and as appropriate, and review legislation proposed by others. It could and should have a lively interest in funding and in cost effectiveness.

For the Library of Congress to perform properly the functions of the *de jure* National Library, certain assumptions must be made. Adequate funding has been mentioned. So has the guidance and advocacy that a permanent Commission could afford. A third assumption, perhaps implicit in the foregoing, is an "economy" of continuous expansion. A static national library is a contradiction in terms. The National Library must continuously expand its collections, its services, its space, and its support. It must also expand its tools—the staff who are to do the intellectual work and, in the electronic age, the machines that are to perform the slave labor. The qualifying standards, like the supply, of the competent people and the machines can only increase as the collections and services grow in size and in complexity.

Congressional Appropriations Committees have in recent years frequently recognized this need for the Library to grow if it is to continue as a dynamic national institution. This attitude must be continuously nourished and justified by evidence from the country that LC's role is both viable and vital to the welfare of the nation's libraries and their users. Also imperative is the wholehearted support of the Joint Committee on the Library and of the parent committees from which its members are drawn—the Committee on House Administration and the Senate Committee on Rules and Administration—for the dual-role concept of "The Library of Congress: The National Library of the United States." The proposed permanent Commission, in other words, would in no sense supplant the Library's traditional relationships with Congress; it would supplement them, bringing nonpartisan, informed advice to the makers of public policy.

OPPORTUNITIES FOR EXPANDED
SERVICES AND ACTIVITIES

A basic characteristic of the Library of Congress in the role of *de jure* National Library of the United States would be that each of the services and activities performed would have both an internal and an external component. Also, the Library would be acting formally—as it does at present informally—in a national setting and on a much larger stage. In certain functions, The Library of Congress: The National Library would be the sole agent, the active agency; in others, it would work as a part of, or with, or through another organization, or organizations, or groups. In terms of its overall responsibilities, it would, as the National Library, act not as a Legislative agency but as an independent Federal agency whose sphere of activity would not be restricted to any one branch but would embrace all branches of the Government, as indeed its services *now* do. In this regard, though it might not have or need to have the title, it would in fact act as, and be, the national library and information service agency.

In the following discussion of opportunities and responsibilities for expanded services and activities that we believe the Library could have as the National Library, it is of course assumed that the basic Library *of Congress* function would remain, and that it would remain basic. Although that aspect of the Library's duties was beyond the scope of inquiry of the National Advisory Commission on Libraries and is therefore not a material consideration in this report, it should be pointed out that the services and activities of our present Legislative Reference Service must keep pace in growth not only with the ever-expanding responsibilities of the Congress but also with the public-service aspects of the Library.

It must also be pointed out that many of the functions described below are interdependent and overlapping and that no attempt has been made here to cross-reference all the interrelationships. Further, when such words as "agency," "center," etc., are used, they should not be construed as names of actual or proposed organizational units but merely as convenient terms for describing functions.

The remainder of this paper is devoted to a sketch of some services and activities that the Library of Congress might expand or undertake if it were formally recognized as the National Library and supported accordingly.

THE NATIONAL ACQUISITIONS AGENCY

The Library would not only develop and maintain comprehensive collections for its own purposes (with special emphasis on the national heritage and with extensive coverage of materials from other nations and cultures), but under such programs as the

P.L. 480 Program and the National Program for Acquisitions and Cataloging (NPAC), established by authority of Title II-C of the Higher Education Act of 1965, and the proposed amendments now before Congress, would also acquire materials for other research libraries and information centers on a worldwide basis, serving, in certain areas, as the agent of the other libraries.

In performing the role of national acquisitions agency, the Library of Congress would:

Extend the National Program for Acquisitions and Cataloging to All Countries and All Types of Materials

Since the spring of 1966 seven overseas offices have been established in Europe, one in South America, and one in Africa. Arrangements with foreign book dealers and with the producers of current national bibliographies have speeded the flow of books and cataloging data to the Library. To date, however, only books available from commercial booksellers have been acquired and these preponderantly from European countries. As soon as feasible, we believe this program should be extended to every country in the world and its coverage broadened to include all types of library materials—periodicals, newspapers, government publications, maps, music, recordings, prints and photographs, as well as current trade books.

Acquire Multiple Copies of Foreign Publications

Under NPAC the Library of Congress would acquire at least one additional copy of hard-to-obtain foreign publications for deposit as a loan set in the Center for Research Libraries. It would be preferable for the Library, as the National Library, to acquire multiple copies, to be placed in a number of strategically located, possibly regional, institutions throughout the United States. Enactment of the proposed amendments to the Higher Education Act would enable LC to take the first step toward implementing this program. The regional depositories should be tied closely to the National Library through a rapid-communications network and should be provided with full bibliographical apparatus which would equip them to serve effectively as regional bibliographical centers. It is expected that experience would demonstrate the advisability of such centers becoming, in some formal way, branches of the National Library, with at least a degree of regulation (for the purposes of standardization, comparability of service, etc.) from the national center, sharing its resources and extending its services far more directly than is at present possible to every state in the Union.

Expand and Modernize the International Exchange Machinery

The exchange of publications between governments and institutions is of ever-greater importance. The existing machinery, with mass shipments of partial or full sets of documents being effected through the International Exchange Service of the Smithsonian Institution, has changed little since the nineteenth century and is badly in need of modernization. The Library of Congress, as the official depository for the publications of foreign governments and as the supplier of United States Government publications to other nations, should, in its role as the National Library, possess the means for assuring more selectivity and should send abroad only the serials and monographs desired by particular foreign libraries and organizations.

Acquire Comprehensively and Bring Under Bibliographical Control Federal, State, and Local Government Publications

No library is now obtaining anything like a complete set of Federal, state, and local documents. Coverage of government publications not from the Government Printing

Office (GPO), many of them of great importance, has been especially poor. Only a portion of the issuances of the states is acquired, and the Library has been able to do little with regard to local (city, county, etc.) publications. The coverage of the GPO's *Monthly Catalog of U.S. Government Publications* and of LC's *Monthly Checklist of State Publications* is very incomplete. There is no comparable catalog or checklist for local publications. There should be a reasonably complete set of all the most important of these publications in the Library of Congress and also in a number of other widely distributed centers in the national-library network.

Based on LC's statutory right to obtain for its collections, and for use in exchange, copies of all Government publications, and with the aid of the Bureau of the Budget, the Library is taking steps that should bring its coverage of Federal documents to near-completeness. As the National Library, it could perfect and enlarge acquisitions arrangements with state libraries, state universities, and other centers to assure complete local coverage of the issuances of state and county governments and of the larger municipalities in each state. A copy of these publications would be sent to the Library of Congress for the national collections. The Library's expanded coverage of governmental documents should make it possible, through cooperative arrangements with the Superintendent of Documents, to transform the *Monthly Catalog of U.S. Government Publications,* as well as LC's *Monthly Checklist of State Publications,* into the comprehensive records they should be. It would also make it feasible for the Library to initiate a current checklist of important United States municipal publications. The growing concern of Congress and the nation with state and urban problems makes a strong collection of such materials necessary for Congressional use, even if there were not other compelling national reasons for their acquisition.

THE NATIONAL CENTER FOR LIBRARY RESOURCES

The archival function is one of the principal duties that research libraries especially owe to the communities they serve and one of the great benefits they render collectively to society, yet it has become popular in some circles to deprecate this service and disparage libraries as warehouses full of musty old tomes. However, no library, not even the Library of Congress with all its vast collections, can be expected to be exhaustively comprehensive in the literature of all fields, all countries, and all periods of history, nor, more particularly, can any one depository hope to possess more than a tithe of such special record materials as manuscripts, rare books, prints, photographs, etc.

Nevertheless, as the National Library in fact, the Library of Congress is already a "library of record." It would therefore be in a good position to take the leadership in systematically creating a national center for library resources, which might be physically decentralized, as previously suggested in regard to foreign materials, but might operate as a regional system under LC's direction and utilize uniform bibliographical control apparatus and rapid communications media. Some of the means by which the archival services of libraries could be improved include:

Extension of the National Union Catalog

The National Union Catalog is already a basic research tool, the effectiveness of which is now being enormously enhanced through the publication of the pre-1956 portion in book form, as mentioned earlier. However, this 600-volume publication—though it will be the largest single publication ever issued—is an author catalog only, covering books of research value held by some 700 major libraries in the United States and Canada. A future task for LC as the National Library would be to publish a catalog of similar proportions arranged by subject, in order that scholars and research workers may have a systematic subject approach as well as an author and title approach to the wealth of materials contained in North American libraries.

Prepare Guides to the Total Library Resources of the United States

The Federal Library Committee has made preliminary studies of the feasibility of preparing a guide to the resources of Federal libraries and is contemplating seeking outside support for such a guide. As the National Library, the Library of Congress should, we believe, take over this effort and expand it to cover the resources of all significant American libraries, both publicly owned and private. The guide—which in practice might well take the form of a number of guides in particular subject areas— would describe the nature of the collections held, their scope, coverage, organization, and availability. It would not be a catalog of individual collections like the *National Union Catalog of Manuscript Collections* but summary in nature. Books, journals, government documents, technical reports, and all other library materials should be covered. It should be the Library's intention to maintain the guide on a current and continuing basis through the use of automated methods.

Serve as a National Center for Research, Guidance, and Information on Preservation Problems

Preservation problems of the nation's libraries, especially those having research functions and serving primarily the community of scholars, are assuming serious proportions. Over the years, some preservation problems have been solved in whole or in part, but many problems remain which require further investigation. Further, certain preservation problems are of such magnitude that they can be undertaken only on a national basis. The Library of Congress is the only agency qualified to assume leadership in this important area, and it has already accepted responsibility for coordinating a program designed to preserve the existing collections of research libraries. Specifically, the Library should undertake the following programs:

1. Establish a preservation research and testing program to conduct fundamental investigations, by means of an appropriate laboratory, covering a wide range of preservation problems: from further studies of the accelerated aging of paper, to methods of paper deacidification, to better methods of library binding, to research on new methods of document restoration, to improved or new techniques for preserving library materials in such forms as sound recordings and motion picture films. Further, such a laboratory should conduct testing on a wide variety of products and materials used in preservation work. Leadership would continue in promoting high standards for photographic reproduction, particularly as related to copying for preservation.

2. Establish a program, similar in part to the present general intern program of the Library, to train selected librarians in the basic philosophies, theories, and techniques of preservation.

3. Conduct a comprehensive program for preserving in microform older materials (particularly those in a deteriorating or brittle state) of research value.

4. Establish a national preservation program to identify and preserve the best copies of research materials. Such a program is required in order to save, for future generations of scholars, those research materials now deteriorating on the shelves of the nation's libraries. The text of these deteriorating materials would be made generally available on microforms. It is important, however, that copies, in the best possible condition, of many publications be preserved in their original form. Such a program may have several aspects, including development of a national underground storage library where materials will be stored under the optimum environmental conditions necessary to assure indefinite preservation, these facilities to include the laboratory and photographic services necessary to insure adequate control and service to the collections. Other aspects of such a program may include designation of particular libraries to serve as official holders of

national-preservation copies, provision of consultative services on suitable storage conditions for such materials, and coordination of a central file of national preservation materials.

THE NATIONAL CATALOGING CENTER

A great many American libraries have long looked to the Library of Congress to perform the services of a national cataloging center. The need of research libraries throughout the country to broaden and deepen this relationship was the motivating force behind the mandate incorporated into Title II-C of the Higher Education Act of 1965, which provided the basic justification for the National Program for Acquisitions and Cataloging and its overseas complement, the Shared Cataloging Program. If this mandate continues over the years to be supported by adequate funding—and we mean here funding adequate for the expanded acquisitions program described above—the Library will be well launched as the national cataloging center.

Among the number of desirable specific undertakings in the cataloging area are the following:

Automate the Catalog-Card Distribution Service

The Library of Congress began in 1901, as a national service, to make its printed catalog cards available to other libraries. In the fiscal year ending June 30, 1967, some 20,000 libraries purchased more than 74.5 million Library of Congress catalog cards; receipts from the sale of cards, book catalogs, and technical publications—income which eventually goes into the United States Treasury—totaled $6,289,000. The cards provide full and accurate descriptions of the titles cataloged, including the subjects covered, indicate the presence of bibliographies, and give two alternative subject classifications, one according to the Library's own system and the other that of the widely used Dewey Decimal Classification. Library of Congress printed cards are increasingly regarded as the standard in this country and abroad. Yet the system of distributing to subscribers is no longer rapid enough to meet the urgent need for libraries for prompt cataloging information. Most of the card-distribution operations would lend themselves to mechanized data processing, with a resultant speeding up and improvement of the service. Although the Library has taken initial steps toward this goal, a full-scale effort, with the required funding, is required to push the conversion to completion with the least possible delay.

Publish a Current National Union Subject Catalog

The product of the Library's cataloging efforts is made available not only through the printing of catalog cards but also in the form of current book catalogs, issued monthly and cumulated quarterly, annually, and quinquennially. The chief of these book catalogs, the *National Union Catalog* (NUC), is now being sent to over 1,700 libraries, both foreign and domestic. With the Library's stepped-up program for the acquisition and cataloging of foreign-language materials, the NUC has become a truly international bibliography. Issued since 1956, it reproduces the cards prepared by the Library of Congress and, in addition, those from nearly 1,000 other cooperating libraries; it also indicates which libraries hold each title. Nevertheless, the utility of this publication is limited by the fact that it provides only an author approach to the holdings of American libraries. The Library of Congress should begin to issue a companion publication which would list by subject all the titles acquired and cataloged by United States and Canadian libraries, thus providing a complete bibliographical service.

A NATIONAL CENTER FOR BIBLIOGRAPHICAL SERVICES

The Library of Congress has long been distinguished for the number, kind, and variety of bibliographical services it has been able to offer to other libraries, to scientists, historians, and other scholars working in many fields. If it had formal status and support as the National Library, the Library of Congress would be in a position to improve and expand its bibliographical activities. Its ability to do so will be enhanced when the Library's automation program has progressed to a point where it is anticipated that it will be possible to retrieve bibliographic information on a subject basis to a greater depth than is now possible, not only from the central catalogs but from the catalogs of special materials. Eventually, it should be possible to compile, through automation techniques, bibliographic information held anywhere in the national library and information system, although such capability is admittedly some years away.

Meanwhile, many libraries will continue to depend upon the book catalogs, and there are many other valuable though less ambitious services which the Library might undertake. Among them are the following:

Provide Systematic Bibliographic Coverage of Non-Western Publications

The publication of the current *National Union Catalog,* and the project to publish in book form the older portion of the *National Union Catalog* on cards, now well under way, go far toward providing adequate bibliographic control over publications in European languages. But neither, unfortunately, covers all publications in Oriental alphabets. There can be no doubt that Asian publications will become ever more important to American interests in the years ahead. The Library of Congress, as the National Library, should therefore complete, bring up to date, and publish its union catalogs of Chinese, Japanese, Korean, South Asian, and Near Eastern publications. Current titles in these and other Oriental languages, with locations, should also be listed in the *National Union Catalog* or a companion publication.

Publish Comprehensive Accessions Lists for All Countries Lacking Adequate Current National Bibliographies

With the expansion of its overseas programs under the P.L. 480 Program and the National Program for Acquisitions and Cataloging, the Library of Congress will be in a position—always provided adequate funding is available—to fill the bibliographical gap which now exists in most of the countries of the world. The lists it already publishes of its accessions under the P.L. 480 Program in Ceylon, India, Indonesia, Israel, Nepal, Pakistan, and the United Arab Republic at present supplement the national bibliographies where they exist and serve as national bibliographies where there are none. In its role as the National Library, LC should undertake, on a continuing basis, comparable lists of its accessions from all countries where the national bibliography is not sufficiently current, detailed, and comprehensive. Where possible, these countries should be encouraged and aided to begin the issuance of such bibliographies on their own. But, until these countries can take over the responsibility and perform it in an adequate fashion, the United States, through the Library of Congress, should, for the sake of its own research community, continue to publish the accessions list.

Create New Bibliographical Tools

The Library's subject classification system, in twenty volumes, is the most extensive in existence and is being adopted by a rapidly increasing number of libraries, both large and of medium size. This trend seems certain to continue. The Library should develop and publish a manual of guidance and instruction in the use of its classification schedules.

Each of the score of volumes making up the Library of Congress classification system is supplied with an index, yet there has been no combined index to the entire classification. Such an index is now being cooperatively developed. It should be published and made widely available.

Each of the author and subject headings used in the Library's catalogs has been established by LC on the basis of investigation. At present this background information is to be found only on cards filed in the Library's Official Catalog, now available only to the staff. If this information were edited and published, it would save other libraries much unnecessary work in establishing the same headings.

The Library's shelflist is, in effect, a classified catalog of all the materials which have been processed and added to its collections. It now exists only in card form. It should be published and provided with an index in order to give other libraries the benefit of a classified (subject) approach to the immense collections of the National Library, thus supplementing the author approach now available through the Library's published catalogs in book form.

A NATIONAL CENTER FOR RESEARCH AND TRAINING IN LIBRARY AND INFORMATION SCIENCE

The movement during the last decade or so for the creation of a national library and information system has brought into sharp focus the need for a central technical authority with responsibilities for the development of standards and techniques applicable broadly to library and information work. For lack of such an authority, we have seen the mushrooming growth of national-system proposals as discussed earlier in this paper, and a variety of schemes for collecting, organizing, and communicating bibliographic and other literature—derived information. If solid progress is to be made toward the development of the kind of national system that is needed—that is, one that will work—the library community must have a mechanism for making its experience and expertise felt in this field which is so peculiarly its own.

The second, and related, need that arises out of this movement and out of the increasing demand for library and information services is the necessity for an adequate supply of personnel, trained and experienced in library and information science. Unless and until such a supply is guaranteed, libraries and information services must expect not only to have to make do with unskilled personnel for the performance of workaday tasks, but to find specialists outside of their profession making the big decisions in the intellectual matters that determine the quality and effectiveness of library and information services.

We believe the Library of Congress, therefore, in its role as the National Library, should have a formal responsibility in the realm of library and information technology and in the training or retraining of professional personnel. The following are some of the kinds of specific tasks it might undertake:

Create a National Technical Processes Service

The Library of Congress has already established a Technical Processes Research Office to serve its own needs. Its functions should be broadened and its services extended on a national scale. It should undertake research projects for other libraries, give a reference and information service in this field, and create and provide all necessary materials relating to automated systems of cataloging, subject analysis, classification, indexing, filing, storage, retrieval, and bibliographical control required to meet the expanding needs of the national library and information system. The recently established Library of Congress Automation Techniques Exchange (LOCATE) serves as a focal point for information on activities in the area of library automation and provides reference services on this information. LOCATE collects reports, manuals, forms, worksheets, flow charts, articles, etc., published or unpublished, that describe automation programs. This service should be continued on a permanent basis and should be broadened in scope to cover all of the foregoing subjects.

Create a National Automated System of Subject Controls

Through the use of computers and photocomposition, the Library publishes successive editions, with monthly supplements, of the list of subject headings used in its catalogs. This is by far the largest of existing lists and is a standard for all American and many foreign libraries. The magnetic tapes used to print the seventh edition of the list have recently been made available for sale to libraries who wish to experiment with them in developing a system of automated and bibliographical controls; edited tapes, stripped of the printing instructions, will also be obtainable. As the National Library, the Library of Congress should, we believe, establish promptly a full-scale, continuing program to increase the depth of its analysis of the subject content of all the types of publications it acquires, catalogs, and, through its bibliographic projects, indexes, and should make the results available in machine-readable form. It should also develop subsystems of subject control to meet the special needs of particular categories of users—for example, the scientific and technical community—and provide them with instructions or codes of application.

Translate the Library's Technical Publications and Bibliographical Tools

As the National Library of the world's most advanced nation (not least in bibliothecal techniques) and in the interest of promoting and facilitating the development of an international information system, the Library of Congress should promote and coordinate the translation of technical publications and when possible make available in machine-readable form its many basic and essential instruments for bibliographical control. These would include the Library's list of subject headings, its own classification system and the Dewey Decimal Classification (edited by the Library of Congress), its filing rules, *Cataloging Service Bulletins,* and all the bibliographical tools mentioned above. These publications should, when possible, be translated into all the principal foreign languages. Provision should also be made for the prompt translation and distribution of revisions.

Train American Librarians

The libraries of the United States, having long regarded the Library of Congress as the *de facto* National Library, have looked to it for leadership and for a wide and increasing range of services on a national scale. Its techniques and procedures, particularly those having to do with acquisitions, cataloging, classification, and bibliography, are recognized as standards to be followed. This trend is an accelerating one, but many librarians at all levels feel a need for a more intimate knowledge of the National Library than can be gained through library schools, reading, or casual visits. Such knowledge is also needed by information specialists who are not necessarily librarians. Also, there is a need to train subject specialists in charge of special collections in libraries who are not necessarily or even likely to be technical librarians and information specialists. The Library of Congress should establish a large-scale program for bringing members of the staffs of United States libraries and all other kinds of information personnel to the Library for intensive training in its methods and technical processes, including LC's programs for handling special materials.

Train Scholars to Administer Research Collections

Beginning in 1968, the Library of Congress and the George Washington University will offer an affiliated doctoral program in American Thought and Culture, with emphasis on research in organizing and handling library materials.

Doctoral candidates in the fields of American civilization, or of civilizations to which American culture is related, will study with scholars on LC's staff, who will offer courses and supervise research. Instruction will be offered both at the Library and at the University.

The program will help meet a national need for scholarly administrators in research libraries, particularly in regard to special collections. It will also enrich graduate study by bringing students into broader but more intimate contact with the unique collections of the Library of Congress. Such a program could be expanded to include other subject specialties.

Train Foreign Librarians

In a shrinking world, the National Library of the United States has at least implied responsibilities that extend far beyond the boundaries of this country. The Library of Congress should, in cooperation with other government agencies, coordinate and promote a massive systematic program for the training of foreign librarians in American library techniques, with emphasis on the bibliographical procedures, broadly interpreted, of the Library of Congress. Foreign librarians at all levels should be brought to the Library of Congress for intensive instruction and Library officers should be sent, on request, to foreign libraries to give courses and conduct seminars in existing libraries and to aid in the establishment of new libraries and library services.

THE NATIONAL CENTER FOR DATA ON SERIALS

For the past several years, the Library of Congress, together with other libraries and interested organizations, has been studying the possibility of establishing a control-data program for the improved handling of journal literature. The periodical is often called the lifeblood of research, yet it is a form of literature that has long been a serious problem for libraries and information services, professional societies and publishers, as well as users. The problem was considered at some length by a task force of the Committee on Scientific and Technical Information (COSATI) and a study was made of the feasibility of creating a broad-based, national, journal-control project. The report, made by the Information Dynamics Corporation, concluded that the project, while feasible, would not be inexpensive, would have to be computer-based, and would require the cooperation of many libraries, especially the Library of Congress, the National Library of Medicine, and the National Agricultural Library. The report, although not specific on the matter, clearly pointed to the Library of Congress as the agency best qualified to manage, house, and operate the project. The Library agreed and presented a plan of attack on the problem.

A small beginning has recently been made with funds provided by the National Library of Medicine, the National Agricultural Library, the National Science Foundation, the Library of Congress, and the Council on Library Resources, Inc. A phased project, looking toward a system design, is being carried out by the Library's Information Systems Office, with the cooperation of the Processing and Reference Departments. It is expected that, eventually, large-scale funding on a continuing basis will be required, but the activity is certainly a proper one for the National Library.

Such a national serials data program would offer libraries and other organizations concerned with serial literature a variety of bibliographical and management information. One major benefit of the program would be the ability to produce a fourth edition of the *Union List of Serials* (and future revisions) by computer methods. The third edition excluded many categories of serials (government publications, administrative reports, newspapers, law reports and digests, international conferences and congresses, etc.) that the national serial data program might well include. The program will also provide a ready method for updating information (the third edition of the *Union List* is already out of date as a record of both listings and holdings). Another by-product of the serials program would be the ability to produce *New Serial Titles,* which is more inclusive than the *Union List* but omits newspapers and certain other categories of publications, by machine methods.

The national serial data program was originally conceived as a current service oriented particularly toward science and technology. The Library of Congress from the outset insisted that it must, at least eventually, be extended to all subject fields. As the National Library, LC would, of course, also wish to extend the coverage backward in time, and to other than United States holdings, so that the program would at maturity become in effect an automated, worldwide union list of serials, old and new, that could be maintained on a current basis.

A NATIONAL TECHNICAL REPORTS CENTER

A subset of the serials control problem that is perhaps more exasperating and challenging than any other is the control of technical reports, materials in near-print form that are not considered publications, that receive limited distribution, but that contain the valuable results of current research, much of it done on a contract basis. The Library has in its general and special collections approximately a million such reports, and is receiving on a current basis from Government, industrial, and academic sources in this country and abroad upwards of 50,000 new reports a year—and the figure is growing. Most of these receipts are kept, uncataloged, in a special collection, serviced mainly through the use of finding aids issued by the producer organizations, although certain important series are cataloged and added to the Library's general collections.

Many other groups, within and outside the Government, have struggled with this hard-to-handle form of literature, which is of critical importance to the research and development community not only in the United States but around the world. The Government has established, from time to time, special agencies to deal with the problem—the Office of Technical Services, the Armed Services Technical Information Agency, the Defense Documentation Center, and, most recently, the Clearinghouse for Federal Scientific and Technical Information—but no definitive solution has been found. Attempts have been made to afford local access, not only to industrial but also to academic users, through regional depositories, but these have failed for economic and other reasons.

The Library of Congress has had long experience with the technical-report problem but has been without a mandate to assert the leadership that a solution would require. As the National Library, however, the Library should, we believe, have the responsibility for acquiring all significant literature and for offering whatever range of services users need. This responsibility could be effectively discharged if the legal and funding basis could be provided for the Library to assume and broaden the functions now assigned to the Clearinghouse for Federal Scientific and Technical Information in the Department of Commerce.

THE NATIONAL REFERRAL SERVICE IN ALL FIELDS

Five years ago, with National Science Foundation funding, the Library established the National Referral Center for Science and Technology. This Center has the threefold function of inventorying all United States information resources relating to science and technology, of publishing general and special book-form directories of such information resources, and of providing, in-house and by mail, responses to requests for referral information. The Center does not answer bibliographical or substantive questions, but through its inventory of resources, refers users to the persons, organizations, or services best able to render expert assistance.

The referral service technique is not a new one in information transfer; it is rather an attempt to categorize and systematize a service that libraries had long provided in a more or less haphazard way. The Library believes that the Referral Center has proved its value and that it should be a permanent feature of the Library's service. To achieve maximum effectiveness, however, it should be extended to cover information resources in all fields of scholarship and endeavor.

Through the efforts of the State Technical Services programs, administered by the Department of Commerce, impetus has been given to the development of a considerable number of local and state referral activities pertaining to industrial and commercial enterprise. Similar developments might well take place in other spheres of interest. At present a basic service of LC's National Referral Center is to serve as the central clearinghouse through which not only individual information resources, but also these local and state referral centers, are brought into fruitful contact with each other and with the nationwide complex of potential users.

THE FOCUS OF A NATIONAL INTERLIBRARY LOAN SYSTEM

The Library of Congress has provided a national service over many years through its participation in a nationwide interlibrary loan service. Materials from the Library's collections that are not at the moment in demand by Congress and the rest of the Government, and that cannot be obtained otherwise, are now lent to other libraries in this country and abroad when there is a genuine scholarly need. With the improvement of facsimile transmission methods and other means of electronic reproduction, the availability of the Library's research collections can be and undoubtedly will be augmented, although there is the difficult problem of copyright, discussed later in this paper.

Plans for making available additional copies of books received through the operation of Title II-C of the Higher Education Act are under discussion, as already noted, and may result in regional deposit collections and a further extension of the interlibrary loan service for these publications.

A NATIONAL RESEARCH AND INFORMATION CENTER

Through its many reference and bibliographical services, the Library of Congress has long served as a national research and information center. If it is to do this on a more formal basis as the National Library, it must intensify certain of its activities and, concomitantly, increase and improve the quality of its staff of specialists. Among other services, it should, beyond what it is now doing, provide:

1. Assistance and guidance in the use of the Library's collections. This kind of service should constitute a model for other libraries in the country. Orientation courses, seminars, and publications programs should be increased and expanded; individual advice and help from the Library's specialists should be made more freely available; and vastly improved physical facilities, especially for visiting scholars, should be provided.

2. Information about and from the Library's collections. Providing bibliographical information about the Library's collections through guides, calendars, registers, descriptive bibliographies, checklists, contributions to union lists and catalogs, etc., is a traditional responsibility that, with adequate staff, can be considerably expanded. Providing substantive information from the Library's collections (abstracts, reports, indexes, etc.) to the scholarly community, as is now done for the Federal Government on transferred funds, would be a logical extension of the Library's national responsibilities.

3. Information about the collections and services of other libraries, which constitute segments of the nation's total resources for research, should be collected and disseminated.

4. Data about all other kinds of information resources throughout the world should be made available through directories of research activities, rosters of special competence, biobibliographies, etc.

The above services could be best carried out through a congeries of centers in LC that would combine and coordinate the various information, bibliographic, and referral functions now carried on in varying degrees by the divisions of the Reference Department. Although traditionally a part of normal, though limited, reference service, these functions could be much better adapted to meet national needs if they were regrouped and greatly expanded in depth. As stated above, the success of the National Referral Center for Science and Technology is a good indication of the direction in which information and referral centers should move. The need for bibliographic centers, as expressed by various professional groups (with one such operation recently funded by a foundation) is further evidence of this trend. The final shape of the centers must be left for future development but the following pattern is envisaged. A series of centers on the various geographic areas and cultures of the world: the United States of America, Canada, Hispanic America, the Orient (possibly with five subdivisions), Slavic and Central Europe, Africa, Western Europe, and Australia and the Pacific Islands.

The United States of America

The Library's collections on American civilization are unexcelled; in manuscripts, maps, music, prints, photographs, and in all other forms of research material, the collections are unequalled in depth and in scope. The Library has also a tradition of high-level scholarship.

Because of its unequalled holdings, its bibliographic and scholarly competence, and its responsibilities to American scholarship, existing programs should be expanded and extended in scope and new means devised for exploiting the Library's treasures. Among these should be mentioned: publications (in modern edited texts or in facsimile reproduction) of some of the basic primary resources for study of American civilization; descriptive guides to the holdings of LC's major custodial divisions relating to American civilization; descriptive guides (some in the form of exhibit catalogs) to LC resources for specific topics of research in American civilization, particularly those resources which are separated for custodial purposes in different divisions of LC; bibliographic lists of publications in one or more of the disciplines comprising American civilization or of the total field; abstracts of studies in American civilization (rather than mere enumerative bibliographies); descriptive guides to the state of the literature, a selective and discriminating discussion of recent publications of studies in American civilization; and union catalogs and registers of holdings of special research materials in American civilization not provided for in existing publications.

It will be evident that some of these activities are also being carried on elsewhere (e.g., under the auspices of the National Historical Publications Commission); wherever this is true, the center would play a referral role, developing lists of work in progress as well as registers of material worthy of editorial or bibliographical attention. In addition to its referral role, the center would participate and cooperate with other parts of the Library and with institutions engaged in related bibliographical and publication activities, seeking to facilitate and supplement, certainly not to duplicate or supplant. It would also be the focal point for participation in such graduate-study activities as the above-mentioned program in cooperation with George Washington University.

Other Areas of the World

As in the case of the United States of America, the Library has collections on the civilization and culture of other areas that are in some cases unique, and in most respects overwhelming. In Chinese and Japanese, for example, the collections cannot be equalled in this country or, in some aspects, elsewhere. Most of the area collections had their inception long before other research libraries (with a few exceptions) anticipated or recognized the needs by the Government and the scholarly community that became obvious in the 1930's and urgent thereafter. Recognition of the national character of the Library's area collections has been borne out by the grants and endowments given to the Library for their exploitation over a period of several decades. Their full potential, however, has yet to be realized. This could be approached most effectively by concentrating bibliographical and information activities in centers of the kind described here. Programs could include compilations for the Asian, Near Eastern, Slavic, and African areas similar to the highly useful *Handbook of Latin American Studies;* union catalogs and listings of specialized language materials, one example of which is the *Monthly Index of Russian Accessions;* union lists of newspapers and periodicals; and other bibliographical undertakings to bring under control the unique holdings of the Library of Congress, as well as to make known resources existing in other collections.

Coordination of bibliographical activities throughout the country would be a major responsibility of these centers. Close cooperation with scholarly and professional groups, research libraries, and foundations should be carefully worked out, and the centers would play an important referral role in respect to bibliographical and other scholarly work in progress, as well as to information about publications in their spheres of interest.

Finally, the centers would answer needs for substantive information and for expert assistance in using the Library's collections, and would continue to develop the collections. Here again, the services and staff would require considerable expansion, including additional competence to carry out the selection responsibilities necessary to the enlarged acquisitions program described earlier in this paper.

Just as the subject matter of a discipline does not have rigid boundaries, it is recognized that all knowledge cannot be divided nationally or regionally. Many of the programs suggested above would require joint efforts by two or more centers. Union catalogs and bibliographies of nonbook material—for example, sound recordings, motion pictures, maps, music, and prints—would not necessarily be limited to the products of a single country or area. This, however, is an administrative problem, the solution of which will lie in close coordination of the work of the centers and of the various custodial divisions.

Center for Science and Technology

Of all the disciplines, science lends itself least well to national or regional treatment. While a country's scientific achievements may be an integral part of its culture, they are usually so closely related to similar activities in other nations that undesirable fragmentation would result if a national or regional approach were adopted. Hence a separate center for science and technology (including some of the social sciences) seems preferable for information and referral purposes.

The appropriateness of such a center in the Library of Congress requires little argument. With its vast science collections (the largest in the world), with its access to conventional publications through the immense acquisitions machinery mentioned above, with its ability to procure technical-report literature on a scale unequalled in any other library, and with its years of experience in giving a national bibliographical service to other Government agencies, the present Science and Technology Division, along with the National Referral Center for Science and Technology which it administers, is an eminently logical choice for performing the functions of a national information and referral center for science and technology.

The nature of the scientists' information needs, the heavy use of current materials, the greater availability of professional and commercial abstracting and indexing sources than for any other subject area, and the presence of many highly specialized information and document centers in the Government and elsewhere would require a center that would differ somewhat from the others. Its functions would be to:

1. Provide expert advice and assistance (locally or remotely) in the use of the Library's collections, largely through computerized methods. Directly by means of consoles, or indirectly through machine-produced bibliographies, reviews, evaluation reports, etc., the center's specialists would fill the role of both teacher and researcher working in and through the collections and computer stores of the Library for the benefit of individual scientists.

2. Provide expertise in the development of new bibliographic control services, such as a National Union Catalog of Scientific and Technical Monographs and a National Serial Data Service for Science and Technology (as a subset of the overall serial data program), to name only two of the many tools needed to bring under control the Library's enormous collections in science and technology, regardless of form. This service would be largely for other scientific and technical centers in the national system.

3. Develop and plan for the development of the Library's science and technology collections, especially in respect to unpublished and difficult-to-acquire scientific reports and other materials not available through conventional channels.

Exactly where this center would fit in the national science and technology information system, and the characteristics of its relationship to other information centers in the Federal Government, must await the results of further study. Whatever the outcome, the basic concept should not be changed—that of a national service given by a highly skilled group doing the intellectual work that only people can do, while the machines do the rest. This will require augmenting the present staff, speeding up automation studies, and installing the most efficient system and equipment. (The foregoing statement applies to the other centers as well, but is singled out here for mention because of the greater urgency for automating science information resources.)

A PUBLISHING CENTER

A greatly strengthened Publications Office, capable of handling the products outlined in this paper would be necessary. The Library's obligation to produce work of a high level of scholarship, similar to that found in a university, is a real one and should be supported by a publishing program equal to that of a university press of a similarly high level. The aids to research prepared by the projected centers would demand the best in editing, production, and promotion. The imprint, "The Library of Congress: The National Library of the United States," should be a silent witness to the excellence of the institution's publications.

A national library should not only publish bibliographic aids to scholarship, but also facsimiles of maps, manuscripts, prints, entire books, and similar rare and unusual items in its collections, to say nothing of educational and teaching materials to be used in the schools. Such a program, to be of value to the nation, calls for careful planning and preparation, imagination, scholarly attitudes, and technical excellence. It would cut across many subject and geographic areas if quality reproduction of the riches of the national treasurehouse are to be seen and used by the scholar and owned and appreciated by the public.

Equally important is the Library's responsibility to make available, to libraries and to similar institutions, quickly and in appropriate form, the results of LC's technical and experimental programs—surveys and studies in such fields as preservation, microreproduction, and automation. Also, if the Library is to make the nation as a whole aware not only of the sources of our national heritage but also the vast resources available to American minds, it must engage in a program for the publication of descriptive, scholarly sound, but popularly written booklets about the Library itself, its special collections, special services, and special programs.

The wide range and the size of the potential publishing program demand close coordination, not only within the Library but with the two other national libraries, other agencies, institutions, scholarly presses, professional associations, and publishing firms. The Library at present carries on its publishing through a program that, on paper, is centralized administratively, but, of necessity, is largely decentralized in fact.

LC's Publications Office should cooperate with the Preservation Office and with such Government agencies as the Government Printing Office (GPO) and the National Bureau of Standards in testing and developing advances in paper, binding, printing, and the graphic arts. It should make use of permanent-durable paper for appropriate publications and encourage its use in the publications program of Government agencies, other libraries, and at least the scholarly presses. Computer applications to printing promise improvements in schedules and, it is to be hoped, in quality as well as in reduced costs. The effect of the revolution in printing will be especially pronounced in bibliographic publications, notably in the so-called technical publications. Nonbibliographic publications, however, will also be affected. Already the Library has produced some publications through the application of computer technology, and it must continue to keep up with and apply these advanced methods in its publication program.

A CENTER FOR PHOTOCOPYING

Because of the scope and unique nature of many of the collections of the Library of Congress, it has a responsibility to make these collections available to the research community. Many scholars cannot visit the Library personally, or if they do they often want to retain portions of their research documentation in a form for later restudy. A copying service is necessary for making these valuable resources more widely available.

Essential requirements of copying service include: a broad range of copying techniques to satisfy a variety of needs; products of the highest technical quality; reasonably rapid response to requests; costs comparable to similar services elsewhere but consistent with quality; and reasonable accessibility to collections, consistent with legal restrictions and preservation objectives.

The Library has done much in the past to meet these requirements, but in pursuing national objectives it could expand this service further as new copying techniques are developed. Continued efforts are made to maintain currency in operations and to keep costs down. Financial support from sources other than sales may be required, however, in order to continue to serve specialized copying needs without excessively high prices.

ADMINISTRATION OF THE UNITED STATES COPYRIGHT LAW

The Copyright Office, one of the Library's six departments, in addition to performing the functions summarized earlier, has for the last ten years been working on a major revision of the copyright law. The act now in force is essentially the 1909 statute. Some features of the revision bill, which has passed the House of Representatives and is now before the Senate Judiciary Committee, are of special concern to libraries and to their users.

The revision bill contains, for the first time, a statutory declaration of the fair-use doctrine. What has finally emerged as Section 107 of the House bill (H.R. 2512) consists of two interrelated sentences. The first states that fair use is not an infringement and cites "criticism, comment, news reporting, teaching, scholarship, or research" as examples of the purposes for which fair use is permitted. The second sentence lists four major factors, distilled from the court decisions, to be considered in determining what fair use is: "(1) the purpose and character of the use; (2) the nature of the copyrighted work; (3) the amount and substantiality of the portion used in relation to the copyrighted work as a whole; and (4) the effect of the use upon the potential market for or value of the copyrighted work." This does not "change, narrow, or enlarge" the doctrine in any way, according to the report on the bill.

The bill as passed by the House contains a specific exemption permitting manuscript collections to be reproduced under certain circumstances. Unpublished works—in which the author and his heirs now, under the common law, have literary property rights with no time limit—will, for the first time, be governed by the statute. Because it was argued that a limited right to reproduce unpublished collections (photographs, motion pictures, and sound recordings, as well as manuscripts) in archival and manuscript repositories would not harm a copyright owner's interests but would be a positive aid to scholarship and would permit the making of security copies, Section 108 of H.R. 2512 provides that they may be reproduced under certain circumstances. There must be no "purpose of direct or indirect commercial advantage" and commercial reproduction must be for "preservation and security" or for "deposit for research use" in another "nonprofit institution" that has "archival custody over collections of manuscripts, documents, or other unpublished works of value to scholarly research." This would permit photographic or electrostatic reproduction but not reproduction in machine-readable form for use in an information storage and retrieval system. The report on the bill makes it clear that this provision of law could not be used to justify copying if the donor had placed specific restrictions upon this.

The change in the duration of copyright has also been a matter of considerable discussion. The present term is 28 years from date of publication, with renewal for another 28 years being possible. The new act provides for a term running for the author's life (from the date his work is written) and for 50 years after his death. For anonymous works and for "works made for hire," which include corporate authorship, the term would run for 75 years from publication or 100 years from creation of the work, whichever is shorter. For manuscripts and other unpublished works, the new term would be the same as for published works—life plus 50 years, or, if the author were unknown, copyright protection would expire when the manuscript was 100 years old.

The provision for a term of the author's life plus 50 years is, to the author, the most important single feature of the revision bill. From the point of view of administration, the most compelling reason for adopting this term is that it is the same as that provided for in the laws of nearly all the developed countries of the world.

Of particular relevance to automation and its possibilities for enhanced bibliographic and information services is the input of copyrighted works into a computer system and their output from such a system. The bill as passed by the House makes no special rules for such input or output. Under the general provisions, the permission of the copyright owner would be required, except where the copying is of the limited nature allowed as fair use. Recently, however, the matter has become a major issue. Since it is generally agreed that computer-based systems for the dissemination of the content of copyrighted works are some years in the future and that the copyright problems in this area cannot now fully be foreseen, a bill (S. 2216) has been passed in the Senate to establish a National Commission on New Technological Uses of Copyrighted Works, under the chairmanship of the Librarian of Congress, to study the problems and to make recommendations within three years on the use of copyrighted material in information-transfer systems. The recommendations of such a commission will be of major concern to librarians and information scientists and will influence the course that facsimile transmission will take. Meanwhile, it is likely that proposals for a temporary moratorium on liability for the use of copyrighted materials in computer-based systems during an experimental period will be considered in the context of the revision bill.

ADMINISTRATION OF THE NATIONAL LIBRARY PROGRAM FOR THE BLIND AND PHYSICALLY HANDICAPPED

The Library of Congress should continue to provide library service, through a network of cooperating regional libraries, for all residents of this country who cannot use ordinary printed materials because of physical handicaps. The Library's Division for the Blind and Physically Handicapped operates the model and demonstration library, which gives direct service to the District of Columbia and supplements the activities of the cooperating regional libraries with its large collections and professional staff.

The Division regularly prepares and distributes bibliographic aids to facilitate use of its resources. It is the national training, certifying, and coordinating center for volunteers who supplement purchased resources by transcribing into braille, recording on magnetic tape, typing books in large print, or who repair sound producers. It maintains a central listing of such volunteer resources.

The Division is the national reference and referral center for information on all aspects of library service to physically handicapped persons. It conducts ongoing research, development, and testing in reading media suitable for persons who cannot use conventional printed materials. It cooperates closely with all agencies and organizations interested in physically handicapped individuals and continuously sponsors or participates in conferences, seminars, and other meetings to ascertain needs and improve services.

Planning is now under way to utilize electronic production of braille, to apply the techniques of compressed speech and aural indexing in recordings, to use projected microfilm, to encourage the production of large-print publications, and to provide rapid communication not only by telephone but by means of networks of teletype and amateur radio. These steps will lead to the development of needed reference and scholarly collections and services which do not as yet exist. They will also extend the program to a far greater percentage of eligible persons than is now possible by enabling any handicapped individual to read in a form specifically adapted to his needs.

With each of the states soon operating its own regional library to serve blind and handicapped readers in its area, each will look to the National Library for reading resources, leadership, guidance, coordination, and assurance that every phase of library service will be provided through the best available technological and professional competence.

A NATIONAL CENTER FOR CULTURAL ACTIVITIES

For many years, through the generosity of private donors, the Library has maintained an endowed Chair of Poetry in English and has provided poetry readings, dramatic productions, lectures on music and literature, conferences, festivals, and symposia on literary and other matters, chamber music concerts, and festivals. The concerts and many lectures, poetry readings, and discussions have been made available to the nation through various radio outlets. At present, programs are available only to a limited radio audience, and sound recordings can be provided for educational purposes only to a limited extent. Cooperative ventures in educational television have been possible on even more rare occasions. Eventually, with adequate endowments or appropriations, all these programs should be available nationally on tapes, kinescopes, or recordings, enabling listeners and viewers across the country to benefit. In an advisory and consulting capacity, the Library's specialists in literature, music, and the arts should continue to develop close liaison and communication with the National Foundation for the Arts and the Humanities and with the numerous privately endowed foundations engaged in supporting cultural programs that are national in scope.

The Library also presents in its buildings exhibits of scholarly excellence but designed to have wide appeal for the million and a half visitors who come to LC each year. Catalogs of the most important exhibits are published to extend the educational and informational value of these displays. Loan exhibits are also prepared so that the American people may have an opportunity, at present quite limited, to enjoy directly and to benefit from the rich collections of their national library. An expansion of this program has already been planned. The availability of extensive exhibit space in its own buildings, once the Madison Building has been completed, will permit the Library to resume an active exhibit program in Washington, which, in turn, will nourish the loan-exhibit program.

IMPLEMENTATION

For the vision described in the foregoing pages to become a reality, certain very hard concrete steps must be mounted and, in some cases, surmounted:

1. The first requirement for effective implementation of the proposed national library and information service would be not only across-the-board support of such a proposal by the National Advisory Commission on Libraries but also

continued support by a permanent commission. This permanent commission's most influential service might well be to provide a voice that would speak in universal accents for the needs of all the people and of "all seasons"—for what is past (and has historical value) as well as for what is (and has great urgency) and what may be (and holds great promise).

2. The next requirement is legislation that would formally recognize the Library of Congress as also the National Library of the United States. The language of such legislation should convey the intent of Congress in a manner so lucid and unequivocal as to command the adherence and support of future Congresses for our dual role. The Joint Committee on the Library, which "considers proposals concerning the management and expansion of the Library of Congress," is the proper Congressional body to take up such legislation and, it is to be hoped, to sponsor it and its objectives with conviction and enthusiasm.

3. Support being in the positive sense the most critical problem of the transition of the Library of Congress from the *de facto* to a *de jure* as the National Library, mammoth efforts must be made to overcome the notion that the price tag on the National Library is an integral part of the price tag for the operation of the Congress of the United States. This notion cannot be overcome solely from Washington, but the voters of America in every county in the country must be made aware of the benefits that accrue to them personally from the National Library. Their sense of pride in such a national treasure must be touched. The library and information community must also be made even more acutely aware of its National Library. And the scholarly world, which realizes its stake in the welfare of the National Library, must also accept its responsibility to mobilize support for it. Until such widespread appreciation and support is evident, the National Library may not be adequately funded.

Direct appropriations, no matter how generous, should not preclude arrangements for gifts, grants, or transfers of funds for specified national objectives. Cooperative arrangements with other Government agencies, foundations, libraries, and library associations would not only have to continue but be considerably expanded.

Today, the three national libraries—the Library of Congress, the National Library of Medicine, and the National Agricultural Library—have voluntarily organized themselves into a consortium to coordinate their automation efforts and to make their systems compatible on the national level. They are also cooperating on the national Serials Data Program, among others. The major objective is the creation in LC of a computer-controlled data bank to serve the entire nation.

For the future, similar consortia can be envisaged. Libraries cannot forever stay out of the business of collecting and servicing informational materials limited to data. There are at present several Government agencies concerned with the collection, processing (as machine records), and servicing of data, and the Library of Congress should be tied to them in a more or less formal relationship. An initial consortium for the acquisition and processing of data records might consist, for example, of the Library of Congress, the Smithsonian Institution (SI), the National Bureau of Standards (NBS), and the Environmental Science Services Administration (ESSA). NBS operates the National Standard Reference Data Center, ESSA has the National Oceanographic Data Center, and SI operates the Astrophysical Observatory. But data do not exist alone in the form of such formal collections, reduced to computer stores. They are also produced in ordinary print and near-print form. For example, LC's Photoduplication Service accepts, for retention and for servicing by photocopying, accumulations of data that individual scientists have compiled in a form too voluminous or otherwise unsuitable for publication in the normal scientific literature.

Similar consortia would need to be formed in fields other than science and technology, for example, in the arts, the humanities, and in the social sciences. There are already, in existence or evolving, consortia among libraries for one purpose or another. University libraries—at present, Chicago, Stanford, and Columbia—have formed relations that may contribute to the development of the national library and information system. Although these are operational groupings, there are other possible forms of association for still other purposes. A number of organizations are devoted to library research. Where once there was only the Council on Library Resources, there are now the Institute for Library Research and other emerging activities. In its own research work, the Library of Congress as the National Library would assuredly need more or less formal association with these organizations and even closer relations than it now has— and they are already multitudinous—with the research-oriented committees of the major library associations, such as, the American Library Association, the Association of Research Libraries, the Special Libraries Association, the American Documentation Institute, and others.

If the Library of Congress is to be the kind of national library outlined in this paper, there must be a high degree of coordination of activities with libraries and other information centers. It goes without saying that all will have to be adequately funded and staffed if a truly national network of library and information centers is to emerge during the remainder of this century. The quality and quantity of professional staff will have to be greatly augmented and the recommended permanent National Commission on Libraries and Information Science will be needed to help provide the requisite influence and inspiration. Time, too, is an important element. Obviously, not all of the foregoing services could be inaugurated immediately, nor could they be operational overnight. The Library of Congress, however, recognizing its limitations but attempting honestly to assess its potentialities, believes that with widespread support, adequate funds, and the talented staff it has always been able to attract, it can provide the leadership expected by the library and information scientists in the national effort to control and disseminate information.

CHAPTER XI

THE UNITED STATES OFFICE OF EDUCATION: PROGRESS AND POTENTIALITIES OF ITS LIBRARY PROGRAMS[1]

by the Staff of the Division of Library Programs,
Bureau of Adult, Vocational, and Library Programs,
United States Office of Education

Education has the basic goal of maximizing human potential. The basic concept that education is a lifelong process was slow in being generally accepted. Libraries, with their organized sources of knowledge and information, are essentially an integral part of the education system while a citizen is in school and in college and a continuing tool after his formal education is ended. The development, extension, and improvement of libraries are essential factors in the educational program of the nation. Federal assistance to libraries provides a great opportunity to advance the whole reach of education through libraries.

OFFICE OF EDUCATION RESPONSBILITIES AND ORGANIZATION

The Office of Education is one of the major agencies of the United States Department of Health, Education, and Welfare. Perhaps a better understanding of the philosophy of the Office and its involvement with library affairs can be obtained through a brief description of the larger unit. This context appears below, followed by a discussion of library-related programs and significant areas for further development.

The establishment of the Department of Health, Education, and Welfare (HEW) by Congress in 1953 grouped together the "human concerns" of the Federal Government and provided a voice in the President's Cabinet. Today, the over 250 HEW programs authorized by the Congress touch the lives of almost every American every day. The Department has the second largest expenditures of any agency in government to carry out its mission to strive toward the elimination of *all* the conditions that stunt individual growth or impair human dignity. Today the Department disburses about $47 billion annually. The amounts vary somewhat each year, but the breakdown is as follows: $33

---

[1] *This paper, specially written for this book in fall 1968, was coordinated by Ray M. Fry, Director, Division of Library Programs. At the time this paper was written the Division was officially known as Division of Library Services and Educational Facilities, and it included the Educational Television Facilities Branch, since moved out of the Division and retitled the Educational Broadcasting Facilities Program. No copyright is claimed for chapter 11.*

billion in social security payments from the trust funds, $7 billion in public assistance, $4 billion for education, and $3 billion for health. More than 90 cents out of every dollar appropriated to the Department is spent by states, cities, academic institutions, nonprofit agencies, and others.

The century-old Office of Education is the only Federal agency solely concerned with education per se. It is the recognized agency of the Federal Government charged by legislation of Congress to administer educational functions of the Federal Government. Although the basic mission of the Office, "to promote the cause of education," has remained unchanged since its establishment in 1867, there have been significant changes since that time in the conception of our citizens of the role of its Federal Government in the area of education. The Office seeks to improve the quality of education and to make educational opportunities available to all Americans. It provides assistance for building schools, training teachers, providing scholarships, and conducting research to strengthen and expand the role of education in American life.

The growth of the Office of Education, although it was performing important tasks, was slow until the 1950's. With the passage by Congress of the National Defense Education Act (P.L. 85–864) and of the Elementary and Secondary Education Act of 1965 (P.L. 89–10), expansion became very rapid. After the signing of this last-named act, which authorized an appropriation of $1.3 billion for the first year, President Lyndon B. Johnson instructed a White House task force to study the organization of the Office of Education and to develop recommendations.

The reorganization, based on the work of the task force, was put into effect by the Commissioner of Education on July 1, 1965. The former three major bureaus which were functionally organized—the Research and Development Programs, Educational Assistance Programs, and International Education Programs—became four major bureaus based primarily on levels of education: Bureau of Elementary and Secondary Education; Bureau of Higher Education; Bureau of Adult, Vocational, and Library Programs; and Bureau of Research. A National Center for Educational Statistics was established, reporting directly to the Commissioner, in order to centralize all statistical staff and services of the Office.

In January 1967, a Bureau of Education for the Handicapped was created to strengthen and coordinate activities in behalf of the handicapped. A sixth bureau, the Bureau of Educational Personnel Development, was established in February 1968. Its main responsibility is the administration of the Education Professions Development Act (P.L. 90–35), which seeks to improve the quality of teaching and to help meet critical shortages of adequately trained educational personnel.

An Institute of International Studies was established as a major component of the Office on March 25, 1968, headed by an Assistant Commissioner for International Education and Director of the new Institute. The Institute has responsibilities for international education programs funded at approximately $30 million annually. The establishment was another step toward carrying out the program of action in international education outlined by President Johnson in his special message to Congress on February 2, 1966. Part of the program was embodied in the International Education Act of 1966, which was signed into law by the President on October 29, 1966. As of this date, the Act has not been funded.

Lastly, a significant action was the appointment of a Special Assistant for Urban Education by the Commissioner of Education in April 1968. Responsibilities of this position include the promoting of comprehensive action proposals that focus the energies of the Office of Education on areas of national concern in large cities. This is an example of the organizational flexibility of the Office in meeting changing situations.

Over twenty new education laws have been passed since mid-1965 to strengthen and improve all areas from higher education to noncommercial television. These laws have brought the number of major programs administered by the Office of Education to more than eighty and the agency's total budget to $4 billion. (For a summary of current legislation, see Appendix E.)

LIBRARY-RELATED PROGRAMS

The historical development of the Office of Education programs which have either direct or indirect implications for library services is indicative of the growth of the Federal interest in libraries. In this development, the period 1867–1937 can be defined as an exploratory phase which would end with the establishment of a Library Services Division in 1938.

Although the original staff of the Office of Education comprised the posts of Commissioner and three clerks as contrasted to a present-day staff of over 2,900, the Office's concern for libraries goes back to the 1870's when it published its first library surveys. In 1876, it published a monumental 1,200-page report titled *Public Libraries in the United States: Their History, Condition, and Management,* a landmark in librarianship in this country.

The interest in a separate library unit in the Office of Education began in the early years. In annual conferences the American Library Association expressed concern that proper attention be given to library interests in the Office. In 1919, hearings were held on H.R. 6870 and S. 2457 to provide for the establishment of a division of library service.

A developmental phase, 1938–64, highlighted by the passage of the Library Services Act (LSA) in 1956, began with the appropriation provided by the Congress in the late 1930's for the establishment of a Library Services Division in the Office of Education. This division—the name and its place in the Office's organization varied from time to time—began operation on January 2, 1938, with a staff of some four professional and three clerical staff members. There were few changes in the number of these employees until early in 1957. It is interesting to note the wording on the appropriation act (1936 49 Stat. 1797) for the Office of Education which first included funds (a $25,000 budget) for this new unit. It states in part:

> For making surveys, studies, investigations, and reports, regarding public, school, college, university, and other libraries; fostering coordination of public and school library service; coordinating library service on the national level with other forms of adult education; developing library participation in Federal projects; fostering Nation-wide coordination of research material among the more scholarly libraries, inter-State library cooperation, and the development of public, school, and other library service throughout the country. . . .

Carleton B. Joeckel in a report, *Library Service,* Staff Study No. 11, prepared for the Advisory Committee on Education (published by the Government Printing Office in 1938) noted:

> The creation in 1937 of a Library Service Division in the United States Office of Education was an event of great significance in the history of Federal relations to libraries. It marked the entry of the Federal Government into a field of educational activity which, though not entirely new in precedent or in principle, is largely new in emphasis. Prior to the establishment of this Division, there was no Federal office directly responsible for leadership in a Nation-wide program of library development. The new unit will serve as a Federal library headquarters and will provide a national focus for library interests.

In the period from the creation of the Division until the passage of the Library Services Act (P.L. 597, 84th Congress) in 1956, the greatest stress was placed on the collection and analysis of library statistics and consultative and coordinating services. A pattern of library statistics was established which resulted in separate nationwide surveys on public school, academic, and public libraries. Twelve nationwide studies were conducted (four in each of the three areas of library service) in intervals of five, six, or seven years.

Early in 1957 the library function of the Office was elevated to Branch status as a result of the passage of LSA. (This pioneer program authorized $7.5 million per year for five years to provide grants to the states for the further extension of public library services to areas of less than 10,000 population which had no public library services or which had inadequate libraries.) To aid in the administration of the program, three library extension specialists were added to the Branch staff. The staff was again increased in 1964 when the Act was amended to include urban as well as rural areas, and a Title II was added which provided for grants to the states for the construction of public libraries. To administer more effectively this new legislation, now titled the Library Services and Construction Act (LSCA), a separate LSCA Section was established in the Library Services Branch with the addition of a chief, three more extension specialists, and a small unit for reporting purposes. The LSCA was extended in 1966 for five years, through fiscal year 1971, and two new titles were added: Title III (Interlibrary Cooperation) and Title IV (Specialized State Library Services). These last two titles became the responsibility of the reorganized library program which is described in the following paragraphs.

The major reorganization of the Office of Education which took place in July 1965 designated the principal library unit which had existed under various titles since its establishment in 1938 as the Division of Library Services and Educational Facilities. It was placed in the Bureau of Adult, Vocational, and Library Programs. In addition to its responsibilities for the Library Services and Construction Act, the administrative responsibilities for Title II-A (College Library Resources) and the library training portion of the Higher Education Act of 1965 were also given to the Division.

A very significant change occurred in 1967 with the shifting of the operational decision-making for the LSCA program from Washington to the nine regional offices of the Department of Health, Education, and Welfare. Library Services Program Officers, under the supervision of the regional Office of Education directors of the Adult, Vocational, and Library Programs, are responsible for the administration of the state grant programs under LSCA. These program officers have been delegated authority for reviewing state plans and projected programs of activities under the LSCA state grant programs. This has resulted in more efficient, more rapid, and more understanding review of state plans and programs, thus enhancing the consultant role of the program officers with the states. These same staff people are also available for regional consultant services connected with the two titles of the Higher Education Act mentioned above. The development of overall policy and programs is retained at the headquarters level in the Division of Library Services and Educational Facilities.

An organizational change in the library program of the Division of Library Services and Educational Facilities formally established three new branches in May 1967—the Library Program and Facilities Branch having consultative and policy responsibilities for LSCA, the Library Training and Resources Branch with responsibilities for Titles II-A (College Library Resources) and II-B (Library Training) of the Higher Education Act, and the Library Planning and Development Branch, an overall library planning branch with staff representing all types of libraries. Later in the same year, an additional branch was created—the Library and Information Science Branch with leadership responsibilities for the effective training and utilization of library and information sciences manpower. These four library branches with a fifth branch, the Educational Television Facilities Branch, responsible for the administration of a noncommercial educational television facilities grant program, make up the present Division as of fall 1968.

In the July 1965 Office of Education reorganization, the administration of Title II (School Library Resources, Textbooks, and Other Instructional Materials) of the Elementary and Secondary Education Act of 1965 was placed in the Bureau of Elementary and Secondary Education. At this same time, responsibility for the administration of the library research and demonstration portion of Title II-B of the Higher Education Act of 1965 was placed under the Library and Information Sciences Research Branch, a unit of the Division of Information Technology and Dissemination in the Bureau of Research. Although there is at this time no formal administrative device specifically established for cooperative library services planning and action between the three bureaus, there are many examples of close cooperation. Incidentally, it should be pointed out that under the library research and demonstration program, Bureau of Research staff in the nine regional offices administer the Small Project Research Program, which is designed to support significant small-scale research projects. As with the LSCA program, the overall policy responsibilities are in the Washington office.

In addition to these briefly described programs of the three Bureaus—of Adult, Vocational, and Library Programs; Elementary and Secondary Education; and Research—the bureaus of Higher Education, Education for the Handicapped, and Educational Personnel Development, as well as the Institute of International Studies, have direct or indirect implications for librarianship. The Bureau of Higher Education administers the Higher Education Facilities Act of 1963, which, by providing grants and loans for the construction and improvement of undergraduate and graduate academic facilities, has been of tremendous assistance in college and university library construction in the past years. Other titles of the Elementary and Secondary Education Act, administered by the Bureau of Elementary and Secondary Education—particularly Title I (Educationally Deprived Children) and Title III (Supplementary Centers and Services)—have included programs which have had great impact on library services. The same bureau also is responsible for Title III of the National Defense Education Act which provides grants to assist in the purchase of books (other than textbooks) and audiovisual materials and equipment for elementary and secondary school use in specified fields.

The staff of the Division of Library Services and Educational Facilities—particularly the staff of its Library Planning and Development Branch—have seen, as part of their responsibilities, the necessity of being aware of all programs with implications for libraries, making appropriate information available to the library profession and informally coordinating programs relating to libraries. Representing all types of libraries and library education, the Division staff also works cooperatively with the staff of the National Center for Educational Statistics in connection with the compiling and issuance of library statistics.

The Office of Education also has an Educational Materials Center, organizationally a part of the Division of Information Technology and Dissemination of the Bureau of Research. The Center's collection of some 15,000 reference items includes the latest texts used by elementary and secondary school students and their teachers, as well as children's literature found in school and public libraries. The collection is the result of cooperation between the American Educational Publishers Institute, the Children's Book Council, and the Office of Education. It receives support from the Agency for International Development, the Department of State's Bureau of Educational and Cultural Affairs, and the Office of Education.

The clearinghouse for Library and Information Sciences of the United States Office of Education's Educational Resources Information Center (ERIC) program, a responsibility of the Bureau of Research, is one of the specialized clearinghouses that make up a nationwide comprehensive information network for the field of education. This clearinghouse, located at the University of Minnesota, is responsible for the acquisition of documents on the operation of libraries and information centers, the technology used to improve their operations, and the education and training of librarians and information specialists.

In the same way that today's libraries are evolving institutions, the library-related programs of the Office of Education have developed, usually in response to different situations and approaches in education and librarianship. Beginning with the rural Library Services Act of 1956 with a first year appropriation of just over $2 million, the Office has had to expand its existing library program in order to administer complex programs aiding the library and information sciences with total Federal funding of over one hundred times this initial appropriation. It has not been easy. An overall staff effort has been required far beyond the formal staffing of the previously described "library" units. The Office will continue to examine critically its administration of all the library-related programs, with the determination to advance the quality of librarianship at all levels by all possible means. (See Figures 11.1–11.4 for placement of the library programs and for organizational charts of HEW and the Office of Education.)

SIGNIFICANT AREAS FOR FURTHER DEVELOPMENT

There is some trepidation in marking out rather arbitrary areas in which Office of Education staff see the possibility of the Office offering some degree of national assistance to librarianship in the future. Primarily, it can be done only on the basis of what its library-related programs have accomplished in the past. There is some degree of overlapping in the various areas, but this in itself is not bad. Areas and library programs should be interrelated. They should reinforce each other in striving for common goals. The library research and demonstration program is an example of an Office of Education program which can make a contribution to almost every area. It would be extremely difficult to point out all of the possibilities.

It can be noted that there are areas—international librarianship is an excellent example—in which the Office of Education, as of this time, actually has few activities. Nevertheless, it is included with the thought that this is an area in which the Office will be moving in the future. The Office of Education is the recognized educational agency of the Federal Government. It has an obligation to be concerned with international librarianship as one aspect of its concern with education in other lands. There is reason to believe that this concern will not decrease in the future; indeed, it will increase.

The potentiality of growth in all of the areas is, of course, contingent upon Congressional and Executive actions. There should be confidence, however, that our Nation is moving in the direction of supporting more adequate library and information services at all levels of government. With this in mind, there is value in outlining some aspects of this general direction such as will be done in this section. Five, ten, or twenty-five years from now, we may be in a better position to know more exactly what is the role of the Office of Education in library development. At this time, all of us can and should plan for a future which undoubtedly will have even more significant opportunities and problems than we have today.

RESOURCES

One of the most substantial contributions of the existing Office of Education programs presently assisting library development has been in the area of resources—by providing Federal grant assistance in the purchase of books and other library materials, primarily for school, public, and academic libraries. The acquisition, organization, and maintenance of collections is a common activity for all libraries, and all libraries have been affected by the increased cost of library materials and the proliferation of book titles. *The National Inventory of Library Needs* (Chicago: American Library Association, 1965) noted a national shortage of over 390 million volumes with a cost figure (without discount) exceeding $1.6 billion if public school, academic, and public libraries were to meet American Library Association collection standards. There is little doubt that the cost of books and other library materials will remain as a major expenditure of United States libraries for many years in the future. An estimated projected library budget for library materials and binding for 1974–75 for public school libraries, college and university libraries, and public libraries has been given by the Office of Education as $504.7 million.

The Office's legislative programs providing the greatest Federal grant assistance in the acquisition of library materials have been the Elementary and Secondary Education Act of 1965 (ESEA), the Library Services and Construction Act (LSCA), and the Higher Education Act of 1965 (HEA).

Title II of the ESEA, which provides funds to the states for the purchase of school library resources, textbooks, and other instructional materials has provided the largest Federal contribution to date for the purchase of library materials, with Congressional appropriations of approximately $306.5 million for the three-year period 1965–68. Of the different types of materials eligible for acquisition under this title, library resources have been given the highest priority by most approved state plans.

Of the other titles of the same act, Title I (Educationally Deprived Children) and Title III (Supplementary Centers and Services) have included library services aspects— many undoubtedly representing a considerable purchase of library materials—which have been of significance in the past years. An analysis of Title I activities for fiscal years 1966 and 1967 showed that some 3.3 million children participated under library services projects each year with total expenditures in the library category of $45.3 million in fiscal 1966 and $42.3 million in fiscal 1967. An examination of the funded Title III projects in the first year of the program found 83 projects in 36 states concerned with school libraries and instructional materials centers. In the second year there were 177 such projects. Many school libraries have also been aided in the purchase of library materials through Title III of the National Defense Education Act of 1958, which is designed to strengthen instruction in critical subjects: science, mathematics, modern foreign languages, history, civics, geography, economics, English, reading, and industrial arts.

The Library Services and Construction Act, as of this time, has brought new or improved library services to an estimated 85 million people. Its greatest impact on the acquisition of library resources has been through Title I which provides funds for books and other library materials, salaries, equipment, and other operating expenses. In a ten-year period (fiscal years 1957–66) this title resulted in an expenditure for $108.2 million for books, pamphlets, periodicals, and other related materials in public libraries from combined sources. This amount represented 27 percent of the total expenditures under state plans under Title I.

In connection with the 1966 amendments to LSCA, Title III (Interlibrary Cooperation) is resulting in a multiplication of the usability of collections of books and other materials of individual libraries. In the future, the joining together of libraries of all types into networks of service will yield dividends in greater resources for library users, reduce duplication, and permit the use of the newer and expensive communication devices.

Title IV (Specialized State Services) will help to meet the learning needs of the institutionalized and physically handicapped—people too often neglected in library service. In 1966, it was noted that only about one million volumes were available for more than 206,000 inmates of penal or correctional institutions. By accepted standards, this number of inmates should have some 2.1 million professionally selected volumes.

Under this title, Federal assistance is authorized to the physically handicapped who are not institutionalized. Here again, a great deal of material will be purchased, particularly special material. Based on data from several sources, there are some 2 million persons in the United States who cannot read ordinary printed books, magazines, and newspapers because of poor eyesight or other physical factors which make them unable to manipulate such materials.

Title II-A (College Library Resources) of the Higher Education Act of 1965 is the major Federal program aiding institutions of higher education in the purchase of library materials. This title assists in the acquisition of books, periodicals, documents, magnetic tapes, phonograph records, audiovisual materials, and other library materials for use in academic libraries. In the first three years of this program, fiscal years 1966–1968, Federal grants totaling more than $57 million have been made to colleges and universities.

The awarding of grants is made under different categories as follows: basic grants cannot exceed $5,000 and may be made to all qualified applicants; supplemental grants may be awarded to colleges and universities with demonstrated institutional needs related to lack of library resources and other special circumstances; grants for special purpose include: (1) Type A grants, which help meet needs for quality in the educational resources of institutions; (2) Type B grants, which meet special national or regional needs; and (3) Type C grants, which help combinations of institutions meet special needs in establishing and strengthening joint-use materials. There are matching requirements for the basic grants and the special purpose grants. In awarding special purpose grants, priority is given to institutions that are members of combinations of colleges and universities that need special assistance in setting up and strengthening joint-use library facilities. An actual example of how grants have been awarded in these various categories can be seen by the fiscal 1968 awards. A total of 3695 basic, supplemental, and special purpose grants amounting to $24,509,219 were approved by the Office. The number of grants and amount of funds in each category follows: (1) 2,111 basic grants totaling $10,294,709; (2) 1,524 supplemental grants totaling $10,764,524; and (3) 60 special purpose grants totaling $3,449,986, which represent 19 Type A grants totaling $895,059; 9 Type B grants totaling $558,924; and 32 Type C grants totaling $1,996,003.

This account does not describe in detail the extent of the thrust of Federal programs in aiding the acquisitions programs of our libraries. In brief, it can be said that recent Federal legislation has greatly increased available funds for books, other instructional materials, and binding in academic, school, and public libraries starting with fiscal 1966. It has provided strength to back-up collections such as the library collections of the state library agencies. Funds under Title I of LSCA helped in strengthening many of these collections. Perhaps mention should be made of Title II-C of the Higher Education Act, administered by the Library of Congress with funds transferred from the Department of Health, Education, and Welfare. Under this title, the Librarian of Congress is charged with the following responsibilities: (1) acquiring, so far as possible, all library materials currently published throughout the world which are of value to scholarship; and (2) providing catalog information for these materials promptly after receipt, and distributing bibliographic information by printing catalog cards and by other means. Research funds under Title II-B of the Higher Education Act have aided many projects concerned with the acquisition, organization, and use of knowledge and information, using new approaches and techniques. This is an example of the interrelationship of programs striving for common goals.

What does the future hold for these Federal programs? The actions of Congress, of course, are crucial. It can be said, however, that a core of experience has been built in programs aiding library resources in this country. This can be the basis for expanded programs in later years.

SERVICES AND CONSTRUCTION

In the case of the Library Services and Construction Act, very few pieces of legislation were given such a broad mandate and opportunity to benefit their recipients. Title I (Public Library Services) funds may be used for salaries and wages, books and other library materials, library equipment, and general operating expenses. Most of the activities carried out under approved state plans may be classified in one of these general categories: organizing larger unit library systems; strengthening the state library agency; recruitment, scholarship, and training programs; surveys of various types; public information efforts; and development and extension of special services. Program results have been impressive. Over 600 bookmobiles were purchased during fiscal years 1957–67. An estimated 85 million persons are now living in areas receiving new or improved public library services under 1968 state plans.

Funds under Title II (Public Library Construction) can be used for the construction of new buildings, for additions to existing buildings, and for the renovation or purchase of existing buildings. Some 1,000 construction projects were approved by the states under state plans during fiscal years 1965–67. Title III (Interlibrary Cooperation) has unlimited possibilities for cooperation between all types of libraries. Title IV, parts A and B, focus on the services and special materials required to meet the library services needs of the institutionalized and the physically handicapped. Although the impact of the LSCA grant programs has been far in excess of the amounts of Federal funds involved as of this time, there is still much to be done. Millions of people are still without access to adequate public library service. There is particular need for the expansion and improvement of public library services and facilities for disadvantaged persons of all ages.

The Higher Education Facilities Act of 1963, which provides grants and loans to assist in the construction and improvement of undergraduate and graduate academic facilities, has been of tremendous assistance in college and university library construction over the years. The three titles of the act are designed to aid the states in financing the construction and improvement of laboratories, college classrooms, libraries, and other academic facilities.

An indication of the extent of funding for academic library construction under this act in past years can be seen by statistics reported in the 1968 edition of the *Bowker Annual of Library and Book Trade Information*. Some 230 grants totaling approximately $77.5 million were made to assist library construction projects under Title I in fiscal 1967. Under Title I, grants of up to 40 percent of project development cost may be awarded to public community colleges and public technical institutes; grants of up to one third of the development cost may be awarded to all other undergraduate institutions. Under Title II, facilities grants of up to one third of cost may be awarded for graduate school facilities or for cooperative graduate centers. Eight grants totaling $5.2 million were awarded under this title for library construction in fiscal 1967. For the fiscal year period, 1965–67, a grant total of 43 grants amounting to $41 million were made under Title II. Title III authorizes loans for construction of both undergraduate and graduate academic facilities. Approximately 80 loans totaling over $48.5 million were awarded in fiscal 1967 for assistance in library construction.

There are certainly many other Office of Education programs with direct implications for library services. They would include such programs as: Title I of ESEA with its programs for the disadvantaged; Title III of ESEA supporting supplementary educational centers, including literacy programs for adults; Title I of HEA strengthening community services projects; and Title II-B of HEA assisting library research and demonstration programs.

What is needed in the future is further refinement of library goals, statistics, and program information. The Office of Education will be making increased efforts to strengthen the impact of all of these programs. Efforts will also be continued to add a library component to as much existing and planned Office of Education legislation as possible.

PLANNING AND CONSULTATIVE SERVICES

In general, there is a lack of proper emphasis on planning and development in library and information services at all levels of government. The Federal Government has a particular necessity for the identification of needs and trends, for overall planning, and for evaluation activities. There must be appropriate coordination and correlation among types of libraries and levels of government. National systems covering all areas of knowledge must be planned and designed. Results of existing programs must be evaluated and further tested. Proposals that would meet critical needs and problems must be drafted and submitted for possible future library legislation.

The need of library planning was considered when a Library Planning and Development Branch was established in the Division of Library Services and Educational Facilities as a unit that would have responsibility for the development and improvement of *total* library and information services. Its professional staff, representing all types of libraries, acts together in developing legislative proposals and in coordinating relationships with other Federal agencies and with professional organizations. The staff works closely with all Office staff who are connected with library-related programs, including HEW regional office staff. In effect, this branch, aided by the LSCA, Title III (Interlibrary Cooperation) program and the HEA, Title II-B research program will be able to accomplish a great deal to better the present compartmentalization of library services in our country.

To aid in decision-making for overall planning, the staff of the Library Planning and Development Branch is concerned with the application of the Planning-Programming-Budget System (PPBS) to library programs. Because of this system, better decisions can be made on the allocation of resources among alternative ways to attain objectives in library programs at all levels of government.

Significant library program issues which have engaged the library specialists of the Office of Education during the past years include the following:

1. How can public libraries best serve the disadvantaged urban population? Toward this end what changes, if any, should be made in Federal programs aiding public libraries?
2. How can the concept of networks for knowledge be coordinated with the initial establishment of library systems achieved under Titles I and III of LSCA?
3. How can city libraries serving as regional and national resource centers convert to and acquire the new communication and retrieval equipment? What would be the costs and benefits of such conversion?
4. How can the state library agencies be strengthened to better respond to the multiple needs of library users, particularly the metropolitan users?

These are typical of the problems that need examination, planning, and direction. With the present organization and staffing, the Office of Education is now in a position to move forward in a national effort to bring total library services to all citizens.

The concern of the Office in connection with its consultative services has been to work cooperatively with the various levels of government and types of associations and organizations. Particular stress is placed on working with the state library agencies in helping them to meet questions that have often come up in other areas of the nation. This is particularly true in problems arising from providing library services to the disadvantaged. This area of concern requires a wide knowledge of a range of Federal programs, several of which may provide the necessary resources and assistance. As a broad objective, the Office of Education is interested in assisting school, college, university, research, state, special, and public libraries in developing and carrying out their full responsibilities in achieving standards of service to their respective users.

The headquarters and regional library specialists of the Office form a staff which is specialized in the best techniques and methods of operation in librarianship. Their backgrounds furnish a wealth of specialized knowledge which can collectively be brought to bear on difficult problems. As an example, there is only one college and university library specialist in the Office of Education; however, a quick check of the other professional staff connected with library-related programs reveals that some 50 percent of this staff has, at some point in their careers, worked in college or university libraries.

Over the past ten years, it has been perceived that a good method to use in providing answers to significant problems in librarianship is through workshops, institutes, and conferences on problems of national and regional significance. Either independently or in cooperation with another agency or with an association, the Office plans and conducts such activities. An example of such a conference is that on statewide long-range planning for libraries which was held in Chicago in September 1965. Library specialists, planning experts, and education administrators were called together for pertinent papers, panel discussions, and general question periods. The conference papers were then published by the Office of Education and made available through the Superintendent of Documents as a source of information to all concerned with the crucial questions of statewide planning.

The document clearinghouse which has been established by the Bureau of Research in library and information sciences as a significant part of the Office's Educational Resources Information Center (ERIC) program can be considered as one aspect of the Office's "consultative services" which undoubtedly will be expanded through new techniques and operations in future years. In essence, the Office hopes always to keep its activities flexible enough in this general area so that future problems can be dealt with in the most appropriate manner.

MANPOWER

It has been evident over the past years that the many aspects of manpower needs in library and information services represent an extremely critical situation today. It was estimated in the American Library Association's *National Inventory of Library Needs* that, according to accepted standards, some 100,000 additional professional librarians were needed for mimimal service in public, school, and academic libraries.

Of particular concern to the Office of Education has been the great area differences in the nation in the availability of library education. With the passage of time, it has also been noted that the personnel needs have changed. There is an increasing need for specialists in a range of fields, for increased staff in connection with legislative programs such as the growing number of programs for the disadvantaged, and for a greater number of school library staff trained in the use of new media. Existing Federal programs providing scholarship and training assistance have had to attempt to meet the backlog of critical shortages as well as to attempt to meet future and more sophisticated library requirements. The state library agencies, with all of their added responsibilities, are in particular need of qualified personnel.

The library and statistical specialists of the Office have long been interested in questions of library manpower. Specific staff worked extensively on the library manpower data in the *National Inventory of Library Needs* (Chicago: American Library Association, 1965), which has been mentioned previously. In 1966, the Office issued a study, *Library Manpower: Occupational Characteristics of Public and School Librarians* (Washington: U.S. Government Printing Office, 1966). Staff members also prepared the background paper, "Library Manpower," for the American Library Association's 1967 annual conference program in San Francisco. In a recent organizational change in the Division of Library Services and Educational Facilities, a new Library and Information

Science Branch was established; it is specifically focused on all aspects of library and information science manpower. This is an important step in progress for the future.

Title II-B (Library Training) of the Higher Education Act of 1965 authorizes grants to institutions of higher education to assist them in training persons in library and information science. Such grants may be made for fellowships, traineeships, or institutes for library personnel. A primary objective of the fellowship program under Title II-B is to produce more qualified persons to fill staff vacancies in library education. The opportunity for additional persons to participate in graduate education at the doctoral level is an attempt to provide more faculty for library schools. The manpower shortage of librarians can best be met by the expansion of our educational and training resources.

A four-year analysis of this scholarship program shows that a total of 1,941 fellowships has been awarded during the four years of the operation of this program by the Office. The breakdown of this total follows: 1966–67, 139 (52 doctoral, 25 post-master's, 62 master's); 1967–68, 501 (116 doctoral, 58 post-master's, 327 master's); 1968–69, 709 (168 doctoral, 47 post-master's, 494 master's); and 1969–70, 592 (193 doctoral, 30 post-master's, 369 master's).

Title II-B also provides for Federal assistance for institutes for training in librarianship. For three years prior to fiscal 1968, institutes for school librarians were conducted under Title XI of the National Defense Education Act. Beginning in fiscal 1968, under the authority of Title II-B of HEA, institutes are now conducted for academic, public, and special librarians as well as school librarians. More than 3,000 persons will receive training in librarianship during the summer of 1969 and the 1969–70 academic year at 92 institutes throughout the country. This "continuing education" aspect of librarianship must be encouraged. It is possible through this legislation.

Other programs of the Office of Education have done much for the training of librarians. State plans under Title I (Public Library Services) of the Library Services and Construction Act, since its beginnings as the rural Library Services Act of 1956, have often included provision for scholarship aid for the education of public librarians.

School librarians, in particular, have been assisted under such programs as the "Experienced Teacher Fellowships" and "Prospective Teacher Fellowships" programs under Title V–C of the Higher Education Act. Other Office of Education programs which have had implications and use for librarians have been Faculty Development Programs under Title VI–B of the Higher Education Act and certain programs under Title I (Community Service and Continuing Education Programs) of the same act. The Education Professions Development Act may also present opportunities for librarianship. This act has been described as the most far-reaching legislation ever granted to the Office for the training of the entire range of school personnel. All of these programs present very distinct possibilities of assisting in this very critical area of library manpower. It should also be mentioned that there have been training opportunities for library personnel under such legislation as the Economic Opportunity Act of 1964 and the Vocational Education Act of 1963.

Other important aspects of Office of Education concern with library manpower that have implications for the future are research studies which are presently being funded under the library research and demonstration program under Title II-B of the Higher Education Act. Another research project with important implications is that which is being conducted by the University of Maryland's School of Library and Information Services on the identification of manpower requirements, and the educational preparation and the utilization of manpower in the library and information profession. Other studies often are directly related to the many aspects of library manpower that require constant study and assessment.

In summary, training and education, from preschooling to continuing education, have been designated by Congress as the responsibility of the Office of Education at the

Federal level. As the activities of the Office expand, in the same manner so will the Office's specific interests grow in the area of education and training of librarians and information specialists.

RESEARCH AND EVALUATION

The Office of Education through its Bureau of Research seeks to improve education through support of a variety of research and related activities. This support is awarded under a number of legislative authorizations. Under Title II-B (Library Research) of the Higher Education Act of 1965, Federal grant and contract assistance is authorized for research and demonstration projects to improve libraries and training in librarianship; to develop new techniques, systems, and equipment for handling and distributing information; and to disseminate information derived from such research and demonstrations.

Under this program, as with the other research programs of the Office of Education, the concern is that Federally supported research be applied for the public good. Full utilization is based on four mutually supported processes: (1) dissemination activities, (2) prototype development and pilot operation, (3) demonstration, and (4) implementation. With its increasing interest in the application of research that translates research into usable form, planning is going forward for the issuance of a series of practical targeted publications as a substitute for the usual reports.

The Office plans in the future to focus attention on topics such as the following:

1. Refinement in projections for library and information science manpower requirements, specifications of role performance for emerging occupations in these fields, and the training prerequisites for these roles.
2. Development of empirically validated curricula for the education of persons for emerging roles in librarianship and information sciences, employing where possible individualized and multimedia approaches to learning.
3. Prototype development and operational testing of an undergraduate library, employing as fully as possible microform and the latest technological advances in the communications industry.
4. Tests of several ways of combining library resources with classroom teaching.
5. Operational tests of methods for integrating outputs from information systems such as Medical Literature Analysis and Retrieval System (MEDLARS), Educational Resources Information Center (ERIC), and National Aeronautics and Space Administration (NASA), etc., with academic library resources.
6. Operational tests of the feasibility of statewide or regional networks employing centralized cataloging and bibliographic control, on a computer time-shared basis, to eliminate or greatly reduce present duplicative and costly efforts.

The nine Office of Education regional offices now administer a program particularly designed to support significant, small-scale educational research projects and to encourage faculty members of small institutions as well as large schools to participate in research. To qualify for the program—called Small Project Research—proposals must meet two basic requirements: the total Office of Education investment must be not more than $10,000, and the project must have a capability of being completed within a period of eighteen months. This program is unique in that it is a regionally administered research program. This approach allows the researcher and the reviewer a better opportunity to examine closely each other's aims and purposes. If the proposal is approved, a contract is negotiated at the regional level.

The Educational Resources Information Center of the Office of Education is the first national information system to serve education. ERIC stores the full texts of documents on microfilm, makes the documents available at nominal cost in pamphlet or microfilm form, and publishes announcements of all new acquisitions. Each center is manned by experts in the subject matter involved and by specialists in modern information retrieval techniques. A monthly journal entitled *Research in Education,* issued by the Office, includes abstracts of all research supported by it, listing the author, location of study, and length. The task of establishing a clearinghouse for library and information sciences has been given to the Center for Documentation and Information Retrieval at the University of Minnesota. The work of this clearinghouse has great potential for the future.

Twenty research projects were funded by some $1.8 million in Federal funds in fiscal 1968 under Title II–B of the Higher Education Act. One of the projects involves a study of the use of computers and automated procedures at major Federal libraries and information centers, including the National Library of Medicine and installations of the Atomic Energy Commission and the Department of Defense. The study, to be made by the Information Dynamics Corporation, will provide an overview of existing Federal facilities, successes and problems, and patterns of development in using automated information systems, and reasons for employing such systems.

In another project, the Office of Education will seek to evaluate the effect that Federal funds have had upon the development and expansion of public library services under the Library Services and Construction Act. During the past twelve years, more than $500 million in Federal, state, and local funds have been expended for public library services under Title I of LSCA. Of this total, about $166 million were Federal funds. This evaluation will be done by the System Development Corporation of Santa Monica, California. Representative programs will be analyzed in eleven states scattered throughout the nine regions of HEW. This is an example of the increased consideration being given to evaluation of existing Federal grant programs in library services and library education. A new position of Evaluation Specialist was established in the Division of Library Services and Educational Facilities. This person works with appropriate Office of Education staff to perform a variety of duties in connection with evaluation of the Division's grant programs.

The research and demonstration program is one that can have tremendous effect on the development of librarianship and information science in this country. It has particular value in a field which at this time is in such a great period of change.

STATISTICS

Successful functioning of library systems and library education depend on high-quality planning and management which, in turn, depend on high-quality information. A good library-statistical-data information system can make a substantial educational and social contribution in our nation.

A National Center for Educational Statistics was established in 1965, reporting directly to the United States Commissioner of Education, in order to centralize all statistical staff and services of the Office of Education. This unit is responsible for developing the statistical program for the Office, for coordinating information-gathering activities, and for providing assistance in application and use of automative data-processing systems and services. Stress in this unit is on service to the consumer.

A satisfactory library statistics program involves many factors such as: (1) availability of the essential data and cooperation of the respondents; (2) practical use of the data to administrators, to the public, and to Congress; (3) validity, accuracy, and comparability of the data; (4) frequency of compilation and promptness of issuance of data; and (5) adequacy of funding of the program.

Changes in the National Center for Educational Statistics in the past months indicate that library statistics will receive increased attention in the future. A Library Studies Branch has been activated in the Division of Statistical Operations. The appointment of a new Assistant Commissioner for Educational Statistics in May 1968 gives indication that greater stress will be placed on the practical use of statistics.

The Office of Education is extremely interested in the development of a definitive plan for library statistics. Staff of the Center and of the Division of Library Services and Educational Facilities, as well as other library specialists of the Office, are cooperating with the American Library Association in the development of such a plan. At the same time—showing how the various Office of Education programs can act together—a special project with implications for a nationwide plan, "Systems Analysis of Library and Information Science Statistical Data," is being funded under Title II-B of the Higher Education Act. This research project, which has the Wharton School of Finance and Commerce, University of Pennsylvania, as contractor, will provide the necessary factual information needed for planning purposes. The establishment and implementation of a master plan for library statistics holds great promise for the future.

STATE-LOCAL-FEDERAL RELATIONSHIPS

There will be no solution for the great problems facing us today unless ways are found of mobilizing the talents and resources from all sectors of our life today. In practice, this means close and effective working relations between the different levels of government as well as with the private sector. It means relationships which would not only preserve, but indeed strengthen, the autonomy of state and local government and private-sector institutions. Secretary of Health, Education, and Welfare Wilbur J. Cohen several years ago (*HEW Indicators* May 1966) expressed the situation in these words:

> We must strive for a social structure that is at once more diversified and more interdependent—a more truly pluralistic society. Diversity and interdependence must be buttressed by intelligent cooperation between business and government, and more effective governmental cooperation among the local, State, and Federal levels.

Of particular concern to the development of our nation's library and information services at this time is the changing role of the state library agencies. The tasks before them under existing library legislation is overwhelming. They include the necessity for total library planning on a statewide basis, the development of many types of library systems, and the responsibility for bringing library services to citizens who previously had little or no service. One state librarian expressed it as follows,[2]

> The trend is clear and inexorable; the state library agency, or some other agency if the library fails, must take responsibility for planning and coordinating the re-sources, information, and financing of library service of all kinds and to all special groups. . . . Knowledge expansion and information flow require systems, and systems require coordination. Here is where we find ourselves; here is where the action is.
>
> In our future we can see computer-based information data banks, research net-works à la EDUCOM, and instant satisfaction of information and/or book needs on a statewide basis. We see patients of hospitals and inmates of prisons being assisted in their rehabilitation through the ministrations of librarians and their wares. We see professional staffs of these and other institutions being provided with the last word in their respective subject areas. We see the blind and handicapped en-joying the same library advantages as the sighted and whole.

Although faced with these expanding responsibilities, the state library agencies are, in terms of the brief period of time in which they have assumed major responsibility, young developing institutions. They have, under the Library Services and Construction Act, taken severe burdens in developing library service, always under the pressure of responding to the increasingly complex information needs of state government. The response to all of the challenges has been magnificent. There is little doubt that in future years the state agencies will be able to provide a strong foundation for nationwide networks of knowledge.

The Office of Education—through LSA LSCA and other Office of Education

2 *Ernest E. Doerschuk, Jr. "Finding the Mix of Services,"* Wilson Library Bulletin (*April 1968*), p. 802.

library legislation—has developed an effective and cooperative relationship with the state agencies. The matching principle, which has been followed in the Library Services and Construction Act, has stimulated state and local participation and has benefited all members of the partnership. The regionalization of the Federal administration of LSCA is another step forward in the development of a partnership of the different levels of government in the provision of public services to meet library and information needs that transcend local and state boundaries.

The Office of Education's relationship with the states will be of special importance in any future activities under a national plan for library statistics. With the close cooperation with the states in previous compilations of library statistics, a base has been provided that has potential of being useful in providing a framework for obtaining a true picture of the status of national library services.

NETWORKS

One of the most serious problem areas in the development of library and information services of all types is that involving coordination and cooperation between libraries. An ultimate goal is to achieve a nationwide system of service which can be responsive to the legitimate demands from a user of one type of library through use of the resources of another library. The Office of Education, through its activities and grant programs, has encouraged the development of library systems. State programs under the original Library Services Act of 1956, and its continuation in the Library Services and Construction Act, resulted in a significant increase in the number of systems as well as growth in the establishment of state agency regional branches. Numerous library surveys were financed with grant funds to provide a sound factual basis for library planning and development. Grant funds, in many cases, assisted the state library agencies in sponsoring conferences on statewide library development.

Title III (Interlibrary Cooperation) was added to the Library Services and Construction Act by Congress in 1966. Under this title, funds may be used to establish and maintain cooperative networks of libraries at the local, regional, state, or interstate level for the systematic and effective coordination of the resources of school, public, academic, and special libraries and information centers. At this time, more substantially funded state programs are going into effect—the initial Federal funding was for planning purposes only, and the indications are that this legislation will have a very substantial impact on network development.

Another Office program which will have an impact on the development of networks is that under Title II–A (College Library Resources) of the Higher Education Act of 1965. The entire program under this title supports stronger libraries which can assist in the development of systems; however, the special purpose type grants B and C are specifically awarded to institutions of higher education to encourage joint use and interlibrary cooperation. Type B grants are given to assist institutions to meet special national or regional needs in the library and information sciences. Type C grants are awarded to institutions which are members of combinations of institutions of higher education which need special assistance in establishing and strengthening joint-use facilities. Some $2.9 million in Federal funds were awarded for special purpose type grants B and C in fiscal 1968.

The Higher Education Amendments of 1968 include a new title, "Networks for Knowledge," to the Higher Education Act which authorizes the Commissioner of Education to enter into grants and contracts to encourage colleges and universities to share their technical and other educational and administrative facilities and resources through cooperative arrangements. Authorizations for this program are $340,000 for fiscal 1969 for planning, $4 million for fiscal 1970, and $15 million for fiscal 1971. At this stage, the implications of this title for the development of library networks is uncertain. Certainly the library specialists of the Office are concerned with how the concept embodied in this new title can be best coordinated with the initial strengthening and establishment of library networks achieved under the other library programs of the Office of Education.

The Bureau of Research is placing major emphasis on the development of library networks and information centers. Varied research projects directly or indirectly related to this area are being funded under Title II–B (Library Research) of the HEA. Many of the institutes under Title II–B (Library Training) also focus on systems. Among the institute topics funded in fiscal 1968 were: system analysis as applied to libraries, automation of the bibliographical services for libraries based on Project MARC (Machine Readable Catalog), and computer-based library information systems. In connection with program activities under Title II (School Library Resources) of the Elementary and Secondary Education Act, there has been an increase in the number of school library districts and in centralized processing and materials centers. It can be seen that all of the library-related programs, with little or no exception, are providing impetus to the development of networks.

A factor that can never be ignored in planning for library and information networks is consideration of the strengths and weaknesses of the state library agencies. They play a key part in the total picture of library development. Although these agencies have been greatly strengthened during the past decade, principally under the LSCA, they still lack the status, the staffing, and the resources to play their roles effectively. The Office of Education, because of its long and fruitful record of close cooperation with the state library agencies, is prepared to work closely with the states in the crucially needed development of national networks.

SERVICES TO THE DISADVANTAGED

A national objective of the Office of Education is to bring equality of educational opportunity to every citizen. Although there can be many types of handicaps, at this time there is a special concern for those economically and culturally depressed in our large urban cities. How can libraries be made relevant to the wants of the urban ghetto population? The answer to such a question is not easy. It requires not just the appropriation of Federal funds, but the thinking and the dedication of all levels of government. The library profession—in its associations, in its library education, and as individual librarians and administrators—must be truly concerned in discovering new approaches and techniques.

Here again, as in other national problems, the Office has, through its library-related programs, attempted to provide effective Federal assistance in bringing books and information services to the disadvantaged. The various titles of the Elementary and Secondary Education Act—particularly the first three titles—have provided millions of dollars of aid to depressed urban areas. Although Title II (School Library Resources) is not focused directly on this problem, this title has provided great financial assistance to the states that have large numbers of deprived people.

Many states have included special projects for the economically and culturally disadvantaged under Title I (Public Library Services) of the Library Services and Construction Act. However, it must be faced that even greater funding would be required under this title to begin to bring really measurable results. Ways of adding a dimension of service to our "have-not" citizenry under this legislation could include the following: youth employment in urban public libraries, organized and continuous preschool and child-parent programs, intensified service to teenagers, adult education programs, and storefront neighborhood library center demonstrations.

Another approach which can be expanded in future years is appropriate library training through the institute program under Title II–B (Library Training) of HEA. Current fiscal 1968-funded institutes in this area under this title are library service to the disadvantaged (University of Arizona), expanding public, school, and academic library service to the culturally and economically disadvantaged (Our Lady of the Lake College, San Antonio, Texas), and team approach to improvement of library services in elementary schools serving disadvantaged youth (Washington State University).

Research projects under Title II–B of HEA represent another approach to determining how library services can best be brought to the disadvantaged. Two such major projects are the University of Wisconsin's project, library materials in service to the new adult reader, funded in fiscal years 1967–68, and the University of Maryland's formally titled project, "A New Approach to Educational Preparation for Public Library Service: An Experimental Program in Library Education for Work with a Specialized Clientele," funded in fiscal years 1967–69. This type of project has high priority for funding by the Office of Education, as it represents an area which can be greatly aided by controlled experimental activities and by a wide range of techniques and operations.

Staff of the Division of Library Services and Educational Facilities in the Office of Education have had a responsibility in the past years in calling the attention of the profession to a great variety of legislative programs aiding the disadvantaged which have implications for librarianship and in acting as a constant source of information on these programs. The listing of all such programs is not possible in this paper. A few examples are the Economic Opportunity Act of 1964, the Public Works and Economic Development Act, Demonstration Cities and Metropolitan Development Act of 1966, and the National Foundation on the Arts and Humanities Act of 1965.

Indications are that the emphasis that has been placed on Federal assistance to the institutionalized and the physically handicapped will undoubtedly be continued in the years to come. The chief programs to aid these categories in the area of library services are through Title IV (Specialized State Services) of LSCA. This title has two parts: A: State Institutional Library Services, and B: Library Services to the Physically Handicapped. The first part helps to remedy the deplorable deficiency of library services in most state institutions. The purpose of the second part is to reach the physically handicapped who are too often an invisible part of the community served by a library. Such library services to the handicapped who are not institutionalized remain to be developed through the coordinated efforts of a wide variety of libraries, agencies, and organizations. Surveys have been made; planning has gone forward under both parts of this title. The years ahead offer an opportunity to meet the challenge of bringing library services to these categories of the disadvantaged.

INTERNATIONAL EDUCATION

Education has become an increasingly important part of our national foreign policy in promoting international cooperation and understanding. Our schools and colleges are rapidly increasing their efforts to inform students about other countries and to improve competence in foreign languages and area studies. The Office of Education is not only concerned with providing information on education in other countries to interested institutions and organizations in the United States, but it also provides services, advice, and leadership in many other aspects of international education. The office supports national action and policy abroad and is also concerned with training programs for foreign educators, exchange of teachers, and the recruitment of teachers and administrators for overseas assignments. The Office works closely with the Department of State and with the United Nations Educational, Scientific, and Cultural Organization (UNESCO) and other international organizations in relation to educational programs at the international level.

Previous mention has been made of the establishment of the Institute of International Studies in the Office of Education; its full range of activities is contingent upon the implementation of the International Education Act of 1966. This legislation has direct implications for library and information services. It does authorize the expenditure of Federal funds for "teaching and research materials and resources" for graduate-level area study programs, and it has been noted by one librarian deeply involved in international librarianship that "certain provisions of the act could also be interpreted to permit the exchange of librarians and travel by American librarians for the purpose of collection development."[3]

At present, the library-related programs of the Office of Education that provide grant assistance in purchasing library and instructional materials are making a definite contribution to aiding our knowledge and understanding of foreign countries. These would include the Elementary and Secondary Education Act, the National Defense Education Act, the Library Services and Construction Act, and the Higher Education Act. Although not properly classified under this section, mention might also be made of the growing concern in the Office for the education problems of the Mexican-Americans and all Spanish-speaking minority groups. This is reflected in the Office's library-related programs, not only through the funding of special projects such as those under Title I of the Library Services and Construction Act, but also through activities of the Division of Library Services and Educational Facilities whose staff is working with other Federal Government units, library associations, and state agencies in this area.

The Department of Health, Education, and Welfare has had interest and concern with the Government Advisory Committee on International Book and Library Programs. This committee was established in October 1962 by the Secretary of State, under the authority of the Fulbright-Hays Act (P.L. 87–256), to advise the Federal Government on the policies and operations of its overseas book programs and to achieve closer cooperation between United States commercial book publishers and Government activities in foreign countries. The Department of State responded to recommendations on the need for greater coordination within the Federal Government on its book programs overseas by creating, in July 1966, an Interagency Book Committee on International Book and Library Programs. This Committee, which includes an HEW member (presently a staff member of the Office of Education's Division of Library Services and Educational Facilities), has discharged its coordination purpose by developing an official Government-wide policy of international book and library programs and the development of guidance policies for its implementation by United States officials overseas.

Increasingly, our nation's libraries will become international institutions, and library components will become a part of our Government's commitments in international education agreements. It will follow that the Office of Education will necessarily become more involved with international library exchanges and activities. The Office of Education will certainly never be in the position of having all knowledge of international library problems and developments. However, it must be sufficiently involved and informed so that it can determine a relationship of these problems and developments to the situation in our own country. Further experience and research will be required before there can be a precise definition of the role of the Office of Education in the library field as it relates to library education.

The Office also has responsibility in seeing that adequate and current data and information on American librarianship is available to foreign countries. To accomplish this, it will undoubtedly be necessary that appropriate Office of Education staff must take the initiative in areas in which previously the Office played no part. Essentially, the Office's resources must be used in meeting important problems in librarianship—no matter whether these problems appear first in this country or overseas.

COHERENCE IN FEDERAL PROGRAMS

Carleton B. Joeckel, the author of *Library Service*, Staff Study Number 11, which was prepared for the Advisory Committee on Education in 1938, noted on page 47 of

[3] M. D. Shepard, "*International Dimensions of U.S. Librarianship,*" ALA Bulletin (*June 1968*), p. 702.

the study that the newly established Library Services Division in the Office of Education "will serve as a liaison agency for library interests in all phases of the Federal Government, both in Washington and in the field." Later, on pages 89 and 90, Dr. Joeckel states: "The Federal Government should synthesize and correlate its own departmental library functions and should expand and extend its technical and bibliographic services to the maximum limit of their potential usefulness. Through its library agency in the Office of Education, it should take an active part in the development of library services throughout the Nation."

This report was made many years before the passage of the Library Services Act in 1956, which was the forerunner of greatly expanded Congressional legislation aiding all types of libraries and library education. The criticism has been made that the passage of library legislation has been largely uncoordinated and that the actual administration of the legislation has been assigned to too many different units of the Federal Government.

As background, the Office of Education has as its basic mission "to promote the cause of education." As part of its long-range interest in American education, the Office has responsibilities for coordinating the many aspects of Federal educational activities and for acting as a source of information and advice for decision-making activities of the Federal Government in the area of education. The Office should also be the agency for measuring the Federal impact of education.

The planning for adequate library service for the nation's citizens must be an integral part of the planning for education in general. In the same way that the Office of Education should be the catalyst for the total thrust of Federal efforts and activities in American education, so should the library-related units of the Office serve as a catalyst for Federal efforts aiding American librarianship. The Division of Library Services and Educational Facilities has a unique position within the Office because of its support and leadership role in connection with the improvement of libraries and library education.

The Division's specialized staff must have full knowledge of the other Federal grant programs and services for libraries and librarians—whether administered in the Office of Education or in other Federal agencies. A continuing responsibility of the Division is to make its services available to the staffs of any Federal agencies administering library-related programs. The Division serves as a clearinghouse of information for all Federal programs aiding librarianship.

At the same time, the Division's leadership responsibility in helping state agencies, other appropriate organizations and agencies, and library and educational associations must be broadened and intensified. Its complete staff of specialists, representing all types of libraries, must look into the future and plan together efficiently from a national vantage point with all agencies and organizations whose goals identify with those of the Office of Education.

PUBLIC INFORMATION AND UNDERSTANDING

There has been greater understanding by our citizens over past years that there are national problems that require a national solution. But there has been no even progression toward the attainment of overall goals. The cause of librarianship has been greatly hindered because the necessary facts, along with examples of good services and results, have not been presented effectively.

Our citizens must know why knowledge is crucial in an open society and must understand that our libraries have a truly significant part to play in making information and ideas easily available. Local governments have too often failed to make their library needs known to their communities. State governments, all too often, have not supported their state library agencies at a level proportionate to the responsibilities of these agencies. Specifically, the essentially educational and cultural nature of libraries need legal, financial, and organizational recognition.

Basically, what is needed is public understanding that library services cut across all education, that these services are a necessity which require support and cooperation at the various levels of government in order to heed the demands of the future. *Total library service*—which should be user-oriented—is now within the realm of possibility because of our great advances in technology and in communication.

The full development of our nation's library services requires informed public opinion. The Office of Education has played a role in developing public understanding of the needs of education through many of its activities—through its advisory role with other Federal agencies and through its concerns and responsibilities with education at the different levels of government and with colleges and universities. The Office reports directly on the condition and progress of education. Aspects of the grant programs, national conferences and workshops, as well as many cooperative programs—all are a means of increasing information and knowledge of the significance of education.

The Office of Education has recognized the need of focusing attention on the conditions and progress of library and information services in our country and will continue in this activity. It has done this through the actions of its library specialists, through sponsored conferences and meetings, and through cooperative activities. However, this does represent an area in which much remains to be done in advancing the development of library services. The Office recognizes this need and will continue its efforts in the years ahead in seeing that the requirements and the progress required in the overall development of library services are brought before the public in the most effective manner.

CONCLUDING STATEMENT

In direct proportion to current needs, there has necessarily been a marked increase in the complexity and scope of activities in the area of library and information services in the United States. Nevertheless, there is a considerable degree of possible coherence in librarianship through the relationship of libraries and library services to education.

The Office of Education does have a unique role in the educational structure of the nation. It is the one Federal educational agency which represents not a part but the totality of national interest in education. Libraries are essentially an integral part of the educational system; they are significant for people of all ages and at all levels of educational attainment. It follows that the planning for adequate services for all of the nation's citizens must be a part of planning for education in general. What is needed at this time is a greatly intensified effort to integrate library planning and development with the improvement of education at all levels.

This paper has outlined the development of the library-related programs of the Office of Education and the placement of these programs in the structure of the Office. Greater stress has been placed on the potential areas for further development in library and information science. The present range of support available from Office of Education programs does provide crucial assistance to librarianship. The Office, through its experience with these varied programs and through its philosophy of state-local-Federal relationships, is in a strong position to administer expanding national programs which could include: (1) state library agencies as key agencies in future networks of knowledge and information, and (2) broad concepts of information extending beyond the scientific and technical fields.

The Office of Education is the only Federal agency with planning units with no grant program responsibilities yet concerned with overall development in librarianship— namely, the Division of Library Services and Educational Facilities' Library Planning and Development Branch, for all library services and the Library and Information Science Branch, for library education and training. The first branch, with specialists for each type of library has responsibility for surveying and assessing national library needs and Development Branch, for all library services, and the Library and Information library services, focused on the users and potential users of such services. The Office's planning for the future is based on the premise of strong state library agencies with appropriate status within their state governments. In the future, the states will have to move more than ever into the area of interstate cooperation.

With its stress on service, the Office is not committed to any particular media of information in the broad field of library and information science. Through the appropriate actions of Congress and the Executive Branch of the Federal Government, it can quickly respond to changing situations. It is free to move in direction with the development of new approaches and techniques.

Even a crystal ball cannot help in clearly foreseeing the future of librarianship. We can only conjecture. The Office of Education does hope to provide leadership in the development of the best possible system of library services for a nation dedicated to the maximum fulfillment of each individual.

FIGURE 11.1

ORGANIZATION OF DEPARTMENT OF HEALTH, EDUCATION, AND WELFARE (1968)

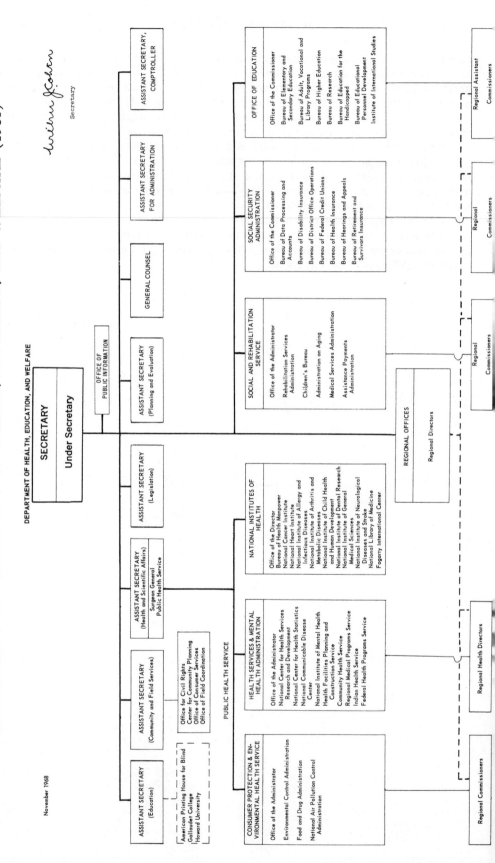

FIGURE 11.2

DISTRIBUTION OF REGIONAL OFFICES OF THE DEPARTMENT OF HEALTH, EDUCATION, AND WELFARE
(1968)

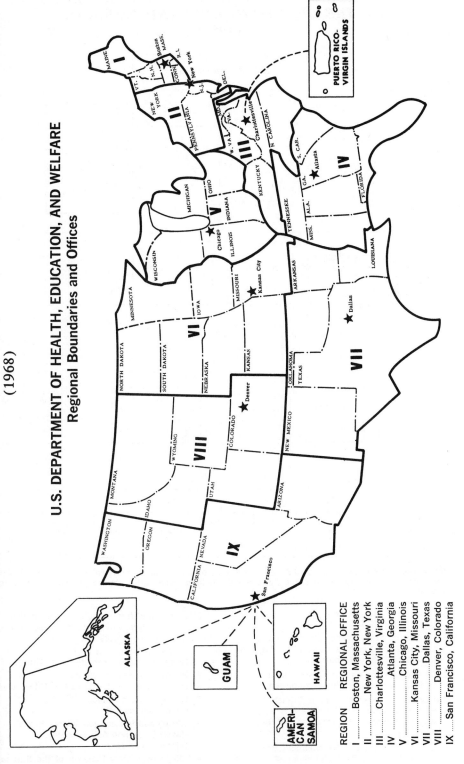

U.S. DEPARTMENT OF HEALTH, EDUCATION, AND WELFARE
Regional Boundaries and Offices

REGION   REGIONAL OFFICE
I .... Boston, Massachusetts
II .... New York, New York
III .... Charlottesville, Virginia
IV .... Atlanta, Georgia
V .... Chicago, Illinois
VI .... Kansas City, Missouri
VII ...... Dallas, Texas
VIII ..... Denver, Colorado
IX ...... San Francisco, California

FIGURE 11.3

*LIBRARY PROGRAMS IN THE U.S. OFFICE OF EDUCATION, BY THE OPERATING UNIT AND PROGRAM**
(1968)

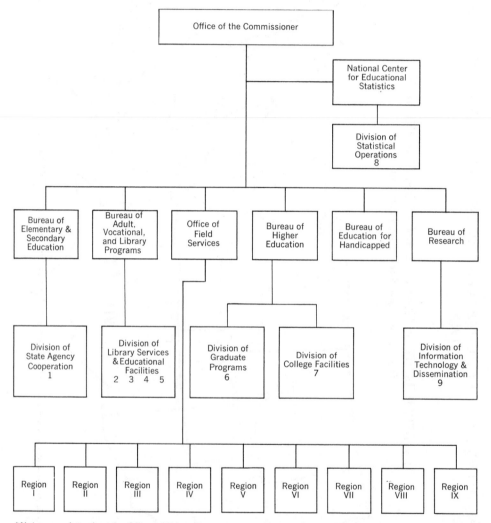

*Not a complete chart for Office of Education, presents only location of library-related programs. In 1969 the Division of Library Services and Educational Facilities became the Division of Library Programs. See Fig. 11.4.

PROGRAM CODE

1. Division of State Agency Cooperation
   Elementary & Secondary Education Act, Title II (School Library Resources)

2. Library Services and Facilities Branch
   Library Services and Construction Act

3. Library Resources & Training Branch
   Higher Education Act, Title II-A & B
   (College Library Resources and Library Training)

4. Library Planning and Development Branch
   (Consultative, Advisory and Planning Services by type of library)

5. Library and Information Science Branch
   (Consultative, Advisory and Development Services for Library Education)

6. Graduate Facilities Branch
   Higher Education Facilities Act, Title II

7. Program Operations Branch
   Higher Education Facilities Act, Titles I and III

8. Library Studies Branch
   (Library Statistics)

9. Library and Information Science Branch
   Higher Education Act, Title II-B,
   (Library Research)

I-IX Regional Library Program of the Bureau of Adult, Vocational, and Library Programs

FIGURE 11.4

ORGANIZATION OF DIVISION OF LIBRARY PROGRAMS (1969)

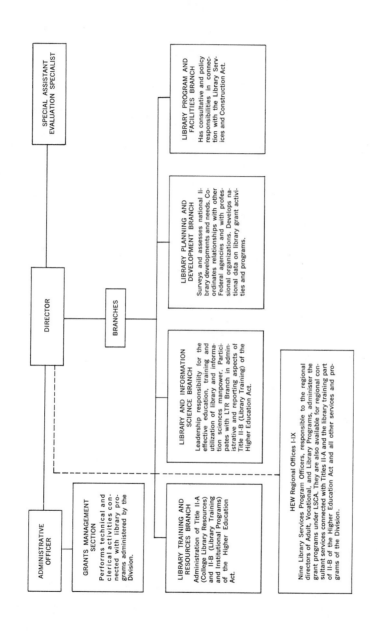

PART IV

Fulfillment of a National Policy Through Evolving Responsiveness to User Needs

CHAPTER XII

LIBRARY SERVICES FOR THE NATION'S NEEDS: THE REPORT OF THE NATIONAL ADVISORY COMMISSION ON LIBRARIES[1]

by the Commission Membership

FOREWORD

When President Lyndon B. Johnson appointed the National Advisory Commission on Libraries in 1966, he gave it a demanding task, and one with urgent as well as enduring aspects. He asked the Commission to consider the nation's library structure, the nature of the present and wisest possible future involvement of Federal support in the development of national library and informational resources, and the most effective shaping of those resources to our common need as we can picture it over the next decade. This third concern of the Commission has been for resources of every kind, and needs at every level. We know very well how difficult it is to relate Federal and local, public and private sources of support and definitions of purpose, but we have tried to suggest some of the ways in which that crucial job can be done.

Our recommendations will be understood best, I think, by seeing them as they result from our basic concern for adequate library resources. This concern may in its turn seem simple or self-evident until we look at the history of libraries and the needs of this country in the late twentieth century—needs which grow equally from the individual citizen and the large corporation, the pioneering university and the complex Federal agency. The historical growth of libraries is a vivid commentary on our problems today, in fact, for we see at major periods in the past the development of one or two particular kinds of library. Today we have the whole array of libraries alive at once; our world demands this variety, while our achievements and our great need grow from it. We are Alexandrian or Renaissance citizens in our development of great book and manuscript collections which range across the past of Western culture; we are Roman or Baroque

---

[1] *Chapter 12 is the entire basic text of the Report of the National Advisory Commission on Libraries (July 1968). Appendixes A–D of this book present Commission documents and contain lists of the witnesses who offered testimony, and organizations which submitted useful special studies. Many other individuals in one way or another contributed to the efforts of the Commission. It is appropriate here to mention our particular thanks to Dr. Frederick H. Wagman, Director, University Library, University of Michigan, whose preliminary compilation of written material at the request of the Commission served as indispensable resource for discussions at its final meetings and enabled the distillation of content for the December 1967 preliminary Report and the present Report to be completed within the limited time available. Finally, the Commission wishes to thank the officials and agencies of the Federal Government, whose cooperation has been most helpful from the beginning.*
No copyright is claimed for chapter 12 and appendixes A-D.

in many of our superb private and personally shaped libraries; we are medievalists in our development of libraries for specialized fields of learning; and we continue the public or national traditions of the eighteenth and nineteenth centuries in our great Federal, municipal, and university libraries. Just as we have an astonishing range of demands on our libraries, so we have range in the kinds of library we create and support.

But what in fact do we mean by a library? We must ask this elementary question, because we are surrounded, almost overwhelmed, by the tangible fact of libraries. We take their meaning, like their existence, too much for granted. That existence and meaning are best understood, perhaps, by realizing what libraries are *not*—not warehouses of books and manuscripts, not collections of reading-rooms, and not sets of reading devices. Any library is instead a particular kind of meeting-place, and it grows from certain major attributes of the human mind and spirit. It is not a neutral spot, not passive, and yet it does not have restrictive purpose or direction as a thoughtful radio or television show does. A library differs from other systems of communication, indeed, precisely because its value and power emerge from the use which we as individuals choose to make of it.

A library—great or small, privately or publicly supported—has two major and unique functions. First, it makes possible meetings of mind and idea which are not limited by our normal boundaries of time, space, and social or economic level. An effective library gives us the option of moving to the far side of the world, to the fifth century B.C., or to the company of prophets and princes. And we do all this, not by the transient means of fantasy, but by the enduring power of our own human awareness. We can become more than we were; we can, if we wish it, increase our individual stature as well as our public effectiveness.

To say this is to suggest the second great function of a library. It is the institution in our society which allows and encourages the development, the extension of ideas—not their passive absorption, but their active generation. Here our image of the conventional reading-room may interfere. We picture a hundred silent, inert figures, and forget that each is making some active reckoning with all that he thought to be true before he confronted a new range of ideas or conditions. He may be more active at that quiet moment, in fact, than at any other time in his life. The technical means of his encounter may be a record, a tape, a film, a print-out or—most radical of all—a book. Libraries are not bounded by means; they will and should employ any means to achieve their ends.

At a time of great technical virtuosity it is important to realize that in the predictable future new means of information storage and retrieval will not displace the book. Nor will they lessen the need for materials, buildings, or skilled staff. Instead they will extend and supplement what we now have, and our investments during the next decade must take equal account of the enduring purposes of libraries and the diverse emergent means of strengthening them.

Clearly, of course, libraries cannot achieve their ends for the illiterate or the indifferent. They are dependent on teachers, writers, parents to set interest alight, but they are the means of meeting the interest, and giving it range beyond those who first stirred it. This creative center which is a library should not be defined by the adequacy of its space, equipment, and collections alone, but by the adequacy of its people—those who first teach the mind to inquire, and those in the libraries who can show it *how* to inquire. The librarian of today and tomorrow must have many technical and professional skills, but above all he must have skill with people. He is a teacher whose subject is learning itself, and his class has no limits on age, field of study, or degree of competence. The national policy which we propose is as a result based equally on the need for skilled and sensitive people, bold and yet imaginative technical means, and support from every sector of the economy as well as every major level of government.

DOUGLAS M. KNIGHT
Chairman, National Advisory Commission on Libraries
President, Duke University

A. THE COMMISSION'S CHARGE

In the executive Order of September 2, 1966 [see appendix A-1], the National Advisory Commission on Libraries was charged to:

(1) Make a comprehensive study and appraisal of the role of libraries as resources for scholarly pursuits, as centers for the dissemination of knowledge, and as components of the evolving national information systems;

(2) Appraise the policies, programs, and practices of public agencies and private institutions and organizations, together with other factors, which have a bearing on the role and effective utilization of libraries;

(3) Appraise library funding, including Federal support of libraries, to determine how funds available for the construction and support of libraries and library services can be more effectively and efficiently utilized; and

(4) Develop recommendations for action by Government or private institutions and organizations designed to ensure an effective and efficient library system for the Nation.

The Commission tried conscientiously to meet these charges. In particular, it attempted a broad look at the complex roles of libraries in relation to user needs in a changing society, and it developed some recommendations for structural adaptations that can foster evolutionary development and enable continuing, coordinated study and action in the years ahead. The Commission's conclusions with respect to major objectives and its five specific recommendations for realizing these objectives are the basic subject matter of this Report. Sections B through D present the rationale for the Commission's response to point 4 in the Executive Order.

Here in section A, however, it seems appropriate to comment on the response of the National Advisory Commission on Libraries to the first three points set forth in the Executive Order.

In some areas the Commission feels it would be presumptuous to make premature judgments on the basis of current evidence, but even in these cases some tentative judgments can be made. The discussion that follows touches on many areas, including some still confused by questions affecting the philosophy, administration, and financing of library and information services for the nation's needs. Tackling the imponderables is part of the job ahead.

EVOLVING RESPONSIVENESS TO USER NEEDS

With respect to point 1 in the original charge, the National Advisory Commission on Libraries approached its appraisal of the role of libraries in several ways. It arranged to hear a variety of testimony [see appendixes C and D]; it sponsored several major studies on basic aspects of the roles of libraries—notably the System Development Corporation report on *Technology and Libraries* and the American Council of Learned Societies' study *On Research Libraries* [*see appendix B*]; and its members have discussed the issues at some length and familiarized themselves with many of the other major studies that fall into this general area. As a result of this effort, the Commission has reached a number of conclusions that have led to its specific recommendations.

The Commission believes that libraries are both essential and major elements in providing resources for scholarship in almost all fields of knowledge, in serving as centers for the dissemination of knowledge, and in serving as components in the evolving national information systems. The library role in these matters is in fact so critical that the Commission believes that libraries serving these purposes must be significantly strengthened. This increased strength will require a variety of different approaches and techniques; Federal support, long-range planning, and better coordination are all urgent requirements.

In the Statement by the President accompanying the Executive Order, three serious questions were asked about the future of our libraries. One of these was quite similar to the item in point 1 of the Commission's charge about the role of libraries as components of evolving national information systems. It asked:

What part can libraries play in the development of our communications and information-exchange networks?

In considering the role of libraries in national information systems and in communications and information-exchange networks, the Commission found many uncertainties, often further complicated by semantic confusion and a tendency to polarize conventional written information and scientific and technical data. The National Advisory Commission on Libraries favors resolving the uncertainties through multiple but coordinated planning and experimentation. It urges an evolutionary development responsive to user needs, whether it is simple interlibrary cooperation or a highly technical communications system. Some points supporting this conclusion appear to be already evident.

Libraries are reservoirs of information whose means and ends of distribution are determined by the function the information is to serve in the hands of the user rather than by some abstract set of values inherent in the term "library" itself. Similarly, one cannot evaluate electronic and computer-processed information stores except in terms of improving the function of the ultimate user of this information.

The requirements for effective library and information access for students, scholars, and practitioners in various disciplinary areas and at various levels display sharp and complex variations. Consequently, sweeping generalizations with respect to user needs are likely to be misleading through incompleteness and inaccuracy. For example, some misunderstandings exist because the need for books has now been joined by needs for information in other formats. In some technical fields traditional books may be playing a decreasing role as reservoirs of information. In other fields the need for traditional literary information may actually be increasing. But in all fields the needs are multiple and are likely to become more so as new multidisciplinary relationships emerge and develop simultaneously with further highly specialized needs.

At the beginning levels of formal education, we find that the close adaptation of elementary school libraries to the functional needs of changing teaching patterns has made the book only one of many information resources handled by the information center of the elementary school. It is at other levels within the formal educational system—the secondary school, college, and university levels—that library needs are most evident and least satisfied. Here the more traditional understanding of the library asserts itself and a wide variety of measures will be needed, including more collaborative efforts among these libraries, to insure their long-range effectiveness. As for academic research, the library responses to these needs display, even where there appears to be great strength, severe stresses and great unevenness in access.

The roles of the public library are changing. The relative inefficiency of completely self-planned instruction and the increasing availability of organized instruction within the community have decreased the function of the public library as the university of the poor. Nevertheless, as educational demands upon the public library by the educational system itself increase, and as the sophistication of the community increases, the public library becomes an essential element within the community as an information reservoir for multiple user groups.

It follows from the foregoing paragraphs that naturally evolving systems that clearly serve the needs of users should be given support in their own right at this time. No one can perceive the final nature of communications and information-exchange networks, nor the quality of a national information system—with a single exception. The exception is that such a system will finally be made up of a large number of highly specialized individual components, each one of which should be designed to serve the needs of a defined user group.

The specialized libraries, such as the National Library of Medicine, one of our three existing national libraries, can therefore be looked upon as important models of how a library alters or develops its role and activity to serve a defined group—in this case the medical scientists and practitioners. The National Library of Medicine also engages in cooperative activities. Likewise the largest of our national libraries, the Library of Congress, has demonstrated many kinds of cooperation with other units, thus exemplifying how the understanding of the need of response to a user group (e.g., the Congress) does not exclude sensitivity to cooperation with the larger whole.

Libraries badly need support in establishing new means of intercommunication and cooperation. Only after this kind of support of the existing order has been established can it be reliably estimated what the role of these units is in the evolving national information system.

To summarize, then, and to place the Commission's response to the very broad point 1 of its charge in somewhat clearer focus, the following observations are relevant here. These are shared by members of the Commission and recur many times throughout this Report in various contexts.

First, in order to improve the access of our society to information, the Commission believes the basic necessity is to foster development by an evolutionary process. An example is the application of technology, which can play an extremely important role in improving library and informational operations; the Commission does not presently see a technological solution that will make either the printed book or the library itself quickly obsolete—nor does it see any near-term system that will inexpensively provide instant access to all knowledge at any location.

Second, if the present unsatisfactory situation, described particularly in section C of this Report, is to be improved, the Commission believes there should be augmented Federal support for: (a) national or regional resource collections and services for infrequently used research materials in a carefully planned pattern; (b) nationally oriented indexing, cataloging, abstracting, and other bibliographical services; (c) basic and applied research in library operations and in the intellectual problems, technology, and economics of information transfer and dissemination.

Third, it is apparent that public, school, and academic libraries will all be obligated to change many of their methods of work, their interrelationships, and some of their roles and objectives in the years ahead. If these libraries are to be responsive to contemporary and future requirements, the Commission believes that changes will have to take place at a much faster rate than has heretofore been the case. To effect more rapid rates of change and response, funds, among other things, will be required that are not now available.

Fourth, there are, and there will continue to be, many information dissemination and data-handling functions that may be handled in part or entirely outside the walls of traditional libraries—e.g., indexing, abstracting, literature evaluation, synthesis, and computer or other means of access to extensive economic, sociological, scientific, and other data banks. These services are of great importance in insuring effective access to the resources collected, organized, preserved, and made available primarily through libraries—especially those of a scholarly research nature.

Fifth, the Commission believes that the nation's library and other information systems will continue to be a shared responsibility of Federal agencies, the states, municipalities, educational institutions, and many other public and private organizations. No monolithic Federal or other centralized administrative control seems either feasible or desirable. There will have to be many different kinds of information systems and working relationships among a variety of institutions if we are to provide effective access to relevant information for our society. New systems, roles, and relationships are likely to emerge at very different rates of speed in response to widely varying user needs.

Finally, it should be stated here that the tasks of analyzing the needs, planning, setting standards, allocating resources, measuring performance, and coordinating efforts will be difficult and complex in the years ahead. Effective progress will require the sustained effort of the present Commission's recommended ongoing National Commission on Libraries and Information Science working with Federal agencies, the national libraries, and many other institutions, groups, and individuals.

THE FRAGMENTATION OF EFFORTS

The second of the President's charges required the National Advisory Commission on Libraries to "appraise the policies, programs, and practices of public agencies and private institutions and organizations, together with other factors, which have a bearing on the role and effective utilization of libraries."

In an effort to accomplish this appraisal, a number of the special studies referred to earlier were planned by the Commission to concentrate on the various kinds of libraries and the different public agencies involved. These studies by competent authorities included one on the Federal Government and libraries by Duke University; one on state libraries and library agencies by Nelson Associates, Inc.; one on research libraries by the American Council of Learned Societies; three on undergraduate and junior college libraries, public libraries, and school libraries, respectively, all by Nelson Associates, Inc.; and one on special libraries by the American Documentation Institute. The Commission also heard testimony from representatives of all types of libraries, from Federal and state agencies concerned, and from library associations.

It is impossible to present any reliable appraisal of the policies, programs, and practices of even a single type among the multitudinous agencies and institutions that are involved in giving library and information services to the American people. An overriding conclusion, however, evident from all the studies and hearings, is that there is an extremely wide range in both the character and the adequacy of library services and library resources. The incomparable holdings of the great university libraries contrast starkly with the nearly empty shelves of new community colleges and similar institutions. Residents of some large cities and affluent suburbs enjoy a wealth of library services denied to residents of most rural areas. The schools of suburbia are likely to have superb libraries, the schools of urban and rural slums none at all—at least until the Elementary and Secondary Education Act of 1965 (P.L. 89-10, P.L. 89-750) began to offer assistance. What kind of library service an American has available to him may have the widest possible variation, depending on his means and where he lives. In general, the areas of greatest poverty and social need and the institutions confronting the most critical social and educational problems are those with the least adequate library services. Where such great efforts are required to induce nonusers of library services to become users, we face a great lack.

More detailed appraisals of particular strengths and weaknesses are reflected in the definitions of objectives and the recommendations for action that make up the ensuing chapters of this Report. A forthcoming book planned by the Commission and based on

Commission materials, including a number of the special studies, will attempt a further analysis of the multiplicity of users and uses of library and information services [see the chapters in Part I of the present volume]. Surely one of the primary tasks of the present Commission's recommended ongoing National Commission on Libraries and Information Science will be broad planning toward understanding and coordinating the present fragmented situation.

In the Statement by the President accompanying the Executive Order establishing the National Advisory Commission on Libraries, there was a question, somewhat related to point 2 in the charge but directed toward the fragmentation of Federal efforts:

Are our Federal efforts to assist libraries intelligently administered, or are they too fragmented among separate programs and agencies?

As mentioned above, there are many current complexities in evaluating and even identifying some of the programs and the relationships between them. The Commission clearly believes that coordination of and cooperation between the organic units of the whole body of library efforts, both within the Federal Government and supported by it, are inadequate. Such a body needs a central nervous system. In pursuing this analogy, it is important to emphasize that a central nervous system is the servant of the organs— that each has its own independent and discrete function on behalf of the whole. The central nervous system cannot substitute for the function of the organ, but the function of the organ serves the whole body only when it is coordinated.

For this reason the National Advisory Commission on Libraries does not recommend that one of the organic units—for instance the largest of the national libraries, the Library of Congress—should dominate all of the other organic units in this coordination. Rather, the Commission recommends that a body roughly analogous to that serving the National Library of Medicine as its Regents should be established as a Board of Advisers to the Library of Congress, and that an institute should be established within the Office of the Secretary of Health, Education, and Welfare to coordinate developmental efforts. The brain of this system is that overall planning and advisory agency, the National Commission on Libraries and Information Science, already referred to several times here in section A.

The present Commission believes that, within this system it has recommended, the haphazard fragmentation of efforts can be circumvented and the strength of diversity maximized.

SOURCES AND USES OF FUNDS

The third point in the charge to the National Advisory Commission on Libraries was to "appraise library funding, including Federal support of libraries, to determine how funds available for the construction and support of libraries and library services can be more effectively and efficiently utilized." Attention was further directed to the following question from the President's Statement:

Are we getting the most benefit for the taxpayer's dollar spent?

The pitiful incompleteness and tardiness of library statistics, and their lack of comparability, make it impossible to give specific quantitative responses to this series of questions. No one knows precisely, or even with close approximation, what the total present library expenditures of the nation are, or even what the Federal contributions to those expenditures are—nor can even approximately reliable specific estimates be made of the costs of remedying the serious deficiencies in library service that we all know exist.

Estimated needs suggest extensive expenditures in order to approach the various sets of standards adopted by the American Library Association (ALA). According to figures supplied to the Commission by the United States Office of Education in June 1968, it would require a lump sum expenditure in 1968 of $1.6 billion to stock school libraries optimally. Just to make up the backlog of space required to construct centralized public school libraries where they did not exist in 1961 would require $2.145 billion. Space requirements for replacement and new growth for public libraries have been estimated at $1.132 billion for the period 1962–75. As for academic libraries, available figures compare present trend with optimum trend over the total period 1962–75: $1.945 billion compared with $9.891 billion for books and materials, $120 million compared with $360 million for new construction.

Obviously such large amounts are beyond immediate achievement, but the estimates afford some general measure of the magnitude of the financial problem that lies ahead in the development of library services. The present Commission has not attempted to make its own specific estimate of the dollar needs of libraries—in part because the members have not found it possible to evaluate existing standards and do not believe an adequate factual basis for a reliable estimate exists, and in part because any estimate would quickly be made obsolete by changing needs and costs—but primarily because the principal need is to create machinery for continuing examination of changing library needs, for devising means of meeting them, and for determining priorities and costs. This would be the task of the permanent National Commission on Libraries and Information Science proposed in this Report.

It already seems perfectly clear, however, that the need for additional financial support for our libraries is great at present and will grow rapidly in the future. Population growth, our more extensive educational commitments, the rapidly increasing role of research, the greater complexity of our society, and our determination to achieve a massive improvement in the educational and vocational status of the poorer and less-educated among our citizens will join to require very substantial increases in the quantity and quality of library services.

The present Commission has explored possible means of reducing the unit cost of library service to offset in some degree the total financial impact of the need for greatly increased services. Interlibrary cooperation, the establishment of interlibrary networks, and the more extensive employment by libraries of new information technology have all been considered in this connection. As other sections of this Report indicate, the Commission believes that all of these developments have great potentialities for library service and should be vigorously pursued. Their value, however, will almost certainly rest in making it possible for us to have library services of a form and scope now unattainable—for example in making the holdings of the great research libraries more realistically available to users in smaller communities and institutions—rather than in reducing the cost of services. In reality, the effective employment of these new devices and methods will itself require a large additional investment of funds.

The unit cost of library services is, in fact, almost certain to rise substantially over the foreseeable future. Three fourths or more of the cost of library service consists of salaries. These will undoubtedly rise steadily as the general wage and salary level of society rises with higher productivity. Indeed, the acute shortage of professional personnel is likely to drive library salaries up even faster than the general salary level. The absence of opportunities to increase man-hour productivity comparable to those available in industry, coupled with increases in salary rates, will produce substantial and inescapable increases in unit costs. This is the same problem the nation faces in connection with increasing costs of education and medical services.

Since the principal reason for the steady increase in the cost of library services, as of other social services, is the rising affluence of the country, the means exist to meet these costs. It is inescapable, however, that these should be met from sources of public income that rise hand-in-hand with increases in the gross national product. Public libraries and school libraries are now financed primarily from local real estate taxes, which are inelastic and respond very slowly to increases in national income; many college and university libraries are heavily dependent on endowment income and student fees, which are also capable of only limited increase. The role of state support for many of these types of libraries has been substantially enlarged and should be further increased as a partial response to the inflexibility of other sources of support. Even state income, however, based as it is largely on low income taxes and sales taxes, responds relatively slowly to rises in the general productivity and is critically low in just those states especially in need of large-scale expansion of library services.

For all these reasons, the Commission believes that over the coming decade very large increases in Federal support of libraries will be necessary and, indeed, inescapable. Even if this necessity did not exist, however, there would be ample justification for an increase in the Federal component of library support. The problem of research libraries is peculiarly a national one; we need to develop national centers of research collections, national backstopping facilities to improve access to research materials, national plans for coordination, national catalogs and bibliographies, and other apparatus that will improve the accessibility of relevant information. The employment of the newer information technology in libraries—including research to develop its applications, the formulation of uniform or compatible information storage and retrieval systems, and the creation of library networks—are also inescapably national problems whose solutions require national participation and support.

Even on the level of local school and public libraries, there is a great and distinct national interest. Especially with a population so mobile as that of the United States, the whole nation must have a concern for the level of educational and informational services throughout the country. Illiteracy, ignorance, limited education, and lack of vocational skills, and other poverty-engendering deprivations, wherever originating, spread their impact by migration and otherwise throughout the country. Library development is an essential element in such national objectives as the elimination of poverty and the achievement of rapid social and economic development, and it requires and deserves national support.

As for the effective utilization of funds already available for the construction and support of libraries and library services, it should be pointed out that, during the life of the Commission, the Federal contribution to libraries had just been greatly expanded under the Elementary and Secondary Education Act of 1965 and the Higher Education Act of 1965 (P.L. 89–329, P.L. 90–35, P.L. 90–82), and appropriate procedures and staffing were still being worked out. There was some inevitable confusion, and it is too early to reach dependable judgments about the efficiency of the Federal program. In general, however, the Commission hopes that the administration of these acts may be moving toward the quite high level of efficiency already achieved in the administration of the Library Services and Construction Act (P.L. 88–269, P.L. 89–511, P.L. 90–154) and the library components (Titles III and XI) of the National Defense Education Act (P.L. 88–665).

There are, however, some fundamental weaknesses in the present pattern of Federal library support:

a. It is given under a large number of different acts in addition to the four mentioned above. Some such diffusion is inevitable, and even to some degree desirable since it would be unwise to pull library components out of many different Federal programs and put them into one act, thus separating library support from the objectives it is intended to serve. But there is substantial overlapping and lack of coordination among these different acts at present, and they have not been planned as part of a comprehensive whole.

b. There is no program of Federal support for research libraries as such.

c. There is no central program for the development of the newer information technology and its application to libraries.

    d. Although manpower is a most critical library problem, Federal support has been almost wholly given to buildings and materials, with limited support for training and almost none for salaries.

    e. Effective employment of Federal funds within the states, especially for school and public libraries, and effective state support both depend on strong state library planning and administrative services, which do not always exist.

The National Advisory Commission on Libraries has stated in this Report a number of conclusions and recommendations to strengthen these aspects of Federal support. Particularly relevant in this respect are the permanent National Commission on Libraries and Information Science to undertake broad central planning toward coordination; a central Federal Institute of Library and Information Science for research and development; aid to research libraries as well as other libraries; improved manpower recruitment, training, and utilization; and strengthening of state libraries. The Commission believes the adoption of these approaches would substantially improve both the efficiency and the effectiveness of library funding and the use of Federal funds.

THE CRITERION OF SOCIAL VALUE

In retrospect, examining the objectives and recommendations presented in this Report in relation to the original charge, the National Advisory Commission on Libraries believes that questions now unanswered will yield to the diverse approaches and interlinked continuing bodies recommended. There clearly already are, and will continue to be, many challenging problems for the scrutiny of the continuing National Commission on Libraries and Information Science—the very fact that the present Commission, in only the few months since completion of its preliminary Report, has developed additional conclusions and recommendations for the present Report is encouraging evidence of the validity of the commission function in overall planning and advising.

One theme emerges throughout all the activities of the National Advisory Commission on Libraries since its first meeting in November 1966. This is a strong social-benefit awareness, a service orientation that pervades every existing and conceivable library and information function. Perhaps it is not too soon to propose the criterion of social value as the most important in decision-making—whether for broad central planning, more specific planning, or immediate problem-solving. We should look at the value to our people and our culture that accrues from the activities of the user whose functions are to be enhanced by improved availability of library and information services. A library can be understood only as it enhances a socially valuable function, one of which—and one that all libraries can enhance—is the personal intellectual and ethical development of every individual in our society. The variety of the other socially valuable functions determines the need for variety in kinds of libraries.

In this spirit of social awareness, the National Advisory Commission on Libraries developed its recommendations for a National Library Policy, presented in the following section.

B. A NATIONAL LIBRARY POLICY

    RECOMMENDATION: That it be declared National Policy, enunciated by the President and enacted into law by the Congress, that the American people should be provided with library and informational services adequate to their needs, and that the Federal Government, in collaboration with state and local governments and private agencies, should exercise leadership in assuring the provision of such services.

Increasingly over the years the need for a national library policy has become apparent—a policy which could permit plans that take into consideration the needs for library service of the American people as a whole. Recent developments which have profoundly affected not only the supply and the use of informational materials, but also the way in which information is used, have made the recognition of this need inescapable.

As long ago as circa 1730, when Benjamin Franklin and his youthful colleagues were establishing what was perhaps the first communal library in the American colonies, he gave expression to the basic principle of modern library service. By "clubbing our books to a common library," he wrote, each member had "the advantage of using the books of all the other members, which would be nearly as beneficial as if each owned the whole." Today, some Americans share the use of collections of millions of volumes, while others still lack access even to meager and deficient library facilities.

By the end of the nineteenth century the country possessed many thousands of academic, public, and other libraries, all based on Benjamin Franklin's principle of clubbing. These libraries were all more or less self-sufficient institutions, necessarily limited by their local resources, but providing important services to local communities of users. But the need for more broadly based services was already recognized and growing, and interlibrary lending, union catalogs, and other products of interlibrary cooperation were responding to this need.

During the next fifty years, however, it became clear that the library needs of the country could not be met merely by cooperation between independent units having local responsibilities. Several of the state governments led the way in developing regional library services organized around their state libraries, while increasingly through the period the libraries of the country were taking advantage of central services—of which the Library of Congress catalog-card system is the archetype—for reducing their costs and increasing their effectiveness. Finally, in 1956, in the Library Services Act (P.L. 597), Congress took a major step to enable the Federal Government, in collaboration with the states, to extend public library services to that third of the nation's population, mainly in rural areas, that still lacked them.

That Act was just in time. Since 1956 the accelerated momentum of events has made cumulative demands upon the libraries of the country which they were quite unprepared to meet, but the experience gained under the Library Services Act has proved invaluable for suggesting methods for meeting library problems.

It is now clear that library services are needed, to greater or less extent, directly or indirectly, by the entire citizenry of the country. Such services are increasingly essential for education, scholarship, and private inquiry; for research, development, commerce, industry, national defense, and the arts; for individual and community enrichment; for knowledge alike of the natural world and of man—in short, for the continuity of civilization on the one hand and increasingly for the preservation of man's place in nature on the other.

It is also now clear that these needs can no longer be met by spontaneous independent institutions having merely local responsibilities and claiming merely local support, no matter how willing they may be to assist. Indeed, these institutions through the years are persistently further and further from self-sufficiency and increasingly dependent upon the services of external bodies—public and private, state and Federal, domestic and foreign—without which their costs would skyrocket and their services diminish.

A principal reason for this exists in the sheer mass of new information continuously being added to the existing stock as a result of the ceaseless probings of scholarship and research—information which is requisite for the increasingly complex activities of civilization and of modern communities, yet which is beyond the capacity of individual libraries to acquire, organize, store, search, and make available for service. For the efficient handling of this information, a system of specialized agencies is needed. Elements of such an arrangement actually do exist, but on an unplanned and spontaneous basis. The situation requires rationalization through the execution of careful plans in the national interest.

There are other reasons why libraries can less and less attempt to serve as self-sufficient entities but must more and more derive strength from membership in regional or national systems or networks. One of these is the increasing mobility both of people and of industry—a mobility that tends not only to diversify, but also to intensify the demands upon local libraries for specialized materials. Another is the enormous increase in personnel costs that all service organizations, including libraries, are forced to sustain, costs that compel them wherever possible to substitute mechanisms and automatons for manual operations. A special aspect of this process is the inevitable impact of electronic technology on information transfer—a process already under way in the development of methods for storage of information in electronic memories, processing by computer, distribution by wire or microwave, and service to the consumer by telefacsimile or cathode-ray-tube display.

To avoid haphazard and fragmented response to the inevitable forces of a changing society, a national plan is required that can be used to guide the next steps of all participants toward a recognized and achievable goal of adequate library service to all Americans. Because of the deep involvement of the Federal Government as producer, processor, and user of information, and because this is a matter closely touching the national welfare, the leadership of the Federal Government is essential to the success of any plan.

A prerequisite to the development of such a plan is a clear enunciation of the policy on which the plan is to be based. In consequence, the first recommendation of the National Advisory Commission on Libraries, on which all its further recommendations rest, is that it be declared National Policy, enunciated by the President and enacted into law by the Congress, that the American people should be provided with library and informational services adequate to their needs, and that the Federal Government, in collaboration with state and local governments and private agencies, should exercise leadership in assuring the provision of such services.

THE INTERNATIONAL DIMENSION

A National Library Policy for meeting the needs of our own citizens does not preclude an international awareness and responsibility. In fact a national policy statement on international book and library activities already exists—it was approved by the President on January 4, 1967. [See appendix F–1.B.] Subsequent directives to Government agencies have further elucidated this policy for the encouragement of education through exchanges of books and of teachers and students, fostering indigenous book publishing and distribution facilities, support for programs of library development, training programs for library personnel, liaison between American and foreign libraries, increased exchange of reference and bibliographic information, and joint undertakings in the development of library technology.

The National Advisory Commission on Libraries shares the enthusiasm of the library profession toward achieving these goals and urges the appropriation of funds to implement the International Education Act (P.L. 89–698). The Commission also commends the idea of a clearinghouse at the Library of Congress to which foreign scholars and libraries might apply for needed publications.

The contribution of our library profession and our libraries to the improvement of international relations over the years has been noteworthy. Their acquisitions programs have attempted to develop rich resources of information from all parts of the world to meet the ever increasing needs of our citizens. They have aided in the work of creating understanding of our society and our policies by making publications of the United

States available to libraries abroad. They have participated on a continuing basis in the work of international library associations and of the United Nations Educational, Scientific, and Cultural Organization (UNESCO) in its program of fostering education and librarianship abroad, and they have helped restore libraries ravaged by war and natural disasters.

Today, when it is clearly in our national interest to help the emerging countries develop progressive educational systems and provide a basis, through education and knowledge, for peaceful coexistence in the community of nations, the American library profession can—through participation in both publicly and privately supported efforts— make a greater contribution than ever before.

The United States can demonstrate to the world that we support our convictions regarding intellectual freedom by providing free access to all types of information and all shades of opinion for all citizens. Our libraries can strive to become a vital positive force in the social and intellectual reconstruction of a broadening and changing society. The National Advisory Commission on Libraries believes that the basic first step for the Federal Government is to state a National Library Policy toward the provision of services truly adequate to the nation's needs.

C. OBJECTIVES FOR OVERCOMING CURRENT INADEQUACIES

In order to fulfill the National Policy and provide library and informational services adequate to the nation's needs, current inadequacies must be faced. The purpose of this section is to discuss some areas where objectives are needed: where existing deficiencies threaten to undermine the success of any coherent development into the future. These deficiencies already severely limit or deny effective access to libraries and relevant knowledge for many individuals, but the situation can and must be remedied. A variety of complex responses and changes are required, and these responses and changes need to be developed in a sustained, consistent, and evolutionary manner over a period of time—and with a substantial degree of Federal leadership and participation. The National Advisory Commission on Libraries recommends that immediate national attention be given to six broad and fundamental objectives. The long-range development of an adequate library and information system will be dependent to a large degree on the achievement of these objectives.

FORMAL EDUCATION AT ALL LEVELS

OBJECTIVE: Provide adequate library and informational services for formal education at all levels.

First of all, we must reduce some serious current deficiencies in those libraries serving not only every level of formal education, but also the increasingly blurred boundary lines between these levels.[2] School library deficiencies, labeled "a national disgrace" by former Commissioner of Education, Francis Keppel, have truly serious consequences for our entire system of education. The habit of reading, skill in reading, and skill in identifying and using pertinent information are vital in the learning process, in dealing with concepts, in making wise judgments, in pursuing a vocation or profession, in extending the frontiers of knowledge, and in the liberation and extension of the mind of man.

---

2 *As evidenced, for example, by such phenomena as advanced-placement credit for college-level courses taken in high school and early-entrance programs to professional education.*

Recent Federal legislation has already had visible impact on elementary and secondary school library development, in part by encouraging much greater local effort in library improvement. Nevertheless, and in spite of differences from one system to another, the needs of our schools in general for books and other library materials, for adequate physical facilities in which to house libraries, and for staff are so enormous that continued Federal assistance is necessary. The Commission believes that appropriations for school library resources should be increased as soon as possible to at least the full amount authorized by the Elementary and Secondary Education Act of 1965 (P.L. 89–10, P.L. 89–750). At this time some school buildings have no libraries in any sense of the word; too often meager materials are housed with notable inadequacy. Provision for libraries should be made mandatory in any Federal legislation supporting the construction of new school buildings or the expansion of existing buildings that do not already have adequate library facilities. It should be noted that libraries in schools serving educationally deprived children appear to be extremely deficient, and it would be advisable to bolster the library assistance provided by the Elementary and Secondary Education Act with supplementary legislation to help solve this problem in our large cities where so many disadvantaged children reside. To provide for a more efficient use of materials, equipment, and personnel, local and state school library agencies should be further encouraged to form community and regional systems to provide centralized consultation and acquisitions and processing services for school library materials.

The implementation of a national plan to raise elementary and secondary school libraries to full and continuing adequacy will require far better data on school libraries than are now available. Investigations should also be undertaken on the relative cost and utility of the various types of library materials, which are often indistinguishable from instructional materials; on differing patterns of service, supervision, and library organization; on appropriate standards; on the various means of coordinating school library districts to provide centralized consultant, processing, and materials-evaluation services; and on the means of stimulating the production of special library materials for students and preschool children in disadvantaged or bilingual communities, where children lack the preschool preparation and relative linguistic and cultural sophistication of children from middle-class American families.

One of the most complex problems that will have to be resolved in any national planning for genuine adequacy of library service to the total span of education relates to the difficulty of coordinating the various library agencies that serve high school and college students in urban areas. Because high schools, urban colleges, and junior colleges are often remote from areas where many of their students reside, and because it is frequently difficult and costly to provide the maintenance services necessary to keep the school library open evenings and weekends, and because the school collections are often inadequate to the needs, students have been resorting to their local public libraries in such large numbers as seriously to overload the public library. Coordination of public library directors, teachers, school principals, and various librarians within different geographic jurisdictions is not an easy administrative matter, but evidence suggests that there is a serious lack of such coordination even within areas where the jurisdictional boundaries of the public library and school library systems coincide. New thinking and planning are critically needed regarding the distribution of responsibility and financial support to the various types of libraries within each region if we are to serve the increasing demands of formal education.

As college enrollments have increased since World War II, we have witnessed an almost phenomenal increase in the number of junior and community colleges. In no other type of institution serving higher education are library shortcomings so glaring. The great majority of library collections of junior colleges are considered substandard, and a high percentage of the libraries of four-year colleges are also weak. Of all the difficulties that beset the college library, the most visible is that of inadequacy of library buildings. The Higher Education Facilities Act of 1963 (P.L.88–204 as amended) has been a tremendous stimulus and support for college library construction. Substantial amounts have been granted under this Act for undergraduate college library buildings, but in many instances the combination of Federal aid and local resources has led only to an alleviation of the pressing immediate need for more library space, and not to solutions viable for long periods.

The National Advisory Commission on Libraries believes it to be of great national importance that the libraries serving the undergraduate students and faculties of our two-year and four-year colleges, and also the undergraduate colleges in our universities, be equipped and staffed to do their jobs with full adequacy. To help achieve this goal, the Commission believes that sums appropriated under the authority of the Higher Education Act of 1965 (P.L. 89–329 P.L. 90–35, P.L. 90–82) to strengthen the collections of college libraries should be increased substantially, and in the administration of grants for this purpose, special attention should be given to improvement of the collections of the two-year and four-year colleges that are most seriously in need. Additionally, the limitation on grants for the construction of academic library buildings under the Higher Education Facilities Act of 1963 should be raised to permit a Federal contribution of three fourths of the construction cost, as provided, for example, in the Medical Library Assistance Act (P.L. 89–291).

For long-range college library development, plans should be developed for centralized services to college libraries in acquisitions, processing, and storage of little-used material; in effecting cooperative arrangements that will give college students and faculty members efficient bibliographic and physical access to the resources of research libraries; in arranging for advisory services to college librarians, especially with respect to the utilization of technological aids to library work; and in persuading the states and other responsible agencies that adequate libraries are essential rather than marginal or optional facilities.

As formal education progresses into graduate and professional schools of the university and the continuing education of practitioners, the informational needs become more complex and the boundary lines between education and research become blurred. Inadequacies in serving the nation's research needs are discussed later in this chapter under other objectives, but it is appropriate to point out here that a dynamic relationship exists between all the areas for which the National Advisory Commission on Libraries has identified inadequacies and suggested objectives.

THE PUBLIC AT LARGE

OBJECTIVE: Provide adequate library and informational services for the public at large.

Serving the informal educational needs at all levels might well be the stated function of the only libraries to which the undifferentiated general public has access today—the public libraries. There are inadequacies here too, and there are strong arguments for overcoming these in order to strengthen the health of our democracy.

The public library reaches the entire population as does no other aspect of library service. Parents of preschool children rely on it for the picture and storybooks that are the child's first introduction to the mystery of reading. Elementary school children go to the public library for books when school is out and during vacation, as do high school students, who also use it for assistance in homework and term papers. Urban college students living at home find the public library more convenient than their college libraries. Adults rely on it for recreation and continuing education. Businessmen may turn to it for practical information, as do housewives, craftsmen, and hobbyists. The larger public libraries are major research resources. More recently we have turned to the library as one of the social agencies needed to assist in liberating the prisoners of urban ghettos from ignorance and poverty. For all men and women, it is the one place through which they may reach the world's collected informational and intellectual resources.

Yet, important as the public library is, there are few social services so unequally provided to the American people. Residents of some cities can command the resources of enormous institutions holding many hundreds of thousands, or even millions, of volumes. At the other extreme, some twenty million Americans, largely in rural areas, have no public library service at all, and some ten million more have access only to very small libraries with very inadequate collections and little or no service from professional librarians. Indeed, only residents of cities of substantial size or of areas served by well-sustained county or regional library systems are likely to have access to reasonably adequate library service. It is essential that measures be taken to extend at least basic local public library service to every American. The encouragement of library systems, interlibrary loans, and other similar approaches can give everyone ultimate access to all the library resources he needs.

The unequal distribution of service is not the only inadequacy. Even where public library service is available, indeed even in some of the better-served cities, it is usually far below any reasonable standard of adequacy. More than two thirds of all public libraries fail to meet American Library Association (ALA) standards as to the minimum adequate size of collections, and not one in thirty meets ALA standards for per-capita financial support.

There are a number of other quite critical problems in current public library services. One is the heavy burden of high school and college student use of the public library. This pressure will in part be relieved as the educational libraries are strengthened. But students turn to the public library not only because of its relative strength, but because of its convenience. This motive will not be lessened by the improvement of a high school library, for it may still be closed on evenings and weekends, or by the improvement of a college library that may be distant from a student's home. Diverting students away from the public library would deprive them of definite conveniences. The desirable objective would be to assist the public library in developing the means to meet the pressure and serve the student better. Public libraries need to be included in programs of assistance to educational libraries.

Another special problem, shared by many urban services, arises from the fact that patterns of public library service in metropolitan areas by no means correspond to the pattern of local governmental jurisdiction. In particular, the public library of the central city may be called on to render service to residents of the entire metropolitan area, without any financial support from suburban jurisdictions. The situation is doubly complicated when the metropolitan area, as in several of our large cities, extends across state lines. Further means of support and coordination must be found.

Still other problems stem from the fact that the nature of the informational and reading needs of the residents of core cities has radically changed in the last decade, so radically as to require substantial changes in the outlook, collections, and services of the core-city branches of urban public libraries if they are to become effective instruments in the attack on poverty, ignorance, and semiliteracy. The public libraries require assistance, financial and professional, in equipping themselves to meet these new needs.

One of the principal tasks of the National Commission on Libraries and Information Science, proposed in section D, should be to develop a national plan, calling on Federal, state, and local sources of support for making adequate public library service available to all Americans. Such a plan should give special attention to the problems of large cities with difficult educational problems, of metropolitan areas with multiple jurisdictions, and of rural areas entirely or almost entirely lacking public library services.

The planning should give attention to the coordination of school, college, and public library services. It should consider arrangements for the maximum use of cooperative library systems, and assure compensation to larger or more specialized libraries—public or private—when they give service to such systems that extends beyond the demands of their normal clientele. The National Advisory Commission on Libraries believes the plan should provide for substantially increased levels of support on a matching-fund basis.

The term "public library" includes county libraries serving townships without libraries, or with very inadequate ones, and state libraries. State libraries support the public library system in their respective states and provide assistance to school libraries. They are entrusted, usually, with planning state library systems and with the administration of state aid to public libraries. In some instances they are required to provide legal collections and other resources necessary for the work of state government. The deficiencies some state library agencies face are so severe that one recommendation of the National Advisory Commission on Libraries is specifically directed to this problem area.

RESEARCH IN ALL FIELDS AT ALL LEVELS

OBJECTIVE: Provide materials to support research in all fields at all levels.

A third broad national goal must be the development and implementation of a plan that will insure that the nation has the research resources required for its increasingly complex informational and research needs. The publication of new books and new editions of older titles (exclusive of Government publications, dissertations, pamphlets, and most subscription books) doubled between 1950 and 1966. The growth of knowledge and the phenomenal increase in its use is reflected not only in the increased production of books, but in the proliferation of such information-bearing records as journals, research reports, dissertations, microfilms, audiorecordings, and other materials. Increases in the use of all publications are difficult to assess, but a recent report states that the use of scientific literature has been increasing by 12 to 17 percent per year. In addition, there are major new areas of research concern (such as Asia, Africa, the Middle East, and Eastern Europe) requiring acquisitions programs for large quantities of material that are very costly, very difficult to acquire, and very expensive to catalog and organize for effective use.

The increase in research conducted by universities and sponsored by Federal and state agencies, corporations, and foundations, has made demands upon university libraries that have not been satisfied by either the growth of library collections or staffs. All agencies of government, foundations, industries, and other organizations that subsidize research by contracts, grants-in-aid, fellowships, and other means should be made aware of the greatly augmented burden on the library that their grants and subventions commonly entail. This should be taken into account in the planning of grants and programs. Continuity of such funding is critically important.

Although many libraries share in carrying the burden of acquiring, organizing, and servicing this vast body of material for the nation, the principal burden at the present time falls upon a relatively small number of university libraries, the three great national libraries (the Library of Congress, the National Library of Medicine, and the National Agricultural Library), and a number of very large public libraries and privately supported research libraries. Rapid increases in the costs and scope of required publications and of the staffs for handling them, as well as the added means for sufficient space, are severely straining the very limited resources of all these institutions. Existing programs of Federal assistance are not in general addressed to the development or the accessibility of research materials. It is essential to develop and fund a more systematic and comprehensive national program to assist these libraries in the acquisition, organization, housing, and servicing of materials likely to be of research value to the nation.

Research, basic or applied, requires source materials and itself produces new informational output—this is true of the arts and humanities as well as the natural and physical sciences, the social and behavioral sciences, and many technical areas. As society continues to demand both new knowledge and more rapid application of knowledge for its own betterment, the proliferation of information may defeat its own purpose unless adequately recorded, acquired, and available for use.

BIBLIOGRAPHIC ACCESS

OBJECTIVE: Provide adequate bibliographic access to the nation's research and informational resources.

It is not enough simply to acquire research and informational resources. To insure that their existence and relevance will be known to those who need them, an adequate apparatus for indexing, cataloging, abstracting, and evaluating their content must be developed.

The work of bibliographic organization of vast collections of books and other materials, and of providing the tools that permit any user to determine their location quickly, grows in complexity with every volume added to the collections and with the proliferation in the sources, the subjects, the languages, and the forms in which pertinent materials appear. Under the Higher Education Act of 1965 (P.L. 89–329, P.L. 90–35, P.L. 90–82), funds totaling $3 million were provided in 1967 to enable the Library of Congress to expand its acquisitions and cataloging program in an effort to provide cataloging data for any foreign book that an American library might purchase. This appropriation has now been increased substantially and the program, if sustained, may prove to be the most far-reaching service to scholarly and many other national bibliographic needs of all Federal library undertakings.

At present the technology of electronically storing, updating, querying, and transmitting bibliographic data is emerging. In section D, the National Advisory Commission on Libraries sets forth its recommendation for a vigorous program of research and development leading toward national networks that will provide better access to improved bibliographic and related services.

Bibliographic access to the content of the many thousands of journals and research reports in our libraries is inadequate and uneven. There is no agency: (1) to initiate and develop national technical standards that could help to insure coverage of all journals contributing to the total research effort; (2) to coordinate the work of various association-supported, governmental, and commercial enterprises; and (3) to assist in determining priorities in funding.

Despite the seeming wealth of service of all kinds to assist in providing bibliographic access to information in the sciences and technology, several deficiencies in the present pattern are obvious. Except for medicine, agriculture, and the Library of Congress, the responsibility of the Government agencies for coverage is naturally based primarily on the particular objectives and literature requirements of the agency. The commercial services respond only to demonstrably large-scale need in special fields, and the work of the various scientific associations is not well coordinated. As a consequence, there are both extensive overlapping of effort and tremendous gaps in coverage. Moreover, a proprietary attitude in both the Government agencies and the scientific societies as regards their bibliographic products is a natural consequence of their desire to satisfy the special requirements of their users.

There is no direction by any national agency concerned with the total information problem. As separate services proliferate, grow, and succeed, the prospect for standardization and compatibility diminishes. There is clearly a need for national planning and coordination to insure, for all subject fields, including the humanities and social and behavioral sciences, adequate systems of bibliographical control.

PHYSICAL ACCESS

OBJECTIVE: Provide adequate physical access to required materials or their texts throughout the nation.

Plans to strengthen national holdings of research resources and their effective subject or bibliographical control must also provide for effective physical access to the texts themselves. Even the largest research, university, corporate, or Federal library cannot hope to achieve self-sufficiency, despite the fact that it must possess library resources adequate for all but the most unusual needs of its staff or constituency. As the college library looks to the university library in its locality, so must the university library depend on the holdings of other institutions and the national libraries to satisfy requests for publications that it has not acquired. The public library, in turn, may look to state library agencies, other public libraries, or to academic libraries for materials needed by readers.

The demands for research information extend far beyond the requirements of scholars employed at universities. Industry must be able to draw upon the resources that our university libraries offer, since the duplication of their holdings in the depth and extent necessary for many industrial research purposes is almost inconceivable. Moreover, the needs of governmental agencies at all levels, of the professions, of the private scholar, all require access to research and other information not necessarily available in the immediate vicinity. Means must be found to make the full text of documents available in some suitable form and at locations convenient to all users, with minimum delay and at manageable and equitably distributed costs. The problems of physical access are likely to be further complicated in future unless efforts are made to discourage the continued use of book paper with a rapid rate of deterioration.

The present cooperative arrangements between libraries to make materials available are slow and inefficient and are costly to the relatively small number of libraries that are called upon to provide a major part of this service without recompense. Furthermore, the present difficulties in the way of interinstitutional physical access to publications forces research and other libraries, at high cost, to acquire, catalog, and house large amounts of little-used materials. These costs might be significantly reduced if new and effective patterns of joint physical access to materials can be developed. It is apparent that national, regional, and state planning is needed to facilitate physical access to publications generally, utilizing any technological aids that it is feasible to employ.

Such planning will obviously entail: (1) support from Federal, state, and other sources for improvement of interlibrary loan and copying services, which the research and certain other libraries can no longer provide gratuitously at high cost to themselves; (2) the establishment of regional library networks and of resource libraries to serve them; and (3) support for agencies, such as the Center for Research Libraries, which should have Federal assistance in their efforts to serve research and informational needs in all parts of the country. Finally, it will be important in the public interest, whether under the present copyright law or any revision that may be adopted, that arrangements for the protection of copyright proprietors do not unreasonably hinder access to and use of information.

LIBRARY MANPOWER

OBJECTIVE: Provide adequate trained personnel for the varied and changing demands of librarianship.

Recent analyses undertaken by the library profession, as well as the testimony of almost all witnesses before the National Advisory Commission on Libraries, indicate that the problem of manpower shortage in our libraries is of such critical severity as to merit its being singled out for special mention. All estimates of the number of professional personnel needed to fill existing vacancies and for normal attrition of staff in public, academic, and special libraries exceed the number of librarians graduated each year by the forty-five accredited schools of librarianship in the United States and Canada. With respect to the provision of librarians qualified for positions in elementary and secondary school libraries, the situation is even more unsatisfactory.

Before the library profession can hope to enroll the requisite number of persons for training in the schools of librarianship, a variety of obstacles must be overcome. First, librarianship should be made more attractive as a career for men as well as for women. As is true of most professions in which women predominate at the lower and middle levels of responsibility, the prestige of librarianship as a whole is lower in the public view than it deserves to be, and the financial rewards are less tempting than in many other professions that require professional education. General public ignorance of the variety of interesting specialized career opportunities within the broad field of librarianship also makes recruitment difficult. A further handicap is the discrepancy between the status, salaries, and fringe benefits accorded the librarians of many academic institutions and those available to their colleagues employed in teaching and research. Finally, there is a long tradition of recruitment for librarianship among only the humanistically oriented college students. Too few scientifically oriented young people understand that the profession of librarianship embraces all categories of specialists who mediate between the sources of recorded information and the people who need access to information in all subject fields and at all levels of sophistication.

A second major obstacle is the inadequacy of the forty-five accredited graduate schools of librarianship in the United States and Canada with respect to financial support for staff and physical facilities. It is not known how many qualified applicants for library training may be lost for this reason. To complicate matters still further, all schools of librarianship contend with a shortage of qualified teachers, with a scarcity of fellowships to encourage the advanced study requisite for the preparation of future faculty, and with inadequate support for workshops, institutes, and other programs to enhance the competence of librarians already employed and help them adjust to changing demands. Equally important is the inadequacy of support for working librarians who wish to take advantage of opportunities for specialized training or advanced training when these do exist.

Paralleling these dilemmas is the slowness of the library profession itself in achieving agreement regarding the nature and extent of education or training needed for employment in the various specializations of librarianship, and in enlisting more fully the aid of the various disciplines of the social, behavioral, and applied sciences in preparing library science students for the changing requirements of library management and for the evolving role of the library in our society.

The resolution of library and information science manpower problems will be and Information Science should give high priority to an exploration of professional should undertake a program of ongoing research in librarianship in order to improve functional efficiency and facilitate the establishment of the variety of training programs needed now and in the future. Research in library education itself should be encouraged, as well as curricular experimentation.

Second, library administrators should employ every effort to make all professional library work intellectually and socially challenging to retain the best minds that enter the profession.

Third, the Federal Government, which has already acknowledged its responsibility for the improvement of library service under its constitutional mandate on the general welfare, should assist the profession through a number of undertakings. The United States Office of Education should analyze the library personnel situation on a regular basis, compare it with standards established by itself or the library associations, and publish its findings. It should, further, maintain a clearinghouse of information on all innovations in library education and training and on all efforts of libraries to make more efficient use of personnel. Further, the Office of Education should provide advisory aid to library schools, library associations, and others interested in recruiting people to library work in adequate numbers to carry out the various existing and emerging specialized tasks required.

To assist the library profession, the proposed National Commission on Libraries and Information Science should give high priority to an exploration of professional education and training, including experimentation with alternate modes of library training. The Commission should assist also with achieving improved salary scales and providing better promotional possibilities to make librarianship more attractive as a career.

Finally, Federal assistance in developing library personnel should be provided: (1) by direct aid to schools offering graduate and undergraduate training, postgraduate in-service training, and refresher courses; (2) by aid in the publication of suitable texts for such training; (3) by support of special programs to train potential teachers of librarianship; and (4) by greatly increased provision of funds for fellowships for undergraduate, graduate, and special library training.

CONCLUSION

These, then, are six areas where current inadequacies exist, and future inadequacies are foreseen unless all participants in the management and use of information can look to coherent national planning and coordinated research and development. The nation's needs for library and information service can be expressed in terms of the need to serve formal education, the public at large, and research of all kinds. The need to provide appropriate ways of locating information (bibliographic access) and acquiring it for use (physical access) is basic. Manpower is a pervasive and very urgent problem area. The six interrelated objectives discussed above form the context for the recommendations of the National Advisory Commission on Libraries set forth in section D.

D. RECOMMENDATIONS FOR ACHIEVING THE OBJECTIVES

In order to serve the needs of education at all levels, the general public in all its diversity, and research in all fields of knowledge, the problems of access to continually burgeoning information and efficient utilization of manpower must be resolved. Some dilemmas are immediately pressing and can be handled by immediate action. Other dilemmas are foreseen as still emerging over the transition period to the long future, and thus provision must be made for constant adaptation to inevitably changing needs and improved understanding of these needs. The National Advisory Commission on Libraries believes the five recommendations discussed below provide both a sound base for the future and a realistic means of coping with current inadequacies.

NATIONAL COMMISSION ON LIBRARIES AND INFORMATION SCIENCE

RECOMMENDATION: Establishment of a National Commission on Libraries and Information Science as a continuing Federal planning agency.

In order to implement and further develop the national policy of library services for the nation's needs, the most important single measure that can be undertaken is the establishment of a continuing Federal planning agency. It is noteworthy that almost all representatives of library, scholarly, scientific, and other professional associations who testified before the National Advisory Commission on Libraries gave high priority in their recommendations to the creation of such a Federal planning agency. The present Commission's efforts to analyze current and future national library needs, assess the strengths and weaknesses of existing library resources and services, and evaluate the effects of library legislation, leave the members with the absolute conviction that the goal of library adequacy will be achieved only as a consequence of long-range planning and fostering of the evolutionary process of library development. This will require taking advantage of present and emerging knowledge in information science; it will require encouraging and exploiting future research.

The proposed National Commission should be charged with the responsibility of preparing full-scale plans to deal with the nation's library and information needs, and for advising the Federal Government and other agencies, institutions, and groups—both public and private, with respect to those needs. It should be empowered to conduct, or have conducted, such studies and analyses as are necessary for the fulfillment of its responsibilities; it should have ready access to information relevant to its purposes from other Government agencies concerned with library and information services; and it should be empowered to recommend legislation which is needed to enhance and strengthen the nation's library and information services.

The National Commission should be established by the Congress. Its members should be appointed by the President with the advice and consent of the Senate. The National Commission should report at least once a year to the President and to the Congress on its activities, recommendations, and plans in the areas of its responsibility and concern. This report should be published.

The present National Advisory Commission on Libraries recommends that this proposed National Commission on Libraries and Information Science be constituted of not more than fifteen private citizens of distinction. This group shall include, but not necessarily be restricted to, persons competent in the library and information science professions. The Chairman should be appointed by the President from among its members. A rotating, staggered membership is suggested so that individuals serve for a term of five or six years.

To accomplish its complex and broad mission the National Commission should be provided with a staff adequate in number and strong in expertise, and with funds sufficient to enable it to exercise the extensive research and planning functions which will be necessary if it is to provide sound advice to the President and the Congress. A suggested location appropriate for the National Commission on Libraries and Information Science is in the Office of the Secretary of Health, Education, and Welfare.

THE LIBRARY OF CONGRESS: THE NATIONAL LIBRARY OF THE UNITED STATES

RECOMMENDATION: Recognition and strengthening of the role of the Library of Congress as the National Library of the United States and establishment of a Board of Advisers.

The National Advisory Commission on Libraries believes that the role of the Library of Congress as the National Library of the United States should be recognized and strengthened, and it specifically recommends:

1. That the Congress define the responsibilities of the Library of Congress as follows: (a) to serve as the principal reference and research arm of the Congress, thus serving the nation through this body; (b) to assemble, maintain, and provide national availability for comprehensive national research collections of materials from all countries and in all fields of knowledge, except those for which the National Library of Medicine and the National Agricultural Library

have accepted responsibility; (c) to catalog these materials promptly and offer its catalog cards for sale to other libraries; and (d) to provide basic national bibliographical, reference, and copyright services. The Commission suggests that these functions of the Library of Congress, already largely exercised in fact, should be further recognized by adding an appropriate phrase to its title, so that its formal designation would be: "The Library of Congress: The National Library of the United States."

2. That a Board of Advisers to the Library of Congress be created. Its chairman and members should be drawn from the public, including scholarly and research organizations, the scientific community, universities and colleges, and research librarianship, and they should be appointed by the President of the Senate and the Speaker of the House of Representatives. The recommended functions of this proposed Board of Advisers are to review the Library's operations and services and to advise the Librarian of Congress—and, as desired, the appropriate Committees of Congress—on matters that would assist the Library in the development of its collections and the performance of its national services. The Board should be required to prepare and submit an annual report to the Congress and to the Librarian of Congress. This report should be published.

The rationale for the Commission's inclusions lies chiefly in the fact that, by far-reaching legislation and generous appropriations over the last seventy years, the Congress has created in the Library of Congress perhaps the greatest of the world's national libraries. It has the principal national research collections in most fields of knowledge, except of course those served by its two companion national institutions, the National Library of Medicine and the National Agricultural Library. It is a source of last resort to which other libraries can turn for interlibrary loans and for microfilms of materials. It provides a means of acquisitions, for other libraries' collections as well as for its own, of public documents and other research materials not available through the book trade, especially from Asia, Africa, Latin America, and Eastern Europe.

The catalog cards of the Library of Congress provide a basis for the catalogs of most American libraries. The Library houses and maintains the *National Union Catalog,* one of the greatest and most nearly indispensable of our bibliographical tools. The publication of its own catalogs in book form has provided a major reference resource for libraries here and abroad. Many of its other bibliographic services have become essential to research libraries and to scholars. Since 1948 the Library of Congress has published the best continuing bibliography of Russian books compiled outside the Soviet Union. It edits the indispensable *National Union List of Serials* and publishes regularly a list of new serial titles received by principal American and Canadian libraries. It provides the subject apparatus for the national listing of doctoral dissertations, maintains a *National Register of Microcopy Masters,* and publishes a *National Union Catalog of Manuscript Collections.*

The Library of Congress performs many other national services as well. It is the chief agency in providing braille and "talking" books for the blind. It has undertaken major responsibility for a national program to preserve the physically deteriorating book stocks of libraries. On a contractual basis it has provided a major bibliographical and documentation service to a number of Federal agencies concerned with scientific and technological research.

The Library of Congress in general, and in their respective fields the National Library of Medicine and the National Agricultural Library, have the ultimate in comprehensive national research collections and provide national bibliographical services that are absolutely indispensable to research and scholarship in many fields and to the whole system of American research libraries. Comprehensive as the collections and bibliographic services of the Library of Congress now are, however, they need further strengthening in a number of areas.[3] This strengthening of the Library of Congress through provision of a Board of Advisers, definition of the Library's responsibilities, and recognition of the role it already plays as a great national library is the main thrust of the Commission's recommendations here.

It is a great credit to the wisdom and vision of the Congress that the Library of Congress has been so responsive to many needs. Today all the nation's requirements for library services are becoming so complex that the Library, which has never had a charter or basic constituent act defining its responsibilities, must be formally recognized for its national role and provided with advisers that can help to steer its future responsiveness.

The National Advisory Commission on Libraries does not recommend that the Library of Congress have responsibility for the development, administration, or co-ordination of a national library system or for the administration of programs of library assistance or grants such as those carried on by the United States Office of Education, the National Science Foundation, and other agencies. That would be a deterrent to its main function as a national library. The Commission believes that the indispensable role of the Library of Congress is in the development and availability of its unmatched collections and in its unique cataloging and bibliographic services. These should be strengthened in every possible way.

FEDERAL INSTITUTE OF LIBRARY AND INFORMATION SCIENCE

RECOMMENDATION: Establishment of a Federal Institute of Library and Information Science as a principal center for basic and applied research in all relevant areas.

The National Advisory Commission on Libraries recommends that a Federal Institute of Library and Information Science be established to become a principal national center of research on library and information science in all its aspects. The Institute should have as one of its major responsibilities the system engineering and technical direction involved in the design and implementation of an integrated national library and information system, but the mission of this proposed Institute must range beyond matters of technological development and application to research into the changing needs of information users and the effectiveness of libraries and information systems in meeting these needs.

This recommendation is based on the striking contrast between the serious inadequacies of the nation's libraries and the rapid progress in the technology of information transfer. One of the great challenges of our day is to apply new technology to the operations of our libraries and thereby give each individual in our society easy and comprehensive access to the information resources he needs to make his work competent and his life meaningful.

The Commission recognizes that this goal will not be achieved by a single sweeping innovation, but rather by a succession of technical advances, some already within reach, others attainable by short-term efforts, and some approachable only through prolonged research activities. The times at which elements of new technology are introduced into specific libraries will also vary with the type of library service. Books and card files will be the mainstays of most small libraries for many years to come, but the large research libraries and a few special libraries will press for the earliest possible exploitation of new developments. Ultimately, the new technology will provide effective links from all information resources to all information users.

---

[3] *This is true, for example, in connection with the previously mentioned acquisition and prompt central cataloging of foreign research materials not available through normal trade channels. To a considerable extent, this must now be accomplished through the transfer of funds appropriated to the United States Office of Education under Title II-C of the Higher Education Act of 1965 (P.L. 89–329) and the transfer of foreign currencies accumulated under Public Law 480.*

The uses of microfilm and document copiers are already familiar to every serious library user, even to some elementary school pupils. In the near future, gradual reduction in the costs of microfilm duplicates and full-size paper copiers will make on-demand duplication compete even more with traditional circulation of books and other materials in responding to many kinds of readers' needs. At a later time, as communication costs come down, we shall also see a more extensive adoption by libraries of telefacsimile transmission to distant users.

Of greater potential importance for future libraries than any past technical innovation will be the utilization of high-speed digital computers and their associated information-handling equipment, for the employment of computers in libraries has already led to high hopes for improved access to informational resources, in spite of the exponential growth of knowledge. Computers will most likely be applied to library operations in three successive stages. The computer has already demonstrated its usefulness as a rapid and efficient accounting device for the control of such library functions as acquisitions, circulation, serial records, and binding, as well as for general business operations; this is the first stage. Second, we are witnessing the initial successful attempts to apply the computer to bibliographic operations. The third and most exciting stage of computer involvement, which we are only beginning to approach, is the interaction between the library and the on-line computer community, in which a time-shared central computer is used as a general intellectual tool by many users working simultaneously at different terminals in a network. Development work is now in progress on the transmission of bibliographic data in such networks and on the more formidable problem of storing and transmitting the full text of documents.

In the course of time, different local networks will be interconnected and we shall see the emergence of regional, national, and international information-transfer networks. What we know today by the term "interlibrary cooperation" will be superseded by a much more fluid pattern of providing access to distant users without preventing concurrent access by local users. The evolution of these networks is the brightest promise of the new technology for libraries, but there are many technical, economic, and other problems that must be resolved before such networks can be operational.

The realization of all that is implied in this array of new technology can be achieved only by a substantial program of research and development. This Commission urges that the Federal Government should actively promote research and development in all aspects of technology as it relates to libraries and information transfer. To this end, the proposed National Commission on Libraries and Information Science should develop an integrated plan of support and cooperation involving the various Federal agencies now sponsoring such research and development work. Such a plan would greatly aid the continuation and strengthening of the current grant and contract program, which involves research and development projects at universities, private and public libraries, nonprofit research and development organizations, professional societies, and private companies.

The major Federal Institute recommended by the National Advisory Commission on Libraries can play an important role in the over-all plan. This Institute should itself undertake multidisciplinary research, development, and prototype application of all types of new technology as they relate to library and information science activities. Its program should be built on a foundation of basic research efforts directed toward better tools for the analysis of library and information requirements, quantitative measures for judging the value of existing systems and services, and an understanding of the relative value of various information-transfer media and of the role of interactive systems.

Supported by such basic investigations, the major research and development activities of the program should aim for further multidisciplinary efforts to improve library work—for example: (1) through applications of new technology for purposes of saving labor, improving speed and accuracy, maximizing convenience and dependability, reducing costs, and performing tasks previously impossible; (2) through more effective devices for organizing, storing, transmitting, displaying, and copying information; (3) through more effective organization of manpower and service units; (4) through superior understanding of the theoretical foundations of library work and of the storage, organization, and communication of knowledge; (5) through understanding, based on comprehensive studies of both users and nonusers of libraries, both as to their library requirements and also the reasons for nonuse; and (6) through the resolution of legal problems, such as those relating to the photocopying of copyrighted material.

The apex of the overall plan for research and development should be a system of interconnected libraries, established as a prototype network, a model for information transfer by advanced techniques. Such a network, after attaining full operational success, would become the first step in the evolution of an integrated national library system. The National Advisory Commission on Libraries recommends that the proposed Institute should be given the system engineering and technical direction responsibilities for the design and implementation of such a system.

In all planning of technological applications in library work, in all library network or systems planning, a crucial element is the development and application of national standards for the compatibility and convertibility of data systems and techniques among libraries. The proposed Institute should take a leading part in bringing about such standardization.

Administratively and organizationally, the Government can choose among many different patterns in establishing a research and development Institute of the type here contemplated. It is recommended that this Institute be established within the Office of the Secretary of Health, Education, and Welfare. It may be helpful to point out that the models that were prominent in the Commission's thinking were the National Institutes of Health and the National Laboratories of the Atomic Energy Commission.

UNITED STATES OFFICE OF EDUCATION

RECOMMENDATION: Recognition and full acceptance of the critically important role the United States Office of Education currently plays in meeting needs for library services.

Recent legislation and Federal appropriations providing for: (1) major research programs that greatly accelerate the growth of new knowledge, and (2) additional massive support for education at all levels place new and large responsibilities on the Office of Education. Its task would become even greater with the adoption of the National Advisory Commission on Libraries' proposals for a National Policy on library services for the nation's needs, the creation of a nationwide library network, and the widespread use of technological aids to improve library services.

The Commission recognizes the steps which the Office of Education has taken during this past year to strengthen and to increase the efficiency of its operations. The proposed organization of the Office's activities that affect libraries must focus on the most critical library problems: programs, professional education, facilities, research, planning, and development. In addition, the National Center for Educational Statistics must be in a position to collect on a continuing basis the pertinent and adequate library data—urgently required and not now available—for an appraisal of present programs and formulating plans for the future. But to carry out these key functions, the Office's staff must immediately be strengthened. The Commission urges the approval without delay of support for professionally trained, experienced people, with supporting staff, to serve in the library programs of the Office, particularly within its Division of Library Services and Educational Facilities. To provide the essential overall leadership, the National Advisory Commission on Libraries specifically recommends the appointment of an Associate United States Commissioner for Libraries, responsible directly to the Commissioner of Education.

With its library and information services programs properly organized and staffed, the Office of Education would be in a far better position to administer present and impending Federal legislation and to conduct efficiently more extensive activities on behalf of the libraries. It could then plan, extend, and coordinate, at the national level, all types of library services for schools, colleges, continuing and adult education, public libraries, research, industry, government, and other agencies. In doing so, it would assist greatly in providing the service to libraries so vital in our time.

The critically important role of the Office of Education in meeting the nation's need for services in support of libraries must be clearly recognized and fully accepted by the Federal Government.

STATE LIBRARY AGENCIES

RECOMMENDATION: Strengthening state library agencies to overcome deficiencies in fulfilling their current functions.

Because state library agencies are unable to fulfill their current role adequately, far less their participative role in new joint ventures toward the objectives discussed in section C, state library agencies must be strengthened. This can best be done at this time by amendment of the Library Services and Construction Act (P.L. 88–269, P.L. 89–511, P.L. 90–154) authorizing aid specifically for such agencies to enable them: (1) to overcome staff shortages; (2) to provide better consultative services to public libraries; (3) to offer special information and library services to state government; (4) to insure that a full range of library services is offered to the handicapped and disadvantaged; (5) to initiate and encourage research into library problems; and (6) to coordinate library planning for total library service. These are the areas where serious deficiencies currently exist.

In the long-range development of state-related library services, the principle of state matching should be retained. The National Advisory Commission on Libraries believes that Federal programs should give increasing attention to the building and strengthening of regional and interstate library programs where these appear to respond more effectively and efficiently to library needs.

CONCLUSION

The five recommendations discussed above are the result of the deliberations of the National Advisory Commission on Libraries from its establishment by Executive Order September 2, 1966, through June 1968. They are intended to provide structural innovations and realignments for a planned and coordinated approach to society's changing needs in the years ahead, as well as immediate actions to solve immediate problems. The order of presentation and relative length of descriptive text do not imply order of importance. All are major recommendations. Some relate to all the objectives discussed in section C; others relate more to one objective than another. All are aimed toward fulfillment of the National Policy presented in section B:

RECOMMENDATION: That it be declared National Policy, enunciated by the President and enacted into law by the Congress, that the American people should be provided with library and informational services adequate to their needs, and that the Federal Government, in collaboration with state and local governments and private agencies, should exercise leadership in assuring the provision of such services.

Appendixes

APPENDIX A

COMMISSION DOCUMENTS

This first division of appendixes A through F of *Libraries at Large* consists of formal documents relating to the National Advisory Commission on Libraries and its Report. Appendix A–1 reproduces the President's Statement and the Executive Order. Appendix A–2 is the formal list of Commission members. Appendix A–3 reproduces the two letters of transmittal that accompanied the Report.

APPENDIX A–1

TEXT OF THE PRESIDENT'S STATEMENT AND THE EXECUTIVE ORDER ESTABLISHING THE PRESIDENT'S COMMITTEE ON LIBRARIES AND THE NATIONAL ADVISORY COMMISSION ON LIBRARIES

1. STATEMENT BY THE PRESIDENT

Our nation is providing better education to more citizens today than ever before. The result of this expanding effort in education is a rising demand for information—and a tidal wave of new information touching every aspect of our lives: health, education, jobs, national defense, goods and services, transportation, communications and environmental use.

But merely piling up valuable new knowledge is not enough; we must apply that knowledge to bettering our lives.

In our effort to do this, we depend heavily upon the nation's libraries. For this reason, the Federal Government will spend, next year, more than $600 million in the library field.

But money alone cannot do the job. We need intelligent planning and advice to see that our millions are spent well. We need to ask serious questions about the future of our libraries:

What part can libraries play in the development of our communications and information-exchange networks?

Are our Federal efforts to assist libraries intelligently administered, or are they too fragmented among separate programs and agencies?

Are we getting the most benefit for the taxpayer's dollar spent?

To help answer these questions, I have signed today an Executive Order creating the National Advisory Commission on Libraries, composed of distinguished citizens and experts.

I have asked the Commission to appraise the role and adequacy of our libraries, now and in the future, as sources for scholarly research, as centers for the distribution of knowledge, and as links in our nation's rapidly evolving communications networks.

I have also asked the Commission to evaluate policies, programs, and practices of public agencies and private organizations—and to recommend actions which might be taken by public and private groups to ensure an effective, efficient library system for the nation.

I believe that this new Commission, aided by public and private efforts, will bring real advances in our progress toward adequate library service for every citizen.

Dr. Douglas Knight, president of Duke University in Durham, North Carolina, will serve as the Commission chairman.

The other members are:[1]

Proposed Membership for the National Library Commission:

Douglas M. Knight, President of Duke University—CHAIRMAN
Verner Clapp, President, Council on Library Resources
Herman Fussler, Library, University of Chicago
Carl Overhage, M.I.T., Cambridge, Massachusetts
Theodore Waller, President, Teaching Materials Corporation, New York (resigned December 28, 1966)
Wilbur Schramm, Director, Institute for Communication Research, Stanford University
Launor Carter, Senior Vice President, System Development Corporation, Santa Monica
Caryl Haskins, Carnegie Institution, Washington, D.C.
William N. Hubbard, Jr., Dean, University of Michigan Medical School, and Chairman, EDUCOM
Alvin Eurich, President, Aspen Institute for Humanistic Studies, Colorado
Stephen Wright, former President of Fisk University, Nashville, Tennessee
Harry Ransom, Chancellor, University of Texas, Austin
Carl Elliott, former Congressman from Alabama
Estelle Brodman, Medical Library, Washington University, St. Louis, Missouri

2. EXECUTIVE ORDER NUMBER 11301

By virtue of the authority vested in me as President of the United States, it is ordered as follows:

Section 1

Establishment of Committee. (a) There is hereby established the President's Committee on Libraries (hereinafter referred to as the "Committee").

(b) The membership of the Committee shall consist of the Secretary of Health, Education, and Welfare, who shall be the Chairman of the Committee, the Secretary of Agriculture, the Director of the Office of Science and Technology, and the Director of the National Science Foundation, and may include, in addition, the Librarian of Congress who is hereby invited to be a member of the Committee. Each member of the Committee may designate an alternate, who shall serve as a member of the Committee whenever the regular member is unable to attend any meeting of the Committee.

Section 2

Duties of the Committee. (a) The Committee shall:

(1) Appraise the role of libraries as resources for scholarly pursuits, as centers for the dissemination of knowledge, and as components of the Nation's rapidly evolving communications and information-exchange network;

1 *See appendix A–2 for the final official list of Commission membership.*

(2) Evaluate policies, programs, and practices of public agencies and private institutions and organizations with reference to maximum effective and efficient use of the Nation's library resources; and

(3) Develop recommendations for action by Government or by private institutions and organizations designed to ensure an effective and efficient library system for the Nation.

(b) Such recommendations shall take into account the final report of the National Advisory Commission on Libraries established by Section 3 of this order, which report shall be transmitted to the President with the recommendations of the Committee.

Section 3

Establishment of Commission. (a) To assist the Committee in carrying out its functions under Section 2 of this order, there is hereby established the National Advisory Commission on Libraries (hereinafter referred to as the "Commission").

(b) The Commission shall be composed of not more than twenty members appointed by the President, none of whom shall be officers or full-time employees of the Federal Government. The President shall designate the Chairman of the Commission from among its members.

(c) The Commission shall meet on call of the Chairman.

(d) Each member of the Commission may be compensated for each day such member is engaged upon work of the Commission, and shall be reimbursed for travel expenses, including *per diem* in lieu of subsistence, as authorized by law (5 U.S.C. 55a; 5 U.S.C. 73b–2) for persons in the Government service employed intermittently.

Section 4

Duties of the Commission. (a) The Commission shall transmit to the Committee its independent analysis, evaluation, and recommendations with respect to all matters assigned to the Committee for study and recommendations.

(b) In carrying out its duties under subsection (a), above, the Commission shall:

(1) Make a comprehensive study and appraisal of the role of libraries as resources for scholarly pursuits, as centers for the dissemination of knowledge, and as components of the evolving national information systems;

(2) Appraise the policies, programs, and practices of public agencies and private institutions and organizations, together with other factors, which have a bearing on the role and effective utilization of libraries;

(3) Appraise library funding, including Federal support of libraries, to determine how funds available for the construction and support of libraries and library services can be more effectively and efficiently utilized; and

(4) Develop recommendations for action by Government or private institutions and organizations designed to ensure an effective and efficient library system for the Nation.

(c) The Commission shall submit its final report and recommendations to the Committee no later than one year after the date of its first meeting, and shall make such interim reports as it deems appropriate for improving the utilization of library resources.

Section 5

Federal departments and agencies. (a) The Committee or the Commission is authorized to request from any Federal department or agency any information deemed necessary to carry out its functions under this order; and each department or agency is authorized, consistent with law and within the limits of available funds, to furnish such information to the Committee or the Commission.

(b) Each department or other Executive agency the head of which is named in Section 1(b) of this order shall, as may be necessary, furnish assistance to the Committee or the Commission in accordance with the provisions of Section 214 of the Act of May 3, 1945 (59 Stat. 134; 31 U.S.C. 691), or as otherwise permitted by law.

(c) The Department of Health, Education, and Welfare is hereby designated as the agency which shall provide administrative services for the Commission.

Section 6

Termination of the Committee and the Commission. The Committee and the Commission shall terminate ninety days after the final report of the Commission is submitted to the Committee.

LYNDON B. JOHNSON
THE WHITE HOUSE, September 2, 1966

APPENDIX A–2

MEMBERSHIP OF
THE NATIONAL ADVISORY COMMISSION ON LIBRARIES

Chairman
Douglas M. Knight
President, Duke University, Durham, North Carolina

Vice Chairman
Frederick H. Burkhardt
President, American Council of Learned Societies, New York, New York

ESTELLE BRODMAN, *librarian and professor of medical history,* Washington University School of Medicine, St. Louis, Missouri

LAUNOR F. CARTER, *vice president and manager,* Public Systems Division, System Development Corporation, Santa Monica, California

VERNER W. CLAPP, *consultant,* Council on Library Resources, Washington, D.C.

CARL ELLIOTT, *attorney at law,* Jasper, Alabama

ALVIN C. EURICH, *president,* Academy for Educational Development, New York, New York

MILDRED P. FRARY, *director of library services,* city schools libraries, Los Angeles, California

HERMAN H. FUSSLER, *director of the university library and professor in the graduate library school,* The University of Chicago, Chicago, Illinois

MARIAN G. GALLAGHER, *professor of law and law librarian,* University of Washington, Seattle, Washington

EMERSON GREENAWAY, *director,* Free Library of Philadelphia, Philadelphia, Pennsylvania

CARYL P. HASKINS, *president,* Carnegie Institution of Washington, Washington, D.C.

WILLIAM N. HUBBARD, JR., *dean,* University of Michigan Medical School, Ann Arbor, Michigan

DAN LACY, *senior vice president,* McGraw-Hill Book Company, New York, New York

MRS. MERLIN M. MOORE, *supervisor of economic education,* State Department of Education, State Capitol, Little Rock, Arkansas

CARL F. J. OVERHAGE, *professor of engineering,* Massachusetts Institute of Technology, Cambridge, Massachusetts

APPENDIX A–3

LETTERS OF TRANSMITTAL

THE SECRETARY OF HEALTH,
EDUCATION, AND WELFARE
Washington, D.C. 20201
October 3, 1968

THE PRESIDENT
The White House
Washington, D.C.

Dear Mr. President:

The Report of the National Advisory Commission on Libraries established in September 1966, by your Executive Order Number 11301, is attached. The Report has been reviewed by the members of the President's Committee on Libraries.

The Committee found it a highly stimulating report, containing numerous ideas which would strengthen the role of libraries in our society. It reflected the painstaking and energetic efforts of the Commission to look at the varied problems confronting libraries and librarians as they seek to supply a variety of services in the midst of growing demands.

Libraries are the keepers of our history and our culture. But they are not merely storehouses for the relics of the past, but meeting places for people and ideas, vital partners in our system of education.

The Committee urges a wide distribution of the Report. Its recommendations should be considered and discussed by individuals and groups at Federal, State and local levels, both in and out of the library community. It should encourage all of these groups as they make plans for even more effective services.

Respectfully yours,
Wilbur J. Cohen
CHAIRMAN, PRESIDENT'S
COMMITTEE ON LIBRARIES

NATIONAL ADVISORY COMMISSION
ON LIBRARIES
Suite 6800 West
200 C Street S.W.
Washington, D.C. 20204
July 1, 1968

THE HONORABLE WILBUR J. COHEN
Secretary, Department of Health,
  Education, and Welfare
Chairman, President's Committee on Libraries
Washington, D.C.

Dear Mr. Secretary:

In accordance with the Executive Order of the President of the United States, we are pleased to transmit to the President's Committee on Libraries the recommendations of the National Advisory Commission on Libraries. The Commission believes that its six broad objectives for the transitional and future development of library and information services can be achieved responsibly and realistically through the structural and organizational recommendations set forth in these pages.

The Commission has tried diligently to meet its charge as set forth in Chapter 1 of this Report. We have met eleven times as a full Commission to discuss library problems and potentials as perceived by a most interesting diversity of viewpoints represented by our membership. We have heard formal testimony and had informal discussions with technological experts, librarians, people from government and private agencies, and a variety of users and producers of both conventional literary material and newer forms of informational transfer. Regional hearings were held in communities throughout the country by members of the Commission to ascertain the people's library needs at the grass roots of our nation. Special studies on a number of relevant topics, in most cases specially commissioned by us, were submitted to the Commission and contributed to our deliberations on problems and issues. Already, areas for vital new research are evident.

On the basis of deliberations through early December 1967, the Commission had agreed on its recommendations and reached some basic conclusions on fulfilling the national policy we recommend for library services appropriate to the needs of the people. We presented these conclusions and our specific recommendations in a preliminary Report dated December 1967. Since then, the Commission has prepared a chapter analyzing its response to the President's charge, completed a statement on library manpower for Chapter 3, and made certain other refinements and modifications in the five basic recommendations now set forth in Chapter 4.

The work we have started can continue most meaningfully through the combined efforts of many existing and evolving entities, coordinated by the overall planning efforts of our recommended National Commission on Libraries and Information Science. There must be continuing, coordinated study and action in the years ahead—it is an ongoing, never-ending venture. Because the results of all the activities of the present Commission can continue to provide resource on library and information science and service in the future, we are supplementing our Report with a forthcoming volume which will be based on a variety of materials and data, including the special studies, in an attempt to synthesize and document a complex set of problems and issues.

At this time, it is our hope that the President's Committee on Libraries will study our Report and commend our proposals for action to the early attention of the President and the Congress. The problems are urgent. A sound beginning can be made.

Sincerely yours,
Douglas M. Knight
CHAIRMAN, NATIONAL ADVISORY
  COMMISSION ON LIBRARIES
President, Duke University

THE SPECIAL STUDIES

This second division of the Appendixes is devoted to explanatory material on the special studies commissioned by the National Advisory Commission on Libraries in 1967. As indicated in Table B–1, these studies provided basic raw material for this resource book; a number of them appear *in toto,* specially revised and updated to constitute chapters or sections of chapters in the topical sequence.

BACKGROUND

One of the most ambitious endeavors undertaken by the National Advisory Commission on Libraries was to call for more than a dozen special studies on a wide range of subjects. Social science, history, political science, economics, information science, education, and library science were only some of the disciplines contributing to the studies—all of which were performed within the limited space of a few months.

Most of these special studies, commissioned by or made available to the Commission, contributed at least partially to Commission decision-making, although there was by no means a total endorsement of every position or recommended action in even the most highly acclaimed studies. All have been made available to the United States Office of Education for consideration for the Educational Resources Information Center (ERIC), and some may appear elsewhere in addition to the versions that appear here in *Libraries at Large.* In the form in which they were accepted by the Commission, these studies are in the public domain.

The list in Table B–1 includes those special studies the Commission judged to be relevant to the problems with which it was concerned and worthy of serious consideration, although a few are of mostly descriptive value. Incomplete studies and those deemed to be of little or no immediate relevance to Commission decision-making, in the form in which they were submitted, are not included in Table B–1.

ERIC INFORMATION

Many of the materials of the National Advisory Commission on Libraries are available in their original form from the ERIC Document Reproduction Service (4936 Fairmont Avenue, Bethesda, Maryland 20014). For the information of interested scholars, the following list includes pertinent data on the special studies in the select list and on the Commission Report itself.

1. Technology and Libraries: ED 022 481; microfiche, 75¢; hard copy, $6.68
2. On Research Libraries: ED 022 480; microfiche, 50¢; hard copy, $3.76
3. The Impact of Technology on the Library Building: ED 018 147; microfiche, 25¢; hard copy, 56¢
4. The Federal Government and Libraries: not on ERIC list
5. American State Libraries and State Library Agencies: ED 022 486; microfiche, 25¢; hard copy, $1.56
6. Social Change and the Library: 1945–1980: ED 022 483; microfiche, 50¢; hard copy, $4.40
7. On the Economics of Library Operation: ED 022 525; microfiche, 75¢; hard copy, $6.80
8. The Use of Libraries and the Conditions That Promote Their Use: ED 022 489; microfiche, 50¢; hard copy, $4.88
9. Special Libraries: Problems and Cooperative Potentials: ED 022 482; microfiche, 50¢; hard copy, $5.04
10. School Libraries in the United States: ED 022 485; microfiche, 50¢; hard copy, $3.16
11. Undergraduate and Junior College Libraries in the United States: ED 022 487; microfiche, 50¢; hard copy, $4.28
12. Public Libraries in the United States: ED 022 484; microfiche, 50¢; hard copy, $2.80
13. Libraries and Industry: ED 022 488; microfiche, 75¢; hard copy, $6.00
*** Library Services for the Nation's Needs: Toward Fulfillment of a National Policy: ED 020 446; microfiche, 50¢; hard copy, $3.04

TABLE B-1

SELECT LIST OF SPECIAL STUDIES

	TITLE OF STUDY	AGENCY CONDUCTING STUDY	APPEARANCE IN *Libraries at Large*
1.	Technology and Libraries	System Development Corporation	Chap. 7, Sec. C; App. F-3.C
2.	On Research Libraries*	American Council of Learned Societies	Chap. 3, Sec. A.1, A.2; Chap. 6, Sec. A; Chap. 7, Sec. A; Chap. 8, Sec. C; App. F-3.A
3.	The Impact of Technology on the Library Building*	Educational Facilities Laboratories	Chap. 7, Sec. B
4.	The Federal Government and Libraries	Duke University	Chap. 8, Sec. A, B; Chap. 9, Sec. B; App. F-1.A, F-1.B
5.	American State Libraries and State Library Agencies	Nelson Associates, Inc.	Chap. 9, Sec. A
6.	Social Change and the Library: 1945–1980	National Book Committee	Chap. 1; Chap. 2, Sec. A.1, C.1, C.2
7.	On the Economics of Library Operation	Mathematica	Chap. 5; App. F-2
8.	The Use of Libraries and the Conditions That Promote Their Use	The Academy for Educational Development, Inc.	Chap. 2, Sec. A.2, B.1, B.2, C.2
9.	Special Libraries: Problems and Cooperative Potentials	American Documentation Institute	— — —
10.	School Libraries in the United States	Nelson Associates, Inc.	Chap. 2, Sec. C.1
11.	Undergraduate and Junior College Libraries in the United States	Nelson Associates, Inc.	Chap. 2, Sec. C.2
12.	Public Libraries in the United States	Nelson Associates, Inc.	— — —
13.	Libraries and Industry	Programming Services, Inc.	— — —

* Not financed or only partially financed by the Commission but offered to ERIC. On Research Libraries will also be published by The M.I.T. Press.

APPENDIX C

THE REGIONAL HEARINGS

Appendix C to *Libraries at Large* consists of important material relating to the regional hearings held by the National Advisory Commission on Libraries during 1967, one of which is reported in detail in section C of chapter 9. This Appendix is divided into two sections: Appendix C–1 presents background material and summary data; Appendix C–2 lists the witnesses recorded as testifying at each hearing.

APPENDIX C–1

BACKGROUND FOR THE REGIONAL HEARINGS

Another project of the National Advisory Commission on Libraries was designed to acquire information on the people's needs for library and informational services. This was the series of regional hearings, held during the summer and early fall of 1967, at which subcommittees of Commission membership heard testimony from a variety of citizens, businessmen, professional people, farmers, white-collar and blue-collar workers, students, teachers, parents, and local, state, and national officials in communities of varying size throughout the nation. There was testimony representing the blind, the aged, and virtually all religious and ethnic groups in America.

The results contributed particularly to the Commission's consensus on the objective to "provide adequate library and informational services for the public at large" and on the recommendation for strengthening state library agencies. The need to solve library problems by effective manpower utilization was pervasive throughout all the hearings. (See chapter 9, especially section C.)

Table C–1.1 summarizes the who, when, and where of the regional hearings. The number of witnesses differs slightly from the listing in the July Commission Report itself due to a rechecking of the record and the receipt of additional transcript.

TABLE C–1.1

SUMMARY DATA ON
THE REGIONAL HEARINGS

LOCALE	DATE 1967	NUMBER OF WITNESSES
St. Louis, Missouri*	April 12	7
Tampa, Florida	September 8	31
Great Falls, Montana	September 11	34
Portland, Oregon	September 13	38
Anchorage, Alaska	September 15	24
Nome, Alaska	September 16	11
Bismarck, North Dakota	September 18	42
Wilkes-Barre, Pennsylvania	September 22	23
Baton Rouge, Louisiana	October 4	51
Lubbock, Texas	October 6	47
Pikeville, Kentucky	October 20	70
Tucson, Arizona	October 27	26

* This earlier meeting was actually held before the series of regional hearings was established.

APPENDIX C–2

LIST OF WITNESSES AT THE REGIONAL HEARINGS

TAMPA, FLORIDA (SEPTEMBER 8, 1967)

WITNESSES:

ELMO ELLIS, *past state chairman,* National Library Week, and *general manager,* WSB Radio, Atlanta, Georgia

JOHN CHAMPION, *president,* Florida State University, Tallahassee, Florida

JAMES A. PINSON, *newspaperman,* Waycross, Georgia

MRS. WAYNE BEVIS, *president-elect,* Congress of Parents and Teachers

MRS. CLYDE COVENTRY, *chairman of the board,* Waycross Public Library, Waycross, Georgia

LEROY COLLINS, *former governor*

CHESTER H. FERGUSON, *attorney, chairman,* Board of Regents, Florida State System of Higher Education

JOSEPH MILLS, *director,* Adult and Vocational Education, Pinellas County, St. Petersburg, Florida

LLOYD ANDERSON, Tampa Electric Company, representing *chairman of the board,* Tampa Electric Company

JAMES FAIR, *businessman,* Tampa

JOHN S. ALLEN, *president,* University of South Florida

GEORGE EMANUELLE, *director of Medical and Social Services,* Florida Council for the Blind

DOUGLAS MANNHEIMER, *eighth-grade student*

LOUIS DE LA PARTE, JR., *state senator,* Florida

JOSEPH CRENSHAW, *superintendent of education,* Florida

GILBERT L. PORTER, *special assistant to the deputy superintendent of schools,* Dade County, Florida

FRANCES HATFIELD, representing Dr. Myron Ashmore
FANT THORNLEY, *librarian,* City of Birmingham, Alabama
KATHY LUTRICK, *recreational therapist,* Hillsborough County, Florida
PAT WILLIAMS, *librarian,* Tampa
CARLOS TAYLOR, *assistant superintendent,* Pinellas County Public Schools, Clearwater, Florida
EDWARD HIRSHBERG, *professor,* University of South Florida, Tampa
DEBE NIGELS, *librarian intern*
MRS. JAMES D. BRUTON, JR., *chairman,* State Library Board, Plant City, Florida
JOHN BLANK, *principal,* Azalea Elementary School, St. Petersburg, Florida

Letters of Testimony from the following people were read at the hearing:
MRS. NATHAN S. RUBIN
SAM M. GIBBONS, *member of congress*
ROBERT L. F. SIKES, *member of congress*
A. SYDNEY HERLONG, *member of congress*
CHARLES E. BENNETT, *member of congress*
JAMES A. HALEY, *member of congress*

GREAT FALLS, MONTANA (SEPTEMBER 11, 1967)

WITNESSES:

J. J. MCLAUGHLIN, *mayor,* Great Falls
HERBERT JACOBSON, *architect,* Helena, Montana
MRS. LOUIS FLOERCHINGER, *trustee,* Conrad Public Library, Conrad, Montana
HAROLD WENAAS, *superintendent of schools,* Great Falls
WILLIAM BAILLIE, *attorney, chairman,* Montana Library Commission, Great Falls
MRS. F. J. ALLAIRE, *housewife,* Great Falls
MRS. DENNIS MOLLANDER, *housewife,* Great Falls
CONSTANCE LOHSE, *trustee,* Valier Public Library, Valier, Montana
B. D. MACE, *president and general manager,* Montana School Equipment Company, Billings, Montana
SARAH KERR, *retired home-demonstration agent,* Baker, Montana
MRS. GERALD ANDERSON, Dayton, Ohio (*librarian, wife of Air Force man stationed in Montana*)
MRS. RICHARD GRIFFING, *housewife,* Great Falls
LEROY STAHL, *writer,* Great Falls
WILLIAM STARLING, *director,* Southside Action Center, Great Falls
VERA PRAAST, *housewife, freelance writer,* Great Falls
HELEN BERTELSON, *public relations, administration,* Prudential Life Insurance Company of America, Billings, Montana
MRS. W. A. CORDINGLY, *housewife,* Great Falls
MRS. LEO C. GRAYBILL, *former member of State Library Board,* also, *former member of Great Falls Library Board,* Great Falls
MRS. N. H. BROWNING, *housewife,* Belt, Montana
MAYNARD OLSEN, *assistant superintendent of schools,* Department of Public Instruction, Helena, Montana
DON GIBSON, *county commissioner,* Dawson County, Glendive, Montana
Panel of: J. J. McLaughlin, William Conklin, R. D. Warden
INEZ HERRIG, *librarian,* Lincoln County Library, Libby, Montana
GEORGE JAMES, *board member,* Lincoln County Library, Libby, Montana
BRANSON STEVENSON, *library user,* Great Falls
MRS. W. L. HILL, *housewife,* Great Falls
MRS. REISSING, *librarian,* Cascade, Montana
MRS. RICHARD L. ELLIS, Great Falls
MRS. R. D. WARDEN, *chairman,* Public Library Board, Great Falls
MRS. JACOBS
MISS ANHAULT
MRS. LONGWORTH

PORTLAND, OREGON (SEPTEMBER 13, 1967)

WITNESSES:

JAMES M. GLEASON, *chairman,* Multnomah County Board of Commissioners, Portland

LEE C. JOHNSON, Eastern Oregon College, representing Tom McCall, *governor of Oregon*

DONALD STERLING, *editorial editor,* The Oregon Journal, Portland

RUTH DASILVE, *student,* Portland State College (letter of testimony read)

ROSS MORGAN, *senator from Oregon*

BRYON YOUTZ, *professor and acting president,* Reed College, Portland

FRANK M. WARREN, Board of the Library Association of Portland, Portland

CHARLES HODDE, *chairman,* Pacific Northwest River Basin Commission, Vancouver, Washington

HERBERT F. MUTSCHLER, *president,* Washington Library Association, representative of Daniel J. Evans, *governor of Washington*

MRS. CHARLES BOGUE, *member,* Gig Harbor Library Board, Gig Harbor, Washington

MRS. EARL D. BROWN, *housewife,* Lummi Island, Washington

CARL HINTZ, *director of libraries,* Oregon System of Higher Education, Portland

IRVING LIEBERMAN, *director,* Washington University School of Librarianship, Seattle, Washington. (also, *member,* Washington State Library Commission.)

WALTER MORRIS, *PTA president,* Portland Model School, Portland

STORY BIRDSEYE, *judge,* Superior Court of the State of Washington, Bellevue, Washington

MARCIA ERICKSON, *assistant superintendent,* Multnomah County Schools, Portland

MARYAN REYNOLDS, *state librarian,* Olympia, Washington

W. G. LOOMIS, *director,* State Department of Vocational Education, Salem, Oregon

MARY BUSTERUD, *member,* Oregon State Library Board of Trustees, Portland

MARY E. PHILLIPS, *librarian,* Portland Public Library, Portland (statement read)

GEORGE M. MARTIN, *attorney,* Yakima, Washington (statement read)

J. WALTER BARHAM, *city manager,* City of Coos Bay, Oregon

COLLEEN ROBERTSON, Buckman Community Action Committee, Portland

RUTH WATSON, *librarian,* Public Library, Coos Bay, Oregon

IRENE MCHALE, Portland Public Schools, Portland

WILLIAM J. LINDEMAN, *retired naval officer,* Puget Sound, Washington

FATHER JOSEPH BROWN, *librarian, chairman,* Department of Library Science, University of Portland and *president,* Oregon Library Association, Portland

MRS. L. T. HAAS, *housewife,* Yakima, Washington

JACQUELYN JURKINS, *librarian,* Multnomah County Law Library, Portland

MRS. BRUCE COOMBS, *president,* American Library Trustee Association, Yakima, Washington

PHYLLIS HOCHSTETTLER, Portland (statement read)

NATHAN BERKHAM, *library user,* Portland

JUNE SMELSER, *librarian,* David Douglas High School, Portland

MRS. FOREST RIEKE, School Board Number One, Portland

ROY E. LIEUALLEN, *chancellor,* Board of Higher Education, Salem, Oregon (statement read)

ELOISE EVERT, *state librarian,* Portland (statement read)

ANCHORAGE, ALASKA (SEPTEMBER 15, 1967)

WITNESSES:

ELMER RASMUSON, *mayor,* Anchorage

ERNEST GRUENING, *senator from Alaska*

JOHN ASPLUND, *chairman,* Greater Anchorage Area Borough, Alaska

GEORGE SUNDBORG, *administrative assistant to Senator Gruening*

EVANGELINE ATWOOD, *author, historian, past chairman,* Committee to Promote Statehood for Alaska

JOHN BUCHOLD, *director,* Anchorage Community Action Program

MRS. BERNARD STURGELEWSKI, *chairman,* Borough Library Study Committee

DON DAFOE, representing President Wood of the University of Alaska

PAUL MCCARTHY, *archivist,* University of Alaska, also representing President Wood

BLANCHE MCSMITH, *president,* Anchorage Chapter, NAACP and *former member,* Alaska
legislature
FRED MCGINNIS, *president,* Alaska Methodist University
ELVIRA VOTH, *assistant professor,* Anchorage Community College
TOM PILIPHANT, *superintendent,* Bureau of Indian Affairs, Anchorage
YULE KILCHER, Homer, *user,* Alaska
CARLISLE KRAMER, *superintendent of schools,* Greater Anchorage Area Borough
HERBERT HILSCHER, *president,* Cook Inlet Historical Society
BETTY SMITH, *president,* Soldatna Library Board, Soldatna, Alaska
FRANCES JONES, *librarian,* Fairview Elementary School, Anchorage
MARILYN SCOTT, representing the Alaska Education Association
CHRIS TOWER, *student and library user,* Anchorage
O. THOMAS BEIRNE, *editor, publisher,* Alaska Northern Lights, *instructor in English,
elementary*
ELLIE BITTNER
SALLY MONSERRUD, Anchorage Community College

NOME, ALASKA (SEPTEMBER 16, 1967)

WITNESSES:

SHARON SOBOCIENSKI, *president of the Library Association*
MRS. ROBERT (PHYLLIS) DAVIS, *secretary-treasurer,* Nome Public Library
M. ANNE PARKS, *librarian,* Nome High School
JOYCE RAE CLARK, *librarian,* Nome Grade School
SARAH JAMES, *librarian,* Beltz School
GEORGE WHITE, *superintendent,* Beltz School
ROBERT DAVIS, *district superintendent,* Bureau of Indian Affairs
LESTER BRONSON, *former member,* Alaska Legislature
PAT WEATHERBY, *member of library board*
GEORGE SUNDBORG, *administrative assistant to Senator Ernest Gruening*
ALLAN DOYLE, *mayor of Nome*

BISMARCK, NORTH DAKOTA (SEPTEMBER 18, 1967)

WITNESSES:

STEWART SCHLIFF, *chairman of the library board,* Fargo, North Dakota
VERA E. BOLLINGER, *former teacher,* Valley City, North Dakota
GRACE CARLSON, *city superintendent of schools,* Lakota, North Dakota *member,* Re-
gional Library Board, Lakota
MRS. HELMER DAHLEN, *member,* Regional Library Board, Michigan, North Dakota
MRS. ARTHUR HARP, *library board member,* Williston, North Dakota
MRS. HAROLD WEYRACH ⎤
ANNE LASSEY   ⎬ PANEL (*library board members,* northwestern North
CAROLINE JONES   ⎦   Dakota counties)
BERNICE ASHBRIDGE, *Burleigh County auditor,* Bismarck
BROTHER PAUL NYQUIST, *librarian,* Assumption Abbey, Richardton, North Dakota
GLENN RESELL, *superintendent,* Unity School District, Petersburg, North Dakota
GENE KOTASKA, *superintendent,* Michigan School District, Michigan, North Dakota
MRS. NORMAN MARTIN, *library user,* Bismarck
MRS. FREEMAN WEBBER, *library user,* Harvey, North Dakota
VIOLET BAILEY, *librarian,* Harvey, North Dakota
MRS. HENRY JOHNSON, *library user,* Sioux County, North Dakota
ESTHER HAMPLE, *superintendent,* Burleigh County Schools, Bismarck
DON PEARCE, *president,* North Dakota Library Association, and *librarian,* University of
North Dakota, Grank Forks, North Dakota
DAN RYLANCE, *archivist,* University of North Dakota, Grand Forks, North Dakota
RITA JOHNSON, English teacher, Bismarck High School, representing the North Dakota
Education Association
GENEVIEVE BURESH, *school library director,* State Department of Public Instruction,
Bismarck, North Dakota

MRS. BRUCE VAN SICKLE, citizen working for libraries, Minot, North Dakota
HELGA OLSON, *librarian,* Bismarck High School
ART LENO, *library user,* Bismarck
MRS. WILLIAM MILLS, Bismarck Library Board
GRACE BACON, *state president,* North Dakota Federation of Women's Clubs, Minot, North Dakota
LYDIA HEPPERLE, representing American Association of University Women, Bismarck
THELMA KLININGSMITH, *county superintendent of schools,* Mandan, North Dakota
LOIS ENGLER, *librarian,* Bismarck Junior College
RICHARD WOLFERT, *librarian,* Bismarck Public Library
FREDA HATTEN, *director,* State Library, Bismarck

Letters of testimony from the following people were read at the hearing:
W. E. NELSON, *library user,* Manfred, North Dakota
DEAN WINKJER, *attorney,* Williston, North Dakota
SUE PODENSKY, *freelance writer,* Edgeley, North Dakota
W. M. BEEDE, *library user,* Williston, North Dakota
MRS. HARVEY G. VAN EREM, *library user,* Jamestown, North Dakota
MRS. RAY GABBERT, *citizen and parent,* Harvey, North Dakota
HARRIET BURCHILL, *high school librarian,* Harvey, North Dakota
GEORGE H. HASLER, *library user,* Edgeley, North Dakota
EILEEN BOWLINGER, *library user,* Harvey, North Dakota
BARBARA COWLES, *medical library consultant,* Bismarck
ELEANOR P. GRAHL, *library user,* Bismarck

WILKES-BARRE, PENNSYLVANIA (SEPTEMBER 22, 1967)

WITNESSES:
WALTER C. WOOD, *superintendent,* Wilkes-Barre City School District
GEORGE H. STRIMEL, WVIA-TV, Channel 44, Wilkes-Barre
JEAN ROMMEL, Pennsylvania Division, American Association of University Women, Swarthmore, Pennsylvania
H. LEROY MARLOW, PENNTAP, Pennsylvania Technical Assistance Program
MRS. JOHN VIVIAN, *board member library trustee,* Dallas, Pennsylvania
MRS. LELAND HAZARD, *chairman,* Governor's Advisory Council on Library Development, Pittsburgh, Pennsylvania
MRS. WILLIAM THOM, *library user,* Wilkes-Barre
MRS. WARN MENHENNETT, *board member,* Chester County Library, Cockranville, Pennsylvania
ANDREW HOURIGAN, *attorney at law,* Greater Wilkes-Barre Chamber of Commerce
MRS. EDWARD SCHECHTER, *author,* Kingston, Pennsylvania
ELEANOR CAMPION, *director,* Union Library Catalogue of Pennsylvania, Philadelphia, Pennsylvania
JOSEPH W. BARR, JR., *Secretary,* Department of Community Affairs, Harrisburg, Pennsylvania
MRS. RICHARD D. GROSS, *secretary,* Huntington Valley Library Board, Huntington Valley, Pennsylvania
JULE AYERS, *minister,* First Presbyterian Church, Wilkes-Barre
JEANETTE F. REISMAN, *state senator,* Pennsylvania Eighteenth District, Easton, Pennsylvania
MARY ELIZABETH ALLEN, *reference librarian,* Warren, Pennsylvania
MRS. N. H. MEYER, Plymouth Library Board, Plymouth, Pennsylvania
GEORGE BIERLEY, *director,* Pennsylvania State Extension Center, Wilkes-Barre
MRS. HORACE KRAMER, *community worker,* Wilkes-Barre
ERNEST DOERSHUCK, *librarian,* State of Pennsylvania, Harrisburg Pennsylvania
MARGARET MARY FISCHER, King's College Library, Wilkes-Barre
NAN SCHIOWITZ, *student,* Elementary School, Wilkes-Barre
BETSEY SCHREDER, *librarian,* VA Hospital, Wilkes-Barre

BATON ROUGE, LOUISIANA (OCTOBER 4, 1967)

WITNESSES:

EDWARD STAGG, *director,* Council for a Better Louisiana, representing Governor John J. McKeithen

JOHN BLACKWELL, *library user,* Baton Rouge Industries for the Blind

GEORGE NECK, *library user,* New Roads, Louisiana

SAM H. JONES, *former governor of Louisiana*

J. W. BROUILLETTE, *former director,* General Extension Division of Louisiana State University, Baton Rouge

FRANK A. BAILEY, JR., *superintendent,* Ruston State School, Ruston, Louisiana

T. HARRY WILLIAMS, *professor of history,* Louisiana State University, Baton Rouge

MAX NATHAN, *attorney at law,* New Orleans, Louisiana

RENE CALAIS, *assistant superintendent,* St. Martin Parish School Board, St. Martinsville, Louisiana

WARREN E. DIETRICH, *president,* Webster Parish Library, *former president,* Louisiana Forestry Association, Minden, Louisiana

HUEL D. PERKINS, *chairman,* Music Department, Southern University, Baton Rouge

MALCOLM F. ROSENBERG, *assistant superintendent for instruction,* Orleans Parish School Board, New Orleans, Louisiana

E. J. OURSO, *insurance businessman,* Donaldsonville, Louisiana

CASS S. HOUGH, *president,* Daisy-Heddon Company, Rogers, Arkansas, representing Governor Winthrop Rockefeller

THE REVEREND H. WARREN BLAKEMAN, JR., *associate pastor,* First Methodist Church, Baton Rouge

KAY ROGERS, *housewife and library user,* Laplace, Louisiana

C. C. LEE, *high school English teacher, consultant to Pell City Public Library,* Pell City, Alabama

AL POLLARD, *president,* Brooks-Pollard Company, Little Rock, Arkansas

R. A. COX, *former superintendent of schools in Arkansas,* Harrison, Arkansas

THE REVEREND SHERMAN WILLIAMS, *member of the legislature of Arkansas,* Little Rock, Arkansas

MRS. I. C. OXNER, *trustee,* Southeast Arkansas Regional Library, *former member,* Arkansas State Library Commission, McGehee, Arkansas

MARGARET DIXON, *managing editor,* "Morning Advocate," Baton Rouge

EDWARD J. STEIMEL, *executive director,* Public Affairs Research Council of Louisiana, Inc., Baton Rouge

ALEX P. ALLAIN, *attorney at law, chairman,* Library Development Commission, *member,* St. Mary Parish Library Board, Jeaneratte, Louisiana

BERNARD SLIGER, *dean of academic affairs,* Louisiana State University, Baton Rouge, representing also, Edward G. Holley, *director of libraries,* University of Houston, Texas

THE REVEREND J. D. CANFILL, *episcopal minister,* Port Allen, Louisiana

OGBA OKORIE, *chairman,* Physics Department, Southern University, Baton Rouge

JOSIE MAJOR, *student,* Southern University, Baton Rouge

MRS. MARVIN MILLER, *housewife and library user,* New Orleans, Louisiana

W. D. ROSS, *dean,* College of Business Administration, Louisiana State University, Baton Rouge

SANDRA ROGERS, *student,* Capitol Senior High School, Baton Rouge

ROBERT J. AERTKER, *superintendent,* East Baton Rouge Parish Schools, Baton Rouge

S. H. MCDONALD, Office of Legislative Auditor, State Capitol, Baton Rouge

ALBERT TATE, *judge,* 3rd Circuit Court of Appeals, *visiting professor,* Louisiana State University Law School, Ville Platte, Louisiana

INA GREMILLION, *student,* Highland Elementary School, Baton Rouge

DARLENE CELESTINE, *student,* Westdale Junior High School, Baton Rouge

LOUISE PEARSON, *retired office worker, library user,* Baton Rouge

IONE HILL, *supervisor of elementary education,* State Department of Education, Baton Rouge

E. C. MCGEHEE, *library user,* Lake Charles, Louisiana

DANNIS SMITH, *student,* Louisiana State University, Baton Rouge

TERRY TYNES, *student,* School of Library Science, Louisiana State University, Baton Rouge

A. I. WARRINGTON, *library user,* Division of Employment Security, Baton Rouge

MRS. EDWARD LAMBREMONT, *student,* Louisiana State University, School of Library Science, Baton Rouge

GENORA C. WIRE, *student,* Louisiana State University, School of Library Science, Baton Rouge

LEWIS MOHR, *salesman,* Motorola Communication, Baton Rouge

INEZ ALLEN, *teacher,* Glen Oaks High School, Baton Rouge

V. W. WILLIAMS, JR., *principal,* Arlington Elementary School, Baton Rouge

MRS. C. E. BLANCHARD, *principal,* Sherwood Forest Elementary School, Baton Rouge

LUBBOCK, TEXAS (OCTOBER 6, 1967)

WITNESSES:

GROVER MURRAY, *president,* Texas Technological College, Lubbock

W. D. (DUB) ROGERS, JR., *mayor of Lubbock*

NAT WILLIAMS, *superintendent of public schools,* Lubbock, married to a former librarian

JAMES L. LOVE, Diboll, Texas, recipient of American Library Association's 1967 award for the Outstanding Librarian Trustee in America

JACK PAYNE, *president,* American State Bank, Lubbock

S. M. KENNEDY, *vice president for academic affairs,* Texas Technological College, Lubbock

MARIE SHULTZ, *director,* Field Services Division of the Texas State Library, Austin, Texas

MRS. A. W. YOUNG, *member of library board,* Lubbock

E. C. STRUGGS, *retired school principal,* Lubbock

ARCH G. LAMB, *county commissioner,* Lubbock

MRS. EDWARD D. OLIVER, *library user,* Brownwood, Texas

MARY BOYVEY, *library consultant,* Texas Education Agency, Austin, Texas

DAVID HENINGTON, *president,* Texas Library Association

MRS. JOHN C. MCLARTY, *president,* City-County Library Board, Lubbock

FATHER THOMAS MCGOVERN, Christ the King School, Lubbock

RYLANDER, *former employee of U.S. Congressman George Mahon,* Lubbock

HEENAN JOHNSON, *dentist,* Lubbock

JIM REYNOLDS, Lubbock Independent School District, Lubbock

AUBREY GREEN, Department of English, Lubbock Christian College, Lubbock

MRS. JOHN A. ANDERSON, *president,* League of Women Voters, Lubbock

SUZIE STERLING, *senior high school student,* Lubbock

JOANN JOHNSON, *senior high school student,* Lubbock

BROOKS TOWER, *junior high school student,* Lubbock

MRS. DUANE P. JORDAN, library user, Lubbock

SUZANNE CRAIN, *student,* Texas Technological College, Lubbock, *president,* Association of Women Students

RODERICK SHAW, *judge,* County of Lubbock

GWEN WHITAKER, *senior high school student,* Lubbock

JANIE HARRIS, *student,* Texas Technological College, Lubbock

DORA MONCIVIAS, *student,* Lubbock

JACQUELINE THOMAS, *student,* Lubbock Senior High School

BARBARA HEATH, *junior high school student,* Lubbock

JOEL ARMSTRONG, *student,* Lubbock Junior High School, Lubbock

MARIE WALKER, *former practicing librarian,* Lubbock

MRS. ALEXANDER S. KLINE, *housewife,* Lubbock

FLOYD HONEY, *director of Federal projects,* Lubbock City Schools, Lubbock

MRS. W. E. HOLDEN, *member,* Texas Fine Arts Commission

MRS. WILLIAM B. ARPER, *vice president,* Texas Libraries Trustees Association and *president,* Library Friends, Lubbock

JEAINE WAGNER, *bookseller,* Lubbock

LOLA BETH GREEN, *English professor,* Texas Technological College, Lubbock

FRANK MULLICAN, *principal,* Maedgen Elementary School, Lubbock

OLIVE BOONE WHEELER, *professor,* Teacher Education Program, Texas Technological College, Lubbock

MINA W. LAMB, *professor,* Technical Field of Home Economics

WILLARD F. WILLIAMS, *chairman,* Department of Agricultural Economics, Texas Technological College, Lubbock

NANCY S. BOZE, *professor* School Education, Texas Technological College, Lubbock

MRS. HARRY UNDERWOOD, *housewife,* Lubbock

STANLEY FUDELL, Special Education Department, Texas Technological College, Lubbock

TRAVIS TYER, *librarian,* city and county of Lubbock

PIKEVILLE, KENTUCKY (OCTOBER 20, 1967)

WITNESSES:

CARL D. PERKINS, *U.S. Congressman*

MRS. J. W. AMMONS, Fulton County Library, Fulton, Kentucky

W. C. HAMBLEY, *mayor of the city of Pikeville*

GEORGE STREET BOONE, *Kentucky lawyer,* county seat of Todd County, Elkton, Kentucky

MRS. GEORGE HART, *library user,* Murray, Kentucky

MAX HURT, *retired executive,* Kirksey, Kentucky

ROBERT KIMBALL, *president,* Auburn Hosiery, Russellville, Kentucky

ALICE CONNEALLY, *secretary and library user,* Louisville, Kentucky

MRS. WILLIAM O. BROOKS, *library user,* Winchester, Kentucky

MRS. J. D. DOBBS, *library user,* London, Kentucky

REBECCA CAUDILL, *author of* "My Appalachia," *library user,* Urbana, Illinois

TOM WILSON, *mayor of Paducah, Kentucky*

EARL KAUFFMAN, *director,* Council on Aging, University of Kentucky, Lexington, Kentucky

MRS. JAMES GADBERRY, Paducah Area Public Library, Paducah, Kentucky

MRS. LASCA B. MARTIN, *librarian,* Metcalf County Library, Edmonton, Kentucky

SALLY PATTON, *library user,* Livermore, Kentucky

CAROL HUNT, *registered nurse,* Fordsville, Kentucky, *library user* representing Mrs. Lillian Langford, Berry's Lick, Kentucky

MRS. JOHN SEATON HUFF, *bookmobile project worker,* Louisville, Kentucky

MRS. DONALD FOOSE, Library Science Department, University of Kentucky, Lexington, Kentucky, representing: John W. Oswald, *president;* George Provensky, *faculty;* Lora K. Martin, *faculty;* Charles Evans, *faculty*

CHARLES COX, *library user,* Industries for the Blind, Louisville, Kentucky

DARRELL HALL, *library user,* Industries for the Blind, Louisville, Kentucky

MRS. T. D. WINSTEAD, *housewife and library user,* Rineyville, Kentucky

BUENA HOWELL, *librarian,* Breathitt County, Kentucky

JANICE HOLT GILES, *library user,* Knifely, Kentucky

MRS. BARRY BINGHAM, *chairman of bookmobile program,* Louisville, Kentucky

JULIA BENNETT ARMISTEAD, *board of trustees,* Knoxville Public Library, Knoxville, Kentucky

JULIA ANN ARMISTEAD, *library user,* Knoxville, Kentucky

MRS. W. J. GUNDIFF, *library user,* Columbia, Kentucky

LARRY TUCKER, *lawyer and library user,* Cynthiana, Kentucky

MRS. NASH LANKFORD, *library user,* Lebanon, Kentucky

JANE BARBER, *library user,* Springfield, Kentucky

SISTER MARY SODELBIA, *Washington County teacher,* Kentucky

J. M. BOSWELL, Cumberland College, Williamsburgh, Kentucky

EDWARD J. KELLEY, *state senator,* Kentucky

GRACE JESSE, *library user,* Plummers Landing, Kentucky

CLARA SHAW, *library user,* Whitesburg, Kentucky

MRS. GEORGE GRAY, *library user,* Louisville, Kentucky

FRANCES F. ADAMS, *library user,* Louisa, Kentucky

MRS. M. D. BAILEY, *library user,* Paintsville, Kentucky

TOMMY REYNOLDS, *bookmobile librarian,* Johnson County, Paintsville, Kentucky

MRS. CARL BOYLEN, *library user,* Carrolton, Kentucky

HELEN LAWSON, *driver of bookmobile,* Shelby County, Waddy, Kentucky

MRS. ROY HARDESTY, *library user,* Eminence, Kentucky

J. I. MEYER, *minister,* Pikeville

JAMES B. STEPHENSON, *circuit judge,* Pikeville

MRS. A. J. HEABERLIN, *library user,* Corbin, Kentucky

ELEANOR SIMMONS, *director of library services,* Jefferson County Board of Education, Louisville, Kentucky

THOMAS H. JOHNS, *president,* Pikeville College, Kentucky

MRS. DON WARD, Hazard, Kentucky, representing Mr. Vernon Cooper, Hazard, Kentucky, *library users*

PAULINE HERN, *library user,* Lynch, Kentucky

MRS. ELLIS GORSUCH, *library user,* Cumberland, Kentucky

LILLIAN OLINGER, *library user,* Hazard, Kentucky

BILLIE SUE WHITE, *student,* Hazard, Kentucky

MRS. E. P. GRIGSBY, *library user,* McDowell, Kentucky

LOTTIE CODY, *library user,* Hindman, Kentucky

LAURA COMBS, *library user,* Sassafrass, Kentucky

MRS. RALPH MINIARD, *library user,* Hazard, Kentucky

RICHARD PARSONS, *former teacher and worker for Republic Steel,* Pikeville, Kentucky

NORMA JOHNSON, *library user,* Frankfort, Kentucky

LAWRENCE BROWN, *library user,* Stearns, Kentucky

JOSEPH JUSTICE, *library user,* Pikeville

MRS. LON B. ROGERS, *library user,* Pikeville

CAROL MAY, *student,* Buchanan County, Virginia

MARGARET WILLIS, *state librarian,* Pikeville

TUCSON, ARIZONA (OCTOBER 27, 1967)

WITNESSES:

GEORGE SPARKS, *professor of speech,* University of Arizona, Tucson

F. ROBERT PAULSON, *dean,* College of Education, University of Arizona, Tucson

ROBERT M. HAMMOND, *president,* Tucson Library Board, Tucson

SIDNEY W. LITTLE, *chairman,* Library Subcommittee on Municipal Bonds and *dean,* College of Architecture, University of Arizona, Tucson

MRS. W. D. KELLEY, *state president,* League of Women Voters, Tucson

ANNA MARIE KORN, *student,* Rincon High School, Tucson

JOHN ASHWOOD, *director,* House of Neighborly Service, Tucson

SID DAWSON, *junior high school teacher,* Tucson

ADELBERTO GUERRERO, *Spanish instructor,* University of Arizona, Tucson

JOHN P. FRANK, *attorney,* Tucson

ELBERT BROOKS, *assistant superintendent of schools,* Tucson

GRACE T. STEVENSON, *library consultant,* Tucson

MRS. SAM GODDARD, *wife of former governor of Arizona,* and *member* volunteer group called "Libraries Limited"

A. COVEY, *librarian,* Arizona State University, Phoenix, Arizona

JANE PETERS, *librarian,* Pinal County Free Library, Florence, Arizona

JOHN F. ANDERSON, *director,* Tucson Public Library, *president,* Arizona State Library Association, *president-elect,* Southwestern Library Association, *chairman,* Arizona Survey Advisory Committee

SISTER THOMAS CLARE, *teacher,* Tucson

DAVID BISHOP, *librarian,* College of Medicine, University of Arizona, Tucson

KATHARINE MATCHETT, *librarian,* Motorola, Inc., Phoenix; *president,* Special Library Division of the State Library Association

HASMON HARRISON, *member of school board,* District Number One, Tucson

JAY DUNN, *student,* Townsend Junior High School, Tucson
MURVISE ODOM, *member,* Arizona Survey Advisory Committee, Tucson
DON GRISWOLD, *assistant dean,* Graduate School of Information and Library Service, State University of New York at Buffalo, New York
CHARLES WASHBURN, *library user, banker, accountant,* Tucson
RALPH BERGSTON, *retired advertising, merchandising, and marketing executive, library user,* Tucson
MRS. COOLEY, Arkansas State Library Agency

ST. LOUIS, MISSOURI (APRIL 12, 1967;
PREDECESSOR OF THE REGIONAL HEARINGS)

WITNESSES:

FRANCIS B. O'LEARY, *librarian,* Medical Center, *associate professor,* St. Louis University, St. Louis
BETTY DUVALL, Florissant Valley Junior College, St. Louis
JOHN ABBOTT, *librarian,* Southern Illinois University, Edwardsville, Illinois
RALPH McCOY, *director of libraries,* Southern Illinois University, Edwardsville, Illinois
F. RANDLE, *librarian,* Southern Illinois University at Carbondale, Illinois
CHARLES TAYLOR, *librarian,* St. Louis Public Library, St. Louis
JEAN PENNINGTON, Washington University, St. Louis

APPENDIX D

THE COMMISSION MEETINGS

The Members of the National Advisory Commission on Libraries convened formally on eleven occasions to hear testimony, to converse with both witnesses and guests, and to deliberate among themselves on a broad range of topics relevant to the study of library and informational services for the nation's needs. A list of these meetings of the full Commission appears below. The titles of the witnesses who gave formal testimony and of the guests who visited are shown as they were at the time of each meeting.

I.   NOVEMBER 30, 1966 (WASHINGTON, D.C.)

GUESTS:

S. DOUGLASS CATER, JR., *special assistant to the President*
HAROLD HOWE II, *commissioner of education*
LOUIS HAUSMAN, *assistant to the commissioner of education*
JEROME N. BLUESTEIN, *administrative officer,* Office of the Commissioner of Education

II.   JANUARY 7 AND 8, 1967 (NEW ORLEANS, LOUISIANA)

WITNESSES:

An informal meeting was held on January 8 with representatives of the Association of Research Libraries Liaison Committee and the Committee on National Library–Information Systems. There is no transcript of this meeting.

III.   FEBRUARY 13, 1967 (WASHINGTON, D.C.)

WITNESSES:

BURTON W. ADKINSON, *head,* Office of Science Information Service, National Science Foundation
SCOTT ADAMS, *deputy director,* National Library of Medicine
ANDREW A. AINES, *technical assistant,* Office of Science and Technology, and *acting chairman,* Committee on Scientific and Technical Information (COSATI) of the Federal Council for Science and Technology (FCST)
FOSTER E. MOHRHARDT, *director,* National Agricultural Library

IV.   MARCH 5 AND 6, 1967 (NEW YORK, NEW YORK)

WITNESSES:

KATHLEEN MOLZ, *editor, Wilson Library Bulletin*
JEAN CONNOR, *director,* Division of Library Development, New York State Library
EDWARD G. FREEHAFER, *director,* New York Public Library

FRANK L. SCHICK, *director,* School of Library and Information Science, University of Wisconsin (Milwaukee)

BILL M. WOODS, *executive director,* Special Libraries Association

FRANK E. MCKENNA, *president,* Special Libraries Association

LESTER E. ASHEIM, *director,* Office for Library Education, American Library Association

JOHN M. CORY, *executive director,* New York Metropolitan Reference and Research Library Agency

JOHN A. HUMPHRY, *director,* Brooklyn Public Library

PAUL WASSERMAN, *dean,* School of Library and Information Services, University of Maryland

ERIC MOON, *editor, Library Journal,* R. R. Bowker Company

V.   APRIL 18 AND 19, 1967 (CHICAGO, ILLINOIS)

WITNESSES:

American Library Association Representatives:

MARY V. GAVER, *president*

DAVID H. CLIFT, *executive director*

American Library Association Panel Members:

RALPH U. BLASINGAME, *associate professor,* Graduate School of Library Science, Rutgers University

KEITH DOMS, *director,* Carnegie Library of Pittsburgh

FRANCES B. JENKINS, *professor,* Graduate School of Library Science, University of Illinois

MARION A. MILCZEWSKI, *director,* University of Washington Libraries

FREDERICK H. WAGMAN, *director,* University of Michigan Library

Other Witnesses

EILEEN THORNTON, *librarian,* Oberlin College

HAROLD G. JOHNSTON, *director,* Detroit Metropolitan Library Project

GENEVIEVE M. CASEY, *state librarian,* Michigan State Library

GERTRUDE E. GSCHEIDLE, *chief librarian,* Chicago Public Library

JESSE H. SHERA, *dean,* School of Library Science, Western Reserve University

DON R. SWANSON, *dean,* Graduate Library School, University of Chicago

RALPH H. PARKER, *dean,* Library School, University of Missouri

JAMES L. LUNDY, *president,* University Microfilms

JAMES G. MILLER, *principal scientist,* EDUCOM

VI.   MAY 22 AND 23, 1967 (WASHINGTON, D.C.)

WITNESSES:

Present from the Library of Congress:

L. QUINCY MUMFORD, *librarian of Congress*

JOHN G. LORENZ, *deputy librarian of Congress*

ELIZABETH E. HAMER, *assistant librarian*

MARLENE D. MORRISEY, *executive assistant to the librarian of Congress*

PAUL L. BERRY, *director,* Administrative Department

LEWIS C. COFFIN, *law librarian*

ROY P. BASLER, *director,* Reference Department

WILLIAM J. WELSH, *acting director,* Processing Department

MARVIN W. MCFARLAND, *chief,* Science and Technology Division

ABRAHAM L. KAMINSTEIN, *register of copyrights*

LESTER S. JAYSON, *director,* Legislative Reference Service

PAUL R. REIMERS, *coordinator of information systems*

Other Witnesses

ALICE BALL, *executive director,* United States Book Exchange

GERMAINE KRETTEK, *associate executive director,* American Library Association, and *director,* ALA Washington Office

EDWIN CASTAGNA, *chairman,* Legislation Committee, American Library Association

PAUL HOWARD, *executve secretary,* Federal Library Committee

HENRY J. GARTLAND, *director of libraries,* Veterans Administration

BURTON E. LAMKIN, *chief,* Library and Information Retrieval Branch, Federal Aviation Administration

HUBERT E. SAUTER, *deputy director,* Clearinghouse of Federal Scientific and Technical Information

MELVIN S. DAY, *deputy assistant administrator,* Office of Technical Utilization, National Aeronautics and Space Administration

EDWARD J. BRUENENKANT, *director,* Division of Technical Information, U.S. Atomic Energy Commission

WALTER C. CHRISTENSEN, *staff assistant for scientific information,* Department of Defense

Representatives from the Office of Education

HAROLD HOWE II, *commissioner of education*

GRANT VENN, *associate commissioner,* Bureau of Adult and Vocational Education

LEE BURCHINAL, *director,* Division of Research Training and Dissemination

RAY FRY, *director,* Division of Library Services and Educational Facilities

EUGENE KENNEDY, *chief,* Library and Information Science Research Branch

ALEXANDER MOOD, *assistant commissioner,* National Center for Educational Statistics

MORRIS ULLMAN, *chief,* Adult, Vocational, and Library Studies Branch

VII.   JUNE 25 AND 26, 1967 (SAN FRANCISCO, CALIFORNIA)

GUESTS:

MARYAN REYNOLDS, *librarian,* Washington State Library

LUCILE NIX, *library consultant,* Georgia State Department of Education—Public Library Unit (Library Extension Service)

CARMA LEIGH, *librarian,* California State Library

VIII.   SEPTEMBER 6 AND 7, 1967 (WASHINGTON, D.C.)

GUESTS:

CAROLYN I. WHITENACK, *associate professor,* Library and Audiovisual Education, Purdue University

MARY HELEN MAHAR, *chief,* School Library Section and *acting chief,* Instruction Research Branch, U.S. Office of Education

WILLIAM KNOX, *vice president,* McGraw-Hill, Inc.

J. LEE WESTRATE, *senior management analyst,* Bureau of the Budget

LOUIS B. WRIGHT, *director,* Folger Shakespeare Library

IX.   OCTOBER 9, 10, AND 11, 1967 (WASHINGTON, D.C.)

GUEST:

BARNABY C. KEENEY, *chairman,* National Endowment for the Humanities

X.   NOVEMBER 27 AND 28, 1967 (WASHINGTON, D.C.)

XI.   MAY 1, 1968 (NEW YORK, NEW YORK)

LIBRARY-RELATED LEGISLATION[1]

by *GERMAINE KRETTEK*
Director
and *EILEEN D. COOKE*
Associate Director
American Library Association Washington Office

Four major Federal grant-in-aid programs are authorized to help develop and improve various types of library service throughout the nation: the Library Services and Construction Act (LSCA); the Elementary and Secondary Education Act (ESEA), Title II; the Higher Education Act (HEA), Title II; and the Medical Library Assistance Act (MLAA). In fiscal year 1968 (July 1, 1967—June 30, 1968), the funds authorized to implement these programs totaled $357.77 million—$114 million under LSCA; $150 million under ESEA II; $72.77 million under HEA II; and $21 million under MLAA. Considering that it was only a little over a decade ago that Congress first came to recognize that it was in the national interest to help improve and expand library services and to make them more widely available to people in all walks of life, that $357 million authorization represents a dramatic and gratifying accomplishment.

Back in 1956 when the first library program was enacted (the Library Services Act, forerunner of LSCA) with an authorization of $7.5 million, to contemplate a soaring increase in Federal aid of nearly 500 percent twelve years later would have seemed an impossible dream indeed. However, it should be pointed out that recognition of the significant role of libraries and their seeming rush of success was not achieved without proportionate grass-roots efforts. It took some thirty years of dedicated work to establish the importance of libraries as essential elements in sound educational programs. In addition, a contributing factor was the changing role of education, with emphasis on the need for lifetime learning rather than a terminal period of fact finding.

Also, in considering the increasing amounts authorized, it must be firmly borne in mind that authorizations are not appropriations. Authorizations merely set the ceilings at which programs may be funded; appropriations, which provide the money to operate programs, may and often do fall considerably short of the authorized ceilings. For example, although $357.77 million was authorized in FY 1968 for the above library programs, in the final appropriations process, $210,993,000 was actually made available for expenditure, an amount $146,777,000 below the authorization.

---

[1] *FY 1968. This summary was prepared especially for this book in fall 1968.*

PRINCIPAL PROVISIONS
OF THE MAJOR LIBRARY PROGRAMS

LIBRARY SERVICES AND CONSTRUCTION ACT
(PL 89-511, AS AMENDED)

First established in 1956 as a rural public library program, and subsequently extended and expanded four times, this legislation is designed to help meet the urgent and essential library needs of the people of the United States in the fields of education, science, technology, business, culture, and everyday living. It covers all ages and all levels of educational attainment and economic status.

Title I: Public Library Services

Authorization: $35 million for FY 1967; $45 million, FY 1968; $55 million, FY 1969; $65 million, FY 1970; and $75 million, FY 1971.

Matching-grant funds may be used for books and other library materials, library equipment, salaries, and other operating expenses. The minimum state allotment which must be matched is $100,000 for each of the states, Puerto Rico, and the District of Columbia, and $25,000 each for American Samoa, the Trust Territory of the Pacific Islands, Guam, and the Virgin Islands. The floor year for matching purposes is the second fiscal year preceding application.

In the case of all titles, the state library administrative agency is responsible for drawing up and submitting the required plans for library development and specialized state library services suited to the needs of the state and local communities.

Title II: Public Library Construction

Authorization: $40 million for FY 1967; $50 million, FY 1968; $60 million, FY 1969; $70 million, FY 1970, and $80 million, FY 1971.

The basic allotment is $80,000 for each of the states, Puerto Rico, and the District of Columbia, and $20,000 each for American Samoa, the Trust Territory of the Pacific Islands, Guam, and the Virgin Islands. The Federal share of the expenses of administering Title II programs is paid out of Title II allotments rather than deducted from Title I funds as the LSCA of 1964 authorized.

Title III: Interlibrary Cooperation

Authorization: $5 million for FY 1967; $7.5 million, FY 1968; $10 million, FY 1969; $12.5 million, FY 1970; and $15 million, FY 1971.

This section provides for the establishment and maintenance of local, regional, state, or interstate cooperative networks of libraries. The basic allotment is $10,000 each to Guam, American Samoa, the Trust Territory of the Pacific Islands, and the Virgin Islands, and $40,000 to each of the other states. The Federal share for fiscal 1967 was 100 percent, with no matching funds required. Thereafter, matching was to be 50 percent. However, LSCA Amendments of 1967 (PL 90–154) postponed the matching requirement until fiscal 1969. Administration costs are also included.

Interlibrary cooperation is defined as the establishment and operation of systems or networks of libraries—including state, school, college and university, public, and special libraries—working together to provide maximum effective use of funds in providing services to all library users. Such systems may be designed to serve a community, metropolitan area, region within a state, or may serve a statewide or multistate area. Requirements for participation include:

Provisions for coordination of supplementary services

Appropriate allocation of costs

Assurance that every appropriate local or other public agency in the state is given an opportunity to participate

Criteria for evaluation and assignment of priorities by the state agency

Establishment of a statewide council, broadly representative of professional library interests and of library users, to act in an advisory capacity to the state agency.

Title IV: Specialized State Library Services

Designed to assist the states in providing greatly needed specialized state library services. It is in two parts:

A: State Institutional Library Services

B: Library Services to the Physically Handicapped

Part A: State Institutional Library Services

Authorization: $5 million for FY 1967; $7.5 million, FY 1968; $10 million, FY 1969; $12.5 million, FY 1970; and $15 million, FY 1971.

This provision authorizes grants to the state library agencies for five years to strengthen library services to: (a) inmates, patients, or residents of penal institutions, reformatories, residential training schools, orphanages, or general or special institutions or hospitals operated or substantially supported by the state, and (b) students in residential schools for the handicapped (including mentally retarded, hard of hearing, deaf, speech impaired, visually handicapped, seriously emotionally disturbed, crippled, or other health-impaired persons who by reason thereof require special education) operated or substantially supported by the state.

Under this section the basic allotment is $10,000 each to Guam, American Samoa, the Trust Territory of the Pacific Islands, and the Virgin Islands, and $40,000 to each of the other states. No matching funds were required in fiscal 1967; thereafter, the Federal share was to be determined on a per capita income basis, as under Section 104, but LSCA Amendments of 1967 (PL 90–154) postponed the matching requirement until fiscal 1969.

The basic purpose of this part is to extend the benefits of public library service to those persons who are unable, because of their institutional confinement, to use regular community library facilities. The responsibility for such service has long been clearly recognized as resting with state library agencies, but lack of funds has prevented the satisfactory meeting of this need.

Part B: Library Services to the Physically Handicapped

Authorization: $3 million for FY 1967; $4 million, FY 1968; $5 million, FY 1969; $6 million, FY 1970; and $7 million for FY 1971.

This part authorizes payments to states for five years to encourage the establishment or improvement of library services to the physically handicapped, including the blind and the visually handicapped. Such service is interpreted as the provision of library service through public or other nonprofit libraries, agencies, or organizations, to physically handicapped readers certified by competent authority as unable to read or to use conventional printed materials. Plans are approved by the Commissioner of Education in consultation with the Librarian of Congress where appropriate. (See also, Library of Congress Books for the Blind and Handicapped [PL 89–522].)

With the exception of fiscal 1967, when the Federal share would be 100 percent, matching-grant funds were to be available to the states as under Title I, Section 104, including costs of administering such program plans. However, LSCA Amendments of 1967 (PL 90–154) postponed the matching requirement until fiscal 1969. No part of these grants can be applied, directly or indirectly, for construction or land acquisition. The basic allotment is $5,000 each to Guam, American Samoa, the Trust Territory of the Pacific Islands, and the Virgin Islands, and $25,000 to each of the other states.

ELEMENTARY AND SECONDARY EDUCATION ACT (TITLE II) (PL 89-10, AS AMENDED)

School Library Resources, Textbooks, and Other Instructional Materials

A five-year program initiated in fiscal 1966 to make grants available to states to acquire school library resources, textbooks, and other printed and published instructional materials for the use of children and teachers in public and private elementary and secondary schools. The legislation is aimed at remedying some of the deficiencies existing in these materials in the nation's schools.

Authorization: $100 million for FY 1966; $125 million, FY 1967; $150 million, FY 1968; $162.5 million, FY 1969; and $200 million, FY 1970, plus not more than 3 percent of the amounts for payments to outlying areas.

Main Provisions

Any state desiring grants under this program must submit to the Commissioner of Education a state plan which sets forth a program for the acquisition of resources and the administration of same based on the criteria specified in the law.

To insure that this legislation will furnish increased opportunities for learning, books and materials supplied by Title II must not supplant but must supplement those already being provided.

Library resources are defined as books, periodicals, documents, audiovisual materials, and other related library materials.

The amount used for administration of the state plan for any fiscal year may not exceed 5 percent of the Title II payment to the state or $50,000 whichever is greater.

Allocations to the 50 states and the District of Columbia are based on the number of children enrolled in public and private schools within the state in relation to the number enrolled in all states and the District. Funds also are allotted to the outlying areas of the nation and to Department of Defense and Bureau of Indian Affairs schools.

Materials are made available within the state on the basis of the relative need of children and teachers for school library resources, textbooks, and other instructional materials.

Other ESEA titles offer opportunities for library participation even though they do not include a specific library provision.

HIGHER EDUCATION ACT (TITLE II) (PL 89-329, AS AMENDED)

College Library Assistance and Library Training and Research

Title II of HEA is designed to improve college libraries and the quality of library service throughout the nation by providing grants for: (1) acquisition of books, periodicals, and other library materials by colleges and universities; (2) training of all types of librarians; (3) research and demonstration projects, including the development of new ways of processing, storing, and distributing information; and (4) aiding the Library of Congress to acquire and catalog additional scholarly materials published throughout the world.

Part A: College Library Resources

Authorization: $50 million each for FY 1966, 1967, and 1968; $25 million, FY 1969; $75 million, FY 1970; and $90 million, FY 1971.

Provides grants to institutions of higher education for books, periodicals, documents, magnetic tapes, phonograph records, audiovisual materials, and other related library materials (including necessary binding). Eighty-five percent of the sum appropriated for any fiscal year is for *Basic and Supplementary Grants;* the remaining 15 percent is for *Special Purpose Grants.*

Basic Grants of up to $5,000 may be approved by the Commissioner of Education for eligible institutions of higher education and for each branch, located in a community different from its parent institution. To qualify for a basic grant, the previous level of expenditure for library programs must be maintained, in addition to matching the grant money on a dollar-for-dollar basis. An exception is made for new institutions which are eligible for these grants in the fiscal year preceding the first year in which students are to be enrolled.

Supplementary Grants: From the remainder of the 85 percent not used for basic grants, up to $10 per full-time student (or the equivalent) may be given in supplementary grants to institutions which have a minimum basic grant in excess of $1,500.

Special Purpose Grants are to be made by the Commissioner to help meet institutional, regional, or national library needs, either in a single college or in combinations of colleges. Maintenance of the previous level of library expenditures is required as well as matching every $3 of Federal grant money with $1 from the institution.

An eight-member Advisory Council on College Library Resources is authorized to assist the Commissioner in establishing criteria for making supplemental and special purpose grants.

Part B: Library Training and Research

Authorization: $15 million each for FY 1966, 1967, and 1968; $11.8 million, FY 1969; $28 million, FY 1970; and $38 million, FY 1971.

Sec. 223 provides grants to institutions for the *training* of persons engaged in or about to engage in the practice of librarianship in public, school, academic, or special libraries, supervisors of such personnel, and professional personnel to train librarians. Regular sessions, short-term programs and institutes, with stipends and allowances for travel, subsistence, and other expenses, are authorized. Beginning in FY 1968, institutes for school librarians previously financed under the National Defense Education Act (NDEA) were transferred to this program.

The Commissioner may make grants only upon application by these institutions and only upon finding that their library training programs will substantially increase nationwide library training opportunities.

Sec. 224 provides *research and demonstration* grants to institutions of higher education and other public or private nonprofit agencies, institutions, and organizations to improve libraries and library training, including development of new methods and equipment for processing, storing, and distributing information.

The Commissioner is authorized to appoint a Special Advisory Committee of not more than nine members to advise him on matters of general policy concerning research and demonstration projects.

Part C: Strengthening College and Research Library Resources

Authorization: $5 million for FY 1966; $6,315,000 for FY 1967; $7,770,000 for FY 1968; $6 million for FY 1969; $11.1 million for FY 1970; and $11.1 million for FY 1971.

This section authorizes the Commissioner to transfer funds to the Librarian of Congress for the purpose of acquiring all library materials which are of value to scholarship and of providing and distributing catalog and bibliographic information promptly.

As with ESEA, other HEA titles offer a number of possibilities for library participation.

MEDICAL LIBRARY ASSISTANCE ACT (PL 89-291)

This program was established to help remedy the deficiencies of medical libraries and authorizes $105 million over the five fiscal years 1966–1970. The law authorizes the Surgeon General of the Public Health Service with the advice of the National Medical Libraries Assistance Advisory Board to award grants-in-aid for the following programs:

1. A four-year program for the construction and renovation of medical library facilities, which will provide grants to pay nonprofit institutions up to 75 percent of the costs of constructing health science library facilities.

Authorization: $10 million for each of the four fiscal years 1967–1970.

2. A five-year program to finance: (a) Training of medical librarians; *authorization:* $1 million each year, FY 1966–1970. (b) Special scientific projects; *authorization:* $500,000 each year. (c) Research and development in medical library science and related fields; *authorization:* $3 million each year. (d) Improvement and expansion of the basic resources of medical libraries; *authorization:* $3 million each year. (e) Development of a national system of regional medical libraries; priority will be given to those medical libraries having the greatest potential of fulfilling the needs for regional medical libraries, based on area needs, adequacy of the library being considered, and the size and nature of the population to be served; *authorization:* $2.5 million each year. (f) Support of biomedical scientific publications of a nonprofit nature up to three years; *authorization:* $1 million each year.

3. A five-year program to establish branches of the National Library of Medicine where the Surgeon General determines that: (a) There is no regional medical library adequate the serve such areas; (b) there is need for a regional medical library, based on criteria prescribed in Section 398 of the law; (c) there is no medical library which can feasibly be developed into a regional medical library according to the provisions of Section 398.

Authorization: $2 million each year, to remain available until expended.

OTHER FEDERAL LAWS
WITH LIBRARY IMPLICATIONS

In addition to the four basic library programs, there are several acts of great importance in providing specialized library assistance, and there are more than a dozen other Federal laws that have library implications:

Appalachian Regional Development Act (Title II)
(PL 89-4, as amended)

Section 214 authorizes supplementary grants-in-aid to assist economically depressed areas in Appalachia in meeting matching-fund requirements under other Federally aided construction programs, such as LSCA Title II; NDEA Title III; and the Higher Education Facilities Act. Altogether, eligible projects might be granted up to a total of 80 percent in Federal funds.

Beirut Agreement (PL 89-634)

This is a joint resolution to give effect to the agreement for facilitating the international circulation of visual and auditory materials of an educational, scientific, and cultural character, approved at Beirut in 1948. It removes import duties from audiovisual materials to be used for educational purposes.

Demonstration Cities and Metropolitan Development Act (PL 89-754)

Title I: Comprehensive City Demonstration Programs provides supplementary grants-in-aid to enable cities to plan and develop comprehensive model city programs. In combination with other Federal grants-in-aid (e.g., LSCA, Title II) up to 80 percent of costs could be Federally financed.

Title II: Planned Metropolitan Development provides additional Federal grants to both state and local bodies for metropolitan development projects, including libraries, as incentives for comprehensive metropolitan-wide planning. The grants would be conditioned upon meeting the requirements specified in Sec. 205.

Title VII: Urban Renewal amends the Housing Act of 1949, to encourage urban renewal. It authorizes the Secretary of Housing and Urban Development (HUD) to credit certain local expenditures as a local grant-in-aid if the project was begun within three years of enactment of the Demonstration Cities and Metropolitan Development Act (November 3, 1966). The allowance would be 25 percent of the cost of the facility, or $3.5 million, whichever is less.

Depository Library Act (PL 87-579)

This act provides for a class of libraries in the United States in which certain Government publications are deposited for the use of the public. Currently, there are 979 depository libraries, 38 of which are regional. There may not be more than two regional depositories in each state, and to be so designated, the libraries must already be designated depositories. In addition to fulfilling the requirements for regular depositories, they must receive and retain at least one copy of all Government publications made available to depositories, either in printed or microfacsimile form (except those authorized to be discarded by the Superintendent of Documents).

Economic Opportunity Act (PL 88-452, as amended)

Title I: Youth Programs, Title II: Urban and Rural Community Action Programs, and Title VIII: Volunteers in Service to America (VISTA) seem to offer the best opportunities for library involvement. Although there is no specific provision for library participation, libraries have cooperated in projects under Head Start, Neighborhood Youth Corps, Job Corps, New Careers Program, Community Action Programs, and VISTA.

Federal Property and Administrative Services Act (Sec. 203,J,3) (PL 87-786)

Public libraries became eligible for the Federal surplus real and personal property program when the Federal Property and Administrative Services Act of 1949 was amended in October of 1962.

Florence Agreement (Educational, Scientific, and Cultural Materials Importation Act of 1966) (PL 89-651)

This removes tariff duties from books, scientific instruments, and other educational and cultural materials.

Higher Education Facilities Act (PL 88-204, as amended)

Under this act, Federal grants and loans are available to institutions of higher education for the construction of various academic facilities, including libraries. Construction of college and university libraries accounts for over one fifth of the building project grants annually.

Housing and Urban Development Act (Title VII) (PL 89-117)

Section 703 grants can be made to local public bodies to finance neighborhood facilities, so, although not spelled out in the law, a multipurpose community center might include an area for a public library branch.

International Education Act (PL 89-698, as amended)

This two-year-old law was designed to strengthen United States graduate and undergraduate programs in international studies. However, as of October 1968, no funds have yet been appropriated to implement these programs.

Library of Congress Books for the Blind and Handicapped (PL 89-522)

This provides special reading materials and equipment for the visually and physically handicapped through regional libraries.

Mutual Education and Cultural Exchange Act (PL 87-256)

The program is conducted as an important part of official United States cultural relations: to increase mutual understanding between the people of the United States and the people of other countries by means of educational and cultural exchange, to promote international cooperation for educational and cultural advancement, and to assist peaceful relations between the United States and other countries. Librarians are among the foreign specialists who visit the United States under the auspices of this program.

National Defense Education Act (Title III) (PL 85-864, as amended)

This provides matching grants and loans to strengthen instruction in critical subjects in elementary and secondary schools. Funds may be used to acquire laboratory and other special equipment, audiovisual materials and equipment, and printed and published materials (other than textbooks), and for minor remodeling.

National Foundation on the Arts and the Humanities Act (Secs. 12 and 13) (PL 89-209, as amended)

Section 12 of this act provides for the acquisition of books and audiovisual equipment and materials to strengthen instruction in the arts and humanities fields and serves as a counterpart to the NDEA Title III program. Section 13 authorizes teacher training institutes in these same fields. In addition, through grants, contracts, or training proposals administered by either the National Endowment for the Arts or the Naional Endowment for the Humanities, it appears likely that special libraries, departmental libraries, and fine arts collections in selected branch libraries of large public and university systems might qualify for financial assistance.

Older Americans Act (PL 89-73)

This authorizes Federal grants to states to stimulate communities to develop a variety of services for the elderly, and authorizes funds for the study, development, and evaluation of techniques that can assist the aged to enjoy wholesome and meaningful lives. Library service to nursing homes, to senior citizen centers, and various other activities involving participation by older people are likely prospects for project grants.

Public Broadcasting Act (PL 90-129)

This act extends the Educational Television Facilities Act for three years, establishes a public broadcasting corporation to improve the quality of educational and cultural programs, and authorizes a study of instructional TV. The findings of this study will have indirect, if not direct, implications for library services of all types. The study will be concerned with the relationship of facilities such as broadcast, closed circuit, community antenna television, instructional television fixed services, and two-way communication of data links and computers to each other and to other educational materials and devices. It also is to address itself to the role of these facilities in disseminating educational programs, data, and information to all the people in the United States.

Public Works and Economic Development Act (Title I) (PL 89-136)

Similar to the Appalachian program, Title I of this act provides supplementary grants-in-aid to other depressed areas to assist them in matching Federally aided construction programs such as LSCA Title II, NDEA Title III, and Higher Education Facilities Act.

State Technical Services Act (PL 89-182, as amended)

This matching-grant program aims to promote and disseminate the findings of science and technology for the wider use of commerce and industry; libraries equipped to serve the special information needs of such patrons may be interested in participating in the Special Merit Program authorized by this act and administered directly by the Department of Commerce. The other grants are administered in the various states by agencies designated by their governors.

RECENT AND FUTURE TRENDS

Congress has demonstrated its concern over the nation's varied and growing needs in an increasingly complex society by developing a startling array of grant-in-aid programs. Federal spending for these programs has stepped up from less than a billion dollars in 1946 to nearly $15 billion in 1966, and it is expected that the figure will quadruple by 1975.

However, the Legislative and the Executive Branches of Government, as well as powerful national groups, are now taking a new and hard look at the proliferation of Federal programs with an eye toward possible consolidation. In the future, many categorical aid programs may be fused with block grants and possibly with revenue-sharing, paving the way to general aid to education.

On an upward trend in both the Executive and Legislative Branches is the theme of creative federalism. Its aim is to improve the quality of life for all Americans through creative and efficient administration and utilization of available resources. In a 1966 memo to his Cabinet, President Lyndon B. Johnson said: "The basis of creative federalism is cooperation." If Federal aid programs are to achieve their goals, more than money alone is needed, he said. "These programs . . . should be worked out and planned in a cooperative spirit with those chief officials of State, county, and local governments who are answerable to their citizens. . . . Our objective is to make certain that vital new Federal assistance programs are made workable at the point of impact."

The Bureau of the Budget, at the direction of the President, started an intensive effort to launch the planning, programming, and budgeting system (PPBS) in the management of executive departments and agencies. The purpose was to demonstrate the potential of PPBS for improving intergovernmental planning and for strengthening and modernizing the management procedures of state and local government.

According to a survey cited in the latest report (October 1967) of the prestigious Advisory Commission on Intergovernmental Relations (ACIR):

> With the increase in the number and magnitude of grants, the belief has grown among State and local officials that Federal aid has led to greater Federal interference, especially in purely administrative matters, and is tending to exert a less stimulative and more coercive impact.
>
> Concurrently, there has come a growing acceptance of the grant-in-aid principle, but accompanied by a desire for a number of specific reforms in the system— including greater flexibility in organizational, personnel and fiscal reporting requirements; greater uniformity in matching and apportionment formulas; broader categories; improved intra-agency, inter-agency and interlevel coordination; and greater certainty and better timing in Federal grant funding practices.

Among the recommendations in the two-volume report of ACIR is a revised system of Federal aid to states and cities—now covered by 379 separate grant programs—

including for the first time completely "untied" grants to be used at the states' discretion. They say some problems should continue to be covered by categorical grants. However, in areas such as education, the proliferation of programs should be consolidated into block grants with the states free to spend the money as they see fit in the general area of concern. Another of the ACIR recommendations is to strengthen the State Executive and Legislative Branches as effective partners in the Federal system. However, the ACIR recommends that the states themselves provide adequate funds and staff to improve the fiscal and program coordination of Federal categorical grants; they oppose the use of Federal grant funds to provide staff or facilities for the immediate office of the governor.

What weight the ACIR findings and recommendations will carry remains to be seen. Also, when it comes to speculating about the future of Federal aid for education and for the further development of essential library programs, the recent national presidential election and the subsequent shift in Administration philosophy must be considered as an essential factor.

In any event, it would seem that the greatest emphasis in future education legislation will be on programs that help to solve the crucial problems of our time, especially in relation to the crisis in the cities, the unmet needs of the culturally and economically deprived citizens, and the need for full-scale implementation of the comprehensive early-childhood education programs. This prognosis is based on the assumption that Federal legislation is not developed in a vacuum but rests on the clearly defined state and community needs that affect the nation as a whole. Therefore, it is only logical to assume that any new Federal library legislation will be evolved, supported, and enacted only if the proposed library activities will be in the national interest and will help to serve those needs which Congress and the Administration consider most essential and most urgent.

Recognizing the impact of library programs on the cultural, educational, and economic development of this nation, and the growing need for improved library services and more informational material for all people—from the darkest ghetto to the highest level of research—the American Library Association will continue its efforts to help libraries gear their services to the ever-changing national needs and to maintain the necessary support at all levels to meet this country's library needs.

APPENDIX F

SUPPLEMENTARY PAPERS

With any book designed as basic resource for a varied audience on a subject as broad as *Libraries at Large,* the supplementary material—sometimes highly specialized and technical and often quite elementary—can be for some readers the most valuable content of all. A collection of such materials appears here in appendix F, with the hope that it will provide not only factual data for the inquiring specialist, but also both basic introductory information and continuing study material for the novice and the generalist.

Appendix F–1 is a monograph in itself on "The International Dimension," a subject the National Advisory Commission on Libraries considered of vital importance in the years ahead, although a detailed consideration of this area could not be accomplished in the limited time available. Appendix F–1 is divided into two sections: F–1.A is a narrative discussion; F–1.B is a compilation of supporting documents.

Appendix F–2 supplements chapter 5 with statistical data and other technical information on the economic analysis presented in that chapter. Appendix F–2 is divided into sections A, B, and C.

Appendix F–3 supplements chapter 7 on the subject of technology. Perhaps no other single topic of concern to the library world has received so much attention—or has been the cause of so much misunderstanding. For this reason appendix F–3 presents descriptive material at considerable length. It is divided into sections A, B, C, and D.

APPENDIX F–1

THE INTERNATIONAL DIMENSION[1]

by CRAUFURD D. GOODWIN
Vice Provost for International Studies
Duke University

A. THE INTERNATIONAL INVOLVEMENT OF AMERICAN LIBRARIES

THE PROBLEM

Background

The growth of interest in international affairs in the United States since World War II has been spectacular. At least four factors explain this development. First, the war itself brought the American people forcibly into contact with the rest of the world to an extent which was quite new and in sharp contrast to the isolation of the 1930's. The war effort created an urgent need for expert knowledge of foreign languages and cultures and stimulated establishment of some of the earliest area studies programs at American universities on such crisis areas as the U.S.S.R. and Japan.

Second, the decline in power and influence of other world powers, such as Great Britain and France, created a leadership vacuum into which the United States quickly moved. The American Government became the acknowledged primary force in the Western world with need for a sophisticated foreign policy to cover all countries of the world. This need created pressures on trained manpower not only within the Department of State but throughout the community where demands arose for consultant experts on foreign affairs, interpreters to the public, and critics.

The third factor which generated interest in foreign affairs was acceptance by the United States in the years after World War II of responsibility to assist the less fortunate countries of the world with social and economic development. Initial success with reconstruction in Western Europe and Japan gave an atmosphere of heady optimism to the early years of this effort, but repeated setbacks in attempts at modernization of non-Western areas generated skepticism and recognition of need for extensive research in foreign areas, particularly in the social sciences, as a guide to action.

Fourth, a factor closely linked to the first three factors was a growing recognition of and dissatisfaction with the parochialism of the American educational system. Educators and students alike became increasingly aware after World War II that curricula in all fields of knowledge were incomplete which did not incorporate the experience of the whole of mankind. American research workers began to find in the rest of the world a laboratory for study with data not only of particular but of general interest. In countries of the world where the frontiers of knowledge were well within sight, the challenges for research were particularly great. At the same time, Americans who studied abroad

[1] *From* The Federal Government and Libraries, *one of the special studies commissioned by the National Advisory Commission on Libraries in 1967. This paper was prepared in summer 1967 and is based on material current at that time.*

found their appreciation of and insight into their own environment substantially extended.

Implications for American Libraries

American libraries at every level have been affected by the surge of interest in world affairs. The literature and contributions to knowledge of scholars in other countries have become of increasing interest to readers in the United States. For public libraries, it has been necessary to develop general collections which will satisfy the changing tastes of the broad reading public. Liberal arts colleges have been called upon to develop minimum teaching collections on portions of the world on which hitherto they had little or no material. The great reference and university libraries have faced enormous tasks in attempting to develop comprehensive collections for use of research scholars, an objective requiring not only selective acquisition and processing of a flood of current materials but development of retrospective collections.[2] Some rough indication of the magnitude of the problem of merely maintaining through current acquisitions library collections on world affairs can be gained from statistics on world book publication gathered by the United Nations Educational, Scientific and Cultural Organization (UNESCO). These show that more than 90 percent of the new books and more than 70 percent of the daily newspapers published in the world each year are produced outside North America. The United States is far below the U.S.S.R. in the publication of book and pamphlet titles and only slightly ahead of the United Kingdom, the Federal Republic of Germany, and Japan.[3]

Some of the problems facing American libraries as a result of United States involvement abroad may be viewed merely as parts of the broader phenomenon of library growth and are not examined in detail here. These include needs for more space, more trained staff, more reference service, and more administrators. In the following section of this paper, the nature of some of the *special* problems raised by the international dimension are set forth, together with attempts which have been made to overcome these problems. This is followed by a discussion of the philosophy of participation by the Federal Government in the international activities of American libraries; some possible directions for the future are proposed.

Descriptions of programs and categories of programs in this paper are intended to be representative rather than exhaustive. Because the National Advisory Commission on Libraries was concerned specifically with library development in the United States, greatest attention is paid here to international activities that relate directly to the central domestic responsibilities of American libraries rather than to those activities which may have the greatest impact on development in new nations, world literacy, or other external problems.

EXPERIENCE TO DATE

Programs to develop the international role of American libraries, despite considerable overlap, can be grouped under four general headings: acquisitions, technical processing, bibliography and access, and book and library programs abroad.[4]

---

2 *The report of a recent conference to discuss the special impact of regional studies on libraries is Tsuen-Hsuin Tsien and Howard W. Winger,* Area Studies and the Library *(Chicago, 1966).*
3 UNESCO Statistical Yearbook, 1965 *(France: United Nations, 1966), pp. 431, 445, 525. UNESCO statistics contain an unknown mixture of book and pamphlet titles for most countries, whereas the United States figures represent only book titles published by regular publishing houses. The standardization of UNESCO publishing statistics on the basis of a recommendation in November 1964 will probably require several years to put into effect in all the reporting countries.*
4 *Useful general works on this subject include: James E. Skipper, "National Planning for Resource Development,"* Library Trends *(October 1966), pp. 321–34; and an unpublished "Memo on Library Aspects of President Johnson's Proposed Program on Free Flow of Books," by an Informal Group of Librarians (Chairman, Luther H. Evans) (November 7, 1965), mimeo.*

Acquisitions

Farmington Plan

The first major attempt of American libraries to cooperate in solving problems of foreign acquisitions was the Farmington Plan which began operations in 1947.[5] The purpose of the Plan at its inception was to "make sure that one copy at least of each new foreign publication that might reasonably be expected to interest a research worker in the United States would be acquired by an American library, promptly listed in the *National Union Catalog,* and made available by interlibrary loan or photographic reproduction."[6] The Association of Research Libraries has administered the Plan through approximately sixty of its participating members which accept responsibility to acquire and catalog for the *National Union Catalog* material from specific geographic and subject areas identified in the Library of Congress classification system.

Officials of the Association have emphasized repeatedly that the Plan should be characterized by its objective and "is not to be identified with any specific methods of allocation, acquisition, or distribution." Nevertheless, a pattern of operation has been firmly established. Book dealers in selected foreign countries are charged to identify, acquire, and distribute to designated American libraries books that fall within the scope of the Plan. Until book acquisitions began under P.L. 480, full costs of the program, with the exception of some initial operating costs, were borne by recipient libraries, and every effort was made to keep costs at a minimum. Books costing more than $25 were not supplied automatically, and certain fields, such as children's books and music, were excluded. The Plan began with European coverage but has expanded to other areas of the world.

The Farmington Plan has encountered a number of major difficulties in its operation: the vagaries of depending on foreign book dealers, especially those outside Western Europe; the difficulty of identifying with confidence the items which "might reasonably be expected to interest a research worker in the United States"; reluctance of participating institutions to bear mounting costs of the program, particularly in more esoteric subject areas; exclusion of certain important subject and geographic areas (such as Eastern Europe) from the Plan; and, of greatest importance, increasing doubts about the relative priority of the problem set up for solution by the Plan. The Farmington Plan was a product of the war and the immediate postwar period, when international studies were viewed as exotic endeavors, primarily of strategic interest, in which one university could not be expected to have many participants and to undertake more than a small fraction of coverage. Recently, conditions have changed. There has been widespread acceptance of the principle that world affairs have a central place in education and research. Accordingly, the task of seeing that every piece of significant foreign material is held somewhere in America has become subsidiary to the need to build a large number of collections with breadth as well as depth.[7] Spontaneous interest in library collections of some non-Farmington areas has resulted in adequate coverage without the shared responsibility.[8]

5 *For discussions of the purposes, history, and success of the Plan, see Edwin E. Williams,* Farmington Plan Handbook: Revised to 1961 and Abridged (*Association of Research Libraries, 1961*); *and Robert Vosper,* The Farmington Plan Survey: A Summary of the Separate Studies of 1957–1961 (*Urbana: University of Illinois Graduate School of Library Science, 1964*). *Current information on the Farmington Plan and other cooperative library activities is contained in the serial publication* Farmington Plan Newsletter, *prepared by the Association of Research Libraries' Farmington Plan Committee.*
6 *Williams,* Handbook, op. cit., *p. 8.*
7 *The original task was performed quite effectively under the Plan, particularly for Western Europe; see Vosper, op. cit.*
8 *A recent study shows that coverage in the United States of material from Poland, which is outside the Farmington Plan, is at least as large as that for most countries included in the Plan. See André Nitecki, "Polish Books in America and the Farmington Plan,"* College and Research Libraries (*November 1966*), *pp. 439–48.*

To compound the difficulty of continuing the Farmington Plan philosophy, the buildup of interest in international studies has caused many of the larger libraries to experience mounting internal pressure on their collections and to take a correspondingly reduced part in schemes of interlibrary loan. Inability of the Farmington Plan to cope with burgeoning interest in Africa, Asia, and Latin America, has been indicated by vigorous library activity in area study associations on these parts of the world during the late 1950's and 1960's.[9] The Farmington Plan Committee, probably in response to a survey conducted of the Plan's operation by Robert Vosper and Robert L. Talmadge, modified its activities in the 1960's and included a new emphasis upon the need for duplication of important materials in major libraries.

The acquisitions program of the Library of Congress under P.L. 480 and Title II-C, of the Higher Education Act of 1965 (outlined below) has in substantial measure been a natural successor to the Farmington Plan. It has also, however, largely ended the need for the Plan in its present form.

Public Law 480

In 1961 American libraries undertook their first program of cooperative acquisitions with Federal support, using "surplus" counterpart foreign currency, a source of financing that was employed successfully shortly after World War II to initiate the Fulbright Program. The origin of the funds was the Agricultural Trade Development and Assistance Act of 1954 (P.L. 83-480) which provided for sale to certain needy countries of surplus agricultural commodities for which payment would be received in "blocked" local currencies.

An amendment was made to the Act in 1958, entitled Section 104n, which authorized the Library of Congress to process and deposit in appropriate locations such materials as they could acquire with appropriations under the Act. The first funds were appropriated in 1961 for acquisitions in India, Pakistan, and the United Arab Republic. In 1964, Indonesia and Israel were added, and recently coverage was extended to Yugoslavia, Nepal, and Ceylon. Recipient libraries were selected on the advice of a special committee and generally were the locations of major area study programs. Token contributions of $500 were required from each participant institution, and special arrangements were made for centralized and cooperative cataloging. The Library of Congress established acquisition centers in the countries covered by the project and published regular accessions lists which, for several of the countries involved, are the nearest thing to national bibliographies. A microfilming program for newspapers and foreign gazettes has been incorporated into the original project.

Proposals have been made to extend the P.L. 480 program to several additional countries, but an obvious limitation on further expansion will be dependence upon the availability of counterpart funds.

Latin American Cooperative Acquisitions Program

The Latin American Cooperative Acquisitions Program (LACAP) was organized in 1960, in response to the findings of the Seminars on the Acquisition of Latin American Library Materials described below, as an attempt to overcome through cooperative use of private enterprise the problems of communication faced by American libraries in acquisitions from Latin America. Under this program, more than thirty cooperating libraries received a steady flow of printed material currently published in Latin America from the commercial bookseller Stechert-Hafner, Inc., which selects, acquires through agents in Latin America, and distributes materials through its New York office to cooperating institutions on a general order basis. In some cases, orders are limited by subject or geographic area. Current acquisitions average about 2,500 titles per year at a total annual cost of $9,000.

[9] *See Williams,* op. cit., p. 20.

LACAP has been of particular assistance to American libraries with heavy specialization in Latin American studies. However, libraries wishing to be more selective in their purchases may order from catalogs of LACAP materials in stock at Stechert-Hafner.

Programs of the Association of Research Libraries

In addition to the Farmington Plan, the Association of Research Libraries has operated, stimulated, or coordinated several cooperative acquisitions programs. For example, the Foreign Newspaper Microfilm Project has some sixty subscribers and makes available about one hundred forty newspapers on microfilm; The Scholarly Resources Development Program, Contemporary China, is a comprehensive effort to improve library holdings on this particular country.[10]

Cooperative Africana Microform Project

The Cooperative Africana Microform Project (CAMP) is an example of a response to a pressing need expressed by scholars in the African Studies Association. "The purpose of the project is to acquire, at joint expense, microfilms of important but expensive or scarce Africana for the joint use of the participants . . ."[11] Materials for the project are acquired and stored by the Center for Research Libraries in Chicago.

Other Programs

The obvious gains from cooperative acquisition of foreign library materials have led to the establishment of a variety of *ad hoc* programs, ranging from a short-term gathering together of a few institutions to formal arrangements for large-scale sharing among consortia. One of the most successful of these programs is the National Council for Foreign Area Materials administered by the New York State Education Department.

Technical Processing: Centralized Cataloging

The need for centralized cataloging of foreign materials was recognized in testimony on the Higher Education Bill of 1965, particularly in light of the proposed support for college and university library development in that bill in the amount of $50 million.[12] It was pointed out that while the holdings of foreign materials in American libraries were growing rapidly to answer the needs of an increasing body of scholars, these libraries were seriously handicapped by the enormous task of processing foreign materials, many of which were in an unfamiliar form and language. At the same time, substantial and increasing duplication of effort was occurring as more and more libraries attempted to carry out identical processing operations simultaneously. Title II, Part C, was accepted as an amendment to the Higher Education Act of 1965 with authorization through HEW for a total of $19 million over three years.

In brief, II-C charges the Library of Congress with the responsibility of (a) acquiring, so far as possible, all library materials currently published throughout the world which are of value to scholarship; and (b) providing catalog information for such materials promptly after receipt, and using for exchange and other purposes such of these materials as are not needed for the Library of Congress collection.[13]

---

10 *The Association of Research Libraries,* Minutes of the Sixty-Ninth Meeting, January 8, 1967 (*Washington, 1967*), p. 69 and pp. 54–62.

11 *James F. Kane, "Cooperative Africana Microform Project,"* Farmington Plan Newsletter, *Number 25 (May 1967), pp. 1–3.*

12 *A specially effective statement was presented by William S. Dix on behalf of the Association of Research Libraries;* Congressional Record: Senate (*May 19, 1965*), pp. 10587–8.

13 *For descriptive information and comment about what the Library of Congress has come to call the National Program for Acquisitions and Cataloging (NPAC), see L. Quincy Mumford, "International Breakthrough,"* Library Journal (*January 1, 1967*), pp. 79–82; John W. Cronin, "The Library of Congress National Program for Acquisitions and Cataloging," Libri 16 (1966), pp. 113–17; John W. Cronin, John M. Dawson, William S. Dix, and James E. Skipper, "Centralized Cataloging at the National and International Level," Library Resources and Technical Services 11 (Winter 1967), pp. 27–49; Jerrold Orne, "Title II-C, A Little Revolution," Southeastern Librarian (October 1966); the special issue of Library Trends entitled "Cooperative and Centralized Cataloging," 16 (July 1967).*

The zeal, imagination, and speed of the Library of Congress in getting the centralized cataloging program under way have been extraordinary. A debt of gratitude is owed by the American reading community to the Library of Congress staff and to Messrs. John Cronin and Edmond Applebaum who have directed the program. A host of problems have been faced and solved. The first tasks consisted of selecting the material which could reasonably be described as of value to American scholars and finding persons to catalog it. Wisely, the decision was made to undertake as much of the operation as possible abroad and to take advantage of work done in foreign libraries. For acquisition, book dealer agents were asked to make initial selection of material. For cataloging, national bibliographies have been used where available, usually in printers' copy stage. Acquisitions and cataloging centers have been established around the world, and P.L. 480 offices have been used where they exist. To supplement selections by foreign book dealers and offices abroad, the Library of Congress accepts recommendations from its Washington staff and also receives from cooperating libraries copies of order forms for current foreign material. Works which have not been cataloged or ordered already are immediately ordered by air mail, and frequently are processed by the time the initiating library has received its copy.

Experiments are in progress to make available the results of centralized cataloging in machine-readable form. Efforts are also under way to expand the number of foreign centers from the nine in operation as of June 1967.

Reception of the centralized cataloging program has been overwhelmingly favorable. Sir Frank Francis, Director of the British Museum, predicted that the program will lead to "the most important breakthrough in the realm of information since the elaboration of rules for cataloging. . . ."[14]

The Farmington Plan and the P.L. 480 Program pointed up with special urgency the long-standing need in the United States for a program of shared cataloging of foreign materials analogous to the program for processing domestic publications. The program of centralized cataloging which is now in effect, however, is far more than merely a response to this need. This program has signaled a new philosophy of Federal assistance to the international collections of American libraries, not merely through the back door with funds from a foreign assistance Act, but as part of a broad effort to support American higher education. Title II-C of the Higher Education Act of 1965 has indicated acceptance of the principle that library collections worldwide in scope are not an exotic luxury, superfluous if duplicate copies exist elsewhere, but are central to the intellectual activity of America and, therefore, are deserving of continuing support in depth.

All the benefits of the centralized cataloging program are not yet fully apparent, but undoubtedly they are many. First, the speed with which American scholars have access to foreign materials, both through their own libraries' collections and interlibrary loan, is greatly increased. Second, substantial economies are bestowed upon American libraries in reduced cataloging costs and released staff time for processing retrospective material.[15] Third, through accessions lists published by the Library of Congress, approximations to national bibliographies are provided for parts of the world in which none had existed hitherto. Worldwide uniformity in cataloging procedure is encouraged by this development. Fourth, as a by-product of the primary objective of the program, substantial technical and bibliographical assistance is provided to countries around the world which can and do make use of the new services. Fifth, and perhaps of greatest long-run significance as suggested above, a model has been provided for Federal participation in American library development in a manner which is satisfactory to all partici-

---

14 *Mumford, "International Breakthrough,"* op. cit., *p. 81.*
15 *See the evidence on this point supplied by several major American libraries as reported by the Librarian of Congress in Hearings before a Subcommittee of the Committee on Appropriations, House of Representatives, Ninetieth Congress, First Session,* Departments of Labor and Health, Education, and Welfare Appropriations for 1968, Part 6, pp. 77–86.

pants and is conspicuously successful in its results. A path has been cleared for international library cooperation on a scale only dreamed of in the past.

Bibliography and Access

A variety of different agencies have helped to answer the need for bibliographies of foreign materials.

Library of Congress

With funds from private as well as public sources, the Library of Congress has been able to provide numerous bibliographical tools of great use to scholars of foreign areas. To mention only two examples from many, the Library's Hispanic Foundation issues a valuable bibliographical series, including the annual *Handbook of Latin American Studies* (published since 1936).[16] In recent years a number of specially important bibliographies on Africa have been issued.[17]

An important service the Library of Congress performs which has both bibliographic and acquisitions features is operation of a Center for the Coordination of Foreign Manuscript Copying to serve as a clearinghouse for all American photocopying of original materials abroad.

Association of Research Libraries

The Association has been active since its inception in encouraging and preparing foreign area bibliographies. Well known examples are the publications of the Farmington Plan area subcommittees.[18] Specially significant are efforts of the Coordinating Committee for Slavic and East European Library Resources (Cocoseers).

United Nations Educational, Scientific and Cultural Organization

Under its constitution, UNESCO is charged to "maintain, increase, and diffuse knowledge." The main obstacle in its way in achieving these objectives has been shortage of funds. The organization from the beginning has opposed the notion of a World Bibliographical Center, but it has undertaken important individual bibliographical tasks such as the bibliography of works in translation *Index Translationum* begun in 1949.[19] Two specially useful bibliographical publications are *UNESCO Bulletin for Libraries* and *Bibliography, Documentation and Terminology* (bimonthly, in four languages).

In accordance with its mission, UNESCO must confine its attention to tasks that are truly international in scope, such as worldwide directories of indexing and abstracting services, and national bibliographies and manuscript collections. UNESCO supports, through grants, bibliographical efforts of international councils of scholars in single disciplines or groups of disciplines. It is important to note, however, that the bibliographical objectives of UNESCO are not always identical to the needs of the American reading community.

Organization of American States

The Pan American Union, as General Secretariat of the Organization of American States (OAS), through its Columbus Memorial Library, its Inter-American Library Development Program, and other substantive offices, together with the specialized organizations of the OAS in such fields as agriculture, health, statistics, history, and geography, provide a wide variety of evaluative bibliographies of books published in Latin America. It produces an index to Latin American periodicals and has ready to go to press a bibliography of Latin American bibliographies.

16 *A recent grant from the Ford Foundation announced on January 10, 1967, has made possible continuation of this series.* See LC Information Bulletin 26, No. 3 (*January 19, 1967*), pp. 51–2.
17 Farmington Plan Newsletter, *No. 25 (May 1967), p. 9.*
18 *Association of Research Libraries,* Minutes of the Sixty-Ninth Meeting, January 8, 1967 (*Washington, 1967*), pp. 94–101.
19 *See Herbert Coblans, "Bibliographic Organization at the International Level,"* Wilson Library Bulletin (*April 1966*), pp. 733–7.

The Pan American Union operates an annual Seminar on the Acquisition of Latin American Library Materials (SALALM) whose main concern is with resolving problems facing libraries in acquiring publications from Latin America and one of whose chief objectives has been bibliographic improvement.[20] A particularly weak aspect of foreign materials bibliography has been evaluative selection lists for schools and public libraries. Here the Pan American Union has taken pioneering steps, both as a consequence of its interest in Latin American studies and from concern with the reading needs of Spanish-speaking residents of the United States.[21]

Committee on Scientific and Technical Information

The Committee on Scientific and Technical Information (COSATI) of the Federal Council for Science and Technology has as one of its functions facilitation of access to scientific and technical information produced outside the United States.[22] A special panel on International Information Activities was established (sponsored by the National Aeronautics and Space Administration) to make recommendations in this field. The panel is reported to be working on a United States policy for the exchange of magnetic tapes, microforms, and other bibliographic tools with foreign countries and is "producing guidelines for domestic distribution of these media." In general the panel "serves as a Federal central information and coordination point for international scientific and technical information activities of the Executive Branch of the U.S. Government."

In 1965 a COSATI Task Group submitted a report entitled *Recommendations for National Document-Handling Systems in Science and Technology* which led to agreement by the Federal Council that "the Director of OST (Office of Science and Technology) will initiate, on an exploratory basis, the operation of a central mechanism which will provide a comprehensive, coordinated program to insure the acquiring, cataloging, and announcing of the significant worldwide scientific and technical literature." A study of such a mechanism was then initiated in 1966.

COSATI has undertaken programs to improve knowledge of and access to translations of social science literature. The Clearinghouse for Federal Scientific and Technical Information (in the Department of Commerce) operates the Joint Publication Research Services, which is said to produce "some 80 to 90 percent of the social sciences translations generated in the United States."

Miscellaneous Public and Private Organizations

Area studies associations, professional associations, various departments of the Federal Government, and private publishers such as the R. R. Bowker Company *with Libros en Venta* (a list of books in print in the Spanish language) have made significant bibliographic contributions.[23] But these efforts have been sporadic, largely uncoordinated, and inadequate overall.

[20] *See* Working Papers of the Seminars on the Acquisition of Latin American Library Materials: List and Index, *Cauadernos Bibliotecologicos No. 22 (Pan American Union, Washington, 1964); Carl W. Deal,* A Report of Bibliographic Activities, 1965 . . . , *XI SALALM Working Paper No. 3 (Pan American Union, Washington, 1966); and* Publicaciones Del Programa De Fomenta De Biblioteces Y La Bibliografia En La America Latina, De La Union Pan Americana *(Pan American Union, Washington, April 1967, mimeo); and* Progress Report on the Seminars on the Acquisition of Latin American Library Materials, 1967, *XII SALALM Working Paper No. 1 (Pan American Union 1967).*

[21] *See Marietta Daniels Shepard,* Selection Aids on Latin America for Primary and Secondary School Libraries, *Cuadernos Bibliotecologicos No. 32 and Supp. (Pan American Union, Washington, 1966); and statement by Mrs. Shepard on S. 428 prepared for the Special Subcommittee on Bilingual Education of the Senate Committee on Labor and Public Welfare, June 16, 1967 (mimeo).*

[22] *See* Activities of the Federal Council for Science and Technology: Report for 1965 and 1966 *(Washington: Executive Office of the President, 1967), pp. 28–30; Richard E. Barry, "Committee on Scientific and Technical Information Coordinates Inter-Agency Information Systems,"* Navy Management Review 12 *(April 1967), pp. 3–14; and Andrew A. Aines, "The Promise of National Information Systems,"* Library Trends 16 *(January 1968), pp. 410–8.*

[23] *See Mary C. Turner, "Libros en Venta,"* Library Journal *(June 15, 1964), pp. 2561–2; and Daniel Melcher, "Goals in National Bibliography," ibid., pp. 2556–9. See also, for example, the selected bibliographies of East European Educational Materials published by the U.S. Office of Education.*

Book and Library Programs Abroad

United States book and library programs overseas have grown steadily since World War II as part of the overall commitment to foreign assistance.[24] Until recently, however, these have been uncoordinated both in the public and private sectors. Moreover, although book and technical assistance programs to libraries abroad can be, and in a few cases are, related closely to development of American libraries, this potential is largely unfulfilled.

At least seven principal government agencies have taken an active part in book and library assistance.[25] The Agency for International Development has provided extensive book aid to most of the countries in which it operates, through contracts, direct assistance, and until recently through assistance to the United States Book Exchange. Recipients have been mainly educational institutions and departments of foreign governments. The Department of State, through the Conference Board of Associated Research Councils, administers the International Education Exchange Program (Fulbright and Smith-Mundt Acts) which makes available a few American librarians for temporary posting abroad.

The Library of Congress and the other national libraries (the National Agricultural Library and the National Library of Medicine) provide a variety of services: advice and exchange of materials directly to libraries of other countries; bibliographical guides for developing libraries; and study programs for foreign librarians visiting the United States.[26] The Peace Corps includes librarians among its volunteers and makes available small quantities of materials for the programs of its personnel. The United States Information Agency maintains USIS libraries in most countries of the world, and these provide important services to a wide range of readers, albeit with a strong propaganda bias and limitations on types of materials which may be stocked. This agency also sponsors some training activities for foreign librarians and makes outright book gifts to some institutional libraries abroad. The Department of Health, Education, and Welfare provides a variety of services to foreign librarians. The Smithsonian Institution distributes its own publications abroad and operates the extensive program of book exchange entitled International Exchange Service.[27]

Various international organizations to which the United States makes substantial contributions assist library development. OAS, with its specialized organizations, has been especially active as a stimulator of improvements. The Pan American Union carries on a comprehensive program for the development of libraries in Latin America. It publishes manuals and bibliographies, organizes seminars, and provides short-term consultants, fellowships, and other services.[28] UNESCO has offered a wide range of library aid both direct and indirect.[29]

[24] *For recent surveys of these programs see Miles M. Jackson, Jr., "Library Development Abroad,"* Library Journal *91 (March 15, 1966), pp. 1354–61; Ray E. Hiebert, ed.,* Books in Human Development *(Washington, 1965); and "International Book Programs,"* Bowker Annual of Library and Book Trade Information *(New York, 1967), pp. 71–8.*

[25] *A summary of these activities, from material prepared by the staff of the Interagency Book Committee in October 1966, is attached in appendix F–1.B.*

[26] *A description of "United States Department of Agriculture International Information Activities," prepared by Blanche L. Oliveri is attached in appendix F–1.B, which also contains a statement from National Library of Medicine.*

[27] *A description of this program is: J. A. Collins, "The International Exchange Service,"* Library Resources and Technical Services *10 (Summer 1966), pp. 337–41.*

[28] *The report of a meeting organized by the Library Development Program of the Pan American Union to assess Latin American book needs is, Elaine A. Kurtz, "The Round Table on International Cooperation for Library and Information Services in Latin America,"* Special Libraries *56 (November 1965), pp. 667–8. "The Inter-American Program of Library and Bibliographic Development of the Organization of American States: A Statement of Principles and Practices" is attached in appendix F–1.B.*

[29] *A survey of UNESCO assistance programs related to libraries, documentation, and archives was prepared for the Organization's twentieth birthday.* UNESCO Bulletin for Libraries *20 (September– October 1966). A summary is on pp. 257–76.*

A large number of private organizations in the United States have been active in varying degrees in the library assistance field.[30] The International Relations Office of the American Library Association was established in 1956 with a grant from the Rockefeller Foundation to render direct and indirect assistance to libraries in the developing countries.[31] Missionary bodies, such as the Christian and Missionary Alliance and the United Board of Christian Higher Education in Asia, have traditionally provided book and library assistance as part of their wider programs. Similarly, American foundations with special interest in foreign assistance have extended library support, notably the Asia Foundation, the Carnegie Corporation of New York, the Ford Foundation, the W. K. Kellogg Foundation, and the Rockefeller Foundation. The United States Book Exchange, Inc., has been a most successful means of distributing abroad surplus books and periodicals from the United States (more than two and one half million in thirteen years). Unfortunately, funding for the international program of this organization was terminated by the Agency for International Development in 1963, and its operations are now limited mainly to relations with foreign libraries which can pay their own fees.

Until recent years, there has been very little coordination or cooperation among American book programs abroad or foreign assistance programs with library development in the United States. In 1962, the Secretary of State established a Government Advisory Committee on International Book Programs under authority of the Fulbright Hays Act "for the purpose of advising the Government on the policies and operations of its various overseas book and library programs and of serving as a liaison between the Government and the book industry and library profession to achieve closer coordination of public and private book and library activities overseas." Originally this body consisted only of publishers and constituted little more than a voice from the book trade. In October 1966, however, three of the publishers on rotating membership were replaced by two educators and a librarian to give the body a wider focus.

A second move to improve coordination of United States book and library programs abroad was the formation in July 1966 of an Interagency Committee on Books, chaired by the Assistant Secretary of State for Educational and Cultural Affairs. A National Policy Statement on International Book and Library Activities, issued by the President in January 1967 (copy attached in Appendix F-1. B), was the result of collaboration between the Interagency and Advisory Committees. Despite instructions in the subsequent "Directive to Government Agencies for Implementation of the National Policy Statement on International Book and Library Activities" (copy attached in Appendix F-1. B) "to further a greatly increased inflow of foreign books and materials," these two committees have continued to devote their attention predominantly to book programs of the United States Government and have made little attempt to coordinate their actions with either private assistance programs or the developmental efforts of American libraries. Discussions currently in progress for establishment of an American based "International Book Institute" may help to remedy this deficiency. Multinational organizations of libraries and librarians (e.g., IFLA and FID) have not in the past been notably successful in accomplishing either significant cooperation or coordination.[32]

---

[30] *More than a hundred public and private organizations and agencies carry on assistance programs in Latin America alone. See* Final Report of the Round Table on International Cooperation, *1965, Vol. II.*

[31] *Lester Asheim, director of the International Relations Office from 1962 until 1966, has offered some reflections on his experiences and tasks in his book* Librarianship in the Developing Countries *(Urbana, 1966). (Mr. Asheim has also described the work of the Office in a statement to the National Advisory Commission on Libraries, March 6, 1967.)*

[32] *See Edward Carter,* International Organization in Librarianship and Documentation, *made for the Council on Library Resources, Washington, 1958.*

Worldwide Services of American Libraries

Many of the programs of American libraries and related agencies, including some of those described above, are of substantial value to libraries and their users in other countries. To mention only a few examples, the Library of Congress provides printed catalog cards to libraries around the world. The II-C program has now substantially extended the scope of this service. The Atomic Energy Commission (AEC) has accepted the world community of nuclear scholars as its constituency. The Agency describes the program as follows:[33]

> Since 1947 the Atomic Energy Commission has operated a unique information system designed to collect, analyze, and disseminate all published nuclear information on a worldwide basis. In addition to publishing *Nuclear Science Abstracts,* the only abstracting and indexing service devoted exclusively to nuclear science, the AEC distributes its unclassified technical reports to nearly 100 depository collections abroad.

The National Library of Medicine has also been active. For a description of their international functions, see appendix F–1.B.

THE FUTURE

Philosophy of Federal Government Participation in International Programs of American Libraries

All of the holdings of American libraries are a vital national resource that must be husbanded and developed in the same way as the nation's educational system. However, substantial involvement of the Federal Government specifically with international programs is warranted for at least three special reasons.

First, because at this time in United States history, it is in the national interest to have all segments of the population more familiar with international affairs. At one end of the population spectrum, highly trained experts are needed to administer and advise concerning United States foreign policy and activities abroad, both public and private. In times of crisis, thorough understanding of a foreign area can become vital to the national security; such understanding and the library tools to support it can seldom be gathered after the crisis has begun.

At the other end of the population spectrum, the citizenry itself must be enabled to understand and to make enlightened judgments concerning the complex events that occur in a world of ever-diminishing size. Legislators, journalists, and the average voter must be provided with the information needed to make decisions concerning international problems.

At the center of the spectrum, the American educational system must be enriched at all levels to take advantage of the full range of human knowledge and experience through foreign library acquisitions. Strengthening of the international dimension of American libraries is an essential step toward a reduction in the parochialism of American life and culture to match the recent change in this country's foreign relations.

Second, because books and libraries are valuable tools in the worldwide process of social, political, and economic development to which the United States is committed. It is now apparent that extensive research must be undertaken by American and foreign scholars in all fields of knowledge before solutions can be found to many of the most difficult problems of modernization. At home, holdings of foreign library materials are the essential source of raw data and the repository of the findings of foreign scholars that make this research possible. Abroad, books, in addition to being the research base

---

[33] *Statement from the AEC entitled "International Cooperation in Nuclear Science Information." The memorandum goes on to suggest that "a broad cooperative program" for an articulated international network of information centers should replace the heavy world dependence on the United States.*

of these foreign scholars, are a direct means of bringing skills and incentives to persons in other lands who are totally unfamiliar even with the notion of progress. Books and libraries are essential to improvement of formal school systems and of programs in adult education.

Third, because Federal funding is a practical means of accomplishing the most pressing tasks of development of international collections in American libraries. In no other area of library activity is cooperation and centralized performance of key functions more essential than in relations with foreign areas. In part, Federal participation in international programs can be justified as a means of encouraging activities that yield public benefits (as outlined above) in addition to the private benefits to the institutions that operate the libraries. This is the same rationale used for Federal aid to education generally. In addition, however, many of the tasks that will be presented to individual American libraries by their international relations in the years ahead can be accomplished effectively *only* with cooperative effort, carried out either directly by the Federal Government through its various agencies or by private organizations with Federal support. Because of the high costs of many of these programs of national significance, it will be a case of Federal support or none at all.

Some of the efforts at cooperation undertaken by the Federal Government in the past have been described above. Set forth below are certain new types of programs and extensions of current programs that appear to this writer to be urgently required.[34]

Strengthened Role for the Library of Congress as the National Library

Increased participation by the Federal Government in the international programs of American libraries presupposes a growing role of leadership for the Library of Congress. In fact, even if not in name, the Library of Congress must become in the international area a true national library, accepting responsibility for support of the libraries of the nation. The two traditional functions of the Library of Congress, as a service department to the Legislative Branch of Government and as a lender of last resort to the scholarly community, can be strengthened rather than weakened by performance of the functions of a national library. But these new functions of leadership and assistance, which have been growing rapidly *de facto* in recent years without a formal change of status, must now be recognized as of equal importance in their own right to the older functions of the Library of Congress. The pattern for more effective leadership by the Library of Congress in international cooperation among American libraries has been provided already by the centralized cataloging and P.L. 480 programs. Examples of new and extended activities in the international area that the Library of Congress should perform as the national library are as follows:

Extension of
the Centralized Cataloging Program

The centralized cataloging program of the Library of Congress is one of the most successful innovations in the history of American libraries. Not only does this program, as described above, improve substantially the speed of access to and breadth of coverage of foreign materials for American scholars, but it has saved American libraries large amounts of catalog costs and use of precious staff time. The desirability of extending this program to portions of the world not now covered, as recommended by the Librarian of Congress and included in proposed amendments to the Higher Education Act of 1965, is manifest. It would be possible also for the program to be extended to some retrospective material.

---

[34] *Some of the proposals set forth here are similar to those listed under "Library Exchange" by the Committee on Culture and Intellectual Exchange which reported to the White House Conference on International Cooperation in 1964–65. See* Library Journal *91 (January 15, 1966), p. 221.*

Extension of
Cooperative Activities of Library of Congress Centers Abroad

The centers now operated in many parts of the world by the Library of Congress under the centralized cataloging and P.L. 480 programs, and others which are contemplated, should be given substantial extended authority and support to cooperate in the development of library collections throughout the United States. New functions of these centers might include the following types of activities.

There might be shared acquisition for American libraries of current material, particularly ephemera and Government publications, in countries where the publishing industry and book trade are not highly developed. Where Government assistance was not provided, payment for material would be made by participating American libraries to the Library of Congress on special or blanket order. Where exceptionally small press runs are encountered, as in the case of some government publications in the newer countries, xerox copies might be supplied by the centers to American libraries. In some areas, cooperation between private firms and the Library of Congress (such as that taking place in Latin America at this moment) would be a successful technique of effecting shared acquisitions.

Provision is made in the proposed amendment to Title II-C, of the Higher Education Act of 1965 for purchase of two or more copies of items included in the shared cataloging program, the second copy to be deposited in a central lending institution such as the Center for Research Libraries in Chicago. The admirable principle implicit in this proposal—that at least one extra copy of foreign material should be available to American scholars outside the Library of Congress in a "library of last resort"—is similar to that which lay behind the Farmington Plan. This principle is still valid for some items of narrow interest, but for the large amount of material that is of broader interest, it is no longer adequate. The philosophy of the Farmington Plan was a product of the 1940's, when foreign research was still largely peripheral to American scholarship; it is an anachronism today as a guide to policy in the burgeoning international studies of the 1960's. No longer can one or two library collections of foreign material available on interlibrary loan be seen as answers to the rapidly increasing numbers of scholars working on foreign areas. Instead, closer to forty or fifty major balanced foreign area research libraries must be contemplated, with close cooperative relationships to smaller college and university collections in their regions. The Library of Congress, if provided with adequate funding, might contribute in a significant way through its centers abroad to the development of these regional library centers. Failure of the Federal Government to assist in the advancement of the international collections of American libraries will not prevent this development from taking place, but it will inhibit and limit it in scope.[35]

The foreign centers of the Library of Congress should act as cooperative collection and filming units to deal with manuscript and rare retrospective published material acquired by American libraries. This service, which would be a natural development from the past and present Library of Congress activities (particularly under P.L. 480), would yield several major benefits to United States and world scholarship. Many documents would be rescued and preserved for recorded history which appear at the moment to be destined for oblivion. Political turmoil, climate, and simple neglect are playing havoc with many of the world's most precious records, and unless an agency such as the United States Government joins private American citizens and libraries in an acquisition and film project of major proportions, this heritage will be gone forever. At present, individual American scholars and libraries are undertaking extensive filming and collecting activities, but in a relatively haphazard and uncoordinated fashion. More extensive

---

35 *It is reported that the possibility of shared acquisitions by the Library of Congress has been explored by representatives of the Association of Research Libraries,* Farmington Plan Newsletter, *No. 25 (May 1967), pp. 6–7.*

government participation in these activities would eliminate costly duplication, reduce film costs to scholars, and permit undertakings, such as filming of entire foreign archives, which are impossible for individuals acting alone. There is some hope for developing more effective foreign acquisitions and processing through private enterprise, but massive improvements must surely come from the Federal Government.

It is not the task of this paper to examine how the status of the Library of Congress might be altered so that this institution could perform more effectively its role as a national library. The proposal here is merely for an extension of this role. Whether the Library of Congress carries out its tasks of leadership and coordination in the international area through a substantial increase in its own activities, through administration of a program budget using the services of other public and private agencies, or through other techniques, the tasks still need to be performed.

Preparation of Bibliographies of International Materials

In recent years, American scholars and educational institutions at all levels have become actively interested for the first time in international affairs. This interest is partly spontaneous and partly inspired by such statements of policy as the President's Smithsonian address and such pieces of legislation as the International Education Act of 1966.

A major obstacle, in many instances, to pursuit of this interest by Americans through use of books, periodicals, and other library materials has been ignorance of what items are most worthwhile from among the plethora that are available. The small college which starts a course in non-Western civilizations, the large university which begins an area studies program, a public library which decides to broaden its foreign holdings, and a scholar who suddenly decides to extend his interest outside the United States cannot easily find analytical and descriptive bibliographies to guide them.[36] School, college and university libraries are especially deficient in this regard. Frequently, the faculty members at those institutions that move quickly to broaden their curricula are themselves newcomers to international studies and are of little assistance as guides to acquisitions. Even institutions which already have strong collections increasingly find relevant faculty members unreliable as advisers, or disinterested, or absent from campus at critical periods.

Reviews in learned journals are seldom useful in gaining a notion of priority of importance. *Choice* has thus far restricted its reviews to American publications. Occasional *ad hoc* bibliographical guides to foreign material have been published by professional societies and other groups, but without regularity or dependability.[37] A model for the type of periodical publication which is required to provide current bibliographical information in international studies is the experimental journal published from 1954 to 1962 by the Johns Hopkins University Department of Political Economy entitled *Economic Library Selections Series*.

In order for American libraries to develop intelligently their international holdings and for American readers to make proper use of these holdings, provision should be made for the Library of Congress, in its capacity as the national library, to prepare adequate annotated bibliographies.[38] These should take two forms. First, there should be periodic lists of minimum international library holdings for various specified purposes—such as a liberal arts college interdisciplinary course in African studies, a university graduate program in the social sciences on Southeast Asia, or a general public

---

[36] *This bibliographical problem was discussed at a recent conference at Douglass College. See Shirley Stowe, "Look to the East,"* Library Journal 91 *(August 1966), pp. 3645–6.*
[37] *See an account of "Bibliography: Current State and Future Trends. Part II,"* Library Trends 15 *(April 1967), pp. 601–919.*
[38] *A plan for preparation of bibliographies of this type for Latin American universities, institutions which frequently are in no greater need than their North American counterparts, is described by Mrs. Shepard of the Pan American Union in* Choice 3 *(December 1966), p. 887.*

library collection on world affairs; bibliographical items should be described briefly, along with the source from which they may be purchased, and should be given priority ratings. Second, a serial publication such as *Choice* should be published for international materials, including those in foreign languages, so that scholars and librarians may have a professional guide to current acquisitions.

Bibliographies for international studies could be prepared and published either directly by the Library of Congress, or through Federal support to private organizations such as the American Council of Learned Societies, American Library Association, Association of Research Libraries, SALALM, and the individual professional and area studies associations. In any case, the consultative services of scholars in the individual fields should be utilized fully to guarantee acceptance and authority.

Coordination of Library Assistance Abroad with Development of International Collections at United States Libraries

An outline description of programs of library assistance abroad has been provided above. Whether these programs should be extended is a consideration of foreign policy and beyond the scope of this paper. However, certain aspects of programs that involve relations with institutions abroad have a direct impact on American libraries themselves. In particular, staff and material exchange arrangements and affiliation programs can be, and in some cases have been, of substantial benefit to domestic institutions. The utility of the exchange of library materials is self-evident. Frequently, exchange with foreign libraries is the cheapest and most effective means of acquisition for American libraries.

Exchange of staff has more subtle effects. Service abroad has been one of the most successful techniques of reducing the parochialism of United States college and university faculties. This method has been used only in the smallest way to effect the same process in American libraries. More directly, temporary secondment to a foreign library enables an American librarian to gain skills and personal connections that are valuable in development of his own collections at home. Efforts should be made to recognize this relationship more fully and to capitalize upon it. In particular, Federal Government agencies responsible for library assistance abroad should be charged with responsibility for keeping these dual objectives in mind. At the very least, full compensation should be provided to cover all out-of-pocket costs of American libraries in assistance to foreign libraries and visiting librarians. But, in addition, exchange programs should be aimed toward development of libraries and of library collections at both ends of the exchange.

Miscellaneous Special Services

Frequently, as a result of their foreign collections, urgent problems arise for American libraries that require prohibitive expenditure or excessively complicated cooperative machinery for solution. One example is the present need for special support of the training of librarians familiar with exotic languages. Another is the occasional need for preparation of such low-circulation publications as *The Current Digest of the Soviet Press*. Publication of the *Current Digest* has been accomplished in recent years with some difficulty through the American Council of Learned Societies (ACLS) and special contributions from subscribers. Such a task could have been accomplished more sensibly by the national library.

An excellent example of how the Library of Congress may use its great prestige and strategic location to obtain foreign material which might otherwise be unobtainable to scholars is the recent exchange of microfilm of archival records with the Soviet Union.[39] In general, the Federal Government should maintain flexible machinery in the Library of Congress or elsewhere to respond where urgent and demonstrated need exists.

[39] *See* LC Information Bulletin *25 (May 26, 1966), pp. 262–3.*

SUMMARY AND CONCLUSION

The widespread interest and involvement of the American people in world affairs have created enormous new problems for United States libraries. These problems center around acquisitions, technical processing, bibliography, and foreign assistance. Mounting pressures upon American libraries have led to a variety of cooperative efforts to meet these problems, and in several programs, agencies of the Federal Government have demonstrated exceptional imagination and leadership. Increasingly, by action and public statement, Congress and the Executive have indicated they recognize that the international collections of American libraries are significant national resources that deserve public support. The centralized cataloging program of the Library of Congress has illustrated dramatically the type of assistance that can and should be provided.

In planning for new programs of aid to libraries in the international area, it will be most important for the Federal Government to keep a clear view of certain basic principles which have emerged from recent developments. These are as follows:

1. International studies in the United States are not now, if they ever were, a superfluous appendage of American culture and education. They are of critical significance to the national interest.
2. Library support for international studies can no longer consist merely in providing for ultimate access to foreign material at remote repositories. Adequate and convenient library collections are as essential to international studies as laboratories are to the sciences.
3. Significant benefits can be gained by American libraries through Government assistance to cooperative activities in development of foreign area collections. The Federal Government has a major potential for service as well as a responsibility.
4. The most significant contributions can be made where centralized machinery of Government exists with authority specifically to carry out services to the library community of America. Most criticisms against the library agencies of Government, including the Library of Congress, have been of timidity and lack of enthusiasm for the tasks of leadership and cooperation. Indications are that these charges will end when agencies have been provided with a clear mandate and adequate financial support.

B. SUPPORTING DOCUMENTS

The seven documents appearing here are those referred to in the preceding paper, "The International Dimension," by Craufurd D. Goodwin. These selections were chosen by the author as important supplements to the text.

BIBLIOGRAPHIC NOTE

In preparation of the paper appearing as Appendix F-1. A, I carried out an informal survey of the recent book and periodical literature on the subject. A helpful bibliographical source for this purpose was the serial publication *Library Literature*. Some of the more useful items consulted are listed in footnotes to the paper.

In addition to examination of relevant literature, I held interviews with a number of persons specially competent in the field. These included:

Duke University
    Dr. Benjamin E. Powell, Librarian
    Miss Gertrude Merritt, Assistant Librarian
American Library Association
    Mr. David Hoffman, Assistant Director
    International Relations Office

Council on Library Resources
    Mr. Verner Clapp
Association of Research Libraries
    Mr. Donald Cameron, Executive Director
Library of Congress
    Dr. L. Quincy Mumford, Librarian
    Mr. John Lorenz, Deputy Librarian
    Mrs. Elizabeth Hamer, Assistant Librarian
    Mr. John Cronin, Director, Processing Department
    Mr. Edmond L. Applebaum, Assistant Director, Processing Department
National Agricultural Library
    Mrs. Blanche L. Oliveri
Office of Education
    Mr. Paxton Price
    Mr. Otto Schaler
Department of State
    Mr. Fred W. Shipman, Librarian
    Miss Frances Coughlin (telephone conversation)
Pan American Union
    Mrs. Marietta Daniels Shepard, Associate Librarian
Committee on Scientific and Technical Information
    Colonel Andrew Aines (through Colonel Aines' Secretary), Chairman

Several of these persons were generous enough to comment upon a first draft of the paper. However, none of them is responsible for anything in it.

CRAUFURD D. GOODWIN

SUMMARY OF BOOK AND LIBRARY ACTIVITIES BEING ADMINISTERED BY MEMBERS OF THE INTERAGENCY BOOK COMMITTEE
(Based on information dated 10/10/66)

AGENCY	MISSION	INVOLVEMENT IN INTERNATIONAL BOOK AND LIBRARY ACTIVITIES	APPROXIMATE BUDGET (in millions) LEVEL FOR FY 1966
Department of State	Improve and strengthen international relations of U.S. through educational and cultural exchanges. Promote international cooperation. Strengthen ties with other countries by demonstrating educational and cultural developments and achievements of the people of the U.S.	A. Administers programs which exchange approximately 50 grantees (students, teachers, specialists, etc.) each year in field of library science. B. Funds U.S. contribution to UNESCO which carries on a number of programs to promote the free flow of books.	$ .25

AGENCY	MISSION	INVOLVEMENT IN INTERNATIONAL BOOK AND LIBRARY ACTIVITIES	APPROXI- MATE BUDGET (in millions) LEVEL FOR FY 1966
Agency for International Development	Promote U.S. foreign policy by assisting peoples of the world in their efforts toward economic, social and political development.	A. Assists in establishing and expand- ing overseas book industry capa- bilities through technical assistance grants and loans for writing, print- ing, publishing, and distributing books abroad. This includes the training of approximately 100 persons yearly.	$4.4
		B. Overseas distribution of U.S. books (especially textbooks) and related educational commodities in the basic professions and trades and the learned disciplines. Such books are generally placed in book collections and libraries of institu- tions and organizations involved in development activities.	4.4
Department of Health, Ed- ucation, and Welfare	Increase U.S. re- sources of foreign publications, espe- cially those involving subjects of concern to HEW. Increase foreign ac- cess to our own col- lections.	A. Utilizes PL 480 funds to translate foreign medical journals into Eng- lish.	.5
		B. National Library of Medicine col- lects and disseminates published materials, bibliographic and other specialized information in the field of medicine; promotes interlibrary loans and exchanges publications on a one-for-one basis with over 800 foreign libraries and institu- tions; publishes the *Index Medicus,* most comprehensive index of its kind in the world, sending over 2,300 copies to overseas libraries through purchase or exchange; and provides Medical Literature Analysis and Retrieval System (MEDLARS) tapes at cost to international institutions able to provide regional research facilities.	
		C. The Office of Education adminis- ters an Education Materials Cen- ter which maintains an up-to-date display of some 15,000 texts and children's books for use of visiting foreign and American educators.	
Library of Congress	Facilitate all coopera- tive activities, both national and interna- tional, relating to books, library services and techniques, area	A. Establishes official and institutional agreements with governments and organizations all over the world for the exchange of publications. In FY 1966, under its international exchange program, distributed	

AGENCY	MISSION	INVOLVEMENT IN INTERNATIONAL BOOK AND LIBRARY ACTIVITIES	APPROXI- MATE BUDGET (in millions) LEVEL FOR FY 1966
	studies, and informa- tion transfer.	more than a million publications at a value exceeding one million dollars to foreign institutions, re- ceiving in return 500,000 mono- graphs and serial issues from abroad.	
		B. Utilizes PL 480 funds to acquire books and materials abroad, and is initiating under Title II-C of the Higher Education Act, a worldwide purchasing program, as well as a shared but centralized cataloging program.	$ .3
		C. Cooperates with other countries in establishing acceptable interna- tional bibliographic standards.	
		D. Shares knowledge with other coun- tries concerning application of computer technology to the con- trol of library materials and to information retrieval.	
		E. Administers Jointly-Sponsored Li- brarian Project for the Department of State. Also renders facilitative assistance to more than 300 for- eign librarians annually.	
Peace Corps	Help the peoples of interested countries and areas in meeting their needs for skilled manpower.	While it is not Peace Corps' policy to offer material aid to foreign countries, the following Peace Corps programs help Volunteers in establishing or ex- panding school and community li- braries in the developing countries:	
		A. Booklocker Program—in FY 1967 200 technical booklockers in 125 how-to-do-it titles will be distrib- uted to regional offices and 4,200 booklockers will be distributed to volunteer households to serve as reading materials for Volunteers and as libraries for their local friends and students.	.4
		B. *Peace Corps—USIA Donated Books Program.* In FY 1966 Peace Corps Volunteers distributed 66,- 000 books donated by American publishers to USIA. These books are used to develop the libraries of communities and schools where Volunteers serve.	
		C. *Peace Corps Librarians*—In FY 1966, 13 Volunteers served as full-time librarians in secondary schools and 15 in universities. In addition, a substantial number of Volunteers served as school or	.25

AGENCY	MISSION	INVOLVEMENT IN INTERNATIONAL BOOK AND LIBRARY ACTIVITIES	APPROXI- MATE BUDGET (in millions) LEVEL FOR FY 1966
		community librarians as part of their assignments or in extracurricular projects.	
Smithsonian Institution	Promote the increase and diffusion of knowledge among men.	Two major objectives of the Smithsonian for its international book program are: A. Dissemination abroad of its own published works (100,000 publications were distributed in FY 1966). B. Exchange of current publications with foreign institutions (in FY 1966 the International Exchange Service received approximately 1,388,000 packages of material from over 400 domestic organizations for shipment abroad, some 1.2 million of these going to foreign libraries. About 56,000 packages were received from abroad, about 52,000 from foreign libraries).	$ .200 .114
United States Information Agency	Promote better understanding of U.S. among peoples of the world. Strengthen cooperative international relations.	A. Utilizes all available book production, distribution, and promotion techniques which lend themselves to varying circumstances. Books are caused to be produced in English and translation in standard and simplified texts; in hard covers, paperbound, and serial form; and by any manufacturing process, locally available, which has most practical application to the immediate circumstances. Books are distributed commercially, by donation and presentation to individuals and institutions, and by library loans. Books are promoted by exhibits and displays; by book review publications; by radio, television, and press output; by lectures, discussion forums, and individual conversations; and by stimulating and assisting the development of local production and distribution mechanisms. These techniques are financed by use of appropriated dollars, U.S.-owned foreign currencies, private contributions, and by joint undertakings with book publishers in the U.S. and abroad. B. Supports 223 American libraries and reading rooms in 84 countries and 129 Binational Center Librar-	5.9

ies. In FY 1966, 230,165 American books were purchased and shipped abroad to these libraries.

C. Administers the Information Media Guaranty (IMG) program which guarantees the convertibility of soft currencies for the sale of American books—largely educational—in seven dollar-short countries where markets would otherwise be closed to them.

UNITED STATES DEPARTMENT OF AGRICULTURE INTERNATIONAL INFORMATION ACTIVITIES

Presented by Blanche L. Oliveri before the
Committee on Scientific and Technical Information
Washington, D.C.
July 26, 1967

The statutory authority for information activities of the Department of Agriculture is stated in 5 U.S.C. 511 and 514:

The Secretary of Agriculture shall procure and preserve all information, the general design and duties of which shall be to acquire and diffuse among the people of the United States useful information on subjects connected with Agriculture, in the most general and comprehensive sense of the word. . . .

The Secretary of Agriculture shall procure and preserve all information concerning agriculture which he can obtain by means of books and correspondence, and by practical and scientific experiments, accurate records of which experiments shall be kept in his office, by the collection of statistics, and by any other appropriate means within his power. . . .

The first Commissioner of Agriculture in outlining the primary program for the new department included "Establishing an agricultural library and museum. In this Library the most valuable works would gradually accumulate by exchange, gift, and purchase, forming a rich mine of knowledge."

There are a number of different agencies within the Department of Agriculture which deal with international information activities. The Foreign Agricultural Service disseminates information abroad through its participation in trade centers, trade fair exhibits, and other market development activities, although that part of the information which is scientific and technical is negligible. That Service, as well as the Economic Research Service, prepares reports of USDA studies and surveys which could be extremely helpful to potential investors. The agricultural attachés of United States Embassies are utilized to disseminate information and to procure publications. Every new appointee or attaché on a home visit receives a current indoctrination on the Department's information needs and particularly on the National Agricultural Library's needs and services. In addition, they serve as a reference source for questions or inquiries within less developed countries where published answers to specific questions are not available.

The International Agricultural Development Service has responsibility for general administration and coordination of the Department's responsibilities and activities in foreign assistance and training programs, including those under Sections 301 and 302 of the United States Information and Educational Exchange Act of 1948 (22 U.S.C. 1451–1452); the Foreign Assistance Act of 1961, PL 87–195, as amended by the Foreign Assistance Act of 1963, PL 88–205; and PL 87–256, the mutual Educational and Cultural Exchange Act of 1961; and in developing and maintaining effective relationships with international and U.S. organizations in planning and carrying out such programs. . . .

All agencies of the Department, and particularly the Office of Information which acts as a distribution point for most Department publications, disseminate single copies of Department publications to requestors from abroad. All other requests are referred to the National Agricultural Library.

The Director of the Library serves as the Secretary's agent for carrying out Departmentwide responsibilities relating to Library and science information activities. His authority is outlined in Titles 1 and 2 of the USDA Administrative Regulations.

From the date of its inception, the Library of the Department of Agriculture served as a national library and during the centennial year the Secretary of Agriculture renamed it the National Agricultural Library. In so doing, he implied that the Library exercised international responsibilities even though there is no explicit legislation which directs it to serve persons other than those in the United States.

In the 1965 COSATI Report on International Data Exchange, it was stated:

A review of the scientific and technical information exchange program of the Department of Agriculture revealed an aggressive, well-conceived systematic approach and in some respects a model program for other federal agencies to follow.

As a matter of policy, all USDA publications exchange arrangements with foreign government, organizations or individuals are made by the National Agricultural Library. Material acquired by the Library is in the field of agriculture, biology, and creative sciences. Publications disseminated in the exchange are those issued by the Department of Agriculture. A total of about 200,000 pieces is being sent annually to other countries. The return flow brings the USDA about 216,000 pieces annually; about 18,000 titles are listed.

The Department's Office of Information prepares a subject interest *List of Available Publications,* a list which the National Agricultural Library cites as representative of a series being utilized in the exchange program of USDA. Prominently displayed at the beginning of the list is the statement: No publication issued by the Department of Agriculture will be sent regularly to any foreign government, organization or private agency, unless exchange arrangements have been made by the Director of the National Agricultural Library of the Department of Agriculture. . . .

Hence it is clear that this agency has set up control mechanisms to preclude competitive and duplicative efforts in the Department of Agriculture. Only individual requests for a one-time exchange between authors or an exchange of reprints may be handled outside the framework of formal arrangements.

At the time the above information was written the National Agricultural Library had approximately 7,000 arrangements with foreign organizations for the exchange of publications and information. At the present time we have 9,500. Exchange arrangements are expanded and developed continuously as knowledge about new opportunities is received through correspondence, personal contacts, and examination of bibliographical literature.

In addition to our exchange program, information concerning all publications relating to agriculture and the agricultural sciences is disseminated through the *Bibliography of Agriculture, Pesticides Documentation Bulletin,* and Special Bibliographies. Over 2,000 copies of the *Bibliography of Agriculture* are distributed monthly, about a third of which are sent without cost to foreign sources; 104 foreign institutions or organizations are on the mailing list for the Bulletin with more than 1,200 going to domestic organizations and institutions. Our *Dictionary Catalog* and our *Monthly Catalog* are both published by a commercial publisher, and separate figures for domestic and foreign subscriptions are not currently available.

We lend separates and monographs to foreign libraries in accordance with our interlibrary loan policy and furnish photostat or microfilm copies of articles, etc., in the Library collection through individuals, agencies, firms, and libraries in other countries. A nominal fee is charged for these copies.

Approximately 25 percent of our total paid photocopy business is carried on with foreign organizations or institutions. Orders come from all over the world. A survey of three months' duration made in 1963 revealed that Antarctica was the only continent not using our photocopy service. Our Bee Culture Library also carries on a translations exchange program with the Bee Research Association, Gerrard's Cross, Bucks, England.

The National Agricultural Library cooperates with the Library of Congress in its shared cataloging (Title 2c) and PL 480 Programs and performs training of foreign nationals through the Agency for International Development. We work closely with Food and Agriculture Organization of the United Nations on exchange of publications and information. We establish repository libraries for USDA, land-grant universities, and experiment station publications and assist in the establishment of agriculture libraries in developing nations in cooperation with universities engaged in technical assistance programs.

The Department of Agriculture is represented on the United States National Committee for the International Federation for Documentation by the Director of the National Agricultural Library who has chaired the committee since 1965. Other international organizations with which we work closely are the International Association of Agricultural Librarians and Documentalists, the International Federation of Library Associations, and similar groups. Our Director and other USDA staff members have served as delegates and lecturers to innumerable scientific and professional meetings throughout the world. A representative of the International Agricultural Development Service serves as secretary of the Washington Chapter, Society for International Development, and as Chairman of the International Committee, Agricultural College Editors.

While the Library has no direct access to PL 480 funds, it does utilize the PL 480 translation program centered in the National Science Foundation. We have an item in the 1968 budget requesting PL 480 funds for the specific use of the National Agricultural Library. With the cooperation of the Library of Congress, arrangements have been made with several cooperating university libraries in a program to acquire the agricultural publications for which they have no use. Presently we are arranging with the Library of Congress to share a full set of PL 480 publications acquired by the Library of Congress with the National Library of Medicine and the Center for Research Studies.

At the present time the Library is examining its international responsibilities and expects to apply the knowledge which is developed in evaluating its future international responsibilities and programs.

THE INTER-AMERICAN PROGRAM OF LIBRARY AND BIBLIOGRAPHIC DEVELOPMENT OF THE ORGANIZATION OF AMERICAN STATES: A STATEMENT OF PRINCIPLES AND PRACTICES[40]

I. Guide-Lines for the Program

At no time in history has access to information and knowledge found in printed form been so essential to the resolution of social and economic problems as it is at the present. No problem in Latin America, taken as a whole, is more serious than that of the low educational level of the population and the high rate of illiteracy. The difference between literacy and illiteracy, however, is not merely in knowing how to read, but in reading. To remain functionally literate, both the adult and the child must have reading materials at hand—at his own reading level, and in quantities sufficient to permit him to keep in practice and to encourage him to read.

It is the goal of the Library and Bibliographic Development Program of the Organization of American States to place books and other printed materials within the reach of the peoples of the Americas in their own language, as they are needed, and to carry out essential activities of both general and specific nature in the areas of book production and distribution, bibliographic control, and library services in order to achieve that goal.

Books are an integral part of the life-long educational process. Books (including journals, and other printed materials), both those for general cultural and informational reading and those of a textbook or technical manual nature, are required today at all levels of education from pre-school through university technical training, and advanced study, in the languages of the countries. Social and economic progress follow fast upon an increase in the intellectual level of the population achieved both through formal study in class and in continued seeking for information and knowledge. Conversely, if there is no increase in the intellectual level of the people, social and economic progress cannot be attained. Scientific and technical research and progress, moreover, depend upon availability of the latest information as well as data of an historical nature found in printed sources.

The first specific aim of the Library and Bibliographic Development Program of the OAS is to seek rapid improvement in the book trade in the Americas, to eliminate existing barriers to the free flow of information across hemispheric borders, and to assure the publication and distribution of books in the languages of the countries at the reading level required by the population, as an effective means of assuring the elevation of the intellectual and cultural level of the people.

However, to know what has been published is essential as a basis for determining what should be published in terms of textbooks, technical manuals, reference books, and books for general reading. This calls for improved methods of recording new publications and for increased bibliographic control over what has been and is being published, and where it can be secured either for purchase through a book dealer or for use through a library. The second aim of the Library and Bibliographic Development Program is to seek to achieve adequate bibliographic control of the publishing output of Latin America.

Libraries are found to be the most efficient and economic means thus far devised to make printed materials available to the largest number of people at the least cost. The

[40] *Cuadernos Bibliotecologicos No. 11 (English). (Washington: Pan American Union, General Secretariat, Organization of American States, 1962). UP/0.2, II/III. 11, 1962 (reprinted 1966, with revised list of publications); original: English; limited distribution. This series is prepared in the Columbus Memorial Library, Department of Cultural Affairs, Pan American Union, Washington, D.C. 20006.*

Library and Bibliographic Development Program, as a third aim, encourages the application of methods, procedures, and techniques known to be effective in library organization and services and in all kinds of libraries.

This means that the activities of the program are governed by the problems and needs which are common to the small collections of books for children and young people found in hundreds of thousands of school libraries which either do or should exist, to small and large popular and public libraries which either number or should number in the tens of thousands for services both to the literate population and to barely literate adults and children, to the thousands of libraries which either do or should exist in institutions of higher learning and specialized training, to the potential thousands of research libraries of government agencies, scientific and technical institutions, banks and other commercial and industrial establishments, and to the national libraries and archives guarding the cultural patrimony of their countries, created to render service to entire nations.

The terms of the Act of Bogotá of 1960 specifically point out the need for the improvement of institutions of learning and for immediate attention to the illiteracy problem, and for extended technical assistance on the part of the OAS to aid individual countries in resolving their specific problems in these areas. Institutions of learning cannot be improved and people made functionally literate without books.

II. Activities of the Program

That the improvement and extension of library and bibliographic services in the Americas should be a normal function of the Pan American Union, as secretariat of the OAS, has been reiterated by inter-American conferences and meetings of the Inter-American Cultural Council. A five year work program to meet increasing demands from member states for aid to their libraries, proposed by the Secretary General to the Council of the OAS in 1956, was accepted in principle and translated into work programs as funds permitted since 1958. The activities of the Library and Bibliographic Development Program, although based directly on the recommendations of the Third Meeting of the Inter-American Cultural Council in 1959, take into account subsequent developments, including the call made by the Act of Bogotá and President Kennedy's proposed Alliance for Progress.

The principal continuing activities of the Office of Library Development have not been changed substantially since the inception of an expanded program in 1958. Minor shifts in orientation of some activities have occurred to adjust to past accomplishments and serve newer needs, and to cover these specific yet general aspects: 1) Promotion of the professional training of librarians; 2) advisory services; 3) manuals and technical aids; 4) stimulation of bibliographic compilation and standardization; 5) improvement of the book trade and international exchange of publications; 6) information and documentation services; and 7) promotional and administrative services.

They may be further described in the following terms:

Improvement in Professional Training of Librarians.

To advise and assist member states in giving academic and technical training to librarians, bibliographers, and documentalists, for the purpose of organizing and administrating, in an efficient manner, the school, public, scientific, technical, and research libraries, and to give advanced training to a group of directors and professors in library schools.

Advisory Services.

To give advisory services and technical assistance to member states for the improvement of library services, establishment of national bibliographic, documentation, and exchange centers; to make recommendations in relation to techniques, services, library materials and personnel; to aid member states in analyzing their library and bibliographic needs, and to organize, in accordance with requests from member states, technical missions for the Program of Direct Technical Assistance of the OAS.

Manuals and Technical Aids.

To make available manuals necessary to the Latin American countries for uniform organization and administration of different library systems; to promote adoption of uniform techniques for the efficient organization of libraries, and better cooperation among the same; to encourage the adoption of universally accepted bibliographic standards.

Stimulation of Bibliographic Compilation and Standardization.

To encourage better bibliographic recording of current production of publications, through promotion of compilation and issuance of various kinds of national and international trade bibliographies of commercial and noncommercial publications, lists of current journals, periodicals, official publications, and required periodical indexes; to stimulate national bibliography, current and retrospective; to promote compilation of specialized bibliographies and lists of other reference tools; to offer member states advice and assistance in creation of national bibliographic centers, union catalogs and lists; to work toward hemispheric integrated bibliography through cooperative efforts and aid in training personnel, and to encourage adoption and use of accepted bibliographic standards for these purposes.

Improvement in the Booktrade and International Exchange of Publications.

To promote improved and expanded production and marketing methods of book publishing in the Americas; to stimulate publication and distribution of low-cost editions of children's books, books for new literates, and other publications in the languages of the member states needed for eradicating illiteracy and raising the intellectual level of the peoples; to foster the free flow of publications between the nations of the hemisphere; to encourage ratification of international agreements and to effect necessary inter-American agreements aimed at fostering the free flow of publications, the international exchange of publications, and copyright protection; and to promote the creation of national exchange centers and the legislative and administrative means of effecting exchanges.

Information and Documentation Services.

To obtain those documentation services necessary to inform and provide effective assistance by the OAS for improvement of libraries and bibliographic services in member states; to serve as an information center for specialists in the OAS concerned with the production of books and with libraries; to develop a systematic program of informational publications and coordinate all publications activities of the library development program so as to disseminate information on current trends, techniques, and professional activities in library and bibliographic fields; and to experiment with documentation methods for recording and retrieving information on books, libraries, and bibliography so as to be able to advise other offices of the PAU in maintaining similar services in their fields of specialization.

Promotional and Administrative Services.

To coordinate activities of the library development program and other programs of the OAS aimed at improving library and bibliographic services and booktrade expansion; to collaborate with professional associations, philanthropic foundations and international organizations, as well as government agencies engaged in improving library and related services; to prepare necessary background documents for conferences and organs of the OAS; to promote national planning for library, bibliographic, and documentation services, on school, university, research, government and popular levels.

III. *Objectives of the Library and Bibliographic Development Program*

In general terms, the objectives of the Library and Bibliographic Development Program are, we repeat, to place books and other printed materials within the reach of all the peoples of the Americas, in their own language, as they are needed, and to carry out essential activities of both general and specific nature in the areas of book production and distribution, bibliographic control, and library services in order to achieve this goal. In specific terms, the objectives may be defined as the following:

Through programs of technical advisory and informational services to libraries, bibliographical centers, government and educational authorities and philanthropic foundation officers, through translations and compilation of manuals and other publications required, through provision of advice to member states in library planning and development, and through provision of services for the improvement of library science teaching and the preparation of essential textbooks and other teaching materials, to promote the increase of libraries and the adoption of standard techniques for their efficient organization; to contribute to the professional preparation of librarians, bibliographers, and documentalists; to encourage improved methods of bibliographic control, techniques, and services; and to stimulate publication and more adequate distribution of books needed in the languages of the member states through improvement of the booktrade and the elimination of booktrade barriers.

The degree to which the OAS, in a very few years, has succeeded in its stated objectives to place books and other printed materials within the reach of the peoples of the Americas, would be difficult to measure. It is obvious, however, that no more than a bare start has been made toward reaching the ultimate goal of giving to every citizen of the Americas the chance to read.

[A list of publications appears at this point in the original document.]

NATIONAL POLICY STATEMENT ON INTERNATIONAL BOOK AND LIBRARY ACTIVITIES

In his message to Congress of February 2, 1966, the President said, "Education lies at the heart of every nation's hopes and purposes. It must be at the heart of our international relations." Books, by definition, are essential to education and to the achievement of literacy. They are also essential to communication and understanding among the peoples of the world. It is through books that people communicate in the most lasting form their beliefs, aspirations, cultural achievements, and scientific and technical knowledge.

In the United States and other developed countries, where there has been the opportunity for a long time to emphasize education and books, there have been created vast resources of printed materials and other forms of recorded knowledge in all fields of human endeavor. In the United States, a great complex of library systems has emerged, serving ordinary citizens as well as students and scholars. In the developing countries, where more than two-thirds of the world's population live, there is an acute need for the books essential to educational growth and general social progress, and for libraries which can enable these nations more easily to acquire and use the technology of the modern world. The United States Government declares that it is prepared, as a major policy, to give full and vigorous support to a coordinated effort of public and private organizations which will make more available to the developing countries those book and library resources of the United States which these countries need and desire.

The total needs of the developing countries with regard to books cannot be adequately filled by assistance from the outside; nor, under present conditions, can they be filled from local resources. From a long-range point of view, the establishment of viable book publishing and distributing facilities in the developing countries and regions is essential. It shall therefore also be the policy of the United States Government to encourage and support the establishment of such facilities.

The utility of books goes beyond their contribution to material progress. The free and full exchange of ideas, experiences and information, through books, is indispensable to effective communication between people and nations, and has a unique role to play in the enrichment of the human spirit. Recognizing this, the United States Government is further prepared, as a major policy, actively to promote the free flow of books and other forms of recorded knowledge.

The task of filling the world's need for books and of achieving an adequate exchange of books among the nations is immense. No single institution or agency and no single government can hope to accomplish it alone. It is therefore essential that all agencies of Government concerned in any way with international book and library programs assign to these a high priority. It is further essential that they coordinate their book and library efforts with those of other pertinent government agencies and private institutions. Agencies will propose to the President for transmittal to the Congress any requirements for new legislation or special funds to carry out this policy. All agencies of Government, under the direction of the Department of State, should actively seek to cooperate with other governments on a bilateral or multilateral basis in the achievement of these objectives.

The Assistant Secretary of State for Educational and Cultural Affairs has the responsibility for coordinating United States Government efforts in this field.

1/4/67

DIRECTIVE TO GOVERNMENT AGENCIES FOR IMPLEMENTATION OF THE NATIONAL POLICY STATEMENT ON INTERNATIONAL BOOK AND LIBRARY ACTIVITIES

I. To carry out the foregoing policy, agencies are directed to develop specific courses of action, within the framework of their financial resources and statutory responsibilities, to accomplish the following goals:

A. To ensure that the book and library assistance programs of all federal agencies contribute on a coordinated basis to the broad objectives of educational growth and peaceful progress in the developing countries by such activities as:

(1) assisting in the development of textbooks and supplementary reading materials for indigenous school systems;

(2) expanding programs for distributing and supporting the publication of low-priced editions of American books, including textbooks and source materials, in English and in translation;

(3) establishing, under local auspices, English and indigenous language rental libraries and bookstores for high school and college students;

(4) providing graded reading materials for new literates in local languages or English;

(5) providing books to support the basic professions and trades and the learned disciplines, theoretical and practical;

(6) providing funds and technical assistance to establish viable indigenous book publishing and distributing facilities;

(7) contributing to the development of greater professional competence by increasing the number of exchange and training programs for book publishers, librarians, textbook writers and editors, and persons engaged in related activities;

(8) supporting a program of library development, in cooperation with the U.S. publishing industry, U.S. libraries, library organizations and institutions, to include:

    (a) assistance in adapting to local conditions and needs the most advanced library technology;

    (b) overall "collection development" programs by cooperating institutions in the U.S.;

    (c) counseling on library development;

    (d) sizeable expansion of the present Smithsonian program to provide core libraries overseas with U.S. journals and serial publications;

(9) initiating a major training program for library personnel, to include:

    (a) strengthening of existing national and regional library schools, plus refresher and in-service training and selected work-study training in the U.S.;

    (b) development of additional regional library schools, with provision of scholarship funds;

    (c) instruction in the application of modern technology to library practices.

B. To encourage and directly support the increased distribution abroad of books studying or reflecting the full spectrum of American life and culture by:

    (1) expanding U.S. book "presentation" programs and otherwise facilitating gifts of books abroad;

    (2) encouraging cooperative ventures between U.S. and overseas publishers for the publication of American books abroad, in translations or in inexpensive English-language reprints; and

    (3) increasing the number of American libraries and bookstores overseas.

C. To further a greatly increased inflow of foreign books and materials including journals, microfilms, and reproductions of art, music, folklore, archival and manuscript collections, to U.S. libraries through the use of PL 480, appropriations under Title II-c of the Higher Education Act of 1965 and other funds.

D. To stimulate and support a much more extensive exchange program in books and related materials between U.S. and foreign libraries, museums, educational and research institutions.

E. To encourage closer liaison between American and foreign libraries, greater exchange of reference and bibliographical information, and closer collaboration in the development of information storage and retrieval and computer utilization programs.

F. To support, as appropriate, measures designed to lower or eliminate tariff barriers, exchange restrictions and other impediments to the free flow of books and related educational materials.

G. To provide greater support to the efforts of the U.S. book industry toward the attainment of these goals.

II. The Department of State, in consultation with appropriate agencies, is directed to ensure:

A. That activities of U.S. Government agencies are coordinated in such a way that Government resources will be used with the greatest efficiency and economy.

B. That the actions of the U.S. Government take into account the activities of private institutions and of the American book industry in the international book and library field.

C. That specific actions are tailored to conditions in specific countries or regions.

III. In seeking any new legislation or additional funds, agencies, in consultation with the Department of State, should make appropriate proposals to the President through normal legislative clearances and budgetary channels.

1/4/67

INTERNATIONAL ACTIVITIES OF THE NATIONAL LIBRARY OF MEDICINE

In addition to the comprehensive international functions of the Library of Congress, the two other National Libraries, the National Library of Medicine and the National Agricultural Library, in their respective fields of interest, have developed specialized international programs. Both of these institutions have assumed responsibility historically for the bibliographic management of the literatures of their fields, encompassing the broad areas of acquisition of materials, of cataloging, and of indexing the specialized journal literatures in depth.

Since 1879, the National Library of Medicine has published indexes and bibliographies, international in scope and use. It may be said that by virtue of this long-standing tradition, the medical sciences have been better served bibliographically than any other area of science. The *Index Catalogue* of the Library of the Surgeon General's Office, for example, was a combined book catalog and index which published three million references to the international literature of medicine between 1880 and 1956.

The latest form of this traditional enterprise is the published *Index Medicus,* which is computer-produced and has international usage. MEDLARS (Medical Literature Analysis and Retrieval System), which is used to produce the *Index Medicus,* its cumulation and other indexes, is a large operationally successful system, which serves two purposes: (1) the photocomposition of indexes and catalogs, and (2) the provision of machine searches by subjects. The system now contains 950,000 citations to the international biomedical journal literature, 60 percent of which are from outside the United States. It now accomplishes 400 subject searches monthly.

Through a planned program for decentralizing the search function, the National Library of Medicine is sharing this innovational system with universities in the United States. It is developing plans for a national network of libraries and information centers to utilize nationally the retrieval capabilities of a second-generation MEDLARS system. The implications of the introduction of machine-search technology in the research library community are far reaching.

MEDLARS is in process of becoming an internationally used information retrieval system. The United Kingdom Department of Science and Education has funded MEDLARS functions at the National Lending Library for Science and Technology in Boston Spa, and the University of Newcastle-upon-Tyne, for a three year introductory period. The British system is now operational. The Swedish Medical Research Council has funded a project at the Karolinska Institut in Stockholm, which will provide search services to Scandinavian countries. Two international organizations, the World Health Organization and the Organization for Economic Cooperation and Development (OECD) are in process of training individuals to service European countries and international health purposes. Through sharing responsibility for indexing internationally and providing searches from a tape-store of bibliographic data, MEDLARS has become a prototype of an American system shared internationally to the benefit of world health.

Centralized Cataloging

Since January 1966, the National Library of Medicine has been using MEDLARS to prepare a published bi-weekly *Current Catalog* of books received. This catalog, which cumulates every quarter, is widely used by the medical libraries for both procurement and cataloging purposes. The National Library of Medicine now has taped records of approximately 65,193 titles. Although minor variations between the format of the National Library of Medicine's *Current Catalog* and the Library of Congress' MARC exist, the National Library of Medicine, as it approaches its second-generation system, has indicated its desire to achieve a common cataloging standard for machine systems with the Library of Congress and the National Agricultural Library.

Public Law 480 Programs

Using authority under Public Law 480 (Section 104K as distinguished from Section 104N, utilized by the Library of Congress), the National Library of Medicine has developed international programs involving the creation and production of abstracts, translations, and critical review papers in Israel, Jugoslavia, and Poland. The products of such cooperative programs are distributed through medical libraries to the American health community. These programs exist to improve the communication of foreign research results to the American biomedical community.

International Interlibrary Loans

The National Library of Medicine was a leader among the American research libraries in substituting photocopies of scientific articles for the interlibrary loan of volumes. Historically, it has made no distinction between overseas photo-loan service and domestic. Approximately 15 percent of its 150,000 loans go outside the United States yearly. The indefinite extension of international photo-loan service is detrimental to medical library development in other countries. In the interest of encouraging self-sufficiency, the National Library of Medicine has acted to encourage the development of regional libraries outside the United States. Working with the Pan American Health Organization and the Commonwealth Fund, the National Library of Medicine has assisted in the planning of a Regional Medical Library for South America to be located in São Paulo, Brazil. This Library would serve to backstop libraries in the South American republics, and would reduce the volume of direct services currently provided by the National Library of Medicine.

Cooperation with the Agency for International Development

While lacking authority to engage in direct foreign assistance, the National Library of Medicine cooperates with the Agency for International Development (AID), through provision of services and benefits to institutions and libraries in AID countries and to the staffs of AID missions. These services range from the provision of interlibrary loans, reference, and MEDLARS search services, to consultation in medical library development. In the latter category, for example, the National Library of Medicine staff has participated in a medical library survey in Korea and assistance to the University of Saigon.

Training

The National Library of Medicine for many years has accepted trainees from institutions from outside the United States through both governmental and private international exchange of persons programs.

As MEDLARS becomes increasingly international, requirements for the training of foreign nationals in systems takeover have increased.

APPENDIX F–2

LIBRARY ECONOMICS

by *STANLEY W. BLACK*
Princeton University

A. AN ECONOMIC MODEL OF LIBRARY OPERATION

INTRODUCTION

In recent years economic decisions have made increasing use of mathematical models describing the structure of the problem at issue. With the aid of such models it often becomes possible to determine, to some reasonable degree of approximation, the optimal decision, i.e., the best of the alternatives available to the decision-maker. At least one such model relating to the operation of the libraries has already appeared in the literature.[41] This represented an engineering approach dealing with such particular issues as the average rate of decline in a book's annual circulation as a function of its age and the relation to spatial dispersion of library resources. This appendix deals with some broader issues relating to the overall operation of the library and some of the variables that affect it. In appendix F–2.B, the conclusion of the discussion of the model itself, there are presented some empirical findings which have been derived with its aid. The material presented in appendixes F–2.A, B, and C is supplementary to chapter 5.

The purpose here is to describe briefly and analyze the short-run and long-run characteristics of a simple model of a library. Definitions will be made in such a way that the model can be interpreted as applying either to a public library, a school library, or a college or university library, although the structural parameters will presumably be quite different for these different types of libraries.

The library, regardless of type, is conceived as primarily a producer of "circulation," defined broadly to include in-library use of reference facilities, microfilm, etc. The revenues available to the library are spent on a combination of skilled labor services, purchase of ancillary processing equipment, and the maintenance and expansion of a stock of "books," again defined broadly to include periodicals and microfilm in this simple model.

The librarian chooses the division of his revenues between expenditures on wages and salaries, books and other library materials, and purchase of ancillary equipment in such a way as to maximize circulation subject to the revenue constraint. The analysis produces a supply of circulation function and a shadow price variable which represents the implicit cost of borrowing a book. This cost is essentially the reciprocal of the marginal increase in circulation from an extra dollar of revenue.

A demand for circulation function is also introduced, making demand a function of population served (or number of students served if a school), income per-capita (or total school revenue per student if a school), and the implicit cost of poorer service, faster recall of books, and smaller chance of finding a desired book which result from a lower amount of revenue.

---

41 *See F. F. Leimkuhler, "Systems Analysis in University Libraries,"* College and Research Libraries *(January 1966), pp. 13–8.*

Equating demand to supply, we find the equilibrium implicit cost of borrowing, the revenue which the library must receive to provide the equilibrium level of services, and the equilibrium levels of circulation, labor services, rate of book purchase, and rate of purchase of ancillary equipment. Each of these solutions is in terms of the structural parameters of the model and the exogenous variables: population, income per-capita, wage rate, and book price.

Next it is assumed that each of these exogenous variables grows at some specified constant rate (differing for each variable). Steady growth solutions are then obtained for the rates of growth of revenue, circulation, book stock, and labor input.

The model could be extended to deal with the existence of a constraint on storage space, obsolescence of books, and technical progress in library operation.

With perfect data available, it would be possible to estimate both the parameters of the model and the rate of growth of the exogenous variables. In fact, it appears that some data on the rates of growth are available, but that assumptions may be required for at least some of the parameters of the model.

THE ECONOMIC MODEL

The library is assumed to be able to produce a maximum circulation (C_t) per time period with a given stock of books (B_t), input of labor services (L_t) and processing equipment (V_t). The particular form of the circulation function specifies diminishing marginal productivity to additional amounts of any one input, holding other inputs constant. Increasing returns to scale are expected. Specifically, our circulation function is taken to have the form

(1) $\quad C_t = A \; B_t^\beta \; L_t^\lambda \; V_t^\theta.$

Since only equilibrium growth is being studied here, demand will grow at a constant foreseen rate, and no excess capacity will be kept to satisfy fluctuations in demand. Books are assumed to depreciate at a constant percent δ per unit time, so that the average life of a book is $1/\delta$. The growth rate of the book stock (which is a variable in the growth part of the model) is assumed to be g. Thus the rate of book purchase per unit of time is $(g + \delta) B_t$, providing for both expansion and replacement. The percent rate of purchase of processing equipment is taken as ξ per unit time, so that purchases are ξV_t. The wage rate is w_t, book price q_t, equipment price s_t, and total revenue is R_t. Thus the librarian's job is to maximize (1) subject to the constraint

(2) $\quad w_t L_t + q_t(g + \delta) B_t + s_t \; \xi V_t \leqq R_t$

The maximization is accomplished with the aid of a Lagrange multiplier μ_t, which in the solution equals the partial derivative of C with respect to R. The optimal levels of B, L, and V for given R are

(3) $\quad B_t = \dfrac{\beta}{q_t(g + \delta)} \left(\dfrac{R_t}{\beta + \lambda + \theta} \right)$

(4) $\quad L_t = \dfrac{\lambda}{w_t} \left(\dfrac{R_t}{\beta + \lambda + \theta} \right)$

(5) $\quad V_t = \dfrac{\theta}{\xi s_t} \left(\dfrac{R_t}{\beta + \lambda + \theta} \right).$

The supply of circulation as a function of R is given by substituting (3), (4), and (5) into (1) to get

(6) $\quad C_t = A \left(\dfrac{R_t}{\lambda + \beta + \theta} \right)^{\lambda + \beta + \theta} \left(\dfrac{\beta}{q_t(g + \delta)} \right)^\beta \left(\dfrac{\lambda}{w_t} \right)^\lambda \left(\dfrac{\theta}{\xi s_t} \right)^\theta$

In addition, the value of the Lagrange multiplier μ_t can be obtained from

(7) $\quad \dfrac{C_t}{\mu_t} = \dfrac{R_t}{\lambda + \beta + \theta}$.

Substituting (7) into (6), we obtain the supply of circulation as a function of $1/\mu_t$, which is interpreted as the implicit cost of borrowing a book:

(8) $\quad C_t = A \left(\dfrac{1}{\mu_t}\right)^{\frac{\lambda+\beta+\theta}{1-\lambda-\beta-\theta}} \left(\dfrac{\beta}{q_t(g+\delta)}\right)^{\frac{\beta}{1-\lambda-\beta-\theta}} \left(\dfrac{\lambda}{w_t}\right)^{\frac{\lambda}{1-\lambda-\beta-\theta}} \left(\dfrac{\theta}{\xi s_t}\right)^{\frac{\lambda}{1-\lambda-\beta-\theta}}$

This interpretation can be obtained by noticing that $\partial C/\partial R$ in (6) is equal to μ_t as given in (7). Thus $1/\mu_t$ is the number of dollars it costs to supply an extra unit of circulation per time period.

Demand for Circulation:

It seems clear that the actual level of circulation produced by any library will depend on the interaction of supply conditions and available revenue with demand conditions, even though no market exists to ensure market clearing. It is assumed that higher demand relative to revenue is reflected partly in increased circulation and partly in a higher implicit cost of borrowing, i.e., through lower μ [see equation (7)]. This has the result of lowering demand through a price elasticity term. The demand function is assumed to be of the form

(9) $\quad C_t = A' \ P_t^\epsilon \ y_t^\nu \left(\dfrac{1}{\mu_t}\right)^{-\eta}$,

where P_t is population, y_t is income per capita. The effect of a higher implicit borrowing cost makes itself felt as longer waiting time to obtain a desired book, quicker recall, and other forms of reduced service.

Equilibrium Solution:

By equating (8) and (9) we can solve for the equilibrium implicit borrowing cost as a function of P, y, q, w and s. Substituting back into (9) we find the equilibrium level of circulation C. Then using (7) we determine the revenue per period required to provide the equilibrium amount of service. This solution turns out to be, letting $\phi = \eta + (1-\eta)(\lambda + \beta + \theta)$:

(10) $\quad R_t = (\lambda + \beta + \theta) \ A'^{\frac{1}{\phi}} A^{\frac{\eta-1}{\phi}} P_t^{\frac{\epsilon}{\phi}} y_t^{\frac{\nu}{\phi}} \left(\dfrac{\beta}{q_t(g+\delta)}\right)^{\frac{\beta(\eta-1)}{\phi}} \left(\dfrac{\lambda}{W_t}\right)^{\frac{\lambda(\eta-1)}{\phi}} \left(\dfrac{\theta}{\xi S_t}\right)^{\frac{\theta(\eta-1)}{\phi}}$

Equilibrium Growth:

The relationship between the equilibrium rates of growth of endogenous variables and the exogenous variables is obtained by letting the exogenous variables grow at specified rates and substituting them into (1) to find the required rate of growth of R_t. This amounts to assuming that plans are formed and realized in such a way as to satisfy the equilibrium conditions in every time period along a path of equilibrium growth.

The assumed behavior of exogenous variables is

(11) $\quad \begin{aligned} &P_t = P_o \, e^{\rho t}, \ y_t = y_o \, e^{\gamma t}, \ w_t = w_o \, e^{\omega t}, \\ &q_t = q_o \, e^{\kappa t}, \ s_t = s_o \, e^{\sigma t} \end{aligned}$

The unknown behavior of endogenous variables which will be solved for will be described by

(12) $\quad \begin{aligned} &B_t = B_o \, e^{gt}, \ C_t = C_o \, e^{ht}, \ L_t = L_o \, e^{lt} \\ &V_t = V_o \, e^{\xi t}, \ R_t = R_o \, e^{rt}, \ \dfrac{1}{\mu_t} = \dfrac{1}{\mu_o} \, e^{mt} \end{aligned}$

Inserting these definitions into (10) yields the rate of revenue growth

$$(13) \quad r = \frac{\rho\epsilon + \gamma v + (1 - \eta)(\beta\kappa + \lambda\omega + \theta\sigma)}{\phi}$$

Using (3), (4) and (5) we then find input growth rates

$$(14) \quad g = r - \kappa, \, l = r - \omega, \, \xi = r - \sigma$$

Combining (14) with (1), we get the rate of growth of circulation

$$(15) \quad h = (\beta + \lambda + \theta) r - \beta\kappa - \lambda\omega - \theta\sigma = 1/\phi \, [(\lambda + \beta + \theta)(\rho\epsilon + \gamma v) - \eta(\beta\kappa + \lambda\omega + \theta\sigma)]$$

By (7), the rate of growth of $1/\mu$, the implicit borrowing cost is

$$(16) \quad m = r - h = 1/\phi \, [(1 - \lambda - \beta - \theta)(\rho\epsilon + \gamma v) + \beta\kappa + \lambda\omega + \theta\sigma]$$

A Special Case:

By making a few additional strategic assumptions, the growth path solution we just obtained can be considerably simplified. Let us assume constant returns to scale in the circulation function (1), or $\lambda + \beta + \theta = 1$ and also that the elasticity of demand with respect to population is unity ($\epsilon = 1$). Then we can show that revenues grow at the rate

$$(17) \quad r = \rho + v\gamma + (1 - \eta)(\beta\kappa + \lambda\omega + \theta\sigma)$$

and the implicit cost of borrowing grows at rate

$$(18) \quad m = \beta\kappa + \lambda\omega + \theta\sigma \quad \text{so that (17) is the same as}$$

$$(19) \quad r = \rho + v\gamma + (1 - \eta) m.$$

The rate of growth of circulation becomes

$$(20) \quad h = \rho + v\gamma - \eta m.$$

Results (18)–(20) are exceedingly easy to interpret. The implicit cost of borrowing grows at a weighted average of the rates of increase of wages, and equipment costs. Revenues grow at the rate of population growth plus income elasticity times rate of per-capita income growth plus one minus the price elasicity times the rate of growth of implicit cost of borrowing. Circulation grows at the rate of population growth plus income elasticity times per capita income growth less price elasticity times rate of growth of implicit borrowing cost.

B. STATISTICAL ANALYSIS OF LIBRARY COST AND THE MODEL OF APPENDIX F-2.A

OPERATING COSTS OF PUBLIC LIBRARIES

This section offers an interpretation of public library data in terms of the economic model of libraries described in appendix F–2.A. The data considered here concern libraries in cities of size 50 to 100 thousand and 100 thousand and over, from 1954 to 1959. We are interested in the relation of circulation to the input of books and personnel. Operating costs consist mainly of salary costs and book-purchase costs. These costs are related to circulation through the shadow price concept of the implicit cost of borrowing, which has previously been shown to represent the marginal cost of circulating an extra volume, on an equilibrium growth path.

From 1954 to 1959, the average annual rate of increase of circulation in libraries serving populations of 50,000 and over has been 5 percent per year. Over the same period the book stock of these libraries has grown an average of 2.8 percent per year. Library staff has increased only 2.6 percent per year. These figures clearly imply either substantial increasing returns to scale or technological progress which allows a given circulation figure to be supported with less inputs of books and manpower.

Total operating expenditures rose nearly 7 percent a year over the 1954–59 period, just matching the growth in personal income generated by a 5.1 percent increase in per-capita disposable income and a 1.9 percent a year rise in population. Expenditures have grown this rapidly because of a 3.5 percent to 4 percent rate of increase in book prices and salaries, with salaries perhaps rising a bit faster than book prices. These price and wage increases, when combined with the increases in book stock and labor input cited earlier, accounted for most of the 7 percent of increase in expenditures.

The rate of increase of the implicit cost of borrowing a book was 2 percent a year over the period. This is equivalent to the rate of increase of expenditures per unit of circulation, which is the rate of increase of expenditures (7 percent) less the rate of growth of circulation (5 percent).

On the basis of the 7 percent of total expenditures and the 3.5 percent to 4 percent rate of growth of costs per unit of input, one would expect on a straight Cobb-Douglas model of circulation to have inputs increasing at above 3 percent a year; see equations (3) and (14) of the library model. If, however, embodied technological progress is taking place, this would reduce the expected rate of growth of physical inputs as long as the rate of growth of *effective* labor input or book stock exceeds 3 percent.

RETURNS TO SCALE

Several attempts have been made to estimate the parameters of the assumed "circulation function"

$$C_{it} = A \, B_{it}^{\beta} \, L_{it}^{\lambda} \text{ or } \log C_{it} = \log A + \beta \log B_{it} + \lambda \log L_{it}$$

between circulation (C) and inputs of labor (L) and book stock (B). The subscripts on C_{it} refer to circulation in year t of libraries serving populations of size i. The survey data collected by the United States Office of Education cover the years 1954 to 1962 and libraries serving cities of size 35,000 to 50,000; 50,000 to 100,000; and 100,000 and over, for a total of 20 observations. Table F–2.B.1 below summarizes the results of these efforts.

Equation (3) in Table F–2.B.1 is the logarithmic form of the circulation function above with dummy variables added to reflect two serious changes in definition of the sample. Although the overall fit of the equation as measured by R^2 of .91 is very good, the coefficients of the chief variables of interest, labor input (L) and book stock (B), do not appear to be significantly different from zero. This is indicated by the size of the coefficients being less than their respective standard errors, shown in parentheses below the coefficients. The statistical reason for this result is a high degree of multicollinearity indicated by the correlation of .99 between the two explanatory variables L and B.

The true implications of equation (3) are revealed by dropping either of the two closely related explanatory variables, as is done in equations (1) and (2). Here we find the same overall fit as measured by R^2 and coefficients for either B or L which are over seven times their respective standard errors.

The question which then arises is how are we to interpret these results? It turns out that the correlation of .99 between B and L can be expressed approximately as

$$L = (.2265 \times 10^{-3}) \, B \text{ or } \log L = \log(.2265 \times 10^{-3}) + \log B$$

Substituting the latter equation into equation (3) gives

$$\log C = \text{constant} + \text{dummies} + (1.008 - .066) \log L,$$

so that $1.008 - .066 = .942$ is an estimate of the *sum* of the coefficients $\beta + \lambda$. This is the same sort of result as obtained by assuming log L = constant + log B to begin with and substituting into the logarithmic form of the circulation function to derive an estimating equation such as (1) or (2). In all three equations we are estimating the *sum* of the coefficients $\beta + \lambda$. And in all three cases we come out with point estimates that are not significantly different from unity. Thus the hypothesis of constant returns to scale cannot be rejected.

Having failed to estimate the coefficients β and λ from the regressions above, our next step is to use the cost-minimization equations from the library model to estimate their ratio. This ratio, together with knowledge that the sum of the coefficients is approximately unity, can be used to determine point estimates of the coefficients themselves.

The ratio of the equations minimizing cost with respect to book purchases and labor input is

$$\frac{\beta}{\lambda} = \frac{q(g + \delta)B}{wL} = \frac{\text{book purchase costs}}{\text{wage and salary costs}}$$

For the public library data, the overall average ratio of book purchase costs to wage and salary costs is .216. The average ratio for libraries serving populations of size 100,000 and over is .177, while the averages for size 50,000 to 100,000 and 35,000 to 50,000 were .235 and .261, respectively. There appears to be a clear tendency for books to become more important relative to labor as size decreases. From these data, it is inferred that the ratio $\beta/\lambda = .2$, approximately. This together with $\beta + \lambda = 1$ implies $\beta = .167$, $\lambda = .833$.

TECHNICAL PROGRESS

These estimates can be used to provide a residual estimate of the impact of technical improvements and other factors influencing the efficiency of library service. Let us modify the circulation function to allow for neutral technical change of 100 u percent per year, or

$$C_t = Ae^{ut}B_t^{.167}L_t^{.833}.$$

This implies

$$\log \frac{C_t}{B_t} = \log A + ut + .833 \log \frac{L_t}{B_t}.$$

Now the data show staff per volume owned, L/B, roughly constant from 1954 to 1959 for libraries serving cities of size 50,000 and over. Over the same period circulation per volume owned rose at an average annual rate of 2 percent per year. Thus it appears that $u = .02$ for this period, at least. A 2 percent per year rate of "technical progress" may appear a bit high for public libraries, especially since new techniques must often be embodied in new machines or new personnel who are familiar with the new methods. As a check, another set of assumptions which are not inconsistent with the data imply $\beta + \lambda = 1.2$, $\beta = .2$, $\lambda = 1$, $u = .014$. Thus increasing returns to scale reduce the estimated rate of technical progress to about 1.5 percent per year.

THE DEMAND FUNCTION

It has not been possible to estimate the parameters of the demand function (9) but it is possible that the income and price elasticities both equal unity, on the likely hypothesis that the population elasticity is equal to one. For then the rate of growth of circulation per capita, at 3 percent, should equal the income elasticity times 5 percent less the price elasticity times the 2 percent rate of increase in the implicit cost of borrowing.

An exceedingly shaky projection might be built on this analysis. A reasonable projection of personal income by the Commerce Department suggests that if the unemployment rate is 3.5 percent in 1975, personal income per capita will grow an average of 4.5 percent a year from 1965 to 1975. The Census Bureau's B-Series population projection shows 1.4 percent a year growth over this period. A continued 2 percent increase in unit costs of circulation (i.e., implicit cost of borrowing) together with unitary price and income elasticities would imply a 4 percent rate of growth of circulation, 6 percent growth in expenditures, and only 1.75 percent rates of growth of book stock and labor input. This of course ignores backlogs of unmet needs and considers only equilibrium growth at a given level of service. Notice that expenditures are projected to grow at the same rate as total personal income, 6 percent.

Alternative elasticity assumptions that are also consistent with the 1954–59 record are an income elasticity of 1.2 together with a price elasticity of 1.5 or an income elasticity of .8 and price elasticity of .5. The first of these alternative assumptions yields a forecast for rate of circulation growth of 3.8 percent per year from 1965 to 1975. The second yields a projection of 4 percent a year circulation growth. Thus the projection is not too sensitive to the choice of parameters, but rather reflects the slower projected rate of growth of population and per-capita income.

The implication of these projections appears to be roughly equal rates of growth of personal (and national) income and library expenditures. Given the tax structure, libraries will probably be able to maintain their share of growing income. These conclusions, however, are based on rather shaky data for a relatively short time period.

TABLE   F-2.   B.1

REGRESSION RESULTS: PUBLIC LIBRARIES SERVING CITIES OF SIZE 35–50,000; 50–100,000; 100,000 AND OVER (1954–1962)

(1) $\log C = 10.0 + .027\,D_1 - 7.11\,D_2 + .955 \log L$
    $(1.15)\quad(.24)\qquad(.58)\qquad(.13)$
    $R^2 = .91,\ F_{3,\,16} = 55.7$

(2) $\log C = -1.35 - .100\,D_1 - 7.31\,D_2 + 1.16 \log B$
    $(2.69)\quad(.24)\qquad(.60)\qquad(.16)$
    $R^2 = .91,\ F_{3,\,16} = 55.4$

(3) $\log C = 10.56 + .034\,D_1 - 7.10\,D_2 + 1.008 \log L - .066 \log B$
    $(43.07)\quad(.54)\qquad(.97)\qquad(3.61)\qquad(4.39)$
    $R^2 = .91,\ F_{4,\,15} = 39.1$

CORRELATION MATRIX

	C	D_1	D_2	L	B
C	1.00				
D_1	−.21	1.00			
D_2	−.78	.25	1.00		
L	.23	.06	.36	1.00	
B	.17	.13	.41	.99	1.00

C = Circulation
D_1 = Dummy for 59, 60, and 62 for change in sample and
     addition of county and regional libraries
D_2 = Dummy for 62 for cities of 100,000 and over to allow for
     inclusion of New York Public Library Reference Department
L = Library staff
B = Book stock

C. DESIGN OF THE COLLEGE AND UNIVERSITY LIBRARY SAMPLE AND OTHER DATA SPECIFICATIONS

As already noted, our usable data consisted exclusively of figures relating to public libraries and to college and university libraries. The latter were themselves composed of two series, one, for the years 1960–66, relating to colleges and universities as a whole, and a second longer series constructed by us from a substantial sample of libraries.

The public library data (for cities with a population of 50,000 or more) were obtained from the following two series of pamphlets:

U.S. Department of Health, Education, and Welfare, Office of Education, *Statistics of Public Library Systems in Cities with Populations of 100,000 or more,* and a similar series . . . *In Cities with Populations of 50,000 to 99,999.*

Though there are some data in these fiscal series, from fiscal 1945 through to fiscal 1962, 1954 to fiscal 1959 inclusive were chosen as the basis for this study since

(a) There were changes in sample size after 1959 (to include county and regional libraries and the Reference Department of the New York Public Library).

(b) The data for periods preceding 1954 were later "updated" to make them comparable to the post–1954 data.

(c) The first substantial data available for both population breakdowns were for Fiscal 1954 (for the smaller population categories comparable data are not present until even later years).

The figures for total all college and university libraries appear in the American Library Association, *Library Statistics of Colleges and Universities, 1965–66, Institutional Data,* 1967, pp. 6–9. These data (for 1959–60 to 1964–65) were compiled by Theodore Samore for U.S. Office of Education, *Library Statistics of Colleges and Universities. Institutional Data.*

The sample of colleges and universities was chosen in accord with statistical principles designed to assure a representative and relatively reliable breakdown of expenditure figures.[42] Thus large institutions are sampled heavily to minimize sampling error arising from the large variance in expenditure breakdowns between institutions. Liberal arts colleges were sampled heavily because of their large numbers. The sample size chosen was one hundred institutions reporting to the Association of College and Research Libraries (ACRL), from which data were obtained for the nine years from 1950 to 1959. An additional five years was added from the Federal Government and ACRL publications from 1960 to 1966 (excluding 1965).

The proportions in the last column of Table F-2. C.1 were chosen on the basis of the relative size of libraries shown in column 3 and their relative numerical importance given in column 2. This was done on the grounds that the standard deviation of operating expenditures is likely to be proportional to the size of institution.

---

[42] *The college and university library sample for the fiscal years 1951 to 1959 was taken from a series of statistical studies conducted by the statistics committee of the Association of College and Research Libraries of the American Library Association and published annually in the January issues of the* College and Research Libraries.

The data for the years, 1959–60 to 1964–65 were derived from a series of annual surveys, U.S. Department of Health, Education, and Welfare, Office of Education Library Statistics of Colleges and Universities, *Part 1,* Institutional Data.

The data for 1966 were obtained from the continuation of this series by the American Library Association, Library Statistics of Colleges and Universities, 1965–66, *Institutional Data, 1967.*

The actual institutions sampled were chosen with the aid of a random number table from the 1950 list of schools reporting to the ACRL. Replacements were chosen for schools that dropped out of the sample. Since the sample size varies between about 75 and 100 because of reporting variations, no meaningful total figures can be derived from the sample. It is thought, however, that for the aggregate of colleges and universities the sample will give useful information on the breakdown of expenditures, expenditures per student, and expenditures per unit of input.

As a quick check on the accuracy of our sample of colleges and universities, we compared our results for 1960 to 1966 (on a per-unit input basis) to those of the American Library Association (ALA). The ALA, during these same years, published not only institutional but aggregate data for all college and university libraries in the continental and outlying United States. This comparison gave us further confidence in our results, as Table F-2. C.2 illustrates.

TABLE   F-2.   C.1

CONSTRUCTION OF SAMPLE

TYPE OF SCHOOL	NO. OF SCHOOLS IN 1960 UNIVERSE	APPROX. % OF TOTAL NO.	1960 MEAN OPER. EXPEND.	SAMPLE PROPORTION
University	150	10	680	42
College	760	47	160	47
Teachers college	195	12	83	6
Technical inst.	53			
Junior college	526	31	25	5
		100		100

TABLE   F-2.   C.2

COMPARISON OF SAMPLE OF 100 COLLEGES AND UNIVERSITIES
VS
TOTAL ALL COLLEGES AND UNIVERSITIES

ITEM	1960		1961		1962	
	SAMPLE OF 100	TOTAL ALL	SAMPLE OF 100	TOTAL ALL	SAMPLE OF 100	TOTAL ALL
Total exp./vol. owned	.752	.777	.864	.840	.872	.913
Exp. for salary & wages per vol. owned*	.473	.476	.498	.516	.532	.553
Exp. for books & material per vol. owned*	.203	.231	.244	.256	.254	.280

ITEM	1963		1964		1965	1966	
	SAMPLE OF 100	TOTAL ALL	SAMPLE OF 100	TOTAL ALL	TOTAL ALL	SAMPLE OF 100	TOTAL ALL
Total exp./vol. owned	.937	.991	1.031	1.084	1.141	1.225	1.208
Exp. for salary & wages per vol. owned*	.563	.605	.603	.639	.660	.705	.674
Exp. for books & material per vol. owned*	.288	.302	.309	.348	.378	.387	.419

* For our sample of 100 college and university libraries:
Exp. for salaries and wages includes staff salaries and student salaries.
Exp. for books & material covers only books.

APPENDIX F–3

LIBRARY TECHNOLOGY

A. MACHINE-READABLE CATALOG COSTS

In this appendix to section A of chapter 7, we shall assume a computing system with 12 tape drives operating at 90,000 characters per second and with a relatively slow memory of about 300,000 8-bit characters. On-line secondary storage is not required. (An IBM 360/40 with these characteristics would cost about $3 per minute during the prime shift, including operators and air-conditioned space.)

We shall also assume that the catalog consists of five million cards of 300 characters each. These are stored on 80 reels of magnetic tape with 60,000 cards per reel. Thus each reel contains about 18 million characters. (We have assumed a 2,400-foot reel packed at 800 characters per inch with a packing efficiency of about 80 percent.) Since the cost of a reel is about $60, the total cost of the magnetic tape is about $5,000.

Since a pass over one 2,400-foot reel at a rate of 112 inches per second takes 4 minutes and costs about $12, a pass over the entire catalog would take about 5 hours and cost about $1,000.

A union catalog is simply a merging of its constituent catalogs. We assume that most of the decisions about whether two cards represent the same document can be made by a sophisticated computer program, so that expert human handling of the remaining difficult cases would not be unduly burdensome. If the number of libraries in the union is less than 10 (which we assume to be the maximum available merge ratio), then a single merge pass will suffice and the cost will be $12 for each reel of the union catalog.

To sort the catalog, we first sort each reel separately and then merge. The time required to sort a single reel is essentially four times the time required to read or write it; the cost would be about $48. In our example two merge passes would be required, each occupying 4 minutes per reel and costing $12 per reel. Thus the total time for sorting and merging would be 24 minutes per reel, and the total cost would be $72 per reel. For a much smaller catalog (less than 10 reels), one merge pass would suffice, and the cost would be $60 per reel. For a larger catalog (more than 100 reels) three merge passes would be required, and the cost would be $84 per reel.

For microform publication, we have taken estimates for the Stromberg-Carlson 4060 microfilm printer. It has a font of about 100 characters including both upper and lower case roman letters. The font can be produced in four sizes at rates varying from 30,000 to 90,000 characters per second. Special characters not in the font can also be drawn directly from digital descriptions of their shape. Thus the machine can accommodate the odd symbols which occasionally occur and can accommodate foreign alphabets. Assuming a speed of 50,000 characters per second, about 10 hours of printer time would be required to make a microfilm copy of the catalog.

Assuming 200 card images per foot of 16mm microfilm, about 30,000 feet are needed for the catalog. This presents material at about a 20:1 reduction. At $5 per hundred feet cost for processed microfilm, the film cost is $1,500.

For a paper copy, we assumed a density of 40 cards per page and a reproduction cost of 3 cents per page.

These estimates can easily be incorrect by a factor of 2. We doubt that more accurate predictions are possible.

MAX V. MATHEWS AND W. STANLEY BROWN

B. STUDY PARTICIPANTS

THE EDUCATIONAL FACILITIES LABORATORIES CONFERENCE

(See section B of chapter 7)

Baker, William O. *Vice President for Research, Bell Telephone Laboratories*
Blackburn, Robert *Chief Librarian, University of Toronto*
DeGennaro, Richard *Associate Librarian for Systems Development, Harvard University*
Ellsworth, Ralph *Director of Libraries, University of Colorado*
Fussler, Herman *Director, the University of Chicago Library*
Gores, Harold B. *President, Educational Facilities Laboratories*
Hayes, Robert M. *Director, Institute for Library Research, University of California at Los Angeles*
King, Jonathan *Vice President and Treasurer, Educational Facilities Laboratories*
Licklider, J. C. R. *Consultant to Director of Research, Thomas J. Watson Research Center of IBM at Yorktown Heights, New York*
Lowry, W. K. *Manager of Technical Information Libraries, Bell Telephone Laboratories*
Mason, Ellsworth *Director, Hofstra University Library*
Mathews, M. V. *Director, Behavioral Research Laboratory, Bell Telephone Laboratories*
Netsch, Walter A., Jr. *Skidmore, Owings & Merrill, architects, Chicago*
Rooney, Walter J., Jr. *Curtis and Davis, architects, New York*
Singer, Ira *Assistant Superintendent, West Hartford Public Schools*
Swinburne, Herbert H. *Nolen, Swinburne and Associates, architects, Philadelphia*
Toan, Danforth *Warner, Burns, Toan and Lunde, architects, New York*
Ulveling, Ralph A. *Director, Detroit Public Library*
Weinstock, Ruth *Research Associate, Educational Facilities Laboratories*

THE SYSTEM DEVELOPMENT CORPORATION REPORT TEAM

The report appearing in section C of chapter 7 was prepared by members of the Information Systems Technology Staff, with the assistance of other System Development Corporation staff members. Chief contributors to the report were:

Donald Black
Harold Borko
Carlos A. Cuadra (Principal Investigator)
Ann W. Luke (Research and Technology Division)
Jules Mersel
Frances Neeland
David R. Pascale
Arthur Teplitz (Defense Systems Division)
Robert F. Von Buelow (Research and Technology Division)
Everett M. Wallace

The report team had the benefit of guidance and criticism from a Monitoring Committee appointed by the Commission, as well as from a number of other interested colleagues. Such assistance is gratefully acknowledged.

C. SUPPLEMENTARY MATERIAL FROM THE SDC REPORT[43]

COMPUTER TECHNOLOGY RELATED TO THE LIBRARY
Computer Systems

Within a short span of fifteen years, intensive development work has brought about truly amazing increases in capacity and decreases in cost for computer systems. An extremely wide range of computers and associated equipment is now available, with various configurations spanning a purchase range from $6,000 to $10,000,000.

This section briefly reviews the status of computer technology as related to library systems, highlights particularly important trends in such technology, and provides a prognostication of the state of the art in five to ten years.

A computer system consists of hardware (the equipment) and software (the programs and instructions). The earlier computers had much less hardware capability than those being marketed today, and with additional software, could perform many of the same tasks now being performed primarily by hardware. Supplying these capabilities in the form of hardware adds to the speed of operation, and thus reduces the cost of operating the computer, though it raises initial costs of hardware.

The hardware of the computer consists of five segments (see Figure F–3.C.1): (1) central processing units; (2) main memories; (3) mass memories; (4) peripheral (input/output) devices; and (5) terminal devices. Each of these is discussed below.

Central Processing Units

The central processing unit (CPU) is that portion of the computer complex that actually processes the information, e.g., performs computations, comparisons, etc. The amount of computational capability built into the CPU involves an engineering compromise between two alternatives: (1) giving the computer user something inexpensive, but requiring him to expend a large amount of effort to use it, and (2) providing him with a more complex and expensive machine that requires him to expend less effort to use it for those applications for which it is intended. Capabilities that are not built directly into the CPU must be provided by computer programs.

Most CPUs have been built for problems of scientific computation or business-data processing, rather than for problems of library automation. Nevertheless, these units are more than adequate to handle any of the problems of library data processing. The barriers that stand in the way of library automation are not technical inadequacy of the CPU, but price, lack of adequate software, too little peripheral memory capacity, or limitations in the input/output equipment.

In addition to being able to operate very rapidly, present-day CPUs have a number of features that make them more adaptable to library automation than their predecessors. A particularly important feature, increasingly common in today's CPUs, is the external interrupt capability. With this feature, external devices such as the teletypewriter can cause the central processor to suspend its operation momentarily to read a character, and then return to its previous operation. A multiplicity of terminals can thus be operated simultaneously in this fashion by a large number of persons, each using the

[43] *Appendix F-3. C is supplement to section C of chapter 7. This material was prepared in November 1967 by the System Development Corporation report team.*

FIGURE F–3.C.1

MAIN COMPONENTS OF A COMPUTER SYSTEM

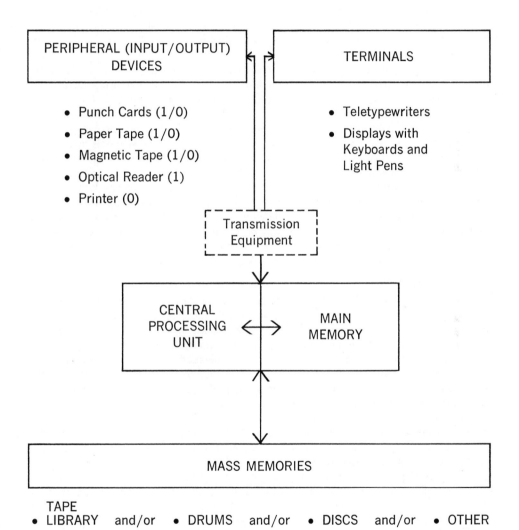

computing capability and the data files of a centralized system in his own particular way. Such multiple use is known as time-sharing.

Another important feature of present-day CPUs, necessary for time-sharing, is called memory protection. With this feature, each of the many simultaneous users can operate with the assurance that another user cannot alter, or even read, his program, if the latter is a consideration. This feature can be extended to protect data as well, and lends itself to systems that can operate with sensitive or classified information.

Main Memories

Computer storage (memory) includes a wide range of storage media that differ in the relative speed and ease with which the CPU can obtain information from them. The fastest, most easily accessible, and most expensive storage is called main memory or internal memory.[44]

A large percentage of present-day main memories are made of arrays of magnetic cores. Within the past fifteen years, with improvements in manufacturing techniques, core memories have increased in speed from a 10-microsecond cycle time for performing one operation to a 1-microsecond cycle time. During the same period, the cost has dropped from over $1 per bit to the present approximately 25¢ per bit, and it is not unreasonable to expect cost to decrease to only a penny a bit.[45] Since a typical large computer may have from one- to five-million bits of main memory, this is an important factor in the overall cost of the system.

It is doubtful that another order of magnitude in speed improvement will occur in core memories in the next decade. Other types of main memory devices are emerging, including thin films, integrated circuits, plated wire, laminated ferrites, cryogenic devices, and others. It is difficult to say which will be the most successful. Most of the newer types are more expensive than cores, but have a speed advantage. However, even today's *internal* storage is generally adequate for handling library problems.

Mass Memories

Mass memory—or bulk storage devices—provide large stores of accessible data for computer systems. Present-day memories of this category include magnetic drums, discs, and various forms of magnetic tape. Some of these can store up to 10^{12} bits, at a fraction of the cost of core memory storage.[46] The penalty for this greater capacity and lower cost is time. Information generally has to be read from external storage into internal storage before it can be handled by the CPU. External storage requires milliseconds for access, rather then microseconds (as in the case of core memories).

Magnetic tapes are considered here as falling into the category of mass storage devices. However, their use as such is decreasing year by year as faster-access storage such as drums and discs becomes larger and cheaper. Magnetic tape was the first form of computer storage. It has many advantages, perhaps the foremost being that it is the least expensive of the many forms of storage. It is also easy to store; the only limit is that of space required to maintain the reels in a library-like stack. In addition, magnetic tape (as well as the punched card) has the virtue of almost universal readability by a multitude of different machines. Where readability is not directly possible, it is usually easy to translate from the form required by one machine to the form required by another.

[44] *"Memory" and "storage" are used interchangeably here.*
[45] *Bit stands for "binary digit," the elementary unit of information stored and processed by a computer. Ordinarily, six bits are required to represent one character or symbol, if the number of symbols is limited to 64.*
[46] *This is the file size mentioned in the King report in connection with cataloging the information at the Library of Congress. It is the equivalent of 40,000 reels of magnetic tape, or 33 billion English words. (Hereafter storage capacities and costs will be discussed in terms of English words rather than bits. The arbitrary but reasonable rule will be followed that 30 bits = one word in binary form, not binary coded decimal.)*

The main disadvantage of magnetic tape is its relatively slow speed. Even if the tape is already mounted on one of the tape-handling devices associated with the computer, one has to wait for the tape wheels to rotate so that the desired portion of information is in position to be read by the computer.

Up to five minutes may be required to pass from beginning to end of a tape. Often one must wait for location of the tape and manual placement of the tape on the machine. In spite of such limitations, magnetic tape is still considered so versatile that almost all computer systems provide for a number of tape drives. Thus, it is likely that magnetic tape will remain the major backup storage for the large amount of information that is required for library operation.

Present-day tapes have recording densities over fifty words per inch, and a typical 2,400-foot tape can hold the equivalent of over one million English words. This data can be transferred at a rate of about 50,000 words per second. Both density and speed will probably double within ten years. The present cost of tape storage is only about .015 cents per word, which is far cheaper than discs or drums.[47] If the user can tolerate the relatively slow access time, which may be as high as several minutes, magnetic tape is the medium to use.

Drum storage has been in use almost as long as tape storage. Magnetic drums were originally used as internal storage on the earlier computers and some inexpensive computers still use them.

Drum storage has the advantage of requiring a much smaller access time than tape. The fastest drums have an access time of less than .01 seconds and can transfer words at virtually the same rate as core memory. One generally never needs to wait longer than one drum revolution in order to get the data that are required.

Drum storage is, in one sense, a compromise between main memory storage and tape storage. Drum capacity (up to 333,000 words) is smaller than tape capacity, but greater than that of main memories. The access time is slower than main memories, but faster than tape. Storage cost is on the order of 3¢ per word, far less than core storage but greater than tape.

One deficiency that drum storage has in comparison to tape storage is that the device itself cannot be disconnected from the computer: drum storage stays with the computer and presumably has its information removed when the next problem or task is run. However, drums are seeing substantial use in time-sharing computers and will undoubtedly continue to be important for some time.

Use of magnetic discs for storage came next in the development of computer storage media. The disc device looks somewhat like a jukebox, with many discs contained in a stack. The amount of time to get information from a disc is roughly the same as that for getting it from a drum, once the desired disc is accessed by a reading head. In general, discs have slower access than drums because one may have to wait for the reading head to be applied to the proper disc. (Some machines reduce this problem by having more than one reading head available.) Discs make a good compromise between drums and tapes, both in terms of capacity and speed. The cost for storage is roughly the same as that of drums (about 3¢ per word). It is unlikely that this cost will ever drop to that of magnetic tapes (.015¢ per word).

A recent development in discs gives them a much greater advantage over the original disc-like external storages. This is the development of the disc pack, which allows a small group of discs to be removed from the computer in the same way that a magnetic tape can be removed. Thus, the advantage of nonserial accessibility of the disc is married

---

[47] *Evaluating the cost per bit of magnetic tape is difficult. One reel of magnetic tape costs only $25, but the tape drive and part of the controller must also be amortized, and the access time must be considered. If access is restricted to a mounted reel (resulting in an access time of several milliseconds to three or four minutes), one cost will be derived. If access time were five or six minutes, which would include mounting a reel, the apparent cost would drop by two or three orders of magnitude. The former case has been considered here.*

to the advantage of being able to remove discs when the machine is to be used for other purposes. In fact, many new computer systems have been sold without tape-handling capability at all, with total reliance on disc packs. The disc pack will be important for holding the generally changing data required for the operation of libraries.

Other forms of mass memory are being developed or produced. One type that has the highest capacity, and lowest cost per stored word, is the "photoscopic" disc, which is a photographic, read-only memory. These devices, with capacities up to 33 billion words, could be generally available in the next few years at a cost of about .03 cents per word. Since they are not magnetic, updating a disc is a photocopying operation and takes longer than updating a magnetic drum or disc—minutes rather than seconds. However, photoscopic discs are ideally suited to operations involving a relatively stable kind of information, such as dictionaries or authority files that must be consulted frequently. Libraries have many such files.

Research and development are continuing on associative, or "content-addressable," memories. If economical associative memories could be developed, they would have important applications in libraries, where the retrieval of entries could be based on coincidence of a part of an input or query pattern with a part of the stored reference patterns. Associative memories are still in the laboratory stage, and it seems unlikely that adequately large ones will be available within the next five to ten years.

Peripheral (Input/Output) Devices

The punched card—a popular storage medium in the precomputer era of electric accounting machinery—continues to be the main input for some kinds of data. It has some advantages over other types of input which may never be overcome. One of the chief ones is that a small portion of a program or set of data may be added, deleted, or changed conveniently.

On the other hand, punched-card equipment is extremely slow for input and output to a computer. Thus, it is inadequate for handling large quantities of data. In addition, most punched-card equipment provides for only 64 characters. This tends to suppress the type of information that is carried by different type fonts in libraries. The distinction between upper case and lower case is usually lost. Some punched-card machines will handle larger character sets, but these are generally available only on special order.

Paper tape has long been used in communications and has found good use as a cheap input/output medium in computer systems. Many of the smaller computers have used this as the prime means for entering programs. Punched paper tape overcomes some of the drawbacks of the punched card. It is usually created on a typewriter-like device and can repersent the full set of characters found on typewriters. The ease of keyboarding and of inputting paper tape to the machine is comparable to that of punched cards, and on output, one gets typescript with the full range of typewriter characters.

Paper-tape readers and punches can be associated with (and even interchanged with) teletypewriter keyboard-printer devices. They are able to transmit messages rapidly and accurately, and they can store messages and send them on request of the computers to which they are attached. Use of paper tape as an input device will probably increase as time-sharing terminals become more prevalent.

Paper-tape output is quite slow, because it is character-by-character, rather than card-by-card (as with punched cards) or line-by-line (as with computer line-printer). It is fragile, compared to cards, and also relatively difficult to search. Since it is a serial medium, one may have to scan the entire tape, character by character, to find a particular item. In this respect, it is much less satisfactory than a properly arranged file of punched cards.

Magnetic tape has been referred to above as a form of external storage for the computer. It also lends itself naturally to being an input/output medium. Since the early 1950's, there have been devices for keyboarding information directly onto magnetic tape. Such devices are as easy to use as punched paper tape for purpose of input. In addition, magnetic tape has been the natural form of output from computers for many years. Some high-speed printing devices work directly from magnetic tape. High-speed typesetting is possible from magnetic tape, e.g., devices produced by Photon, Mergenthaler, etc.

Another class of input/output equipment includes the typewriter or typewriter-like devices. These are discussed below under terminal devices, since they are particularly adaptable to an on-line mode of operation.

Optical readers are rather specialized computer input devices, intended primarily for preparing massive amounts of text for computer processing.

Many of the speculations on future library automation involve the assumption that there would be a computer-readable version of the text of documents. Since early language-processing research required little text, most researchers were content to have material keypunched for the computer, at about 1 cent per English word. This would be very expensive, of course, for large-scale conversion of library holdings. Calculations showed that few, if any, of the developments in large-scale information processing would reach the point of economic feasibility unless a much less expensive technique was discovered for putting already printed text into computer-readable form. This conclusion led to the development of the optical reader, or, as it is sometime called, the optical scanner.

Optical readers scan pages of print and write what has been read onto magnetic tape, punched cards, or directly into the computer memory. Current readers have widely varying capabilities and prices. Some that sense marks (not characters) cost about $20,000. Others that can sense a variety of fonts, and even a limited amount of handwriting, cost from $200,000 to $500,000.

Considerable progress is being made in optical-scanner technology. Ten years ago the only fonts that could be read were highly stylized and, although readable by people, unnatural in appearance. Later advances allowed optical character readers to read a few typewriter fonts, and at present some character readers can read several fonts, printed or typed, with high speed, accuracy, and economy, provided there is unsmudged text on clean paper, properly placed. Although there are predictions that in ten years almost any document will be readable by machine, general-purpose text readers will probably not be available that soon.

The optical scanning technique is useful as a substitute for keypunching, and it will probably be more so for libraries or other organizations that either have a sufficient volume of suitably prepared information to be able to afford their own optical character reader, or can conveniently send the material to a service bureau. Keyboarding could be done on ordinary typewriters (with a standardized typeset) by people trained as typists, instead of being done on more expensive punched-card, paper-tape, or magnetic-tape equipment. It is unlikely, however that it will be useful or economical to libraries as a technique for reading the bulk of present holdings, even if that were desirable.[48]

The high-speed line printer is the usual means of printing output from a computer. Such printers operate at over 1,200 lines per minute, each line of which can be over 130 characters wide. The quality of print turned out by high-speed printers is usually poorer than that produced by typewriters, and it is considerably poorer than the quality of any formally printed material. In part, this lack of quality stems from the fact that most printers are only equipped to turn out upper-case letters, numerals, and a few special

---

[48] *The ideal situation is one in which keyboarding is done only once for any given item. Since the publisher of a book or report must keyboard it, it would be a great convenience to have a machine-readable output of that keyboarding. Even without machine-readable tapes or optical readers, a few libraries are attempting to make one keyboarding serve several purposes, e.g., order preparation, in-process lists, catalog and production, circulation control, etc.*

characters. Printers with both upper- and lower-case letters have become available, but all of them are somewhat slower than the equivalent standard upper-case-only printers.

Terminal Devices

The previous section was concerned with input/output equipment used in an "off-line" manner. In the off-line approach to the use of the computer, human interaction with the machine is foregone in order not to slow down waiting for the much slower-reacting human. The devices discussed here are intended for use in situations where the man and the machine interact in real time. Since the matter of data transmission is closely related to the use of terminals, it will be touched on briefly here.

For many years now, there has been interest in providing techniques for human interaction with the computer while it is operating. Current techniques attempt to preserve some element of the computer's great speed by having many persons coupled to the computer at the same time. Two general classes of equipment are currently being used. One is the relatively inexpensive typewriter-like device. The other is the much more expensive and sophisticated console with a cathode-ray tube.

The most commonly used terminals are keyboard devices, e.g., typewriters. The input rate depends on the user's skill, which is well within the 14.8 characters per second allowed by the transmission line. Output is likewise limited, but there are lines that allow transmission at more than 14.8 characters per second. In that case, output speed is limited by the terminal, which is commonly about 10 characters per second (approximately 100 words per minute), although there are special terminals that will accept about 20 characters per second.

There are a variety of modems (modulator-demodulators) available for coupling teletypewriter terminals to telephone lines. The most common are those provided by the telephone companies themselves. Another device, which has come into popularity within the last year, is the audiocoupler. This permits the connection of a teletypewriter to a computer via telephone. The main advantage of this technique is that the device is portable. It is not yet as reliable, however, as a permanent connection via data set (input/output interfaces between telephone lines and the computer or terminal). The pushbutton on a touch-tone telephone is also seeing some use for input to a computer.

Terminals may be connected to a computer either by leased line or by a dial-up service. With a leased line, the connection is always available and the quality of transmission is likely to be somewhat better. The dial-up service is more economical, unless the terminal has a very high usage factor. For example, a leased line across the country for a teletype would cost about $3000 per month. A dial-up service would have to be used over 100 hours a month to cost an equivalent amount.

One of the advantages of typewriter-type equipment is that it is relatively inexpensive. The cheapest send-receive teletypewriter (Model 33) can be purchased for $470, a price that is not likely to change drastically in the next few years. Other keyboard-type terminals (not common-carrier) cost up to $3,000. Another advantage is that typewriter-like devices require little training in their use. Also, they can be located thousands of miles or even a continent away from the computer. The low-capacity lines needed to use the teletype have already been installed for other (commercial) reasons. The primary disadvantages have to do with output. Speed is limited because of the mechanical slowness of a one-stroke-at-a-time device, and the variety of output is restricted to those characters found on typewriters or teletypewriters.

The next most common type of man-machine interactive terminal is the cathode-ray-tube (CRT) display console. CRTs can be divided into two categories, based on vastly different prices and capabilities.

The cheaper CRTs are relatively small devices—about the size of a 14-inch TV—with an alphanumeric keyboard and perhaps some other control buttons. The keyboards function much the same as typewriter keyboards, providing direct input to the computer or causing a character to be displayed on the face of the CRT, or both. Some consoles have considerable editing capability, permitting a message to be composed and displayed, enlarged, shortened, altered, rearranged, etc., before it is transmitted to the computer.

The display usually allows only alphanumeric characters, but some of the terminals have a limited graphic capability, permitting the display of bar charts and the like. A typical number of displayed characters is 1,000 per display controller. Each controller can drive a number of CRTs, and the 1,000 characters are divided equally among the consoles. The quality of the image is poorer than the printed quality received through a teletypewriter. One compensation for this reduction of quality is the fact that a full screen of print can be placed in front of the user almost instantaneously.

Most of these consoles are made to operate remotely from the central computer, but at each remote site a display controller device is required. Since these controllers are made to drive a number of terminals, the cost of any isolated terminal must also include a controller. Considering a system where controllers are adequately utilized, this class of display console (with its amortized share of the controller) costs about $6,000 to $7,000.

Much work is being done on the development of cheaper CRT terminals, and by the end of the next decade they should be down to the price of a commercial TV set. Another approach in reducing the cost of a CRT terminal is the development of a communication method whereby the display controller can be centrally located, or the development of a practical storage tube that does not require continuous transmission of data (as does TV).

Present-day communication links for display consoles of this type can use telephone lines of voice-grade quality. Here again, a variety of data sets are available. The most popular of these are products of the common carriers. Private lines having an adequate bandwidth (e.g., send 300–400 characters per second) cost about twice as much as telegraph lines. Dial-up service closely approximates that of telegraph (teletype), i.e., a transmission speed of 14.8 characters per second. Although these speeds are likely to increase, they will not approach the speeds of dedicated lines.

The more sophisticated consoles in the second group cost from $25,000 to $200,000 apiece. These devices have larger tubes (19 to 23 inches) and can present more data. They have curve-drawing and other graphic capabilities, and have light pens that can be used as switches (triggered by displayed data) or as pens for drawing curves on the CRT, plus numerous other characteristics. Some of the more elaborate display consoles have the capability of mixing computer-generated data with rear-projected slide or film-strip images. These may even be in color.

No attempt to locate these consoles remotely from the computer has been made, except experimentally. Effective use of this kind of console requires a high rate of information transfer between console and computer, and common practice has been to limit the distance to one or two thousand feet. For longer distances, microwave links or video cables—with their inherently high costs—must be used to provide connection lines with sufficient bandwidth. An alternative is to use a small peripheral processor at the remote site and communicate between processors with a slower and less expensive channel (2 KC may well be adequate).

Another type of output terminal that has seen some limited use and has shown promise for application is the audio response unit. Designs range from devices that store a limited number of words to those that synthesize output messages from a stored vocabulary of words, or even synthesize words from stored phonemes. (This latter device is not commercially available.) A typical device can hold over 60 individual message segments of 1.6 seconds duration. This is probably inadequate to synthesize the variety of messages most library systems might require. Another audio response device has a vocabulary of 127 words; still another provides for a large vocabulary to be stored in "digitally coded voice." The latter system requires a million bits to store 750 words. Both of these devices are quite expensive—in the $30,000 to $50,000 range.

One manufacturer has developed a family of equipment that permits converting pictures to digital data and transmitting them to a computer. The reverse process is also possible, i.e., synthesizing a picture from digital data transmitted from a computer. The major advantage of this system is the speed with which it operates. It will, for example, allow transmission of printed material in 8-point or larger type at a rate of about 10 quarto pages per minute. Without involving the computer, the device could convert, transmit, and reproduce text at an acceptable rate over a moderately priced transmission line, such as Telpak A.

PROCEDURAL TECHNOLOGY RELATED TO THE LIBRARY

Introduction

There are a number of applications of data-processing equipment that are much more dependent on the solution of conceptual problems than on hardware. We will refer to this group of applications as "procedural technology," to distinguish them from the kinds of technology discussed elsewhere in Appendix F–3.C. It is important to note that even though the equipment and procedural technologies are necessarily interrelated, they do not necessarily develop at the same rate.

Most of the procedural technologies discussed in this appendix are computer-oriented, although a great many manual and mechanical techniques are also utilized to make specific library operations more efficient. They include photographic systems of various types, as well as edge-notched, punched-card, and "peek-a-boo" card systems. All have their place in library technology. However, it seems fairly clear that computer technology has greater potential for the immediate as well as for the more remote future of libraries.

Each of the technologies discussed in this section is considered to have some degree of potential applicability to library systems. The objective here is to define and discuss each procedure in sufficient detail to indicate the bases for statements and conjectures made in the main body of the report presented in section C of chapter 7. As will become apparent, the various procedures discussed are interrelated.

Document Storage and Retrieval

Document storage and retrieval is concerned with methods for organizing and managing collections of documents (recorded information) to facilitate their recovery as they are needed. Defined in this general way, document retrieval is hard to distinguish in principle from the kind of activity that libraries have performed for centuries. (It also shares many aspects of business record-keeping.) What distinguishes the field from more conventional library operations is the reliance upon mechanical and electronic aids and associated procedural technology.[49]

The terms "data management" or "data retrieval" are often used to refer to storage and retrieval operations in which the records are not documents but more discrete, often numerical, items. Invariably, such data are stored in highly structured and formated files for ease of handling. This is not usually the case in document files, which consist of variable-length records with different kinds of textual data. Inventory records and stock market quotations are examples of data files. Success in processing such highly organized files antedates and still outdistances achievements in document handling. There are differences as well as significant similarities in the processing techniques used in both of these

---

[49] *The term "information storage and retrieval," originally introduced to describe the kinds of activity we are discussing, is ambiguous and does not help to distinguish between retrieving a* document *or document citation and retrieving* information *or data contained somewhere within the* document.

activities. However, in this discussion, document storage and retrieval systems, rather than data retrieval systems, will be the main concern.

A few specialized techniques that are closely related to the problems of document storage and retrieval (such as automated indexing and automated classification) are discussed separately below for purposes of emphasis and clarity.

Systems designed for purposes of document storage and retrieval include several key processes: (1) analyzing of incoming material to create some representation that may be stored in the file; (2) storing the material and its representation in appropriate files and arranging for their later manipulation, as needed; (3) analyzing of information requests and converting them into a search prescription; and (4) searching the file to match the prescription against the stored data, to provide relevant responses. Some document storage and retrieval systems—particularly those tailored to handle standing requests for various kinds of information—are referred to as "selective dissemination" systems. Conceptually, selective dissemination is a service that can be performed by any comprehensive document storage and retrieval system, and should be considered as an integral part of such a system rather than a separate entity.

The state of the art in each of the four basic processes listed above is sufficiently different to warrant the following separate discussion for each.

Operational information systems, even those with a very high degree of automation, do not presently use computers for analyzing and preparing representations of documents. This is because it has not yet proved possible to build into computer programs all of the kinds of considerations that human document analysts and indexers bring to their decisions. Although there has been nearly a decade of interest and work in automatic indexing, abstracting, and classification for providing representations of documents, there is not yet a satisfactory capability of identifying automatically those aspects of a document that need to be preserved in the representation.

A basic technical problem is that all analysis and representation involves a subtle and often unconscious process of comparison with other documents being processed or already in the store, or with previously expressed user needs. No adequate means have yet been developed to provide such information to the computer system.

Despite this problem, a degree of success has been achieved with relatively simple tools such as permutation indexes, in which individual key terms in a document title are automatically alphabetized by the computer and the terms, plus title context, listed as an aid to document search. This level of representation has not proved adequate to meet the search needs in most document storage and retrieval systems, since the index consists only of words actually used in the title, and there are no vocabulary controls.

Another technique in which something like automatic representation can be done is the so-called "full-text indexing," in which the computer makes a concordance of all of the "content" terms in a document and their location in the text. Such systems are already technically feasible for the production of concordances. They can be useful in those instances where one can afford to store full text in a computer and where one requires the capability to search on the basis of any term mentioned in the text. There are few, if any, installations in existence where full-text indexing is in operational use.

Although automated data-processing techniques can be used to provide a number of valuable aids for document analysis and for the preparation of representations, at present such functions still remain in the province of the skilled librarian.

Document systems are concerned with two kinds of storage files—those that store the document itself, and those that store the document representation. These two files may be kept separate or merged; most systems keep them separate. Some document storage and retrieval systems maintain a microform file of their holdings, but this is not for processing by the computer itself.

In no operational system is the full text of all the documents in the collection stored in the computer for search and retrieval, because: (1) it would be expensive and time-consuming to code all this information; (2) graphs and photographs would be very difficult to code; (3) computer storage facilities are expensive and limited—even magnetic tape files would not be large or cheap enough; and (4) most importantly, such full-text storage is of unproven value for operational systems.

One potential advantage of having the full text of a document available in machine-readable form for computer processing is that an automated analysis of the document could be made and representations of the document could be prepared. However, as was pointed out, automated document analysis is still in the research stage. On the other hand, considerable progress has been made in using the computer to manipulate more limited sets of representation data, such as accession numbers, titles, authors, citations, etc. Such document representations can be sorted, reordered, restructured, displayed, and otherwise processed in many ways, depending on the capabilities built into the particular computer program. Although there is a great deal of current activity and discussion on file organization and data management, most of it is focused on questions of the economics and efficiency of particular techniques, or on the best means to take advantage of changing hardware capabilities. In this vein, one area currently receiving attention is that of generalized data-management systems, i.e., computer programs and procedures that permit one to create, merge, or restructure new and existing files within an existing programming system without extensive reprogramming. Most data-management systems have not been mainly concerned with the manipulation of natural language text or unformated data, but there is a trend toward consideration of text-processing and editing features for such systems.

The primary advantages of generalized data-management systems are that: (1) the same basic programming system can be used by any of several information facilities (for example, libraries), with each facility using only those aspects of the program that address its particular requirements; and (2) any given facility can modify its processing procedures without needing to rebuild an entirely new, special-purpose program. The primary disadvantage of such generalized systems is that they are larger and more complex than special-purpose programs and therefore less efficient and more costly to operate on the computer. Operational efficiency is traded for general utility. To date, the applications to library problems have generally been of this generalized type, and therefore have been less efficient for this specific application than if a specialized program had been written for each application.

Like the analysis of documents, the analysis of information requests is largely a human activity in most document storage and retrieval facilities. The user generally provides some kind of description of the kinds of information he is seeking; sometimes a reference librarian or information specialist must review the request, perhaps in consultation with the user, and convert it into a set of terms that he thinks will be most likely to retrieve documents relevant to the user's needs. The task of automation here is to convert written requests into an effective set of search terms without the help of a human intermediary. This has not been achieved yet in an operational system. However, the automation of this area may be less difficult than document analysis, if for no other reason than that information requests are much shorter and therefore require much less condensation and conversion to provide suitable search avenues to a file.

One type of arrangement that promises to be fairly successful is to have the user communicate his information needs directly to the computer via an input typewriter console. At present, such arrangements constrain users to communicate in specific "authorized" subsets of English. However, promising research is under way to provide better computer "understanding" of less restrictive subsets (e.g., natural English) or to permit an interactive "negotiation" or "interpretation" of the query. The latter efforts are still in the research stage, and have not yet provided tools for operational use.[50]

[50] *Some already operational systems allow the user to specify search terms, on line, to the computer. These systems are not considered to involve request analysis, in the literal sense.*

The manner in which a file is searched is highly dependent on both its original mode of organization and the kind and configuration of storage media available. Here, the procedural and equipment technologies are very closely interrelated.

There are two basic file-organization strategies that can be used in document storage and retrieval systems: the unit record file and the inverted file. In the *unit file,* each document record (e.g., citation, index terms, and, perhaps, abstract) maintains its integrity. The standard library catalog card is an example of the unit file.

Until the development of the coordinate indexing system, most libraries used a set of *unit* cards, such as Library of Congress cards, for main and added entries, including subject headings. In the card catalog the *unit* subject-heading cards are usually arranged by authors for the subsets of each subject.

In contrast to the unit cards, with classification numbers (call numbers) as well as all the descriptive information and tracings on each card, coordinate indexing cards are simply subject-term cards with only document-accession numbers posted on them. They are called *inverted* cards and their files are referred to as *inverted files.* This system was developed for report literature and journal articles. Separate files are maintained for other indexes to the document collection, e.g., author index and source index.

Both unit-card and inverted-card files can be used for computer storage and retrieval. Each system has its own advantages and disadvantages. The unit record file system must add approximately five new records (filed by author[s], title and subject[s]) for each new document added to the collection. The inverted file grows much more slowly, since only the *new* document numbers need to be posted on existing records. A new record needs to be created only when a new index term is authorized. However, the other indexes to the inverted file continue to grow.

Recent studies have shown that, for automated retrieval systems based on magnetic tape as the storage medium, the use of an inverted file may hinder rather than enhance retrieval, and further, the index itself must be constantly updated, thus making maintenance operations more complex. Also, more time is required to purge the file or modify terms applied to an entry.

When one moves to more rapidly accessible storage media that are not limited to sequential access (e.g., discs, drums, and core memory), the difficulties with the inverted file are substantially reduced. How, precisely, to take best advantage of rapid-access storage media for more efficient search is currently the object of considerable interest and work, with several techniques of file organization, data addressing, and data association vying for favor. The best conclusion that one may draw at this point is that many alternative techniques of file organization and search are available for a particular installation, and the primary questions are those of efficiency, not capability.

The most difficult search problem, from the standpoint of systems that deal with documents, is to locate relevant information in the computer file having a description that is different from that expressed in the query. This problem is, of course, exactly the same for manual systems as it is for computer-based systems. However, the computer has been demonstrated to offer some special capabilities for dealing with this problem. For instance, one can develop and store a fairly large thesaurus and/or authority list in a computer file so that translations can be made automatically between the query and the contents of the file. Thus, a single term used by a requestor (or the librarian) can be expanded into a set of related terms to enhance the likelihood of covering relevant material. Should some of the terms used in the query not be authorized index terms in the particular system's vocabulary, the computer can—in many instances—make the translation to legitimate terms automatically. Such capabilities are already in operational use, and more powerful capabilities are well within range.

In the next five to ten years, we may expect to see substantial, continued improvement in techniques for document storage and retrieval, quite apart from the advances in equipment technology and linguistic knowledge on which (in part) they ultimately depend. There will almost certainly be acceptably efficient computer aids to human indexing and classification, using machine-readable inputs that are provided by optical readers or that are by-products of publication. Techniques of file organization and search, currently lagging behind equipment technology, will probably keep up reasonably well with the increasing demands placed on them by the very large files that new equipment techniques are providing. Too, the present somewhat embryonic techniques for direct interaction with the file—already accepted in the intelligence community and increasingly mentioned in "libraries of the future" discussions—can be expected to become relatively commonplace in research-type libraries that can afford some degree of computer assistance.

Although many technical problems must be overcome to make substantial improvements in document storage and retrieval techniques, the most serious problems may be those of cost rather than those of technical feasibility. Thus, the widespread applicability of document storage and retrieval techniques is heavily dependent on the degree to which success is achieved in providing cheaper and more powerful computer equipment.

Automated Classification

Most libraries in the United States use some kind of classification system (either the Library of Congress or the Dewey Decimal scheme). The basic purpose of such systems is to group together textual objects that are conceptually related.

The purpose of automated classification techniques is to use computers to subdivide a mass of materials into organized groups, to improve the efficiency of searching. There are two aspects to automated classification: (1) defining the groups that constitute the classification scheme and (2) assigning materials to particular groups.

The basic objective of current research and development in automated classification is to optimize the grouping of documents for computer-based storage and retrieval and to assign each document to its proper group or groups by using programs that substitute computer manipulation—in whole or in part—for human judgment. A secondary, but nevertheless important, objective is to have the capability to detect changes in the character of the collection (automatically) and, accordingly, to modify and update the classification scheme and the document assignments.

Thus far, studies have shown that computers can be used to generate classification categories that look reasonable and that have a moderate amount of agreement with categories created by human classifiers on the same material. Studies have also shown a moderate amount of agreement between human and computer sorting of documents into prescribed categories. (It must be remembered that humans show only a moderate amount of agreement with each other on such tasks.)

A basic procedure commonly employed in generating an automated classification scheme is to compare a list of words or word pairs from (or representing) each document with a similar list from every other document in a collection, and to use various mathematical and statistical sorting techniques to construct a number of categories that encompass the full range of material and yet permit a reasonable subdivision. The second step, classifying documents into the previously determined categories, is accomplished by preparing a list of "clue words" which best distinguish each category from all others, and then comparing each document against the various clue-word lists for best fit.

Research to date has identified a number of problems that must be solved before automated classification can be accepted as a useful adjunct, much less as a serious competitor to conventional classification systems:

1. A problem inherent in any classification method based upon the words used in the document is that there is not a one-to-one correspondence between the exact

words in the document and what the document is about, or in what it is saying about the subject matter. Whereas humans can see the same concept in many alternative sets of words, present automated classification techniques are closely tied to the particular words the documents happen to use. Providing the computer with an adequate repertoire of word-concept translations may not be impossible, but it is difficult and has not yet been demonstrated.

2. A second problem is that there are many different ways of conceiving of, and measuring, document similarity. Each has proponents, but an intelligent choice cannot be made until evaluation criteria are better developed.

3. A third problem has to do with the size of the document collection that can be automatically classified. Most experiments have used only a small data base of a few hundred documents. There is now some indication that the data base can be enlarged, but this still has to to be demonstrated in practice.

4. A fourth problem has to do with the depth of indexing required to provide inputs to automated classification. The 15 to 30 descriptors ordinarily required exceed by far the number applied to documents in operational systems. Unless *automated* indexing has preceded the automated classification, the costs for the latter might be too large for practicality.

5. A fifth problem has to do with computer costs. Comparison of each document with every other document, for purposes of generating classification schemes, involves large amounts of computation. As the number of documents to be processed increases, computation time and dollar cost increase geometrically, thus making the classification of large numbers of documents quite impractical. Some recent breakthroughs in processing strategy offer promise of shifting the cost from an exponential to a linear increase. Using these new algorithms, generating a classification system for 10,000 documents would require approximately 20 minutes on a modern high-speed computer and would cost around $250. Thus, automated classification is no longer entirely ruled out—on the grounds of cost—for some kinds of automated libraries and information facilities.

6. Finally, there is the problem that no generally accepted methods have yet been developed to evaluate the products of automated classification efforts or to indicate whether one method gives "better" results than the other. Although there are promising research leads in this direction it is worth noting that there have been few systematic attempts to evaluate, or to compare, various manual classification systems such as LC, Dewey, or UDC on an operational, as opposed to a theoretical, basis.

Because of these kinds of problems, use of computer-generated classification schemes is not yet appropriate for most libraries or even for most semiautomated retrieval systems. In addition to the fact that the relative merits of automated classification are yet to be demonstrated, there is the fact that all libraries presently use one or more existing conventional classification systems, and their personnel and patrons would require extensive training to reorient themselves toward computer-generated, adaptive classification systems. The cost of data generation and programming is also, for the moment, a prohibitive factor. For the present, exploratory use of computer-derived classification categories is desirable primarily where documents are already deeply indexed, and where either the existing schedule is not considered satisfactory or there is no classification schedule at all, e.g., with:

- specialized collections of current technical reports on the leading edge of science and technology,
- specialized collections of current technical reports being produced by a particular organization,
- specialized collections of information whose basic character is constantly changing so that new trends need to be identified and the organization of the data modified,

- accumulations of documents by individual researchers or small projects for their specialized, and often temporary, needs.

On the other hand, use of computers to place documents into classification categories that have already been established is not nearly so far off. Given a set of human or machine-derived terms representing what a document is "about," computer techniques may—in the next two or three years—prove adept at assigning the documents to appropriate classification categories. If the current classification assignments are regarded as correct—i.e., as an acceptable criterion—for evaluating computer assignments, a year or two of experimentation should make it clear whether an acceptable level of accuracy can be developed for the computer.

The need for all forms of automated text-processing techniques, including automated classification, will increase as collections grow and as more materials become available in machine-readable form. Regardless of the fact that costs per unit of computer input and processing are dropping each year, it will continue to be inefficient and wasteful to search complete files where there is the possibility of subdividing the file and searching within a small set of documents or document representations. In addition, it seems likely that progress will continue to be made in solving the technical problems mentioned above.

The status and value of automated classification are sufficiently uncertain to make predictions of use hazardous. It seems very unlikely that automatically generated classification schemes will supplant existing ones. They may find some use as an adjunct to etablished schedules, perhaps helping the library staff to notice possible new perspectives and providing alternative paths for the users to "browse." On the whole, the best prediction one can make at the moment is that computer-generated schemes will be used infrequently and primarily as a means of sensitizing the system periodically to changes in the character of the collection. Obviously, this use will be more prevalent in new or rapidly changing collections, of the sort presently found in information centers, rather than in conventional libraries.

Looking ahead to 1975, one may expect to see some large libraries regularly developing or receiving machine-readable data on some percentage of their inputs, and using automatic classification techniques to suggest assignments to the human classifiers. This kind of a joint, man-machine document assignment may have considerable promise. Although the detailed analysis performed by the computer may help humans notice new concepts or relationships, present text-processing techniques do not, and perhaps cannot ever, use all of the information context that a human brings to the classification situation. Thus, the idea of man-machine cooperation offers interesting possibilities for classification. A moderate amount of research attention to this possibility might permit use of even present-day automated classification programs.

Automated Indexing

The term "automated indexing" refers to several different computer-based procedures, all of which share the feature of providing some means of subject access by a searcher to particular documents. The simplest kind of automated indexing is that done in connection with document titles. The most complex kind attempts either to extract appropriate index terms from documents, or uses the words in the document as a basis for assigning still other, more appropriate index terms.

Most of the interest in automated indexing has been in connection with technical information systems, rather than libraries. This is largely because such systems are oriented toward information retrieval, a function that relatively few libraries emphasize. However, some—and perhaps all—automated indexing techniques have strong potential for library operations.

Although there is still controversy about the relative merits of automatically produced indexes of titles, compared with subject indexes prepared by humans, there is little doubt that title indexes are already useful search tools, and no doubt whatever that they are relatively inexpensive to produce.[51] A list of 4,000 titles, for example, requires approximately 50 minutes on a large modern computer to be converted into a KWIC-type index. Including time for keypunching or other preparation, and given an existing program (of which there are many), total costs for such an index are under $1,500. Computer costs for these indexes go up in roughly linear fashion with the number of titles. Current research on KWIC-type indexes is concerned with refinements of the technique, with extension to nontitle material, and with questions of effectiveness. The effectiveness of KWIC indexes is heavily dependent on the adequacy of the titles themselves; accordingly, pressure is growing for authors to use representative, rather than fanciful, titles.

The automatic selection or assignment of index terms from text, originally viewed with optimism some years ago, is increasingly recognized to be a difficult challenge. Early hopes that individual content words used with high frequency in a document would identify adequately what the document is "about" having given way to recognition that high-quality indexing is *concept* indexing, and at the very least, needs to consider syntactic and semantic factors, i.e., both the order and the context of words. Many current studies are attempting to meet or circumvent this problem.

Fully automatic indexing is a desirable goal, but it does not yet seem within reach, a fact which has led to increasing interest in computer-*aided* indexing, i.e., a man-machine cooperation in indexing. A current example is the use of a computer to select candidate indexing terms from the text of a book, and to organize these by frequency of occurrence (i.e., into a permutation-type index) so that the final selection can be made by a trained indexer. This is a classic and important example of using a computer to perform a task for which it is eminently suited, while still taking full advantage of special human capabilities in making the final selection.

Other important uses being explored for computer-aided indexing are those in which a computer acts as clerk-verifier-editor-monitor of human indexing activity and as a recorder of such activity data as requests sought under a given term, the number of times users enter the system with a term not in a glossary, etc. Such activity data can be an invaluable guide in the design (by humans) of a consistent, user-oriented indexing language. Full capability to provide such useful *aids* to human indexing is already well within the current status and requires only some developmental activity to be readily available. However, the economic value of providing computer-produced aids to indexing has not yet been demonstrated. Studies are needed to compare the unit cost and quality of indexing when using completely manual and computer-aided indexing procedures.

The permutation technique, already firmly established and widely used, could be very useful for quite a number of library operations. For example, in acquisitions, one of the biggest drawbacks to a conventional file of outstanding orders is that there is only one entry per item. Both staff and patrons, in seeking to find what is on order in a library, often ask for a particular item by other than the entry that has been used in the order file. A KWIC-type index of the order file could be most useful here, particularly for monographic series or for volumes of conference proceedings with multiple authorship or sponsorship.

Within three to five years, one may expect to see widespread use of computer aids to indexing in most information facilities that have access to a computer. Many of the uses will be of the monitoring variety that help system personnel to be aware both of their own linguistic practices and those of their clientele. Computer programs for such monitoring are relatively small, simple, and inexpensive; the bookkeeping is done behind the scenes, and a printed output may be required only at infrequent intervals.

---

[51] *The most commonly used is referred to as a KWIC (Key Word In Context) Index.*

Policy changes in technical journals, particularly in the engineering field, require more authors to suggest a set of index terms at the time they submit their articles for publication. These terms may be printed along with the article, with or without modifications. If this policy becomes more prevalent (and there is every indication that it will), the task of the journal indexers will shift in emphasis from the selection or assignment of terms to the more intellectually demanding task of insuring quality. If this occurs, the role of automatically producing indexing aids (computer-suggested index terms similar to author-suggested index terms) may become increasingly important.

Within the same period, one may also expect to see some information systems in which index terms are either suggested or directly supplied through computer analysis of text. (This is, of course, economical only in those instances where the text has already been prepared in machine-readable form as a by-product of some operation, e.g., publication.) Although present-day index-term extraction does not appear to compete in quality with the best human indexing, expected advancements in the understanding of language and of human indexing itself seem very likely to support a gradual but steady increase in the acceptability of computer-selected index terms. Given a parallel growth of machine-supported thesauri and authority lists, one can foresee, by 1975, a number of systems—particularly specialized technical information systems—that will rely heavily on the assignment of index terms from automated analysis of text, with a final review by a supervising indexer.

Book indexing can also be done prior to publication. Library of Congress catalog card numbers are already assigned in this manner, and the concept could be expanded to include subject indexing performed as a service for the benefit of all libraries. Indexing and cataloging of books is not likely to be affected in the near future by automated indexing, for such indexing is shallow and would not benefit greatly from a computer analysis of the entire text.

Machine Translation and Automated Abstracting

Machine translation, or MT as it is commonly called, aims to use computer processing to translate texts from one language into another in order to make the contents of foreign-language documents more accessible and usable. Automated abstracting, as the name implies, attempts to prepare condensed representations of documents by computer processing rather than by human analysis. These topics are treated together because they involve processing of the full text of documents and the use of statistical, syntactic, and semantic tools.

Although work in MT started out optimistically several years ago, the analysis of language has proved to be much more difficult and complex than was anticipated. Machine translation of sorts can be accomplished by using a large internally stored dictionary and largely word-by-word techniques, but the results achieved by this method are, for the most part, not very satisfactory, either in terms of readability or in terms of accuracy. The acknowledged disappointments in practical applications have helped to shift emphasis from translation per se to basic research in linguistics.

The current status in automated abstracting has undergone almost no change for the past several years. After an enthusiastic start in the early 1960's, most of the effort has come to a halt because of severe and discouraging conceptual and technical problems. The basic premise on which automated abstracting work was founded is that certain parts of documents—usually sentence units—carried the essence of the total document message and that, by using statistical techniques based on word frequencies, one could identify these sentences and assemble them into an abstract. Early work floundered somewhat on the same problems of comparative evaluation experienced in automated indexing and automatic classification. It was also discovered that statistical cues alone were not sufficiently powerful to select all the "best" sentences, a finding that led to efforts to prescribe good clue words to be up-weighted, other words to be down-weighted, and additional nonstatistical criteria (e.g., the position of the sentence in the document) for sentence selection.

Quite apart from whether or not the "best" sentences were located for the abstract, there is the additional problem of automatically organizing them into a coherent piece of prose. Since there has not been, and does not yet exist, a capability for the reliable generation of contextually meaningful sentences, current automated abstracting techniques can only string together sentences extracted from the text. Although there has been some degree of acceptance (or tolerance) shown for such rough-reading products in experimental applications where the need for current awareness overrode the demand for elegance of expression, even here there has been a gradual erosion of acceptance. No relief for this particular problem is in sight at the present time.

Producing an automated abstract of a journal article, given a machine-readable record, would require roughly one-half minute of computer time on a large, modern computer and would cost about $4.00 in a batch-processing operation. This figure assumes that no sentence-generating capability is necessary.

The future of automated abstracting is highly problematical. Any increments of improvement, at our present state of knowledge about language and language processing, can be expected to be very small. Any substantial progress in automated abstracting must await a breakthrough in other language-processing techniques, particularly in understanding sentence context and concepts that are expressed by groups of sentences but are not *in* any particular sentence. Furthermore, since some technical journals, as well as elements of the Department of Defense, are requiring that an author-produced abstract be submitted along with the article, the need for an automated abstracting capability may be diminishing.

Looking ahead to 1975, any substantial *independent* progress in automated abstracting that would make the use of those techniques attractive to most libraries cannot be foreseen. Although the required breakthrough could conceivably come, it does not seem prudent to count on it, particularly since abstracts do not now play, nor do they seem likely to play, an extensive role in most library operations.

A similarly gloomy prognosis must be made for fully automated translation. Significant advances will have to be made in computational linguistics before the quality of either MT or automated abstracting can be improved to the extent of achieving general acceptance.

Question-Answering Systems: Retrieval of Information

Up to this point, consideration has been given to document storage and retrieval systems and those aspects of automated language processing that are related to the storage and retrieval of documents and their representations. From some users' point of view, the ultimate retrieval system is one in which they ask questions and receive answers—not documents. Automated question-answering systems are designed to provide this kind of service.

Question-answering systems are of particular interest to libraries, inasmuch as they provide a rather direct analogy to the reference situation. The basic approach is to store the reference material in the computer, search through it in response to a question, and output an answer, i.e., a very small amount of highly relevant data.

The degree to which question-answering systems can be considered already an accomplished fact depends on one's definition. If one has highly structured *data,* such as are contained in airline schedules or census material, and if one asks questions in a prescribed and simple format (e.g., "fare, Chicago/New York"), question-answering is a *fait accompli* and has been so for several years. If, on the other hand, the file contains text, and if the user is allowed to express his question in ordinary English and expects a well-formulated answer, then fully automatic question-answering is a distant goal.

There is one kind of system, already being used in an experimental way, that combines the question-answering approach with ordinary reference retrieval, i.e., providing the user with references rather than answers. The system simply takes the "content" terms in the question as subject descriptors and performs a search accordingly. The questions are not screened or formalized, as they are in a typical reference retrieval systems such as MEDLARS. The system does not have the capability for "understanding" the question in a semantic sense.

The reasons for this are much the same as those for machine translation. For a computer (or, indeed, for a human) to deal with language in a way comparable to the expectable range of human understanding, a great deal of information is needed—information about the grammatical structure of the question and the text, about the meanings of words in the particular context, and about the world. Knowledge that humans take for granted (e.g., San Francisco is a city in the United States) needs to be deliberately programmed into a question-answering system in order to get a reasonable response. While research progress is being made in providing all three of these kinds of information (syntactic, semantic, and real-world) to computer systems, it is becoming apparent that *high-quality* natural-language question-answering from usefully broad content domains is subject to as many difficulties as fully automated mechanical translation, and may be as many years away. However, there are a number of researchers working at such systems, and this should help to accelerate progress.

Question-answering systems could prove to be a very valuable aid and support for the reference librarian. Considering today's technology, and the machine's limited capability to "understand" questions, such systems would operate best when used by reference personnel rather than by the library patrons. The latter might have such a limited knowledge of the file and such a variety of question-asking expressions that it would be impossible for any current question-answering system to interpret them adequately. However, reference personnel who were cognizant of the file and the acceptable question format might make good use of machine-readable files.

On the other hand, there is the knotty problem of deciding which material to store in machine-readable files. The sizable costs of preparing and storing any significant amount of textual material or a sizable "data base" in a computer, together with the infrequency of questions on any given material, make it unthinkable for a typical library to have all of its reference material in computer form. For the present, question-answering technology is most realistically considered in terms of a system in which many libraries are sharing not only the computer time but the reference material (including cost of storage) as well.

Although automated question-answering, in the most elegant sense, is probably technically more difficult than machine translation, we may expect by 1975 to see a great many instances of its use. Both the desire and the capability for communicating with the computer in natural language will continue to grow. With steady improvements based on linguistic research and experience from current embryonic question-answering systems, one may expect to find some level of question-answering capability in many reference facilities. Even if many of the expected technical improvements in question-answering systems do not materialize, there will still be many such systems in operation, because computer support will be increasingly inexpensive and accessible; less-than-elegant systems will provide some useful service; and a new generation of librarians, information specialists, and patrons in technical libraries will have learned, to some extent, how to communicate with computer-based systems.

Computer-Aided Instruction

The term "computer-aided instruction" (CAI) refers to a number of techniques for using computers to assist in communicating information to learners. These techniques were originally developed in an educational context, but they are now seen to have a broader applicability than was first recognized. CAI techniques are presently being developed as instructional adjuncts to computer-based systems with other than an educational purpose.

The feasibility of using a computer as a teaching machine was first explored around 1959. Since that time, a number of computer-aided instructional systems have been developed, most of them experimental but a few of them in operational use. Equipment at terminals for students often includes typewriters, random-access film-projection devices, and, less typically, cathode-ray-tube display devices. Equipment has recently been shown that can display rear-projected slides on the face of a cathode-ray tube, thus eliminating the requirement for all CRT display material to be computer-*stored*. Equipment and techniques for audio response and interaction are not nearly as far along. Random-access tape recorders are in general use, but they are not as efficient as workers would like. There is some research under way to have the computer "recognize" speech and to generate speech, either by using prerecorded words or phrases or by using a set of rules to convert stored speech sounds into meaningful speech patterns. Such systems already exist, for example, at the New York Stock Exchange.

Three major problems barring widespread use of CAI are currently commanding attention. The first is the technical, or equipment problem. Although computer-system capabilities are generally quite adequate for today's needs, computers need to become more reliable, particularly for on-line operations where "down time" is a nuisance, in addition to being costly. Improvements are also necessary in computer programming for time-shared systems (the only kind of system that permits several persons to use the system simultaneously).

The second major problem involves semantics. It is concerned with the precision with which desired meaning can be conveyed between the learner and the system. Thus, one must decide whether to use, for any given communication, an audio or visual mode, and when and how to switch from one to the other or to use both of them simultaneously (redundantly). One must also learn how to prepare and program instructional material that makes some concessions to individual differences among learners without being unacceptably expensive. Preparing such material is presently slow and costly; a single two-hour lesson may take several months to prepare. Of course, once prepared, such a lesson can be widely used.

The third problem has to do with effectiveness. To date, studies on the effectiveness of various aspects of CAI are somewhat inconclusive, in part because adequate evaluation criteria and methods have not been devised yet, and in part because the effectiveness of CAI appears to be very situation-dependent. Thus, valid generalizations are difficult to make.

Because of a lack of reliable information on effectiveness, it is not fruitful to discuss questions of CAI cost-effectiveness at this time. It has repeatedly been remarked that the present costs of CAI are prohibitive for all uses except research. However, this need not necessarily be the case, where either (1) the CAI is an adjunct to an operational system that does a highly related job (e.g., acquisitions control or circulation), or (2) where CAI shares the machine with some other unrelated function such as payroll or cost accounting.

Granted an increasing use of computers in libraries, both for technical processes and for reference services, CAI can play an important role. On-the-job training of new library personnel, both professional and clerical, is a demanding task that all libraries face periodically and most face continually. By adding instructional components to the computer programs used for various aspects of technical processes, the library can shift *some* of the teaching burden from experienced library personnel (already in short supply) to the computer. CAI can also be useful in helping library patrons to learn how to use the particular library's resources or to conduct some kinds of reference searches.

By 1975, one may expect to see a large number of CAI-type facilities in many libraries, particularly those in an educational or research setting. The library college concept, which attempts to shift emphasis in college libraries from archival functions toward direct education, is a forerunner of what is likely to be an increasingly accepted concept of service. In line with this concept, some colleges and universities are already planning or building study carrels equipped with input/output equipment for more direct contact between the student and the information store. Unless library personnel are to add a sizable training load to their regular library duties, they must—and undoubtedly will—take advantage of the opportunity for the system to help students learn how to use the library more effectively.

Within a very few years, one may expect to see CAI-type programs developed in connection with most operational programs for support to technical processes in libraries. For many people, the most desirable and effective method of learning how to deal with a computer-based system is to sit down at the console and learn by doing. CAI-type programs can bring some measure of efficiency to this process and help to avoid both unnecessary frustration from blind fumbling or excessive dependence on experienced library personnel. By 1975, it will probably be rare to find any significant degree of computer support without also finding a CAI element as an adjunct.

RELATED EQUIPMENT AND MATERIALS TECHNOLOGY

Introduction

This section describes several kinds of equipment, materials, and techniques, other than those primarily associated with computers, that bear on library operations, present of future. Topics discussed are: microform technology, reprography, publication techniques, physical handling and storage, transmission of materials, and lasers and holograms. The status of each of these is briefly described, together with possible applications.

For some materials, equipment, or techniques, there is general information available on costs; where this is so, it has been provided to suggest orders of magnitude. It should be understood that these general figures will not necessarily apply to particular equipment operated in particular circumstances. In some instances, meaningful cost information is not available, or was not readily available at the time of this report.

Microform Technology

Microforms come in many sizes and shapes. They are available both as microreductions on opaque sheets, enlarged for viewing by reflection, and as transparent films through which light is passed into an enlarging mechanism. Microfilm is available both in rolls and in individual sheets. Until quite recently, the roll form has been prevalent in libraries and in newspaper operations. However, unit record sheet film, referred to as *microfiche,* or simply *fiche,* has been receiving increasing attention and emphasis as the most effective microform for reports and as potentially the most valuable form to replace paper copies of bound volumes.

During the past decade, the use of microforms has undergone another radical change. Initially, microfilming was thought of as a technique for space reduction in some special libraries or in connection with the need for preservation of materials in scholarly libraries. This was true both for files that were going to be stored away for safekeeping and for the preservation of much more fragile documents, such as newspapers. However, microforms are now beginning to be used as a medium of communication, much as books and report literature are used.

The widespread use of microfiche has coincided with the beginning of a new library concept within the Federal Government—that of a distributing, rather than a circulating, library or information facility. Documents are not to be returned; they are to be kept or discarded. Such a concept is quite practical with microforms. The Defense Documentation Center, NASA, and the Federal Clearinghouse for Scientific and Technical Information are currently distributing reports in fiche forms, and the United

States Office of Education has announced its intention to make fiche available on material of interest to those concerned with educational resources. The cost savings in fiche are apparent from the fact that the Clearinghouse sells a hard copy document for $3.00 and can sell a fiche for 65¢. The price holds, whether the document can be contained on only one fiche or requires six, seven, or eight for example. The United States Office of Education intends to distribute fiche at 9¢ each.[52]

The microfiche standards created by the Federal Government through COSATI (the Committee on Scientific and Technical Information) have gone a long way toward eliminating the earlier confusion and incompatibility that resulted from having many forms. The fiche produced under these standards are 4 x 6 inches, with a 19:1 reduction ratio. The initial sheet (or fiche) of each document has title, author, and other such information on the top edge of the fiche printed in a size enabling it to be read by the unaided eye. The remainder of the fiche consists of 5 rows, each representing 12 document pages. If additional fiche are needed in order to represent the full document—as they are for nearly any book—the succeeding sheets contain 6 rows of 12 pages, rather than 5 rows. Thus, considerable reduction is achieved without losing the capability of handling individual documents as units.

With the production and distribution of information in microform, it was necessary to create usable, inexpensive microform readers. It is now possible to obtain good desk-top readers for microfiche for under $100, roughly the price of a portable typewriter. Thus, it no longer need be housed only in the library; one can easily have a reader in one's office. Better readers are, of course, available at higher prices, extending past $1,000. The more expensive of the readers provide the capability of producing hard copy and provide a means for libraries to either circulate or distribute copies. The fiche remains with the library, while hard copy or a second fiche is produced to be carried away. There is some question as to whether using even the most expensive current readers is as acceptable as viewing hard copy, when one has to read for many hours of the day. However, their convenience and other advantages override some of their limitations.

At present, the film handling in most microfilm filing systems is done manually. Most files are not of sufficient volume to warrant automated or semi-automated mechanized handling. Only during the past few years have manufacturers directed product research and development efforts in this area, because some microfilm files are becoming quite large. Microfiche edge-sensing by mechanical or magnetic processes is used for quick retrieval of a single fiche and also subsequent transport to readers, cameras, or reproducers. The Houston Fearless Card system also automatically selects the desired image on the selected fiche through the use of X-Y coordinates. Roll film has retained its importance in those areas where the size of the document greatly exceeds the capacity of a single fiche, e.g., parts catalogs. In addition, if a portion of film is to be chosen by some means other than visual examination, then roll film provides an easier mechanical procedure for reaching the proper frame on the film. Several devices exist for searching reels mechanically and retrieving via motorized transports. Use of roll film in cartridge form will probably increase, for a period, in special library applications. However, it seems probable that within the next five to ten years, the dominant microform for library applications will be the microfiche sheet.

Within the past two years, much effort has been devoted to developing color microfilm. The primary difficulty has been the low resolution qualities of existing color film as compared to black-and-white film. For many applications, color must be precise, and present color film is inconsistent in color rendition. In addition, it fades, even in controlled conditions, and because of its construction is very sensitive to scratching, surface

---

[52] *This price is unofficial as of November 1967 and subject to change. Also note that it does not represent cost to USOE, but only selling price to the recipient.*

damage from handling and dirt, and loss of color images from the layering of color gelatins.

Since color microfilm is just coming out of research into development, there is presently little in the way of processing equipment for duplicating microfilms or for printing from the color film. However, automatic processing equipment exists now for mass-production handling of color films; microfilming equipment for black-and-white film can usually handle color film; viewing devices usually have color-corrected lenses; and printing equipment often can reproduce the color image in black and white. Microfilm costs vary widely in different organizations and in different parts of the United States. A summary of current *average* costs is presented in Table F–3. C. 1.

With a predictable large increase in the use of microforms, we may expect to see significant improvements in microform technology over the next ten years, both in the materials available and in the equipment for processing and storing it. Most of the needed improvements may not require any technological breakthrough. For example, although increasingly large sizes of microfilm files demand more sophisticated microfilm-handling hardware, this will probably come through concentrated product engineering that utilizes the principles of existing electronic and mechanical developments. This type of development effort, along with procedural breakthroughs in computer-based information retrieval, can lead to more and better computer-controlled systems that can automatically manage large-scale microfiche and/or microfilm reel files.

We can also expect to see increasing development of equipment and procedural technology that permits direct information *transfer* between microimage and computer subsystems. One manufacturer, Stromberg-Carlson, has announced a soon-to-be-available (November 1967) system capable of direct transfer from magnetic tape to microfiche utilizing a CRT display at a rate of 5 fiche per minute. Furthermore, the system will incorporate a hard-copy printer, producing 11- x 14-inch material, electrostatically, at an output rate of 60 feet per minute. A sizable amount of attention will continue to be paid to the microfilm itself. The storage problem is also likely to be reduced, quite apart from technological changes, by adherence to the storage standards set by the National Bureau of Standards (NBS) and industrial photographic firms. Adherence to the NBS standards requires conscientious microfile management but should pay valuable dividends. One development that will probably occur during the next five years is the perfection of a stable color microfilm. Too, continued research into undersirable chemical phenomena related to film (silver-halide, Diazo, Kalvar, etc.) aging is likely to lead to less severe storage requirements.

Ultramicroform technology is being vigorously developed by at least one or two manufacturers. Ultramicroform uses reductions of 150 or 200 to 1 instead of the commonly accepted reduction of 19 to 1. The advantages of ultramicroform come from the ability to place more information on a single sheet; this is also its disadvantage. Few documents are large enough to require a full sheet; thus, they share it with other documents. The ultrareduction, however, does allow for extremely inexpensive reproduction, if a large number of copies are to be made. This fact has led to a proposal for the creation of a thousand libraries of one million books in ultramicroform. Such a library would not only be inexpensive from the point of view of the amount of storage required to house it; far more importantly, it would be comparatively inexpensive to create the holdings. The expense of cataloging, creation of retrieval techniques, etc., need only be incurred once.

The initial investment required to implement this proposal would be close to $300 million. However, the sparseness of libraries of million-book size makes the proposal important, for providing an economically feasible way of satisfying the need for great libraries, not only within the United States but throughout the world.

The proposal of million-book library replicated a thousand times assumes that all

TABLE F-3. C.1

MICROFILM COST COMPARISONS
(As of 1967)

ITEM	Cost in $*		REDUCT. RATIO	# / Fiche		# OF IMAGES PER UNIT	Cost per Image		Storage Req./100,000 Pages		
	ORIG. MICRO-FILM	DUPE. MICRO-FILM		ROWS	COLS.		ORIG.	DUPE.	UNITS OF MICRO-FORM	LINEAR INCHES FOR UNITS	LINEAR INCHES FOR ORIG.
BLACK & WHITE											
A. Roll Film						(100' roll)			(# reels)		
1. 35mm Roll-normal	22.00	6.50	16×	—	—	550	.040	.0118	180	360	1200
Hi density	72.00	6.50	16×	—	—	1,800	.040	.0042	56	112	1200
2. 16mm Rotary	60.00	6.00	24×	—	—	2,400	.025	.0025	42	84	1200
Planetary	100.00	6.00	24×	—	—	2,400	.042	.0025	42	84	1200
B. Fiche						(per fiche)			(# fiche)		
1. COSATI	1.75	.12	19×	5	12	60	.029	.0020	1,670	16.7	1200
2. NMA	2.10	.12	24×	6	14	84	.025	.0020	1,190	11.9	1200
3. Library STD	7.50	.12	50×	13	30	390	.019	.0003	256	2.6	1200
4. HR-1	300.00	1.00	120×	30	70	2,100	.143	.0005	48	0.5	1200
5. HR-2	300.00	1.00	150×	40	80	3,200	.094	.0003	32	0.3	1200
COLOR											
A. Roll Film											
1. 35mm	85–125	75.00	16×	—	—	550	.254–.227	.136			
2. 16mm	125–150	40.00	24×	—	—	2,400	.057–.063	.017			
B. Fiche											
1. COSATI	7.50	5.00	19×	5	12	60	.125	.0830			
2. NMA	10.50	5.00	24×	6	14	84	.125	.0590			
3. Library STD	48.75	5.00	50×	13	30	390	.125	.0128			
C. Aperture Card											
1. 35mm	0.357	0.357	16×	2	2	4	.089	.089			
2. 16mm	0.193	0.193	24×	2	4	8	.024	.024			

* Includes labor, film, and processing.

libraries would have the same *base* collection. Of course, the concept of the uniform library is not restricted to ultramicroform. It can also be applied to regular microform. In either case, the concept grows more exciting when it is coupled with the possibility of a computer tie-in for information retrieval.

Another advanced library concept involving microforms is represented by a project at M.I.T. and scheduled for operation in about two years. Documents are to be stored on microfiche, and the fiche will be retrieved by computer, viewed with a television camera, transmitted to one of many remote locations, and presented for reading.

Some interest is currently being expressed in microfiche with a reduction ratio of about 50:1. This is less ambitious than the ultramicroform approaches but it has some desirable features for library applications. The fiche would consist of about 13 rows of 30 images each. The title block could contain appropriate normal-reading indexing material, a classification code, title, author, acquisition number, publisher, number of pages, number of fiche, etc., in the same manner, and to the same degree, as the 19X fiche. However, the capacity of the image area would be 390 pages, permitting handling of from 60 to 80 percent of all monographs on a single fiche. (The COSATI fiche handles only 60 images, thus requiring 6 to 7 fiche for a 300-page book.)

Some feel that the potential advantages of a 50X fiche may impel equipment manufacturers and others to advocate this as standard within the next two to five years. One production advantage of the 50X fiche is that unlike other ultramicrofiche it could be produced in a single step, as 45X reductions are currently being done. Another advantage over other ultramicrofiche is that, apart from modification in the frame-locating mechanism of readers, current fiche equipment and techniques for duplication, filing, retrieving, etc., should be capable of handling a 50X fiche quite satisfactorily. Then, too, good reading and printing capabilities should be more easily obtainable than with the 150:1 or higher ratios.

Another microform with considerable potential is microprint.[53] Microprints are opaque and are produced by a printing (not photographic) process. The microprints use either the 19X or 24X reduction ratios and can be produced by standard printing techniques at an approximate cost of 2¢ each. One great advantage of microprints is that they do not have an emulsion; therefore, there are no problems with scratches. However, use of microprints has been limited because of the difficulties of reading and reproducing opaque materials with current equipment. Their use could be enhanced with development of viewers and reader-printers that provided quality equivalent to that obtained with the transparent microfiche.

Reprography

The term "reprography" refers to the reproduction and replication of graphic materials. The term is fairly new and comprehends not only conventional printing techniques, including letterpress, offset lithography, and intaglio printing, but also the burgeoning field of copying (duplication). The gradual erosion and blurring of the traditional distinction between printing and copying led to the new designation.

Traditionally, printing has been most efficient at high volumes, while copying has been most efficient at low volumes. Also, both the quality of printing and skill requirements for printers have been much higher than for copying. However, we are seeing an increasing convergence of these characteristics. Copies are becoming increasingly more capable of handling larger runs with less degradation of output quality. Printing devices are becoming more efficient at low volumes.

Present reprographic techniques are already so efficient, rapid, inexpensive, and acceptable from the standpoint of quality that there is no doubt about their utility in libraries. Present-day discussions of the subject usually concern how much one should pay for a particular amount of quality.

---

[53] *Microprints are not new, and are in common use in libraries. They still have not fulfilled their true potential of very low cost publication.*

To provide a useful frame of reference for understanding reprography costs in relation to library services, we performed a cost analysis of several representative techniques and situations.

Copier Processing

Copier quality is such that it can be used only for line work at this time. (However, a few companies have announced availability of a halftone attachment for their copiers.) Copiers can accept color input but cannot reproduce the color. Since the economics of halftone copiers are not now known, only line work was assumed for the costing exercise. Three copier cost sets were used in the analysis:

a. Xerox 2400. This is electrostatic printing, at the rate of 2,400 copies per hour, from single sheets of paper.[54]

b. Copyflo. This is electrostatic printing, from 35mm roll film, at speeds of 1,200 copies per hour.

c. Copier. This encompasses both the gelatin-dye-transfer and the diffusion-transfer-reversal processes. Average speed is 1 page copy per minute (64 seconds).

Offset Printing

Line printing involves plate preparation and printing using offset printing presses. Plates may be paper or metal. The paper plates prepared using electrostatic processes are adequate for line work only. Photo-direct and negative-to-plate processes can be used to provide graphic arts quality on line work, and can handle halftone and color work as well. For the 17 x 24-inch size presses, it is assumed that negative-to-plate processing is used for the plates, and that four separate pages are run simultaneously. Four separate cost sets were used:

a. with electrostatic plate.

b. with photo-direct plate.

c. with negative and metal plate.

d. with negative and metal plate, handling four pages at a time.

Printouts from Microfiche

The specialized equipment found in reader printers (to handle copying in conventional image sizes stored on fiche) provides capabilities for line-work reproduction almost equal to that for copiers. Halftone images may be reproduced that are satisfactory for reading and comparable to photo-direct plates used for printing. Color may be stored on fiche and reproduced either in black and white or in color, although close color registration is not alway obtained from current equipment. Three sets of fiche-printer combinations were priced (costs for generating a plate from microfiche are comparable to the costs for generating a plate from paper reproducibles; therefore, no separate costs are shown for printing from microfiche):

a. Fiche created and printed using a reader-printer, such as Recordak Magnaprint, Itek, or 3M Filmac, with the corresponding photographic paper.

b. Duplicate fiche used with the aforementioned reader-printers.

c. Duplicate fiche used with the EL-4 printer and dry silver paper.

Letterpress and Silk-Screening

Since costs for letterpress and silk-screen printing and processing depend on volume and quality requirements of a particular task, and since the feasibility point for letterpress involves copy preparation as well as printing, this process was not included in the costing exercise.

Printing and copying costs are dependent primarily on the quantity of pages, the

---

[54] *All production rates given here are maximum obtainable, but may be unreachable in normal operations because of handling problems, need to reload, etc.*

number of copies of each page, the material to be printed, and the equipment used. The comparisons in Table F–3.C.2 are based on copy requirements from 1 to 5,000 pages (impressions). The assumption is made that the machine is fully utilized. This makes it possible to ignore the initial cost of the printing equipment (shown in the right-hand column) for purposes of the analysis. Approximate equipment costs are given only for a comparison of the relative size of the basic investment required. When the equipment is fully utilized, its cost contributes a negligible amount to the per-page cost figures for copies. Thus, the numbers in Table F–3.C.2 cover primarily materials and labor. It is understood that individual figures in this table can vary for many reasons associated with a particular installation's operations. Details of specific assumptions necessary to produce these figures are omitted, in the interest of brevity.

The quality and capabilities of copiers, fiche and other microfilm readers, multilith equipment, etc., have been increasing steadily, and this trend can be expected to continue. It is reasonable to assume now that within five to ten years, the following conditions will prevail:

1. Copiers will be economically competitive with offset equipment through 100 copies, and may be competitive through 200 copies of a page. They will be able to reproduce color, halftones, and massive solids as well as fiche readers can display them today.

2. The quality of offset printing will be superior to its present quality, make-ready time will be further reduced, and plate-making from microforms will be more widely used than presently. The ability to handle very high quality printing will be common.

3. Fiche reader-printers will be vastly improved, with cost per impression from fiche-to-paper printers dropping below 1.5¢ per page and perhaps reaching as low as 1¢. Use of color will gradually increase in the first five years, and in the following five to ten years will become widespread and economically competitive with black and white.

4. Development of electrostatic printers, using fiche as the source document, will be the dominant development in the fiche reader-printer and printing field.

5. Printing directly from optical storage devices, magnetic tape or holographic devices, and from ultramicrofiche will obtain a state about equal to that of reader-printers today.

6. Printing from digital data on magnetic tape, or from thermoplastic microimages can achieve major importance. The growth of the Stromberg-Carlson film devices and the development of electron beam recording, etc., indicates the potential of these developments. Cost for generating a page image on microfilm is estimated at 2–5¢ per page. Direct printout from CRT to bond copy is reported to be competitive with offset printing, although copy quality is not as satisfactory.

7. Optical preparation of copy for high-quality graphic arts material under the control of computers (photocomposition), already very practical, will increase rapidly in applications and usefulness. The current price for text material is about $11 to $25 per page, while graphical material, such as flow charts, wiring diagrams, etc., runs closer to $50. The price of processing, and of obtaining microfilm output for subsequent printing, should drop to about $5 to $7 per page, and even less for producing microprints. (This compares favorably with hot-type costs of from $10 per page and up.) Distribution of the microfilm output from this kind of process is scheduled to start within a year or two in some organizations.

Publication Techniques

Several developments in publication technology hold promise for libraries. The most important is probably computer-managed printing, including photocomposition. Also important is the production of massive amounts of textual material in machine-

TABLE F-3. C.2

PRINT COST COMPARISONS
(As of 1967)

ITEM	1ST COPY PLATE, OR FICHE COST IN DOLLARS	IMPRESSION COST	Total costs per number of copies indicated											RANGE OF ESTIM. EQUIP. COSTS PER MONTH
			1	5	10	20	50	100	200	500	1,000	2,000	5,000	
COPIERS														
A. Xerox 2400*	.021	.021	.021	.105	.210	.420	1.05	2.10	4.20	—	†			$1,100/mo.
B. Copyflo	.029	.029	.029	1.45	2.90	5.80	—	—						800
C. Copier	.130	.130	.130	.650	1.300									250
PRINTING														
A. Multi-paper plate	.250	.0075	.258	.288	.325	.400	.625	1.000	1.750	4.000	7.750	15.250	37.750	4,000
B. Photo-direct	.600	.0075	.608	.638	.675	.750	.975	1.350	2.100	4.350	8.100	15.600	38.100	4,000
C. Negative & plate	2.000	.0075	2.008	2.038	2.075	2.150	2.375	2.750	3.500	5.750	9.500	17.000	39.500	4,000
D. 17 × 24 in.‡	2.000	.0019	2.002	2.009	2.025	2.050	2.125	2.250	2.500	3.250	4.500	7.000	14.500	10,000
FICHE														
A. Orig. fiche & photo-print	.030	.080	.110	.430	.830	1.630	4.030	—						1,200
B. Dupe fiche & photo-print	.003	.080	.083	.403	.803	1.603	4.003	—						1,200
C. Dupe & dry silver	.003	.030	.033	.153	.330	.660	1.650	3.300						300–400

* Averaged over typical month's operation in a medium-sized company.
† Dashed lines indicate that there is no economic merit in considering this means further.
‡ Proportionate cost per 8½- x 11-inch page.

readable form, as a byproduct of the publication process. This means that not as much reliance need be placed on progress in developing optical readers; such progress has been rather slow.

The publishing industry has long made use of punched paper tape for the transmission of news copy. In the past few years punched paper tape has also seen heavy use as an input to typesetting machines. More recently, computers have been introduced into the publication operation, to reduce the cost of line justification and hyphenation, and many typesetting machines are now being run by the tape output produced by the computer.

Computers are also being used to prepare high-quality reproduction masters at high speed with electro-optical techniques. The process is referred to as "photocomposition." Early photocomposition devices contained many fonts, on one or more optical plates. Light was passed through a character onto photographic film, lenses being used to obtain the proper size for the character and to place it in the assigned position on the film. These techniques produced extremely high-quality print—as good as any hot-lead device —but there was a serious mismatch with computer speed, fewer than 10 characters per second being set.

Some effort has been made to achieve greater speed by reducing the number of characters available for printing purposes, sacrificing some degree of quality for speed. The latest techniques attempt to achieve *both* high quality and great speed. Light, instead of being passed through individual characters, is created electronically in the proper character shape as an emission from a cathode-ray tube. Although quality is not as high as the quality of the characters etched onto the photographic plates, the speeds now achievable are commensurate with computer speeds. The printer of this type presently used by the Government Printing Office is capable of setting a full page in five seconds.

Developments in photocomposition are important to libraries not only because they need machine-readable text, but because—quite apart from advanced text-processing techniques—most libraries have a constant printing requirement. The National Library of Medicine, for example, sponsored research on one of the processes described above, and uses it for the publication of *Index Medicus,* a guide to the medical literature.

One can expect to see continuing improvement in photocomposition devices. The Government Printing Office is scheduled to install, sometime in 1967, a photocomposition device with a character set of 1,024 characters and operating speeds of up to 600 pages per hour. This device is felt to represent a major advance in automated print composition.

The advent of the computer and, to some extent, photocomposition, has spurred suggestions for a return to the publication of book-form catalogs. Many libraries feel that if a card catalog were available in many places other than just the standard card catalog area, the library would receive wider use. Replication of the card catalog itself is not economically feasible. With text in machine-readable form, the production of such catalogs is not technically difficult. But if the library once translated its card catalog into machine-readable form, it would be easy to use the computer to update the machine-readable form of this catalog. This machine-readable record could be used to drive some kind of printing device (line printer or photocomposition) to create an updated version of the book catalog. Very large library collections would require many volumes to contain the catalog record. Since no really large library has its entire catalog in machine-readable form, it is not yet clear what problems will exist for large computer-produced book catalogs that need to be kept up to date, say, on a monthly basis. Other questions concern the number of copies of a catalog required to service users without delays, length of life of a heavily used book catalog, etc. Such questions need to be explored before it will be clear how extensive will be the impact of publication technology on library procedures.

Physical Handling and Storage

The book is currently the primary kind of information carrier used in libraries. Because books require physical handling and storage, considerable attention has been given by manufacturers and librarians to the development of aids for these functions.

Materials-handling installations that have been successful in the library are those in which selected library activities are viewed as being similar to those of the wholesale drug and sundries distributors. Their situation requires filling many requests (orders) for small quantities of small items of irregular shape, size, and weight. Libraries have very successfully used containers and baskets in connection with vertical lifts, conveyors, chutes, and pneumatic tubes. These devices move standard-size receptacles *after* a human handles the books and decides on their destinations. Among the libraries effectively using existing technology in this manner are Detroit Public Library (conveyors, tubes, and lifts), UCLA Library (the same, including an underground tube connecting two distant buildings), and the Technological University Library at Delft, Holland. The latter is a fairly advanced operation of this sort, but it serves only for delivery of books to patrons, not for reshelving.

One new product line, announced in 1966 by the Library Bureau of the Sperry Rand Corporation's Remington Rand Office Systems Division, appears to have considerable promise as a tool for library stack management. It is called the RANDTRIEVER and was originally designed for storage and retrieval of letter-sized document folders in "original-document" filing systems. Basically, the RANDTRIEVER is an automated warehousing system. Items requiring physical retrieval are housed in open-top metal containers large enough to hold 15 letter-size filing folders. Each container is stored in a unique, seven-digit-coded shelf location. Attached to each container is a machine-sensible punched card containing its shelf location code. Shelving modules may be as high as 22 feet, or 20 levels of containers. A moving vertical "master column" extracts and replaces containers, then delivers them to and receives them from one-way conveyors linking the storage area to the control stations. Control station operator consoles accept keyboard, punched-card, or tape inputs for retrieval.

The manufacturer has one system in operation for display purposes at the plant facility. Two have been sold, but are not yet installed; both are for record-keeping rather than library applications. The cost range quoted by the manufacturer is $2.25 per linear inch of shelving. This is quite high, but it may be justified when evaluated in terms of long-range amortization and savings. Clearly, cost justification for this type of system is possible only in high-volume, high-usage collections.

Several aspects of books limit the prospects for substantial automation of physical handling—for example, the variety of sizes, shapes and weights, and the absence of uniform or repetitive handling of each item. Nevertheless, the outlook for automation is not hopeless, because: (1) some devices have been successfully installed in the library; (2) there are ways of tailoring library operations to satisfy some of the physical requirements for automation; and (3) there are some promising materials-handling products of the future.

Countless mixes of existing equipment and procedural technology might be very effectively used for physical handling of books, without unnecessary adverse trade-offs in service to the user. For example, today's technology *could* offer a system with the following characteristics:

- Books stored in closed or open-top metal containers having unique shelf location
- Computer record-keeping of container locations
- Computer-controlled display of bibliographic and/or abstract data by either microfilm or cathode-ray tube (to provide browsing)

- Mechanical retrieval and reshelving along with conveyor transportation (eliminating the need to "subject-store" books)

The above features are all within the state of the art and require no advances in equipment technology, although admittedly the cost would probably be rather high. It seems likely, however, that existing equipment technology and minimal refinement of existing procedural advances could provide significant operational improvements in some libraries.

On the basis of observation of current developmental work in mechanical materials handling, some projections can be stated for product trends for the next five years that will have application to library book handling. The general approach to materials-handling engineering is likely to be more systems oriented. We may expect to see more installations in which handling equipment, storage equipment, sensors, control devices, and computers will interact under computer monitoring. The computer will be able to manage not only the movement and storage processes, but also related inventory data management functions.

Some of these developments will be founded more on procedural advances than on equipment advances. However, there are several specific hardware advances that can contribute to high-level system performance in library book handling. For example, magnetics will be more widely used in the development of sensing devices. Items such as book covers or book containers can be uniquely magnetized for automated identification. The processes in which the payoff for libraries would be the greatest are selecting, sorting, distributing (flow direction), counting, and storing. (Magnetics may also see more use in protection against theft.)

The next ten years will probably also see the development of automatic self-loading equipment designed to handle units such as book containers. Outside the library world, unit-load equipment is not new, nor is its use in automated systems. Mechanized storage rack systems under automatic and semiautomatic control already exist for both palletized and special-shaped goods. Equipment such as the overhead stacker crane is presently operational in such systems. This type of equipment is suspended from overhead monorail or track networks. Its movement is controlled by commands from work station consoles or machine-processable cards, tapes, etc. Floor-running, rack-running (shelf), and overhead-running stackers could be tailored for library use.

The development of improved handling equipment for moving, storing, and locating will require comparable development of control devices and associated instrumentation related to sensing, switching, and directing material flow. Sophisticated electronic, electromagnetic, and electromechanical control devices are being developed and used for industrial material-handling applications, and they presumably will be adaptable to library systems through concentrated product engineering.

The matter of care and preservation of printed materials continues to receive attention. Research efforts concerning the chemical and physical characteristics of paper deterioration have pinpointed the principal cause as acidity in paper itself. The most notable research in this area is that of W. J. Barrow, under sponsorship of the Council on Library Resources. Paper deteriorates not only because of the presence of acid, but also because of the reaction of the paper's acidic chemical content to environmental factors such as temperature, humidity, and air impurities. For example, conditions in a geographic area having high humidity and sulfur dioxide in the air result in a deteriorating sulfuric-acid reaction in the paper. Research efforts have shown that controls for air-purification, lower storage temperatures, and humidity can prolong the life of paper, regardless of acid content. It has been estimated that unused, non-acidic, manufactured papers, when stored at about 15°F. and 51 percent humidity, can have a life expectancy of up to 400,000 years. The life expectancy of a deacidified used book stored at 34°F. is 600 years and 4,000 years if stored at −2°F.

The technology of caring for existing printed materials should be discussed in terms of preservation vs. restoration. Preservation involves chemical deacidification by spraying the printed page with a magnesium bicarbonate solution to neutralize the paper's acid. The cost for this process is about $2 per volume. Complete restoration involves removing the binding, bathing each page in the solution, laminating the pages, and then rebinding. Costs are usually based on a square-inch basis, since printed materials other than books are also processed. However, a 400-page volume of average page size would cost around $40 to restore.[55] At least two firms now specialize in this service. Most libraries could not presently afford the equipment and skills necessary for such operations; those wishing to restore documents would do best to obtain the services from outside.

The problems of caring for deteriorating books have been addressed by the Association of Research Libraries (ARL), with financial support by the Council on Library Resources, Inc. ARL has endorsed a proposal whereby a Federally supported central agency (newly created or to be established within an existing agency) would insure the physical preservation and low-temperature storage of at least one example of every deteriorating record. Such an agency would also insure either microform or full-size photocopies of deteriorating materials. The cost of the proposed system is estimated at $7.25 per volume.

The cooperative interaction of the library community, the paper industry, and the Federal Government will lead toward stepped-up activity in two areas. First the development of paper of more enduring physical characteristics will be a major developmental effort. Advances in chemicals used for sizing and other mill processes have already occurred, and improved processes will reduce the cost of more durable paper. Further Federal support will probably be needed to accelerate the growth of preservation and restoration of existing printed materials.

Transmission of Materials

Both current and projected library operations involve tranmission of materials from the storage location to the user. This can be achieved by local transportation, the United States mails, or by other techniques such as television or facsimile transmission. Each has technical and cost advantages and disadvantages. Some techniques raise difficult legal issues as well, for example, when published material is transmitted from one computer store to another. The present discussion is restricted to technical and cost issues, particularly as related to some of the more advanced techniques.

The controlling factors in the selection of the transmitting and receiving equipment include the material to be transmitted, the quality of transmission desired, the available interconnections (telephone lines, cables, broadcast, etc.) between transmitting and receiving equipment, and the cost of the interconnections. Typical interconnecting links are standard telephone, telegraph, and teletype circuits; private telephone voice lines; broad-band computer-to-computer circuits; special-purpose television circuits; and microwave relay.

The factors to be considered in planning a library application using transmission equipment as an integral element of the system include:

1. The storage medium for the document (hard copy, microfilm, magnetic tape or disc, in image form, or in digital data form, etc.).
2. Number of access stations and distances between the access stations and the central store.
3. Number of documents to be stored.
4. Simultaneous access requirements (i.e., how many users will be looking at the same document at one time), or total transmission load at one time.

55 *"Putting New Life in Old Volumes,"* Publishers Weekly *188 (July 19, 1965)*, pp. 115–8.

5. Quality requirements of document—number of characters, illustrations, half-tones, size of page image, size of type face, etc.

6. Image form desired at output station, e.g., hard copy, microform, image only, or a combination.

7. Cost.

A comparison of current transmission speeds, based on a page characteristic of 60 characters per line and 50 lines per page (a total character count of 3,000) shows that teletype and facsimile (or long-distance xerography) require approximately 220 seconds for the transmission of one page. In contrast, it takes only 1/30 of a second per page for video transmission.

Both the speed and quality of transmission are a function of available bandwidth. Work of the standards committee on image transmission has established a resolution scale, based on examination of 8-point type material, as follows:

> 100 lines/inch — unsatisfactory
> 135 lines/inch — marginal
> 190 lines/inch — fair

Present equipment on voice-grade lines produces about 96-line resolution. It is estimated that it takes about 6 minutes to transmit one page at 100 lines; 11 minutes at 135 lines; and 22 minutes at 190 lines. Hence, the cost per page increases 370 percent to obtain a 90-percent increase in quality. Costs, on this limited basis, increase 3 times as fast as the quality.[56] However, there is considerable promise in long-distance xerography. Although one study showed a discouragingly high cost ($7.26 for transmitting and reproducing a 10-page document over a 75-mile distance), the technique produces better quality reproductions than ordinary facsimile.

For a given library application, costs per image, per operating hour, etc., can be determined only in relation to a particular configuration of equipment. However, some rough guides to current costs can be given:

1. *Books:* Mailing costs per book are about 10¢ per book (based on a 4¢/lb. library rate). Time for "transmission" is about 120 hours (5 days). Cost of reproduction (full-size hard copy) of a book of 300 pages can be estimated at $6.30.

2. *Fiche:* Mailing costs for 5 fiche are 5¢ for first-class mail. Time for transmission is about 48 hours (2 days). Costs of reproducing a set of 5 fiche (into more fiche) can be estimated at $0.75.

3. *Facsimile:* Facsimile equipment costs for 96-line resolution are approximately $1,800 per month for both transmitting and receiving equipment (assuming one receiving station). Time per page is about 6 minutes, and cost for telephone time can be estimated at $1.50. Printout in hard-copy form is about 8¢ per page. Assuming usage of 170 hours per month, costs for equipment and telephone lines would average about $2.75 per page for cross-country transmission.

4. *Video:* Video equipment costs for 500-line resolution are approximately $18,000 for transmitting equipment, $12,000 for receiving equipment (buffer, display refresher, and display), and about $100,000 per month for rental of a coaxial cable linking points 3,000 miles apart (assuming $35 per mile per month). Transmission speed is at 30 pages per second. If we assume that reading speed is 10 seconds per page, and buffer capability is one page, the transmission requirement is one page every 10 seconds. Costs for that page can be estimated at 3¢ for equipment, and 16¢ for line charges, or 19¢ per transmitted page. Any reproduction of the video image can be accomplished at conventional prices at the receiving facility, or at a hard-copy printout price maximum of 8¢ per page.

56 *Morehouse, H. G.* Telefacsimile Services Between Libraries with the Xerox Magnavox Telecopier, *a study prepared for the Council on Library Resources, Inc. (Reno, Nevada: University of Nevada Library, December 20, 1966).*

None of these prices include maintenance of equipment and supplies for that equipment. Maintenance of the video equipment can be extremely expensive, perhaps 25 percent of the yearly equipment costs.

In general, one can say that fiche provide the lowest cost per page transmitted and that video equipment, while providing low per-page costs, does require a large capital investment. (However, costs for line charges in a video system can be reduced from the maximum distance cost of 16¢ per page to an estimated cost of one cent per page for short-distance transmission.) It is clear that a cost-effectiveness study, including some analysis of the relative value of information obtainable within 48 hours, versus, say, one second, certainly must form a part of any planning for the improvement of library service.

In general, it is expected that both the accuracy and the data-transmission rates of various kinds of telecommunications equipment will increase in the near future.[57] Communications satellites, which are currently in a development and testing phase, can also be expected to have some potential as a medium for transferring documentary information. What is not yet clear is whether there will be sufficient integration of the various kinds of transmission media and networks to serve the purposes of a more highly integrated library network. Even though an organization (the National Communications System) was established in 1963 to help coordinate the planning and optimized use of Federal telecommunications resources, there does not yet exist a truly integrated, compatible Federal telecommunications network.

Several programs are under way to develop working systems for retrieving from a central store, transmitting the image to a different location, and viewing the image at that location. For example, one objective of Project Intrex is to provide unlimited access to the M.I.T. library collection of one million books. There is to be:

guaranteed rapid access to the entire data base (i.e., full text) from every console,

rapid transmission of the data on request (at ½ second per page), and

high-quality displays, including engineering drawings, mathematical expressions, foreign languages, and special symbols.

The system is intended to have the ability to advance page images (turn pages) of the book being read, by button action at the remote receiving console, and to supply supplementary hard copy or microfilm, if needed.

Several other organizations are also working along somewhat similar lines. RCA is requesting permission to experiment with newspaper or book-page image transmission, using standard commercial television channels, and modified home TV sets. Use of the set for viewing text images is not expected to make the set unusable for conventional TV. Bell Telephone is working toward establishment of regional data centers for engineering drawings, which will be available on demand to each of the engineers and draftsmen within that region. The Navy Department's Bureau of Ships has installed a system for transmission of maintenance data from shore to ship, using microwave relay techniques.

On the assumptions that more and more serials will be published in microfiche form and that portions of the report-type literature will be almost completely microfiche, it seems feasible to equip *some* local libraries with remote consoles, using video displays. Present techniques and equipment could be utilized to provide a significant number of local libraries with up to 100 display and inquiry stations. These stations would have to be located within about .2 mile from the computer, to avoid special coaxial lines and booster circuits. With a concerted effort, it would be possible to convert 40 to 60 percent of the nation's libraries to the use of remote display stations within 10 years. Needless

---

[57] *Brown, George W., et al.* EDUNET (*New York: John Wiley & Sons, 1967*).

to say, the source documents would also have to be converted within the same time limits to provide compatibility between old and new materials.

It also seems feasible to provide video communication links between local and regional libraries. If, later, regional libraries could be linked, it would be possible to view documents, with minimum delay, from any repository within the network. Transmission costs from a regional library to another regional library, and then through a local library to a local viewer, can be estimated to be somewhat under 30¢ per page. If the image were put on microfiche at the receiving library (or at any point on the circuit) at about 3¢ per page, *subsequent* viewing costs would be quite minimal. The quality of the images thus obtained is difficult to predict; it would be worth some experimentation here to provide a better basis for speculation.

In spite of the promise of this new technology, it seems unlikely that, for the next ten years (or longer), libraries will, or should, expect the dominant storage medium to be other than books and the dominant transmission medium to be other than the United States mail. This is the one existing network that can support the materials transmission needs of all libraries, regardless of the extent to which they choose to cooperate, amalgamate, or join in an integrated national system.

Laser Technology and Holography

The laser contains a material that can be handled in such a way that its energy is released at one time (rather than in random sequence), and at nearly the same wavelength (color). Furthermore, and particularly important from the standpoint of future library technology, the light is coherent, or, from the wave-theory point of view, inphase. This coherence causes two important effects: The first is that light is emitted in a narrow beam, which makes the laser potentially useful as a data-transmission carrier. The second is that it can be used for a type of photography known as holography, which provides the ability to record many items, or many views of a single item, on a single, small surface.

The advent of laser technology promises a tremendous increase in what, before satellites, had been thought of as an already overcrowded communication capacity. The nearly instantaneous transmission of information over a distance is dependent upon electromagnetic radiation, that is, light and radio waves. The four primary ways of transmitting such information over long distances have been: (1) through the use of electromagnetic radiation, propagated through the space between the receiving and transmitting stations; (2) through coaxial cable; (3) by point-to-point microwave relay (which in functional terms is equivalent to transmission by coaxial cable); and (4) by piping the electromagnetic radiation through cylinders known as wave guides. The first technique requires use of a certain band within the electromagnetic spectrum, and no one else can use this band within the energy range of the emitted radiation without causing interference for both himself and the other sender. The other three techniques are more directional and use much narrower channels, but they are also much more expensive to use.

The advantage of the laser beam is that it provides a *wireless* straight cable, on which it seems possible to impose signals. These signals can be carried along the surface of the earth or by repeat transmission from satellites. Though the results of laser research have been exciting and promising, the work is still experimental and there are many problems still to be solved in the modulation of the laser beam so that it can carry information. We still do not know when this experimental work will have advanced the techniques to the point where they will be useful and economical for library applications.

Holography, the other aspect of the new laser technology that may have important results for libraries, is quite different from regular photography. The result of regular photography is a picture that one observes by looking at the plane surface of a photographic plate. In holography, one looks through the plane of the plate, so to speak, and sees an image on the other side of the plate. The image is presented as if it were a real object, that is, the image is seen three-dimensionally. If one looks from a particular vantage point, one part of the image might block out another part. As one changes the angle of view, by moving one's head or the plate, one can see what had previously been blocked.

The hologram is produced by recording onto the photographic plate the wave lengths (technically, the interference patterns) reflected from the object being illuminated by coherent light. Reading out is, in a sense, simply the reverse process: the plate is illuminated by the same wave length (color) as when the picture was taken, and one has the same effect as seeing the original scene. For library purposes, this has many potential uses. One is in storing multiple images on one photographic plate. This is, of course, something that can already be done—though with a radically different technique —on microforms. It can also be accomplished with the new but untried technique of multiplex photography. However, a few investigators believe that the hologram has very great potential for high-density storage and retrieval applications.

A more novel use of holograms in libraries would be for the storage of color pictures of three-dimensional objects. Each hologram plate would contain many views of the object, seemingly from different angles, but actually taken with one exposure of the plate. If this technique were perfected and made economical, one could well imagine greatly improved collections, in libraries, of representations of statuary and other three-dimensional works of art.

It is important to note that there are many research and engineering problems to be solved before holograms can be used in libraries. We have no way, as yet, of predicting when these problems will be solved. Thus, the techniques to be considered for the immediate future are the more conventional methods of photography discussed in previous sections.

BIBLIOGRAPHY

1. ABELSON, PHILIP H. "The Human Use of Computing Machines." *Science,* 153 (15 July 1966) p. 253.
2. ADAMS (CHARLES W.) ASSOCIATES, INC. *The Computer Display Review.* Cambridge, Mass., 1966, 1 v. (loose-leaf).
3. *Advances in Programming and Non-Numerical Computation.* 1st edition. Symposium Publications Div., Pergamon, Oxford, 1966, 218 p.
4. AMERICAN LIBRARY ASSOCIATION. LIBRARY TECHNOLOGY PROGRAM. *Annual Report* (Eighth) Chicago, 1967, 31 p.
5. *Annual Review of Information Science and Technology,* ed. by Carlos A. Cuadra. Interscience, 1966 — (Volume 2, 1967)
6. AUERBACH CORPORATION. *DOD User Needs Study, Phase 1,* Final Technical Report 1151-TR-3, 2 vols. Philadelphia, Pa., May 1965.
7. AVRAM, H. D. & B. E. MARKUSON. "Library Automation and Project MARC. An Experiment in the Distribution of Machine-Readable Cataloging Data." In: *The Brasenose Conference on the Automation of Libraries, Oxford, Eng., 30 June–3 July 1966. Proceedings* . . . Mansell, London, 1967, p. 97–127.
8. BALLOU, HUBBARD (Ed.) *Guide to Micro Reproduction Equipment:* 1966 Supplement. National Microfilm Assoc., 1966, 127 p.
9. BARNES, ROBERT F. *Mathematico-Logical Foundations of Retrieval Theory: General Concepts and Methods.* Center for the Information Sciences, Lehigh Univ., Bethlehem, Pa., Nov. 1965.
10. BARNETT, MICHAEL P. *Computer Typesetting: Experiments and Prospects.* The M.I.T. Press, Cambridge, Mass., 1965, 245 p.
11. BEASLEY, KENNETH E. "Social and Political Factors." *ALA Bull.,* 60 (Dec. 1966) p. 1146, 1151–1155.

12. BECKER, JOSEPH & ROBERT M. HAYES. *Information Storage and Retrieval: Tools, Elements, Theories.* Wiley, New York, 1963, 448 p.
13. BELL, G. & M. W. PIRTLE. "Time-Sharing Bibliography." *Proc. IEEE,* 54 (Dec. 1966) p. 1764–1765.
14. BENJAMIN, CURTIS G. "Computers and Copyrights." *Science,* 152 (8 Apr. 1966) p. 181–194.
15. BENNETT, EDWARD, EDWARD C. HAINES, & JOHN K. SUMMERS. "AESOP: A Prototype for On-Line User Control of Organizational Data Storage, Retrieval, and Processing." In: American Federation of Information Processing Societies. *AFIPS Conference Proceedings, vol. 27, Part 1; 1965 Fall Joint Computer Conference.* Spartan Books, Washington, D.C., 1965, p. 435–455.
16. BLACK, DONALD V. (Ed.) *Progress in Information Science and Technology.* Proceedings of the American Documentation Institute; 1966 Annual Meeting, October 3–7, 1966, Santa Monica, California. Adrianne Press [Woodland Hills, Calif.] 494 p.
17. BLAINE, THOMAS. *Technique of Advertising Production.* Prentice Hall, New York, 1964.
18. BLEIER, ROBERT E. *Treating Hierarchial Data Structures in the SDC Time-Shared Data Management System* (TDMS). System Development Corp., Santa Monica, Calif., 15 Feb. 1967 (SP-2750).
19. BLUNT, CHARLES R., ROBERT T. DUQUET, & PETER T. LUCKIE. *A General Model for Simulating Information Storage and Retrieval Systems.* HRB Singer, Inc., State College, Pa., Apr. 1966, 178 p. (Report No. 352.14-R-2) (AD-636 435)
20. BOBROW, DANIEL G. *Problems in Natural Language Communication with Computers.* Bolt Beranek and Newman, Inc., Cambridge, Mass., Aug. 1966, 19 p. (Report No. Scientific-5, BBN-1439) AFCRL 66-620 (AD-639 323).
21. BOOZ ALLEN APPLIED RESEARCH, INC. *Study of Mechanization in DOD Libraries and Information Centers.* Bethesda, Md., Sept. 1966 (AD-640 100) 1 volume, various pagings.
22. BORKO, HAROLD & H. P. BURNAUGH. "Interactive Displays for Document Retrieval." *Inform. Display,* 3 (Sept./Oct. 1966) 47–90.
23. *Bowker Annual of Library and Book Trade Information.* R. R. Bowker Co., New York, 1967 (edition).
24. BRANDHORST, W. T. & PHILIP F. ECKERT. *Guide to the Processing, Storage, and Retrieval of Bibliographical Information at the NASA Scientific and Technical Information Facility.* Documentation Inc., College Park, Md., 156 p. (NASA CR-62033).
25. BROWN, GEORGE W., et al. *EDUNET.* John Wiley & Sons, New York, 1967.
26. BUCKLAND, L. F. *Machine Recording of Textual Information During the Publication of Scientific Journals.* (Report on Work Done During Period January 1, 1963 to May 30, 1965) Inforonics, Inc., Maynard, Mass., 30 May 1965, 70 p. (NSF Contract 305).
27. CALIFORNIA. UNIVERSITY, SANTA CRUZ. *Specification for an Automated Library System.* Santa Cruz, Calif., 1965, 122 p.
28. CARTER, LAUNOR F., et al. *National Document-Handling Systems for Science and Technology.* John Wiley & Sons, New York, 1967.
29. CARTWRIGHT, KELLEY L. & RALPH M. SHOFFNER. *Catalogs in Book Form: A Research Study of Their Implication for the California State Library and the California Union Catalog, with a design for Their Implementation.* Institute of Library Research, Berkeley, Calif., 1967, 1 v. (various pagings).
30. CLEVERTON, CYRIL, JACK MILLS, & MICHAEL KEEN. *Factors Determining the Performance of Indexing Systems.* ASLIB Cranfield Research Project, Cranfield, Bedford, Eng., 1966, Vol. 1, Part 1, 120 p.; Vol. 1, Part 2, p. 121–377; and Vol. 2, 299 p.

31. CLINIC ON LIBRARY APPLICATIONS OF DATA PROCESSING. *Proceedings, 1966.* University of Illinois, Graduate School of Library Science, Urbana, 1966, 218 p.

32. COATES, E. J. "Scientific and Technical Indexing." *Indexer,* 5 (Spring 1966) 27–34.

33. CONNORS, THOMAS B. "ADAM—A Generalized Data Management System." In: American Federation of Information Processing Societies. *AFIPS Conference Proceedings, Vol. 28; 1966 Spring Joint Computer Conference.* Spartan Books, Washington, D.C., 1966, p. 193–203.

34. CRAEGER, WILLIAM A. & DAVID E. SPARKS. *A Serials Data Program for Science and Technology.* (Final Report to the National Science Foundation) Information Dynamics Corp., Reading, Pa., 1965, 169 p.

35. CREATIVE RESEARCH SERVICES, INC. *The Use of Data Processing Equipment by Libraries and Information Centers.* A Survey Prepared for the Documentation Division, Special Libraries Association and the Library Technology Program. American Library Ass., Chicago, 1966, 160 p.

36. CRONIN, JOHN W., et al. "Centralized Cataloging at the National and International Level." *Libr. Resour. Tech. Serv., 11:1 (Winter* 1967) p. 27–49.

37. CRONIN, JOHN W. "The Library of Congress National Program for Acquisitions and Cataloging." *Libri,* 16:2 (1966) p. 113–117. SP-2516).

38. DALTON, PHYLLIS I. "Special Libraries and State-Wide Plans for Library Service." *Spec. Libr.,* 57 (Oct. 1966) 589–591.

39. DAVIDSON, LEON. "A Pushbutton Telephone for Alpha-Numeric Input." *Datamation,* 12 (April 1966) 27–30.

40. DAVIS, RICHARD A. & CATHERINE A. BAILEY. *Bibliography of Use Studies.* Graduate School of Library Service, Drexel Institute of Technology, Philadelphia, Pa., March 1964, 438 p. (AD-435 062).

41. DOYLE, LAUREN B. *Breaking the Cost Barrier in Automatic Classification.* System Development Corp., Santa Monica, Calif., 1 July 1966 (Report No. SP-2516)

42. DREW, D. L., et al. "An On-Line Technical Library Reference Retrieval System." *Amer. Doc.,* 17 (Jan. 1966) p. 3–7.

43. EBERSOLE, J. L. "An Operating Model of a National Information System." *Amer. Doc.,* 17 (Jan. 1966) 33–40.

44. ENGEL, JAN. & ARTHUR M. ELDRIDGE, JR. "A New Device for Versatile Display Systems—The Electrostatic Storage Display Tube." In: *7th National Symposium on Information Display: Technical Session Proceedings.* Society for Information Display, Boston, 1966, p. 31–34.

45. FISCHER, MARGUERITE. "The KWIC Index Concept: A Retrospective View." *Amer. Doc.,* 17 (Apr. 1966) p. 57–70.

46. FLANNERY, ANNE & JAMES D. MACK. *Mechanized Circulation System, Lehigh University Library.* Center for the Information Sciences, Lehigh Univ., 11 Nov. 1966, 1 v. (Library Systems Analysis. Report No. 4).

47. FREISER, LEONARD H. "The Civilized Network . . ." *Libr. J.,* 92 (15 Sept. 1967) p. 3001–3003.

48. GENERAL ELECTRIC COMPANY. TECHNICAL MILITARY PLANNING OPERATION (TEMPO) (1) *The Deacon Project,* Final Report 65 TMP-69. (2) *Phrase-Structure Oriented Target Query Language,* Final Report, Vol. 1 and 2, 65 TMP-64. Santa Barbara, Calif., Sept. 1965.

49. GENTILE, J. RONALD. "First Generation of Computer-Assisted Instructional Systems: An Evaluative Review." n.p., n.d.

50. GIULIANO, VINCENT E. & PAUL E. JONES. *Study and Test of a Methodology for Laboratory Evaluation of Message Retrieval Systems.* Interim Report. Decision Sciences Lab., Electronic Systems Div., Air Force Systems Command, U.S. Air Force, L. G. Hanscom Field, Bedford, Mass., Aug. 1966, 183 p. (C-65850; C-66257) (ESD-TR-66-405).

51. GRUENBERGER, FRED (Ed.) *Computer Graphics—Utility/Production/ Art.* [Graphics Symposium, University of California, Los Angeles, 1966] Jointly Sponsored by Informatics, Inc. and the University of California at Los Angeles. Thompson Book Co., Washington, D.C. and Academic Press, London, 1967, 225 p.

52. HARVEY, JOHN (Ed.) *Data Processing in Public and University Libraries. Combined Proceedings of the Drexel Conference [s] on Data Processing in University Libraries . . . and in Public Libraries . . .* Spartan Books, Washington, D.C., 1966, 150 p.

53. HATTERY, LOWELL H. & GEORGE P. BUSH (Eds.) *Automation and Electronics in Publishing.* Spartan Books, Washington and New York, 1965 (American University. Technology of Management Series, vol. 3. Paul W. Howerton, General Editor).

54. HATTERY, LOWELL H. "Computers, Typesetting, Printing, and Publishing." In: American Data Processing, Inc. *Computer Yearbook and Directory.* Detroit, Mich., 1966, p. 196–206.

55. HAWKIN, WILLIAM R. *Copying Methods Manual.* American Library Ass., Chicago, 1966.

56. HAYES, ROBERT M., et al. "Economics of Book Catalog Production." *Libr. Resour. Tech. Serv.,* 10 (Winter 1966) p. 57–90.

57. HAYS, DAVID (Ed.) *Readings in Automatic Language Processing.* American Elsevier, New York, 1966, 202 p.

58. HENDRICKS, DONALD D. *Comparative Costs of Book Processing in a Processing Center and in Five Individual Libraries.* Illinois State Library, Research Series No. 8, Springfield, Ill., 1966, 89 p.

59. HERBERT, EVAN. "Information Transfer." *Int. Sci. Technol.,* No. 51 (Mar. 1966) p. 26–37.

60. HINES, THEODORE C. & JESSICA L. HARRIS. *Computer Filing of Index, Bibliographic and Catalog Entries.* Bro-Dart Foundation, Newark, N.J., 1966, 126 p.

61. HOBBS, L. C. "Present and Future State-of-the-Art in Computer Memories." *IEEE Trans. Electron. Comput.,* EC-15 (Aug. 1966) p. 534–550.

62. HOBBS, L. C. "Display Applications and Technology." *Proc. IEEE,* 54 (Dec. 1966) p. 1870–1884.

63. HOLZBAUR, FREDERICK W. & EUGENE H. FARRIS. *Library Information Processing Using an On-Line, Real-Time Computer System.* International Business Machines Corp., System Development Div., Poughkeepsie, N.Y., 7 Dec. 1966, 47 p. (TR 00.1548).

64. HUMENUK, STANLEY. *Automatic Shelving and Book Retrieval: A Contribution Toward a Progressive Philosophy of Library Service for a Research Library.* (University of Illinois Thesis, 1964).

65. HUSKEY, H. D. "On-Line Computing Systems: A Summary." In: Burgess, E. (Ed.) *On-Line Computing Systems.* American Data Processing, Inc., Detroit, Mich., 1965, p. 139–142.

66. *The Impact of Technology on the Library Building.* Educational Facilities Laboratories, New York, 1967, 20 p. (One of the Series of Studies Sponsored by the National Advisory Commission on Libraries).

67. INTERNATIONAL BUSINESS MACHINES CORPORATION. *Generalized Information System Application Description.* IBM Corp., Technical Publications Dept., White Plains, N.Y., 1965, 42 p.

68. INTERNATIONAL FEDERATION FOR DOCUMENTATION. *Proceedings of the 1965 Congress;* 31st Meeting and Congress, Washington, D.C., October 7–16, 1965. In cooperation with the American Documentation Institute. (ADI Proceedings, Vol. 2) Spartan Books, Washington and Macmillan, London, 1966, 264 p.

69. JACKSON, EUGENE B. *The Use of Data Processing by Libraries and Information Centers.* (extracts from): *An Interpretation of Creative Research Services, Inc.,* Report (unpublished report) 1967, 44 p.

70. JORDAN, ROBERT T. *The Jordan Plastic Book Box.* (unpublished report) 1966.

71. KASHER, ASA. *Data-Retrieval by Computer; a Critical Survey.* Hebrew Univ., Jerusalem, Israel, Jan. 1966, 72 p. (Technical Report No. 22 to Office of Naval Research, Information Systems Branch) (AD-631 748).

72. KENT, ALLEN. *Textbook on Mechanized Information Retrieval.* 2d ed. Interscience, New York, 1966, 371 p. (Library Science and Documentation, Vol. 3).

73. KESSLER, M. M. "The MIT Technical Information Project." *Phys. Today,* 18 (Mar. 1965) p. 28–36.

74. KING, GILBERT W. *Automation and the Library of Congress.* A report submitted by Gilbert King and others. Library of Congress, Washington, D.C., 1963, 88 p.

75. KNOX, WILLIAM T. "National Information Networks and Special Libraries." Spec. Libr., 57 (Nov. 1966) p. 627–630.

76. KOZLOW, ROBERT D. *Library Automation Project; A Report on a Library Automation Project Conducted on the Chicago Campus of the University of Illinois.* Supported by the National Science Foundation, Grants 77 and 302, 1966. 1 v., various pagings (University of Illinois, Report).

77. KUNEY, J. H. *Computer Typesetting as Input to Information Systems.* Paper presented at the International Computer Typesetting Conference, University of Sussex, Eng., July 14–18, 1966.

78. KUNO, SUSUMU. *Computer Analysis of Natural Languages.* Presented at Symposium on Mathematical Aspects of Computer Science; American Mathematical Society, New York, April 5–7, 1966.

79. "The Library of Congress Automation Techniques Exchange (LOCATE) has been Established in the Information Systems Office . . ." *Libr. Congr. Inform. Bull.,* 25 (17 Nov. 1966) p. 720.

80. LICKLIDER, J. C. R. *Libraries of the Future.* Based on a study sponsored by the Council on Library Resources, Inc., and conducted by Bolt, Beranek and Newman. M.I.T. Press, Massachusetts Institute of Technology, Cambridge, Mass., 1965, 219 p.

81. LINDGREN, H. C. "Creativity, Brainstorming, and Orneriness." *J. Social Psychol.,* 67 (Oct. 1965) p. 23–30.

82. MALONEY, ROY T. *Portable Microvisual Systems.* Lederer, Street and Zeus, Berkeley, 1966, 125 p.

83. MARKUS, JOHN. "State of the Art of Computers in Commercial Publishing." *Amer. Doc.,* 17 (Apr. 1966) p. 76–88.

84. MARKUSON, BARBARA EVANS. "Automation in Libraries and Information Centers." In: *Annual Review of Information Science and Technology,* Vol. 2, 1967, p. 255–283.

85. MARKUSON, BARBARA EVANS. "System Development Study for Library of Congress Automation Program." *Libr. Quart.,* 36 (July 1966) p. 197–273.

86. MARON, M. E. *Relational Data File I: Design Philosophy.* RAND Corp., Santa Monica, Calif., July 1966, 23 p. (P-3408).

87. MASSACHUSETTS INSTITUTE OF TECHNOLOGY. PROJECT INTREX. *Semiannual Activity Report.* (Period ending 15 September 1967) Cambridge, Mass., 49 p. (PR-4).

88. MILLER, JAMES G. "EDUCOM: Interuniversity Communications Council." *Science,* 154 (28 Oct. 1966) p. 483–488.

89. MOREHOUSE, H. G. *Telefacsimile Services Between Libraries with the Xerox Magnavox Telecopier.* A Study Prepared for the Council on Library Resources, Inc. Univ. of Nevada Library, Reno, Nev., 20 Dec. 1966, 54 p. (CLR-314).

90. NATIONAL ACADEMY OF SCIENCES—NATIONAL RESEARCH COUNCIL. AUTOMATIC LANGUAGE PROCESSING ADVISORY COMMITTEE. *Language and Machines; Computers in Translation and Linguistics.*

National Academy of Sciences—National Research Council, Washington, D.C., 1966, 124 p. (Publication 1416).

91. NATIONAL SCIENCE FOUNDATION. OFFICE OF SCIENCE INFORMATION SERVICE. *Current Research and Development in Scientific Documentation, No. 14.* Washington, D.C., 1966, 662 p. (NSF-66-17).

92. *National Symposium on Information Display, 7th, Boston, 1966.* Society for Information Display, Boston, Mass., 1966.

93. NEW YORK STATE UNIVERSITY. STATE EDUCATION DEPARTMENT. DIVISION OF EVALUATION. *Emerging Library Systems; The 1963–66 Evaluation of the New York Public Library Systems.* Feb. 1967, 1 v., various pagings.

94. OHRINGER, LEE. *Progress in Computerized Typesetting.* Univ. of Pittsburgh, Computations and Data Processing Center, Pittsburgh, Pa., 1965, 14 p. (AD-618 077).

95. OPTNER, STANFORD L. *Systems Analysis for Business and Industrial Problem Solving.* Prentice-Hall, Englewood Cliffs, N.J., 1966, 116 p. (Prentice-Hall International Series in Industrial and Management Science. W. Grant Ireson, Ed.)

96. OVERHAGE, CARL F. J. & JOYCE HARMAN (Eds.) *INTREX; Report of a Planning Conference on Information Transfer Experiments, September 3, 1965.* M.I.T. Press, Massachusetts Institute of Technology, Cambridge, Mass., 1965, 276 p.

97. POOL, ITHIEL D., et al. *Computer Approaches for the Handling of Large Social Science Data Files.* Progress Report M.I.T. Center for International Studies, Cambridge, Mass., Jan. 1967.

98. "Putting New Life in Old Volumes." *Publ. Week.*, 188 (19 July 1965) p. 115–118.

99. REES, ALAN M. & DOUGLAS G. SCHULTZ. *A Field Experimental Approach to the Study of Relevance Assessments in Relation to Document Searching.* Formal Progress Report No. 3 (1 July - 31 Dec. 1966) Center for Documentation and Communication Research, School of Library Science, Western Reserve Univ., Cleveland, Ohio, 1966, 11 p.

100. ROGERS, FRANK B. "MEDLARS Operating Experience at the University of Colorado." *Bull. Med. Libr. Ass.*, 54 (Jan. 1966) 1–10. (see also the Bulletin for Oct. 1966, p. 316–320.

101. RUBINOFF, MORRIS (Ed.) *Toward a National Information System; Second Annual National Colloquium on Information Retrieval, April 23–24, 1965, Philadelphia, Pennsylvania.* Sponsored by Special Interest Gorup on Information Retrieval, Association for Computing Machinery; Moore School of Electrical Engineering, Univ. of Pennsylvania; Delaware Valley Chapter, Association for Computing Machinery. Spartan Books, Washington, and Macmillan, London, 1965, 242 p.

102. SALTON, GERARD. "A Document Retrieval System for Man-Machine Interaction." In: Association for Computing Machinery. *Proceedings of the 19th Annual Conference, Philadelphia, 1964,* p. L2. 3–L2. 3–20.

103. *Scientific American,* Issue for September 1966.

104. SHARP, J. R. *Some Fundamentals of Information Retrieval.* London House & Maxwell, New York, 1965, 224 p.

105. SHAW, J. C. JOSS: *A Designer's View of an Experimental On-Line Computing System.* RAND Corp., Santa Monica, Calif., Aug. 1964, 36 p.
    Also published in: American Federation of Information Processing Societies. *AFIPS Conference Proceedings, Vol. 26, Part 1; 1964 Fall Joint Computer Conference.* Spartan Books, Washington, D.C., 1964, p. 455–464. p. 455–464.

106. SIMMONS, R. F. *Answering English Questions by Computer: A Survey.* System Development Corp., Santa Monica, Calif., Apr. 1964 (SP-1556)

Slightly revised version published in: *Commun. ACM,* 8 (Jan. 1965) p. 53–70.

107. STANFORD UNIVERSITY, CALIFORNIA. LIBRARY. *Bibliographic Automation of Large Library Operations Using a Time Sharing System (Project BALLOTS)* Proposal to the U.S. Office of Education, 1967. [Awarded as a project by the USOE (Project No. 7–1145)].

108. STEVENS, MARY E. (Ed.) *Statistical Association Methods for Mechanized Documentation; Symposium Proceedings, Washington, 1964.* U.S. Dept. of Commerce, National Bureau of Standards, Washington, D.C., 1965, 261 p.

109. STEVENSON, C. G. "Checklist for Evaluating Technical Libraries and Technical Information Centers." *Spec. Libr,* 58 (Feb. 1967) p. 106–110.

110. STEWART, BRUCE. *The Serials Mechanization of the Texas A & M University Library.* A Paper Presented at the First Texas Conference on Library Mechanization, Austin, March 23–24, 1966. n.p., 1966, 13 p.

111. SWANSON, DON R. *Studies of Indexing Depth and Retrieval Effectiveness.* Progress Report No. 1. Graduate Library School, Univ. of Chicago, Ill., Feb. 1966, 17 p.

112. SYSTEM DEVELOPMENT CORPORATION. *Experimental Studies of Relevance Judgments: Second Progress Report and Third Progress Report.* Carlos A. Cuadra, Principal Investigator, Santa Monica, Calif., 1 July 1966, 53 p. (TM-3068) & 20 Jan. 1967, 68 p. (TM-3347).

113. SYSTEM DEVELOPMENT CORPORATION. *Experimental Investigations of a Method for Analyzing Document Representation: Progress Report.* Robert V. Katter, Principal Investigator. Santa Monica, Calif., 9 Aug. 1966, 113 p. (TM-3090).

114. THOMPSON, FREDERICK B. "English for the Computer." In: American Federation of Information Processing Societies. *AFIPS Conference Proceedings, Vol. 29; 1966 Fall Joint Computer Conference, November 7–10, San Francisco, Calif.* Spartan Books, Washington, D.C., 1966, p. 349–356.

115. UHR, LEONARD (Ed.) *Pattern Recognition: Theory, Experiment, Computer Simulations, and Dynamic Models of Form Perception and Discovery.* Wiley, New York, 1966, 393 p.

116. U.S. AIR FORCE. SYSTEMS COMMAND. ELECTRONIC SYSTEMS DIVISION. *Advanced Programming Developments: A Survey.* Bedford, Mass., Feb. 1965, 101 p. (ESD TR-65-171) (AD-614 704) Prepared in Cooperation with Computer Associates, Inc., Wakefield, Mass.

117. UNSTEAD, CHARLES R., et al. *Compatible Automated Library Circulation Control Systems.* Redstone Arsenal, Alabama, Apr. 1967, 174 p. (AD-653 591).

118. U.S. LIBRARY OF CONGRESS. INFORMATION SYSTEMS OFFICE. *A Preliminary Report on the MARC (MAchine-Readable Cataloging) Pilot Project.* Washington, D.C., 1966, 101 p. see also chapter 16.

119. VERHOEFF, J. "The Delft Circulation System." *Libri,* 16:1 (1966) 1–9.

120. ZINN, CARL. *Computer Assistance for Instruction: A Review of Systems and Projects.* Center for Research on Learning and Teaching Univ. of Michigan, Ann Arbor, 1966, 63 p. (CAIS Report O1O).

INDEX